Archaeology and Humanity's Story

Archaeology and Humanity's Story

A BRIEF INTRODUCTION TO WORLD PREHISTORY

SECOND EDITION

Deborah I. Olszewski

New York   Oxford
Oxford University Press

Oxford University Press is a department of the University of Oxford.
It furthers the University's objective of excellence in research, scholarship,
and education by publishing worldwide. Oxford is a registered trade mark of
Oxford University Press in the UK and certain other countries.

Published in the United States of America by Oxford University Press
198 Madison Avenue, New York, NY 10016, United States of America.

For titles covered by Section 112 of the US Higher Education
Opportunity Act, please visit www.oup.com/us/he for the latest
information about pricing and alternate formats.

Library of Congress Cataloging-in-Publication Data
Names: Olszewski, Deborah, author.
Title: Archaeology and humanity's story : a brief introduction to world
   prehistory / Deborah I. Olszewski.
Description: Second Edition. | New York : Oxford University Press, [2019]
Identifiers: LCCN 2019015781 (print) | LCCN 2019019992 (ebook) | ISBN
   9780190930134 (e-book) | ISBN 9780190930127
Subjects: LCSH: Prehistoric peoples. | Antiquities, Prehistoric.
Classification: LCC GN740 (ebook) | LCC GN740 .O48 2020 (print) | DDC
   930.1—dc23
LC record available at https://lccn.loc.gov/2019015781

9 8 7 6 5 4 3 2 1
Printed by LSC Communications, United States of America

In memory of my good friend, Harold L. Dibble
(July 26, 1951–June 10, 2018) and all the years of "Forward into the Past"

Brief Contents

Table of Contents

CHAPTER 5 Hunting, Gathering, Foraging, Farming, and Complexity *130*

Part 3 On the Threshold of Political Complexity *169*

CHAPTER 6 Prehistoric Europe North of the Mediterranean *170*

CHAPTER 7 The North American Southwest 202

CHAPTER 8 Eastern North America 242

CHAPTER 14   Andean South America and the Inka Empire   *412*

CHAPTER 15   Mapungubwe and Great Zimbabwe in Africa   *446*

Preface

Archaeology provides the evidence for the story of all humanity. The long time depth of this record and its worldwide coverage offer us a view of change and diversity over the tens, hundreds, and thousands of millennia that mark the human presence on planet Earth. The goal of this book is to convey a sense of the processes that occurred, why these changes may have taken place, and how human groups created relationships that allowed them to navigate both their social and their natural worlds.

Some of our earliest ancestors likely would not be recognized by us as human, but many of the challenges they faced were ones that continued to be significant to later modern human groups. A number of the important watershed events were linked in part to dietary shifts. For our earliest ancestors, these included eating more C_4 plants compared to the C_3 plants that our closest living relatives, the common chimpanzees and bonobos, eat. By doing so, these earliest ancestors expanded into a new econiche. Some of these early ancestors also began to incorporate more meat in their diet (another new econiche), which provided a rich food source to supply energy to the very energy-expensive brain. Along the way, the innovation of using sharp-edge stone artifacts gave our ancestors advantages in procuring meat and marrow from animal bones and eventually weapons with which to hunt. Of course, there were many other later technological innovations, such as hafting stone artifacts, the invention of spear throwers and the bow and arrow, and the knowledge of how to manufacture basketry and, later, how to fire clay to make pottery vessels, among many others.

One of the major economic transitions/dietary shifts, however, was the advent of food-production economies. Some human groups in the late Pleistocene and early Holocene epochs in both the Old and the New Worlds began to manipulate certain plants and animals in ways that led to their domestication. Whereas early farmers and pastoralists faced their own sets of challenges such as droughts, floods, and insects, generally speaking, food-production economies had the potential to create surpluses, which are a type of "wealth." How these surpluses were used by communities could vary significantly. In some groups, surpluses were shared, whereas in other groups, particular individuals and their families eventually gained increased access to surpluses. When this happened, there was potential for the development of "elites" who not only accumulated more surpluses but also became more powerful in terms of authority and decision-making for others. In a number of cases, through a variety of social processes, these elites became established as rulers, and the societies they led became increasingly politically complex. This type of transition often was marked by the development of features such as social classes and bureaucracies, and the polities are those we call kingdoms, states, and empires. Several of this book's chapters focus on these politically complex societies.

Organization and Themes

The intent of this book is to provide undergraduate students and the public with an overview of human prehistory and early history, as well as case studies for several societies that are examples of social complexity and of political complexity. By taking a case study approach, attention is paid in some detail to particular places and points in time at the expense of coverage of all past societies, processes, and events. This approach has the benefit of not overwhelming the reader with everything that is represented in the archaeological record, particularly because such coverage within one book either would require a rather lengthy presentation or would result in just the briefest of mentions for each site and event.

The book is organized into several parts as follows. Part 1 ("The Basics of Archaeology") contains one chapter. This part presents information on archaeological method and theory, dating, and issues such as "Who Owns the Past." In Part 2 ("Prehistory Before Political Complexity"), there are four chapters. Chapter 2 ("Humanity's Roots") discusses the earliest human ancestors in the interval from 7 to 1 million years ago and the origins of stone tool technology. Chapter 3 ("Becoming Human") provides information on later ancestors who began the series of out of Africa movements that led to populating the Middle East, Europe, and Asia. It also includes discussion of the origins of modern humans and of modern human behaviors. Chapter 4 ("A World of Modern Humans") examines the hunting–gathering–foraging groups of Later Stone Age Africa and Upper Paleolithic Europe. It provides information about modern human expansion into Australia/New Guinea and into the Americas, as well as materials on Paleoamericans. Chapter 5 ("Hunting, Gathering, Foraging, Farming, and Complexity") deals with events at the end of the Pleistocene and in the Early Holocene in the Old and New Worlds. These include discussion of the origins of food-production economies and some of the social consequences of these new lifeways. The concepts of social and political complexity are discussed in the context of the example of Hawai'i, as are examples of interpretive frameworks and themes in politically complex societies.

In Part 3 ("On the Threshold of Political Complexity"), there are three chapters. Chapter 6 ("Prehistoric Europe North of the Mediterranean") examines the archaeological background to changes in Europe, especially in the period following the expansion of food-producing economies from the Middle East. It concentrates mainly on the Bronze Age. Chapter 7 ("The North American Southwest") treats developments in the North American Southwest after the introduction of domesticated plants from Mesoamerica. It focuses specifically on the Ancestral Pueblo, particularly Chaco Canyon, but also includes some information on the Hohokam and Mogollon. Chapter 8 ("Eastern North America") examines the North American East where indigenous plants were brought into cultivation but some domesticates were later introduced from Mesoamerica. It highlights Cahokia during the Early Mississippian period.

Part 4 ("Politically Complex Societies") contains seven chapters. Chapter 9 ("Early Dynastic Mesopotamia") discusses developments in the Middle East and uses the Early Dynastic period of Mesopotamia as a case study of political complexity. Chapter 10 ("Pharaonic State and Old Kingdom Egypt") does the same for Egypt, focusing especially on the Old Kingdom period there. Chapter 11 ("Shang China") examines political complexity in East Asia using the Shang period as its case study. Chapter 12 ("The Indus Valley") looks at the Harappan and the processes that led to the Mature Harappan period, especially the context of urbanism. Chapter 13 ("Mesoamerica, the Classic Maya, and the Aztec Empire") provides a case study of early political complexity from the New World using the Classic period Maya. It also includes information on the later Aztec Empire. Chapter 14 ("Andean South America and the Inka Empire") examines the contexts for the appearance of the Inka Empire and provides materials using the Inka as its case study. Chapter 15 ("Mapungubwe and Great Zimbabwe in Africa") does the same for late politically complex societies in southeastern Africa.

In Part 5 ("Epilogue"), there is one chapter. This epilogue recaps the "disappearance" of politically complex entities and some lessons from past societies which are perhaps useful for today's world.

New to the Second Edition

Global Changes
- New chapter (Chapter 6) on Europe.
- New section on the Aztecs in the Mesoamerican chapter (Chapter 13).
- All chapters have been updated to include current research and interpretations, as well as many revisions suggested by reviewers.
- New box feature, "Further Reflections," now appears in all chapters except Chapter 1 and the Epilogue. This feature addresses a key topic or concept that is covered in each chapter.
- Detailed sections on early food production were moved from Chapter 5 to the relevant chapters on Europe, North American Southwest, Eastern North America, China, Mesoamerica, and Andean South America.
- Sections on political complexity, including Hawai'i, were moved from first edition Chapter 15 to second edition Chapter 5.
- Topography was added to map figures throughout.

Chapter by Chapter Changes
- **Chapter 1** ("Acquiring and Interpreting Data in Archaeology"):
  - Reworked section on theory in archaeology

- Table added to show examples of theories and the chapters in which the examples are to be found

- **Chapter 2** ("Humanity's Roots"):

  - New opening image

  - Added nonhoning chewing

  - Reduced discussion of *Ardipithecus ramidus* in main text; see "Further Reflections"

  - Added Lomekwian stone tool industry

  - New box: "Further Reflections: The Place of *Ardipithecus ramidus* in Human Evolution"

- **Chapter 3** ("Becoming Human"):

  - Deleted text and image for Movius Line (a concept now widely disputed re its usefulness)

  - Reorganized and rewrote sections on models for the origins of modern humans

  - Added image on Broca's and Wernicke's areas in the brain

  - Added box: "Further Reflections: Was There an Out of Africa Before 1.9 Million Years Ago?"

- **Chapter 4** ("A World of Modern Humans"):

  - New opening image

  - New images for engravings/painting in Upper Paleolithic caves added for Chauvet and for Altamira

  - New image showing Sahul and Sunda added

  - Moved some mentions of sites to endnotes (e.g., el Castillo) and deleted others (Kostenki12, 17, Kents Cavern, Grotta del Cavallo, Pech Merle, Devil's Lair, Allen's Cave, Huon Peninsula, Kara-Bom, Cactus Hill, Dent, Deborah L. Friedkin site, Lindenmeier)

  - Added sites of Madjebebe, Vilakuav, Carpenters Gap, Bluefish Caves, Wally's Beach

  - New box: "Further Reflections: Megafauna in Australia"

- **Chapter 5** ("Hunting, Gathering, Foraging, Farming, and Complexity"):

  - New opening image

  - Added a second example of a Gobekli Tepe carved T-shape pillar

- Added Shubayqa I and its evidence for early flat bread
- As noted above, detailed sections of food production moved to other chapters, except for the discussion of food production and its background in the Levantine part of the Middle East
- Reorganized/rewrote section "Why Food Production?"
- As noted above, sections on complexity including themes and frameworks, as well as the example from Hawai'i) moved from first edition Chapter 15 to this chapter
- New box: "Further Reflections: Thinking About Food Production"

- **Chapter 6** ("Prehistoric Europe North of the Mediterranean"):
  - New chapter to this edition
  - Boxes include:
    - "Timeline: Prehistoric Europe"
    - "Peopling the Past: Building Stonehenge"
    - "Peopling the Past: Bronze Age Elites"
    - "Peopling the Past: Violence, Ritual or Both in the Bronze Age?"
    - "Further Reflections: Characterizing Social and Political" Organization"
  - Topics covered include:
    - Early Holocene Hunter-Gatherer-Foragers (including Ertebølle)
    - Early Food Production (including Cardial Ware, Linear Pottery, Funnel Beaker)
    - Neolithic Megaliths and Other Monument Building
    - Interpretations of Neolithic Megaliths and Other Monuments in Great Britain
    - Bronze Age Europe
    - Iron Age Europe (Halstatt and La Tène)

- **Chapter 7** ("The North American Southwest"):
  - Added some material from first edition Chapter 5 on precursors to food production
  - Deleted sites (Atl Atl Cave)
  - New box: "Further Reflections: Elite Lineage at Pueblo Bonito"

- **Chapter 8** ("Eastern North America"):

  - New opening image

  - Added some material from first edition Chapter 5 on precursors to food production

  - Deleted sites (Turner)

  - New box: "Further Reflections: Cahokia: Paramount Chiefdom or State?"

- **Chapter 9** ("Early Dynastic Mesopotamia"):

  - New opening image

  - Two new images added: aerial view of Ur and a ziggurat

  - New box: "Further Reflections: Archaeology and Politics"

- **Chapter 10** ("Pharaonic State and Old Kingdom Egypt"):

  - New image added: mastaba

  - New box: "Further Reflections: Egypt's Multiple Rises and Falls"

- **Chapter 11** ("Shang China"):

  - Added some material from first edition Chapter 5 on precursors to food production

  - New images: map showing Neolithic culture areas and oracle bone with writing on it

  - Deleted sites (Haojiatai)

  - New box: "Further Reflections: Consolidating the Western Zhou State Identity"

- **Chapter 12** ("The Indus Valley"):

  - New box: "Further Reflections: Importance of Trade and Exchange Networks"

- **Chapter 13** ("Mesoamerica, the Classic Maya, and the Aztec Empire"):

  - Added some material from first edition Chapter 5 on precursors to food production

  - New images added: Monte Albán plaza area, aerial view of Pyramid of the Moon area at Teotihuacan, a *Spondylus* shell, map of the Aztec Empire, part of the Tlateloco market, stylized portray of the Aztec god Huitzilopochtli, altar with skull carvings at Templo Mayor

  - As noted above, a section on the Aztec Empire was added to this chapter, including:

    - The Triple Alliance

- Aztec Trade and Exchange Networks

- Aztec Social Life

- Aztec Religion and Ritual

- Aztec Warfare and Violence

- New box: "Further Reflections: Historical Documents, the Maya, and the Aztecs"

- **Chapter 14** ("Andean South America and the Inka Empire"):

  - Added some material from first edition Chapter 5 on early food production

  - New images added: *Strombus* shell, aerial view of one of the Nazca lines, different example of a khipu

  - New box: "Further Reflections: Challenges to the State/Empire"

- **Chapter 15** ("Mapungubwe and Great Zimbabwe in Africa"):

  - New opening image

  - New box: "Further Reflections: The Bantu Expansion"

- **Epilogue**:

  - Previously appeared as Chapter 15

  - As noted above, sections on political complexity and on Hawai'i were moved to Chapter 5

  - Retained in this epilogue are the sections: "All Good Things Come to an End" and "Lessons from the Past?"

Features and Benefits

In all of the chapters, several sidebar boxes are provided. Every chapter has a timeline box showing the chronology relevant to that chapter. Each, except the last chapter, also has boxes that feature topics related to "The Big Picture" and to "Peopling the Past." These highlight themes such as methods and frameworks, behavioral strategies, stone and other tool traditions, art and ideology, and social life. Given the scope of the topics covered, the themes and boxes of the early chapters (Chapters 1 through 5) are necessarily different from chapter to chapter, as well as different from those in Chapters 6 on. Finally, all chapters except Chapter 1 and the Epilogue have boxes on "Further Reflections." These treat a variety of topics such as chiefdoms, the importance of "international" trade and exchange to early societies, the family structure of elites, and how elites consolidated their power or legitimacy.

To the extent possible, for all chapters beginning with Chapter 6 in Part 3, each case study has the same set of themes. These include Resource Networks, Trade, and Exchange; Social Life; Ritual and Religion; and Warfare and Violence. Many also have The Written Word. Of course, in some cases, evidence is either not available or these societies did not have certain features. For example, we have not yet deciphered the Indus script, and thus there is not a box on the written word in Chapter 11, whereas for the Inka, theirs was a nonwritten word in the form of the khipu. In some instances, other types of themes are then provided, such as Urbanization for the Indus Valley and Oral Traditions for Mapungubwe and Great Zimbabwe.

The main goal in providing similar themes for all the chapters dealing with social complexity and with political complexity is to have a framework making comparisons between the various case studies easier for the reader. In many cases, there also are analogies given to features in the modern world that are similar in some respects to those of these past societies. These provide a direct connection between us and past groups that help show the relevance of archaeology and its evidence.

A Word About Dates

How dates are shown in the archaeological literature can be quite confusing to the nonspecialist. This is because there are differences in the levels of accuracy; for example, some dates are calendar years, whereas others can be expressed in calibrated calendar years, and still others are absolute dates but not at the level of correlation to calendar years. On top of all this is an additional complexity because of the terms that are used. These can include bp or BP (before the present, which is based on AD 1950 as a baseline), bc or BC (before Christ) or BCE (before the Common Era), and AD or CE. As explained in Chapter 1, to the extent possible, dates in this book are shown/used in the following ways. Prehistory prior to 50,000 years ago is referred to using uncalibrated dates, shown as bp (the small letters indicating that they are not calibrated). For the period between 50,000 and 5000, dates are cal BC (calibrated BC) when appropriate (not all types of dates can be calibrated). From about 5000 to the BC/AD boundary, dates are shown as BC. This is because many of them are from early written records and calendars that can be correlated with the calendric system we use today. Rather than using both the cal BC and the BC standards for the same periods of time, I chose to reduce some of the confusion by using BC for this range of time. Finally, dates after the BC/AD boundary are shown as AD. I have chosen not to use the BCE/CE terminology primarily because this is not as familiar to most readers, and it presents some difficulties for earlier prehistory because this terminology is not used by paleoanthropologists.

Acknowledgments

No book can be written without the comments and critique of the experts who serve as reviewers of earlier versions of the manuscript. Certainly this book has greatly benefited from their insights and suggestions. I thank the reviewers, who include Christopher Barrett, Washtenaw Community College; Peter Bogucki, Princeton University; David Carballo, Boston University; Nancy Gonlin, Bellevue College; Margan A. Grover, University of Alaska Anchorage; Diane K. Hanson, University of Alaska Anchorage; Ryan P. Harrod, University of Alaska Anchorage; Sandra Hollimon, Santa Rosa Junior College; John A. Nadolski, Sierra College; Matthew J. Rowe, University of Arizona; Robert Simpkins, Porterville College; Miriam Stark, University of Hawai'i at Mānoa; Fred Valdez Jr., The University of Texas at Austin; and Pamela R. Willoughby, University of Alberta. I also thank Brian Siegel, Furman University, who sent me corrections as he and his students read through the first edition in his class. I have tried to incorporate as many of their ideas as possible within the framework of how this book is structured. I also thank the members of the Plants, Animals, and People group at Penn Museum for several years of interesting articles and discussions, which greatly informed some portions of this book. In particular, my special thanks to Naomi Miller and Katherine Moore. I also thank my current editor Sherith Pankratz and associate editors Meredith Keffer and Grace Li, and all the students in my Becoming Human and Introduction to Archaeology classes over the years. Thinking about how to introduce them, as nonspecialists, to the magnitude of the materials, explanations, and interpretations of the past was a challenging and rewarding task.

1 | The Basics of Archaeology

CHAPTER 1

Acquiring and Interpreting Data in Archaeology

ABOVE: Excavations at Tor at-Tareeq, Jordan, an Epipaleolithic site.

The British novelist Leslie P. Hartley (1895–1972) began his book *The Go-Between*[1] by observing that the human past was a bit like a foreign country where people did not do things in the same way that we do. The past, however, is both more and less than Hartley's remark suggests. It is more because the human past has a much greater time depth, range of cultural behaviors, and geographical extent than any single foreign country. It is less because we cannot directly or completely see the behaviors of the past as we might if we visited a foreign country and observed the culture(s) there. To develop an informed view of humanity's story given that we do not have firsthand observations of past living peoples and cultures, researchers in archaeology and **paleoanthropology** collaborate with specialists of other disciplines such as chronology, economics, **ethnoarchaeology**, **ethnography**, **geoarchaeology**, history, ancient texts, linguistics, **palynology**, materials conservation, **archaeometallurgy**, and **zooarchaeology** (among others) to find sites, retrieve data, analyze data sets, and interpret archaeological sites, cultures, and regions. This chapter discusses how archaeologists accomplish these tasks, all of which help establish our cultural heritage.

Why Archaeology Is Important

Technological advances in the past several decades, especially the Internet, have accustomed us to having nearly instantaneous access to information about almost everything happening in the world, often as it is occurring. We can watch streaming videos, chat online with people from other cultures, retrieve publications, read blogs, and post our own thoughts and images (of course, not everything on the Internet is accurate). Our unprecedented access to detailed information about peoples' activities, thoughts, and lives around the world, however, is recent. The truth is that most of humanity's story, the story of us and our ancestors, is one that took place in the absence of written records either because writing had not yet been invented or because, after the origins of writing, many groups continued to rely on oral traditions (some still do) rather than written accounts. We should not be lulled, however, into thinking that the written record preserves all features of past cultures, because written records (and even oral traditions) often were and are selective in what they record. Many of the earliest instances of writing, for example, are economic transactions, religious texts, stories of the lives of elite rulers, calendars, or recipes rather than accounts of the activities of everyday people.

Archaeology is the bridge we use to better understand the story of all humanity, both in remote periods and in relatively recent ones, because archaeology has methodologies and theories that focus on acquiring and interpreting evidence with the greatest precision and latitude possible. This evidence can include fossils of human ancestors, stone and metal tools, whole and broken pottery, animal bones, structures, grave goods, plant remains, historical documents, and a host of other cultural and natural materials found at archaeological sites and in the landscapes in which they are situated. The importance of archaeology is that it opens a window into our past by allowing us to collect data, record their precise context, and relate these data to each other at a particular site and to data from other sites of the same and

Paleoanthropology the study of human cultural and biological evolution by archaeologists and biological anthropologists; this term is commonly applied to biological anthropologists studying early hominin fossils.

Ethnoarchaeology a discipline that uses the study of the behaviors of living people to better understand past patterns in the use of cultural materials, site organization, and settlement systems.

Ethnography a subfield of cultural anthropology in which living people are studied using firsthand observation.

Geoarchaeology specialty in which geological analyses are used to aid in the interpretation of archaeological sites, such as the role of natural processes in how site layers form and of the formation of landscapes.

Palynology specialty that focuses on the study of plant pollen to better understand past environments, human impact on environments, human diet, and climate change.

Archaeometallurgy this archaeological specialty concerns the study of how metals were produced and used in the past.

Zooarchaeology the study of animal bones found at archaeological sites. Zooarchaeologists identify the types of animals and their uses to gain information about human behaviors.

different time periods and geographical regions. All of this information is used to examine and interpret the decisions and processes that transformed our ancestors' lives and activities.

Survey and Excavation Methods

One of the basic truths in archaeology is that context is everything. A painted Greek vase might be a beautiful object bringing a viewer aesthetic pleasure. Even a stone tool, such as a spear point, or a fossilized human bone might be an interesting object. But if we do not know its context, that is, not only the site where it was found but also its location within a site, its relationship to other cultural and natural materials found at that site, and whether it was a surface find or was recorded during excavation, it has lost most of its value in helping us understand the past. Precise recording of all information about context is of utmost importance, and archaeology uses many techniques to achieve this goal.[2] All of this is set within research designs that frame the choice of methods, techniques, and multidisciplinary studies for each archaeological project.

Research Design

The set of methods and ideas that archaeologists use in their survey and excavation projects is called a research design. It is based on research questions specific to a given project. We might be interested, for example, in gaining a better understanding of how and why early humans migrated out of Africa, what processes changed hunter–gatherer–forager decisions about what to eat into food-production ways of life in China, or how political organization influenced the types of sites and their distribution in the landscape in Mesoamerica. There are hundreds or thousands of questions that we have about the past, but it is not enough to simply have a question. The research designs that archaeologists use provide frameworks for investigating these questions.

In a research design, questions are placed within a theoretical perspective (read "Theories and Interpretations") that, along with the question, guides the choice of sites, relevant data sets, and methods. In some cases, a research question will help define which areas of the world might be most appropriate for certain types of archaeological research. An obvious case is a research question about the origins of modern humans, which we know from genetic and fossil information is in Africa. Other types of research questions can be investigated in more than one geographical area, for instance, the origins of food-production economies that occurred independently in at least nine world regions (the Middle East, South Asia, China, Southeast Asia, New Guinea, South America, Central America, North America, and Africa).

Whether we conduct investigations at a single site or multiple sites is also a research design choice. Excavations at a single site allow us to examine long-term processes, such as changes in political structure and regional power for a particular city, such as Tikal in Guatemala (see Chapter 13). In other cases, we might need to examine multiple sites to gain a better understanding of how people organized their activities across a landscape. One example of this strategy is research in Chaco Canyon in the North American Southwest, where detailed studies document the timing of the construction of the Great Houses (large pueblos), the import of turquoise and marine shells, and the persistence of many small pueblos (see Chapter 7). All of this work draws on archaeological information previously known about an issue, a time period, and a geographical region.

Although archaeologists carefully collect a variety of information from sites and landscapes, some types of data are more relevant to specific research questions within a research design. If we are investigating the origins of food production, for example, we will be especially interested in recovering evidence for past plant use, changes in human impact on local habitats, and a transition from mobile to settled lifestyles and providing accurate dating. Similarly, if we are examining the origins of modern human behavior, we will find materials likely associated with symbolism (a key characteristic of our behavior today) and innovation (early art, the first bone tools, novel technologies such as spear throwers) to be highly relevant in the interpretation of these origins. In some cases, the data archaeologists collect are used to test assumptions of the research question (read "Theories and Interpretations").

Finding and Recording Sites

Archaeologists often are asked how they find sites, especially those without large, obvious structures such as pyramids, mounds, or standing stones. The most common method is pedestrian survey. The size and scope of these surveys varies, depending on the research questions. A pedestrian survey involves a team of people who space themselves at equal distance intervals; for example, each person is spaced 5 meters (15 feet; many archaeologists use the metric system rather than inches and feet) from the next person. As they walk, they examine the surface and surrounding areas for artifacts (stone tools, broken pottery) and structures (read "The Big Picture: Archaeological Survey in Practice"). This technique is easiest in dry environments with little vegetation to obscure the region surveyed. When archaeologists survey in heavily vegetated areas, they modify their surveys to include methods such as shovel probes, which are small pits dug in the ground at evenly spaced intervals. Shovel probe pits allow them to "see" below vegetation covering the ground surface. Each pedestrian survey records information about the location, artifacts, features, and structures found.

Archaeological sites also can be located using aerial photographs, **remote sensing**, infrared photography, historical documents, and talking to landowners and hikers, as well as sites found during construction and farming. Past human impact on the land, for example, often is easily seen in photographs. An aerial photograph taken from a hot air balloon or a low-flying airplane or drone can reveal former agricultural fields or construction efforts (house foundations or hunting structures that

Remote Sensing uses technology such as satellite images, ground-penetrating radar, and LiDAR (light detection and ranging) to aid in the location of archaeological sites and buried or vegetation covered features of sites.

Archaeological Survey in Practice

Traditional pedestrian surveys focus on locating and recording archaeological sites. The types of sites found and their locations are a guide to long-term processes that affected how people organized their activities. These processes include changes in climate, availability of water, the distribution of wild animals and wild plant foods, erosion of land surfaces and down-cutting by streams, decreased soil fertility resulting from sustained agriculture, and development of political or religious centers. Traditional surveys by **Cultural Resource Management (CRM)** teams on the Goldwater Range in southwestern Arizona, for example, helped indicate how land use patterns shifted from the Archaic to the Hohokam periods (see Chapter 7) based on where sites were found and what types of sites were present (Figure 1.1).

Nonsite pedestrian surveys record sites and cultural materials in the areas between sites.[3] This aids in understanding all the places that people used, including locales that were visited briefly. There are a number of ways to sample nonsite areas. The Abydos Survey for Paleolithic Sites in Middle Egypt, for instance, collected information every 100 meters (300 feet) using a standardized collection area (a 1-meter-radius (3.2 feet) circle). Every sample

FIGURE 1.1
Pedestrian site survey in the North American Southwest.

location was recorded with a Global Positioning System (GPS) unit and cultural artifacts (or their absence) in the circles were recorded in a database in a small handheld computer. All stone artifacts were analyzed for type, form, and length while in the field (Figure 1.2). The Egyptian high desert landscape examined by the Abydos Survey for Paleolithic Sites mostly yields Middle Stone Age artifacts, but earlier periods such as the Acheulian also are present. The combination of data on artifact types and GPS locations allows us to create Geographic Information Systems (GIS) layers, for example, the distribution of the Acheulian compared to sites and samples from other time periods (Figure 1.3).

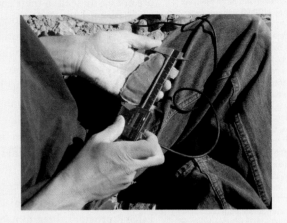

FIGURE 1.2
Using digital calipers to record the dimensions of a stone artifact on the Abydos Survey for Paleolithic Sites, Egypt.

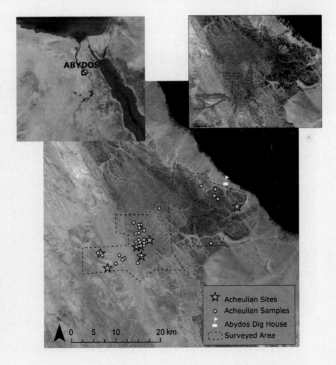

FIGURE 1.3
Data from the Abydos Survey for Paleolithic Sites in Egypt. *Top left*: location of the project area; *top right*: all sites (*red*) and samples (*green*) recorded during the surveys; bottom: the landscape distribution of the Acheulian sites and samples in the areas surveyed.

Cultural Resource Management (CRM) archaeologists who work in the field of CRM have projects that are based on recovering data about areas that will be impacted by new construction or otherwise potentially destroyed. Federal or state-owned lands, as well as federally funded projects, are subject to a number of laws, regulations, and reporting requirements.

UTM Coordinates Universal Transverse Mercator (UTM) coordinates are Easting and Northing numbers that are based on a system of metric grid cells that divide the world. Each Easting and Northing set of coordinates provides an extremely specific geographical location.

Total Station equipment that combines a theodolite (which measures vertical and horizontal angles) with an electronic distance meter (EDM). The EDM uses a laser beam to measure the distance from the total station to an object or point (where a prism is placed). The angles and distance are used to calculate x, y, and z coordinates (Cartesian coordinates) for each point.

Datum a reference point on the ground with known spatial coordinates, sometimes calculated as Easting (x) and Northing (y), as well as elevation (z). One or more datums are established at archaeological sites and used to set up site grids and for precision location measurement of artifacts, animal bones, structures, features, and samples found during excavation at a site, as well as for archaeological survey.

are not easily seen in their entirety while on the ground) (Figure 1.4). Remote sensing techniques, such as ground-penetrating radar and magnetometers, offer ways to see below the surface. Ground-penetrating radar, for example, sends radio pulses into the ground. These pulses bounce back when they encounter changes such as walls of structures, pits, or variations in the type of sediment. The recorded pulses also indicate the depth of the change based on the time it takes the pulse to leave and return. These data can be used to make maps of things not visible on the surface.[4] Magnetometers operate on a similar principle; they measure subtle changes in the magnetic field below ground surface. These subtle changes are caused by the presence of features (buried hearths, ditches, and walls). Heavy vegetation can cover structures and features at archaeological sites, making them difficult to find using pedestrian surveys. A new laser-based remote sensing technology called LiDAR (light detection and ranging) allows archaeologists to "see through" heavy vegetation cover (Figure 1.5).[5] LiDAR provides three-dimensional (3D) images (with x, y, and z coordinates; read "Excavating Sites") of the landscape taken from the air.[6] All changes in the topography or terrain can be seen and identified; one example is the recent discovery of thousands of additional structures near Tikal in Mesoamerica (see Chapter 13).[7]

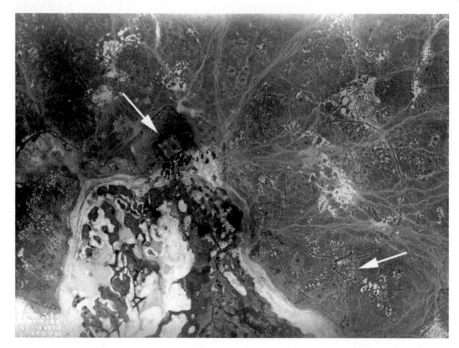

FIGURE 1.4
Use of aerial photography shows features not easily seen at ground level. The structure in the lower right (*lower arrow*) is a desert "kite" site, a type of hunting structure. The black rectangle in the upper left (*upper arrow*) is the Azraq Castle, Jordan (1920s aerial view) (arrows added to original image and input levels modified).

When archaeological sites are found, their location is recorded using GPS units that calculate the longitude, latitude, and elevation (or alternatively, the **UTM coordinates** and elevation). These data can be manually or digitally plotted on topographic maps as well. But a site's location is only one aspect of its context. Most archaeologists also record information about the type of site (stone artifact scatter, broken pottery vessel, cave, dwelling), the kinds and amounts of artifacts present, site size, types of structures (if present), distance to the nearest water source, potential for buried archaeological deposits, and placement (hilltop, floodplain, river bank, or canyon). Most sites and samples of representative artifacts and structures are photographed. Exceptional sites can be revisited and mapped using a **total station**. Digitally plotted sites and other relevant aspects, such as artifact types, can be incorporated into GIS programs, which allow a researcher to examine things such as the distribution of a particular type of artifact and site placement to see whether there might be patterning and how this could be behaviorally interpreted.

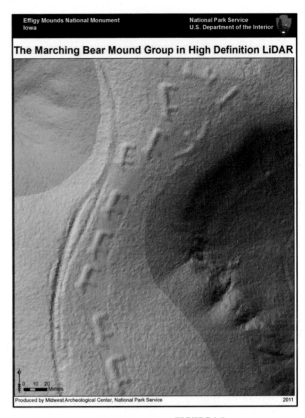

Effigy Mounds National Monument
Iowa

National Park Service
U.S. Department of the Interior

The Marching Bear Mound Group in High Definition LiDAR

0 10 20 Meters

Produced by Midwest Archeological Center, National Park Service   2011

FIGURE 1.5
Use of LiDAR, a remote sensing technique based on laser light analysis, to map a mound site in Iowa in the United States.

Excavating Sites

Once sites with potential for buried deposits are located, one or more that likely can help answer questions in the research design are chosen for excavation. Maintaining precise control over context is just as important in excavations as it is in surveys.[8] The most basic strategy used by archaeologists is to establish two or more **datums** that are used to create a grid over the site. The grid consists of equal-size units, for example, 1 meter by 1 meter (3 feet by 3 feet); each unit has a name.[9] Based on their location at the site and relationship to each other and to structures and features (if present), certain units are chosen for excavation. Alternatively, some archaeologists who work at complex sites with numerous structures and features may choose to excavate mainly within structures and features, each of which has a designated name, for example, Structure 1 or Courtyard 5. These types of sites also use a systematic method of creating units for excavation within rooms, structures, and features.

Although grid systems can be established using a variety of instruments, many archaeologists today use a total station and associated computer software.[10] Most archaeologists prefer to work with positive rather than negative numbers (coordinates). This means that the entire site must be situated within the upper right section of a **Cartesian coordinate system** (Figure 1.6). One advantage of using a total station and its GIS software is that the total station calculates its exact coordinates and elevation every day based on its position relative to the site datums.

Cartesian Coordinate System
a three-dimensional grid system in which horizontal axes (x and y) are combined with a vertical axis (z) to calculate the position of any given point. Each axis is perpendicular to the others. At archaeological sites, the x grid axis often corresponds to north–south and the y grid axis represents east–west. The z-grid axis is the elevation of each point.

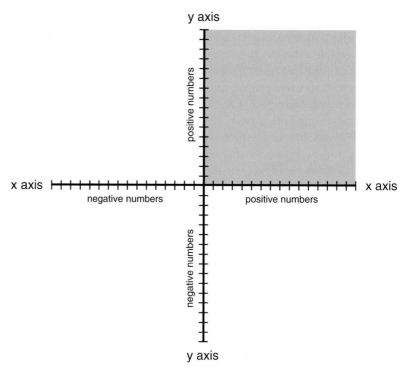

FIGURE 1.6
A Cartesian coordinate system. Archaeologists prefer to use positive numbers to name their grid units. Thus, site datums and the units at the site will be situated in the upper right (*green*) quadrant. Often, the *x* axis reflects W–E and the *y* axis S–N directions.

Stratigraphy the layers or levels at an archaeological site. These can be defined as natural (geological) or cultural and can be used as a relative dating technique in which cultural materials found in deeper levels or layers are older than those in overlying levels or layers.

The grid system establishes a two-dimensional (2D; *x* and *y* coordinates) plan of the site, but in digging a site, we also need a third dimension, the elevation (*z* coordinate). These are used in mapping the structures and features and recording levels (**stratigraphy**) and depth of artifacts and samples we collect while excavating. Although a total station can be used to determine the exact *x*, *y*, and *z* coordinates (called piece-plotting or point proveniencing) of specific artifacts and samples, archaeologists also designate levels, layers, or loci with which the piece-plotted artifacts and samples are associated. Some archaeologists who work at complex sites use a system in which different contexts are given different locus designations, A hearth might be Locus 2, for instance, whereas the sediment below it is called Locus 3, and the wall of the structure in which the hearth is located is called Locus 1.[11] These techniques allow archaeologists to control contextual data in ways that are useful for interpreting activities at sites and sequences in which structures at sites were built and added to during the occupation of the site (read "The Big Picture: Archaeological Excavation in Practice").

The Big Picture

Archaeological Excavation in Practice

The Western Highlands Early Epipaleolithic Project is investigating how hunter–gatherer–foragers used landscape resources in the millennia before the origins of food production economies in the Middle East. One of the sites is a small rockshelter (KPS-75) in west-central Jordan. We established datums and a grid system of 1-meter by 1-meter (3.2 feet by 3.2 feet) units with a total station (Figure 1.7). To gain perspective on the distribution of activities at the site, the units excavated represent contexts inside the rockshelter (N4), immediately in front of the rockshelter (K7, K9, K10, L11, L12, M9, and M10), and downslope (H9) (Figure 1.8).

Crew members excavated with trowels in increments of 3 centimeters within natural levels in 50-centimeter by 50-centimeter quads of each 1-meter by 1-meter unit. In some units, we point provenienced each stone artifact and animal bone larger than 2.5 centimeters with the total station, as well as each bucket of sediment from each 3-centimeter

FIGURE 1.7
Using a total station to record x, y, and z coordinates at site KPS-75, Jordan.

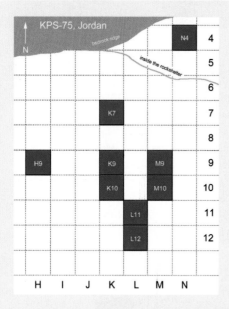

FIGURE 1.8
An example of an alphanumeric grid system. Excavated units are shown in blue, and the grid is in 1-meter increments.

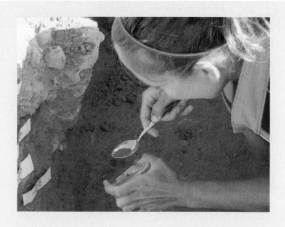

FIGURE 1.9
Collecting a sediment sample for phytolith extraction from the profile of an excavation unit at site KPS-75, Jordan.

increment within each unit quad. In other units, cultural materials from each 3-centimeter increment in each quad were recovered only from each point-provenienced bucket. The sediment from each bucket was screened to recover small artifacts and animal bones. We also collected sediment samples from every natural level in each unit (Figure 1.9); these are processed and analyzed for pollen, phytoliths, and macrobotanical remains.

Point proveniencing allows us to closely examine the distribution of cultural materials across the site and in the different natural levels. This aids in the interpretation of site activities as well as in changes over time. We analyzed more than 94,600 stone artifacts and found, for example, that the way that people made small stone tools called microliths shifted over time. This may be related to changes in hunting equipment and the types of animals pursued by these hunter–gatherer–foragers. Changes in hunting patterns also may have affected the extent to which wild plant foods were collected.

Spit a term used by some archaeologists to describe an excavation unit that has an arbitrarily assigned specific depth and size.

Microfauna this term refers to small animals such as mice, moles, and snails; these small animals are sensitive to changes in local temperature and moisture and thus are valuable indicators of paleoenvironments.

Unless a site is covered by sterile sediment (no cultural materials), most excavation proceeds slowly and carefully using small tools such as masons' trowels, spoons, and dental picks, as well as brushes and a bucket to collect the sediment from each context (a level, layer, locus, or **spit**). In nearly all cases, all the sediment removed from a particular context has a context identification tag and is sieved through small mesh screens. This allows archaeologists to collect many extremely small materials, such as **microfauna**, small beads, and tiny stone artifacts. Many projects also recover small materials using wet screening, in which the sediment in a fine mesh screen is processed by running water through it, making it easier to see artifacts and other materials.

Excavating a site is not only about finding and recording cultural materials, structures, and features. Archaeologists also collect many types of samples that aid in interpreting sites. Some of these are sediment samples that are processed for environmental information (palynology), evidence of plant use (**phytoliths**, **macrobotanical remains**), and sediment-formation processes (geoarchaeology, **geochemistry**) that can be used to understand how a site became a site (**site taphonomy**) and where certain types of activities might have occurred (for example, where domestic animals were corralled). Other useful samples include materials such as charcoal that will provide dates (see "How Old Is It?").

Multidisciplinary Data Sets

Archaeological sites have the potential to yield a diversity of data sets, although for a variety of reasons, not every site produces every type of information theoretically possible. Most sites, however, do contain multiple kinds of cultural and natural data. The best way to investigate, analyze, and interpret these data sets is for archaeologists to work with other archaeologists and with specialists from several other disciplines. This is known as a **multidisciplinary approach**.

Cultural materials from sites can include chipped stone artifacts, ground stone implements, broken or complete pottery, tools of bone or metal, figurines, ancient texts, art, sculpture, textiles, and personal ornamentation. The list is nearly endless, although organic materials often do not preserve over long periods of time (see "Theories and Interpretations"). To this list we can add hearths, roasting pits, ovens, and kilns, as well as burials, mounds, dwellings, storage rooms, courtyards, roads, temples, palaces, and pyramids. All of these were made by our ancestors, and many require special processing and analytical skill sets that aid in their interpretation.

Archaeologists often specialize in certain types of cultural materials. We might, for example, focus on how to classify and interpret stone artifacts or ceramic types and designs or metal tools and ornaments. Each category of cultural material also can be analyzed in much greater detail by specialists in other fields. The edges of stone artifacts, for instance, can be studied for residues such as phytoliths or blood, resulting in a better understanding of the tasks for which specific stone artifacts were used. An analysis of the chemical properties of the clay and temper (materials such as crushed shell, organic fibers, and crushed stone added to clay to keep vessels from breaking during firing) used in ceramics can help us understand the techniques people used to make their pottery and whether certain styles were imported or were locally made copies. At complex sites with many structures, archaeologists work with architects to better understand the sequence of building and rebuilding, as well as structure design. To decipher textual materials, we collaborate with specialists in ancient written languages such as Egyptian hieroglyphs, Sumerian cuneiform, or Maya glyphs.

Phytoliths microscopic plant parts composed of silica or calcium oxalate that have shapes and sizes specific to particular plants; they usually preserve well and can lend insight into plant use, plant foods, and local environments at archaeological sites.

Macrobotanical Remains plant remains that are sometimes recovered from archaeological sites. They can include seeds and wood charcoal and are useful in reconstructing plant use (including plant foods) by earlier people, as well as aspects of local environments.

Geochemistry specialty in which researchers study the chemical composition of artifacts, sediments, and bones as well as participate in laboratory analyses to determine the absolute age of sites.

Site Taphonomy the natural and cultural processes that affect archaeological sites. Natural processes include the actions of animals who might consume animal bones left at a site, the effects of rain and sun on exposed archaeological materials, and erosion. Cultural processes include pit digging by later occupants at a site, reuse of stone artifacts left at a site, and modern-day looting.

Multidisciplinary Approach to interpret the cultural materials and natural features of archaeological sites, site taphonomy, and landscapes, archaeologists collaborate with specialists within archaeology (phytolith researchers, zooarchaeologists, archaeometallurgists, and geoarchaeologists), as well as specialists from other disciplines (architects, materials conservators, geochemists, ethnographers, and chronology laboratories).

Many cultural materials are fragile, especially organics such as wood and textiles. These require the specialized skills of conservators to stabilize and preserve them.

Some types of evidence from archaeological sites were not made by people but are the result of their activities. This includes animal bone (**fauna**), plant assemblages (macrobotanical remains), and phytoliths. Zooarchaeologists specialize in studying the fauna and identify the types of animals, birds, rodents, and reptiles present. They also examine animal bone for burning, traces of use such as polish, cut marks from butchery, and whether some bone was modified into tools. Some of these researchers specialize in identifying fish scales or types of shellfish. Zooarchaeological analyses help determine whether people hunted wild animals or had domesticated stock, whether they focused on animal meat or also processed animal bones for nutrient-rich marrow, and to what extent past groups captured game that required innovative technologies such as traps and snares or made use of freshwater or marine food resources. Similarly, the careful study of macrobotanical remains by archaeobotanists helps archaeologists develop a better understanding of the types of plant foods (wild or domesticated), possible medicinal plants, and plant resources (such as reeds and rushes for bedding, roofing, and basketry) that people exploited. Other evidence for past plant use comes from the study of phytoliths that are extracted from sediment samples or are found on the edges of stone artifacts or on the surface of grinding tools.

Occasionally, archaeological sites contain human bones. Depending on the site type and its age, these can be fossils of early human ancestors or burials of more recent people, and there are many ethical considerations when human bones are found (see "Who Owns the Past?"). Although archaeologists can investigate how people were buried and the distribution of graves at a site, the study of the actual bones is done by specialists in biological anthropology or in **bioarchaeology**. Fossils of early human ancestors before 30,000 years ago tend to be examined and interpreted by paleoanthropologists. Such fossils are rare and often broken into many small pieces. They can require removal of the blocks of sediment in which they are buried and careful excavation in laboratory settings, as well as technical cleaning and reconstruction. Studies of the shape of the bones and other features help identify which group of fossils they represent, for instance, Neandertals versus early modern humans. Human bones found in more recent periods are studied by bioarchaeologists. They identify the age and sex of the human bones; health issues, including diseases; muscular stresses on bones that suggest activity patterns (such as postures used during the hand grinding of grains); prehistoric diet and nutrition; and how and when cavities in teeth became common. Additionally, geneticists sometimes can extract DNA from bone samples; these analyses have provided insights into the relationship of Neandertals to modern humans, as well as into prehistoric migrations such as the peopling of the Americas.

Information about past environments (**paleoenvironments**) also is the result of specialized analyses. Certain large animals, for example, reindeer, indicate that climatic conditions were relatively cold. Our most detailed interpretation of paleoenvironments, however, comes from sources such as microfauna (small rodents and certain tiny snails), which are extremely sensitive to small changes in temperature and moisture regimes, and from the study of pollen (palynology). Palynologists extract

Fauna terrestrial and marine animals, birds, fish, reptiles and amphibians, as well as shellfish and microfauna.

Bioarchaeology specialists in this discipline examine human bones to identify features of individuals and populations. These include health, age, sex, habitual activities, height, diet, and nutrition.

Paleoenvironment the types of environments and habitats characteristic of regions during the past; these developed because of changes in climate, as well as human manipulation of vegetation and animal communities.

pollen grains deposited by plants from site sediment samples. These grains can only be seen with a microscope. Each type of plant produces distinctively shaped and textured pollen grains, which the palynologist uses to determine whether a landscape was forested or open and whether the vegetation cover consisted of plants typical of dry/cool, wet/warm, dry/warm, or wet/cool climatic conditions. In some cases, the types of pollen grains present might suggest that domesticated crops were being grown.

Archaeologists also work with geoarchaeologists who investigate how sediments were deposited at a site, the microscopic characteristics of site sediments (composition and geochemistry), and the formation of the landscape in which a site is located. Geoarchaeological analyses are especially helpful for understanding how sites form and what happens to the sediments at sites over time (site taphonomy), in addition to determining whether some sites or site types have been removed as a result of erosion or other geological processes. Geoarchaeologists also locate prehistoric water sources such as ancient springs and lakes and can determine how river channels have changed over time.

A multidisciplinary approach allows archaeologists to collaborate with a variety of specialists to obtain more comprehensive information about cultural and natural materials present at sites and the activities they represent, understand site distribution across landscapes, and examine site and landscape formation processes. These studies are complemented by specialist data on paleoenvironment and paleoclimate, as well as techniques used to obtain dates for site occupations (see "How Old Is It?").

How Old Is It?

Establishing when occupations at sites occurred is a key component in developing an understanding of social and political organization, the distribution of activities and sites, and the types of cultural materials specific to different time periods, as well as for creating a timeline for the story of our past. Most of us today, however, rarely spend more than a moment thinking about today's date, not only because we have instant access to that information via the Internet or our cell phones but also because we are accustomed to written calendars. Several early complex societies, such as the Maya of Mesoamerica, also had calendric systems. But these types of records do not have great antiquity when we consider that humans and their ancestors have a history and prehistory that stretches back in time some 7 million years.

Relative Dating Methods

Until the twentieth century, archaeologists could date sites and site occupations only using **relative dating** methods (except for some sites for which written records exist, such as ancient Egypt). Relative dating does not provide a calendar year date but aids in building sequences of "older than" or "younger than." The two most common relative dating methods are stratigraphy and **seriation**. Stratigraphy works on a general principle similar to creating a layer cake; the bottom layer is the oldest (the first one deposited) and layers on top of it are progressively younger (Figure 1.10).

Relative dating dating techniques that provide a sequence of "older" and "younger" rather than calendar dates; examples include stratigraphy and seriation

Seriation a relative dating method in which the frequency of artifact types or styles is used to construct a chronology of "older than" or "younger than" based on the popularity of types or styles over time

FIGURE 1.10
Stratigraphic layers at Tor at-Tareeq, Jordan.

By examining cultural materials contained in the different layers of a sequence of layers at a site, archaeologists build a relative chronology of which materials are older or younger than other types of materials. This relative chronology can be used across several different sites as long as each one contains at least a portion of the same sequence (Figure 1.11). One of the most basic of these sequences was called the Three Age System, which noted that tools were first made of stone, then bronze, and then iron.[12] There are some issues with these types of sequences, however, particularly those impacted by site taphonomy (see "Theories and Interpretations").

Seriation works in a way similar to stratigraphy but is based on the popularity of artifact styles over time. If we look at mechanical instruments for writing, for example, we see that manual typewriters, once invented, increased in quantity (popularity) as more and more people used them. The invention of the electric typewriter had an impact on the popularity of manual typewriters, the use of which declined as electric typewriters became the standard. The popularity of electric typewriters then declined when word-processing programs on computers linked to printers became available. Each artifact style thus has a pattern of initial low frequency, followed by a period of peak popularity, which in turn is followed by a return to low frequency or disappearance (Figure 1.12). The beginning and end points of these popularity curves must be anchored in time, which can be done by looking at their position in various stratigraphic sequences.

Absolute Dating methods of obtaining calendar dates for archaeological sites or fossil finds, including dendrochronology, radiocarbon dating, thermoluminescence, optically stimulated luminescence, and potassium–argon dating.

Absolute Dating Methods

Although relative dating methods helped establish temporal sequences, they were (and are) less than satisfying because we had to make educated guesses about the true age of a site. The advent of **absolute dating** methods, which yield dates in years, showed that many of the early educated guesses about the chronology of particular sites and prehistoric cultures were off by thousands or tens of thousands of years. There are now a diverse set of absolute dating methods that archaeologists use, and the choice of which of these is best depends on the types of materials recovered from sites or the near vicinity of sites, as well as how old the site is initially thought to be.

The most precise of these absolute dating methods is **dendrochronology**, which was developed in the early part of the twentieth century by researchers working in the North American Southwest. Dendrochronology, often called tree-ring dating, is based on the principle that trees add a yearly growth ring that varies in thickness depending on whether the year was dry (thin ring) or wet (thicker ring) and that certain types of trees (such as bristlecone pine) more consistently add yearly growth rings. The sequence of thin and thick rings forms a distinctive pattern that can be traced from living trees (for which a known calendar year sequence can be calculated) and matched using overlaps in the pattern to ring sequences in logs used in the construction of ancient structures within certain regions (Figure 1.13). Because the sequence begins with a known calendar year and each growth ring equals one year, the tree-ring sequence is equivalent to a yearly calendar from which the date of cutting a log to be used in building a prehistoric structure can be calculated (see "Pithouse to Pueblo Transition" in Chapter 7 for an example).[13] Dendrochronological sequences, based on certain species of oak trees, also have been developed for parts of Europe.

Dendrochronological dating can be highly accurate, but there are two main drawbacks. First, this dating method can only be used in a small number of world regions and only at those sites with wooden timbers. Second, the sequence is not long, extending only some 8,700 to just more than 12,000 years in the past.[14]

Another absolute dating method used to obtain age ranges for archaeological sites is **archaeomagnetism**. This technique is based on the fact that the earth's magnetic field changes over time. Heating of a fixed feature, such as a clay-lined hearth, to about 650–700°C (1202–1292°F) will align the iron particles in the clay to the position of the magnetic north pole at the time of the firing. Once the orientation of the iron particles

FIGURE 1.11
Example of horizontally laid stratigraphy at the site of Laugerie Haute, France.

Dendrochronology an absolute dating method that provides calendar year dates based on the analysis of tree-ring sequences of thicker and thinner annual growth rings; used in parts of Europe and in the American Southwest, but only extends back in time some 8,700 to 12,000 years.

Archaeomagnetism an absolute dating method that uses variation in the position of the Earth's magnetic pole over time. The orientation of the iron particles in a feature such as a clay-lined hearth align to the magnetic north pole when heated. This orientation is compared to a magnetic north pole sequence to determine an age for the firing of the feature. This technique can be used for sites that are younger than 10,000 years old.

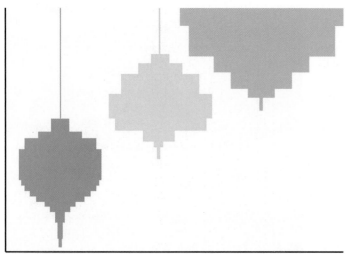

is known, it can be matched to a sequence showing where the magnetic pole was at different points in time. This technique can be quite useful for some sites that are 10,000 years or less in age. Magnetic reversals from the North Pole to the South Pole and back again also have occurred over much greater periods of time. These types of magnetic reversals (or **paleomagnetism**) can be used to date ancient sites prior to 780,000 years ago, when the last major reversal happened (Dmanisi in Chapter 3 is an example).

Several other absolute dating methods are **radiometric techniques**. These are based on the principle that certain

FIGURE 1.12
Example of seriation showing the origins of a technology or style, its peak popularity, and its decline as newer technologies or styles replace it. In this case, manual and electric typewriters continue to be used on rare occasions, although most people now use computer printers and word processing programs.

Paleomagnetism this type of absolute dating technique uses reversals in the magnetic pole of the earth; that is, at some points in time the South Pole was the magnetic pole, whereas at other times, such as today, the North Pole is the magnetic pole. The alignment of magnetic particles in rock can be measured to examine where the magnetic pole was at the time that the layer was deposited. This technique is useful for sites dating to 780,000 years ago and older.

Radiometric Techniques dating techniques that use the principle of a known rate of decay of specific radioactive isotopes into stable isotopes over time; examples include radiocarbon dating and potassium–argon dating.

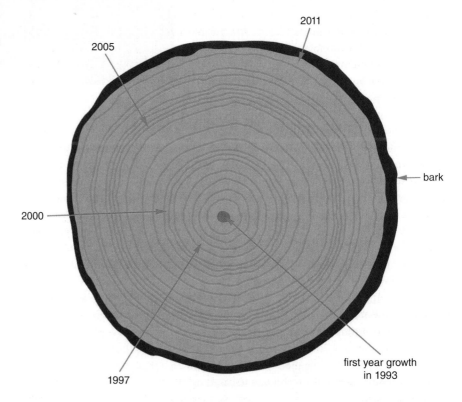

FIGURE 1.13
Example of a tree-ring sequence with one growth ring added each year. Wide tree rings indicate wet years and narrow tree rings show dry years.

radioactive elements have a known rate of decay over time into stable elements. The rate of decay is called a half-life, because half of the radioactive elements will decay into nonradioactive elements within a set interval of time. Each radioactive element has a different half-life. Radiometric techniques yield dates that are associated with a standard deviation. We might get a date, for example, of 10,000 ± 35 years ago. This means that the actual date of the site has a 68% chance of being within one standard deviation (35 years), so within the range of 10,035 to 9,065 years ago, and a 95% chance (two standard deviations or 70 years) of being within the range of 10,070 to 9,030 years ago.

The radiometric technique most people have heard about is **radiocarbon dating** (^{14}C dating). This method uses organic samples, such as wood charcoal, charred seeds, animal bone collagen, shell, or textiles. The major assumption of radiocarbon dating is that while any organism (people, plants, animals) is alive, it contains a ratio of the radioactive isotope, ^{14}C, to stable ^{12}C and ^{13}C isotopes in a proportion that mirrors the frequency of ^{14}C to ^{12}C/^{13}C present in the earth's atmosphere at that time. When an organism dies, it no longer ingests or absorbs ^{14}C and the existing ^{14}C in the organism begins to decay. Organic samples are processed by dating laboratories, where the amount of ^{14}C in a sample is measured. The less ^{14}C there is, the older the sample, and the actual date is the result of calculating how many half-lives have occurred since that organism died. Radiocarbon dating is effective for sites between 400 and 50,000 years ago (many sites have been dated using radiocarbon, see, for example, Chapters 4 and 5)[15].

Another radiometric technique is **potassium–argon dating** (K/Ar), which is useful for dating sites and geological formations that are from 100,000 to tens and hundreds of millions of years ago. The ^{40}K isotope is incorporated into molten rock, and when the rock cools, ^{40}K begins to decay into the stable ^{40}Ar (argon) isotope. Potassium–argon thus is used to date inorganic materials, especially volcanic rocks such as lavas and tuffs, and has been especially useful in providing a chronological framework for the early ancestors of humans (Olduvai Gorge in Chapter 2 is an example). These volcanic beds lie below and above archaeological sites. The sites therefore are bracketed to the time period between the dates of the under- and overlying volcanic beds. Like radiocarbon dating, potassium–argon dates are shown with a standard deviation.

Dates also can be obtained from absolute dating techniques such as **thermoluminescence dating** (TL). This method uses the measurement of light produced by electrons that are trapped in fired ceramics or burned chipped stone artifacts. TL works on the principle that when ceramics or chipped stone artifacts were fired/burned in the past, the "clock" was set to zero because heating to a sufficient temperature releases the trapped electrons in these materials. From that point on, new electrons from ionizing radiation in the sediment surrounding a ceramic or burned chipped stone artifact become trapped in these materials. The TL technique takes these materials and reheats them to release the trapped electrons and measure how much light is emitted. Special devices called dosimeters are placed in a site to measure the ionizing radiation present in the sediment. This information is used in the formula to work out the age of the ceramic or burned chipped stone artifact (when it was fired or burned). TL dating is useful for sites up to about a million years ago (Jebel Irhoud and Schöningen are examples in Chapter 3).

Radiocarbon Dating an absolute dating method that uses the decay rate of the radioactive isotope carbon-14 (^{14}C) to calculate the age of organic materials found at archaeological sites. It can be used to date materials from the past 50,000 years. Because of fluctuations in the amount of ^{14}C in the earth's atmosphere over time, radiocarbon dates must be calibrated (adjusted) to obtain the actual date of a sample.

Potassium–Argon Dating a radiometric dating technique that provides absolute dates based on the half-life decay rate of the radioactive isotope ^{40}K (potassium) into the nonradioactive isotope ^{40}Ar (argon); used in dating inorganic materials such as lava flows or tuff beds in the period from 100,000 years ago to hundreds of millions of years ago.

Thermoluminescence Dating an absolute dating technique that uses the principle of when a stone tool or a piece of pottery was last exposed to heating. Heating releases trapped electrons (light) and sets the clock to zero. After the heating event, ionizing radiation in the sediment of a site bombards the stone artifact or ceramic and electrons begin to accumulate in those pieces. In the laboratory, the electrons can be released as light and measured and then used to calculate when in time that piece was last heated.

Optically Stimulated Luminescence Dating an absolute dating technique in which quartz or feldspar grains are extracted from sediment samples from sites and subjected to laboratory treatment that releases light trapped in these grains. The emitted light, which accumulated from ionizing radiation in the sediment, is measured and used in calculating the last time the grains were exposed to sunlight. The accumulated light represents the period of time since the grains were buried.

Optically stimulated luminescence dating (OSL) also uses light from trapped electrons to calculate age. In this case, single grains of quartz/feldspar from sediment samples are the dated material. When the grains are exposed to sunlight during the site occupation, trapped electrons are released. This sets the OSL clock to zero. Once the grain is buried, it begins to accumulate electrons from ionizing radiation in the surrounding sediment. In the laboratory the light from trapped electrons is released by bombarding a sample with blue or green light. The light emitted by the trapped electrons is measured and used in formulas to calculate the last time that the grain was exposed to sunlight and thus the age of the sediment from that occupation at a site (Pinnacle Point 13B in Chapter 3 is an example). Like TL, OSL is appropriate for sites up to around a million years ago, and both TL and OSL dates have standard deviations (Figure 1.14).

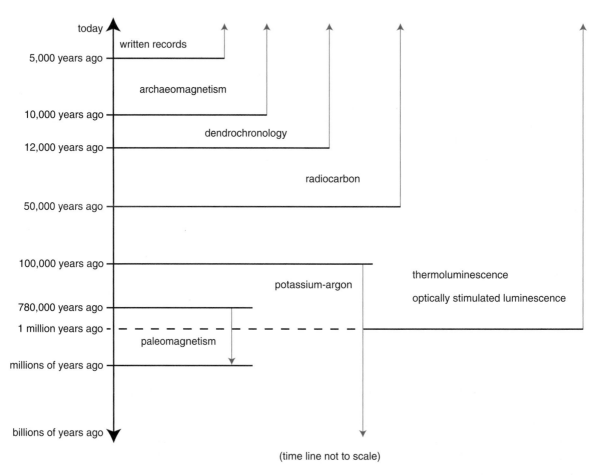

FIGURE 1.14
The range of time that can be dated by each of the absolute dating techniques.

Time Scales in Dating

Absolute dating methods allow archaeologists and others to place sites, artifacts, fossils of human ancestors, and many other finds and behaviors into a time scale. Although this appears to be relatively straightforward, there are several ways of referring to time scales that can seem a bit confusing. The one time scale that everyone knows is the system of AD and BC, which refer to Jesus Christ—AD is *anno Domini* (in the year of our Lord) and BC is before Christ. Some researchers who study the origins of politically complex societies, such as Mesopotamia, prefer to use terms that are not based on a religious figure. In this case, their time scale uses the abbreviations of CE (Common Era) and BCE (Before the Common Era). Essentially, AD = CE and BC = BCE. In this book, we will not use the CE/BCE terms.

For time periods before calendars, the time scales can be shown in BC (or bc) and BP (or bp). In many publications, using capitalized abbreviations means that the dates have been calibrated[16] or can be assigned based on historical sources such as early written documents. As noted previously, the term BP/bp means "before the present" and often is interchangeably used with the phrase "years ago." We know that it is not currently possible to calibrate dates older than 50,000 years ago. This means that archaeologists do not use BC/bc to refer to those time periods but instead use bp or years ago. The BP/bp term is based on assigning a time that is calculated from the baseline date of AD 1950; in other words, AD 1950 is considered the "present." Thus, the time scales that use BC/bc are offset from those using BP/bp by 1,950 years. A date of 10,000 BC, for example, translates into a date of 11,950 BP.

In this book, we will use time scale abbreviations as follows:

- Years ago and bp to refer to uncalibrated periods of time before 50,000 years;

- cal BC (calibrated BC) for the period between 50,000 and 5000 years ago, although not all dates can be calibrated and so those will be referred to as years ago;

- BC for the period between 5000 years ago and the start of the AD calendar;

- AD in the same way that many of us use it today.

Theories and Interpretations

Archaeologists, working with specialists from a variety of disciplines, collect and analyze a wide diversity of data. How we interpret these data depends on our specific research questions and on the theoretical viewpoint that guides our research (see Table 1.1 for examples). Prior to the mid-twentieth century, archaeology was concerned largely with data collection and the description of culture history, rather than explanations for the processes that led to change over time[17] (read "Timeline: The Development of Archaeology"). Since then, several different explanatory theories have been

TABLE 1.1.

Several examples of theoretical frameworks for interpreting the archaeological record.

THEORETICAL FRAMEWORK	CHAPTER	EXAMPLE
Agency	Chapter 5	Kamehameha I's social and political organization
Agency	Chapter 9	Abandonment of Late Archaic period mounds
Agency	Chapter 13	Farmers' role in decline of Harappan
Darwinian Archaeology	Chapter 4	Upper Paleolithic art as communication
Ecological Archaeology	Chapter 5	Younger Dryas theory
Ecodynamics	Chapter 5	Agriculture variables in pre-Contact Hawai'i
Gender Archaeology	Chapter 4	Interpretation of Upper Paleolithic "Venus" figurines
Human Behavioral Ecology	Chapter 5	Eastern North American small seeds use
Human Behavioral Ecology	Chapter 7	Archaic period use of wild vs. domesticated plants
Landscape Archaeology	Chapter 6	Interpretations of the Neolithic landscape in Britain
Networks and Boundaries	Chapter 5	King vs. commoner in Shang China
Niche Construction Theory	Chapter 5	Niche construction theory section and box
Postprocessual Archaeology (cognitive archaeology)	Chapter 15	Oral history–based interpretation of the Great Enclosure at Great Zimbabwe
Processual Archaeology (scientific method)	Chapter 13	Destruction vs. continuity in the Harappan
Scientific Method (biology)	Chapter 3	Peopling the Past: Genetics, Neandertals, and Modern Humans

used by archaeologists. Some of these are briefly examined here and will be seen in action in the chapters that follow.

Understanding the combination of peoples' available technologies, their population size and density (demography), the economic decisions they made in exploiting food resources (subsistence), and how they organized their activities across the landscape (settlement pattern) was the basis of an **ecological archaeology** approach proposed in the 1930s.[18] This perspective recognized that the archaeological record had great potential for examining long-term processes. The decisions that groups made about their settlement, economic, and technological strategies, which were partially responses to their ecological situations, formed a powerful explanatory approach for examining why things change.[19] Considering aspects of ecology continues to play an important role in many explanatory frameworks today (see Table 1.1 for an example).

Ecological Archaeology a theoretical perspective developed in the 1930s to interpret long-term cultural changes in how people responded socially, economically, and technologically to local ecology and changes in local ecology.

By the 1960s, a number of archaeologists came to believe that explanations in archaeology should be amenable to rigorous testing, similar to the hard sciences such as physics or mathematics.[20] This approach is called **processual archaeology** (or New Archaeology), and the use of **scientific method** is an important component. Scientific method involves observations and the creation of hypotheses (ideas) and test assumptions (expected outcomes) based on those observations. The data from the archaeological record are used to assess whether the test assumptions can be falsified. Because the test assumptions can be examined many times with different archaeological data sets, the use of scientific method should lead to refinement of hypotheses so that they more accurately reflect the actual processes leading to change in the past (see Table 1.1 for an example). Ecological aspects have been important in processual archaeology, in particular, the idea that past societies and cultures were systems of interrelated causes and effects. Climate change, for example, creates changes in vegetation that influence gathering and harvesting decisions. These decisions, in turn, affect how people distribute themselves across the landscape, the size and density of population that can be maintained, and the technologies that are subsequently developed.[21] Although the original systems approach is no longer a dominant aspect of processual archaeology, the notion of function (cultural practices develop to serve practical goals) remains important.

The framework of **Darwinian archaeology** (evolutionary archaeology) incorporates the principles of Darwinian evolution (such as natural selection and genetic drift) and applies them to the evolution of cultures.[22] Traits of cultural materials that are functionally beneficial are positively selected because they enhance reproductive success and thus persist (at least for some time) in the archaeological record (see Table 1.1 for an example). Darwinian archaeology does not give much emphasis to cultural influences, such as ideas, or individuals.

Another evolutionary approach, but without the emphasis on Darwinian evolution, is the theories and models offered by **human behavioral ecology** (see Table 1.1 for examples). Many of these focus on costs and benefits as calculated in energy expended versus energy gained. They include prey-choice models, in which decisions are made about which food resources can be most efficiently collected so that the maximum amount of energy is gained. Another human behavioral ecology model is central place foraging, in which round-trip travel costs to resources and back to a home base carrying those resources affect hunter–gatherer–forager decisions about which resources to target. In this case, it may be more efficient to partially process foods before carrying them back to a base camp (for example, shelling nuts so that only the nut meat is carried back). These types of models are used to develop explanations of diversity in human behavior in time and space (see Table 1.1 for an example).[23]

Niche construction theory also is an evolutionary approach adopted from biology.[24] It differs from human behavioral ecology because it treats humans as active in shaping the landscape around them, rather than simply responding to environmental and other changes. Humans manipulate features of the landscape to create a niche (or habitat) in which they can successfully survive. One example of this is when hunter–gatherer–foragers deliberately set fires that burn off the groundcover vegetation. This clearing of

Processual Archaeology a theoretical perspective that uses social, economic, and environmental dynamics to interpret cultural changes over time; it is based on the use of scientific methodology.

Scientific Method the process of gathering information (through observation or experimentation) and using this information to create and test hypotheses (ideas); testing hypotheses allows new information to be added and facilitates corrections that need to be made to the hypotheses.

Darwinian Archaeology (evolutionary archaeology) a theoretical perspective that interprets changes in cultures over time as the result of evolutionary processes, such as natural selection, known from biological evolution.

Human Behavioral Ecology a set of theoretical models, based in ecology, that uses human decisions about resources (including food) and resource use to examine diversity in cultures across geographic space and through time.

Niche Construction Theory the idea that humans actively change or manipulate features of the landscape around them and resources in those landscapes in ways that build a niche or habitat in which they can be successful over long periods of time. It incorporates evolutionary ideas from biology and applies them to humans.

Timeline: The Development of Archaeology

Today:	Broad acceptance by many archaeologists that a variety of theories and approaches can be used to understand the past; availability of numerous absolute dating methods (e.g., ^{14}C, K/Ar, TL, OSL) and technologies (computers, total stations, digital/other types of photography, GPS, GIS).
AD 1980s:	The advent of postprocessual archaeology, which stresses the role of ideas, the actions of individuals, the uniqueness of each past culture or society, and the influence of one's own cultural viewpoint on interpretations of the past.
AD 1960s:	The advent of processual archaeology (new archaeology), with its emphases on explanation (rather than just description), theory, general laws or rules of behavior, and scientific method.
Mid-AD 1900s:	Multidisciplinary archaeological projects become more common; radiocarbon dating is developed.
Early/mid-AD 1900s:	Research is aimed at establishing chronological sequences for different past cultures and societies and at describing these cultures and societies; emphasis is on explaining change over time as the result of migration and the spread of ideas (diffusion); development of dendrochronology.
Late AD 1800s:	The study of living peoples (ethnography), especially those with non-Western technologies, is used as a starting point for understanding peoples of the past; methodical techniques of scientifically excavating sites are developed.
Mid-AD 1800s:	Modern archaeology begins; the great antiquity of the human past is recognized based on observations from geology and the association of stone artifacts with the bones of extinct animals.
AD 1830s:	The Danish researcher, C. J. Thomsen, establishes the Three Age System (Stone Age, Bronze Age, and Iron Age).
AD 1700s:	First excavations, including Pompeii, and the first scientific excavation is performed by Thomas Jefferson in Virginia in AD 1784; he tests ideas about who constructed the earthen mounds found in many parts of the North American Southeast and Midwest.
AD 1500–1700:	Archaeological artifacts and other curious objects are randomly collected and displayed in "cabinets of curiosities." Antiquarians focus on reconstructing ancient life based on artifacts.
Prior to AD 1500:	Various people and groups are interested in their origins as known from oral and, more rarely, written accounts; ancient artifacts sometimes are collected and examined.

the ground promotes the growth of certain plant species that are more attractive as food to game animals, thus increasing the density of animals in these areas and offering more opportunities for successful hunting (see also an example in Table 1.1). Bodies of theory such as human behavioral ecology and niche construction theory exemplify a key goal of processual archaeology, which is to discover general rules and actions that characterize human behavior and to do so in ways that can be tested (scientific method).

For other archaeologists, the sets of generalized rules and the emphasis on ecology and the concept of efficiency (optimization) that characterize processual archaeology are limited because they do not take into account the role that ideas and beliefs have in influencing social–cultural activities and change. By the 1990s, several archaeologists developed a **postprocessual archaeology** approach. This theoretical perspective is interested in the specific history of cultures in the past (see Table 1.1 for an example). It also places more emphasis on the role of symbols and meaning in prehistoric societies, is less interested in scientific method, and believes that our interpretations of the past are not free of our own cultural values.[25] Postprocessual archaeologists argue that there is no single explanation for understanding a particular past society or culture but that multiple interpretations and approaches can best aid in gaining insight into the past. Among the many approaches are agency, landscape archaeology, and gender archaeology.

Postprocessual Archaeology a theoretical perspective that emphasizes the study of particular cultures and their histories, especially the role of ideology and the actions of individuals; it does not stress the use of scientific method.

Agency considers the role that people, as agents, played in deliberately shaping social organization and social change because of the choices they made (see Table 1.1 for examples).[26] There are several approaches within the theoretical framework of agency. In some cases, it is the actions of groups of people (based on social class or gender) that result in how social identity is created. In other cases, the actions of individuals whose life experiences intersect with the larger social processes of their groups allow us to glimpse how the individual is both affected by and affects others. In still other cases, the actions of individuals in attempting to gain social power or prestige, or alternatively, to resist those attempting that gain, produce unforeseen changes in society.

Agency a theoretical perspective that discusses the role of the individual in shaping change in cultures and societies.

In contemporary **landscape archaeology**, the landscape, as well as how it is used, is seen as shaped by the social and symbolic perspectives that people used to create meaning in the world around them; places are culturally meaningful (see an example in Table 1.1).[27] Landscape is not just the physical landscape but the importance that groups of people attached to places and things and the role these places and things played in constructing how people saw the world around them and interacted with it. There is thus a significant cognitive dimension that shaped the perception of the landscape at any given moment in time and the notion that people are active agents. The landscape archaeology theoretical framework can involve studies of settlement (ecology, land use, change over time, and occupations of places), social landscapes, ideological landscapes, and the distribution of archaeological materials across the landscape (a combination of information from sites and nonsites).

Landscape Archaeology a theoretical perspective that uses features of the natural landscape in combination with the placement of archaeological sites and the cultural materials at those sites to better understand potential cultural meanings, symbolism, and ritual in past societies.

In **gender archaeology**, archaeological data can be used to examine which past activities were linked to women as opposed to men, how the role of women was perceived in society, and what these findings mean for gender relations (for an example,

Gender Archaeology a theoretical perspective that examines the roles of women, men, and other genders, as well as their relationships, in prehistory.

see Table 1.1).[28] While gender archaeology has always been associated with the perspective of feminism, its theoretical framework goes beyond examining just women to encompass gender roles that are not those simply of biological male and female (for example, gay, lesbian, and queer studies). Gender archaeology examines social identities in past societies through the study of material culture (the archaeological record) but understands that the social identity of people is not based only on their gender. Instead, it is a complex mix of several variables, for example, sex, status, age, and ethnicity.

It is important to recognize, however, that many archaeologists do not fall squarely into processual or postprocessual archaeology but incorporate aspects of both of these major perspectives into their research.[29] A modern approach using ecology as one aspect, for example, is **ecodynamics**, which focuses on the interplay between the actions of humans and the environment using a complex web of interactions.[30] These include social processes (such as technology or ideology), ecological dimensions (such as changes in population size and density or the relationship between animals and those who prey on them), and nature (such as changes in climate and composition of habitats). One important feature of ecodynamics is that it does not present the story of people as linear but instead as changes that can fluctuate in many directions over time (see Table 1.1 for an example).

Another example of the melding of some aspects of processual and postprocessual ideas is the theoretical framework of **networks and boundaries**. These concepts are useful in the study of the rise of early politically complex polities (see Table 1.1 for an example).[31] The networks might involve power and authority among elites, whereas the boundaries were created by how people conceptualized their political identity or community. At their simplest, networks are much as we think of them today, that is, alliances that individuals make with each other. In the past, such alliances were based on gift exchanges, marriages, shared rituals, and other social mechanisms. Boundaries, on the other hand, relate to how people see themselves as allied to particular groupings within society. This is a feature of our society today, for example, in the contrast between membership in a family (a small bounded grouping) versus membership in a political party (a larger bounded grouping). Some members of a family might be Democrats, others Republicans, and others Independents, but all are members of the same biological family. The power of this theoretical approach is that is shows us that societal groupings and alliances are dynamic and that they are flexible.

Regardless of whether an archaeologist is mainly processual or postprocessual, some aspects of the archaeological record affect their explanations and interpretations equally. Two of the most significant of these data issues are organic preservation and site taphonomy.

We know that certain types of materials, such as stone artifacts and ceramics, are more durable than others because they are inorganic and thus are preserved over long periods of time. Organic preservation, however, is variable, which means that a vast amount of cultural materials and constructions do not survive to be excavated and recorded by archaeologists. The best situations for organic preservation are contexts that are extremely dry (deserts) or extremely cold (permafrost and high altitudes) and

Ecodynamics a theoretical framework that combines social behaviors and natural landscape factors (soil fertility, rainfall, etc.) to understand the processes that led to the development of politically complex societies.

Networks and Boundaries a theoretical framework that examines how networks of power and authority are developed and maintained in complex political societies. These networks integrate with how people create boundaries for their community and political identities.

those that are very wet and lack oxygen (peat bogs; see Schöningen in Chapter 3). In each of these situations, organic materials do not decay as much or as rapidly as they do when exposed to soil acidity (which destroys bone and wood) or microorganisms such as bacteria (which destroy skin and hair). Examples of good organic preservation include the so-called "bog people" who were sacrificed in Europe and preserved in peat bogs, sandals made of plant fibers in the dry North American Southwest (see Chapter 8), and mummies of children in the Andes Mountains preserved due to very cold conditions (see Chapter 14). These exceptional preservation conditions are relatively rare when considered against the long time depth of the archaeological record and against the many places where archaeological remains are found. The rarity of organics means that many things that are valuable data for understanding the past are not available to archaeologists. They include wooden tools and containers, clothing, basketry, cordage, animal hides, seeds, and some types of writing materials (such as papyrus). Even animal and human bone can be rare at archaeological sites.

Aside from issues of organic preservation, the vast majority of archaeological sites are not perfectly preserved snapshots of the past. They are not versions of Pompeii, where a rapid disaster captured a moment in time and preserved it relatively faithfully. Instead, a variety of natural and cultural processes affect the formation of sites (site taphonomy) and therefore our explanations and interpretations of the behaviors represented at those sites. Natural formation processes include burial of sites, erosion, water flow, rodent burrowing, sediment movement, and preservation contexts that do or do not lead to the survival of organic materials. Through careful survey and excavation methodology, we might find, for example, that artifacts at a site have been moved from their original locations by the action of slow-moving water (sheet wash or a gently flowing stream). The distribution of the artifacts thus tells us more about natural processes affecting the site than about activity locales because the artifacts are no longer in situ (in place). Similarly, cultural formation processes—the actions of people both in the past and today—also affect what is found and its distribution at sites. Cultural formation processes consist of a variety of behaviors such as the original activities that deposited cultural materials at a site, digging of pits by later site inhabitants into older archaeological levels for storage or burial, tearing down and rebuilding dwellings and other structures, deliberate burning of sites, and looting and vandalism. Archaeologists must consider all these factors when examining data from sites so that the resulting explanations and interpretations of past behaviors are not based on inaccurate information.

Who Owns the Past?

The archaeological record is our primary source for data relevant to humanity's story, and, at a general level, it belongs to all of us.[32] Many people enjoy exploring cultural heritage—locally, regionally, and globally—by watching documentaries, visiting archaeological sites, reading newspaper and journal articles as well as books, attending public and professional lectures, experiencing museum exhibitions, volunteering on archaeological projects and in museums, and sometimes donating money to support conservation of archaeological sites and their cultural materials.

Because they study humanity's past, archaeologists in particular have an ethical responsibility regarding cultural heritage. Unlike so many portrayals of archaeologists in movies (for example, the Indiana Jones Hollywood series) and other media, we do not search for treasures but instead (as discussed above) focus on recording all the contexts for all materials recovered from archaeological sites. In many cases, the ethical responsibilities of archaeologists include working with conservators and other specialists to help preserve sites that are damaged or deteriorating, establishing protections (such as fencing and legislation) for sites; engaging in discussions with the public about the importance, significance, and protection of cultural heritage; and working closely with native communities to ensure that their concerns are incorporated into surveys, excavations, and presentations of archaeological information from their regions.

Cultural heritage often is thought of as the record of the ancestors of particular groups of people—"our" ancestors. These groups range in size from entire nations to local indigenous (native) communities. At the scale of nations (defined by modern political boundaries), cultural heritage of the archaeological record has been used for many purposes, including tourism, national pride, and various political goals. It is not difficult to find examples of cultural heritage used for tourism—the pyramids at Giza in Egypt, Colonial Williamsburg in the United States, the Parthenon in Greece, Machu Picchu in Peru, the Great Wall of China, and Petra in Jordan.[33] These places also are instances of national pride in the achievements of one's ancestors. And, of course, there are political undercurrents in issues of national pride. The modern country of Zimbabwe, for example, takes its name from one of its greatest archaeological sites, Great Zimbabwe, and the Zimbabwe Culture (see Chapter 15). But during its British colonial period, when it was known as Southern Rhodesia, the cultural heritage of the region, including Great Zimbabwe, was wrongfully attributed to outsiders such as the Phoenicians, Arabs, and the Queen of Sheba (!). These denials of indigenous achievements were political propaganda used by those in power, although archaeological work at Great Zimbabwe in the early 1900s demonstrated that Great Zimbabwe was indigenous. It took many decades until independence was achieved (in 1980) and the cultural heritage of the region could be reclaimed and used to name a new nation.

At the scale of local indigenous communities, cultural heritage also is used to serve many goals. Sometimes these are similar to those of nations—tourism, pride in ancestry, and political. Often, indigenous communities, drawing on a wealth of oral traditions, have interpretations of their past that can differ, for a variety of reasons, from those potentially offered by "outsider" archaeologists. It is easy to see how these differences can sometimes escalate into issues, whether between indigenous communities and archaeologists or between archaeologists themselves.[34] Fortunately, the value of indigenous knowledge, including knowledge about the past, is widely recognized today, and many indigenous communities are actively engaged in archaeology to pursue research about the past[35] (read "Peopling the Past: Indigenous Archaeology"). In some cases, the long-term continuity of indigenous communities within regions and maintenance of many of their traditions means that use of the landscape, identification of special features and sacred places, methods used to extract resources, and aspects of their oral traditions help create a better interpretive bridge to the past. In the North American Southwest, for example, I excavated at a site with a special type of pithouse often interpreted as a kiva (ritual space). As we excavated the kiva, we saw that the bench was painted—dark along the lower portion but with a lighter colored upper panel. In that upper panel were a number of motifs, including a humpbacked figure holding something to its mouth (Figure 1.15). The site is in a region occupied by ancestors of the Hopi and other Puebloan peoples, and it may be that the motif represents the Hopi figure commonly known as a kokopele (see Chapter 7). Although we must be careful about assuming that today's meanings of motifs are exactly the same as those of the past, without information from Hopi oral traditions, it would be impossible to know what this motif might have meant or what its role in social traditions might have been for the people who built and lived at this site in the AD 1200s.

FIGURE 1.15
Probable kokopele images from the LA 17360 site (Ancestral Pueblo), New Mexico. Note the humpbacked complete figure on the right.

Many countries today have laws and regulations that are intended to help protect and preserve cultural heritage. In the United States, for example, there are a series of federal laws including the American Antiquities Act of 1906, the Archaeological and Historic Preservation Act of 1974, the Archaeological Resources Protection Act of 1979, and the National Historic Preservation Act of 1966 (amended in 2000), and each state has a State Historic Preservation Office that oversees compliance with federal and state laws on lands that are state or federally owned or for any project that requires a federal permit.[36] Perhaps one of the most important federal laws, however, is the 1990 Native American Graves Protection and Repatriation Act.[37] This legislation requires consultation with Native American and Native Hawaiian groups about human remains, grave

Peopling the Past

Indigenous Archaeology

The field of **indigenous archaeology** combines archaeological methods and theories with the value and knowledge sets, as well as the concerns, of indigenous communities whose ancestors built on, lived in, and used various places in the landscape.[38] Its most fundamental principles are the recognition that understanding the past is greatly enhanced when it is possible to collaborate and consult with native groups and that the sovereignty of native peoples must be respected when considering the study of cultural materials from their past. One example of this process is from North Hālawa Valley on the island of O'ahu in Hawai'i.[39] This valley contains many sites with house and agricultural terraces, as well as a few *heiau* (temples) and other ritual structures. A Native Hawaiian group, the Women of Hale o Papa, occupied one region of the valley where a *heiau* for women had been recorded. During their stay, they identified several important features near this site that had not been recognized by archaeologists. Many of these features are natural formations, but they hold special significance because of their forms, their *mana* (spirit), and their proximity to the *heiau*. This type of traditional knowledge would not be available to non-Native Hawaiians, including the many archaeologists who worked in the valley. Additionally, the Women of Hale o Papa provided an interpretation for some of the petroglyphs on a boulder near the *heiau* (Figure 1.16). The figures have triangular-shape bodies and bowed legs, which may represent a birthing position and thus a link to the women's *heiau* at the site.[40]

FIGURE 1.16
Petroglyphs of figures with triangular-shape bodies and bowed legs on a boulder near a heiau in North Hālawa Valley, O'ahu, Hawai'i. Note the necklace at the top, left as an offering.

goods, objects of cultural patrimony (items that have continuing importance in the traditions and history of a group, such as ceremonial masks), and sacred objects that are uncovered during excavations on federal and tribal lands, as well as objects and human remains in museum collections. The act creates a mechanism for native groups to present claims, for the claims to be evaluated, and for these human remains and cultural materials to be repatriated (returned) to the affiliated claimant groups.

On the international level, the General Conference of UNESCO adopted the Convention Concerning the Protection of World Cultural and Natural Heritage in 1972.[41] Countries that sign the convention agree to identify and conserve cultural and natural heritage sites; 193 countries had signed as of January 2017. The cultural and natural heritage sites are considered to have universal significance and, as of 2018, there are 1,073 of these sites on the World Heritage List, including Stonehenge (United Kingdom), Swartkrans (South Africa), the Kremlin and Red Square (Russia), Machu Picchu (Peru), Troy (Turkey), Teotihuacán (Mexico), Great Zimbabwe (Zimbabwe), the Great Wall (China), the Taj Mahal (India), and the Statue of Liberty (United States).

Despite the laws, rules, and conventions to safeguard cultural heritage, its destruction occurs far too frequently. In the early days of the recent war in Iraq, for example, more than 12,000 archaeological sites were impacted by looting, and the National Museum of Iraq in Baghdad was stripped of many of its archaeological materials by looters, who stole these objects to sell them. Despite international efforts to track the stolen items, about half were still missing in 2010.[42] Another example is the destruction of the sixth-century monumental standing Buddha statues in the Bamiyan Valley of Afghanistan. These were dynamited by the Taliban in 2001, who considered the statues idols and thus un-Islamic. Looting and vandalism of cultural heritage does not always make the news but is a serious problem worldwide, and it is important that everyone be concerned about protecting, preserving, and conserving archaeological sites. In many cases looting occurs because archaeological materials can be (illegally) sold, and various people dig holes in sites to find objects they believe have monetary value. When these types of activities occur, they result in the loss of vital information about the past because they destroy not only sites but also context for the objects. The destruction of cultural heritage matters to everyone, no matter which country they live in or whose specific cultural heritage is at stake, because each archaeological site (and region) is a nonrenewable resource and a piece of the story of all humanity. There are many lessons we can learn from these pieces of the past, for example, knowledge of traditional agricultural techniques lost long ago but useful again today, or how to plan sustainable cities that can house large numbers of people (see the Epilogue).

Summary

- The methods and theories used in archaeology provide a bridge to understanding the past.

- Archaeological research is guided by research designs that organize the research questions and methods within a theoretical framework.

- Context is a key concept in archaeology because it allows us to precisely place cultural materials, animal bone assemblages, activities, sites, and many other data sets both temporally and spatially. Archaeologists record context in 3D space (x, y, and z coordinates) using technologies such as GPS and total stations.

- Understanding site taphonomy, which is the set of natural and cultural processes that occur during site formation, is critical to developing accurate interpretations of past activities.

- Archaeology is multidisciplinary, and researchers work with specialists in fields such as geology, palynology, bioarchaeology, paleoanthropology, ancient texts, archaeometallurgy, and zooarchaeology, among many others.

- Sites and the materials they contain can be dated with one or more techniques. Relative dating methods include stratigraphy and seriation. Absolute dating methods include calendars and other written records, dendrochronology, radiocarbon, archaeomagnetism, thermoluminescence, optically stimulated luminescence, paleomagnetism, and potassium–argon.

- Archaeologists often use theories originally developed in other disciplines such as biology, ecology, social sciences, and the humanities. Examples of theories include Darwinian archaeology, gender archaeology, human behavioral ecology, agency, ecological archaeology, niche construction, landscape archaeology, ecodynamics, and networks and boundaries. Some of these theories are sometimes grouped into either processual or postprocessual archaeology. Processual archaeology uses scientific method, whereas postprocessual archaeology stresses the influence of the actions and ideas of past peoples on their behaviors.

- The archaeological record represents the cultural heritage of all peoples, past and present. Cultural heritage can be used in many ways, including telling the story of the past history and prehistory of particular groups of people or nations, as well as for tourism. Although there are international agreements plus many cultural heritage laws and regulations in different countries, unfortunately, cultural heritage is not always preserved because of looting and other types of vandalism.

Endnotes

1. Published in 1953.
2. Burke, Smith, and Zimmerman 2008, Hester et al. 2008, and Stewart 2010 give detailed descriptions of archaeological field methods.
3. Other methods include patch-based surveys which are useful in documenting archaeological materials in disturbed contexts such as plowed fields (Snitker et al. 2018).
4. Valdés and Kaplan 2000.
5. Chase et al. 2012.
6. Carter et al. 2016; Gheyle et al. 2018.
7. https://globalnews.ca/tag/mayan-heritage-and-nature-foundation/ (accessed June 11, 2018).
8. See Endnote 2.
9. The name of a unit can be the coordinates of one of the corners; for example, we might use the SW corner of each unit as its name, such as N90, E90 (north and east often are used as the point name because of grid orientation to the north and the fact that the site is situated in the positive [upper right] section of a Cartesian grid system; see Glossary). Alternatively, the total station can keep track of the north and east coordinates, and we can use an alphanumeric system in which grid columns are alphabet letters and grid rows are numeric. In this system, for instance, a unit name could be A10 or D25 (see Figure 1.8).
10. See, for example, McPherron and Dibble 2001.
11. Harris 1989.
12. The Three Age System was published by C. J. Thomsen in 1836 (in Danish) and in English in 1948 as *A Guide to Northern Antiquities.*
13. This method is not as clear-cut as simply counting the rings to arrive at a calendar year. There are various issues (such as when a year is so dry that no annual growth ring is present) that must be worked out, and dendrochronologists must cross-date a sample by comparing it with many other samples from a region (Douglass 1941).
14. Ferguson and Graybill 1983; Friedrich et al. 2004.
15. There are complications in radiocarbon dating, including correcting site organic sample exposure for the radioactivity released into the atmosphere by atomic bomb explosions during World War II and cosmic ray bombardment and the atmospheric effects of the Industrial Revolution in the AD 1800s. Another major consideration is that we now know that the ratio of ^{14}C to $^{12}C/^{13}C$ in the earth's atmosphere has fluctuated over time, which means that a radiocarbon date must be calibrated (corrected) to adjust for the actual calendar year. If the date is not calibrated, the result potentially is wrong by hundreds or a few thousand years. Calibration of radiocarbon dates was initially done using dendrochronology where tree-ring years could be calculated for given rings; the rings were then subjected to radiocarbon dating. This process allowed researchers to develop formulas to correct for ^{14}C fluctuation. More recently, calibration of radiocarbon dates has been extended further into the past (to 50,000 years ago) using methods such as marine sediment varve (layer) counting, glacial ice varves, and uranium–thorium dated corals (Reimer et al. 2013). Dates often are shown in years before the present (using AD 1950 as the baseline). Years before the present are conventionally abbreviated to bp and now cal BP (meaning calibrated BP). It is also possible to calculate and calibrate the dates and express them as cal BC.
16. See Endnote 15.
17. Trigger 2006: 211–313.
18. Steward and Setzler 1938.
19. Steward 1937.
20. For example, Binford 1968, 2001.
21. See, for example, Flannery 1968.
22. Dunnell 1980; Leonard 2001.
23. See articles in Kennett and Winterhalder 2006; Winterhalder and Smith 2000.
24. Zeder 2012: 258.
25. Hodder 1991, 2001.
26. DeMarrais and Earle 2017; Dobres and Robb 2000; Dornan 2002.
27. Anscheutz et al. 2001; Ashmore and Knapp 1999.
28. For example, Arnold 1991; Crown 2000; Geller 2009; Meskell 1999.

29. Hegemon 2003.

30. Fitzhugh et al. 2019.

31. Campbell 2009.

32. See Sabloff 2008.

33. See, for example, Special Issue: Archaeology and Heritage Tourism 2005, *The SAA Archaeological Record*.

34. See, for example, the recent exchange among "outsider" archaeologists about the intellectual role of indigenous interpretations in McGhee (2008, 2010), and the several articles in the Forum section of *American Antiquity* (2010). See also the statement by the Society for Hawaiian Archaeology concerning the special relationship of Native Hawaiians to the archaeological record of the Hawaiian Islands: http://hawaiianarchaeology.org/about-us/ethical-guidelines/ (accessed June 11, 2018).

35. See, for example, Colwell-Chanthaphonh and Ferguson 2007; Dongoske et al. 2000; Grier and Shaver 2008; Preucel and Cipolla 2008; Whiteley 2002.

36. Antiquities Act Centennial Section 2006; see also http://www.nps.gov/history/laws.htm (accessed June 11, 2018) for the federal antiquities acts. State laws can be found on most state websites, for example, for Pennsylvania: http://www.phmc.pa.gov/Preservation/About/Pages/Laws-Regulations.aspx (accessed June 11, 2018).

37. See http://www.nps.gov/nagpra/ (accessed June 11, 2018) for information about this significant federal legislation.

38. Colwell-Chanthaphonh and Ferguson 2007; Nicholas 2008: 1660; Watkins 2000.

39. For discussion on archaeological consultation and collaboration with Native Hawaiians, see the articles in the two special sections of the *SAA Archaeological Record* 2013: 13(1) and 13(2) on Native Hawaiian Perspectives on Archaeology, especially Cachola-Abad 2013 and Uyeoka 2013.

40. Klieger et al. 1998.

41. http://whc.unesco.org/en/conventiontext/ (accessed June 11, 2018).

42. Rothfield 2009; Wegener 2010.

2

Prehistory Before Political Complexity

CHAPTER 2

Humanity's Roots

ABOVE: Olduvai Gorge in Tanzania (Africa), a region that has yielded early hominin fossils and Early Stone Age stone artifacts.

Humanity's story begins 6 or 7 million years ago in Africa, some 3 million years or more before evidence of stone tool use is found. The earliest of the potential human ancestors, whom we know from fragmentary fossils and partial skeletons, were discovered in South, East, and Central Africa. They share a number of skeletal traits with us, some of which are discussed in this chapter. These human ancestors are all extinct, but if we were able to see any of them in life, they would seem much removed from how we look today and from the types of behaviors that we recognize as cultural. The activities that some of these early human ancestors engaged in, however, led to the use of new ecological niches and innovations in ways to extract food resources. It helped that they were quite intelligent, with relatively large-size and complex brains compared to many other mammals. In fact, we might say that their intelligence, like ours today, is one type of evolutionary adaptation that in certain contexts is quite successful. Intelligence can aid in survival and in reproduction so that the genes involved in higher intelligence and other related features are passed on through the generations.[1]

A Word about Classification

Researchers are interested in establishing the relationships between various types of things, including humans and their ancestors. One common way to accomplish this is to use a **taxonomy** (classification system), which contains several different levels of categories from the most inclusive (or broadest grouping) to the most specific (or narrowest grouping). These are based on a taxonomic system originally developed in the AD 1730s. The order called Primates, for example, is a major inclusive category. It consists of humans, apes, Old World monkeys, New World monkeys, and strepsirhines (sometimes called prosimians), which are primitive primates with many ancestral traits (such as their greater reliance on smell and thus a wet rather than a dry nose like we have). Within the Order Primates, the superfamily of **Hominoidea** (a broad grouping) includes humans and their ancestors, as well as apes (gibbons, orangutans, gorillas, common chimpanzees, and bonobos) and ape ancestors (Figure 2.1). The Hominoidea (generically called hominoids) share many physical

Taxonomy a classification system that divides animal and plant groups into categories based on their evolutionary relationships, for example, modern humans/our ancestors and common chimpanzees/bonobos are members of the same subfamily (Homininae) but are different tribes (Panini for common chimpanzees/bonobos and Hominini for modern humans/ our ancestors) within that subfamily.

Hominoidea the superfamily taxonomic category that includes gibbons, orangutans, gorillas, common chimpanzees/bonobos, and modern humans and their ancestors.

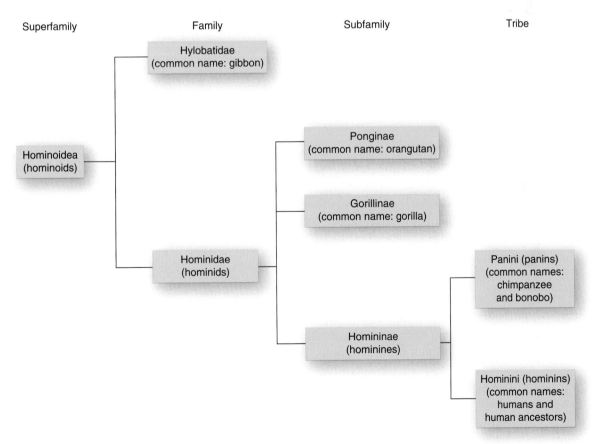

FIGURE 2.1
A taxonomy showing the genetic and evolutionary relationship of humans and apes.

Timeline: Early Hominins

There are several genera and species of fossils that are attributed to the hominins. The exact relationship between each of these species is not easy to determine because they are found in different parts of Africa and can be either roughly contemporary or separated in time. Many paleoanthropologists therefore construct timelines, such as that in Figure 2.2, which minimize attributing ancestor–descendant relationships to these species until larger samples of these fossil groups can be discovered and studied.

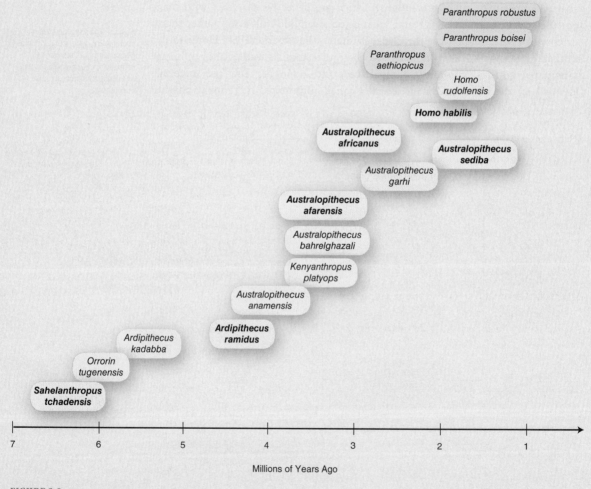

FIGURE 2.2
General timeline of fossil hominins. Note that evolutionary relationships are not implied. Species in bold are discussed in the text. Those shown in blue boxes are an extinct lineage that is not ancestral to modern humans.

and some behavioral traits, and this is why researchers sometimes study living apes to gain insights into the possible behaviors of the earliest human ancestors.

Recent genetic research shows that common chimpanzees and bonobos are the apes most closely related to humans,[2] and as a result, these three are grouped together in the subfamily Homininae. This subfamily is divided into two tribes, with common chimpanzees and bonobos in Panini (or **panins**) and humans and their ancestors in Hominini (or **hominins**).[3] The close relationship between common chimpanzees/bonobos and humans means that many researchers are especially interested in how common chimpanzee/bonobo behaviors similar to ours might be used to interpret the evolution of the human lineage. In discussing humans and their ancestors in this chapter and the next two, we will use the more specific taxonomic categories of **genus** and **species** (a genus can have one or more species.)[4] For humans today, there is only one species within our genus, and we are known as ***Homo sapiens*** (*Homo* is the genus and *sapiens* is the species name). For the panins, there are two existing species. The common chimpanzee is *Pan troglodytes*, and the bonobo is *Pan paniscus*.

Our earliest potential ancestors are members of a grouping generically called the **australopiths**, of which there are several genera (plural of genus) and several species[5] (read "Timeline: Early Hominins"). Because many of the fossils are fragmentary or consist of only a few bones or teeth and because they are found in widely separated parts of Africa, it is often difficult for paleoanthropologists to determine the exact relationship among the different genera and species.

One of the outstanding features of *H. sapiens* is our large and complex brain, which might lead us to think that this characteristic could be used in defining our earliest ancestors in the fossil record. As it turns out, increases in brain size and complexity are a later feature of our evolution. Early fossils, instead, are identified as hominins on the basis of two changes compared to apes. These are bipedalism (see later sections) and **nonhoning chewing**. In an ape, the large, projecting upper canine tooth fits into a gap in the bottom tooth row when the mouth is closed (Figure 2.3). As this happens, the sharp back side of the upper canine hones (rubs) against the sharp

Panin a generic term for the tribe taxonomic category of Panini; it includes the common chimpanzee (*Pan troglodytes*) and the bonobo (*Pan paniscus*).

Hominin the generic term for the tribe taxonomic category of Hominini; it includes humans and their ancestors.

Genus a taxonomic category that includes all similar species that share a common ancestry.

Species a taxonomic category generally based on the biological species concept in which interbreeding natural populations are reproductively isolated from other populations.

Homo sapiens the genus and species name for skeletally modern humans, who first appeared in Africa 315,000 years ago. People living today are members of *Homo sapiens*.

Australopiths a generic term for the subtribe taxonomic category of Australopithecina; it includes genera such as *Sahelanthropus*, *Ardipithecus*, *Australopithecus*, and *Paranthropus*.

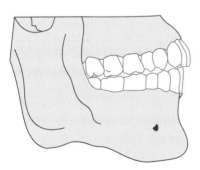

nonhoning chewing (humans and their ancestors)

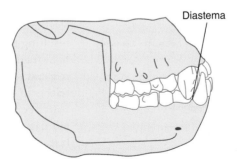

Diastema

FIGURE 2.3
Nonhoning chewing is an early characteristic of the hominins. Apes have a honing chewing complex. In apes, the upper canine tooth fits into a diastema (gap) in the tooth row and sharpens its edge against the premolar tooth immediately behind the lower canine. Hominins do not have large projecting canines and diastemas and do not have canines that sharpen.

honing chewing (apes)

Nonhoning Chewing is characterized by small, nonprojecting canine teeth and no gap in the tooth row, a feature of hominins. This contrasts with apes, where the large projecting upper canines have a sharp edge that hones (rubs) against a sharp edge on the lower premolar behind the canine. Apes use these naturally sharpened teeth to slice through food before they chew it.

Bipedal the use of the lower limbs (legs) to move around when walking or running.

Foramen Magnum the opening in the skull where the spinal column joins the head. The position of the foramen magnum can be used to determine whether a fossil species was a biped or a quadruped.

Chimpanzee-Human Last Common Ancestor the last common ancestor for panins (chimpanzees and bonobos) and hominins (humans and their ancestors), which likely lived sometime between 6.3 and 5.4 million years ago.

front side of the premolar tooth that is behind the canine. Honing helps maintain the sharpness on both teeth so that they can slice food such as fruit or leaves before these are chewed. In the hominins, canines are much smaller and do not project, and the sharp edges of the canines and the premolars are not present. Hominins thus have nonhoning chewing compared to the apes. Honing versus nonhoning chewing has implications for diet differences between apes and hominins and suggests that hominins expanded into new habitats with different types of foods that did not need to be sliced before they were chewed.

Bipedalism and the Earliest Hominins

The earliest hominins are defined (in part) on skeletal features that indicate that they were, or were becoming, habitually **bipedal** (using two legs to move around on the ground as the main form of locomotion). These features include the bowl-like shape of the pelvis (hip bones); the angling of the femur (upper leg bone) from the pelvis to the knee,[6] which results in a knee and foot that are directly under the body's center of gravity; a bony lip on the patella (kneecap) that stabilizes the knee; the joint formed by the tibia and fibula (lower leg bones) at the ankle to provide stability; and specialized feet that include a big toe in line with the other toes. A fossil also can be recognized as a biped from features of the skull, such as a **foramen magnum** (the opening where the spinal column joins with the skull) that is directly beneath the skull, as well as an S-shape spinal column, a shape that helps with weight-bearing stresses (Figure 2.4). This is some of the skeletal evidence that paleoanthropologists use in determining whether a fossil was a biped and therefore likely to be a possible early hominin.

Recognizing the earliest bipedal hominin, however, is a difficult task. One reason, mentioned above, is because the fossil record mainly consists of teeth and fragments of bones. Some of these must be painstakingly put back together and reconstructed to eliminate biases such as deformation of the bone resulting from ground pressure when buried. These bone fragments do not always include the pieces most relevant to determining bipedalism. Another reason relates to the age of some of the fossils. Genetic research comparing the panins to humans suggests that our last common ancestor (**chimpanzee–human last common ancestor**) lived sometime between 6.3 and 5.4 million years ago.[7] It is assumed that the chimpanzee–human last common ancestor was not bipedal and thus the earliest hominins likely will not

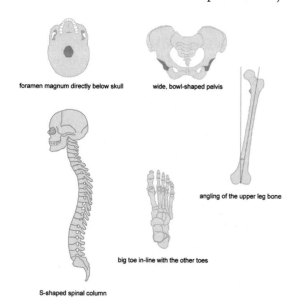

foramen magnum directly below skull

wide, bowl-shaped pelvis

angling of the upper leg bone

big toe in-line with the other toes

S-shaped spinal column

FIGURE 2.4
These are some of the skeletal features that distinguish a habitual biped.

have all the features of fully developed bipedalism. Moreover, the time frame for the chimpanzee–human last common ancestor should mean that no hominin fossil can be older than this, but there are some older fossils that are interpreted by some paleoanthropologists as hominins. One of these is the relatively complete skull of **Sahelanthropus tchadensis**, found in Chad in Central Africa[8] (Figure 2.5). Its context has been dated between 7 and 6 million years ago, but this potential hominin is controversial. The position of its foramen magnum is interpreted by some researchers as indicating bipedalism and thus a hominin status, but others disagree and argue instead that the combination of homininlike and apelike features suggests that S. tchadensis might be related to the chimpanzee–human last common ancestor.[9]

Fossils of **Ardipithecus ramidus** from Ethiopia in East Africa are much more complete. These date to 4.4 million years ago and include a partial skeleton that has allowed detailed study of many anatomical features.[10] Ar. ramidus shows an unexpected mosaic of traits (read "Further Reflections: The Place of Ardipithecus ramidus in Human Evolution"). It has a foot with a grasping big toe, much like the feet of tree-living monkeys, and a flexible back that is not like that of apes or humans, who have a stiff back. These and other features indicate that Ar. ramidus spent time moving around in trees. But, Ar. ramidus does have an upper pelvis that is broader than that in apes, showing that it occasionally moved bipedally when on the ground. Given its combination of arboreal (tree-living) and terrestrial (ground-living) anatomical features, Ar. ramidus was not a habitual biped, as were later australopiths.

Two of these later australopiths are **Australopithecus afarensis** and **Australopithecus africanus**. Au. afarensis is known from Ethiopia, Kenya, and Tanzania in East Africa and lived between 3.7 and 3 million years ago.[11] There are many fossil specimens, including a partial skeleton and a group of fragmented bones and teeth from 13 individuals. There is also a set of preserved footprints, dating to 3.7 million years ago, at the site of **Laetoli** in Tanzania (Figure 2.6). Based on the skeletal evidence and the footprints, Au. afarensis was a habitual biped. It, however, had a somewhat wider bowl-shape pelvis, a greater angling (on average) of the femur from the hip to the knee, and other structural differences in the femur and likely in muscle attachment areas, compared to us. Another distinction between Au. afarensis and modern humans is that Au. afarensis had longer arms and curved finger bones. These are skeletal characteristics indicating behavior that included climbing in trees.

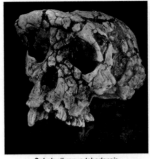

Sahelanthropus tchadensis   Australopithecus africanus

Australopithecus sediba

Homo habilis

FIGURE 2.5
Casts of several of the hominin fossils discussed in the text (casts not shown to same scale).

Sahelanthropus tchadensis a fossil from Central Africa in the period between 7 and 6 million years ago. It is usually described as a hominin, but some researchers argue against this classification, suggesting that maybe it represents a group related to the chimpanzee-human last common ancestor.

Ardipithecus ramidus a fossil hominin from 4.4 million years ago in East Africa, this species has some skeletal features indicating a trend toward bipedalism, but also apelike features such as long arms and monkeylike features in its grasping foot.

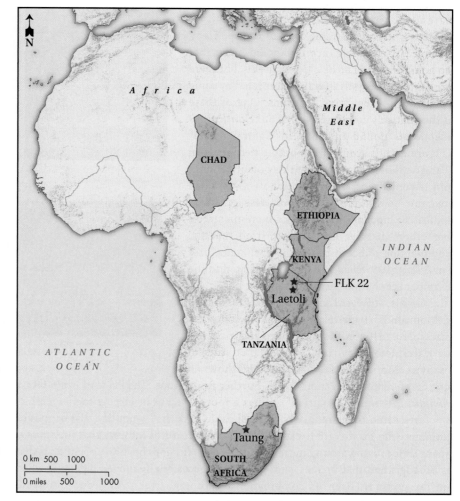

FIGURE 2.6
Fossil sites mentioned in the text. Early hominin fossils have been found in the five countries shown in light brown.

Australopithecus afarensis a fossil hominin dating between 3.7 and 3 million years ago in East Africa. It was a habitual biped but retained long arms and curved finger bones that are apelike traits. There is some evidence indicating sexual dimorphism.

Australopithecus africanus a fossil hominin known from South Africa in the interval between 3.3 and 2.5 million years ago. Although it was a habitual biped, there are some features of the big toe and knee that suggest these areas of the skeleton were still somewhat apelike. Like other gracile australopiths, it also had long arms and curved finger bones, indicating that it spent at least some of its time in the trees.

Laetoli a site in Tanzania that yielded *Australopithecus afarensis* fossils as well as a trail of fossilized footprints attributed to *Australopithecus afarensis*.

Taung a site in South Africa that yielded the first fossil recognized as a human ancestor (in 1925); led to the naming of *Australopithecus africanus* and to the recognition that human ancestors are African in origin.

Fossils of *Au. africanus*, which include the first recognized (in 1925) australopith from the site of **Taung** (see Figure 2.5),[12] are known from South Africa. *Au. africanus*, which dates between 3.3 and 2.5 million years ago, was a habitual biped based on the position of its foramen magnum and its bowl-shape pelvis. Additional fossils found since 1995, however, suggest *Au. africanus* differed bipedally from us in several important ways.[13] A fossilized foot that has been attributed to this hominin appears to show a grasping big toe. Moreover, the upper portion of the lower leg bone at the knee shows features indicating apelike mobility rather than the locked-knee characteristic of most habitual bipeds. Finally, *Au. africanus* had quite long arms and curved finger bones.

Why Is Bipedalism Important?

Most of the early hominins (read "Timeline: Early Hominins") were relatively small creatures ranging in height from 3.3 to 4.5 feet. This variation relates in part to different species of australopiths and in part to size differences between females and males within a species (**sexual dimorphism**). The majority of them (except *S. tchadensis*, *Ar. ramidus*, and some *Au. afarensis* individuals) had large-size brains in the range of 400 to 500 cc (cc stands for cubic centimeters) compared to common chimpanzees, which average 350 to 400 cc. When a ratio of brain to body size is calculated, these early hominins have ratios slightly larger than that of common chimpanzees. There also are many features of early hominin skulls that are distinctive compared to ours; for example, they had low, sloping foreheads, flaring cheekbones, and projecting faces. Although these early hominins differed from us in many ways, they share with us the anatomy for bipedalism.

Sexual Dimorphism differences between males and females, such as (on average) greater weight and height and more visible body hair in males, as well as differences in sex organs.

ADVANTAGES OF BIPEDALISM

Aside from the fact that bipedalism is used to recognize hominin fossils, we might ask why this set of structural features is so important in humanity's story. Quite simply, the mosaic of bipedal adaptations—ranging from *Ar. ramidus* with its monkeylike grasping foot but modified upper pelvis, to *Au. africanus* with its combination of apelike knee and foot with a bowl-shape pelvis, to *Au. afarensis* with its more humanlike knee and foot along with a bowl-shape pelvis—signal increased use of terrestrial habitats. A gradual behavioral commitment to primarily living on the ground and the development of habitual bipedal locomotion had consequences, many of which ultimately were advantageous to early hominins.

One initial idea was that freeing the arms and hands meant that an early biped could use them to manipulate objects and to make tools.[14] Arms and hands not used primarily in locomotion also would be available for carrying objects, food, or infants over longer distances and for throwing things. We now know, of course, that common chimpanzees and some other apes living in the wild, which are primarily quadrupeds with occasional bipedal locomotion, also make and use tools, carry objects over short distances, and throw things.[15] The fact that some apes exhibit these behaviors, however, does not detract from the potential value of freed hands and arms for our earlier ancestors.

Another advantage might be that a ground-living biped, with its upright posture, is better able to withstand heat stresses, especially if it lives in an open habitat such as the savanna grasslands of Africa. This thermoregulation idea suggests that the key to relieving heat stresses from abundant exposure to direct sunlight in an open habitat is caused by two main factors.[16] First, an upright biped exposes less of its body surface to sun rays (and heat) than a quadruped, especially when the sun is highest in the sky around noon. This reduces the heat load on bipeds by about 60%. Second, an upright biped has much of its body farther away from the heat accumulated by the ground surface, and this upright body is exposed to breezes and winds that help carry away some of the heat accumulated by the body. The reduction in heat load by breezes is increased if the biped has less body hair (although we do not know whether early hominins had less body hair). The thermoregulation hypothesis is interesting and would have been an advantage for later hominins. The main problem is that most of the earliest hominins (the australopiths and even some early members of our genus [*Homo*]) appear to have lived mainly in habitats that contained many trees, and as we have seen from their fossils, they retain skeletal features suggesting that arboreal living was in their range of behaviors.[17]

Habitual bipedalism also is thought to have energy and efficiency advantages, although there are many debates concerning the extent to which the earliest hominins were energetically efficient bipeds.[18] These different viewpoints result from the different equations used to calculate energy consumption, from how locomotion behaviors are reconstructed from the fossil evidence, and from which studies of humans and apes are used as the standards for bipedal energy consumption. Studies about locomotor energy efficiency, for example, use the skeletal differences between the australopiths and us, the fact that *Au. afarensis* had a broader bowl-shape pelvis, and differences in features of the femur. There are a number of other ideas suggested by various researchers that are potentially advantageous features of being a biped. Standing and walking upright might give early hominins more constant visual awareness of the presence of dangerous predators such as large cats, particularly over long distances.[19] The ability to carry things plays a role in another model that focuses on male parental care of their biological offspring, which involved carrying food resources to the mothers and infants.[20] All of these views about the advantages of bipedalism, however, still leave us with questions about how early hominins became bipeds.

ORIGINS OF BIPEDALISM

Advantages of bipedalism are sometimes proposed as reasons that bipedalism became important in hominin evolution. Most models for the origins of bipedalism, however, rely not on a single factor but on several variables. These include a combination of changes in climate, habitat, food resource availability, group size, and individual behaviors. To better understand the origins of bipedalism, many researchers have started with what the chimpanzee–human last common ancestor for panins and hominins may have been like, which is somewhat difficult because we have no fossils of the chimpanzee–human last common ancestor. Traditionally, therefore, the anatomy of the chimpanzee–human last common ancestor is assumed to be an apelike skeleton (because both panins and hominins share a number of skeletal features) and chimpanzee–human last common ancestor behaviors are assumed to be similar to those observed in common chimpanzees living in the wild.[21] Generally speaking, the chimpanzee–human last common ancestor would have features such as a short, stiff back, upright posture, and relatively long arms with flexible wrists and shoulders (but read "Further Reflections: The Place of *Ardipithecus ramidus* in Human Evolution"). It also would incorporate occasional bipedal behaviors when feeding, engaging in displays (males for mating rights and females for rights to food resources), carrying and throwing objects, and moving over short distances.

The chimpanzee–human last common ancestor lived around 6 million years ago during the last part of the geological epoch known as the **Miocene**. During the late Miocene, climate became increasingly drier and African areas that once were covered by forests became a more open landscape with wooded regions separated from each other.[22] If the chimpanzee–human last common ancestor was mainly arboreal and used arboreal food resources such as fruits, the reduction in tree cover and larger open spaces between areas of forest would have impacted the availability and abundance of food resources. Under such conditions, **natural selection** (read "Evolutionary Processes") would favor individuals (and, indirectly, groups) that developed behaviors that aided in their survival and their ability to reproduce. One example would be natural selection for increased use of optional bipedal locomotion, possibly to carry food over somewhat longer distances.

One model that uses this baseline reconstruction of the chimpanzee–human last common ancestor and the features of the late Miocene environment in examining the origins of bipedalism focuses on contrasts between group size and daily travel distance.[23] This model assumes that bipedalism is energy efficient for moving over longer distances compared to common chimpanzee **quadrupedalism**. The behavioral changes to compensate for reduced availability of food resources could have taken at least two different forms. In one scenario, a group of chimpanzee–human last common ancestor individuals might have developed behaviors that resulted in a reduction in group size, perhaps similar to the strategies employed by common chimpanzees, which split up into smaller groups when food resources are not particularly abundant. Maintaining a small group size has the advantages that small food patches will be sufficient to provide for the group and that the group need not travel far each day to find adequate food resources. Small groups, however, have disadvantages such as increased danger from predators and decreased success in competition for food resources with large groups. The small-group strategy with its flexibility in splitting up and coming back together depending on available food resources is more likely to retain quadrupedal locomotion and thus would characterize the ancestors leading to modern-day common chimpanzees and bonobos.

The second scenario is one in which a group of chimpanzee–human last common ancestor individuals maintained a large size. This behavioral strategy has the advantages of better protection from predators and increased success in competitions over food resources with smaller groups. A large group, however, will not be able to feed itself adequately at small food patches in the landscape and thus must travel more often and over greater distances, which has an energy cost. If bipedal walking is more energy efficient, then over time, this large group will engage in optional bipedal locomotion more often, and natural selection will favor those individuals with more frequent bipedal behavior. Gradually, the skeletal modifications for habitual bipedalism will become established. This second scenario is the one that characterizes the line leading to the ancestors of humans.

It should be pointed out that while there are many ideas about the origins of bipedalism, it is quite likely that we may never be able to demonstrate which ideas are

Miocene a geological epoch from about 23 to 5 million years ago. The first hominins appear in Africa during the late Miocene.

Natural Selection refers to a major principle of evolution (sometimes called Darwinian evolution) that is based on the individuals who are best adapted to an environment, having the best chance of surviving to reproduce and pass their genes along to the next generation. This process leads to gradual evolutionary change over time, such as the shift from quadrupedalism to bipedalism in the hominins.

Quadrupedalism the use of all four limbs to move around.

the most relevant.[24] This is because these origins do not leave a trace. The traces we have relate to changes in skeletal structures over time but not to the initial reason of "why." Moreover, there appears to be good fossil evidence that the type of habitual bipedalism in early hominins varied between different groups. What this implies is that there were several ways of being a biped that developed in the hominins, rather than one single bipedal hominin lineage.[25]

Evolutionary Processes

There are four major processes involved in evolution, which lead to changes over time in species. Natural selection is based on the principle that certain features (or behaviors) are selected for (positive selection), selected against (negative selection), or are neutral. In positive selection, for example, if an individual has small variations in skeletal structure that make it easier to use bipedal behavior occasionally, this might allow that individual to obtain adequate food for itself. That individual is likely to survive longer and produce more offspring with these small skeletal variations as a result of passing along the gene(s) for those features to future generations. Over time there will be more and more individuals with optional bipedalism because it enhances reproductive success. Becoming a habitual (rather than optional) biped might be an example of further positive natural selection for increased bipedal behavior (and thus changes in the skeleton that enhance the efficiency of bipedalism over time).

A second evolutionary process is **gene flow**. This occurs when individuals from two different groups within the same species mate and produce offspring. Genes from an individual from Group A who moves into Group B and mates with an individual from Group B will add his/her genes to the gene pool of Group B because those genes will be present in the offspring of that mating event. Genes thus "flow" from Group A into Group B. One example of this is interbreeding between Neandertals and modern humans (see Chapter 3).

Genetic drift is a third evolutionary process. It is most easily seen when populations become isolated from one another. If a small group moves to a new area (such as the peopling of the Americas, see Chapter 4), for example, the genes present in that group represent only a sample of the total genes present in the population from which the small group originated. Which genes are present in the small group is totally random. Over time, certain genes can either disappear or become the most prevalent, in part because of who mates with whom and how many offspring each pairing produces.

The fourth process is **mutation**, which is when a change occurs in a gene or when other types of errors occur in chromosomes (long strands of genes). Many mutations are detrimental because they affect critical life-sustaining functions, and these types of mutations are quickly weeded out (negative natural selection) because those individuals who carry them do not live long enough to reproduce and pass the mutation on to future generations. Some mutations, however, are beneficial, and those changes will persist and become prevalent in populations because of positive natural selection. One example of this is a mutation in one gene involved in the complexity of the brain.[26] It occurred about 5 million years ago in the hominin lineage and resulted in the expansion of the neocortex (grey matter) due to an increase in the number of neurons. These changes from this mutation are responsible for the types of cognition (thought) that are unique to us.

"Cousins" in the Early Hominin Lineage

Among the many species of australopiths are several hominin groups that definitely were not on the direct line to humans. They include several species of the genus *Paranthropus*. One group is found in South Africa from 2 to 1 million years ago and others in East Africa from 2.4 to 1.3 million years ago.[27] Frequently called the "robust" australopiths, because they have a greater body mass than individuals of *Au. afarensis* and *Au. africanus*, they also have several specialized skeletal features. Although nearly all australopiths have large premolar and molar teeth, the robust australopiths have enormous premolar and molar teeth; they are sometimes called **megadonts**. Large premolars and molars may indicate much grinding of food as it is chewed, and the amount of time spent chewing food is related to the second specialized feature of *Paranthropus*, a **sagittal crest**. This is a ridge of bone at the top of the skull that runs from the front to the back (a bit like a Mohawk hairstyle). The sagittal crest is associated with exceptionally large and powerful chewing muscles, some of which (temporalis muscle) attach to this bony crest; modern humans do not have this feature. *Paranthropus* also has wide flaring cheek bones resulting in a large gap between the skull and the side of the cheek through which another set of chewing muscles (masseter muscle) passes. *Paranthropus* is interpreted as a habitual biped based on the position of its foramen magnum.

Although *Paranthropus* species are hominins, their suite of specialized features suggests that they had a dietary focus different from the other australopiths and that they were along an evolutionary trajectory that set them apart from the hominin lineage leading to modern humans. The diet of *Paranthropus* thus has been a research interest of several paleoanthropologists, with early ideas suggesting that *Paranthropus* may have focused on eating small, hard foods such as seeds that would require a lot of grinding using their molar teeth.[28] Technological advances now allow us to examine aspects of diet in somewhat more detail. Recent studies using tooth enamel (from which stable carbon isotope ratios, or chemical signatures, can be determined) suggest that *Paranthropus* in South Africa had a varied diet that consisted of a greater emphasis on several foods not eaten on a regular basis by living African apes. These may have included sedges, termites, grass roots, grasshoppers, birds' eggs, lizards, grass seeds, and rodents.[29] But similar diet results also are recorded for the gracile australopith, *Au. africanus*, and would not seem to explain why the robust australopiths were megadonts. More recent studies of *Paranthropus* in East Africa now indicate that these hominins were focused primarily on foods that were low in nutritive value, meaning that they would have spent most of the day eating to gain enough nutrition.[30] Their extremely large premolar and molar teeth and well-developed chewing muscle complex thus reflect a type of diet not shared to any large degree by other australopiths.

The various combinations of skeletal features of most of the hominin fossils discussed previously, as well as several more species discussed later, are characteristic of **mosaic evolution**. This happens when changes resulting from natural selection occur at different rates in some body elements, for example, the fact that many of the

Gene Flow an evolutionary process in which interbreeding between neighboring populations allows genes from one population to enter the gene pool of another population; over geographical space, this transmission of genes from one group to another maintains similarity in the genetic structure of populations that are widely separated from one another.

Mutation changes in genetic material found in genes; most of these are disadvantageous and are subject to negative selection so that they are quickly removed from the gene pool of a population. A few mutations are advantageous and are subject to positive selection, for example, a mutation in one brain gene that led to more neurons that expanded the size of the neocortex and of cognitive abilities in the hominins.

Paranthropus genus name for the robust australopith species found in South and East Africa. These groups have extremely large premolar and molar teeth and massive chewing muscles. Males have a sagittal crest to which chewing muscles attach. These features indicate a low-nutrition diet requiring them to eat most of the day. They are a side branch to the lineage leading to modern humans.

Megadont term often used to describe the enormous premolar and molar teeth of species of *Paranthropus*.

Sagittal Crest a ridge of bone from the front to the back along the top of the skull; one set of chewing muscles attaches to this crest in species of *Paranthropus*, as well as in male gorillas.

Mosaic Evolution represents a situation in which natural selection acts at different rates of change on various parts of the body. One example in the hominins is the combination of habitual bipedalism with apelike long arms and curved finger bones. In this case, natural selection acted earlier on structural changes leading to bipedalism than it did on structural changes to the modern form of the arm and hand.

australopiths have apelike arms and fingers, but clear evidence for habitual bipedalism as well. It is only after 2 million years ago that the long arms and curved finger bones disappear from most hominin fossil populations and bipedal structures become nearly identical to ours (see Chapter 3). The same is true for evidence showing a larger brain size; this change is relatively late in the lineage leading to modern humans.

Tool Use and Manufacture

The biology and behaviors of these earlier hominins can be reconstructed to varying degrees based on their skeletal anatomy and specialized studies of the mechanics of their locomotion and their diets. But none of this speaks directly to the archaeological record, which during these remote periods of time usually means evidence for the manufacture and use of tools and tool-assisted behaviors. Until recently, most of our data about early tool manufacture and use were confined to flaked stone tools (more on these later) because stone is durable and preserves in the archaeological record. Paleoanthropologists, however, have long considered that tool making and use may predate the earliest appearance of flaked stone tools.[31] This perspective is partly based on analogies with living common chimpanzees (as well as other apes and some monkeys) because we know that they make and use various sorts of tools and we assume that our hominin ancestors shared this capability (read "Peopling the Past: Culture in the Prehistoric Record"). Among the tools that common chimpanzees make and use are modified twigs to remove termites from termite mounds so that they can be eaten and rocks and branches to break open nuts and hard-skinned fruits. Organic materials such as wood, however, are unlikely to preserve and be found in the archaeological record.

One organic material that does often survive is bone. At the South African site of Swartkrans, 85 of the 23,000 animal bones have trace evidence of use as tools.[32] These bone tools have a wear pattern and scratches at one end that are similar to wear and scratches on bone tools used experimentally to dig in termite mounds. This suggests that hominins using these tools were extracting termites for food, in a manner similar to common chimpanzees. One difference is that common chimpanzees do not use bone for this task. Although Swartkrans, which dates between 1.8 and 1 million years ago, is younger than the earliest flaked stone tools, the use of bone tools there may indicate that this behavior has deeper roots in time.

Stone Tools

Lomekwian is the earliest known stone tool industry. It dates to 3.3 million years ago and is found in East Africa. The stone artifacts include cores, flakes, anvils, and percussors.

The earliest direct evidence for stone tool manufacture and use comes from the site of Lomekwi 3 (Kenya, East Africa), which dates to 3.3 million years ago.[36] It is named the **Lomekwian** (Early Stone Age period) and includes cores (stone nodules from which pieces have been removed by hammering), sharp-edge flakes (the pieces removed from a core), stone anvils (somewhat flat stones upon which nuts could be placed for cracking open), and percussors (hammerstones used to remove flakes

Peopling the Past

Culture in the Prehistoric Record

One basic way of defining culture is as sets of behaviors that result from social learning and traditions (distinctive ways of doing things). Prior to the 1960s, most researchers believed that cultural traditions were behaviors specific to humans and their ancestors. Field observations of common chimpanzees, bonobos, and even orangutans living in the wild, however, show that these apes make and use tools, learn about tool manufacture and use through observation of other apes in their group, make tools in different ways in different groups (that is, have traditions), and possess systems of social learning that are passed down, usually from females to their offspring.

Common chimpanzees in Assirik (Senegal, West Africa), for example, make termiting sticks from leaves, whereas a different group living in Gombe (Tanzania, East Africa) makes these tools from bark (Figure 2.7); both materials are available in both locations, but cultural traditions are different.[33] Cracking open nuts is done using a stone hammer by common chimpanzees living in Bossou (Guinea, West Africa), whereas those in the Taï Forest (Ivory Coast, West Africa) use either a stone hammer or a wood hammer (branch).[34] One group of orangutans living in Suaq on the island of Sumatra (Indonesia, Southeast Asia) uses modified sticks to probe inside the husks of *Neesia* fruits and detach nutritious seeds contained in them; these seeds are otherwise protected by sharp needlelike projections. These Suaq orangutans learn by observation (social learning); infants learn from their mothers and other tolerant adults. Other orangutan groups living nearby do not have this tradition of tool manufacture and use.[35]

The diversity of traditions across the common chimpanzee groups in different parts of Africa mirrors variability seen in human cultures, and it is thought that these cultural capabilities were within the range of behaviors that were typical of our early hominin ancestors.

FIGURE 2.7
An adult female common chimpanzee using a termiting stick to probe for edible termites in Gombe National Park, Tanzania.

from cores and to crack open nuts placed on anvils). Although there are no associated hominin fossils, this is the time period during which *Au. afarensis* lived, and perhaps it was these hominins who made and used the Lomekwian.

By 2.6 million years ago, **Oldowan** (Early Stone Age period) stone artifacts are found at archaeological sites in East Africa.[37] There are thousands of flaked stone artifacts, including cores and sharp-edge flakes (read "The Big Picture: Oldowan

Oldowan these stone tools appear 2.6 million years ago in eastern Africa. The most common types are choppers, flakes, hammerstones, and scrapers.

Industrial Complex"). Although it may seem to us that these Oldowan (and Lomekwian) stone artifacts are relatively simple, they represent a major cognitive leap for the hominins who made and used them. Flaked stone artifacts, for example, document hominin recognition of the properties of stone. That is, certain types of stone (basalt, quartzite, flint) can be consistently broken to produce flakes with sharp edges. The process of consistently producing flakes is called knapping, and the Lomekwian and Oldowan traditions involve using a hammerstone to hit a cobble so that useful flakes with sharp edges are detached. Not all stone types can be used in knapping because not all have conchoidal flaking properties (a fine-grained microstructure that allows applied force stresses to carry through the stone and result in a flake). This means that early hominins recognized that only certain types of stone were appropriate. Beyond this, early hominins also realized that the angle at which a hammerstone hit a cobble was important in the detachment of a useful flake or a series of flakes. Using the wrong angle results in no detachment of a flake or detachment of thick flakes without useful sharp edges.

The advent of knapping also is important because it shows that earlier hominins understood the value of sharp-edge flakes. Flaked artifacts could be used for tasks such as cutting meat off bones or scraping wood to make it smoother, whereas hammerstones could be used to break open bones for the nutritious marrow that they contain or to crack nuts open. Moreover, the right types of stone are not always present everywhere in the landscape. This means that early hominins had to know where to find the right stone and had to carry it or the cores and flakes they made to other places in the landscape where they could use these stone artifacts. Being habitual bipeds facilitated transport of stones because of freed arms and hands. To engage in this behavior, early hominins likely had a certain degree of planning and foresight, especially because the distances over which these flaked stone artifacts were transported could be up to 15 or more kilometers (9 miles).[38] These distances are much greater than the distances common chimpanzees are known to transport tools or materials for tools, possibly because they cannot walk bipedally for long periods of time.

Despite the obvious advantages of making and using stone tools, some archaeologists argue that this behavior was only occasional (rather than obligatory or habitual) before 1.7 million years ago.[39] This is because we have large gaps in time between the archaeological sites that have these stone artifacts, for example, the Lomekwian at 3.3 million years ago and then nothing until the Oldowan at 2.6 million years ago. Even in the interval from 2.6 to 1.7 million years ago there are not many sites with Oldowan stone tool assemblages. Possibly these gaps mean that we have not yet found more of these sites. Alternatively, it may mean that use of stone tools simply was not very frequent in these remote times, thus the archaeological record is very sparse.

Which Hominins Made and Used Stone Tools?

The recently described Lomekwian flaked stone artifacts at 3.3 million years ago[42] appear in the archaeological record at a time when there are at least four australopith species, including *Au. afarensis* and *Au. africanus*, as potential candidates for stone

The Big Picture

Oldowan Industrial Complex

The Oldowan Industrial Complex represents one of the oldest known flaked stone artifact technologies and dates to 2.6 million years ago. The classification system (typology) for these artifacts was established by Mary Leakey using archaeological assemblages from sites in Beds I and II at Olduvai Gorge, Tanzania.[40] The typology includes tools, utilized pieces, and the by-products of making tools such as flakes (Figure 2.8).

Among the characteristic tools are choppers, spheroids, and scrapers. Choppers are cobbles that have one or more negative scars that represent the removal of flakes. In many other typologies, these forms are called cores rather than tools. Spheroids are cobbles that have some or all projecting ridges removed; the most smoothed are sometimes called "stone balls." Scrapers are flakes or parts of cobbles that have one or more edges showing the removal of small, steep flakes (retouch).

Utilized materials include forms such as hammerstones, which were used to strike flakes off cobbles, and flakes with tiny removals along their edges (which Mary Leakey called "chipping"). The assumption is that chipping along edges might represent damage from the use of these flakes in various activities. By-products are the rest of the assemblage, mainly flakes showing no use (no chipping), as well as unidentifiable fragments of flaked stone artifacts.

Mary Leakey emphasized the importance of choppers as tools in the Oldowan Industrial Complex, but archaeologist Nicholas Toth suggested instead that it was the sharp-edge flakes that likely were the most useful artifacts for various cutting activities.[41] Choppers may have had a role in woodworking tasks.

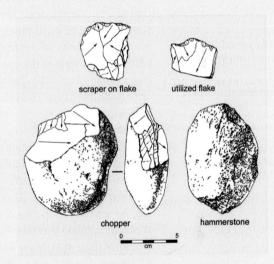

FIGURE 2.8
Examples of Oldowan stone artifacts (arrows indicate the direction in which flakes were removed) (after Leakey 1971).

tool–assisted behaviors. From 3.3 to 2.6 million years ago, there are four to five hominin species, including *Au. africanus*, *Paranthropus*, and early *Homo*[43] (read "Timeline of Early Hominins"). The presence of early *Homo* and Oldowan flaked stone artifacts convinced a number of researchers that it was members of genus *Homo* who made and used stone tools rather than the australopith species.[44] This perspective, however, is complicated for several reasons, including the fact that the 3.3-million-year-old stone tools predate the appearance of the genus *Homo*.

Homo habilis (2.8 to 1.8 million years ago) was first found at Olduvai Gorge in Tanzania (East Africa). This species was defined by Louis Leakey and others in the early 1960s as a member of genus *Homo* because it had a larger brain size and smaller molar teeth than australopiths,[45] although its brain size was only slightly larger (600 cc on average). The larger brain size of *H. habilis* was taken as a rough indicator of likely greater intelligence, and it seemed to many researchers that the appearance of flaked stone artifacts at about the same time was a reflection of this greater intelligence as applied to exploiting food and other resources. The discovery of a partial skeleton of *H. habilis* at Olduvai Gorge in the mid-1980s, however, added a controversial note to our interpretations of this species. The skeleton showed that *H. habilis* had several skeletal features long associated with the australopiths, such as long arms and curved finger bones. There is also a fossil foot that has been interpreted as showing that *H. habilis* had a foot that was still somewhat apelike.[46] The combination of australopith and *Homo* features suggest to some researchers that *H. habilis* should be placed within the genus *Australopithecus* rather than the genus *Homo*.

The discovery of ***Australopithecus sediba*** from the Malapa site in South Africa is another example of the combination of features thought to be australopith-like and genus *Homo*-like.[47] This species had a relatively small brain size (about 420 cc) and long arms and curved finger bones, all of which are australopith features. Its bipedal anatomy, however, was more similar to that of early *Homo*, and *Au. sediba* had small molar teeth, a flatter face, and lacked flaring cheekbones. These are characteristics of genus *Homo*.

All of these early hominins share a generally similar skeletal anatomy (although there are differences as noted above), which might suggest that any one or even all of them (including *Paranthropus*) are good candidates for the manufacture and use of flaked stone artifacts. Regardless of whether we consider them all australopiths or whether one of the species is genus *Homo*, studies of the bones of their hands, where available, indicate that they had grips capable of holding stones and knapping them.[48] Several of these species are found at sites with flaked stone artifacts (a bit later than 2.6 million years ago), but it is not always clear that this association means that a particular species made the flaked stone artifacts at that site. A good example of this difficulty is found at the **FLK 22 site** in Olduvai Gorge,[49] which has flaked stone artifacts, animal bones, and the remains of hominins. The initial discovery in the late 1950s was of *Paranthropus* in association with these archaeological remains, and stone artifact manufacture was attributed to this hominin. This interpretation was overturned a year later when *H. habilis* fossils were found nearby and because of its status in genus *Homo*, the flaked stone artifacts at the site were credited to *H. habilis* instead of *Paranthropus*.[50]

When so many similar and related species are present, and given issues related to site taphonomy (see Chapter 1), deciding whether a hominin found at a site with flaked stone artifacts actually was responsible for making those tools can be complicated, as the FLK 22 example demonstrates. It is probable that we will need a much better understanding of the diets of each of the hominin species to possibly eliminate some of them as knappers and users of flaked stone artifacts. This is because flaked stone artifacts (and hammerstones) would have facilitated access to protein (in the form of meat) and fats (greasy marrow) from animals. Incorporating meat and marrow into the diet is thought to be one of the keystone econiche expansions in the lineage leading to modern humans because this energy-rich diet might have helped in the eventual increase in brain size[51] (more on this later and in Chapter 3). Because hominins do not have dental specializations, such as many carnivores have, that allow easy ripping and tearing of meat or bone-crunching to access marrow, the use of flaked stone tools and hammerstones can act as a substitute for hominin dental disadvantages. Although stone tools also may have been used on wood and plants, their role in meat and marrow procurement is well documented by stone tool cut marks and hammerstone percussion marks on animal bones.[52] If we discover that a particular early hominin species had a more significantly meat- and marrow-oriented diet, then it is more likely that that species is the maker and user of flaked stone artifacts.

The other major consideration about knapping stone is whether the cognitive leap that resulted in an understanding of the mechanics of making sharp-edge flakes, the attributes of different stone types, and where to find appropriate stone sources in the landscape occurred just once or several times. In other words, our perception of whether this was a unique event affects whether we interpret stone knapping as a capability of just one hominin species and its descendants (the lineage leading most directly to modern humans) or a shared ability among the many related hominin species present in Africa 3.3 million years ago. At present we cannot answer this question, although many researchers view the origins of stone knapping as a unique event.

Early Hominin Culture

The term "culture" has a vast number of definitions[53] and is not limited to the behaviors of hominins (read "Peopling the Past: Culture in the Prehistoric Record"). Generally speaking, the archaeological record provides evidence of culture because it contains materials that have been made and used by hominins (such as the Lomekwian stone artifacts from Lomekwi 3 and the bone termiting sticks from Swartkrans). Many researchers also expect that culture includes social learning and traditions that are passed from parents to offspring over many generations. Archaeological sites are a record of these cultural behaviors as they contain cultural materials made and used by hominins, as well as related objects such as animal bones that may represent food resources.

Because of preservation conditions, many of the earliest sites contain only flaked stone artifacts. Other sites also have animal bones, and on rare occasions there are hominin fossils present. Most of these sites appear to represent places in the landscape that were repeatedly visited by hominins. Each time they used a particular spot, they left behind some flaked stone artifacts (and perhaps animal bones), and over time the density of cultural materials at the site increased. This type of pattern suggests that the archaeological sites we find represent favored places. These have been variously interpreted; for example, early explanations suggested that sites were home bases where hominins brought food to other members of the group, which implies that they shared food and had other types of cooperative behaviors.[54] Later interpretations include the idea of safe locales where hominins could bring food resources and spend time making flaked stone artifacts with less danger from lions and leopards.[55] One intriguing interpretation is the idea that early hominins may have deliberately stored stone at certain spots in the landscape.[56] In other words, hominins transported un-worked stone cobbles and flaked stone artifacts to favored locales where these cultural materials were left. Hominins then knew where in the landscape they could go to get stone resources and/or where to take parts of animal carcasses to process for meat and marrow using artifacts from the stored stone at these places.

One early site that has been the subject of much research and varying interpretations is the 1.75-million-year-old FLK 22 in Olduvai Gorge (mentioned previously). It contains thousands of flaked stone artifacts and animal bones from various species, as well as an area with few materials next to a dense cluster of artifacts and bones. When it was originally excavated, it was interpreted as a living floor, where hominins made flaked stone artifacts and used them to butcher the carcasses of animals they had hunted. Some of these activities were argued to have been done in the shelter of a windbreak, represented by the clear area with few materials where the structure would have been built.[57] At the time of this early research, however, consideration of the impact of taphonomic processes on the distribution of materials at sites, as well as on the types of items found, was relatively limited, although the excavator noted that the artifacts and bone were not moved by flowing water.

When issues of site taphonomy at FLK 22 are examined, it is clear that not all the animal bone present at FLK 22 is the result of hominins transporting parts of animal carcasses, especially the bones from elephants and giraffes. Some of the animal bones may be present because lions killed and ate animals here, or the bones may represent natural animal deaths. This is because sites like FLK 22 were attractive not only to hominins but also to other animals, usually because of the access to water or the presence of shade trees. Moreover, there are natural taphonomic processes that could have resulted in the creation of the area interpreted as a windbreak, such as the removal of animal bone by scavenging animals. Alternatively, there are many areas of this site that have few or no cultural materials, so that the relatively clear area next to the dense cluster simply may be an area that was not used.[58] The presence of the flaked stone artifacts, as well as animal bones with stone tool cut and percussion marks, however, does indicate that hominins were obtaining food resources from animal carcasses. Whether this represents hunting or a form of scavenging has been debated (read "Peopling the Past: Hunting versus Scavenging"). The use of meat by early hominins is not surprising given what we know about behaviors in common chimpanzees and bonobos. These species do occasionally hunt small animals such as monkeys, flying squirrels, and bushbabies.[59] Most of this type of hunting and eating of meat is not tool assisted, although one group of common chimpanzees in West Africa uses sticks they sharpen with their teeth to poke into holes in trees to kill and retrieve bushbabies.[60]

Regardless of the exact interpretation of sites such as FLK 22, we can say that early hominins were transporting stone and parts of animal carcasses to various places in the landscape. They revisited these locales often. Each time they brought

Hunting versus Scavenging

The recognition that early hominins were obtaining meat and marrow, based on stone artifact cut and percussion marks on animal bones, created a lively debate about their behavioral capabilities. At the heart of this debate is the question of whether these early members of our lineage were hunters or scavengers of animal carcasses (Figure 2.9). Because of excellent bone preservation, analyses of the animal assemblage at the site of FLK 22 in Olduvai Gorge, Tanzania, has been at the center of this issue.

Mary Leakey, who excavated FLK 22, believed that early hominins were hunters.[61] She based her interpretation on the idea that animal bones found at a site were brought there by hominins for processing. Her view was supported by studies of stone tool cut marks and their specific locations on bones, which suggested that early hominins had access to bones with lots of meat, access that likely meant these animals were hunted.[62]

Not everyone agreed with this viewpoint. Lewis Binford, based on his study of the FLK 22 bone assemblage, suggested that animal gnawing marks on the bones combined with the abundance of animal heads and feet indicated that early hominins were scavenging.[63] These parts of the skeleton do not have much meat but can be broken open for marrow or brains. Early hominins thus were opportunists who found animal carcasses after lions or leopards had killed the animals and eaten most of the meat. The hominins scavenged bone with bits of remaining meat and took them to locales such as FLK 22 to cut off the remaining meat and break

PASSIVE SCAVENGING	ACTIVE SCAVENGING	HUNTING
First Event: a large cat kills an animal and consumes part of the carcass, including most of the available meat.	**First Event:** a large cat kills an animal and begins to eat the meat.	**First Event:** hominins capture and kill an animal.
Second Event: hominins find the abandoned carcass and remove bones with remaining meat and also bones containing marrow.	**Second Event:** hominins chase the large cat away and remove bones with the most meat.	**Second Event:** hominins remove bones with the most meat.
Third Event: hominins transport part of the carcass to a safer location in the landscape, where they cut off the remaining meat and break open most bones for marrow.	**Third Event:** hominins transport parts of the carcass to a safer location in the landscape, where they cut off the meat and break open some bones for marrow.	**Third Event:** hominins transport parts of the carcass to a safer location in the landscape, where they cut off the meat and break open some bones for marrow.
Fourth Event: hominins abandon the site and jackals move in to scavenge the remaining bones and bone fragments.	**Fourth Event:** hominins abandon the site and jackals move in to scavenge the remaining bones and bone fragments.	**Fourth Event:** hominins abandon the site and jackals move in to scavenge the remaining bones and bone fragments.

FIGURE 2.9
Scavenging and hunting models for the Oldowan period.

the bones open for marrow. Binford's research, as well as that of others who looked at the availability of carcasses in the landscape,[64] suggested that early hominins were passive scavengers rather than hunters.

More recently, Manuel Domínguez-Rodrigo,[65] who also studied the FLK 22 animal bones, has argued that the placement of the cut marks on the bones indicates that early hominins had access to limb bones with lots of meat on them and that few bones show percussion marks indicating the breaking of bones to gain access to marrow. Domínguez-Rodrigo suggests that the marrow-focused activity proposed by Binford and others is not supported by the data. Instead, early hominins had early access to carcasses, and this suggests either that they were active (confrontational) scavengers that chased away the lions and leopards that had killed these animals or possibly that some of the food animals were hunted by hominins.

materials into a site (stone artifacts and/or animal bones), they likely also took some stone artifacts away to other places. This type of resource transport is a critical innovation associated with the Oldowan and suggests that hominin behaviors were organized (to some degree) and included planning capabilities.[66] Whether early hominins shared food with each other is a more difficult question to answer. Early hominin behaviors were different from those we see in common chimpanzee groups, but we probably would not recognize these early hominins as human.

Further Reflections

The Place of *Ardipithecus ramidus* in Human Evolution

The fossil group known as *Ardipithecus ramidus* is a good example of scientific method in action. When researchers working with these fossils fully described them,[67] they suggested that *Ar. ramidus* was on the direct lineage to modern humans and that its unusual features meant that we had to rethink the skeletal features and behaviors of the chimpanzee–human last common ancestor. The skeleton of *Ar. ramidus* has many monkeylike characteristics (grasping foot, flexible and long lower back, limb proportions similar to monkeys, and a backward-bending wrist).[68] If *Ar. ramidus* is a direct ancestor of modern humans, then the chimpanzee–human last common ancestor was not apelike. A smaller upper canine, less sexual dimorphism in body size in *Ar. ramidus*, and hidden ovulation (no visible exterior signs such as color changes or swelling of genital regions) in *Ar. ramidus* females acted as part of a suite of behaviors in which males spent less time competing for sexual access to females and instead developed cooperative behaviors. Male *Ar. ramidus* individuals found and carried food resources to females and their young (time spent in optional bipedal locomotion) and in developing pair bonds with particular females. Female *Ar. ramidus* would be likely to pick partners who were successful in providing food, favoring as mates those males who engaged more frequently in optional bipedal walking to carry food. *Ar. ramidus* thus exhibits early skeletal changes (such as the broader upper pelvis) toward habitual bipedality. These ideas are one set of hypotheses for the place of *Ar. ramidus* in human evolution.

Not everyone agrees, however, that *Ar. ramidus* is a direct ancestor of modern humans. Instead, these researchers offer alternative hypotheses for testing. These include *Ar. ramidus* as a hominin side branch to the lineage that led to us, as a lineage more closely related to gorillas, as a lineage more closely related to common chimpanzees/bonobos, or even a fossil group that was a separate cluster of species that was not hominin, gorillin, or panin.[69] How do we scientifically test these various ideas about the place of *Ar. ramidus* in human evolution? One way is to discover more fossils that can

be studied and compared to known fossils. These could come from the time period before *Ar. ramidus* or the interval between *Ar. ramidus* (optional biped) and *Australopithecus afarensis* (habitual biped). One example of this is the discovery of the Bertele foot (Ethiopia, East Africa), which has been put into the genus *Australopithecus*.[70] This is a grasping foot (big toe not in line with the other toes) similar to *Ar. ramidus* but which dates 1 million years later. One interpretation might be that the Bertele foot is from a descendant of *Ar. ramidus* and, if so, might support the hypothesis that *Ar. ramidus* was not a direct ancestor of modern humans. We must, however, await many more fossil discoveries to begin to resolve the debate over *Ar. ramidus*.

Summary

- Paleoanthropologists use a classification system or taxonomy to organize humans and their ancestors into a hierarchy of relationships. This taxonomy also shows the relationships between humans and the great apes, as well as more distantly related species such as monkeys.

- Nonhoning chewing and bipedal locomotion help define humans and their ancestors. They are two of the earliest changes in the hominin lineage and distinguish hominins from the great ape lineages. The earliest hominins were not habitual bipeds, however, because it took time for skeletal changes necessary for full-time bipedalism to become established through natural selection. The specific type of habitual bipedalism characteristic of modern humans appeared about 2 million years ago.

- There have been many ideas or hypotheses about how or why bipedalism originated. These include the advantages of freeing the arms to carry things, exposing more of the body to breezes and wind that would help cool it, sexual selection by females of males who could carry more food as provisions to the female and her offspring, and the possibility that bipedalism was eventually more efficient in traveling longer distances.

- There are many species of early hominins, all of whom are found in Africa. They can be divided into early australopiths (*S. tchadensis, Ar. ramidus*) and later gracile australopiths (*Au. afarensis, Au. africanus, Au. sediba*), robust australopiths (several species of genus *Paranthropus*), and early genus *Homo* (*H. habilis* and one or two other species).

- The species of genus *Paranthropus* are hominins that did not lead to modern humans. *Paranthropus* specialized in plant foods low in nutritive value and would have spent most of their day eating to gain enough energy from food. This can be seen in the cranial features associated with their massive chewing muscle complex and their extremely large premolar and molar teeth.

- The skeletal features of the early hominins indicate patterns of mosaic evolution. That is, natural selection acts on features at different rates of change and at different times. Skeletal evidence for bipedalism thus appears much earlier than increases in brain size or modifications to apelike arms and finger bones.

- Beginning 3.3 million years ago, the first Early Stone Age period stone tools appear in the African archaeological record and are called the Lomekwian industry. By 2.6 million years ago, stone tools are more common; these are called the Oldowan industry and are characterized mainly by choppers, flakes, and a few other forms such as scrapers. These early stone tool industries show that hominins understood the flaking properties of different types of stone. They also show that hominins were transporting stone artifacts over some distance, a pattern of behavior that is not typical of our close relatives, the common chimpanzees and bonobos.

- Stone tools were advantageous to early hominins who lacked specialized teeth for removing meat from animal bones or cracking open those bones for marrow. Whether the hominins were able to hunt large animals or relied instead on scavenging carcasses of animals killed by large cats is still a matter of debate.

Endnotes

1. Bearzi and Stanford 2010.
2. Chimpanzee Sequencing and Analysis Consortium 2005.
3. An older taxonomic system (still in use by some researchers) uses the term hominids to describe humans and their ancestors. This older system does not use the recent genetic information about common chimpanzees and bonobos, and these two apes are seen as more closely related to gorillas than to humans. As a result, there are no tribe taxonomic categories, and the taxonomic category of the family Hominidae (generically hominids) is used to describe humans and their ancestors.
4. There sometimes are subspecies within species.
5. Wood 2005: 23.
6. The technical name is the bicondylar angle, which is the angle formed between a line perpendicular to the bottom of the upper leg bone (femur) and a line representing the shaft of the upper leg bone.
7. However, recent work on generation length in apes has suggested that the time frame for hominin evolution may be longer than previously thought, with a chimpanzee–human last common ancestor in the period between 13 and 9 million years ago (see Hawks 2012; Langergraber et al. 2012).
8. Brunet et al. 2002.
9. Wolpoff et al. 2006: 48; Wood 2002.
10. See the 2009 issue (326(2), October 2009) of *Science*, which contains 11 articles on *Ardipithecus ramidus*.
11. Johanson and White 1979; Kimbel et al. 2006: 135.
12. The anatomist, Raymond Dart (1925), was the first person to recognize that the Taung fossil was an ancestor of modern humans. This was an important observation because it indicated that the origins of modern humans were in Africa.
13. Berger and Tobias 1996; Clarke and Tobias 1995; Harcourt-Smith and Aeillo 2004; McHenry and Berger 1998.
14. Darwin 1981 (first published in 1871).

15. McGrew et al. 2003; Pruetz and Bertolani 2007; Van Schaik 2006; Whiten et al. 2003.

16. Wheeler 1991.

17. However, see Pruetz and Bertolani (2009) for information about how common chimpanzees in more open habitats deal with heat stress and the implications this has for interpreting the behaviors of early hominins.

18. Kramer and Sylvester 2009; Leonard and Robertson 1997; Steudel 1996; Steudel-Numbers 2003.

19. For example, Shreeve 1996.

20. Lovejoy 1981. Lovejoy's hypothesis went further in suggesting monogamous pair bonds between males and females and thus exclusive sexual access to a female by a male, but other researchers criticized this model for early hominin behavior, arguing that monogamy is not characteristic of humans today (Symons 1979) and that greater sexual dimorphism, especially body and jaw size differences, among early hominins would imply nonmonogamous relationships (Richmond and Jungers 1995; but see Reno et al. 2003).

21. But see Sayers and Lovejoy (2008) for a critique of the use of common chimpanzees as models for the LCA; and see Diogo et al. 2017 and earlier publications (Zihlman 1984; Zihlman and Bolter 2015) for arguments suggesting that bonobos are a better model for the chimpanzee–human last common ancestor.

22. Cerling et al. 1991.

23. Isbell and Young 1996.

24. Smith and Wood 2017.

25. Gebo and Schwartz 2006; Haile-Selassie et al. 2012; Harcourt-Smith and Aiello 2004; Harcourt-Smith et al. 2015; Kramer and Sylvester 2009.

26. Florio et al. 2016.

27. Some researchers use the genus name of *Australopithecus* for these robust australopiths.

28. Jolly 1970.

29. Sponheimer et al. 2005.

30. Cerling et al. 2011.

31. Panger et al. 2002.

32. McGrew et al. 2003.

33. Whiten et al. 1999, 2003.

34. Van Schaik 2006.

35. Backwell and d'Errico 2001; they also mention similar results for the South African sites of Sterkfontein and Drimolen.

36. Harmand et al. 2015.

37. Semaw 2000.

38. Leakey 1967, 1971.

39. Shea 2017.

40. Toth 1985.

41. Blumenschine et al. 2012b; Potts 1991.

42. See Endnotes 32 and 33.

43. Although it has not yet been given a species name, a newly discovered fossil of *Homo* from Ethiopia has been dated to 2.8 million years ago (Villmoare et al. 2015). This means either that *H. habilis* extends farther back in time than 2.4 million years ago or that there was an earlier species of *Homo*.

44. For example, Leakey 1971: 280.

45. Leakey et al. 1964.

46. Wood and Collard 1999.

47. Berger et al. 2010.

48. Marzke 1997. Marzke notes that several hand bone features are necessary to confidently assess the structure of the hand with respect to making stone tools.

49. *Zinjanthropus* was the original genus name assigned by Louis and Mary Leakey to what is now classified as *Paranthropus boisei*.

50. Leakey 1971: 280.

51. Bunn 2007; Foley 2002; Milton 2000.

52. Schick and Toth 1993.

53. Kroeber and Kluckhohn 1952; Tylor 1920.

54. Isaac 1978; Leakey 1971; see also Rose and Marshall 1996.

55. Blumenschine et al. 2012a; Isaac 1983.

56. Potts 1984, 1991.

57. Leakey 1971: 49–50; Bunn and Kroll 1986.

58. See Figure 24 in Leakey 1971.

59. Boesch 1994; Ingmanson 1998; Stanford 1998; Telecki 1973.

60. Pruetz and Bertolani 2007.

61. Leakey 1971.

62. Bunn and Kroll 1986.

63. Binford 1988.

64. Blumenschine et al. 1994.

65. Domínguez-Rodrigo 2002.

66. Potts 1991.

67. See Endnote 10.

68. Lovejoy et al. 2009.

69. Harrison 2010; Sarmiento 2010; Wood and Harrison 2011.

70. Haile-Selassie et al. 2012.

CHAPTER 3

Becoming Human

ABOVE: Looking out of the Middle Stone Age and Epipaleolithic site of Contrebandiers Cave, Morocco.

Shortly after 2 million years ago in Africa, a new species of genus *Homo* appears in the fossil record. Within a couple hundred thousand years of their appearance, some of them are the first hominins to migrate out of Africa, eventually reaching China and Indonesia. Later migrations reach Western Europe by 1.4 million years ago. These species of genus *Homo* have our form of habitual bipedalism and brain sizes that sometimes are within the lower range of modern human brain size, features that may have been advantageous in the movement out of Africa. Most archaeologists, however, interpret their cultural behaviors as nonmodern. Sometime around 300,000 years ago, two late hominin lineages of genus *Homo* become recognizable in the fossil record. These are early forms of *H. sapiens* and the Neandertals.[1] The biological origins of and relationships between Neandertals and modern humans have long been debated, mainly using skeletal differences and similarities in the fossils. Recent advances in DNA extraction from fossils, however, have clarified and added to this debate. The archaeological record also has been used, primarily to examine when and where modern forms of cultural behaviors originated and whether Neandertals were behaviorally modern. Discussions of the origins of language as we know and use it today also have been a key factor in assessing the relationships between Neandertals and earlier modern humans. All of these subjects are the focus of this chapter.

Pleistocene Ice Ages

The **Pleistocene** epoch begins 2.6 million years ago,[2] although it is slightly before this that the earliest members of genus *Homo* and the earliest flaked stone artifacts appear in Africa (see Chapter 2). The Pleistocene often is generically called the "Ice Ages" because it was characterized by a series of glacial cycles during which worldwide climate fluctuated between colder and warmer periods (Figure 3.1). The overall trend has been for global climate to become much cooler than it was before 2.6 million years ago. These fluctuations are a result of astronomical processes such as the shape of Earth's orbit around the sun, the wobble of Earth's spin on its axis, and the tilt of Earth's axis,[3] as well as continental drift and ocean current changes. During major cold periods called glacials, significant amounts of water were locked up in the form of glaciers, which in the Northern Hemisphere covered enormous amounts of land. These glacial ice sheets could be as much as 1,500 to 3,000 meters (0.9 to 1.8 miles) thick. In the last major glacial period, around 26,000–20,000 years ago,[4] for example, nearly all of Canada was under two large glacial ice sheets, and all of the Scandinavian countries as well as most of the United Kingdom were buried under

Pleistocene a geological epoch (sometimes called the Ice Ages) beginning 2.6 million years ago and lasting until 10,000 years ago; the first stone tools appear just before the beginning of the Pleistocene.

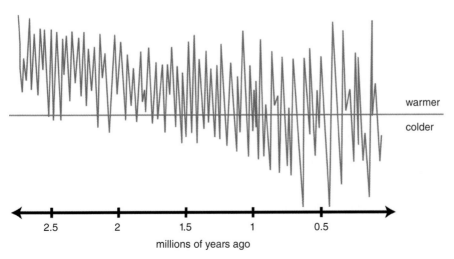

FIGURE 3.1
Climatic fluctuations during the Pleistocene epoch, based on ratios of $^{18}O/^{16}O$.

glacial ice. Removing such large quantities of water from circulation means that sea levels during glacial periods were much lower (more than 100 meters [328 feet] lower in some cases). In many areas of the world, land along coastlines that today is buried under water was exposed and available for hominins to use.

Major glacial periods alternated with major interglacial periods, when worldwide climate became warmer, glacial ice sheets melted, and global sea levels rose. The picture of these changes, however, is complicated because each major glacial period had minor fluctuations between slightly warmer (interstadial) and much colder (stadial) periods. Researchers are able to track these major and minor fluctuations in global climate during the Pleistocene because they are documented by changes in the ratio of two isotopes of oxygen (^{16}O and ^{18}O) that can be measured in the shells of tiny organisms called foraminifera (which make up plankton). When they die, foraminifera become part of the sediments laid down on the bottom of the oceans, and over time the different sediment layers capture the changes in oxygen isotope ratios present in foraminifera shells. Colder periods have less ^{16}O to ^{18}O than warmer periods.[5]

Climatic fluctuations during the Pleistocene had potentially important consequences for hominin populations. Although Africa was not covered by glacial ice sheets, the combination of water locked up as ice in the Northern Hemisphere, plus wind and ocean current changes, meant shifts in rainfall patterns, and this in turn impacted vegetation and animal communities. For vegetation communities, for example, consistently less precipitation might result in shrinkage of forests and expansion of grasslands. As a result, the abundance and types of animals available for hunting or scavenging also varied over time and space. The expansion of African-type grasslands into the Mediterranean part of the Middle East, for instance, meant that grasslands African animal species expanded into the Middle East. Some of the genus *Homo* migrants out of Africa after 1.9 million years ago probably were part of this animal community movement.[6] Additionally, lower sea levels during glacial periods meant that hominins were able to walk to land masses that today are islands, such as Java in Indonesia.

Pleistocene climatic fluctuations were important for the opportunities and constraints encountered by early genus *Homo* groups moving out of Africa and also for later groups of *Homo* moving out of Africa after 800,000 years ago. Changes in vegetation and animal communities in Africa may have resulted in the isolation of some *Homo* populations that ultimately resulted in a speciation event leading to skeletally modern humans (*H. sapiens*). Pleistocene climatic events also may have played a role in the disappearance of the Neandertals (see later discussion).

Early Waves of Out of Africa

Around 1.9 million years ago, fossils in Africa classified as **Homo erectus**[7] appear in the paleoanthropological record (read "Timeline: Later Hominins"). From the neck down, their skeleton is similar to ours, showing that *H. erectus* had a

Homo erectus the earliest hominin in genus *Homo* that is essentially skeletally modern from the neck down; *H. erectus* appears in Africa 1.9 million years ago. They migrate out of Africa around 1.7 million years ago to the Middle East, parts of Europe, Southeast Asia, and East Asia.

modern form of habitual bipedalism. Their skulls, however, differ from ours. Some individuals had a cranial capacity similar to that of the earlier species in genus *Homo*, whereas others (dating somewhat later) had larger brain sizes, ranging from 900 to 1270 cc. All of them had large brow ridges, thick skull bones, sloping foreheads, and a skull shape that was long and low. One of the best preserved examples is the partial skeleton called the "Nariokotome Boy" from West Turkana in Kenya[8] (Figure 3.2). Features of his skeleton have led some researchers to suggest that *H. erectus* could not speak in quite the same way that we do[9] (more on this later).

The Earliest Movement Out of Africa

Not long after *H. erectus* originated in Africa, we find evidence of them in other parts of the Old World. The early groups who migrated made stone tools of the Oldowan Industrial Tradition because these are the types of flaked stone artifacts found at the earliest sites outside of Africa. Some of the first sites in areas beyond Africa are Dmanisi, Sangiran, and 'Ubeidiya (see Figure 3.3).[11]

Dmanisi, in the Republic of Georgia (Figure 3.4), dates to 1.85 to 1.78 million years ago. It contains the remains of early forms of *H. erectus*,[12] animal bones, and Oldowan stone tools, although the context of the site is complicated. Some areas are a combination of hominin and animal fossils, along with stone tools, accumulated together because of geological processes such as water flow that moved these materials from a short distance away and deposited them.[13] The animal bones do not have stone tool cut marks and probably are not the remains of animals hunted or scavenged by the hominins. Recent excavations into the oldest sediments at Dmanisi, however, have uncovered stone artifacts and animal bones that appear to have been part of living surfaces.[14]

Sangiran is on the island of Java in Indonesia (see Figure 3.4) and dates to 1.6 million years ago. This site has hominin remains. Stone tools are present in the Sangiran area but are not directly associated with the fossils.[15] The finds at Sangiran do not represent a living site for hominins, but a locale where their bones were deposited through the action of river water.

'Ubeidiya, located in the Rift Valley in Israel (see Figure 3.4), is slightly younger, at 1.5 million years ago. This site is usually described as a place where hominins carried out various tasks, although tilting of the geological layers has resulted in a reorientation of the site so that the layers are now steeply sloped rather than horizontal (Figure 3.5). There are later types of Oldowan stone artifacts, as well as animal bones with stone tool cut marks and one hominin tooth assigned to early *H. erectus*.[16] Analysis of the animal assemblage suggests that hominins at 'Ubeidiya were hunting horses and deer, which would have grazed in the uplands near the site and then moved downslope to obtain water at Lake Kinneret (Sea of Galilee).[17] This interpretation suggests that hominins leaving Africa may have incorporated more hunting (rather than just scavenging) activities into their behavioral strategies.

FIGURE 3.2
Cast of the skeletal remains of the Nariokotome Boy (*Homo erectus*) from East Africa.

Dmanisi a 1.7-million-year-old site in the Republic of Georgia that contains fossils of early *Homo erectus*, animal bones, and choppers and flakes. It is one of the earliest sites known outside of Africa.

Sangiran a site on Java in Indonesia (Southeast Asia), it contains the remains of *Homo erectus* from 1.6 million years ago.

'Ubeidiya dating to 1.5 million years ago, this site in Israel in the Levantine Middle East is early evidence for the movement of *Homo erectus* out of Africa.

Timeline: Later Hominins

Although species of *Paranthropus* were present in Africa until 1 million years ago (see Chapter 2), modern humans are descended from members of the genus *Homo* lineage (Figure 3.3). Neandertals played a role in our ancestry, but *Homo floresiensis* and *Homo naledi* did not. The period from 2 million to 50,000 years ago witnessed several changes in the technology and typology of stone artifacts (shown in pink) and several periods of movement of hominins out of Africa (shown in red).[10]

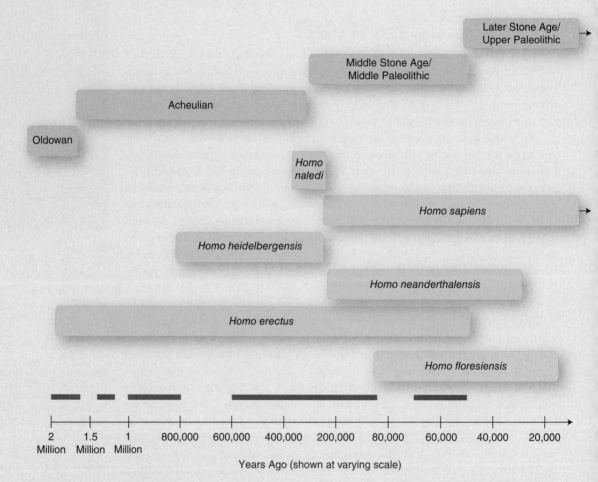

FIGURE 3.3
General timeline of genus *Homo* hominins and stone tool industries (Later Stone Age/Upper Paleolithic will be discussed in Chapter 4). Note that chopper tool industries similar to the Oldowan are present outside Africa until about 400,000 years ago and later, especially in Asia and Southeast Asia. Potential periods of movement out of Africa are shown as red bars. *Homo floresiensis* (*green*) is not ancestral to modern humans.

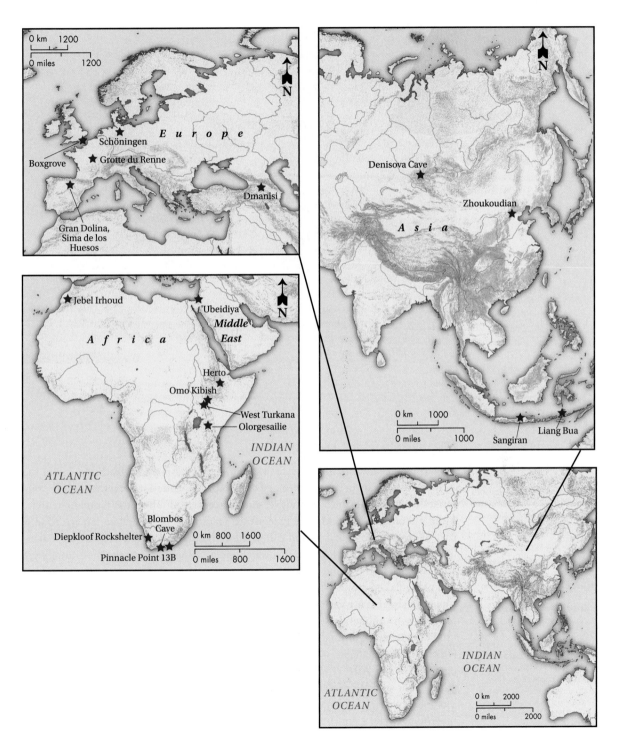

FIGURE 3.4
Location of sites mentioned in Chapter 3.

FIGURE 3.5
The layers at 'Ubeidiya, Israel, have been tilted by tectonic activity.

Meanwhile, Back in Africa

Acheulian flaked stone tool tradition characterized by bifaces such as handaxes. It first appears in Africa 1.7 million years ago, but not in East Asia until 800,000 years ago and in Europe until 500,000 years ago.

Middle Paleolithic a term used for the period between 250,000 and 39,000 years ago in Western Eurasia. The European Middle Paleolithic is associated with Neandertals.

Levallois a special way of knapping a core so that it is shaped in a way that allows the removal of a thin, well-shaped flake. These are known as Levallois flakes and Levallois points and are found in both Middle Stone Age and Middle Paleolithic stone artifact traditions.

Sometime around 1.7 million years ago in Africa, a stone tool tradition called the **Acheulian** appears in the archaeological record. This flaked stone industry is characterized by bifaces, including handaxes and cleavers (read "The Big Picture: Acheulian, Middle Stone Age, and Middle Paleolithic Traditions"). The Acheulian tradition is part of an archaeological period called the Early Stone Age (Africa)/Lower Paleolithic (outside of Africa). When the Acheulian first appears in Africa, hominins were still early *H. erectus* groups. In some instances, some of these groups were making and using flaked stone artifacts that were related to the earlier Oldowan industry. Acheulian bifaces are variously interpreted, particularly handaxes. Some researchers see bifaces as deliberately manufactured shapes (some oval, some pointed) of tools used in butchering animal carcasses. Others interpret bifaces as portable cores from which sharp-edge flakes were struck.[18] What is intriguing is that Acheulian technology is present in Africa for hundreds of thousands of years before it appears in other parts of the Old World. This would seem to mean that Acheulian-using hominins did not leave Africa until very late and that perhaps movements out of Africa in the interval between 2 and 1 million years ago were limited to groups of *H. erectus* who used Oldowan tools.

The Big Picture

Acheulian, Middle Stone Age, and Middle Paleolithic Traditions

The most characteristic stone tool types during the Acheulian are bifaces. These are nodules or large flakes from which flakes have been removed on both sides (faces), resulting in pointed to oval shapes sometimes called handaxes. Another type of biface is a cleaver, which has one end sharpened by the removal of a flake that creates a thin edge on the biface (Figure 3.6). The stone artifact traditions of the Middle Stone Age (in Africa) and the **Middle Paleolithic** (outside of Africa) are present by about 300,000 years ago. Both of these include varying amounts of specially prepared cores and their main removal types. The preparation of the core is called **Levallois** technique and is a way to shape a core by removing flakes in either radial or opposed directions (Figures 3.7 and 3.8). Shaping the core means that a surface is created from which a thin, nicely shaped removal can be made. These removals are known as Levallois flakes and Levallois points. Major differences between the Middle Stone Age and the Middle Paleolithic are that the Middle Stone Age has a variety of bifacial and other stone points, whereas the Middle Paleolithic is characterized by sidescrapers of various types.

A

B

FIGURE 3.7
African Middle Stone Age artifacts: (A) Levallois flake core (*left*), Nubian Levallois point core (*center*), and Levallois point (*right*). (B) bifacial points (from Blombos Cave, South Africa).

FIGURE 3.6
Acheulian bifaces from Africa.

FIGURE 3.8
Middle Paleolithic artifacts: sidescraper (*left*), Levallois flake core (*lower right*), and Levallois flake (*upper right*).

Homo heidelbergensis a later member of genus *Homo* that appears in Africa 800,000 years ago or slightly earlier; they migrate out of Africa and into the Middle East and Europe carrying Acheulian biface technology with them.

Olorgesailie Basin an area in Kenya in East Africa, it contains many important archaeological sites with Acheulian bifaces.

By 900,000 years ago, another hominin is found in the African fossil record. This is the group known as ***Homo heidelbergensis***. They are similar in overall skeletal form to early *H. erectus*, but *H. heidelbergensis* had a slightly larger brain size, ranging from 1,100 to 1,305 cc. This range falls within the lower part of brain size range that characterizes modern humans. *H. heidelbergensis* made and used Acheulian flaked stone artifacts.

There are many Acheulian sites in Africa, including numerous locales in the **Olorgesailie Basin** in Kenya that date between 900,000 and 600,000 years ago (see Figure 3.4). The Olorgesailie Basin has several geological beds that represent different time intervals. Archaeologists thus are able to study changes over time as well as the behaviors of hominins using Acheulian technology across the landscape in a given time interval.[19] This paleolandscape approach uses small test excavations into sites exposed in the geological layers. Study of these sites, in turn, allows assessment of the different habitats available over the landscape at different time periods and the types of hominin activities present at each of these locales. These interpretations are based on the kinds of flaked stone artifacts found and the presence or absence of animal bones. Besides the archaeological sites, sources for stone used in the manufacture of flaked stone artifacts are recorded to examine the distances over which hominins transported stone to sites.

In the geological bed called Upper Member 1, which dates between 992,000 and 974,000 years ago, dense clusters and light scatters of stone artifacts and animal bones were found.[20] The differences in the density of materials indicate that hominins used some locales more frequently or for longer periods of time than other places in the landscape. The high-density locale called Site 2, for instance, has scrapers and sharp flakes associated with cut- and percussion-marked bones of 15 different large animal species. At the site of I3, in contrast, there are numerous bifaces (including handaxes) and other flaked stone artifacts, as well as abundant, fragmented large animal bones.[21] This site is situated near an outcrop of lava that can be used to make stone tools, and the presence of this outcrop is probably the reason that hominins repeatedly visited this place. Dense concentrations of bifaces during Member 1 times are always associated with nearby outcrops of knappable stone. Overall, artifacts and animal bones are relatively continuously represented across the landscape of Upper Member 1, suggesting that the land surface was similar nearly everywhere.[22] This contrasts with later periods where there are large areas where no flaked stone artifacts are found, suggesting that hominins were using the landscape in a different way than during Member 1 times.

Later Movement Out of Africa

It is probable that some hominin groups moved out of Africa in the interval from 1.7 million to 800,000 years ago.[23] These migrations may explain the arrival of hominins in Europe around 1.4 million years ago.[24] Most of the earliest inhabitants in Europe made and used Oldowan stone tools and were associated with Mediterranean habitats rather than living in more northerly parts of Europe. One of the most extensively excavated sites is the **Gran Dolina at Atapuerca** in Spain (Figure 3.9; see also Figure 3.4). *H. erectus* fossils[25] are especially abundant in Layer TD6 (800,000 years ago), where they are found associated with choppers and flakes, as well as bones of horse and deer.[26] Layer TD6 represents a campsite where repeated visits by hominins reflect activities such as making and using flaked stone artifacts and butchering animal carcasses. The stone tool cut marks on the animal bones suggest that hominins had access to abundant meat and they must have either hunted these animals or used active scavenging to take kills away from other animals. All of these activities might be expected given what we know about the behaviors of earlier hominins. What makes Layer TD6 unusual is that the bones of the hominins have the same types of stone tool cut and other processing marks as the animal bones and are found intermixed with the animal bones. This patterning is interpreted to mean that hominins at the Gran Dolina were cannibals who actively hunted other hominins (especially infants and young children), perhaps in the context of defending territories.[27] Once killed, they were butchered and consumed in the same manner as other animals. If this is correct, it is a set of new behavioral strategies, but one that is only occasionally encountered in later hominin groups, including modern humans.

H. erectus groups continued to occupy Asia, where they are found at sites such as **Zhoukoudian** in China (see Figure 3.4). Deposits at Locality 1 here date between 750,000 and 410,000 years ago[28] and contain numerous *H. erectus* fossils, Oldowan stone tools, and bones from water buffalo, extinct giant deer, and horses. Interpretations of this site originally suggested that hominins were hunters (because of stone tool cut marks on animal bones) and that they controlled and used fire. Detailed studies of the sediments thought to represent ash deposits, however, show that the red and dark staining is instead caused by the presence of iron and manganese, respectively.[29] Zhoukoudian also was a focus in the hunting-versus-scavenging debate for *H. erectus*, with some researchers suggesting that Locality 1 represented cave occupations by scavenging animals that alternated with cave occupations by scavenging hominins.[30] Recent

Gran Dolina at Atapuerca a Lower Paleolithic archaeological site in Spain (western Europe) with deposits containing choppers and flakes dating as early as 1 million years ago; fossil hominins (*Homo erectus*) are found here 800,000 years ago with evidence for cannibalism.

Zhoukoudian a *Homo erectus* site in China dating to 750,000 to 410,000 years ago; it has chopper/chopping tools similar to the Oldowan.

FIGURE 3.9
Excavations at the Gran Dolina site at Atapuerca, Spain.

bone taphonomic studies support this alternating-use idea. Some of the horse bone was burned while the bone was fresh, which means that *H. erectus* had access to fire,[31] although no hearths were found.

Sometime around 800,000 years ago, there is a movement of *H. heidelbergensis* out of Africa. These groups took Acheulian technology with them into the Middle East, Europe, and India. They also moved into East Asia (China) because we find Acheulian bifaces there.[32] Oldowan-like technology continued to be used as well. Bifaces, however, do not appear to be common in Southeast Asia. One intriguing possible explanation may be that *H. erectus* there used other materials, such as bamboo, for making sharp-edge tools.[33] Recent experimental archaeology shows that Oldowan-type choppers and flakes have the potential to effectively cut and shape bamboo; however, sharp pieces of bamboo are not good for cutting through animal hides.[34] This might suggest that if hominins were using bamboo as tools, it was for types of tasks not associated with butchery.

The earliest occupations in more northerly latitudes in Europe date to 800,000 years ago. At this time, climate was cooler and characterized by a boreal forest, a novel habitat for early hominins.[35] By 700,000 years ago, warmer climatic conditions of an interglacial phase resulted in a more Mediterranean-like habitat, and England was connected to the rest of Europe by a land bridge (across part of what is now the English Channel).[36] Evidence of hominin activities in England include coastal sites, where Oldowan-like choppers and flakes were used[37] (see Figure 2.7). Around 500,000 years ago, during another interglacial period with warmer conditions and Mediterranean-like vegetation, other coastal areas in England such as **Boxgrove** (see Figure 3.4) contain abundant evidence of Acheulian technology.[38] The majority of the sites at Boxgrove are associated with butchery activities. The refitting of flaked stone artifacts[39] shows that many handaxes were made here, presumably because they and the flakes from them were used for obtaining meat from animal carcasses. Analysis of the animal bones from the Boxgrove sites shows numerous stone tool cut marks and bones fragmented by percussion to acquire marrow.[40] All of this evidence taken together suggests that *H. heidelbergensis* had early access to animal carcasses with abundant meat, and it is likely that they hunted these animals rather than scavenged.

The flaked stone artifacts we find in the Acheulian are not hunting tools, nor are the artifacts associated with nonbiface assemblages during this time period, yet hominins such as *H. heidelbergensis* appear to have been hunters. Our best evidence for their hunting equipment comes from exceptional preservation contexts where wood has been found.[41] One of these sites is **Schöningen** in Germany (see Figure 3.4), which dates to 337,000 to 300,000 years ago.[42] Four nearly complete or complete sharpened wooden spears, ranging in length from 1.8 to 2.3 meters (6 to 7.5 feet), as well as six fragments, were found associated with horse bones that showed butchery marks.[43] These wooden spears, rather than flaked stone artifacts hafted onto wooden shafts, were used by *H. heidelbergensis* when hunting.

It is not yet clear whether *H. heidelbergensis* was able to live continuously in northern latitudes of Europe during glacial times when climate would have been much

Boxgrove a coastal region in England with several sites dating to 500,000 years ago and later. It is the earliest area in northern Europe with the Acheulian tradition. Bifaces are associated with butchery of animal carcasses and rare hominin fossils are identified as *Homo heidelbergensis*.

Schöningen an archaeological site of *Homo heidelbergensis* in Germany, dating to 337,000 years ago, with several wooden spears associated with horse bones.

colder. Some researchers suggest that the early local populations 800,000 years ago may have gone extinct or moved southward to habitats that were Mediterranean.[44] It is not until after 500,000 years ago that the colder glacial landscapes were successfully colonized by hominins both in Europe and in Asia.

Modern Humans, Neandertals, and *Homo floresiensis*

H. heidelbergensis and *H. erectus* were not modern humans in their cranial anatomy or their behaviors. The presence of modern humans and some of their contemporaries such as the Neandertals is most easily seen beginning 300,000 years ago, although we can trace certain skeletal features of these two hominin groups farther back in time. It is natural that many of us are curious about the origins of people who looked and behaved like us. For a variety of reasons discussed later, there are not straightforward answers to many of our research questions. These include figuring out our biological relationship to Neandertals (and other late hominin groups) and deciding what features make modern humans unique or different from other hominin groups. The debate about the origins of modern humans has a long-standing history, which in its most polarized form is the contrast between the Recent Single and the Multiregional Origin models. In some respects, this debate is about whether we consider Neandertals members of a different species (*Homo neanderthalensis*), and thus a different lineage from us (*H. sapiens*), or whether Neandertals are a subspecies (*Homo sapiens neanderthalensis*) who were closely related to us (*Homo sapiens sapiens*). We also will briefly look at a late hominin called *H. floresiensis*, who lived between 100,000 and 60,000 years ago on the island of Flores in Indonesia (Southeast Asia).

Multiregionalism, Recent Single Origin, and Assimilation Models

The original two models for the origins of modern humans are multiregionalism and recent single origins. The easiest way to think about these two models is to treat them as two endpoints of a spectrum, keeping in mind that there are several less extreme versions. The assimilation model is one of the newest ideas about modern human origins. From a biological viewpoint, all these models (and variations of them) have used fossils and then genetics as supporting evidence. Archaeological data also are used, particularly in examining whether different groups of hominins, such as Neandertals and modern humans, were behaviorally similar (read "The Origins of Modern Behaviors"). We will briefly explore the three models in this section.

MULTIREGIONALISM

One of the main assumptions in **multiregionalism** is that all hominin populations were interconnected through the evolutionary process of gene flow (see Chapter 2). Early movements out of Africa by *H. erectus* groups (including

Multiregionalism an interpretive model for the origins of modern humans, it is based on the evolutionary process of gene flow and hypothesizes that modern humans everywhere in the Old World evolved locally from archaic hominins because gene flow kept all populations similar enough to interbreed successfully.

H. heidelbergensis) resulted in the colonization of many regions of the Old World (Asia, Southeast Asia, South Asia, and Europe). Although populations in these regions, as well as in Africa, may have been small in number, most were not isolated from each other. Members of one group mated with those of a nearby group, who in turn mated with members of yet another group (Figure 3.10). The gene pool

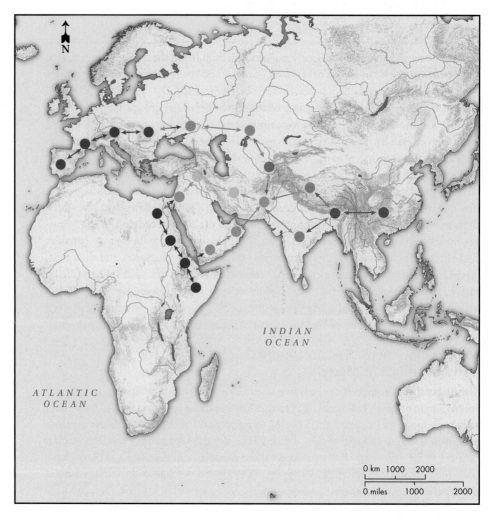

FIGURE 3.10

A simplified diagram showing how populations that are widely separated over geographical space can share genes through gene flow. The bidirectional arrows indicate the flow of genes from one population to the next due to mating between individuals of different populations. Genes thus "flow" from one population to its neighboring populations, with the gradual spread of genes across large geographical expanses.

of a given population thus became a combination of variants of genes from both populations (gene flow), as well as facilitating genetic material "traveling" over geographic space so that all hominins were members of the same species and all contributed to the gene pool, which is the combined set of variations for all genes in a species. In multiregionalism, all hominins have been members of the same species since the first movement out of Africa after 1.9 million years ago.[45] And, all regional hominin populations evolved into modern humans because all were interconnected as a result of gene flow.

Until the late 1980s, hominin fossils were the main source of data for understanding the origins of modern humans and our evolutionary relationships, especially with Neandertals. The morphology (form) of various skeletal elements, as well as measurements of and features on bones, were and are used to distinguish among *H. sapiens*, Neandertals, and late Asian/Southeast Asian *H. erectus*. Multiregionalism emphasizes skeletal continuities in regional populations from earlier forms to living modern humans as evidence to support their perspective.

One example of possibly continuity in skeletal features that multiregional proponents use is from late *H. erectus* populations in Asia and Southeast Asia to *H. sapiens*. This can be seen in East Asian features such as relatively flat faces and a special type of incisor (our front four teeth, top and bottom), which has a thickening of enamel on the back side edges that is called shovel shaped. In Southeast Asia, continuity over time is seen in relatively projecting faces and somewhat flat and sloping foreheads.[46]

RECENT SINGLE ORIGIN

The **recent single origin** model states that anatomically modern humans originated only in Africa and that this speciation event occurred relatively recently (around 300,000 years ago).[47] This model assumes that all earlier hominin populations outside of Africa went extinct, including *H. erectus* in Asia and Southeast Asia, as well as the Neandertals in Europe and the Middle East (Figure 3.11). Early anatomically modern human populations began moving out of Africa before 100,000 years ago, a process that continued until at least 60,000 to 50,000 years ago. The latest movements were of anatomically modern humans who were behaviorally modern. In the single origin viewpoint, modern human groups replaced all existing hominins in areas outside of Africa by 39,000 years ago, except for *H. floresiensis* (see later).

When using evidence from the fossil record, recent single origin proponents stress the disappearance of constellations of skeletal features that characterized earlier regional populations, as well as the African skeletal form that typifies early modern humans outside of Africa and humans today. Constellations of skeletal features that disappear can be seen in the Neandertal example. Neandertals lived in Western Eurasia (Europe, the Middle East, and parts of Central Asia) and are not found in Africa. Neandertals were robust individuals with powerful muscular

Recent Single Origin an interpretive model for the origins of modern humans, based on the idea that modern humans originated only on the continent of Africa and spread from there to other world regions; it hypothesizes that modern humans replaced more archaic hominins living in regions outside Africa.

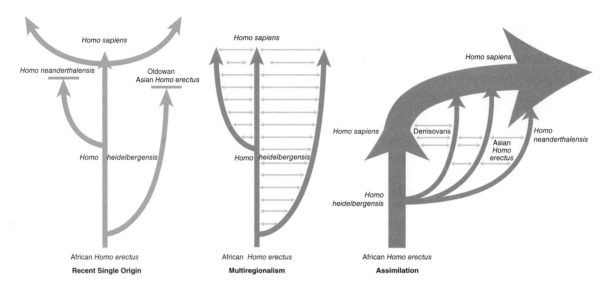

FIGURE 3.11

The recent single origin, multiregionalism, and assimilation models for modern human origins. Blue bars indicate extinction of hominin lineages; yellow arrowed lines indicate gene flow between populations.

development and a brain size similar to us (Figure 3.12). The skeletal features that made them distinctive as a population include a large nasal cavity and their robustness, which are interpreted as biological adaptations to extreme cold stress in glacial Europe.[48] A robust physique would have helped conserve body heat, an obvious advantage during cold periods of the last ice age.[49] Other distinctive Neandertal features include powerful hands, a space between the last molar tooth and the vertical portion of the lower jaw, lack of a chin, large brow ridges, a protrusion at the back of the skull (occipital bun), a skull that was long and low in shape, and a barrel-shape ribcage. No earlier or living modern human groups have this complete set of features, and recent single origin supporters use this as evidence that Neandertals were a separate lineage from modern humans.

The set of skeletal features that characterizes modern humans (*H. sapiens*), on the other hand, is first found in fossil specimens from Africa. The earliest known are from **Jebel Irhoud** in Morocco at 315,000 years ago, with later specimens from **Omo Kibish** (195,000 years ago) and **Herto** (160,000 years ago) in Ethiopia (see Figure 3.4).[50] *H. sapiens* as a group are characterized by globular-shape heads, small faces and small teeth, a vertical forehead, chins, a linear body, and relatively long legs (see Figure 3.12). This body shape and the longer limbs are typical for many tropical and subtropical populations where having more body surface area helps dissipate body heat. The fact that the earliest modern human fossils in the Middle East (dating from 177,000 to 90,000 years ago) and early

Jebel Irhoud the earliest site to yield fossils of early modern humans, at 315,000 years ago. It is in Morocco (northwest Africa).

Omo Kibish a site in Ethiopia (Africa) that yielded fossils of early *Homo sapiens* (skeletally modern humans) dating to 195,000 years ago.

Herto a site in Ethiopia (Africa) that yielded skeletally modern human (*Homo sapiens*) fossils dating to 160,000 years ago.

modern human fossils from Europe (dating after 50,000 years ago)[51] share the tropical/subtropical body type first seen in Africa suggests to advocates of the recent single origin model that *H. sapiens* is a lineage distinct from Neandertals and from contemporary hominins in Asia and Southeast Asia.[52]

In 1987, a study of **mitochondrial DNA** (mtDNA) in living humans gave support to the recent single origin model.[53] Mutations (changes; see Chapter 2) in the genes in mtDNA, which is a type of DNA found outside the nucleus in cells, were examined. mtDNA is almost always inherited only from females; that is, it is passed along from a mother to her sons and daughters.[54] This greatly simplifies the study of mutations over time because mtDNA represents the genetic contribution of just one parent rather than both parents. Based on this study, researchers found that the greatest diversity in mtDNA genes (that is, the most variation caused by mutations over time) exists in African populations, suggesting that they represent the oldest modern human populations.

But mtDNA from living human populations is not necessarily that of ancient populations such as the Neandertals. Fortunately, we have been able to recover ancient mtDNA from several European Neandertals from sites in Germany, Croatia, Spain, and Russia.[55] The results of Neandertal mtDNA studies showed that, on average, they differed from living modern human populations by 35 mutations. This contrasts with an average difference between living modern human populations of 10 mutations. These results were interpreted by many as indicating that Neandertals were quite different from modern humans, and the calculation of an mtDNA clock based on this evidence suggested that Neandertals and modern humans last shared a common ancestor more than 500,000 years ago. This finding was supported by mtDNA analysis from modern human fossils from a site in Italy,[56] which dates to 24,000 years ago. The mtDNA from these modern human fossils showed that they grouped with living modern humans rather than with Neandertals.

ASSIMILATION MODEL

The **assimilation model** also uses evidence from fossil and genetic studies.[57] Assimilation means that there is some continuity in a few skeletal details between different hominin populations, a continuity that also is shown in some genetic aspects. Proponents of this perspective argue that modern humans have a mainly African origin but that once these groups moved out of Africa, they were able to successfully interbreed

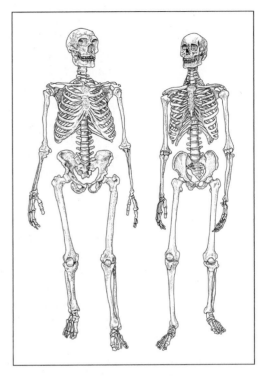

FIGURE 3.12
The Neandertal (*left*) and modern human (*right*) skeletons compared.

Mitochondrial DNA a type of DNA located outside the nucleus in a cell; it is passed down from mothers to their children and represents maternal lineages. It is useful in examining the relationship of Neandertals to modern humans as well as human migration events in prehistory.

Assimilation Model it uses a combination of the fossil and mtDNA evidence indicating a mainly African origin for modern humans in combination with nuclear DNA evidence showing that modern humans interbred with sister lineages such as the Neandertals and Denisovans.

(gene flow) with other hominin populations such as the Neandertals and Denisovans (see later). This perspective thus combines a few elements of the multiregionalism and recent single origin models but also demonstrates that the origins of modern humans are very complex. Fossils from Jebel Irhoud, Omo, and Herto in Africa are accepted as documenting the African origins of modern humans. Neandertals in Western Eurasia and other hominin groups in Central, East, and Southeast Asia are seen as sister lineages to modern humans.

Overall, while the mtDNA studies for an African origin of modern humans are accepted, some researchers wondered what studies of nuclear DNA (passed down from both parents) from Neandertals might show. In 2010, the draft genetic sequence of the Neandertal genome (all the hereditary information or genes) from Neandertal fossils from Croatia, Germany, Russia, and Spain was published.[58] When compared to the genome of modern humans, it is apparent that Neandertals did contribute genes to the gene pool of people living today. But there are interesting nuances. Human populations in sub-Saharan Africa do not have genes from Neandertals, whereas the gene pool of populations outside of sub-Saharan Africa contains Neandertal genes.[59] This suggests that modern humans have a sub-Saharan African origin and that there was no gene flow between Neandertals and sub-Saharan modern humans. The level of interbreeding between Neandertals and modern humans outside of sub-Saharan Africa was low because only 1 to 4% of the modern human gene pool is the result of gene flow from Neandertals. Analysis of several specific genes show that Neandertals had the modern human form of the **FOXP2** gene, which is necessary for human speech production (see "Language").

FOXP2 the human form of this gene regulates the growth and development of the basal ganglia, a brain structure important in motor control and sequencing for bipedalism and for spoken language.

The other example of interbreeding between modern humans and other hominin groups comes from genetic studies of the fossils from **Denisova Cave** in Central Asia (Siberia; see Figure 3.4), which has several layers with fossils. These fossils have been nicknamed the "Denisovans." The oldest fossil is at least 100,000 years old, while the most recent fossil dates to 48,000 years ago.[60] The genetic studies indicate that the Denisovans split from the lineage leading to Neandertals at least 190,000 years ago and thus are a sister lineage to both Neandertals and modern humans. Just like the Neandertals, however, the Denisovans were able to successfully interbreed with modern humans. We know this because there are 4 to 6% Denisovan genes in the gene pool of some modern human populations in the Pacific region, as well as Denisovan genes that help modern humans adapt to living at high altitudes in Tibet.[61]

Denisova Cave genetic analysis of fossil hominin bones found at this Siberian site in Russia indicates that this population is distantly related to Neandertals. The Denisovans interbred with later modern humans because about 4 to 6% of their genes are present in the gene pool of some Pacific region populations.

As a result of the fossil and genetic studies, it now seems likely that the assimilation model for the origins of modern humans is the best current explanation (read "Peopling the Past: Genetics, Neandertals, and Modern Humans"). Modern humans do have a relatively recent origin in Africa, but our sister lineages of the Neandertals and Denisovans were able to interbreed with prehistoric modern humans. Whether we should classify groups such as the Neandertals as a separate species (*H. neanderthalensis*) or as a subspecies (*H. sapiens neanderthalensis*) is still open to debate.

Peopling the Past

Genetics, Neandertals, and Modern Humans

The shifts in scientific interpretation about the relationship of Neandertals and modern humans are a good example of the scientific method in action. The use of skeletal features of Neandertals compared to those of modern humans, as well as aspects of the archaeological record such as presence or absence of evidence for symbolism, led initially to the development of two diametrically opposed theories (Figure 3.13). One of the first independent tests of these ideas came from knowledge gained from mtDNA studies of living human populations and then from mtDNA studies of both Neandertals and modern humans living at about the same time in Ice Age Europe. This genetic evidence was particularly important as support for the recent single origin model because it suggested that Neandertals were a side branch in human evolution. However, genetic data from studies of nuclear DNA in Neandertals later showed that they contributed genes to the gene pool of modern humans living outside of sub-Saharan Africa. This lent support to the gene flow feature prominent in the multiregionalism origin model. As a result, the original diametrically opposed ideas about Neandertals and modern human origins have been combined to reflect a newer hypothesis, the assimilation model, which emphasizes both the recent African origin of modern humans and the contributions of Neandertals and other sister lineages to the gene pool of many living modern people.

Scientific Method in Action

1. Examine Available Data	features of fossils and types of archaeological materials available
2. Develop Hypotheses	recent single origin in Africa OR multiregional evolution into modern humans
3. Test Hypotheses	mtDNA data favors recent single origin in Africa
4. Continue Testing Hypotheses	nuclear DNA from Neandertals and Denisovans is present in modern non-sub-Saharan African populations
5. Revise Hypotheses	modern humans originate in Africa, migrate out of Africa, and mate with other populations
6. Develop New Consensus	some features of the original recent single origin and multiregionalism are both correct; inaccurate features are removed from the models
7. Future Research	more revisions will occur when additional fossil, genetic, and archaeological materials are available in the future

FIGURE 3.13
How the scientific method works.

Isolation and a New Species

When we examine the appearance of anatomically modern human fossils or the early emergence of some Neandertal features in certain European fossils, it is clear that hominin populations were to some extent partially isolated from each other. Through various evolutionary processes[62] (see Chapter 2), these partial isolations resulted in

Homo floresiensis hominins from the island of Flores in Indonesia (Southeast Asia) who lived between 100,000 and 60,000 years ago. Their small stature and small brain size, along with other primitive skeletal features, suggest that they are an isolated population descended from either *Homo erectus* or earlier australopith-like hominins. They overlap in time with *Homo sapiens*.

Liang Bua Cave: an archaeological site on the island of Flores in Indonesia (Southeast Asia) that yielded the remains of *Homo floresiensis*. It also contains animal bones such as the dwarfed, elephant-like, extinct *Stegodon*.

the development of differing skeletal features that characterized the different populations. These partial isolations sometimes can result in speciation events leading to populations such as *Homo floresiensis*.

Excavations at **Liang Bua Cave** on the island of Flores in Indonesia in Southeast Asia yielded several hominin specimens (see Figure 3.4). They are classified as *H. floresiensis* and date between 100,000 and 60,000 years ago.[63] This discovery generated a lively debate with significant implications for our understanding of hominin movements out of Africa, as well as the late survival of hominins that are not us. *H. floresiensis* is unusual for several reasons. It was small bodied, at just more than a meter (3.5 feet) tall with a long, low skull and a cranial capacity (430 cc) that is within the range of the australopiths[64] (Figure 3.14). It was a habitual biped, but the structure of its foot was apelike (flat and long), suggesting that it had a walking gait different from modern humans and also Neandertals, *H. heidelbergensis*, and *H. erectus*.[65] Additionally, *H. floresiensis* had a shoulder structure with a shorter collar bone and an upper arm bone with less of a torsion angle than in modern humans. This resulted in a "shrugged" shoulder more like that found in early *H. erectus* around 1.9 million years ago. The wrist structure of *H. floresiensis* also was more primitive and resembled that of hominins before 800,000 years ago.[66]

Researchers have proposed several different ideas for the mosaic of features seen in *H. floresiensis*.[67] One of these relies on structural abnormalities caused by pathologies such as microcephaly, in which the brain does not develop normally and head size and cranial capacity are small. Another is Laron syndrome, a growth hormone issue that results in short individuals with small cranial capacity. And some researchers have suggested Down syndrome. None of these pathological explanations, however, can account for the complex of features we see in *H. floresiensis*, nor do they explain why the *H. floresiensis* features often are similar to those of earlier hominins.

Another idea is that *H. floresiensis* represents an example of "island dwarfing" of a *H. erectus* population, because there are *H. erectus* in Java about 1.6 million years ago, and by 700,000 years ago on Flores there are fossils that appear to be ancestors of *Homo floresiensis*.[68] Island dwarfing is an evolutionary phenomenon that occurred for some animal populations, such as elephants and hippopotamus on Cyprus in the Mediterranean. These animals became smaller in size when isolated on an island. A smaller body size requires less food and may facilitate survival when

FIGURE 3.14
A cast of the skull of *Homo floresiensis*.

limited food resources are available in an island context. Other animals, such as the extinct *Stegodon* (elephant-like animal), did undergo island dwarfing on Flores, so perhaps that is what we see with *H. floresiensis*. A final explanation is that *H. floresiensis* is a descendant of a group of early hominins (pre–*H. erectus*) who were typically small bodied with small brain size and who left Africa earlier than *H. erectus*. If accurate, this explanation would require that we rethink the "first" out of Africa movement that usually is attributed to *H. erectus* (read "Further Reflections: Was There an Out of Africa Before 1.9 Million Years Ago?").[69]

The Origins of Modern Behaviors

The appearance of skeletally modern populations just before 300,000 years ago in Africa has raised the question of whether these early members of *H. sapiens* were both biologically and behaviorally modern. That is, does the emergence of modern human biology and behavior coincide in time? Researchers also have debated whether our Neandertal relatives had modern behaviors. One of the most difficult aspects of examining these questions is deciding how to define and recognize modern behavior based on the types of evidence available in the archaeological record (read "Peopling the Past: Defining and Identifying Modern Behavior"). Virtually all researchers, however, agree that one of the key features of modern behavior is the use of symbolism (including language).[70]

Another conceptual problem that affects our interpretations of the appearance of modern behaviors relates to the history of archaeological research, which was particularly intensive over the past 150 years in Europe. As a result, we have a detailed European archaeological record, which includes many examples of spectacular finds, such as cave paintings, sculpted figurines, and personal ornamentation (see Chapter 4), that are from sites inhabited by Upper Paleolithic modern humans after 45,000 years ago. Our view of the origins of modern human behavior thus has long been "Eurocentric." We now know, however, that the origins of modern human behaviors are in Africa and have a much greater time depth than 45,000 years ago.

Middle Stone Age Africa

In the past several decades, archaeological research on sites of the **Middle Stone Age** in Africa has yielded clues to the origins of modern human behaviors. The Middle Stone Age begins 300,000 years ago and lasts until 50,000 years ago. Before 200,000 years ago, there is little evidence in the Middle Stone Age to suggest potentially modern behaviors. A few researchers, however, claim that the appearance of flaked stone points of various types indicates that Middle Stone Age people were making complex weaponry that included hafting points onto wooden or other organic spear shafts[78] and that the different points represent styles or traditions of point making (read "The Big Picture: Acheulian, Middle Stone Age, and Middle Paleolithic Traditions"). Style is interpreted as an indicator of symbolic communication and, thus, of modern human behavior.

Middle Stone Age a term for the period between 300,000 to 50,000 years ago in Africa. The Middle Stone Age has evidence for personal ornamentation, art, bone tools, and different types of stone points, as well as the incorporation of shellfish in the diet at coastal sites.

Defining and Identifying Modern Behavior

One of the reasons that defining modern human behavior is difficult is because behaviors, as part of cultural adaptations, can and do vary greatly across the world. This fact makes it problematic to use a list of traits that equate to modern human behavior.[71] How many traits from such a list, for example, are the minimum needed to recognize modern human behavior in the archaeological record? And there might even be ridiculous situations in which applying a trait list to living human groups meant that some of them would not be classified as modern in behavior! The one feature that is agreed on is that modern human behaviors include the use of symbolism.

Archaeologists thus are quite interested in identifying materials that indicate symbolic behaviors, particularly for more remote periods of time. But even these types of materials can be open to debate. One example of this is red ochre, an iron-containing clayey sediment. Powdered red ochre often is found in burials and other symbolic contexts with modern humans of the **Upper Paleolithic** period (see Chapter 4), where we interpret its use as symbolic. Some of the earliest known red ochre, however, is from **Blombos Cave** in South Africa (see Figure 3.4), where a 100,000-year-old kit for grinding ochre into powder was found, as well as an 80,000-year-old ochre piece with incised lines that look like a geometric pattern (Figure 3.15).[72] These discoveries most often have been interpreted as evidence for the use of red ochre in symbolic ways, such as a pigment for body painting or a piece of art in the case of the geometric design on the chunk of red ochre.

FIGURE 3.15
The engraved red ochre piece from Blombos Cave, South Africa.

But is symbolism the only possible explanation for the red ochre at Blombos Cave and other Middle Stone Age sites?

As it turns out, there are other potential uses for red ochre that are not overtly symbolic. Traces of red ochre, for example, have been found on Middle Stone Age stone artifacts that were used as points.[73] In this case, the red ochre is an essential component of the "glue" (called mastic) used to bind a stone point to a wood or bone haft.[74] Other researchers have noted that red ochre might have been used in the tanning process for animal hides because it might act as a preservative.[75] This still leaves us with pieces such as the geometric design on the red ochre piece at Blombos Cave, as well as similar evidence from other Middle Stone Age sites.[76] Even if we decide not to attribute early use of red ochre to symbolic behaviors, perhaps one of the most significant points is noted by Lyn Wadley and her colleagues.[77] They suggest that, because Middle Stone Age peoples recognized the properties of different raw materials such as red ochre and could figure out ways to use these and other materials in complex mastic compounds, this means that their cognitive abilities were like those of people living today.

After 200,000 years ago, we begin to see an accumulation of evidence in the Middle Stone Age that might represent modern behaviors including symbolism. As early as 164,000 years ago, for example, Middle Stone Age people at the coastal site of **Pinnacle Point 13B** (South Africa; see Figure 3.4) expanded their diet to include shellfish.[79] We know that later hunter–gatherer–foragers who had diets including shellfish often were less mobile and had complex social systems, conditions under which symbolic behaviors might be developed or enhanced. The additional presence of ground and scraped red ochre at Pinnacle Point 13B is used to suggest body painting, which would be a form of symbolic communication (but read "Peopling the Past: Defining and Identifying Modern Behavior" for other explanations of red ochre). There also is bladelet technology, which is the knapping of small, linear-shape removals called bladelets from cores. This is a feature that is consistently found in sites after 50,000 years ago that were occupied by modern humans in many parts of the Old World.

Although the symbolic nature or modern human behavior interpretation of the early archaeological materials discussed earlier can be debated, beginning 100,000 years ago there are additional and often clearer examples of features linked to modern human behaviors. Sites in Morocco,[80] as well as Blombos Cave (South Africa), yielded perforated *Nassarius* shells interpreted as shell beads (Figure 3.16). These shells are not modified, but their natural perforations made it easy to string them together or attach them to clothing as personal ornamentation, indicating self-expression or awareness. In addition to more than 65 perforated *Nassarius* shells, dating between 100,000 to 75,000 years ago, Blombos Cave also yielded more than 2,000 pieces of red ochre (many with marks showing use), as well 15 examples of red ochre that are engraved with geometric designs.[81] These pieces of engraved red ochre appear to document abstract representation, one of the fundamental aspects of symbolic behavior. Blombos Cave also has animal bones that have been made into points and

Upper Paleolithic an archaeological term widely used in the Old World (except for sub-Saharan Africa) to represent the period from 45,000 to 9700 cal BC. In Europe, all of the Upper Paleolithic cultures, except for the Chatelperronian, are associated with modern humans.

Blombos Cave a Middle Stone Age archaeological site in South Africa with evidence for symbolic behaviors around 100,000 years ago.

Pinnacle Point 13B a Middle Stone Age archaeological site in South Africa with some of the earliest evidence for potentially modern human behaviors (use of red ochre and diet expansion to include shellfish), dating to 164,000 years ago.

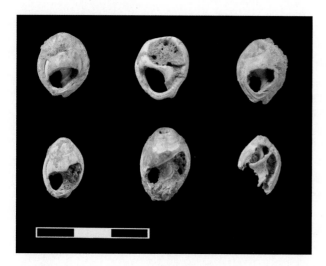

FIGURE 3.16
Examples of Middle Stone Age *Nassarius* shells from Contrebandiers Cave, Morocco. They are often interpreted as shell beads indicating symbolic behavior.

Diepkloof Rock Shelter a Middle Stone Age archaeological site in South Africa with evidence of art in the form of engraved geometric patterns on ostrich egg shell containers that date to 60,000 years ago.

awls.[82] At other sites there are barbed bone points that have been interpreted as harpoons.[83] The use of organic materials such as bone to make tools is believed by many researchers to be a modern human behavior (but see "Middle Paleolithic and Chatelperronian Europe").

Around 60,000 years ago, the engraving technique is extended to other types of materials. At the site of **Diepkloof Rock Shelter** (South Africa; see Figure 3.4), for example, there are 270 pieces of ostrich egg shell that are engraved with hatched lines and other patterns.[84] Ostrich egg shells frequently were used as containers to carry water by later hunter–gatherer–forager groups, and the process of engraving them is much more difficult than carving lines onto ochre (which is soft). Researchers at this site argue that there are four distinct engraved patterns on the ostrich egg shell fragments, suggesting these patterns represent styles (symbols) used in social interactions between people.

The expansion of the diet to include new food resources (shellfish), the emergence of personal ornamentation (perforated *Nassarius* shells) and artistic representation (engraved ochre and ostrich eggshells), the innovation of shaped bone tools (points, awls, and harpoons), and the hafting of stone points onto shafts (composite tools), as well as evidence for long-distance transport of stone raw materials and possibly for styles of flaked stone artifact (points) are a package of features that signal modern human behaviors to many researchers. What is interesting about the African evidence is that all of these innovations do not appear at the same moment in time. Instead, they are sporadically present at different moments in time and over widely separated regions. This suggests that the origins of modern human behaviors are a gradual development of adaptations and technologies that come together as a package sometime around 70,000 to 50,000 years ago, representing cultural mosaic evolution[85] (see the biological concept of mosaic evolution in the glossary).

The movement of this complex of skeletally modern humans with the package of modern human behaviors to other parts of the Old World represents what is sometimes called Out of Africa 2. These later *H. sapiens* leaving Africa 70,000 to 65,000 years ago are thought by many researchers to represent when modern humans and modern behaviors spread and also why modern humans were able to replace nearly all contemporary hominin groups such as *H. erectus* in Asia and the Neandertals in Europe. In this perspective, the adaptations and technologies that characterized later *H. sapiens* gave them cultural advantages that allowed them to outcompete other hominins whose adaptations were more biological. And some researchers have proposed that one of the most important of the modern human adaptations was the result of neural changes in the brain that led to the enhanced communication skills that we know as modern human language, a subject to which we now turn.[86]

Language

Modern human language is a system of communication using abstract symbols represented by arbitrary sounds, gestures, or written signs that are associated with meanings. Although gestural languages, such as American Sign Language, are as complex as spoken languages, we will focus here on spoken language by briefly examining the evolution of speech, the timing of the emergence of modern human speech, and whether hominins such as the Neandertals had our capacity for spoken language.

The ability to produce the complex and diverse array of sounds that characterize modern human languages is the result of a combination of the structure of our throat, how the human brain is organized and wired, and our fine motor control of facial and oral muscles.[87] In the throat, the folds of our **larynx** (voice box) use puffs of air to produce certain sounds, such as vowels, through the creation of vibrations. The tonal quality of these sounds is then produced in the **pharynx** (air space in the throat above the larynx), which is constantly changing in shape during the production of speech sounds. In modern humans, the larynx is positioned low in the throat, creating a long pharynx that permits the diverse variety of speech sounds that humans can make compared to many other animals, even those that are our close relatives such as the common chimpanzees and bonobos (Figure 3.17).

Two regions of the human brain, Broca's and Wernicke's areas (Figure 3.18), have long been recognized as important in human speech. They are found in the left side of the neocortex (gray matter of the brain) and are involved in speaking and understanding language, as well as in understanding the rules (syntax) of building sentences. We now know, however, that Broca's and Wernicke's areas are only part of the story. Structures called the **basal ganglia**, which are located below the neocortex (grey matter) in the brain, are connected by neural circuits to Broca's and Wernicke's areas and to other regions of the brain. The basal ganglia are believed to be the sequencing engine that regulates syntax, thought processes (cognition), and motor control.[88] Such control is extremely important for the sequencing of sound production as sound moves from the larynx through the pharynx and then is further modified by the position of the tongue and the movement of the lips.

Control of facial and oral muscles such as the tongue, although regulated by motor commands sequenced by the basal ganglia, also benefits from the human form of the FOXP2 gene, which helps control the development of neural circuits involved in motor control and cognition. Mutations to this gene result in severe language disorders in which affected individuals do not have the ability to sequence the control of their oral and facial muscles and thus cannot make speech sounds common to

Larynx the "voice box;" an organ in the throat that uses puffs of air to vibrate and produce sounds.

Pharynx the part of the throat above the larynx (voice box); in modern humans, the pharynx is long and this aids in the production of the variety of sounds found in modern languages.

Basal Ganglia a subcortical structure in the brain responsible for motor control and sequencing; it is important in the production of human speech sounds.

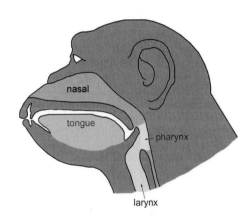

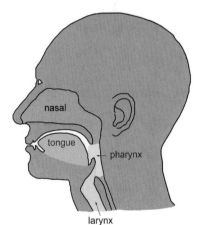

FIGURE 3.17
Comparison of the vocal areas in a common chimpanzee (*top*) and modern human (*bottom*). Note the larger pharynx region and shape of the tongue in humans.

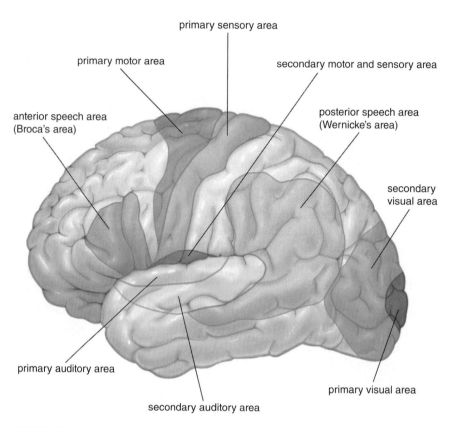

primary sensory area

primary motor area

secondary motor and sensory area

anterior speech area
(Broca's area)

posterior speech area
(Wernicke's area)

secondary
visual area

primary auditory area

primary visual area

secondary auditory area

FIGURE 3.18
Drawing of the human brain showing Broca's and Wernicke's areas.

language, as well as other difficulties.[89] The human form of FOXP2 differs from that of common chimpanzees by two mutations. Based on genetic clocks, these mutations in the human form of FOXP2 are believed to have appeared sometime after 100,000 years ago.[90]

The complexity of speech and language in humans, involving as it does changes to anatomical features in the throat, brain neural circuitry, and mutations in genes, is believed to be the result of gradual evolutionary changes. Similar to the origins of modern human behaviors, it required a long time for each of the necessary anatomical and genetic changes to come together as the package that facilitated modern human speech and language. This gradual development appears to have "kicked off" when our ancestors became bipeds, because the motor control and sequencing functions performed by the basal ganglia are critical to walking and running and thus would have been favored by natural selection.[91] The functions of the basal ganglia, over time, also were used for the sequencing and motor control needed in the production of speech sounds.

The earliest hominins, such as various australopiths, were able to communicate, but their utterances are unlikely to have been speech or language. Some researchers believe instead that protolanguage speech systems were present first among early *H. erectus* populations,[92] but we do not know what this type of speech might have been like because our only comparison is to our own fully developed speech and language systems. Soft tissues that we use to examine the production of speech sounds, such as the larynx and its position in the throat as well as the size of the pharynx, cannot be directly recovered because these soft tissues do not preserve over time. There have been, however, claims for indirect evidence of these anatomical structures and thus whether earlier hominins had the capacity for human speech sounds. This indirect evidence is based on measurements that show the **basicranial flexion** (the shape of the base of the skull), which is thought to reflect whether the larynx is high in the throat, like in common chimpanzees, or low in the throat, as in modern humans. The assumption is that a greater amount of flexion indicates a low position of the larynx. Measurements of the basicranial flexion in *Au. africanus*, *H. heidelbergensis*, and Neandertals shows less flexion than in modern humans and is interpreted as meaning that these hominins did not have the vocal structure to produce the full range of human speech sounds, although this assumption has been challenged.[93] In the case of the Neandertals, assumptions about their lack of the full range of sounds in modern human language also are based on the fact that they last shared a common ancestor with us around 500,000 years ago. As we have seen, however, the results of the study of Neandertal nuclear genes show that they had the modern human form of FOXP2. This may mean that Neandertals had the capacity and the ability for modern human speech and language.

Basicranial Flexion a series of measurements along the base of the skull that have been interpreted as indirect evidence for the length of the pharynx and thus for whether various hominin species were capable of producing human speech sounds.

Middle Paleolithic and Chatelperronian Europe

One of the central questions that remains is the extent to which Neandertals had modern human behaviors, especially evidence that could be interpreted as symbolic. There are several ways to address this issue, including comparisons between Neandertals and skeletally modern humans at different points in time. The archaeological records of Neandertals and early skeletally modern humans (in Africa and the Middle East) prior to 80,000 years ago, for example, share a number of features. Both hominins made and used relatively similar flaked stone tools (although there possibly were several stone point styles in Africa; see previous discussion), had diets often based on large animals (a niche similar to that occupied by social carnivores such as large cats[94]), demonstrated innovation,[95] and buried their dead, at least on occasion (see later discussion). There is one possible example of Neandertal personal ornamentation (use of eagle claws) in Europe at 130,000 years ago.[96] One of the intriguing aspects is that the earliest skeletally modern humans are definitively found outside Africa in only one place, the Middle East.[97] This suggests that their behaviors did not include the range of adaptations and innovations that would have allowed them to live in the colder conditions of Europe, although their flaked stone artifacts included hafted points that likely were parts of thrusting spears such as the Neandertals had.[98]

The picture changes considerably when we examine the archaeological record for Neandertals and skeletally modern humans after 80,000 years ago. As discussed earlier, a few Middle Stone Age sites in Africa have evidence of perforated shells used for personal ornamentation, occasional engraved pieces of red ochre beginning about 75,000 years ago, elaborate carved bone tools such as harpoons, and thousands of pieces of red ochre that may have been ground to create pigment for symbolic uses. After 65,000 years ago some Neandertal sites in Middle Paleolithic Europe contain evidence that suggests they were cognitively capable of the same behaviors that characterize modern humans. Two sites in France, for example, yielded Middle Paleolithic bone tools, and at a site in Russia, Neandertals carved notches into raven bone.[99] Additionally, at one site in France, there are more than 500 pieces of manganese dioxide, a mineral that produces a black pigment; at least half show traces of use.[100] In Belgium, one site has more than 40 pieces of a black pigment that was transported to the site over a distance of 40 kilometers (25 miles).[101] A coastal site in Spain yielded two perforated seashells with traces of red pigment around the perforation and one seashell with traces of several pigments suggesting its use as a container, whereas an inland Spanish site has a seashell with traces of an orange pigment and several pieces of red and yellow colorants (not ochre but other minerals).[102] The perforations on these shells are natural (as is the case with many Middle Stone Age perforated shells), but this does not preclude their use by Neandertals for personal ornamentation. Other late-occurring personal ornamentation at Neandertal sites in France includes perforated or grooved animal teeth (fox, reindeer, and horse), carved ivory ring fragments, and bird bones with consistently spaced notch marks from the **Grotte du Renne** (see Figure 3.4). Grotte du Renne is associated with the Neandertal flaked stone tradition called the **Chatelperronian**, an early Upper Paleolithic industry.[103] Finally, recent dating of cave art at three sites in Spain even suggests that Neanderals may have been painting some caves with simple designs (red lines, red painted mineral deposits on cave walls, and a hand stencil).[104]

Many Neandertal remains have been interpreted as burials,[105] but there is not complete agreement among archaeologists as to whether these are cultural or natural burials.[106] One reason that this is a contentious issue is because many of the Neandertal remains were excavated in the late AD 1800s and early AD 1900s when archaeological methods were not as precise in recording all aspects of contexts. This means that determining whether deliberate pits were dug by Neandertals to bury their dead can be difficult to assess, as is the association of possible burial goods with the skeletons.[107] At one site in France, for example, recent excavations show that a pit in which a Neandertal child was found during early excavations at the site was natural in origin, and other features of the geoarchaeology suggest that the body slumped into the depression and was rapidly buried by natural taphonomic processes.[108] Whether or not Neandertals deliberately buried their dead, it is important to remember that the standards used to assess the validity of burials must be applied not only to Neandertal but also to early modern human burials.

Grotte du Renne a French (western Europe) Middle Paleolithic site with evidence for Neandertal bone tools and personal ornamentation.

Chatelperronian an Early Upper Paleolithic tradition made by Neandertals in France (western Europe); it contains evidence for bone tools and personal ornamentation at sites such as Grotte du Renne.

European Neandertal diets were mainly meat (especially in northern Europe), including extinct large animals such as the woolly mammoth and the woolly rhinoceros, but also reindeer, deer, wild ass, and wild boar. This diet interpretation is based on microwear on their teeth and isotope studies of their bones.[109] A meat-focused pattern also is found in modern humans living in very northern latitudes because colder climates do not favor growth of plant foods that can be directly eaten and digested by hominins, although it would be possible to eat the stomach contexts of animals, which would provide partially digested plant foods.[110] Some researchers have suggested that the robust and muscular bodies of Neandertals, in combination with a biological adaptation to cold stress, may have been energy expensive compared to that of modern humans, with male Neandertals using 4,000 to 7,000 calories per day and female Neandertals 3,000 to 5,000 calories per day.[111] Meat, animal fat, and bone grease and marrow would have helped provide these calories. Neandertal populations, however, also ate pine nuts, moss, mushrooms, grass seeds, tubers, shellfish, birds, hare, land tortoise, and other small game.[112]

Neandertal groups faced several challenges in glacial Europe. These included how to keep warm and the dangers associated with hunting animals such as the woolly mammoth. We have little evidence that Neandertals built substantial dwellings in which they could shelter (as modern humans did when they moved into Europe; see Chapter 4), and researchers suggest that Neandertals had, at most, loose-fitting garments that did not provide as much warmth as tailored clothing (see Chapter 4).[113] Instead, their robust bodies may have biologically decreased heat loss (see "Skeletal Anatomy"). There is evidence from several sites in Europe that Neandertals used fire.[114] Hearths could have provided some warmth, although they seem to be used mainly during warm period rather than cold period occupations (at sites in France). Life for Neandertals appears to have been quite difficult because studies of their bones show that they experienced many head, neck, shoulder, arm, and leg injuries.[115] This damage pattern could be interpreted as the result of using thrusting spears that required Neandertals to be close to the large, dangerous animals they hunted. However, these types of injuries also characterize Pleistocene modern humans in Europe, and the pattern of injuries for Neandertals and modern humans could be the result of hunting accidents, interpersonal violence, or even the fact that the top of the head is a region that is more vulnerable to injury.[116]

When we think about the diversity of modern human cultures in the world today, it should not be surprising to us that Neandertals may have had a culture (or cultures) in which some behaviors were not like those of earlier modern humans, given that these two hominin groups mainly lived in different parts of the world before 70,000 years ago. Whether this can be interpreted as meaning that Neandertals did not have modern behaviors is a difficult question. Some differences between Neandertals and modern humans may be the result of behavioral responses to glacial versus tropical/subtropical conditions and the different habitats in these environments, rather than behaviors that were or were not modern. Not all Neandertals, of course, lived in glacial Europe. There also were populations in the much milder climate of the Middle East.[117] What we should keep in mind is that our interpretations of Neandertals and their activities sometimes are framed in a perspective of "us" versus "them," rather than an integrated understanding of their social behaviors.[118]

Disappearance of the Neandertals

As a skeletally distinct population, Neandertals disappear around 39,000 years ago.[119] Archaeologists used to argue that this occurred because Neandertals could not compete effectively with incoming modern humans, but this perspective is simplistic given what we now know about Neandertal biology and culture (see earlier).[120] Their biological adaptations to cold stress, apparent lack of cultural technologies such as well-built shelters and tailored clothing, high energy requirements, and, quite probably, low population size and density may have led to population crashes that resulted in their extinction,[121] although remember that Neandertal genes are present in non–sub-Saharan African modern human populations today. Such a set of population crashes also might be the result of a "volcanic winter" effect because a series of devastating volcanic eruptions in Italy and the Caucasus Mountains of Russia 40,000 years ago dramatically impacted ecologies from the Mediterranean to Central and Eastern Europe.[122] This might mean that most Neandertal populations disappeared less because of whether their behaviors were modern and more because their small and relatively isolated populations were unable to adjust quickly enough to compensate for considerably fewer food resources.

Further Reflections

Was There an Out of Africa Before 1.9 Million Years Ago?

The debate over *Homo floresiensis* involves questions about whether or not it should be a member of a new species of genus *Homo*, if it represents an example of island dwarfing of *H. erectus*, or even if the individuals are *H. sapiens* suffering from a particular pathological condition. Key to understanding the status of *H. floresiensis* is understanding what its ancestry might be. For those researchers who interpret the combination of unusual features in *H. floresiensis* (see earlier), many of these appear to be similar to an early *Homo* group such as *H. habilis*.[123] If true, one outcome of this hypothesis is that there would have been a migration out of Africa, likely before the appearance of *H. erectus*.

The implications of this idea are quite interesting. If an early *Homo* hominin left Africa around or before 1.9 million years ago, it would have done so using a form of habitual bipedalism that was not modern. We know that the modern form of habitual bipedalism is extremely energy efficient in comparison to nonmodern forms. Traveling over long distances (even over hundreds or thousands of generations of time) with a nonmodern form of habitual bipedalism requires that we rethink our assumptions about the behaviors of hominins with nonmodern habitual bipedalism. Another implication is whether or not an early genus *Homo* group leaving Africa had stone tool technology (probably Oldowan). We generally assume that stone tool technology would have been an important aid in acquiring food (especially meat and marrow, but also plants). But would it have been a necessary condition to successful migration? Perhaps not, given that we know that other animals migrate without needing technology, including hamadryas baboons (monkeys) that crossed the small waterway between the Horn of Africa and Yemen.[124]

Summary

- The Pleistocene epoch, which began 2.6 million years ago, was characterized by numerous climatic fluctuations between colder/drier and warmer/wetter intervals. These have implications for the movement of hominins out of Africa.

- The first movement out of Africa was by *H. erectus* and occurred after 1.9 million years ago. They took Oldowan technology with them and appear to have moved relatively rapidly, with sites appearing in Eastern Europe 1.7 million years ago and in Southeast Asia 1.6 million years ago.

- Hominins reach Western Europe 1.4 million years ago and were characterized by Oldowan technology.

- Acheulian technology develops in Africa 1.7 million years ago, but does not appear outside of Africa until after 900,000 years ago when *H. heidelbergensis* migrated out of Africa.

- The origins of modern humans and their relationship to Neandertals were originally examined by two different sets of ideas. The recent single origin model states that modern humans evolved in Africa and then migrated out and replaced all other hominins in the Old World. The multiregionalism model claims that gene flow between hominin populations over time and space allowed all hominin populations in the Old World to develop into modern humans. These perspectives were based initially on data from fossils and archaeology.

- Genetic analyses of mtDNA and nuclear DNA in modern humans, Neandertals, and the Denisovans now shows that modern humans who migrated out of Africa interbreed with Neandertals and Denisovans because some of their genes are found in living human populations. Thus, the assimilation model that includes a mainly African origin, but with gene flow between modern humans and sister lineages such as the Neandertals and Denisovans, currently explains the origins of modern humans more accurately.

- *H. floresiensis* is a small-bodied hominin in Indonesia with unusual skeletal features. These suggest that this hominin may be descended from Asian *H. erectus*, but in the context of dwarfing seen in island populations of other animals.

Alternatively, these features may indicate that there was a migration out of Africa that was pre–*H. erectus*.

- Identifying modern behavior in the archaeological record is difficult, although most researchers agree that evidence for symbolic behavior is one key characteristic.

- Middle Stone Age Africa has many sites with examples of symbolic behavior, usually recognized from the presence of shells that may have been strung as personal ornamentation, red ochre that could be ground and used for coloring such as body painting, and ochre chunks with engraved lines that may be artistic motifs. Other features include the use of bone to make spear points and harpoons.

- Language is the most fundamental symbolic system of humans. Pinpointing its origin in the paleoanthropological record has been of interest, although this is difficult to do because evidence for the anatomical structures needed is usually indirect. There has been considerable debate about whether Neandertals had language like that of modern humans. We do know that both Neandertals and modern humans have the same human form of the FOXP2 gene, which is necessary for spoken language.

- Neandertals are often portrayed as not having all the features of modern human behavior. However, there is increasing archaeological evidence that they did at least occasionally use personal ornamentation and pigments, especially in the period after 65,000 years ago. Whether they deliberately buried their dead is still an open question.

- The distinctive skeletal signature of Neandertal populations does not exist in modern human populations. This means that Neandertals did go extinct around 39,000 years ago. Suggestions for why this extinction event occurred include the biological adaptations of Neandertals, a volcanic winter effect initiated by volcanic eruptions in Italy and the Caucasus, and their general lack of improvements in cultural technologies to help mitigate the especially cold climatic conditions in Europe after 40,000 years ago. Competition with incoming modern humans may also have been a factor.

Endnotes

1. The generic spelling of Neandertal can also be Neanderthal (with the "h"). This second spelling option comes from how their species name is spelled (*neanderthalensis*). Either generic version is acceptable spelling, but the rules of taxonomy mean that the species name must always be spelled as *neanderthalensis*. The "h" is sometimes dropped in the generic spelling because of changes in spelling rules in the German language that occurred after the discovery and naming of the Neander Valley fossil.

2. Gibbard et al. 2010; however, some researchers prefer to use the traditional date of 1.8 million years ago for the beginning of the Pleistocene (Gradstein et al. 2004).

3. These astronomical processes are known as the Milankovitch cycles, with the wobble on Earth's axis (whether the

Northern or Southern Hemisphere faces the sun) occurring on a 22,000-year cycle, the tilt of Earth's axis shifting back and forth every 41,000 years (an increased tilt means colder winters and warmer summers in the Northern Hemisphere), and the shape of Earth's orbit changing from oval to elliptical to oval about every 100,000 years (Hays et al. 1976).

4. Clark et al. 2009; because most of this chapter deals with a time period prior to 50,000 years ago, to avoid confusion, the Last Glacial Maximum date also is shown in years ago, rather than in the BC time scale.

5. Grootes and Stuiver 1997.

6. Stiner 2002: 7.

7. There is some debate among paleoanthropologists about the species to which these early fossils should be attributed. Some prefer to use *Homo ergaster* to denote early African populations and the term *H. erectus* to signify Asian and Southeast Asian populations who later spread back into Africa (Klein 2009; Wood 2005: 84–93).

8. Walker and Leakey 1993; the official specimen number of this fossil is KNM-WT 15000.

9. MacLarnon and Hewitt 2004.

10. Abbate and Sagri 2012.

11. Antón and Swisher 2004.

12. Some paleoanthropologists do not think that the Dmanisi fossils represent *Homo erectus*, e.g., Villmoare (2018). They suggest instead that these fossils are a sister lineage to *H. erectus*.

13. Gabunia et al. 2001: 161–162.

14. Ferring et al. 2011; Lordkipanidze et al. 2013.

15. Jatmiko 2001; Simanjuntak 2001.

16. Bar-Yosef and Goren-Inbar 1993; Belmaker et al. 2002.

17. Devès et al. 2014; Gaudzinski 2004.

18. Jones 1981; Machin et al. 2007; McPherron 1999.

19. Potts et al. 1999.

20. Potts et al. 1999: 765.

21. Isaac 1977: 40–41.

22. Potts et al. 1999: 780.

23. See, for example, Abbate and Sagri 2012.

24. Bermúdez de Castro et al. 2013.

25. These are called *Homo antecessor* by the excavators (Bermúdez de Castro et al. 1997).

26. Carbonell et al. 1999, 2010.

27. Carbonell et al. 2010.

28. Shen et al. 2001.

29. Goldberg et al. 2001.

30. Binford and Ho 1985; Binford and Stone 1986.

31. Boaz et al. 2004.

32. The Bose Basin in China is one region where early bifaces (handaxes) dating to 803,000 years ago are found (Yamei et al. 2000). Dennell (2016) argues that the "Movius Line" division should no longer be used to separate East Asia and Southeast Asia from Eurasia during the Lower Paleolithic/Acheulian period.

33. Pope 1989.

34. Bar-Yosef et al. 2011.

35. MacDonald 2018; Parfitt et al. 2010.

36. Roebroeks 2005.

37. Parfitt et al. 2005.

38. Roberts and Parfitt 1999.

39. Refitting of flaked stone artifacts involves matching up pieces that fit together, just as we might solve a jigsaw puzzle. By refitting, archaeologists can examine the technology of how stone was worked, the spatial distribution of the pieces that refit (whether they are clustered together in an activity spot or widely scattered), and whether certain items were taken away after they were made. At Boxgrove, for example, refitted groups of flakes sometimes are missing the handaxe from which they were struck, suggesting that the handaxe was carried to another place.

40. Parfitt and Roberts 1999: 399.

41. Wymer 1985.

42. Richter and Krbetschek 2015.

43. Schoch et al. 2015; Thieme 1997.

44. Roebroeks 2005; but see MacDonald 2018.

45. Wolpoff et al. 2000.

46. Shang et al. 2007; Thorne and Wolpoff 2003.

47. Stringer and Gamble 1995.

48. Holliday 1997; Ruff 1993; Steegmann et al. 2002; Weaver 2003; but see Rae et al. 2011, who say that Neandertal nasal and sinus sizes are comparable to those of Pleistocene modern humans and living hunter–gatherer–forager groups such as the Inuit. In fact, the size of these features in Neandertals is less extreme than in the Inuit, suggesting that nasal and sinus size are not cold stress adaptations.

49. This biological adaptation to cold stress is sometimes at- tributed to principles called Bergmann's rule and Allen's rule. Bergman's rule states that a lower ratio of surface area to body mass reduces heat loss (thus, the reason that Neandertals are relatively short and very robust). Allen's rule states that shorter limb size is typical in cold climates, which also reduces surface area and helps conserve body heat (thus, Neandertals had reduced limb size).

50. Hublin et al. 2017; McDougall et al. 2005; Richter et al. 2017; White et al. 2003.

51. Early *H. sapiens* fossils are found at Misliya 1 (Hershkovitz et al. 2018), Qafzeh (Schwarcz et al. 1988; Stringer et al. 1989), and Skhul (Mercier et al. 1993) in Israel.

52. Harvati et al. 2004.

53. Cann et al. 1987. Flaws in the original studies have since been corrected, and more recent mtDNA studies still sug- gest an African origin for modern humans (Ingman et al. 2000).

54. Inheritance of mtDNA nearly always only from mothers is partly because the egg is much larger than the sperm. Thus, sperm carry only nuclear DNA, whereas eggs carry both nuclear and mtDNA.

55. These sites are el Sidrón (Spain), Feldhofer (Germany), Vindija (Croatia), and Mesmaiskaya (Russia) (Krings et al. 1997, 2000; Lalueza-Fox et al. 2006; Ovchinnikov et al. 2000).

56. The site is Paglicci Cave (Caramelli et al. 2003)

57. Smith et al. 1989, 2017.

58. These sites are Feldhofer (Germany), Vindija (Croatia), Mesmaiskaya (Russia), and el Sidrón (Spain) (Green et al. 2010).

59. Sánchez-Quinto et al. 2012.

60. Lu et al. 2016.

61. Krause et al. 2010; Lu et al. 2016; Reich et al. 2011.

62. These processes can include genetic drift (random muta- tions in genes that accumulate over time in a population), which may explain some of the skeletal features of Nean- dertals compared to anatomically modern humans. But the process of natural selection (in which variations of genes can be selected for or against in particular habitats) also was important because it allowed long-term survival of those who were most fit in a given situation. Natural selection likely accounts for the European Neandertals'

biological adaptations to cold stress compared to the Afri- can anatomically modern linear body type with long legs that arose in tropical and subtropical habitats. See also Chapter 2.

63. Brown et al. 2004; Morwood et al. 2005; Roberts et al. 2009; Sutikna et al. 2016.

64. Eckhardt et al. 2014.

65. Jungers et al. 2009.

66. Aiello 2010; Larson et al. 2007; Tocheri et al. 2007.

67. Aiello 2010; Henneberg et al. 2014.

68. Brumm et al. 2016; Huffman et al. 2010; Van den Bergh et al. 2016.

69. Aiello 2010.

70. Chase and Dibble 1987; Henshilwood and Marean 2003; McBrearty and Brooks 2000; see also articles in Mellars et al. 2007 and in Wynn and Coolidge 2010.

71. Henshilwood and Marean 2003; McBrearty and Brooks 2000.

72. Henshilwood et al. 2009, 2011.

73. Lombard 2005.

74. Lombard 2007; Wadley 2005.

75. Wadley 2001; but see Watts 2002 for a critique.

76. D'Errico et al. 2012.

77. Wadley et al. 2009.

78. McBrearty 2007: 136; McBrearty and Brooks 2000: 496–497.

79. Marean et al. 2007.

80. Moroccan sites include Taforalt, Contrebandiers, and Rhafas (d'Errico et al. 2005, 2009). Note that earlier examples of perforated *Nassarius* shells were recovered from Skhul in Israel, where they are associated with early *H. sapiens* between 135,000 and 100,000 years ago (Vanhaeren et al. 2006).

81. Henshilwood 2007; Henshilwood et al. 2009.

82. Henshilwood et al. 2001: 433–434.

83. For example, Katanda, Democratic Republic of the Congo (Yellen 1998).

84. Texier et al. 2010.

85. McBrearty and Brooks 2000: 529–532.

86. Klein 2008: 271–272.

87. Lieberman 2007.

88. Lieberman 2007: 47.

89. Lai et al. 2001; Lieberman 2007: 51.

90. Enard et al. 2002: 871.

91. Lieberman 2007: 52.

92. Lieberman 2007: 52.

93. Laitman and Heimbuch 1982. Note, however, that other research suggests that there are problems with using basicranial flexion to indicate the structure of the throat as well as the size of the oral cavity; for example, Boe et al. 2002 and Lieberman and McCarthy 1999.

94. Burke 2004; Estévez 2004; Marean and Assefa 1999.

95. For example, European Neandertals used bone to retouch stone flakes (Chase 1990), Neandertals used black manganese dioxide (possibly for ritual, tanning hides, or medicinal purposes [Soressi and d'Errico 2007]) and skeletally modern humans used red ochre (possibly for ritual, as a component in the mastic used in hafting flaked stone artifacts, or for tanning hides [Hovers et al. 2003; Marean et al. 2007; Wadley 2001; Wadley et al. 2009]), and both hominins made small flakes using several knapping techniques (Dibble and McPherron 2006; Schurmans 2007).

96. From Krapina, Croatia (Radovčić et al. 2015).

97. See recent claims that early anatomically modern humans also are found in Asia (Lu et al. 2015; Pagani et al. 2016); but see Michel et al. (2016) for issues with Asian fossil finds.

98. Shea 2006.

99. Majkić et al. 2017; Soressi et al. 2013.

100. Pech de l'Azé I (Soressi and d'Errico 2007: 303–306).

101. Scladina Cave (Bonjean et al. 2015).

102. Cueva de los Aviones (coastal) and Cueva Antón (inland) (Zilhão et al. 2010). Recent redating of Cueva de los Aviones suggests it may be as old as 115,000 years ago (Hoffmann et al. 2018a).

103. Zilhão 2007: 26–27.

104. Hoffmann et al. 2018b. But see Pearce and Bonneau (2018) for a discussion of possible issues with this dating.

105. Such as Kebara in Israel (Bar-Yosef et al. 1992), Shanidar in Iraq (Pomeroy et al. 2017; Solecki 1971), and Saint Césaire (Vandermeersch 1993) and Roc de Marsal in France (Bordes and Lafille 1962).

106. Gargett 1989, 1999, for example, believes that all the Neandertal and early skeletally modern human (such as Qafzeh [Vandermeersch 1970], which dates before 90,000 years ago) burials were the result of natural taphonomic processes rather than cultural practices of burial.

107. See Rendu et al. 2014 and Dibble et al. 2015 for contrasting views of the La Chapelle-aux Saints (France) burial.

108. The site is Roc de Marsal (Sandgathe et al. 2011).

109. Bocherens et al. 2005; Lalueza et al. 1996; Richards et al. 2000; Weyrich et al. 2017.

110. Buck and Stringer 2014.

111. Snodgrass and Leonard 2009: 226.

112. Blasco et al. 2016; Boyle 2000; Cortés-Sánchez et al. 2011; Eastham 1989; Henry et al. 2010; Lev et al. 2005; Madella et al. 2002; Power et al. 2018; Rabinovich and Hovers 2004; Stiner et al. 2000: 43–44; Stringer et al. 2008; Weyrich et al. 2017.

113. Aeillo and Wheeler 2003; Gilligan 2007.

114. Dibble et al. 2009, 2017; Pastó et al. 2000; Rigaud et al. 1995.

115. Berger and Trinkaus 1995.

116. Trinkaus 2012.

117. Shea 2003.

118. Davies and Underdown 2006.

119. Higham et al. 2014.

120. Castellano et al. 2014; Villa and Roebroeks 2014.

121. Davies and Gollop 2003; Shea 2008; local population crashes are likely also to have affected modern humans in both the Middle East and Europe.

122. Golovanova et al. 2010; Hoffecker et al. 2008.

123. Argue et al. 2017; Dembo et al. 2015.

124. This was during the interval from 130,000 to 71,000 years ago (Kopp et al. 2014).

CHAPTER 4

A World of Modern Humans

ABOVE: A diorama of now extinct Pleistocene megafauna (sabre tooth cat and mammoth).

From our relatively modest beginnings as a small-bodied, bipedal hominin, one of several different, related hominin lineages living in Africa, modern humans are now the sole surviving hominin lineage. As we saw in Chapter 3, we shared Europe with the Neandertals and East Asia with Denisovans as late as 40,000 years ago and with a relict population in Southeast Asia, called *H. floresiensis*, as late as 60,000 years ago. Modern humans were not necessarily better adapted to some of these landscape contexts than populations such as the Neandertals, but it seems that modern humans may have relied more on cultural behaviors to buffer themselves from the world around them than did the Neandertals. Our cultural behaviors, including the use of symbolism and a relatively rapid rate of technological innovations beginning before 50,000 cal BC,[1] facilitated the spread of later *H. sapiens* populations not only out of Africa but also to previously uninhabited parts of the world such as Australia and the Americas. All of these modern human groups were hunter–gatherer–foragers whose economic strategies relied on wild plant and wild animal foods. In this chapter we will examine some of their activities in Africa, Europe, Australia, and the Americas, including the role of art during the Pleistocene Ice Ages.

Timeline: Hunter-Gatherer-Foragers

The terminology for various areas of the world differs, as shown in this timeline (Figure 4.1). Major peopling events are indicated with red lines, as is the intensely cold Last Glacial Maximum during which many northern areas were covered in glacial ice and worldwide sea levels were more than 120 meters (400 feet) lower than today. In Africa, the Later Stone Age continues in some regions until historic times, whereas the Upper Paleolithic (Europe), Epipaleolithic, and Paleoamerican periods end at about the same time as the end of the Pleistocene Ice Ages, shown by a black line at the top of the columns. The Epipaleolithic period is discussed in Chapter 5.

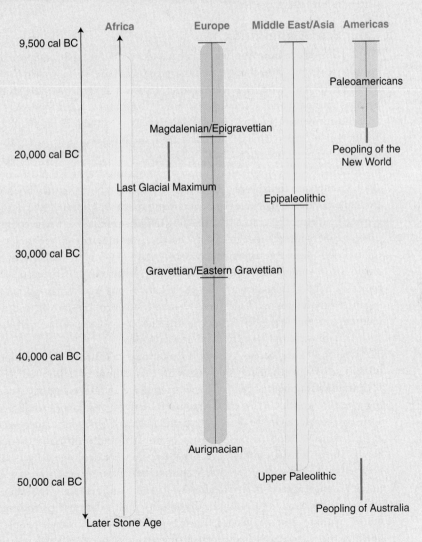

FIGURE 4.1
Timeline showing periods and events in world areas.

Modern Humans as Hunter–Gatherer–Foragers

Modern human behaviors associated with skeletally modern humans, the combination of which originated in Africa (see Chapter 3), spread out of Africa before 50,000 cal BC (read "Timeline: Hunter–Gatherer–Foragers"). These *H. sapiens* populations can be described as socially complex because they used symbolic behaviors in their interactions with members of their groups, with other groups, and the world around them. The archaeological record yields numerous examples of these and other hunter–gatherer–forager behaviors from Pleistocene sites in Africa, Europe, Asia, Australia, and the Americas.

Later Stone Age Africa

Later Stone Age the time period in Africa beginning before 50,000 cal BC; it is characterized by modern humans with modern human behaviors including abundant evidence for symbolism.

During the **Later Stone Age**, which began before 50,000 cal BC, many of the technologies, innovations, and changes in dietary patterns (such as increased fishing and the use of shellfish for food) that were seen sporadically at earlier Middle Stone Age sites became abundant and commonplace[2] (read "Big Picture: Later Stone Age and Upper Paleolithic Technologies and Tools"). There was a shift to making small flaked stone artifacts called microliths, which often are assumed to represent pieces that are combined to create composite tools. One example would be an arrow that had a pointed microlith as the arrow tip and additional microliths as barbs set into a wooden arrow shaft. Composite tools were a significant innovation because they are based on the principle of interchangeable parts. If one microlith was broken, it was removed and replaced with another, rather than having to invest in making a new complete arrow. The concept of interchangeable parts characterizes much of our technology and tools today. Later Stone Age assemblages also contain many bone tools (awls, points, and harpoons in some areas) and symbolic representation (perforated ornaments and rock art). Beyond this, the ways that these Later Stone Age hunter–gatherer–foragers organized their sites and how they used and transported resources in and across the landscape resemble the behaviors of living hunter–gatherer–forager groups in places such as Botswana and Namibia in southern Africa.[3]

Enkapune ya Muto this site in Kenya is one of the oldest Later Stone Age sites in Africa and contains ostrich egg shell beads dating to 40,000 years ago (the dates are on materials that are not calibrated).

One early Later Stone Age site is **Enkapune ya Muto** in Kenya, which dates to 40,000 years ago (the date is on materials that cannot be calibrated) (Figure 4.4). It contains a fragmented animal bone assemblage and flaked stone artifacts including some microliths, a few partially bifacial knives, and lots of small scrapers and scaled pieces[4] (see Grotte des Contrebandiers later). One of the interesting features at Enkapune ya Muto is the presence of finished and unfinished ostrich eggshell beads. The unfinished ones suggest that people were drilling and grinding ostrich eggshell to make beads at the site. Studies of living hunter–gatherer–forager groups in the Kalahari Desert of Africa (Botswana and Namibia) show that they use beads and beadwork as gifts to symbolically solidify their relationships with neighboring hunter–gatherer–forager groups. These types of networks provide people with partnerships that enhance their survival during periods when food resources are limited. The presence of beads at Enkapune ya Muto may indicate that this type of gift-giving social network has great antiquity.[5]

The Big Picture

Later Stone Age and Upper Paleolithic Technologies and Tools

Both the Later Stone Age and the Upper Paleolithic contain many examples of different shapes of microliths (Figures 4.2 and 4.3), although these small tools did not become abundant in Europe, the Middle East, and Asia until after the Upper Paleolithic. Other common stone artifacts were

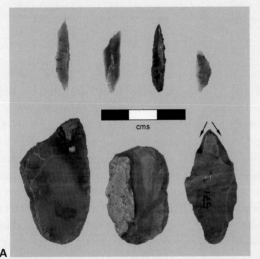

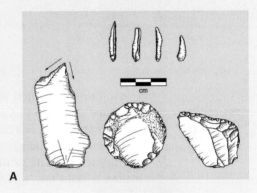

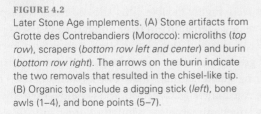

FIGURE 4.2
Later Stone Age implements. (A) Stone artifacts from Grotte des Contrebandiers (Morocco): microliths (*top row*), scrapers (*bottom row left and center*) and burin (*bottom row right*). The arrows on the burin indicate the two removals that resulted in the chisel-like tip. (B) Organic tools include a digging stick (*left*), bone awls (1–4), and bone points (5–7).

FIGURE 4.3
Upper Paleolithic implements. (A) Stone artifacts from Yutil al-Hasa Area A (Jordan): microliths (top row), burin (*bottom row, left*), and scrapers (*bottom row, center and right*). The arrows on the burin indicate the two removals that resulted in the chisel-like tip. (B) Organic tools include Aurignacian split-base bone points such as this one from Trou de la Mère Clochette in France.

endscrapers and burins. Burins are like chisels in that they have a small, sharp edge that could be used for engraving or for fine work on organic materials such as bone and antler. There were many tools made of bone, such as spear points, in both the Later Stone Age and the Upper Paleolithic. The Upper Paleolithic in Europe also had tools made of mammoth ivory (lances) and antler (points).

Innovations included the spear thrower (atlatl), bows and arrows, and composite tools. Based on the abundant numbers of rabbits, foxes, and birds that are found at Later Stone Age and Upper Paleolithic sites, we can confidently assume that these peoples had technologies such as snares, traps, and nets. Fishing and shellfish collecting also became common in the Later Stone Age and the Upper Paleolithic.

Apollo 11 Cave a Later Stone Age site in Namibia in Africa, it contains the oldest known African rock art at 30,000 to 28,000 cal BC.

Some of the earliest rock art in Africa dates to 30,000 to 28,000 cal BC and was found at **Apollo 11 Cave** in Namibia (see Figure 4.4). It consists of rock slabs that have animals drawn on them. These include a possible zebra and a catlike figure that seems to have human hind legs.[6] There are many other rock art sites in Africa, but they tend to date to 10,000 cal BC and later.[7] Because most rock art sites are shallow rockshelters, where natural taphonomic process such as rain and sun can affect painted art, it is possible that many examples of African painted rock art prior to 10,000 cal BC have not been preserved. Based on comparisons to rock art from historic period hunter–gatherer–foragers, some archaeologists suggest that the creation of Later Stone Age rock art images may be related to visions and sensations experienced during trance states produced during certain types of activities, such as intense dancing.[8]

Rose Cottage Cave a site in South Africa with Middle and Later Stone Age deposits. It has several spatially separated activity areas.

The sites of Later Stone Age hunter–gatherer–foragers often reveal careful organization of space, with activities clustered in different parts of the habitation area. In one level (14,300 to 13,100 cal BC) at **Rose Cottage Cave** in South Africa (see Figure 4.4), for example, there are 10 hearths, 4 of which were positioned around a large boulder that may have been used as a windbreak.[9] The abundance of flaked stone artifacts around some of the hearths suggests that stone knapping occurred in these places. At another hearth, ochre and hematite (minerals that can be ground for pigments) were found. Additional clusters of artifacts reveal areas associated with ostrich eggshell fragments, with ground stone tools used for grinding activities, and with animal bone fragments indicating meat processing.

Archaeological evidence suggests that the behavioral strategies of Later Stone Age hunter–gatherer–foragers were highly flexible. This allowed them to respond rapidly to changes such as decreased availability of large animals and various plant foods during drought periods. In this situation, Later Stone Age groups became more mobile, traveling over greater distances more frequently and broadening their dietary choices by capturing smaller animals more often. During periods with wetter conditions, Later Stone Age hunter–gatherer–foragers could return to a less mobile lifestyle and to hunting larger animals more regularly. Larger animals would

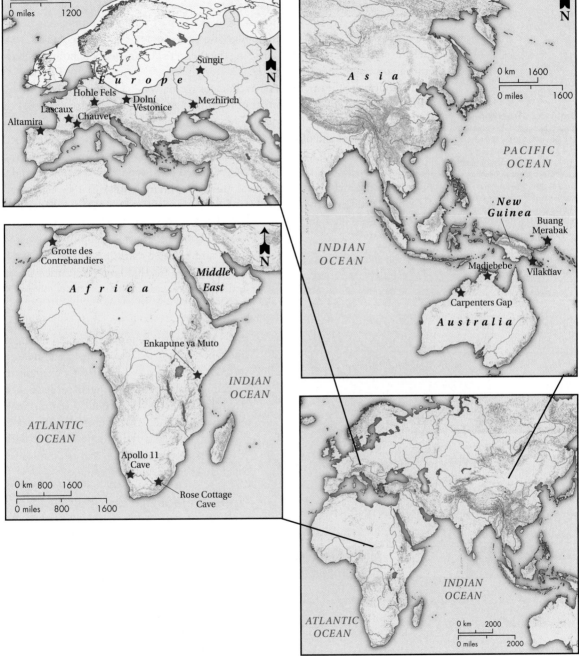

FIGURE 4.4

Locations of sites in Africa, Europe, Asia, Australia, and New Guinea. The pink in Europe represents areas under glaciers.

be more abundant during wetter periods, and if Later Stone Age hunters failed to kill a large animal, there were plenty of other food resources available to use as fallbacks.[10] These types of strategies are based in part on perceptions of costs and benefits involved in hunting and collecting of resources, and archaeologists who interpret strategies in this way are using the theoretical framework of human behavioral ecology (see Chapter 1).

In addition to the microliths that characterize many Later Stone Age flaked stone assemblages from sites in a number of regions of Africa, there are also small flaked stone artifacts called scaled pieces.[11] These are made on flakes or blades (the pieces detached from a core) and often are considered a type of tool. One region where scaled pieces are abundant in Later Stone Age assemblages is northwestern Africa during the period from 19,000 to 9,000 cal BC.[12] These Later Stone Age[13] groups hunted a wide range of animals and their coastal sites also contain shellfish that were gathered and eaten.[14] Studies of the scaled pieces from the site of **Grotte des Contrebandiers** in Morocco (see Figure 4.4) suggest that these may be a type of core rather than a tool[15] (Figure 4.5). That is, people were reusing flakes and blades by striking smaller flakes off them. This meant that larger discarded flakes and blades were used as cores, thus maximizing the use of pieces of fine-grained stone raw materials. This type of strategy might indicate that Later Stone Age groups here did not have frequent access to abundant, good-quality stone. It also serves as a prehistoric example of recycling, that is, transforming discarded flaked stone into a different end product (a core), much as some of us today might take a small plastic food container and reuse it by filling it with paint that we can easily dip a brush into as we touch up a window or door frame.

Grotte des Contrebandiers a site in Morocco with its upper deposits dating to the Later Stone Age where the study of scaled pieces in the flaked stone artifact assemblage suggests that they were used as cores and thus represent an intensive use of stone raw materials that is similar to recycling.

cms

FIGURE 4.5
A scaled piece (*lower*) and small flake from a scaled piece (*top*) from the Later Stone Age deposits at the site of Grotte des Contrebandiers, Morocco.

Upper Paleolithic Europe

It is widely believed that the package of modern behaviors that we see in Africa in the early Later Stone Age moves out of Africa with modern human populations before 50,000 cal BC. In Eurasia, these technologies, tools, and adaptations are classified as the Upper Paleolithic period, which begins around 45,000 cal BC. Historically, the most intensive research has been in Europe, and most of the archaeological cultures that are assigned to the Upper Paleolithic represent the behaviors of modern human groups (rather than Neandertals). These modern human groups moved into Europe during a cold glacial period before 43,000 cal BC, and although they had modern behaviors, they do not seem initially to have been better able to cope with glacial climates than were the Neandertals (see Chapter 3). Studies of early sites of modern humans in Central and Western Europe, who produced the **Aurignacian** archaeological culture, for example, suggest that they used the same type of settlement and hunting strategies as the Neandertals and that perhaps some of these early Aurignacian groups went locally extinct from time to time.[16]

EARLY UPPER PALEOLITHIC

The earliest modern human groups in Europe currently are found in Eastern Europe, at sites in Russia (40,000 cal BC), and also in Western Europe (England and Italy at 43,000 to 39,000 cal BC).[17] In Eastern Europe, these groups were not part of the Aurignacian archaeological culture. Their activities included long-distance transport (>500 kilometers [>310 miles]) of marine shell for making ornaments, use of ivory, antler, and bone to create tools and figurines, and the trapping of small animals (birds, hare, and arctic fox) for food and likely for fur to make warm clothing. After 40,000 cal BC these types of cultural expressions become commonplace throughout Europe.

The exact origins of the Aurignacian archaeological culture remain unknown, but the use of artistic expression by Aurignacian groups is well documented. The earliest modern human cave art includes red dots dating to 39,000 cal BC at a site in Spain (see Chapter 3 for art potentially dating to 65,000 years ago).[18] **Hohle Fels Cave** in Germany (Central Europe) yielded the oldest female human figurine (sometimes called a "Venus" figurine; see later), carved from mammoth ivory, as well as the oldest musical instruments (flutes made of mammoth ivory and of hollow bird bone), all of which are 33,000 cal BC or older[19] (Figure 4.6; see Figure 4.4). The cave of **Chauvet** in France (Western Europe) has Aurignacian paintings of horses, extinct cattle, reindeer, bears, rhinoceros, and panthers that are as old as 35,000 cal BC (Figure 4.7).[20] The earliest eyed bone needles, probably used to sew well-fitting (tailored) clothing, appear by 32,000 cal BC in Russia.[21] Other innovations of the Early Upper Paleolithic include well-constructed hearths lined with rocks to better retain heat, the probable invention of a hand-operated rotary drill that could be used to start a fire, and the construction of artificial shelters that protected modern humans from the weather.[22] All of these suggest the flexibility typical of modern cultural behaviors, including the establishment of social networks.

Early Upper Paleolithic groups were sophisticated hunters of large animals. Sites in Russia, for example, yield abundant reindeer or horse bones suggesting mass kill and butchery events.[23] The reindeer and horses, during separate hunting episodes, may have been forced into

Aurignacian an Early Upper Paleolithic archaeological culture, dating between 43,000 and 33,000 cal BC and associated with modern humans. It is found in Europe and has the earliest evidence for art and musical instruments in this part of the world.

Hohle Fels Cave dating to more than 33,000 cal BC, this Aurignacian (Early Upper Paleolithic) site in Germany (Central Europe) contains the oldest known female figurine ("Venus" figurine) and the oldest known musical instruments (ivory and bird bone flutes).

Chauvet Cave an Upper Paleolithic painted cave in France (western Europe) with the oldest known Aurignacian drawings at 35,000 cal BC; it also has art from later Upper Paleolithic periods.

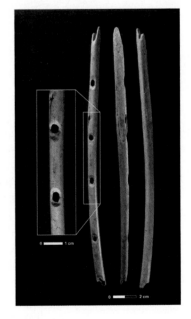

FIGURE 4.6
The bone flute from the Upper Paleolithic Aurignacian perirod at Hohle Fels, Germany.

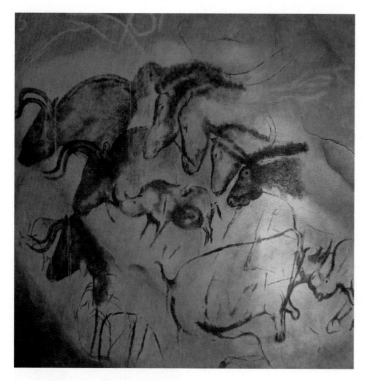

FIGURE 4.7
Replica of bison, rhinoceros, and horses painted on the cave walls at Chauvet Cave, France.

Gravettian/Eastern Gravettian archaeological cultures of the Mid-Upper Paleolithic, dating between 30,000 and 20,000 cal BC and associated with abundant "Venus" figurines, experiments with firing claylike sediments, and some unusual burials; Gravettian is found in western Europe and Eastern Gravettian in central and eastern Europe.

"Mammoth Steppe" a vast dry grasslands set of habitats that characterized the entire region from western Europe to Alaska during the Upper Paleolithic; it supported animal herds such as horses, bison, and mammoth, as well as unusual combinations of plants and animals that are not found together today.

natural traps such as deep ravines where hunters could more easily kill them. People would set up base camps nearby while they used the meat and other products (such as animal hides) from a hunting event. The use of natural traps also is known from Aurignacian sites in France, which have evidence of mass kills of horses.[24] Using features of the landscape as aids in hunting animals is a good example of the ability of modern humans to obtain information, incorporate this knowledge, and problem-solve in new and innovative ways.

MID-UPPER PALEOLITHIC

Although Early Upper Paleolithic hunter–gatherer–foragers were able to solve many of the problems related to living in glacial Europe, during the Mid-Upper Paleolithic, human groups became extremely successful in occupying northerly regions even during the winter when temperatures would have been −20 to −8°C (−4 to 17°F) on average.[25] They do not seem to have lived in the most northerly areas or in Siberia during the Last Glacial Maximum (22,000 to 19,000 cal BC), which was extremely cold.[26] Mid-Upper Paleolithic hunter–gatherer–foragers are classified as **Gravettian** (in Western Europe)/**Eastern Gravettian** (in Central and Eastern Europe); these archaeological cultures begin around 30,000 cal BC.

During the Pleistocene, an unusual combination of plant and animal communities resulted in what is sometimes called the "**mammoth steppe**," which extended from Western Europe eastward to Alaska.[27] This was a vast, dry grassland that provided food for herd animals such as horses, bison, and woolly mammoth. Other large animals included reindeer, woolly rhinoceros, lions, and wolves.[28] The combination of specific plant species of the mammoth steppe and the resulting association of many types of animals are a context not found in today's world.[29] The bottom line is that the mammoth steppe was an incredibly rich habitat for hunter–gatherer–forager groups and is one of several reasons why Upper Paleolithic people in Europe were able to live in areas that otherwise were subject to harsh glacial conditions. The vast open mammoth steppe probably facilitated widespread social networks, aspects of which we can see in art and long-distance transport of marine shells and some types of stone raw materials.

Some of the shelters built by Eastern Gravettian groups included digging the floor level into the ground and using mammoth bone to support the walls and roofs, which likely consisted of animal hides with dirt mounded on top of them. Hearths inside these shelters provided warmth and allowed for relatively long-term stays at base camps, sometimes throughout the winter season. These types of dwellings are found at many sites in Central and Eastern Europe.[30] In some cases, the mammoth bone was collected from successful hunting of woolly mammoth because there is evidence for mammoth kill and butchery sites, especially in Central Europe.[31] The hunting of woolly mammoth, given their large size (they are an extinct relative of elephants), would have required special planning and organization and quite likely the use of natural features of the landscape such as marshy areas where the woolly mammoth would not be able to easily maneuver.

A number of Gravettian/Eastern Gravettian sites are large enough to suggest that they were aggregation sites. These are locales where several groups of hunter–gatherer–foragers repeatedly came together to visit or live for an extended period of time during a year. Archaeological evidence from these meeting points in the landscape allows us a glimpse into the complex social relationships between people in the ice age landscape. A good example of this is the sites from the **Dolní Věstonice** area in the Czech Republic (Central Europe), which date between 30,000 and 27,000 cal BC (see Figure 4.4). Eastern Gravettian people here built shelters that used mammoth bone, hunted various animals for food, and left evidence of early experiments in ceramic technology. This is remarkable because these experiments occurred some 15,000 years before the "origins" and widespread use of ceramics in places such as China and the Middle East. Eastern Gravettians at Dolní Věstonice built small domed or walled kilns to fire loess (sediment that contains clay) that they fashioned into figurines, small balls, and small pellets.[32] The most famous of the figurines is the "Venus" of Dolní Věstonice I (Figure 4.8). Many of the figurines, however, are fragmented because of thermal shock, and this may reflect the experimental nature of this technology during the Upper Paleolithic, that is, people made a lot of mistakes as they tried to figure out the best ways to fire claylike sediment.[33] Despite this Upper Paleolithic use of this innovative technology, these experiments do not appear to have been widely adopted, and this technology was lost for thousands of years.

The sites at Dolní Věstonice also yielded intriguing burials. One of these is a triple burial (dating to 29,500 cal BC), which has two males on either side of a third individual who has been variously identified as either female or male.[34] One of the males is buried face down and the other male has its hands extended into the hip region of the central body. The three people, aged 16 to 25 years old, were buried with a variety of grave goods, including ivory pendants, pierced wolf and arctic fox teeth, fossil shells used for personal ornamentation, and red ochre.[35] What makes the triple burial even more unusual is that the central body has a number of deformities that would have been obvious during the life of this person—one arm and one leg

Dolní Věstonice an Eastern Gravettian (Mid-Upper Paleolithic) set of sites in the Czech Republic in Central Europe, dating between 30,000 and 27,000 cal BC. It contains evidence for early experiments in firing claylike sediment (making ceramics) and exceptional burials.

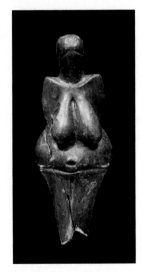

FIGURE 4.8
The fired clay "Venus" figurine from the Upper Paleolithic Gravettian period at Dolní Věstonice, Czech Republic.

are shorter than the matching limbs, and there is bowing of the leg and arm bones.[36] Although it is difficult to assess exactly what the arrangement of these three individuals might have meant in the context of Eastern Gravettian belief systems, the fact that an individual with pathologies is buried in an unusual arrangement may suggest that this person was either an especially valued member of the group or perhaps someone who was viewed negatively.

A similar situation is found at the Eastern Gravettian site of **Sungir** in Russia (see Figure 4.4), which contains a double child burial (dated to 26,800 cal BC), as well as other burials. The children are two males (9 to 10 and 11 to 13 years old) and are buried head to head.[37] Not only is this arrangement unusual, but they are buried with an elaborate array of grave goods. These include more than 10,000 mammoth ivory beads, hundreds of pierced arctic fox teeth, long ivory lances (one about 2.4 meters [8 feet] long), ivory pins and pendants, a polished human upper leg bone packed with red ochre, ivory animal figurines, and abundant red ochre sprinkled over the two bodies. The ivory beads, which represent a massive amount of work to make,[38] likely were sewn onto the clothing in which the children were buried. One child's skeleton has some pathologies, such as the shortening and bowing of both upper leg bones, which would have been visible deformities during his life.[39] The enormous investment in elaborately decorated clothing and other grave goods that accompanied them in death highlights the social complexity of relationships within these Upper Paleolithic hunter–gatherer–forager groups and, like the triple burial from Dolní Věstonice, the possible special status of individuals with physical impairments.

Artistic expression is present in examples of painted cave art, but the Gravettian/Eastern Gravettian is best known for its numerous **"Venus" figurines**, which occur across most of Europe.[40] These female carvings were made from mammoth ivory, antler, loess, and soft stones (limestone and steatite) and are diverse. Some look obese and others quite thin. Some have exaggerated sexual features such as large buttocks, large stomachs, large breasts, or a combination of these. A number of the Venus figurines have indications of possible clothing such as string skirts, belts, and close-fitting caps and sometimes what appear to be elaborate hairdos and jewelry.[41] It is not surprising that archaeologists have offered many different interpretations for this Venus phenomenon. These have ranged from the use of the figurines in fertility rituals to self-portraits to shape-shifting from human to mythical forms to markers of social identity within and between groups of Upper Paleolithic hunter–gatherer–foragers.[42] Given the several thousand years of the Gravettian/Eastern Gravettian, it is probably wise to consider that the meaning of the Venus figurines in the social interactions and rituals of these hunter–gatherer–forager groups may have changed over both time and geographical space. If we apply a postprocessual theoretical framework, it is also important to consider how our present-day assumptions about gender might influence our interpretations of these figurines[43] (read "Peopling the Past: The Role of Art in Late Pleistocene Cultures").

Sungir an Eastern Gravettian (Mid-Upper Paleolithic) site in Russia (eastern Europe) with several spectacular burials including the double child burial that contained mammoth ivory spears, thousands of mammoth ivory beads, red ochre, ivory pendants, pierced arctic fox teeth, and ivory discs.

"Venus" Figurines these female carvings are found throughout Europe during the Gravettian/Eastern Gravettian period of the Upper Paleolithic; the earliest known "Venus," however, is from the Aurignacian period at Hohle Fels in Germany.

Peopling the Past

The Role of Art in Late Pleistocene Cultures

Artistic representations made by prehistoric people during the Pleistocene in many parts of the Old World have fascinated scholars and the public. It is natural that we would like to know what ancient art and its symbols meant to the people who made it. But, as we saw in the Upper Paleolithic Europe section, there can be many different interpretations of the same set of motifs. Another issue is that most interpretations usually assume that the meaning of the motifs does not change over time or even geographical space. When we examine a phenomenon such as the Venus figurines, this might be problematic because the Gravettian was present from Western to Eastern Europe (a distance of more than 3,000 kilometers [1,865 miles]) and for 10,000 years.

One such example of a single interpretation for the Venus figurines describes many figurine details that indicate some stylistic changes both over time and across Europe, but similarities in how some figurine features were created are interpreted as reflecting a widely shared worldview.[44] This analysis suggests that variation seen in the figurines represents a transformation of the female figure to more abstract figures, or what is called "shape-shifting" (Figure 4.9). That is, when you compare the Venus figurines to each other, you see a transition from women to combinations of women and animals to purely abstract nonhuman or spiritual beings. Although this is an intriguing interpretation, it is an example of a "one-size-fits-all" type of explanation. We might ask ourselves whether we should be surprised that people might use similar methods of showing aspects of female figures. After all, there are only so many ways that you can depict recognizable breasts and buttocks. Moreover, the categories that archaeologists create, such as different types of Venus figurines, are not necessarily the same groupings that a Gravettian period person might have used. They might not have classified Venus figurines at all, other than as a female image as opposed to an animal image. This is not to say that archaeologists should not examine the evidence and propose interpretations, but rather that we must be careful in assuming that how we create meaning is similar to how those long-vanished groups created meaning.

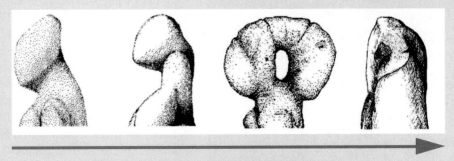

"shift" from female to combined figures to nonhuman figure

FIGURE 4.9
An example of the "shape-shifting" proposed as an explanation of variation in Upper Paleolithic "Venus" figurines.

Magdalenian a Late Upper Paleolithic archaeological culture found in Western and Central Europe from 15,000 to 9,000 cal BC; the majority of Paleolithic cave art and portable art (figurines, etc.) were made during this period.

Epi-Gravettian a Late Upper Paleolithic archaeological culture found in eastern and parts of central Europe from 20,000 to 10,000 cal BC; during this period people recolonized northerly parts of Europe and Siberia.

Mezhirich an Epi-Gravettian (Late Upper Paleolithic) site in Ukraine (eastern Europe) that is a winter base camp; it contains four substantial dwellings built of mammoth bones and tusks, large storage pits, and hearths.

LATE UPPER PALEOLITHIC

The Late Upper Paleolithic begins about 20,000 cal BC, but climate change after 15,000 cal BC and technological innovations in the **Magdalenian**, found in Western and Central Europe as well as in contemporary archaeological cultures in Eastern and Southern Europe such as the **Epi-Gravettian**, facilitated the recolonization of parts of northern Europe and Siberia that had been abandoned by Gravettian/Eastern Gravettian populations during the Last Glacial Maximum. Although Magdalenian groups often are associated with the hunting of reindeer, in fact, they targeted a much wider range of animals, including horse and red deer, whereas Epi-Gravettians hunted mammoth from time to time. One of the most important technological innovations was the use of the spearthrower (atlatl), which was "invented" slightly earlier than the Magdalenian. An atlatl is a device on which a spear can be securely laid, and the atlatl acts as an extension of the arm (a lever) when the spear is thrown (Figure 4.10). This allows for a much farther throwing distance compared to hand-throwing a spear and possibly greater impact force for the spear. The invention and use of the atlatl improved hunting capabilities because it allowed hunters to be farther away from the animals and it delivered a relatively accurately thrown projectile with hide-penetrating power,[45] although use of the atlatl does not seem to have been present in Eastern Europe.[46] Late in the Magdalenian period, there is evidence for bow-and-arrow technology.[47] These early bows were not as effective as much later types of bows, such as the long bow used during the Middle Ages. Other innovations late in the Late Upper Paleolithic are fishhooks and barbed harpoons, suggesting that people were substantially broadening their diets.

During the Epi-Gravettian recolonization of Eastern Europe, we see evidence for sophisticated construction of dwellings that were substantial enough to withstand winter cold. One site is **Mezhirich** in Ukraine (Eastern Europe; see Figure 4.4; 16,000 to 15,000 cal BC[48]), which has four dwellings that were built using substantial amounts of mammoth bone (Figure 4.11). Some of the bones may have come from hunting mammoth, but the different degrees of weathering on the bones suggests that mammoth bone in the landscape also was collected for use. One of the dwellings had a foundation trench with 23 mammoth skulls as well as long bones and hip bones filling the gaps between the skulls, 2 mammoth skulls that were the base for the arched mammoth tusks that formed the entry way into the dwelling, and 35 mammoth tusks that probably were weights to anchor hides stretched over the framework of the dwelling.[49] The dwellings were circular or oval in shape and 3.5 meters (11.5 feet) in diameter.

FIGURE 4.10
Using an atlatl to throw a spear.

FIGURE 4.11
One of the mammoth bone huts at the Upper Paleolithic Epigravettian period site of Mezhirich, Ukraine.

They contained well-constructed hearths for warmth and cooking. Meat storage and garbage pits, as well as other hearths, were located outside the dwellings, as were additional piles of mammoth bones.[50] Based on a study of the hearths, we know that Epi-Gravettian people were using bone as fuel, which is understandable given that the glacial landscape did not contain many trees and thus little wood for fuel. Animal remains at sites such as Mezhirich include arctic fox, which likely was hunted for its fur to make clothing rather than as food (their bones were found articulated [in anatomical position] and not burned).

As we saw earlier, artistic expression was an early feature of modern human cultures of the Upper Paleolithic. The majority of known cave and portable art (figurines and decorated bone and antler tools) dates to the Magdalenian and Epi-Gravettian periods of the Late Upper Paleolithic. More than 240 caves with art in France and Spain are Magdalenian compared to about 40 caves with art from the Early Upper and Mid-Upper Paleolithic.[51] The painted and engraved cave art images are mainly animals, especially horse, bison, woolly mammoth, aurochs, deer, and ibex (a type of wild goat) (Figure 4.12). In some cases, detailed study of images suggests that some animals were shown with seasonal features, such as the length

FIGURE 4.12
The Upper Paleolithic engraved panel of horses at La Chaire à Calvin in France.

of the animal's coat.[52] There also are numerous geometric and other designs such as dots and hands. Less frequent images include leopards, bears, rhinoceros, birds, and humans. Although most of the animal depictions were quite realistic, those of humans tended to be stylized and included what appear to be torsos with no heads, so-called female "vulvae," and the famous "bird-man" from **Lascaux** (see Figure 4.4). The bird-man is a stick figure of a possibly wounded human shown with the head of a bird (perhaps he is wearing a headdress?). Nearby is a staff with a bird's head and a wounded bison with its intestines spilling out.

Lascaux a well-known Late Upper Paleolithic cave art site in France (western Europe); most of the hundreds of images date to the Magdalenian period.

INTERPRETING UPPER PALEOLITHIC CAVE ART

One of the striking aspects of cave art in the Upper Paleolithic is its vast diversity in images and techniques. Numerous types of animals are depicted, sometimes engraved or pecked into cave walls, other times drawn in outline with charcoal, and still other times shown with some of their features filled in, either in monochrome (black or red) or in polychrome (several colors; Figure 4.13). Upper Paleolithic artists used features of the cave walls and ceilings as parts of animals, for example, lumps in the ceiling at **Altamira** in Spain (Western Europe) (see Figure 4.4) are suggestive of the humps on the backs of bison and of bison with their fore and hind limbs curled under them. The bison were painted to integrate these natural features. Animals, human representations including hands, and other designs sometimes are shown alone but often occur in great panels of many animals, some superimposed over one another, and seem to be associated with abstract designs (lines, dots, and grids). The sheer quantity and beauty of Upper Paleolithic cave art has generated enormous interest in how such art might be interpreted, and archaeologists (and others) have proposed a wide variety of ideas.

Altamira a painted cave site in Spain with Magdalenian Upper Paleolithic images including the famous Hall of the Bison.

One of the early interpretations of cave art was that it was "art for the sake of art,"[53] much as we today might go to a museum to see and appreciate the skills of painters and other artists. This is a Western interpretation, however, and postprocessual archaeologists would argue that there might be other, context-specific interpretations that are more appropriate. The location of this art deep within dark caves, in which small flickering lamps would only reveal small portions of engraved or painted walls and ceilings, also does not seem to fit with an interpretation of prehistoric "art galleries" (but see later discussion for rockshelter art).

Another early interpretation was based on the fact that most of the images

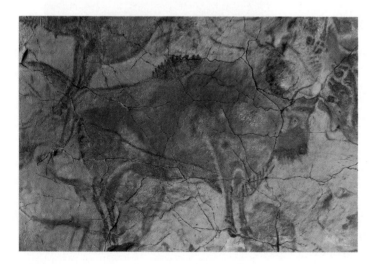

FIGURE 4.13
Polychrome bison painted at Altamira, Spain.

are animals that were hunted for food. This viewpoint became known as the "hunting magic" explanation, which sometimes included "fertility magic" and "initiation rituals"[54] and which suggested that images such as the Lascaux bird-man were ritual specialists. The drawing of the animals was interpreted as a way to magically ensure that an upcoming hunt would be successful, and some of the lines and feathered "darts" that were positioned impacting the body of an animal or nearby it were seen as representing spears to magically kill the animals. There are examples of horses with large bellies, perhaps indicating pregnancy. By drawing a pregnant animal, the artists are thought to be practicing fertility magic, ensuring the long-term survival of the hunted animals. In some cases, the act of drawing these animals was seen as a ritual way of initiating young people (usually thought of as males) into the group of adult hunters. The hunting magic interpretation has much appeal because we know that hunting was an important part of daily life during this period. And, in direct contrast to the art for art's sake explanation, the practice of these "rituals" deep within caves suggests that not everyone participated. Although some aspects of this interpretation might be appropriate to the context of Upper Paleolithic hunter–gatherer–forager groups, there are many images in the caves that do not seem to fit this explanation.

In an effort to include all the types of images (animals, human representations, abstract designs) in Upper Paleolithic cave art in a comprehensive interpretation, some researchers turned to aspects of how the human mind works during altered states of consciousness and what images the mind "sees" during different phases of altered states. This explanation is called "entoptic phenomena," and it argues that all modern human brains experience the same sets of visual images in the same progression. During the first stage, for example, it is common to see geometric patterns; during the second stage, the brain begins to associate various geometric designs with real objects; and during the third stage, the brain sees actual animals, people, and monsters.[55] Altered states can be achieved in many ways—drugs, intense dancing, lack of food, sitting in absolute darkness as in a deep cave—and the entoptic phenomena interpretation argues that cave art images represent the "visions" seen during these experiences.

Other explanations focus more on the use of cave art as a form of communication. That is, its presence and the types of images were used to establish social identities and perhaps as territorial markers.[56] Communication as an explanation is based on identifying different styles that represent different groups of people and is a key element at aggregation sites where these people came together. Communication enhances the survival of groups using social networks or alliances (just as we saw earlier in the Later Stone Age example with one possible use of ostrich eggshell beads). This concept of the adaptive value of art is a feature of the Darwinian archaeology theoretical framework (see Chapter 1). The abundance of cave art in France and Spain, particularly during the Late Upper Paleolithic, is thought to be one outcome of the dense packing of people as they moved south to escape the harshest conditions of the extreme cold of the Last Glacial Maximum. Art was used to form alliances and thus resolve disputes about resources between groups who could not easily move away because of the close presence of many groups and the inhospitable nature of more northern areas in Europe.

We should note that, in recent years, accumulating evidence suggests that Upper Paleolithic people created wall art not only in relatively inaccessible caves but also in the rockshelters where they lived.[57] Like Later Stone Age rockshelters in Africa, those of the Upper Paleolithic in Europe were exposed to sun, rain, and other weather, and most of the art present in these locales has long since disappeared. The traces we do have, however, suggest that wall art was a much more common feature of daily life than the art present deep in caves might suggest. And if wall art was much more widespread and was typical of people's living sites, then single-cause explanations for wall art, especially those that are based in part on its inaccessibility in deep caves, seem less likely to be accurate interpretations for all of Upper Paleolithic wall art.

Worldwide Expansion

Earlier hominins migrated out of Africa several times (see Chapters 2 and 3), but it is the so-called "last" migration out of Africa beginning before 50,000 cal BC that represents the movement of people like ourselves. Some of these groups of modern humans were the first to reach two previously unoccupied parts of the world: Australia/New Guinea and, somewhat later in time, the Americas. As noted in Chapter 2 and earlier in this chapter, during the Pleistocene Ice Ages, glacial periods were characterized by worldwide lower sea levels because of large amounts of water locked up as glacial ice. In some cases, sea levels were 120 to 140 meters (390 to 460 feet) lower than today, and this exposed additional land. These exposed land areas are known today as the continental shelves (submerged), and their presence had important implications for the spread of hunter–gatherer–forager groups into Australia/New Guinea and the Americas.

Australia/New Guinea

The route taken by modern human hunter–gatherer–forager groups out of Africa that eventually resulted in the colonization of Australia/New Guinea is thought by some researchers to be based on coastal habitats.[58] These groups would have originally moved from the Horn of Africa (Ethiopia and Eritrea) across the Bab al-Mandab Strait to Yemen (Figure 4.14). From there, they moved along the southern part of the Arabian Peninsula, the southern portions of Iraq and Iran, and the coasts of India to Southeast Asia. During the Pleistocene, mainland Southeast Asia (Myanmar, Thailand, Malaysia, Cambodia, Vietnam) was linked by exposed land, resulting from worldwide lower sea levels, to many of the islands of Indonesia. This merged land mass is the megaregion known as **Sunda** (Figure 4.15). Hunter–gatherer–foragers could move easily along the coasts of Sunda toward Australia/New Guinea, which were themselves linked together by exposed land in the megaregion known as **Sahul**. The exposed land areas on the northwest coast of Sahul (the portion that is now Australia) made the water distances between Sahul and Sunda

Sunda the merged land masses of many of the Southeast Asia islands (such as those of Indonesia) and mainland Southeast Asia during the Pleistocene; they were connected to each other by land exposed because of lower sea levels.

Sahul the merged land masses of Australia and New Guinea (Pacific region) during the Pleistocene; they were connected to each other by land exposed due to lower sea levels.

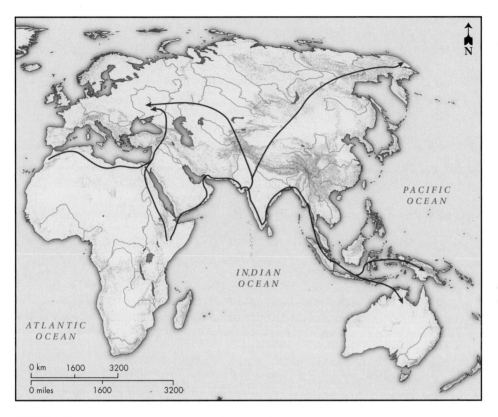

FIGURE 4.14

Simplified map of routes out of Africa taken by modern humans just before 50,000 cal BC. These are based mainly on genetic studies.

much shorter, about 50 to 100 kilometers (30 to 60 miles).[59] The proposed coastal route from Africa to Sahul is supported by genetic evidence (mtDNA, nuclear DNA, and Y-chromosome studies) that shows a close relationship between relict groups in India and Southeast Asia (Malaysia) and Australian Aborigines.[60] Additionally, the coastal route model has been examined using paleoenvironmental data, GIS modeling, and Pleistocene archaeological sites, which suggest that this route to Sahul is a reasonable interpretation.[61]

Hunter–gatherer-foragers using coastal areas as a route likely traveled in paddle-propelled boats from estuary to estuary and planned ahead to make the journeys. Most of this travel would have been relatively easy, because this southern route to Sahul is mainly in tropical areas with similar resources.[62] Estuaries are water areas along the coast that are partially enclosed so that there are freshwater streams or rivers flowing into a water body that has open access to the sea. These are advantageous habitats where fresh water is available in combination with near-shore and marine resources (timber for boats; shellfish, fish, and marine mammals for food).

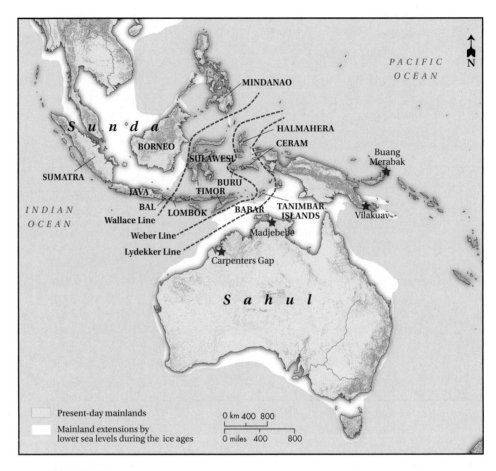

FIGURE 4.15
Showing the Sunda and Sahul regions when sea levels were lower during the Pleistocene, thus exposing more land that connected what are now islands. Areas shown in white are now underwater.

People could have traveled from one estuary to the next by carrying a sufficient amount of fresh water and tools needed for obtaining food as they paddled their boats along the shores. In fact, people could paddle back and forth between different estuaries, thus keeping open a line of communication between neighbors. Once these hunter–gatherer–forager groups were in Sunda, they paddled their way across open water to visible islands, reaching Timor and Timor-Roti (see Figure 4.15). Based on recent analyses of past sea levels, paleoenvironment, and geological data, and because of Pleistocene lower sea levels, there were several small islands (now submerged) present between Timor-Roti and Sahul.[63] These would have been visible and served as an easily paddled route into the Australian part of Sahul. Estimates of the size of this colonizing population, based on calculations from genetic data, range from 72 to 300 people.[64]

Just as in Europe, early hunter–gatherer–forager groups in Australia left evidence of symbolic behaviors, including burials with red ochre, long-distance movement of marine shells and ochre, and examples of rock art.[65] Dates on rock art tend to be late, after 26,000 cal BC, but use of red ochre as a pigment goes back to 65,000 years ago.[66] People colonizing Sahul entered a region where native animals had never before encountered humans, and some archaeologists suggest that humans were responsible for the extinction of a number of different species, especially large animals (read "Peopling the Past: Megafaunal Extinctions" and "Further Reflections: Megafauna in Australia").

The earliest archaeological site in Sahul is **Madjebebe** in northern Australia at 65,000 years ago (the age is too old to be calibrated; see Figure 4.15), some 20,000 years before the disappearance of the megafauna.[67] In its earliest occupation, Madjebebe has a hearth, chipped stone tools, ground stone tools, hatchets, and ground ochre (some of which seem to have been used as "crayons"). The ground stone tools were used to grind seeds as well as some of the ochre. One interesting fact is that hatchets are not known from the areas where colonizing populations originated. This means that these tools were invented by the early colonizers once they reached Sahul. Early sites in the northern portion of Sahul include **Vilakuav** in the New Guinea highlands and **Buang Merabak** in the Bismarck Archipelago (see Figure 4.15).[68] These date between 47,000 and 42,000 cal BC. Vilakuav yielded waisted axes, a type of hafted stone cutting implement useful in forested habitats (analogous to the hatchets from Madjebebe). Analysis of starch grains on stone tools from sites in the same valley as Vilakuav indicates the use of yams. *Pandanus* nut shells (charred) also were found. The cave site of Buang Merabak has a shell midden, which represents the discarded remnants after eating shellfish. Circumstantial evidence suggests that humans at this site may also have exploited bats. Around the same time (47,000 cal BC), sites such as **Carpenters Gap** (western Australia; see Figure 4.15) show the spread of people into more arid and inland areas.[69] Carpenters Gap has hatchets and ochre, as well as a diverse chipped stone tool kit. Its earliest occupation shows that people were exploiting snakes, turtle, lizards, and fish. This type of faunal assemblage indicates that people had a diverse diet, one that was not based mainly on hunting larger animals.

The Americas

The first people to reach the Americas had their origins in the Siberian region of Russia, and genetic evidence (mtDNA and Y-chromosome) suggests that at least some of them came from the Altai Mountains region of southern Siberia.[70] Data from archaeological sites indicate that southern Siberia was first occupied by Upper Paleolithic groups about 45,000 cal BC and that they expanded into northeastern Siberia perhaps as early as 30,000 cal BC.[71] Their movement north may have been facilitated by the development of the mammoth steppe with its vast herds of animals (see Mid-Upper Paleolithic). Some of these Siberian hunter–gatherer–forager groups continued to move eastward and reached the Alaskan

Madjebebe the earliest site in Australia at 65,000 years ago. It documents the early colonization of the Australian part of Sahul.

Vilakuav one of the earliest archaeological sites in New Guinea (Pacific region), documenting the colonization of this part of Sahul at least as early as 47,000 cal BC.

Buang Merabak an early archaeological site in Sahul (Bismarck Archipelago, Pacific region); it has a shell midden and possibly shows the exploitation of bats (42,000 cal BC).

area of the Americas after 25,000 cal BC, as suggested by genetic evidence.[72] During the Last Glacial Maximum (22,000 to 19,000 cal BC), with its extreme cold and dryness, these groups were isolated from populations in Siberia. This isolation period, called the "Beringian Standstill" hypothesis, lasted for 8,000 years or more.[73] During this interval, changes in the mtDNA and nuclear DNA of the groups in Alaska occurred through evolutionary processes such as genetic drift, mutation, and natural selection[74] (see Chapter 2), giving them a unique genetic signature. A number of these unique genetic markers are found in living Native American and First Nations peoples, demonstrating their descent from these earlier groups. At the moment, however, we have only one very early site in eastern Beringia (Canada). This is **Bluefish Caves**, which dates to 22,000 cal BC.[75] Other early Beringian sites (Alaska) date after 13,000 cal BC.[76] Based on dates from a site in South America (see later), we know that some hunter–gatherer–forager groups from the Alaskan region began to expand south into North and South America sometime after 13,000 cal BC. Based on genetic data, the size of the first population that migrated south from Beringia has been estimated to be as few as 250 people.[77]

Two probable routes have been suggested for the peopling of the Americas (Figure 4.16).[78] Historically, the most widely accepted interpretation has been an all-land route in which hunter–gatherer–foragers crossed from Siberia to Alaska over a land bridge called **Beringia** (today this is the waterway known as the Bering Strait because of higher sea levels after the Pleistocene).[79] These groups hunted bison, mammoths, moose, and caribou because these animals also migrated eastward from Siberia to Alaska. When Upper Paleolithic people reached Alaska, however, they were unable to continue onward because of the presence of two large glacial ice sheets, the Cordilleran across western Canada and the Laurentide across middle and eastern Canada. These were joined together during the Last Glacial Maximum and blocked the way south into most of Canada and regions south of Canada. Sometime after 11,000 cal BC, an **"ice-free corridor,"** which ran along the eastern flank of the Canadian Rockies, opened between the Cordilleran and Laurentide glaciers, allowing for southward migration by hunter–gatherer–foragers previously confined to Alaska.[80]

The opening of the ice-free corridor between these two glaciers is relatively late because we know that people were at **Monte Verde** in Chile in South America by 12,600 cal BC (Figure 4.17). Monte Verde is thousands of kilometers south of Alaska, and its early date suggests that some groups of hunter–gatherer–foragers used a coastal route to reach the Americas south of the glaciers.[81] Genetic data also support an early date for people in South America.[82] This coastal route is similar in some ways to the coastal route suggested for the peopling of Sahul; however, the coastal route in the northern portion of the Americas would have been a much colder journey requiring different sets of skills and perhaps technologies. Coast hopping from the Alaskan part of Beringia to south of the glaciers of Canada and

Bluefish Caves a site in Alaska that dates to 22,000 cal BC. It is the earliest site in the Americas and documents the movement of people from Siberia across the Beringian land bridge to the Americas.

Beringia a land bridge that connected Siberia to Alaska during the Pleistocene; when sea levels rose after the Pleistocene, this land bridge was submerged, and the area today is the waterway called the Bering Strait.

Ice-free corridor a term mainly used to indicate the passageway between the Cordilleran and Laurentide glaciers that covered Canada during the Pleistocene; it is widely thought to be a route used during the peopling of the Americas after 11,500 cal BC.

Monte Verde a Paleoamerican site in Chile in South America that is one of the earliest sites in the Americas south of the Cordillaran and Laurentide glaciers covering Canada. It dates to 12,600 cal BC and suggests that some groups followed a coastal route from the Alaskan part of Beringia.

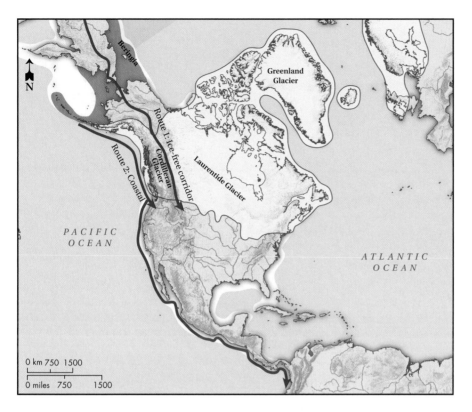

FIGURE 4.16

Two routes proposed for the first peopling of the Americas. Lower sea levels created the Beringia land bridge (areas in white are exposed coastal regions that are now submerged). Regions shown in pink were under glacial ice at the Last Glacial Maximum. The ice-free corridor would have opened between the Cordilleran and Laurentide glaciers after 12,000 cal BC.

the extreme northern United States was possible for two reasons. First, lowered sea levels during the Pleistocene would have exposed continental shelf land along the coasts where people using boats could land and briefly set up campsites. Second, after 15,000 cal BC, as worldwide climate warmed, the Cordilleran glacier began to retreat away from the western coast, opening up additional land areas that facilitated southward travel from Alaska.[83] Once people reached areas south of the glaciers, they could either continue coast hopping down to South America (thus reaching Monte Verde at an early date) or they could land and begin moving east and south in the United States, where we have other relatively early sites such as the **Schaefer Mammoth Site** in Wisconsin (12,800 to 12,200 cal BC) and **Wally's Beach** in Canada (11,300 cal BC); both were occupied before the ice-free corridor opened.[84]

Schaefer Mammoth Site a site in Wisconsin (United States) with dates between 12,800 and 12,200 cal BC; it predates the opening of the "ice-free corridor" and suggests that hunter–gatherers may have entered the Americas south of the glaciers using a coast-hopping route down the western coasts along Alaska and Canada and then spread east and south.

Wally's Beach a Paleoamerican site south of the Cordilleran and Laurentide glaciers covering Canada. It dates to 11,300 cal BC and represents occupation occurring before the ice-free corridor opened completely.

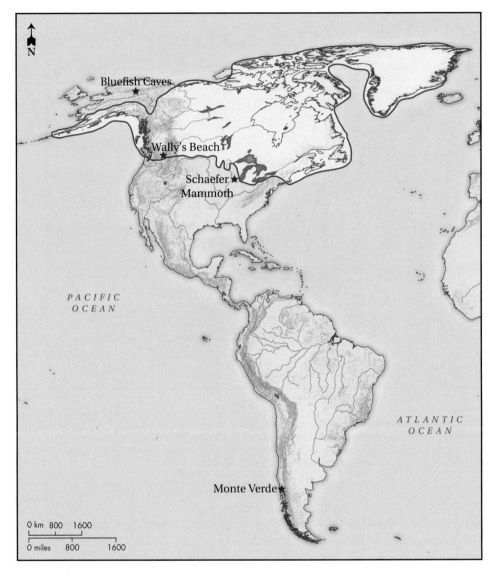

FIGURE 4.17
Some of the pre-Clovis sites in the Americas. Areas shown in pink were under glacial ice during the Last Glacial Maximum. Wally's Beach was occupied after the glaciers began to retreat.

Paleoamerican a term used by some archaeologists to describe the earliest people in the Americas (other archaeologists use the term Paleoindian); their descendants are the Native Americans/First Nations of North, Central, and South America.

Paleoamericans

Some archaeologists use the term **Paleoamericans**[85] to refer to the earliest people in the Americas (Figure 4.18); there also were several later migrations into the Americas, including, for example, the Inuit. The descendants[86] of these several migrations are the many Native American/First Nations groups of North, Central, and

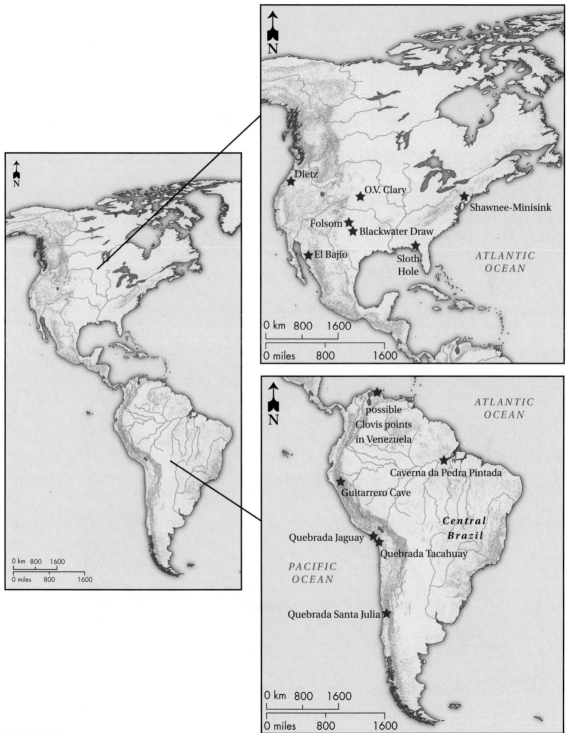

FIGURE 4.18
Paleoamerican sites in the Americas.

Megafaunal Extinctions

If we were able to time travel to North America during the Pleistocene, we would encounter camels, sabretooth cats, lions, giant ground sloths, mastodons, mammoths, and horses among some 35 genera that are now extinct in the Americas.[87] On a similar visit to Sahul during the Pleistocene, we would see 3-meter (10-foot) tall giant kangaroos, a hippopotamus-size wombatlike marsupial, and a sheep-size spiny anteater (echidna) among the more than 20 genera now extinct (Figure 4.19). These animals are called the Pleistocene megafauna (large animals), and the reason(s) for their extinction near the end of the Pleistocene has

been the subject of much debate. The two major explanations are "overkill" by Pleistocene hunter–gatherer–foragers and the effects of climate change on vegetation as the Ice Ages ended.

The overkill hypothesis stresses the impact of hunting on animals that had no prior experience with humans and the so-called timing of the extinctions that some researchers have argued coincides with the first arrival of people in North America and in Sahul.[88] Upper Paleolithic groups in Eurasia, however, hunted woolly mammoth for thousands of years before these animals went extinct there, and there is little evidence for megafauna hunting

FIGURE 4.19
Examples of extinct Pleistocene megafauna.

in Sahul.[89] Moreover, although horses became extinct in the Americas, they survived in Eurasia despite being hunted during the Pleistocene. The best case for possible overkill is from North America,[90] but recent research suggests that climate and vegetation changes, as well as a better understanding of each species' history, are avenues of investigation that may help resolve the megafaunal extinction debate.[91] The disappearance of a vegetation mosaic that included grasslands, forests, and tundra in close association with each other in northern latitudes, as well as increased differences between seasons, for example, likely played an important role in the ability of certain species to survive. And, the megafauna did not all become extinct at the same moment in time; some survived longer by moving farther north. Finally, at least in some cases, hunting by Pleistocene hunter–gatherer–foragers probably placed additional pressure on animals that were already evolutionarily stressed.

South America. Paleoamericans, like their counterparts in Sahul, entered a region with animals that had never before encountered humans (read "Peopling the Past: Megafaunal Extinctions"). The earliest of the Paleoamericans who left traces of their activities at sites such as Monte Verde, Wally's Beach, and the Schaefer Mammoth Site (see earlier) are sometimes called "pre-Clovis" because they predate the well-known Clovis culture (see later). Other related hunter–gatherer–forager groups inhabited Central and South America. These people and later Paleoamerican groups lived during the end of the Pleistocene and the very early Holocene.

Clovis and Related Groups

The **Clovis** culture dates from 11,300 to 10,850 cal BC[92] and is found mainly within the boundaries of the United States. Their distinctive Clovis fluted spear points[93] (Figure 4.20), however, are found in Mexico and possibly in South America.[94] These points were thrown using the atlatl. Although Clovis spear points are found over a large area and appear to represent a set of shared technology and culture, perhaps analogous to the Gravettian/Eastern Gravettian shared tradition of Venus figurines (see earlier),

FIGURE 4.20

Paleoamerican points: Clovis point (*right*) and Folsom point (*left*).

Clovis an early Paleoamerican culture in the Americas, dating between 11,300 and 10,850 cal BC; they made a distinctive, bifacially flaked stone spear point called a Clovis point and are associated with kill and butchery sites of mammoth and other now-extinct animals.

Blackwater Draw Locality 1 a Paleoamerican Clovis kill and butchery site found near the town of Clovis in New Mexico. This is the source for the name of the Clovis culture and the Clovis point.

their distribution is over a geographic region that contains many different types of habitats and most likely represents a number of distinct groups of people.[95] It is important to note, however, that unlike Upper Paleolithic Europe, we have no unambiguous Clovis art except for a few geometric designs on bone and ivory tools.[96]

In the North American Southwest and the Plains, sites such as **Blackwater Draw Locality 1** in New Mexico (see Figure 4.18) are associated with the hunting of extinct mammoth, mastodon, and a bison species (Figure 4.21). Some archaeologists suggest that Clovis hunters may have been responsible for the extinction of these large animals (read "Peopling the Past: Megafaunal Extinctions").[97] However, these are kill sites rather than base camps and probably bias us toward thinking of Clovis groups as strictly big-game hunters. Using archaeological data and models from human behavioral ecology, a number of archaeologists have instead suggested that although Clovis groups hunted large-bodied animals, their adaptations were much broader. That is, they used a variety of food resources, such as deer, rabbits, birds, turtles, and even alligators and raccoons, as well as various plant foods.[98]

FIGURE 4.21
Early excavations at the Paleoamerican Clovis mammoth kill site, New Mexico.

Clovis groups in the western and northwestern United States often are described as highly mobile, but this perspective is tied to the notion that they specialized in big-game hunting. The degree to which these groups were mobile probably depended on the range of resources within the territories they exploited.[99] The **Dietz site** in Oregon (see Figure 4.18), for example, appears to be a place where Clovis groups repeatedly camped as they moved through their territory from one resource-rich area to another. The series of camps at Dietz thus represent a variety of activities and yield artifact assemblages that include materials such as different types of stone from raw material sources located in various parts of the region that these Clovis groups used. Other sites include prehistoric quarries where stone raw material was obtained and knapped. Clovis groups also occasionally stored materials (caches; at least 25 are known), including bone rods, stone points, unfinished stone points, and other stone artifacts.[100] This could be interpreted as a strategy of having artifacts available when the group returned (provisioning the landscape), although a few caches appear to be ritual deposits, based on the quality of the workmanship of the artifacts and their unusual stone raw materials.[101] Blood residue analyses of stone tools in one Clovis cache in Colorado show that four of them were used on sheep, bear, horses, and camelids.[102]

In the eastern part of the United States, Clovis Paleoamericans may have been less mobile overall, in part because of the much richer resources here, including those of the forests. **Shawnee Minisink** in Pennsylvania (see Figure 4.18) is interpreted as a habitation site, indicating longer-term occupation. In addition to fish, Shawnee Minisink also yielded hawthorn seeds, grape, hickory nut shell fragments, hackberry, and blackberry.[103] These would have been supplements to a diet that focused on fish and meat. Other Clovis sites in the eastern United States have yielded evidence for the hunting of mastodon, caribou, beaver, and birds.[104] As in the west, eastern Clovis sites include base camps, kill and butchery sites, quarries, and caches.[105] Clovis Paleoamericans, like their contemporaries in the Old World, made tools of bone, antler, and ivory, although these usually are rare because of preservation issues. One exception is **Sloth Hole** in Florida (see Figure 4.18), a mastodon kill site that is now submerged. In addition to Clovis stone points, there are more than 30 ivory points and many bone tools.[106] This likely indicates that use of organic technologies was much more widespread during the Clovis period than is apparent from the archaeological record.

In northern Mexico, there also are many sites that yield Clovis fluted stone points.[107] These include the **El Bajio** site complex in Sonora (see Figure 4.18). Clovis groups in this area went to El Bajio because of the presence of a local stone raw material source. This part of the complex became a prehistoric quarry. In areas around the quarry, there are places where people knapped the stone into different types of artifacts, including spear points, and other locales that probably were camp sites. Further to the south in Mexico, as well as in other areas of

Dietz Site a series of Clovis Paleoamerican camp locales in Oregon. They are situated near a travel route between several different resource areas and contain artifacts made from various stone raw materials found in different parts of this region.

Shawnee–Minisink Site a Clovis Paleoamerican habitation site in Pennsylvania. It yielded fish and plant remains, suggesting that Clovis diets were much broader than focusing on large animals such as mammoth and mastodon.

Sloth Hole a Clovis Paleoamerican kill site in Florida in the United States. It dates to 11,050 cal BC and yielded more than 30 ivory points.

El Bajio a Clovis Paleoamerican area in Sonora in Mexico. This region contains a quarry for stone raw materials, camp sites, and knapping locales where people made stone artifacts.

Central and South America, evidence for Clovis is much rarer. Most materials are either isolated surface finds of Clovis fluted stone points or of Clovis-like fluted points. The most likely Clovis points in South America are found in Venezuela and in Chile.[108]

This does not mean, however, that Central and South America were mostly uninhabited. Instead, there were non-Clovis Paleoamerican groups living there.[109] **Quebrada Santa Julia** in coastal Chile (see Figure 4.18), for example, is a small hunting camp near a Pleistocene lake. It yielded fluted spear points (not Clovis), a hearth that is radiocarbon dated to 11,000 cal BC, the bones of extinct horse, and stone tools suggesting a range of activities.[110] Coastal Paleoamericans developed a focus on fish and shellfish at sites such as **Quebrada Jaguay** in Peru (see Figure 4.18), which dates to 12,000 cal BC.[111] At both these sites, there are stone raw materials that come from inland sources in the Andes, indicating that these Paleoamerican groups had territories that were larger than just the coastal areas. There also are many Paleoamerican sites elsewhere in South America, for example, at rockshelters and open-air contexts in central Brazil.[112] Archaeological evidence suggests that most of these sites represent groups that were highly mobile and that the sites were short-term occupations. Paleoamerican sites in South America, like those of North and Central America, are characterized by various types of spear points, one of which is called a fishtail point based on its shape (some fishtail points also are fluted).[113] Depending on where they lived, they hunted different types of animals (animals local to those regions), while using a variety of other foods.[114]

Later Paleoamericans

There are many Paleoamerican groups after the Clovis period. They are defined in part by their distinctive stone spear points. Some reflect different chronological periods within the Paleoamerican time frame, whereas others indicate different geographical regions in the Americas. In North America, these include Folsom, Plano, Hell Gap, and Cody, as well as others. **Folsom** groups, for example, lived mainly in the Plains and southern Rocky Mountains regions during the period from 10,800 to 9,800 cal BC.[115] They made fluted stone spear points in which the flute ran almost the entire length of the point (see Figure 4.20). Some Folsom sites have stone artifacts that suggest that the main activity was making stone points.[116] Other Folsom sites are kill and butchery locales (Figure 4.22) associated with the hunting of extinct bison, such as the **Folsom Site** in New Mexico (see Figure 4.18). However, just as Clovis people hunted more than mammoth and mastodon, Folsom groups targeted more than just bison; some sites have deer, rabbits, or mountain sheep. Still other Folsom sites represent longer-term camp sites with a variety of daily activities in addition to bones of extinct bison.[117]

During the late Paleoamerican period, sites such as the **O. V. Clary Site** in Nebraska (see Figure 4.18) show the complexity of Paleoamerican activities and settlement systems.[118] O. V. Clary is a winter habitation site where a Paleoamerican

Quebrada Santa Julia a Paleoamerican site in Chile (South America) that is associated with the bones of extinct horse and fluted spear points. It dates to 11,000 cal BC and represents Paleoamerican traditions that are not Clovis.

Quebrada Jaguay a Paleoamerican site in Peru (South America) that dates to 12,000 cal BC. It contains evidence for the use of maritime resources such as shellfish and fish, rather than an exclusive focus on hunting extinct forms of land mammals.

Folsom a Paleoamerican culture that follows Clovis culture. Folsom dates between 10,800 and 9,800 cal BC. It is characterized by the hunting of extinct bison and is found mainly in the Plains and southern Rocky Mountains in the United States.

Folsom Site a Paleoamerican kill/butchery site of the Folsom culture in New Mexico; it is associated with the hunting of extinct bison.

O. V. Clary Site a later Paleoamerican site in Nebraska. It was a winter habitation with activities such as hide working, food processing (of bison), and possibly hide clothing manufacture.

group lived for several months. It is situated in the bottom of a valley, where people would be somewhat protected from strong winter winds. People hunted bison in the uplands and brought parts of these animals back to the site for food and processing. Stone scrapers with red ochre on them indicate working of animal hides, whereas the presence of numerous bison dew claws likely indicates that people were making or repairing animal hide clothing. The dew claws may have been attached to bison leg hide used for making protective covering for human legs or feet. In the same area, around a hearth, there were bone needles and an awl, which usually are interpreted as tools used for making clothing. Ravens and great horned owls may have been killed, plucked, and skinned to be used as decoration on clothing or to make ritual items such as headdresses. During warmer times of the year, the people living at the O. V. Clary Site would have

FIGURE 4.22
Excavations at the Paleoamerican Jones–Miller Bison Kill site in eastern Colorado.

visited quarries for stone raw materials, hunted and killed bison at kill and butchery sites, and lived at short-term campsites elsewhere in the landscape.

Late Paleoamerican occupations in South America also document the wide variety of subsistence and settlement strategies of these groups. People at **Quebrada Tacahuay** in coastal Peru (see Figure 4.18) continued the strategy of using maritime resources[119] seen earlier at Quebrada Jaguay (see earlier). Around 10,600 cal BC, these groups were hunting several types of seabirds, fishing, and collecting clams and mussels. Many of the bird bones have butchery marks from stone tools, and the small types of fish suggest that these Paleoamericans had fishnet technology. Evidence for Paleoamerican occupations in the Andes Mountains also is present in many South American countries bordering on the Pacific Ocean. One of these is **Guitarrero Cave** in northern Peru (see Figure 4.18).[120] It is situated at 2,580 meters (about 1½ miles) above sea level, and its earliest occupation dates to 10,100 cal BC. Stone artifacts were found with bones from deer, birds, and camelids; this occupation appears to have been short term. In Amazonian Brazil, the site of **Caverna da Pedra Pintado** (see Figure 4.18) dates between 11,000 and 9,000 cal BC.[121] It contains hearths, bird and snake bones, fruits, Brazil nuts, fish, tortoises, freshwater shellfish, and red pigment drops. The red pigment was used to create rock art on the walls of the cave, which includes hands, stick figures, and geometric patterns, which are also found at other Brazilian sites (Figure 4.23).

Quebrada Tacahuay a later Paleoamerican site in coastal Peru (South America). People here continued to focus on maritime resources, especially seabirds and fish.

Guitarrero Cave a site in the Andes in northern Peru in South America. Its earliest occupation dates to the Paleoamerican period when people used the cave for short-term visits.

Caverna da Pedra Pintado a Paleoamerican site in the Amazon region of Brazil. It documents the wide range of foods that Paleoamericans ate and also contains the earliest cave art known in South America.

FIGURE 4.23
Paleoamerican painted images from Serra da Lua, South America. The concentric circle (left, center) may represent the sun setting at the winter solstice, with the figure to the right of it (diving figure with rays off head) as a comet (personal communication, A. C. Roosevelt).

Further Reflections

Megafauna in Australia

One of the debates about Pleistocene hunter–gatherer–foragers is about the extent to which their hunting behaviors had an impact on the disappearance (extinction) of the megafauna worldwide. It is an issue that resonates with us today, as we face challenges of changes to climate, ecologies, and species that human cultural behaviors today and in the recent past are instigating.

The issue of the Pleistocene megafauna extinctions is most easily seen in contexts in which humans entered new regions for the first time, such as Australia. Earlier we saw that people were in the Australian part of Sahul by 65,000 years ago. This means that people and megafauna in Australia overlapped for tens of thousands of years. We also know that humans hunted animals and had excellent technologies with which to do so. What is intriguing about Pleistocene Australia is that there is very little evidence of the hunting of megafauna;[122] even at the one site that has securely dated extinct megafauna bones associated with artifacts, there are no cut marks on the bones.[123]

Should we be surprised by this? Perhaps not—after all, the human population of Australia might have been quite low for a long time, and perhaps we have not yet found those rare kill sites. On the other hand, human behaviors could have impacted the megafauna in ways besides hunting, for example, practices such as using the eggs of now-extinct birds for food.[124] And, like the situation in the Americas, we know that climate changes in the Pleistocene affected vegetation that some megafaunal species relied on.[125] It is quite probable that the reason(s) for the megafaunal extinctions in places such as Australia were due to a combination of factors rather than a situation of "either hunting or climate change."[126]

Summary

- Hunter–gatherer–foragers of the Later Stone Age in Africa and the Upper Paleolithic in Eurasia are characterized by the extensive use of many technological innovations, such as spear throwers (atlatls), bow-and-arrow hunting, traps, snares, nets, and fishnets. This also includes extensive use of small stone artifacts (microliths), which often were parts of composite tools.

- Complex social relationships and networks in the Later Stone Age and Upper Paleolithic are represented by the intensive use of personal ornamentation, as well as art in the form of figurines and cave and rockshelter paintings. These relationships also can be seen in unusual burials in the European Upper Paleolithic, such as those at Dolní Věstonice and Sungir.

- Some of the earliest modern humans to arrive in Europe are recognized archaeologically as the Upper Paleolithic Aurignacian culture. These groups coexisted in Western Europe for several thousand years with the last Neandertals (see Chapter 3).

- The Aurignacian has the earliest modern human cave art, figurines, and musical instruments (flutes) in Europe.

- The Gravettian/Eastern Gravettian Upper Paleolithic in Europe coincides with the "mammoth steppe," extensive use of Venus figurines, and the development of cultural buffers such as tailored clothing that allowed human groups to live in northern parts of Europe during some of the coldest times of the last Ice Age.

- The Magdalenian/Epigravettian Upper Paleolithic period represents a time when human groups were able to recolonize northern Europe after a period of intensive glaciation. These archaeological cultures are associated with the majority of Upper Paleolithic portable and cave art.

- There have been many interpretations of Upper Paleolithic cave art. These include art for art's sake, hunting and fertility magic, entoptic phenomena, and social communication about group identity and territories.

- Some modern human groups migrating out of Africa before 50,000 cal BC eventually reached Sahul. They were the first people to colonize what is now Australia and New Guinea.

- Sometime before 25,000 cal BC, hunter–gatherer–foragers from Siberia began to move into the Alaskan part of the Americas. They are the first people to colonize the New World and are part of the ancestry of living Native Americans and First Nations.

- The first people to reach both Australia/New Guinea and the Americas encountered a situation in which the animals had no experience with humans. Because many of these animals, called the megafauna, became extinct at the end of the Pleistocene Ice Ages, some researchers suggest that human hunting practices were responsible for the extinction events. However, other researchers believe that megafaunal extinctions may have been the result of significant climate changes as well as hunting.

- There are two probable routes for the peopling of the Americas. One is by crossing the Beringia land bridge (caused by lower sea levels) between Siberia and Alaska and then moving south through the ice-free corridor between the Laurentide and Cordilleran glaciers covering most of Canada. Another is a Pacific coastal route in which people may have used simple boats to coast hop from Beringia to south of the glaciers.

- Pre-Clovis sites such as Monte Verde in Chile indicate that some Paleoamericans used the Pacific coastal route to enter the Americas. Slightly later groups may have used the ice-free corridor.

- Clovis culture is a well-known early Paleoamerican tradition characterized by fluted stone spear points. It is found mainly in North America and traditionally has been associated with kill/butchery sites of megafauna such as mastodons, mammoths, extinct bison, camels, and horses.

- South American Paleoamericans, who were contemporary with Clovis culture, not only hunted land animals but also used maritime resources such as seabirds and fish.

- There are many Paleoamerican groups throughout the Americas after the Clovis period. Research on their sites indicates that they continued to broaden their subsistence to include many types of plant foods, land animals, birds, freshwater shellfish and fish, and in some cases maritime resources. Like their counterparts in the Upper Paleolithic of Europe and the Later Stone Age of Africa, Paleoamericans had adaptations that incorporated art and tools made of bone and ivory.

Endnotes

1. All radiocarbon dates with ^{14}C ages of 50,000 years ago and later are shown using their calibrated ages when possible; otherwise, these are shown as years ago. Use of calibrated dates is indicated by cal BC (calibrated or calendric years). Read about radiocarbon calibration in Chapter 1. There are a number of accessible calibration programs, with the current calibration version, IntCal13, explained in Reimer et al. 2013.

2. See, for example, Klein 2008.

3. For example, d'Errico et al. 2012; Dewar et al. 2006; Humphreys 2007.

4. Ambrose 1998; the small scrapers are called thumbnail scrapers.

5. Ambrose 1998: 388.

6. Wendt 1976: 10. Although Wendt describes the painted rock slabs as present in a Middle Stone Age layer at Apollo 11 Cave, the slabs occur near the boundary with the overlying Later Stone Age layer, and the available radiocarbon dates suggest a placement in the Later Stone Age rather than the Middle Stone Age.

7. For example, at Wonderwerk Cave in South Africa (Thackeray et al. 1981) and Coldstream Cave (Rudner 1971) in South Africa; see also Lewis-Williams and Pearce 2004; Parkington et al. 2008.

8. Lewis-Williams 1983: 21.

9. Wadley 1996: 67–68.

10. Bousman 2005.

11. These often are labeled using French terminology, either as *pièces esquillées* or as *outils écaillés*.

12. Bouzouggar et al. 2008.

13. In this region, it is common to use the term Epipaleolithic (or sometimes late Upper Paleolithic) to refer to these groups of hunter–gatherer–foragers.

14. Barton et al. 2005; Camps 1974; Garcea 2010; Lubell 2001.

15. Olszewski et al. 2011.

16. Davis and Gollop 2003; White et al. 2016.

17. Anikovich et al. 2007 for Eastern Europe; Benazzi et al. 2011 and Higham et al. 2011 for Western Europe.

18. The site is el Castillo (Pike et al. 2012).

19. Conard 2009; Conard et al. 2009.

20. Chauvet et al. 1996; Quiles et al. 2016; Sandier et al. 2012.

21. Hoffecker 2005: 188; Hoffecker et al. 2010: 1078.

22. Hoffecker 2005: 189.

23. Hoffecker et al. 2010.

24. One example is Solutré (Olsen 1989).

25. Van Andel and Davies 2003; these glacial-period winter temperatures can be compared, for example, to those of modern-day Germany, which range from −4 to 0°C (24 to 32°F) during the winter.

26. Goebel 1999; Hoffecker 2002.

27. Guthrie 2001; Guthrie and Van Kolfschoten 2000; Zazula et al. 2003.

28. Guthrie and Van Kolfschoten 2000: 17.

29. Guthrie 2001: 553.

30. For example, Dolní Věstonice and Pavlov in the Czech Republic and the Kostenki region in Russia.

31. Shipman 2015; Svoboda et al. 2005.

32. Soffer et al. 1992.

33. Note, however, that Soffer et al. (1992: 272) have suggested that breakage of the figurines was deliberate, being done during ritual performances.

34. Deformities in the pelvis make it difficult to accurately identify the sex (Formicola, 2007: 447).

35. Hillson et al. 2005; Klima 1988.

36. Formicola et al. 2001; these authors also suggest that this individual suffered from an inherited disease (chondrodysplasia calcificans punctata) in which only females survive into young adulthood.

37. Most earlier descriptions of the double child burial state that one is female and one is male, e.g., Formicola (2007). A recent publication by Trinkaus and Buzhilova (2018), however, describes both children as male.

38. Each mammoth ivory bead would have taken about an hour to make (White 2003); it would take a single individual working a 40-hour week (which is not likely during the Upper Paleolithic) nearly five years to make this many ivory beads.

39. Cowgill et al. 2015; Formicola and Buzhilova 2004; Trinkaus and Buzhilova 2018.

40. Amirkhanov and Lev 2008; Mussi et al. 2000.

41. Soffer et al. 2000.

42. McDermott 1996; Mussi et al. 2000; Rice 1981.

43. Nelson 2001.

44. Mussi et al. 2000.

45. Whittaker 2010.

46. Cattelain 1997.

47. The German site of Stellmoor has wooden arrow shafts from about 4,000 years ago (Hoffecker 2005: 194). Microliths (small flaked stone artifacts), however, appear much earlier and often are assumed to be components of arrows.

48. Svezhentsev 1993: 26.

49. Gladkikh et al. 1984.

50. Soffer et al. 1997.

51. Conkey 1984. Painted and engraved caves are mainly confined to Southwestern Europe because this is where the geological formations support the development of caves; Central and Eastern Europe have fewer caves.

52. Castelli 2010.

53. Halverson 1987.

54. Breuil 1952.

55. Lewis-Williams and Dowson 1988; but see Helvenston and Bahn 2003 and Hodgson 2006 for dissenting views about entoptic pheonomena.

56. Barton et al. 1994; Conkey 1985.

57. Bicho et al. 2007.

58. Bulbeck 2007; Erlandson and Braje 2015; Field and Lahr 2005; Lahr and Foley 1994; Norman et al. 2018.

59. Mulvaney and Kamminga 1999: 109–110.

60. Macaulay et al. 2005.

61. Field and Lahr 2005; O'Connor 2007; Ono et al. 2009.

62. Bulbeck 2007.

63. Bird et al. 2018.

64. Bird et al. 2018: 437; Nagle et al. 2017; Tobler et al. 2017.

65. Balme and Morse 2006; Olley et al. 2006; Smith et al. 1998.

66. David et al. 2013: 8; Davidson 2010: S183.

67. Clarkson et al. 2017.

68. Groube et al. 1986; Leavesley and Allen 1998; Leavesley et al. 2002; Summerhayes et al. 2012.

69. Maloney et al. 2018.

70. Lell et al. 1997; Raghavan et al. 2014; Schurr 2000.

71. Goebel 1999; Pitulko et al. 2004.

72. Tamm et al. 2007.

73. Amick 2017; Graf and Buvit 2017; Hoffecker et al. 2014; Tamm et al. 2007. Dental evidence also supports the Beringian standstill (Scott et al. 2018).

74. Amorim et al. 2017.

75. Bourgeon et al. 2017.

76. Potter et al. 2017; Wygal 2018.

77. Fagundes et al. 2018.

78. A third possible route to the Americas involves a sea passage from Europe to the Americas with hunter–gatherer–forager groups using skin boats to travel from northern France along the edge of the glaciers covering most of England and all of Ireland and then along the glacial front stretching from Ireland to the area around Newfoundland in North America, a journey of 2,500 kilometers (1,550 miles) (Stanford and Bradley 2002, 2012). Most archaeologists, however, do not believe that the data support the use of this possible route (for example, Eren et al. 2013; Straus 2000).

79. Goebel et al. 2008; Pitblado 2011.

80. Heintzman et al. 2016; Pitblado 2017; Smith and Goebel 2018.

81. Anderson and Gilliam 2000; Clark et al. 2014; Dixon 2001; Goebel et al. 2008; Pitblado 2011.

82. de Saint Pierre 2017.

83. Goebel et al 2008: 1501; Lesnek et al. 2018.

84. Joyce 2006; Waters et al. 2015.

85. Many archaeologists also use the term Paleoindian, although Paleoamerican is a more acceptable term to some Native American groups.

86. Achilli et al. 2013; Chatters et al. 2014; Raff and Bolnick 2014; Rasmussen et al. 2014.

87. The Spanish reintroduced the horse to the Americas in the AD 1500s.

88. See, for example, Martin 2005 for North America and Diamond 2001 for Sahul.

89. Wroe et al. 2004.

90. Waters et al. 2015.

91. Grayson 2007; Grayson and Meltzer 2015; Guthrie 2006; Wroe et al. 2004.

92. Waters and Stafford 2007.

93. Clovis points are finely made, bifacially flaked stone points with a channel flake, called a flute, running from

the base toward the middle of the point. The channel flake removes some of the point's thickness and likely was a way to thin the point so that it could be hafted onto a wooden, bone, or ivory shaft. It also functioned as a way for the point to absorb shock when hitting an animal, rather than breaking (Thomas et al. 2017).

94. Jackson 1995; Pearson and Ream 2005; Sanchez et al. 2014.

95. Smallwood 2012.

96. Haynes 2002: 158.

97. For example, Martin 2005.

98. Byers and Ugan 2005; Cannon and Meltzer 2004, 2008; Haynes 2002: 177–178; Waguespack and Surovell 2003.

99. See, for example, Pinson 2011.

100. Jennings 2013; Kilby and Huckell 2014.

101. Stanford and Jodry 1988.

102. Yohe II and Bamforth 2013.

103. Gingerich 2011: 132, 134–135.

104. Haynes 2002: 177–178.

105. Haynes 2002: 106–108; Tankersley 1998.

106. Hemmings 2005. There also are rare examples of personal ornamentation, such as beads, as from the Mockingbird Gap site in New Mexico (Holliday and Killick 2013).

107. Gaines et al. 2009; Sanchez 2001; Sanchez et al. 2014.

108. Jackson 1995; Pearson and Ream 2005; Sanchez 2001.

109. Goebel et al. 2008: 1499; Gonzalez et al. 2015; Lohse et al. 2006; Nami 2007.

110. Jackson et al. 2007.

111. Reitz et al. 2016; Sandweiss et al. 1998.

112. Bueno et al. 2013.

113. Morrow and Morrow 1999.

114. Martínez et al. 2016.

115. Collard et al. 2010.

116. Jennings 2012.

117. Wilmsen 1974.

118. Hill et al. 2011; see also Knell and Hill 2012 for settlement diversity in the Cody Paleoamerican complex and Hill 2008 and Kornfield and Larson 2008 for overall Paleoamerican subsistence diversity in the Plains and Rocky Mountains.

119. deFrance et al. 2001; Keefer et al. 1998.

120. Lynch and Kennedy 1970; Lynch et al. 1985.

121. Roosevelt et al. 1996.

122. Johnson et al. 2016; O'Connell and Allen 2015: 78–79.

123. The site is Warratyi Rockshelter (Hamm et al. 2016).

124. Miller et al. 2016.

125. Dortch et al. 2016.

126. Monjeau et al. 2017.

CHAPTER 5

Hunting, Gathering, Foraging, Farming, and Complexity

Hunting, gathering, and foraging, as well as fishing, were the mainstays of subsistence strategies of modern human groups for tens of thousands of years in both the Old and the New Worlds (read "Timeline: Late Hunter–Gatherer–Foragers"). These were successful economic strategies that were characterized by in-depth ecological knowledge about the diverse habitats within the territories used by hunter–gatherer–foragers. In many cases, these groups were highly mobile, with small sites representing short-term stays or limited sets of activities. At other times, when resources were plentiful, some hunter–gatherer–foragers established more permanent settlements where they lived for many months during the year or for a year or more. In this chapter

ABOVE: A Neolithic period sickle. Notice the stone artifacts set into the handle.

we will briefly examine a few of these groups, who in the Old World are classified as the **Mesolithic** or **Epipaleolithic** periods in Eurasia, or the later part of the Later Stone Age in Africa. In the New World, such groups are found during the Archaic period. At the end of the Pleistocene and during the early Holocene, however, some hunter–gatherer–foragers in the Middle East, Asia, the Americas, and Africa became more invested in certain wild plant and wild animal species, which led in some cases to their **domestication** and the origins of food-production economies. Why this key economic transition occurred has long been the subject of archaeological research, and there are a wide diversity of ideas that have been proposed to explain this subsistence shift and the social changes that accompanied it. We will look at some of the theories for the origins of food production at the end of this chapter and discuss social and political complexity, which partially resulted from accumulation of surpluses generated by food-production economies.

Mesolithic an archaeological term used in some parts of the Old World, such as Europe and Asia, to describe late hunter–gatherer–forager groups. The chronology associated with this term varies from region to region. For example, in Europe, the Mesolithic is found between 9600 and 5000 cal BC.

Epipaleolithic an archaeological term most often used to refer to hunter–gatherer–forager groups living in the Middle East in the interval between 23,000 and 9,600 cal BC.

Domestication changes over time in the features of wild plants and animals that made these species more attractive to humans for a variety of reasons. These were genetic changes that were "selected" because of human manipulation.

The End of the Ice Ages

During the Pleistocene, the world was populated by hunter–gatherer–foragers, most of whom had mobile lifestyles. In a few instances and during different time periods in the Pleistocene, some of these groups lived at a single site for longer periods of time, for example, as we saw with some of the Eastern Gravettian occupations in the Dolní Věstonice region in Central Europe (see Chapter 4). The abundance of animal bones at many Pleistocene sites gives us insight into the types of animals hunted, mainly for food, but sometimes also for their furs. These hunter–gatherer–foragers usually did not live by meat alone, and they undoubtedly had a detailed knowledge of many plant foods (and medicines that could be made from plants). Our evidence for their gathering of plant resources, however, is sparse because actual plant remains often are not preserved. Recent analyses of stone grinding tools from sites in Russia and in the Czech Republic (Eastern Europe), however, yielded plant starches, suggesting that by 30,000 to 28,000 cal BC, Upper Paleolithic people were grinding cattail and ferns to make flour.[1]

Humans formed an early close relationship with gray wolves that resulted in genetic changes that led to the domesticated dog. There are many examples of domesticated dogs from Europe (including at Mezhirich in Ukraine; see Chapter 4), the Near East (at sites such as 'Ain Mallaha in Israel; see later), and the Americas after 12,000 cal BC.[2] The domestication process, however, seems to be earlier, with recent evidence from Belgium and Siberia suggesting that domestication leading to dogs was underway by 29,700 cal BC.[3] As large social animals, dogs would have been useful to hunter–gatherer–foragers for protecting campsites from other animals, helping to track or hunt animals,[4] and possibly serving as pack animals to move meat from kill to camp sites or to transport hides/skins used for shelters from one site to another.

Timeline: Late Hunter–Gatherer–Foragers

In today's world, there are few remaining hunter–gatherer–forager groups. During the Late Pleistocene and much of the earlier Holocene, however, these societies characterized all humans (Figure 5.1). In some regions of the world, the activities and economic decisions of some of these groups led to the origins of food production and the domestication of certain plants and animals (timelines for food production economies are shown in Chapters 6 through 15).

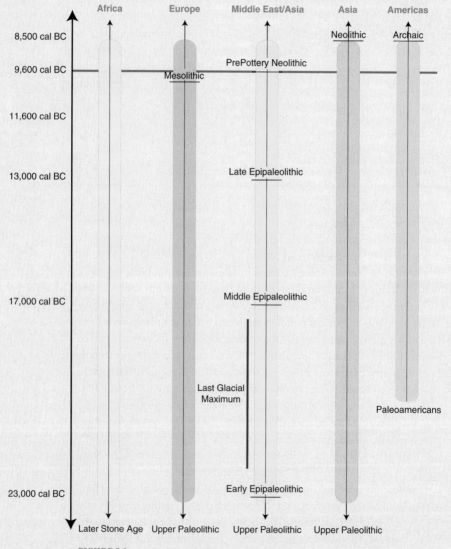

FIGURE 5.1
Timeline of Late Pleistocene hunter–gatherer–foragers and terminology (red line indicates the Pleistocene–Holocene boundary).

The long-term intimate knowledge that hunter–gatherer–foragers had of plant resources and animals—including their domestication of the dog (most likely not intentional in the sense of the modern breeding of dogs)—led in some instances to the domestication of a variety of plant foods and of some other animals after 9000 cal BC. Archaeologically, domesticated plants and animals are recognized as distinct from their wild counterparts because of genetic changes that led to differences in some of their features. Domesticated sheep, for example, are more docile than their wild counterparts and have differences in their horns. Genetic changes in wheat and barley led to seeds that stay on the plant when ripe rather than falling to the ground. Many of these genetic changes were "selected" because of human manipulation of the animals and plants. After all, it is much more advantageous to humans to collect ripe seeds on the stalk than trying to pick them up off the ground, just as it is to have docile animals that are easier to control.

Domestication represented a key economic transition and fundamentally altered social organization, social relationships, and behaviors within and among human groups. For the first time, the world included people who were not hunter–gatherer–foragers and whose use and perception of the landscape were routinely and symbolically different. We will begin by examining hunter–gatherer–foragers in some of these regions and then turn to ideas about the origins of food production and concepts of social and political complexity.

The Old World

People living in the Old World during the end of the Pleistocene and the early Holocene benefited from the effects of worldwide climatic changes on vegetation communities as the Ice Ages ended. The geographical extent of favorable habitats, which contained wild edible plant foods and wild animals, became much larger. For many hunter–gatherer–forager groups life continued as before, with no significant changes in subsistence strategies. This is the pattern we see in Europe and much of Africa. In other regions of the Old World, such as Asia and the Middle East, people's subsistence decisions incorporated changes that eventually fundamentally altered their lifestyles. The timing of this transition differs from region to region. That is, food production economies do not appear in all parts of the Old World at the same moment in time (read "Timeline: Late Hunter–Gatherer–Foragers"). We will examine this transition in detail for the Middle East, as discussed next. Hunter–gatherer–forager groups and their successors in Asia, Europe, Africa, and the Americas are discussed in Chapters 6 to 15.

Middle East

In the Middle East, most archaeologists use the term Epipaleolithic to refer to hunter–gatherer–forager groups during the last part of the Pleistocene, from 23,000 to 9600 cal BC.[5] Our most detailed information comes from the Levant, which is the western or Mediterranean part of the Middle East (Figure 5.2). It includes the

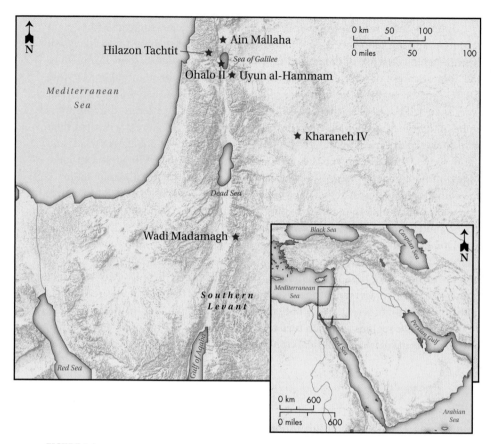

FIGURE 5.2
Epipaleolithic period sites in the southern Levant (Middle East).

modern countries of Jordan, Syria, Lebanon, Israel, and the Sinai Desert of Egypt. The northern part of the Levant includes parts of Turkey. There are numerous named archaeological cultures in the Levantine Epipaleolithic that are distinguished in part by the types of microliths that were made,[6] but rather than using all these names, we will examine them grouped into the Early, Middle, and Late Epipaleolithic periods.

EARLY EPIPALEOLITHIC
The Early Epipaleolithic in the Levant dates from 23,000 to 17,000 cal BC. This interval is quite cool and dry because it is the period of the beginning, peak, and immediate aftermath of the Last Glacial Maximum. For the most part, hunter–gatherer–foragers were highly mobile, living at small sites for short periods of time. They hunted gazelle, onager (a type of wild ass), and aurochs (extinct wild cattle). In the Mediterranean forest areas they also hunted deer, whereas in the rugged hills, they targeted goats and sheep. One example of a small Early Epipaleolithic site is

FIGURE 5.3
The rockshelter at Wadi Madamagh in the Petra region of Jordan. The rockshelter deposits are in
the area with the white sandbags on the surface, which extends to the left behind the juniper tree,
as well as to the right (where the individual is excavating). Wadi Madamagh contains both Upper
Paleolithic and Early Epipaleolithic period deposits.

one that I excavated. It is the rockshelter at **Wadi Madamagh** (see Figure 5.2) in the
Petra region of Jordan and is only 33 square meters (355 square feet) in overall size
(Figure 5.3).[7] Wild goats were the main animal hunted here, probably because this
region is rugged and rocky.[8]

Although climatic conditions were somewhat inhospitable during the Early
Epipaleolithic, there were several favorable situations. These include the Pleistocene lakes and marshes in Jordan and Syria, as well as well-watered areas such as
the Sea of Galilee in Israel. One unusual site is **Ohalo II** on the shores of the Sea of
Galilee (see Figure 5.2).[9] After the Early Epipaleolithic occupation of this site, it was
buried by rising lake levels. This led to excellent organic preservation. The site, which
is 300 square meters (984 square feet) in size, had several brush hut dwellings and
thousands of preserved wild barley and other grass seeds, as well as wild almond,
olive, pistachio, and grape. The organic remains give us an excellent glimpse into the
plant food diet of these hunter–gatherer–foragers, indicating that they were exploiting wild cereal grasses for food at least 10,000 years or more before the domestication

Wadi Madamagh a small rockshelter site in the Petra region of
Jordan (Levantine Middle East).
It has cultural materials of the
Early Epipaleolithic period and an
emphasis on the hunting of wild
goats, which were common in the
rugged terrain in which the site is
situated.

Ohalo II an Early Epipaleolithic
site on the shore of the Sea of
Galilee in Israel (Levantine Middle
East). It contains thousands of
well-preserved organic remains
such as wild cereal grasses. This
demonstrates early and intensive
use of a plant food that became
one of the major domesticates
some 10,000 or so years later.

Kharaneh IV a large aggregation site in the Azraq Basin area of eastern Jordan (Levantine Middle East). It was occupied during the Early and the Middle Epipaleolithic and yielded evidence for long-distance exchange for marine shells, dwelling structures, hearths, burials, and the hunting of gazelle and aurochs.

of cereals. In addition to hunting, people at Ohalo II also fished.[10] There is a burial, and the brush huts, in combination with foods from various seasons, suggest that the people who lived here were able to stay year-round.

Another unusual site is in the Azraq Basin of Jordan, which also contained well-watered situations. **Kharaneh IV** has occupations dating to the Early and the Middle Epipaleolithic (see Figure 5.2).[11] The site is enormous, covering 21,000 square meters (5 acres). Recent excavations in the Early Epipaleolithic deposits yielded evidence for structures, hearths, ground stone tools, red ochre, thousands of pierced marine shells from the Red Sea and the Mediterranean Sea, and millions of stone artifacts including microliths. There are three burials. Groups at Kharaneh IV hunted aurochs and gazelle and collected tortoise. The presence of structures, as well as seasonal information from animal bones, birds, and plant remains, suggests that people lived here for most, if not all, of the year. The site is so large and has such a diverse assemblage, including many different types of microliths and the long-distance transport of marine shells, that it likely was an aggregation site where people from different parts of the Levant came to meet.

MIDDLE EPIPALEOLITHIC

In the interval from 17,000 to 13,000 cal BC, Middle Epipaleolithic groups lived during somewhat warmer and perhaps wetter climatic conditions. Many of them continued to be highly mobile, although the occupation at Kharaneh IV during the Middle Epipaleolithic shows the continued use of this site for aggregation of hunter–gatherer–foragers (read "Peopling the Past: Aggregation Sites in the Levantine Epipaleolithic"). Excavations at the site of **Uyun al-Hammam** in the western highlands of Jordan (see Figure 5.2), on the other hand, document the earliest known cemetery in this part of the world.[12] The site covers 1,000 to 1,500 square meters (2.5 to 3.7 acres) and is near a stream channel. In addition to habitation evidence, there are 8 graves containing 11 humans. This find is significant for two reasons. First, it is the largest number of people buried at a single site during the Early and Middle Epipaleolithic (other sites with burials have only one or two people). Second, it offers an intriguing look into the social complexity of hunter–gatherer–forager groups because some of the individuals buried here have special grave goods. These include tortoise shells, wild goat horns, red deer antler, and partial skeletons of aurochs, deer, and gazelle. One of the most interesting is the burial of a couple of the humans with the skull of a fox and an almost complete fox skeleton. Human–animal associations are frequently found in the Late Epipaleolithic, so the discovery of these at Uyun al-Hammam indicates that these types of rituals or symbolic interactions were established long before the appearance of small village settlements (see "Late Epipaleolithic").

Uyun al-Hammam a Middle Epipaleolithic site in Jordan (Levantine Middle East). It contains a cemetery in which several humans are buried with parts of animals such as tortoise shells, goat horns and deer antler, and foxes. This indicates that human–animal symbolic associations were part of hunter–gatherer–forager societies long before the appearance of settled communities.

Natufian an alternative name for the Late Epipaleolithic period in the Levantine Middle East, dating between 13,000 and 9600 cal BC. During the Early Natufian, which coincided with the climatic optimum, several small village sites were established in the Mediterranean forest area. A return to colder and drier conditions during the Late Natufian corresponds to a return to higher mobility by hunter–gatherer–foragers.

LATE EPIPALEOLITHIC

The Late Epipaleolithic is known as the **Natufian** period and occurred from 13,000 to 9600 cal BC.[14] The earlier part, or Early Natufian (13,000 to 11,000 cal BC), coincided with the climatic optimum—a warmer and wetter period during which the Mediterranean forest, open parkland, and steppe habitats expanded at the expense of

Peopling the Past

Aggregation Sites in the Levantine Epipaleolithic

For much of the Epipaleolithic period, hunter–gatherer–foragers were highly mobile small groups. They had extensive networks with other groups through which items such as marine shell beads and pendants were transported over great distances (Figure 5.4). There are some sites, however, such as Kharaneh IV, where several lines of archaeological evidence suggest that larger numbers of people came together on occasion during both the Early and the Middle Epipaleolithic periods.[13] Kharaneh IV (as noted in the text) has thousands of marine shells from the Mediterranean and Red Seas; there even are a few marine shells from the Indo-Pacific. The sheer numbers of marine shells may suggest a large number of people, whereas the distances to the bodies of water may indicate far-flung interactions between groups and the movement of hunter–gatherer–foragers over long distances when they came together in the Azraq Basin region of Jordan. Other evidence suggesting different groups of people is found in stone artifact types (especially the forms of microliths), some of which are characteristic of the steppic regions of the eastern Levant, whereas others are typical of the western Levant near the Mediterranean Sea. Additionally, the sources for the stone used to make ground stone and some of the chipped stone artifacts are from other parts of the Azraq region. This indicates movement of people across the landscape, bringing their various tool kits with them to Kharaneh IV. Aggregation sites such as Kharaneh IV are important because they document the complexity of social life long before settled villages and food-production economies.

FIGURE 5.4
Examples of shells and shell beads from Area A (Middle Epipaleolithic period) at Kharaneh IV in Jordan.

the desert. This meant that there was a much greater abundance of wild cereal grasses and acorns (both associated with the oak forest), as well as animals such as gazelle. One of key features of the Early Natufian was the establishment of small villages in the Mediterranean forest zone. They ranged in size from 3 to 10 dwellings. Most archaeologists interpret these sites as evidence for year-round residence. In the steppic zone that characterizes much of Jordan, Syria, and southern Israel, however, Early Natufian hunter–gatherer–foragers were more mobile.

The small village sites of the Early Natufian, such as **'Ain Mallaha** in Israel (see Figure 5.2), contain a wealth of archaeological evidence.[15] In addition to dwellings, they have abundant ground stone tools indicating the processing of plant foods, decorated bone tools, small stone sculptures, many burials including some with grave

'Ain Mallaha a Late Epipaleolithic (Natufian period) site in Israel. It dates between about 13,000 and 9600 cal BC and is an example of a small village in the Mediterranean forest region of the Levant.

goods, beads made from marine shells, red ochre, and a host of other materials including the animals they hunted for food. One interesting discovery at 'Ain Mallaha was the burial of an elderly woman with a canid, which is interpreted as a probable domesticated puppy. There are more than 400 known human skeletons or parts of skeletons from burial contexts at Natufian sites; this is the first large population sample from this part of the world. For many decades, archaeologists believed that the unusual archaeological signature of the Early Natufians with their permanent settlements and ritual and social complexity was partly because they were the first people to heavily rely on cereal grasses as part of their diet.[16] Some archaeologists even argued that the behaviors of the Early Natufians were responsible for the domestication of the cereals. However, we now have good evidence that these behaviors were established much earlier during the Epipaleolithic (see earlier) and that hunter–gatherer–foragers continued to exploit wild foods.[17] It is likely instead that the Early Natufians were able to establish villages not because they were agriculturalists but mainly because of the wild cereals and acorns in the Mediterranean forest habitat, as well as plant foods that did not become domesticates, such as club-rush tubers and sedges.[18] Cereal and other grasses ripen during the summer, whereas acorns are available in the fall, and sedges are available year-round. Thus, the collection of these foods does not conflict in terms of scheduling tasks. Additionally, many of these foods can be stored and thereby help offset differences in plant food yields from year to year. Even in the steppic areas, Early Natufians had small settlements such as **Shubayqa 1** (Jordan).[19] Recent discoveries here include the remains of the world's oldest bread (12,650 cal BC). This flat bread (a bit like pita bread) was made of wild wheat and barley, as well as club-rush tuber, which would have given it a nutty flavor.

Beginning about 11,000 cal BC, worldwide climatic conditions worsened with the return of much colder and drier conditions. This had a dramatic effect on Late Epipaleolithic groups, most of whom during the Late Natufian period (11,000 to 9600 cal BC) returned to a more mobile lifestyle, even within the Mediterranean forest. This can be explained in part by the shrinkage of these favorable habitats and a reduced availability of cereal grasses and acorns. Life in areas outside the forest changed less because Natufians in these areas already were highly mobile. Most of the village sites were abandoned, although there was at least one village in the Mediterranean forest area.[20] There also is evidence for continued social complexity in rituals among Late Natufians. This is found at **Hilazon Tachtit** in Israel (see Figure 5.2), which is a small cave with evidence for feasting and the burial of at least 28 people.[21] The feasting involved aurochs and tortoises and appears to have been part of a ritual related to the act of burial (Figure 5.5). Feasting may have been associated with the burial of a disabled old woman. Among the unusual grave

Shubayqa 1 an Early Natufian (Late Epipaleolithic) period site in the Middle East (Jordan). It has the remains of the world's oldest bread at 12,650 cal BC.

Hilazon Tachtit a Late Natufian phase site of the Late Epipaleolithic period in the Levantine Middle East where evidence for an elaborate burial ritual associated with an elderly woman from a hunter–gatherer–forager group was found.

FIGURE 5.5
Excavations at the Late Natufian (Late Epipaleolithic) period site of Hilazon Tachtit, Israel.

goods with her were 50 tortoise shells, an aurochs' tail, part of the wing of an eagle, part of a wild boar's leg, the skull of a marten, and a human foot that did not belong to her. These items possibly indicate that she was a ritual or religious specialist, giving us some insight into social roles within groups of hunter–gatherer–foragers.

Transition to Food Production in the Middle East

As discussed previously, we know that Epipaleolithic groups in the Middle East were intensively using wild plant foods, including barley and wheat, based on macrobotanical and plant starch analyses. This evidence is early, dating around 23,500 to 22,500 cal BC, long before these plant foods were domesticated.[22] The cultural processes leading to the eventual domestication of cereals and other plant foods, as well as animals, however, are not completely understood, although it is during the later Neolithic period that genetic changes in some plant foods and animals led to their domesticated forms (see "Why Food Production?").

The major crops of the Middle East included emmer and einkorn wheat, barley, chickpeas, lentils, and peas. Also domesticated was the bitter vetch, which, unlike the other plant foods, is not a major crop plant today. Traditionally, archaeologists have thought that the domestication of barley and emmer and einkorn wheat occurred in the Levant, possibly in the Jordan Valley and the surrounding region.[23] Some researchers, however, have pointed out that the genetics of the main plant crops and the overlap in their natural distribution in the wild suggests domestication of all of these plant foods occurring in a small region in southeastern Turkey and northern Syria.[24] Indisputably domesticated cereals, lentils, and chickpeas began to appear during the last part of the **Pre-Pottery Neolithic** period, after 8500 cal BC.[25]

In addition to domesticated plant foods, the Middle East is the origin area for the domestication of sheep, goat, pigs, and cattle.[26] The wild goats and wild sheep that are the likely ancestors to domesticated forms are found in rocky and mountainous areas that stretch from southern Turkey (Taurus Mountains) across the northern Levant, east to the Zagros Mountains that form part of the boundary between modern Iraq and Iran, and then farther east to Pakistan. Goats appear to have been domesticated around 8000 cal BC in the Zagros Mountains region, and the earliest domesticated sheep are found at sites in the Zagros and Taurus Mountains. Cattle were domesticated by 7500 cal BC, likely in the relatively wet forests and marshlands present in northern Syria. Pigs, on the other hand, may have been domesticated in southeastern Turkey, between 7000 and 6400 cal BC.[27]

The sites of the Pre-Pottery Neolithic in the Levant date between 9600 and 6250 cal BC and are divided into two major phases—Pre-Pottery Neolithic A and B[28] (Figure 5.6).

PRE-POTTERY NEOLITHIC A

During the Pre-Pottery Neolithic A period (9600 to 8500 cal BC), there are many small sites suggesting a mobile lifestyle that was not too different from the Late Epipaleolithic (Late Natufian). The stone artifacts still include many microliths and other forms similar to those of the Late Epipaleolithic, although the Pre-Pottery Neolithic assemblages

Pre-Pottery Neolithic the earliest part of the Neolithic period in the Levantine region of the Middle East, dating between 9600 and 6250 cal BC. Numerous small and large villages with evidence for complex ritual activities are present. People of the PPN relied heavily on the cultivation of wild plants and the hunting of wild animals, and their economic strategies eventually led to genetic changes characteristic of domestication.

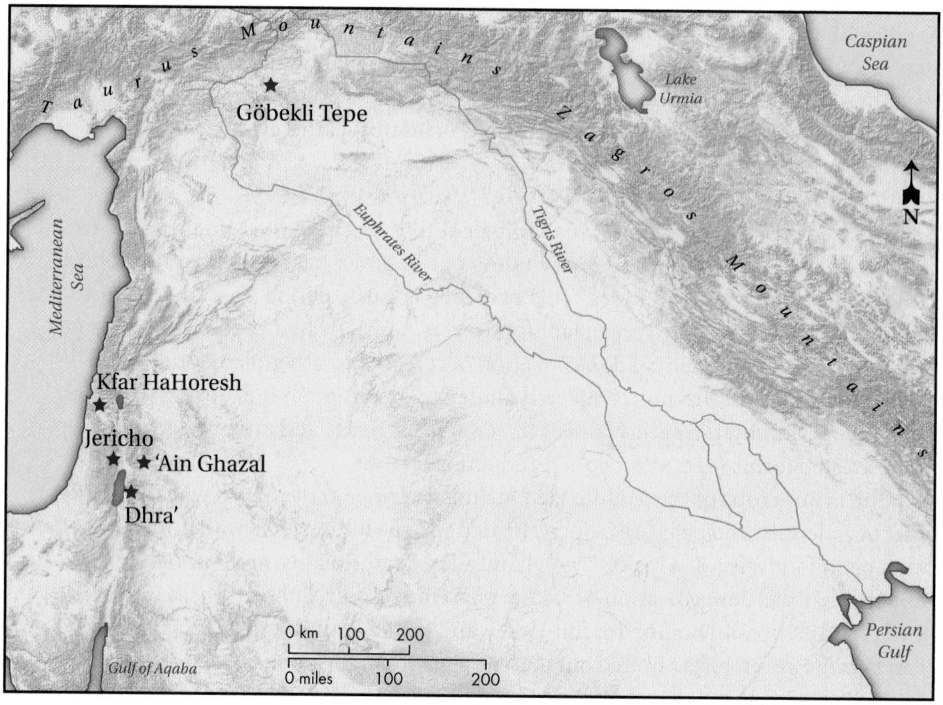

FIGURE 5.6
Pre-Pottery Neolithic period sites, mountain chains, and rivers in the Middle East.

Dhra' a Pre-Pottery Neolithic A site in Jordan. It was a small village with circular stone-walled dwellings that used mudbrick in the construction of the upper portions of each structure.

also have stone arrowheads. Not all sites indicate high levels of mobility, however, because there are locales such as **Dhra'** in Jordan (see Figure 5.6) that have circular houses and that yield abundant ground stone tools, indicating a much greater emphasis on the use of plant foods compared to the Late Natufian. At Dhra', the several oval dwellings were dug partially into the ground and then lined with mudbricks and stone.[29] The use of mudbricks in structures is a new innovation of the Pre-Pottery Neolithic. Population estimates for Dhra' range from 40 to 130 people.[30] They hunted gazelle and birds and collected wild plant foods. Most of these small villages are found in the Mediterranean forest zone, although Dhra' is in a more arid area in the Jordan Valley.

Jericho a large site in the West Bank in the Levantine Middle East, it has many different periods of occupation. During the Pre-Pottery Neolithic A, it was a moderate-size village of circular dwellings that were associated with a monumental stone wall, stone tower, and external ditch. These monumental features are unique for this time period.

One unusual site during the Pre-Pottery Neolithic A is the village at **Jericho** (which also has Natufian, as well as later Pre-Pottery and Pottery Neolithic occupations) in the West Bank (see Figure 5.6). Although the dwellings at Jericho are similar to those at sites such as Dhra', Jericho is much larger and may have housed between 225 and 735 people.[31] Moreover, Jericho has a massive stone wall and a tower situated inside the wall. These are associated with a ditch on the exterior side of the wall.[32] The wall is 3.5 meters (11.5 feet) high, and the tower is 8.5 meters (28 feet) high and 8 meters (26 feet) in diameter. The tower has an internal stairway leading from the base to the top. The exact function of the ditch, wall, and tower has been widely debated by archaeologists, with some proposing that they were built for defense of the village at Jericho. However, there is no evidence at any Pre-Pottery Neolithic A site for defensive structures, nor is there much evidence for the types of violence that would be expected if Neolithic people had to defend themselves. Another suggestion is that the wall and ditch were built to divert flash floodwaters, from the nearby hills, around the village and that the tower was a ritual building such as a shrine or even a structure to view the sunset over the high mountain to the west at midsummer.[33] Regardless of the exact function of these structures at Jericho, their presence indicates a level of social organization and of the management of labor not characteristic of the Epipaleolithic and earlier periods.

Another intriguing site is **Göbekli Tepe** in southeastern Turkey (see Figure 5.6), which is on top of a hill with a good view.[34] It was built during the last part of the Pre-Pottery Neolithic A and continued into the Pre-Pottery Neolithic B period (see later discussion), so that there are several phases with structures. In the late Pre-Pottery Neolithic A, these were oval or circular in shape, whereas in the Pre-Pottery Neolithic B, they were rectangular. The most striking feature of all these structures are the motif-carved, large T-shape stone pillars, each of which is between 3 and 5 meters (10 and 16 feet) tall and can individually weigh up to 10 tons. The images carved onto these include snakes, wild boars, foxes, lions or leopards, wild cattle, gazelle, bears, wild sheep, wild asses, and cranes[35] (Figure 5.7). Each structure seems to have a different grouping of animals. In the circular structures, shorter T-shape

Göbekli Tepe an unusual Pre-Pottery Neolithic A and B site in Turkey. It has structures that incorporate large T-shape pillars. Many of the T-shape pillars are decorated with motifs such as snakes, aurochs, gazelle, felines, and other images. It has been interpreted as a ritual center with each structure being a temple.

FIGURE 5.7

(a) A carved T-shape pillar from one of the structures at the Pre-Pottery Neolithic period site of Göbekli Tepe in Turkey. From top to bottom: wild cattle, fox, crane. (b) A T-shaped pillar (set into a structure bench) with a sculpted animal above animal engraving.

pillars were built into the wall that enclosed the room, which also had a bench, and there were two larger T-shape pillars situated in the center of the room. The later rectangular structures usually have just a couple of undecorated T-shape pillars in the center of the room. This unusual architecture, along with the fact that the entire site was deliberately filled in by Neolithic people, suggested to the archaeologists working there that the site represents a ceremonial locale and that each structure may have been a temple or a way to establish community identities.[36] Other archaeologists, however, pointed out that there is rather a lot of evidence of everyday life in the archaeological deposits, suggesting that people were living at Göbekli Tepe.[37] In this interpretation, features such as the animal grouping specific to each structure might represent family motifs, such as clan symbols.

PRE-POTTERY NEOLITHIC B

During the Pre-Pottery Neolithic B period (8500 to 6250 cal BC), the Levantine region of the Middle East is characterized by numerous villages. Some are small, especially in the steppic to desert areas, such as eastern Jordan. Sites in this type of habitat often have a small number of circular dwellings (Figure 5.8). They sometimes are interpreted as

FIGURE 5.8
A circular dwelling at the Pre-Pottery Neolithic B period site of Wadi Jilat 23, in the Azraq region of eastern Jordan.

reflecting group organization based on nuclear families (mom, dad, and the kids). If this is true, then they might contrast with extended families (nuclear family plus grandparents, married siblings, and their spouses and kids) that may be more typical in the larger Pre-Pottery Neolithic B villages found in more favorable locales.

These larger villages tend to have houses that are rectangular in shape and contain more than one room. One example is **'Ain Ghazal** (see Figure 5.6), which is situated in Amman, Jordan.[38] 'Ain Ghazal was occupied during all of the Pre-Pottery Neolithic B. At its greatest extent, it was 10 hectares (25 acres) in size and had a population between 900 and 2,900 people.[39] Large villages with numerous people were social contexts in which we find increasing evidence for ritual and other special activities. 'Ain Ghazal and Pre-Pottery Neolithic B Jericho, for example, yielded plaster statues of highly stylized people. Some of these are full-body (but not full-size) individuals, whereas others are the upper torso and head. Paint was used to show hair and to emphasize the eyes. At 'Ain Ghazal, these plaster statues were buried in groups, which may represent ritual disposal of special objects when they were replaced by newer images.

Pre-Pottery Neolithic B sites throughout the Levant also are characterized by the special treatment of some individuals after death. These are the plastered skulls of adults (males and females) and children (Figure 5.9), which are found individually and in groups. They represent the removal of the head (minus the lower jaw), cleaning of the bone, addition of a layer of plaster to mold a set of features, and, finally, the use of paint to show hair or beards and emphasize the eyes. In some cases, shells for the eyes are inset into the plaster. This special treatment might represent an "ancestor cult,"[40] that is, a belief in the ability of certain deceased family members to intercede with the spirit world on behalf of the living, although how children would fit into this notion of "ancestors" might be problematic. Perhaps it is more likely that the special treatment of skulls is related to establishing community identity and relationships within that community.[41]

There are many examples of ritual from Pre-Pottery Neolithic B sites (read "Peopling the Past: Ritual in the Pre-Pottery Neolithic"), and this evidence indicates that ritual was an integral part of everyday life, so that we should expect that living spaces also were used for ritual or ceremonial activities.[42] The daily life of people at sites such as 'Ain Ghazal included hunting of wild animals and the collection of wild plant foods, although by the end of the Pre-Pottery Neolithic B, these attain the form of domesticates because of accumulated genetic changes. The amount of cultural materials at the villages is extremely large, as might be expected in places where people lived permanently for hundreds of years. It includes millions of stone artifacts, as well as animal figurines, beads of stone, bone, and shell, bone tools, and ground stone tools. Although no pottery was present, people used unfired earthenware as storage vessels and probably also baskets, as well as building rooms for storing grains and other foods.[43]

FIGURE 5.9
A fragmentary plastered human skull from the Pre-Pottery Neolithic B period at 'Ain Ghazal, Jordan.

'Ain Ghazal a large Pre-Pottery Neolithic B village site in Jordan. It has two caches of plaster statues of humans and also plastered human skulls, figurines, beads, and enormous quantities of artifacts reflecting everyday life.

Ritual in the Pre-Pottery Neolithic

Although there is evidence for ritual activities in the Epipaleolithic period in the Middle East, these become very apparent during the Pre-Pottery Neolithic period. In addition to rooms with special architecture, figurines and other objects, and plastered human skulls that suggest ceremonies of various types at villages such as 'Ain Ghazal, there also are sites that appear to be devoted to ritual. One of these is **Kfar HaHoresh** in Israel (see Figure 5.6), which dates to the middle of the Pre-Pottery Neolithic B period and was a mortuary complex.[44] The site is 0.4 to 0.8 hectares (1 to 2 acres) in size and has several components—a cult area, a funerary area, a production and maintenance area, and a feasting/trash area (Figure 5.10). There is no evidence for everyday life or dwellings, and it is thought that Kfar HaHoresh was used by the people from several villages in the vicinity.

The cult area of Kfar HaHoresh has small, grouped, standing stones, each about 1.5 meters (5 feet) tall. There are a number of hearths lined with stone or plaster. In the production area are low stone platforms, kilns used to make lime plaster, ground stone tools likely used to grind up the limestone for

FIGURE 5.10
One of the plastered surfaces with a stone wall boundary at the Pre-Pottery Neolithic B period mortuary ritual site of Kfar HaHoresh, Israel. Various features such as fire-pits, hearths, ovens, and stelae are associated with these surfaces. The trench (*left*) was excavated to examine the deposits below the plastered surface.

plaster manufacture, stone bowls used during the process of making lime plaster, and evidence for the knapping of stone artifacts. The funerary area has a series of L-shape walls and lime-plastered areas, below which are burials and other deposits. In one case, a large pit filled with ash had bones of humans and animals arranged to create the profile of an animal. In other cases, there are human burials below the lime-plastered surfaces. These can be of individual people or several people buried together; some of the people were buried without their heads. The funerary area also yielded a couple of plastered human skulls and burial of people with animals, especially fox, but also a headless gazelle. The evidence for feasting at the site comes from the abundance of animal bones in the trash (midden) area. The most spectacular is a pit containing bones representing joints of meat of eight aurochs. These were buried and sealed in a pit and then a young male human was placed on top of the pit and his burial sealed with lime plaster. Sometime later, a small area of the plaster was broken open, the young person's skull was removed, and the plaster hole repaired. The animals used at Kfar HaHoresh focus more on aurochs and gazelle (wild) than on goats (managed by people) as found at nearby sites.[45] This likely indicates the special status of wild animals in rituals. Although sites such as Kfar HaHoresh are unusual, they give us insight into aspects of life that held special significance to people during the Pre-Pottery Neolithic period.

For the world regions briefly mentioned below, extended discussion can be found in Chapters 6–15.

Asia

Hunter–gatherer–forager groups in the Asian region include people living in what is now the modern country of China, during what is sometimes referred to as the Mesolithic or Epipaleolithic period, although other researchers prefer to use the term Upper Paleolithic for this entire time range.[46] Like their counterparts elsewhere, microliths were a common part of their stone artifact assemblages.[47] Their sites included longer-term base camps, as well as smaller hunting locales.[48] Their settlement systems were highly mobile, but during warmer climatic periods there was less mobility and people resided at base camps for months and sent out task groups for hunting or other resource collection. What is especially intriguing is the appearance of coarsely made pottery that dates as early as 16,350 cal BC.[49] Technical knowledge about the properties of clay and the ability to shape vessels from it and fire them successfully are a key technology for many food-producing societies. This is because pottery vessels are important for at least two major reasons. First, they are durable containers for storage of seeds for planting, foods, and liquids. They also safeguard the contents from pests such as rodents and insects to a much better extent than a storage basket ever could. Second, pottery vessels mean that foods contained in them can be easily cooked directly over a fire. This is unlike a lined basket or skin container that might be damaged over a direct fire.[50] Stone-boiling (inserting fire-heated stones into a basket or skin container) to cook a stew or other type of meal was no longer necessary. The fact that pottery technology appears so early in China means that hunter–gatherer–forager

Kfar HaHoresh a Pre-Pottery Neolithic B site in Israel in the Middle East. It was a mortuary complex with evidence for burials, plastered skulls, skull removal, feasting, and lime production to make plaster for the burial areas.

groups there had at least one critical element that was important in later food production economies. Rice, pigs, millet (grain), chickens, water buffalo, and yaks were important early Asian domesticates. See Chapter 11 for further discussion.

Africa

As we saw in Chapter 4, the earlier part of the Later Stone Age in Africa is earlier than and contemporary with the Upper Paleolithic in Eurasia. The later part of the Later Stone Age is contemporary with Epipaleolithic period groups in the Middle East, as well as with Mesolithic period hunter–gatherer–foragers in Europe. The advent of food-production economies in Africa was later than in other parts of the Old World, with some groups engaging in strategies that led to the domestication of African plant foods such as millets, sorghum (grain), teff (grain), ensete (root crop), guinea rice, and yams.[51] See Chapters 10 and 15 for further discussion.

Europe

Hunter–gatherer–forager peoples of the Mesolithic period in Europe did not independently develop food-production economies. Instead, domesticated plants and animals were introduced from the Middle East. It took several thousands of years for this new economic strategy to be adopted by local European groups. And, as was the case for Later Stone Age Africa (see Chapter 10), some European hunter–gatherer–foragers initially adopted only some elements of food-production ways of life.[52] See Chapter 6 for further discussion.

The New World

The period of Paleoamerican hunter–gatherer–foragers ended about 8000 cal BC. Archaeologists call the succeeding period in the Americas the Archaic (North America and Mesoamerica) or the Preceramic (South America). Archaic period groups often are described as peoples who more intensively used foods that required processing, such as grinding of wild seeds of many types of plants. Their subsistence economies are thought to be much more diversified and broader in the types of food resources exploited than during the earlier Paleoamerican period, although we do know that Paleoamericans had a broader diet than just hunting large animals (see Chapter 4). In the New World, just like in the Old World, there were several regions where Archaic period groups began to experiment with plants and some animals, which eventually led to the domestication of these species and a fundamental shift in the relationship among people, plants, and animals. These regions include the North American East, Mexico and Central America, and Pacific coastal and Andean South America, among others (see Chapters 7, 8, 13, and 14).

North America

The types of resources used by Archaic period groups varied substantially depending on where they lived. In eastern parts of North America, sometime around 3000 cal BC, gourds were locally domesticated and likely used as containers or possibly as floats on fishnets. Their seeds are quite bitter but may have been processed and eaten.[53] Late Archaic period groups also began to exploit local seed-producing plants (sunflower, marsh elder, and sumpweed) in ways that led to their domestication (see Chapter 8). Some archaeologists have suggested that the processing of large quantities of nuts was an innovation ("bulk processing") that later was applied to the increased use of plants with small seeds, such as sunflowers and sumpweed.[54]

In contrast, Archaic period groups living in the North American Southwest do not appear to have domesticated any wild plants native to the North American Southwest. Rather, beginning about 2100 cal BC, domesticated maize (corn) was introduced from Mexico[55] (see Chapter 7). These Archaic period hunter–gatherer–foragers added maize-cultivation strategies to their relatively mobile lifestyles by planting maize in naturally well-watered areas, such as damp floodplains, and then leaving to take advantage of wild foods and other resources in different parts of the region.[56] When the maize began to ripen, they returned and harvested the crop.

Mexico/Central America

Among the many wild plant foods that Archaic period groups used in this world region were cactus fruits, nuts, squash and gourds, lima beans, Mexican plum, foxtail millet, and teosinte (the wild ancestor of maize).[57] Teosinte is a type of grass, and much of the archaeological work on its eventual domestication centered on its seeds (kernels) because this is what we focus on today with our large-kernel cobs. Other domesticates from this region include turkeys, beans, squash, chilies, and avocados. See Chapter 13 for further discussion of this world region.

South America

Although we will deal mainly with the Andean highlands in Chapter 14, there also were several important developments in the coastal regions of Ecuador, Peru, and Chile. By 6000 to 4800 cal BC, these Archaic period groups were investing time in some cultivation of plants, which included squash and maize (from Mexico/Central America), perhaps growing these domesticates in small gardens.[58] In the Andean highlands, Archaic period people were focused on hunting and managing camelids, two of which became the domesticated llamas and alpacas (used mainly as pack animals). Other important domesticates from South America include potatoes, sweet potatoes, quinoa (grain), guinea pigs (for food), and cotton. See Chapter 14 for more discussion of the Archaic period.

Why Food Production?

Food-production economies were the base on which highly complex and eventually politically complex societies developed (read "Further Reflections: Thinking About Food Production"). These ways of life (plus more recent modern industrialized economies) eventually replaced all but a small number of hunter–gatherer–forager groups, who today inhabit areas of the world that are marginal habitats for domesticated crops and animals (mainly in Australia, southern Africa, parts of Southern and Southeast Asia, and extremely northern latitudes). Food production based on domesticated plants and animals appeared independently in several different areas of the world from 8000 cal BC to AD 0 (Figure 5.11).

Because agricultural surpluses were the "fuel" of earlier socially and politically complex societies, there has been intense interest in the processes that were involved in the transformation from hunting–gathering–foraging to agriculture.[59] Many of the ideas for this transition initially were developed using the Middle East or Mesoamerica (Mexico/Central America) as examples and have tended to emphasize the domestication of plants. As archaeological research gained momentum in other world regions, information from these areas also is used to model the origins of food production involving domesticated species.

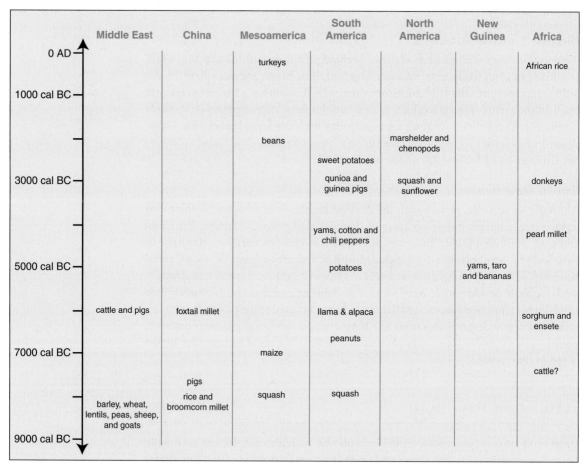

FIGURE 5.10

Some of the plants and animals domesticated in various regions of the world.

Ideas

Many early ideas sought explanations based mainly on one major factor, such as environmental changes, people's knowledge, or population density. One of these is the **"oasis" theory**. This says that the transition to agriculture was sudden, a process called the "Neolithic Revolution."[60] In this model, environmental changes leading to colder and drier climate meant that people, plants, and animals in the Middle East were clustered at oases. The close association at these places quickly led to observational knowledge about plant and animal reproductive behaviors that people used to manipulate plants and animals, resulting in their domestication.

On the other hand, the origin of agriculture in the Middle East could have been a long, gradual process of transition in which environmental changes did not play a large role.[61] People living in the **Fertile Crescent** had long-term knowledge of plants that grew there naturally. The Fertile Crescent is the arc of Mediterranean forest habitat stretching from Jordan/Israel/Lebanon north to southern Turkey/northern Syria and then east and south through the foothills of the Zagros Mountains of Iraq and Iran. Over time, these groups invented technologies such as ground stone tools, which were initially used to process nonfood items such as ochre but eventually were applied to grinding plant foods. These ideas form what might be called the **readiness theory**, that is, it took time for knowledge and appropriate technologies to come together successfully (another example of "mosaic evolution" such as we saw in Chapters 2 and 3) to exploit plants and animals in different ways.

Other archaeologists were influenced by agricultural economists, who predicted that increasing population size and density were major factors in driving agricultural innovations, such as the invention of different types of plows. This is the idea of **population pressure**.[62] It argues that favorable, coastal habitats in the Middle East would be densely occupied. In these situations, hunter–gatherer–foragers would make use of the abundant wild food resources found in these areas. Eventually, these favorable locales would become so packed with people that there would not be enough food for everyone. As a result, some groups would move away to more marginal, inland habitats but would take familiar wild plants with them. To be successful in the marginal areas, hunter–gatherer–foragers invested in deliberately growing these plants, thus leading to their domestication.

More recently, archaeologists have proposed a variety of hypotheses that usually involve several variables, including the role of peoples' decision-making and their social and symbolic activities. Some of these ideas include environmental change as one factor, for example, the **Younger Dryas theory** suggests that a major cold period at the end of the Pleistocene disrupted hunter–gatherer–forager adaptations in the Middle East.[63] Between 13,000 and 11,000 cal BC, climate was warmer and wetter, which facilitated an abundance of wild foods, and some hunter–gatherer–foragers became more settled and established small villages in the Mediterranean forest habitat (see "Late Epipaleolithic"). A return to a cooler and drier climate (Younger Dryas) about 11,000 cal BC resulted in the shrinkage of the Mediterranean forest in favor of the desert and steppe and an overall loss of resource abundance. This helped create

"Oasis" Theory an early idea for the origins of food-production. It assumed this transition was the result of hunter-gatherer-foragers observing features of plants and animals while living at well-watered places. This knowledge was then used to manipulate the animals and plants.

Fertile Crescent a geographical region in the Middle East characterized by the association of Mediterranean forest, wild cereals, and wild sheep and goats. It was a feature used in the readiness theory to explain the origins of food-production.

Readiness Theory an early idea for how food-production arose. It hypothesized a long and gradual transition to food-production that occurred in the Fertile Crescent in the Middle East. This allowed time for technologies such as ground stone to develop and be applied to grinding cereals in an optimal habitat.

Population Pressure an early idea for the origins of food-production, it assumed that population growth drove the need for people to begin to experiment with plants and animals in ways that led to their domestication.

Younger Dryas Theory the rapid cooling and aridity of this late glacial period was used as an explanation for the origins of food production. It assumes that as climate worsened, hunter-gatherer-forager groups began to manipulate plants and animals to assure their availability and abundance.

conditions in which hunter–gatherer–forager behavioral choices led to some groups becoming more mobile with a continued focus on wild foods and to other groups experimenting with wild plant foods and animals in ways that led to their domestication.

The theoretical framework of human behavioral ecology (see Chapter 1) also has been used to understand the behavioral processes involved in the transition to agricultural economies.[64] As noted in Chapter 1, human behavioral ecology hypotheses focus on decisions that people make with respect to the costs and benefits of various strategies available to them, and because these decisions are made by groups and by individuals, human behavioral ecology ideas include the theoretical perspective of agency (see Chapter 1). By examining specific examples of the origins of agriculture, it is possible to apply the human behavioral ecology framework (sometimes with modifications) to many world regions. The domestication of plants with small seeds in eastern North America (**small seed investment**), for example, is a strategy that seems counterproductive, given the high costs and relatively low returns (in terms of energy) when compared to other food resources.[65] When viewed in the context of the seasonal availability of food resources, however, the decision to invest in small seeds can be better understood. This is because small seeds can be processed during the winter, when high-ranked resources such as hickory nuts are no longer available. The time (costs) spent in processing small seeds does not compete with time needed to process the less costly and higher-return hickory nuts. Additionally, because nut harvests are variable in quantity from year to year, collecting and processing small seeds can help offset smaller food returns in a year when nuts are less available.

One variation within human behavioral ecology is the **feasting model**, which is seen as a risk-reduction approach that results in the origins of agriculture in some contexts.[66] Feasts and feasting are found in mobile hunter–gatherer–forager groups, but in the context of complex hunter–gatherers (groups located in resource-abundant areas where it is possible to live in communities that are less mobile), the reciprocal sharing of resources to reduce risk is transformed by several technological and social factors. Among complex hunter–gatherer–foragers, the ownership of resources by individuals is common, and a somewhat more settled lifestyle often involves the accumulation of material goods and of surplus food (seen in the development of storage facilities). Rather than simply sharing food equally among the group to reduce risk, the range of risk-reduction strategies expanded to include experimenting with plants and animals to ensure their abundance, accumulating "wealth" in the form of stored surplus food resources, and using the stored surplus foods to underwrite the costs of feasts. These feasts were rituals used to establish alliances, and they served as "social safety networks" to reduce the risks among and between groups from year to year. Anyone who hosted a feast could expect others to help them out in years that were difficult (risky) for them. Being able to successfully manipulate plants and animals to obtain surpluses eventually resulted in their domestication and continued use in the feasting cycle.

Other archaeologists have proposed a social and symbolic explanation for the origins of agriculture from a postprocessual theoretical framework.[67] In those groups

Small Seed Investment an origins of food-production idea based on ecological habitats in eastern North America. It notes that heavy use of edible small seeds is a seasonal activity that does not conflict with the gathering of other food resources. Manipulation of these small seed producing plants leads to the domestication of some of them.

Feasting Model feasting is a strategy that allows the sharing of food resources and brings prestige to those who host the feasts. It is one possible explanation for the origins of food-production because it hypothesizes that increasing the abundance of certain foods (to be used in feasting rituals) through their manipulation resulted in domestication.

who became more settled, certain aspects of daily life took on additional symbolic meanings, in particular, the **control of nature through its manipulation**. Households and their activities became centered on controlling "wild" nature using social means such as rituals (symbolic behaviors) and food storage, food processing and its technologies, and feasting. In this explanation, people were agents who transformed things that were wild into things that were domesticated and thus controlled.

Although many hypotheses for the origins of agriculture focus on a specific region of the world, occasionally some researchers attempt to explain these origins using worldwide hypotheses. One example is the **hostile Pleistocene theory**, which proposes that sustained agriculture was not possible during the Pleistocene because of extreme and frequent climatic fluctuations.[68] This Pleistocene hostility was due to unpredictable weather patterns, dryness, and smaller amounts of carbon dioxide (CO_2) in the atmosphere, which impacted plant growth because CO_2 is used by plants during photosynthesis. Hunter–gatherer–forager groups would not be able to depend long term on economic strategies that favored plant foods such as wild cereals. During the Holocene, however, climatic conditions greatly improved and plant foods became more abundant and more dependable. Under these conditions, some hunter–gatherer–forager groups began to rely more heavily on and to manipulate the plant foods that became the domesticates that we have today.

Other scholars have argued that we can apply some of the principles of **niche construction theory** from evolutionary biology to help us better understand the origins of domesticated foods.[69] Niche construction theory is based on the fact that animals, including humans, can engage in activities to enhance the productivity of food (and other) resources within their habitats (see Chapter 1). By setting grass fires, for example, some types of vegetation are burned out of areas, encouraging the growth of other types of plants, which may be those eaten by humans or eaten by animals that can be hunted. Humans are agents in this type of "environmental engineering" or niche construction. In niche construction theory, humans are deliberately creating niches and then maintaining those niches over long periods of time. Most importantly, decisions involving plant and animal manipulation occur not in marginal areas or during periods of climatic or habitat stress but when conditions are favorable. This is because people are most willing to experiment with new or changed activities when they have a secure food base and can afford to take losses when some experiments do not work out (read "Big Picture: Niche Construction Theory and the Origins of Food Production").

There are many other ideas, besides those described above, about the origins of food-production economies, and there is ongoing, lively debate about which hypotheses appear to be the most reliable or the most reasonable explanations given the information we have from different world regions. This includes the recent emphasis on genetic studies of domesticated plants and animals compared to the genetics of their wild ancestors.[71] In some cases these have demonstrated where certain species were domesticated and also that independent domestication events of the same species occurred. mtDNA studies of domesticated cattle, for example, which are descended

Control of Nature through Its Manipulation a postprocessual explanation for the origins of food-production. It postulates that people attempted to control wild resources through rituals, food storage, and food processing technologies. This led to domestication as the wild resources were transformed into controlled resources.

Hostile Pleistocene Theory an explanation for the world-wide origins of food-production in the Holocene. It attributes this transition to the fact that climatic conditions during the Pleistocene were not conducive to dependable reliance on plant foods. With less extreme climatic fluctuations in the Holocene, hunter-gatherer-forager groups could manipulate plant foods more successfully, resulting in their abundance and domestication.

Niche Construction Theory the idea that humans actively change or manipulate features of the landscape around them and resources in those landscapes in ways that build a niche or habitat in which they can be successful over long periods of time. It incorporates evolutionary ideas from biology and applies them to humans.

Niche Construction Theory and the Origins of Food Production

Bruce Smith has proposed that the origins of food production can be usefully examined within the theoretical framework of niche construction theory. He argues that all small-size groups have a basic set of features that they apply to choices they make in their behavioral strategies, which he calls cultural niche construction (Figure 5.12). At the beginning of the Holocene, wetter and warmer climate meant an expansion of more favorable habitats with a greater abundance of plant foods and animals. Hunter–gatherer–foragers acquired, used, and passed along to their children traditional knowledge about these resources. In some cases they experimented with certain species of plants and animals. If the results were good, they began to focus more intensively on those species to increase their abundance and availability. Some form of ownership by groups of these enhanced resources was developed, and these wild resources were managed through niche construction activities (weeding or selective collection or hunting). Over time, this focus led to genetic changes in these plants and animals, which made them recognizable as domesticates. The idea of traditional knowledge, or social memory, as a key component also is found in the work of Arlene Rosen and Isabel Rivera-Collazo, who use the framework of a theory of adaptive change.[70] These researchers point to evidence for burning of grasslands and forests to encourage open parklands during the Middle Eastern Pre-Pottery Neolithic A, which would have supported the increased growth of grasses, including cereals. As people focused on fewer species of plants (and animals) and became more settled into smaller regions during the warmer and wetter early Holocene, social pressures from larger and denser populations would have encouraged increased investment in activities leading to domestication during the Pre-Pottery Neolithic B.

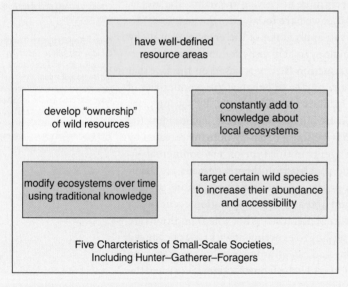

FIGURE 5.12
Cultural variables used in niche construction theory (from Smith 2011).

from aurochs (*Bos primigenius*), show that cattle were domesticated in the Middle East and in South Asia.[72]

Archaeologists are constantly generating ideas about the origins of food-production economies, and there are many discussions about whether this transformation is best understood as differing from region to region because of the social and ecological contexts particular to each place or can be interpreted as reflecting larger scale processes that can be applied to many regions.[73] In the Middle East, which we examined in detail previously, it appears relatively clear that domesticated forms of plants and animals first appear during the last part of the Pre-Pottery Neolithic during the Early Holocene in areas of favorable habitats.[74] This supports the arguments made for the climatic conditions of the Holocene contrasted to the Pleistocene (large-scale processes) and by niche construction theory models (based on the specific social and ecological particulars of the Middle East). Transitions into food-production economies are examined in more detail in Chapters 6 to 15, where they serve as the background to the development of socially and politically complex societies.

Complexity in the Archaeological Record

The eventual establishment of food-production economies helped create conditions in which surpluses could be accumulated and used as wealth to exchange for labor, exotic goods, feasting, and other social demands. When these surpluses became concentrated in the hands of fewer people, some societies that were more or less egalitarian increased in levels of social and political complexity. We saw in Chapter 1 that there are several complicating factors in examining the archaeological past. These include the degree to which archaeological materials are preserved and recovered, how archaeologists define the terminology they use, and the different theoretical frameworks that can be applied to the data. In this section we will look at issues involving complexity.

Social Complexity

All modern humans are socially complex. This is because there are differing social roles and various types of relationships that humans construct with each other and with the world around them. Human societies also are cooperative, with individuals and families working together toward certain goals.[75] So what does it mean when archaeologists use the term **social complexity** to describe a particular group? Generally speaking, the use of this term refers to societies that are no longer egalitarian. In egalitarian societies, such as many hunter–gatherer–foragers, resources are shared more or less equally. There is little private ownership. No one person makes all the decisions or directs others to engage in tasks on a daily basis. This is not to say that there are no differences between people. Some individuals will earn a status, for example, someone who is a good hunter or a person who is well versed in knowledge about medicinal plants. There often are distinctions made between the types of activities that women undertake compared to those of men. Rituals and ceremonies are used to help link people together. Being a member of an egalitarian society is not restricted to hunter–gatherer–foragers but can also characterize people who live in villages.[76] For example, some of the early villagers in the Middle East, Europe, the

Social Complexity a term often used to describe societies that are no longer egalitarian in social structure. There are status and rank differences between people, although relationships usually are still based on kin groups.

North American Southwest, China, Mesoamerica, and South America were likely egalitarian in social structure.

At some point, in some groups, shifts in cooperative behavioral strategies led to certain individuals and their families gaining greater access to resources. These societies are no longer egalitarian but are ranked. Using archaeological data, we see the results of these shifts and identify them as examples of social complexity. They include groups in Europe, the North American Southwest, and the North American East (see Chapters 6, 7, and 8). The exact reasons why these shifts occur are difficult to identify, partly because our chronological control is usually for periods of time that represent generations of people rather than the smaller moments in time when the decisions leading to the changes actually occurred.[77] That is, it is not always easy to identify agents and to apply the theoretical framework of agency (see Chapter 1). Societies that we classify as instances of social complexity have people who are leaders who are often identified as elites. Their status, however, does not allow them to force other members of the group to engage in various activities. This is a concept called "stateless societies."[78] Stateless societies rely on the cooperative behaviors of humans that encourage good behavior rather than "freeloaders." These cooperative endeavors are the result of social norms that are managed through activities such as feasting, cultural taboos, and rituals.

We often recognize the leaders in socially complex societies archaeologically because their burials contain abundant and/or exotic types of grave goods, signaling their unequal access to resources. Village and town sites might contain some residences that are larger or might have areas that are set apart from the rest of the community. These spaces often are interpreted as elite areas. Elite individuals assume greater roles in directing the labor of others, settling disputes, and accumulating agricultural surpluses and exotic materials, and they themselves become focal points of authority, which can be associated with ritual or ceremony (for example, feasting). The degree to which social complexity is expressed by any given group, however, varies from place to place, as we can see in the comparison of Europe and the North American Southwest and East (see Chapters 6 to 8). Why these differences exist might be the result of any number of reasons. Was the aridity of the North American Southwest and its potential agricultural marginality, for example, a reason why groups here appear not to have controlled surrounding regions, which was the pattern in the North American East? Or could these differences instead be a result of how people conceptualized or perceived their relationships with one another and with the landscape? Or are there factors related to how dense and large the population was in a specific place or the degree to which agriculture was managed by elites along with social factors,[79] for example, in comparing the situation in Europe with that of the North American East?

Political Complexity a term used to describe societies for which social classes have replaced kin groups in societal organization. Politically complex societies can be kingdom, state, or empire polities. They usually have one or a few ruling elites, although one exception may have been the Indus Valley in South Asia.

Political Complexity

In this book we will use the concept of **political complexity** to describe societies that were states, kingdoms, and empires. This does not mean that "stateless societies" (socially complex polities, as above) did not have political organization or rulership. Political complexity is, in fact, an extension of social complexity. It can involve the appearance in the archaeological record of evidence for several features.[80] One of these is the expansion of territory under a single ruler. Such expansions are seen partially in the hierarchy of sites that develop, with a primary center, secondary centers, smaller towns and villages, and dispersed faming settlements. Another is the establishment of bureaucrats and bureaucracy through which elite leaders delegate authority and oversight. Yet another is centralized rulership by an elite individual/family who wields political power and sometimes also ritual power. Elite leaders in these "state" societies have power that is associated with being able to force others to do things, which differs from the power of elite leaders in stateless societies (see earlier).[81] A further attribute is that kinship-organized society is replaced by one based on social classes. Other features can be the association of a ruler with the concept of being divine and control of agricultural surpluses and other wealth items.

Using a list of features such as this, however, suffers from one major disadvantage: the fact that not all politically complex societies developed the same set of features, which is a problem recognized some time ago when researchers attempted to apply a set of 10 criteria that had been proposed.[82] Using information from upcoming chapters, we can clearly see this disadvantage. Political complexity in the Indus Valley, for example, did not involve territorial expansion through warfare. Nor was it characterized by a single ruler or by single rulers at the level of important cities/centers such as Mohenjo-daro or Harappa (see Chapter 12). The Mapungubwe and Great Zimbabwe states were based not on territory acquired by warfare but on control of trade and exchange networks through alliances (see Chapter 15). The level of investment in bureaucracy varied considerably from one place to another. The Hawaiian Islands did not have a hierarchical settlement system with primary, secondary, and tertiary centers (see later). This is one reason that it is important to carefully consider the details of the archaeological records of regions when constructing models and theories about the origins of politically complex societies. It also means that archaeologists do not always agree about whether a particular polity was politically complex at the level of a state (for example, Cahokia during the Mississippian period; see Chapter 8).

Social and Political Complexity in Pre-Contact Hawai'i

Here, we examine the terms social complexity and political complexity by looking at the example of pre-Contact Hawai'i,[83] where there are oral traditions of living descendants that can be combined with the archaeological record.

Based on assessment of radiocarbon dates and the use of genealogy from oral tradition, the Hawaiian Islands were first reached by Polynesian voyagers from the Marquesas/Society Islands in Central Eastern Polynesia perhaps as early as AD 860[84] (Figure 5.13). Although oral traditions record at least 24 voyages between these two regions of the Pacific until as late as the AD 1400s,[85] for the most part people living in pre-Contact Hawai'i were relatively isolated. They brought domesticated breadfruit,

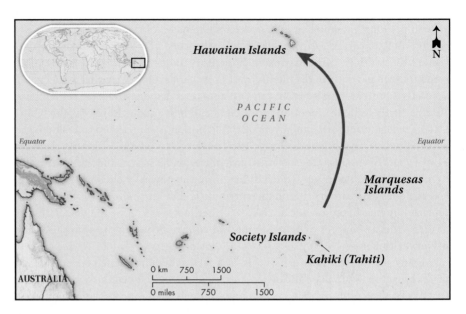

FIGURE 5.13
Map of the Pacific showing voyaging to Hawai'i.

kalo (taro), chickens, dogs, and pigs with them to the islands. These became the basis for their agricultural economy, and they eventually developed aquaculture, using fish ponds to capture and harvest fish.

Hawaiians had divisions of land that stretched from the sea to the inland mountains on the islands; these are called ***ahupua'a***. Because each *ahupua'a* contained a diverse set of resources, each was largely self-sufficient. People lived mainly in the coastal areas but also had residences elsewhere in the *ahupua'a*. This meant that individual people and families moved between places throughout the year rather than living in just one village. As the population grew over time, more and more areas of the islands were colonized. Hawaiian society consisted of chiefs (called *ali'i* in Hawaiian), their families, priests,[86] craft specialists, and commoners. *Ali'i* could be male or female. Each *ahupua'a* was under the control of an *ali'i*, and, like elites elsewhere, the *ali'i* had access to resources on a greater scale than commoners, sometimes nearly exclusive access. The rights to fish from the fish ponds, for example, were held by the *ali'i*, and they controlled when and how often commoners could harvest fish from these structures. Exotic goods included feathered cloaks and feathered helmets, double-hulled war canoes, and finely made *kapa* (bark cloth), all of which were made by craft specialists attached to the households of *ali'i*. Commoners owed labor to *ali'i*, as well as taxes, which were paid in food, such as pigs.[87] Labor commitments were used to build monumental architecture, especially *heiau* (temples), to various Hawaiian gods (Figure 5.14). Hawaiian society was socially complex and politically organized.

Ahupua'a: a division of land in the Hawaiian Islands that includes coastal and inland areas. Each *ahupua'a* was controlled by an *ali'i* (chief) and was essentially self-sufficient in terms of resources.

FIGURE 5.14
A view of part of the stone foundation of the Pu'u o Mahuka heiau above Waimea Bay on the island of O'ahu, Hawai'i.

Ali'i partially based their legitimacy on their descent from chiefs who had voyaged to Hawai'i from Kahiki (Tahiti) and were considered divine, which was reflected in the taboo system associated with *ali'i*.[88] This entailed certain behaviors on the part of others; for example, in the presence of the highest ranked *ali'i,* a person had to lie face down on the ground. *Ali'i* were war leaders and conducted rituals, including human sacrifice, which was introduced to Hawai'i from Kahiki around AD 1350.[89] Some *ali'i* controlled several *ahupua'a*, others controlled larger districts on islands, and later in time there usually were one or two main *ali'i* for an entire island. During periods of social stress, likely caused by shortages of food, *ali'i* fought battles with neighboring rival *ahupua'a*, and the main *ali'i* for an island such as Maui or O'ahu, or the Big Island (which is called Hawaii), also gathered warriors from several *ahupua'a* and sailed in war canoes to neighboring islands to conquer them.[90] Prior to Kamehameha I, however, no single *ali'i* managed to conquer all the Hawaiian Islands. Kamehameha I's success occurred during the Early Contact period.[91]

There are several themes in the story of social complexity in Hawai'i that we will see in later chapters. These include elites who were involved in ritual and/or were considered divine, unequal access to resources, the ability to wage war and control territory, the capacity to direct labor in projects involving the construction of monumental architecture, and hierarchies that included elites, craft specialists, and commoners. These types of features are found in "stateless societies," as well as in states, kingdoms, and empires. Does the story of social complexity in Hawai'i lead to levels of political complexity that can be considered a state? For some researchers, the answer is yes. They argue that by the early AD 1700s (a few decades prior to European Contact), this transition from social complexity to political complexity at the scale of a state occurred.[92] Some of the contributing factors were the eventual appearance of just one (or maybe two) paramount *ali'i* for each island, rank differences within the *ali'i* related to their genealogy, specific birth parents, abilities, and administrative roles at different levels of land control and oversight,[93] and increased control of larger territories and thus greater numbers of people. As we will see, Kamehameha I was able to capitalize on these social and political conditions to eventually control all of the Hawaiian Islands.

The Rise of Political Complexity

Societies characterized by political complexity interpreted as state, kingdom, or empire include both early and late polities.[94] "Early" is used by archaeologists to indicate state-level polities that were among the first to develop in a region. That is, they developed from pre-state contexts. This contrasts with later states because these often were built on the foundations of earlier complex political entities. Old Kingdom Egypt, Early Dynastic Mesopotamia, Shang China, the Indus Valley Harappan, the Classic Maya of Mesoamerica, and Mapungubwe in southeastern Africa can be classified as early state-level polities. We can include late pre-Contact Hawai'i as an early state, although it had only a few decades of existence prior to the arrival of Europeans. Later state-level polities were the Aztec in Mesoamerica, the Inka in South America, and Great Zimbabwe in southeastern Africa. In many cases, although early states developed from pre-state contexts, there was extensive contact—especially through trade and exchange relationships—between different regions where similar developments were occurring. These types of interactions likely played an important role in the origins of early states. We will see this type of process in Mesoamerica, Egypt, Mesopotamia, and the Indus Valley.

Explaining how/why early states emerged from pre-state societies and how they were socially and politically organized is the subject of much archaeological study. A wide variety of theoretical frameworks and processes are used in this research. These include models based on processes such as warfare, territorial expansion, technological advances, economics, ecology and environment, and systems.[95] More recently, frameworks such as agency, cities/urbanization, networks and boundaries, and ideology/cognitive archaeology have been used as explanatory frameworks.[96] Other researchers have examined the rise of politically complex societies as examples of the coevolution of social and political factors.[97] Our goal here is not to discuss all of these varying ideas about the origins of complex political entities but rather to use a few as examples to show how archaeologists integrate data with models. The choice of these examples is not meant to imply that these frameworks can be used to explain the origins of all early states everywhere. Nor does the use of these models for these specific regions necessarily mean that they are the only way to explain the development of state-level polities there.

THE AGENCY AND ECODYNAMICS FRAMEWORKS

Kamehameha I of Hawai'i is one example of how an agent (see Chapter 1) can play a significant role in the formation or maintenance of a state-level polity.[98] Study of Kamehameha I's role is easier to describe because of the wealth of details about him in Native Hawaiian oral traditions and from European written accounts during the Early Contact period. Important decisions made by Kamehameha I included sharing power by creating a council of *ali'i* (chiefs), gaining prominence among other *ali'i* by being successful and aggressive in military campaigns, expanding the amount of territory he controlled in the islands, assassinating his rivals for the position of pre-eminent *ali'i*, and eventually making all the land in the islands royal property. This account of Kamehameha I as an agent, however, does not use much evidence from the archaeological record.

To gain an archaeological perspective that incorporates agency in the sense of social decisions over the long term in the Hawaiian Islands, some researchers integrate the behaviors of people with respect to their landscape and the role of natural processes on that landscape.[99] This approach is ecodynamics (see Chapter 1). Natural processes that impacted agricultural strategies involved the amount of rainfall (especially on the leeward sides of islands, which have less rainfall overall) and the types of soils, their fertility, and whether they could be left fallow. As population grew in the islands after colonization by Polynesians, individuals and groups made decisions that resulted in agricultural intensification to generate enough food to feed people. Intensification is seen archaeologically in an increase in the number of fields and irrigation terracing for crops. These strategies created surpluses that could be used as a form of wealth, especially when surpluses were controlled by the *ali'i*. With large surpluses, social decisions were made to exert control over land in new ways, resulting in the *ahupua'a* system. Control also was achieved through expansion of tributes to agricultural *heiau* (temples), which increased in number over a relatively short period. This is documented archaeologically by meticulous absolute dating that can be used to assign the construction of temples to particular periods. Over time, intensive use of the landscape for agriculture resulted in diminishing amounts of surpluses (especially for dryland farming on leeward sides of islands), and this led to social problems, as described in Native Hawaiian oral traditions. To solve these problems, agents (*ali'i*) made decisions, such as going to war with neighboring *ali'i*, which resulted in more and more territory under the control of a single *ali'i*. To administer larger territories, paramount *ali'i*, such as Kamehameha I, created hierarchies of elites that oversaw land divisions (districts and *ahupua'a*). Such hierarchies were not kin based but social class based. Consolidation of authority in a single individual, power in the hands of elites as a social class, the creation of administrators/overseers, and the separation of commoners from land ownership meant that the Hawaiian Islands became a politically complex polity or state by the early AD 1700s.

THE NETWORKS AND BOUNDARIES FRAMEWORK

The concepts of networks and boundaries (see Chapter 1) are a useful framework for understanding the development and maintenance of early politically complex polities and are ideas applied to the Late Shang period in China (see Chapter 11).[100] Shang China was ruled by a king who used rituals, lineage descent, and human sacrifices to legitimize his power and authority. Evidence from archaeology, writing on oracle bones, and historical sources, however, indicate that the position of the Shang king was much more complicated. That is, he participated in networks of power and authority with other individuals. These networks were based on alliances, rituals, coercion, and exchange relationships. They meant that the king constantly had to reaffirm his position and that his power/authority could be challenged by other elites, both royal and nonroyal. These other elites used the same mechanisms as the king did to achieve power and authority. Examination of networks shows that the king's power and authority were not universal over the Shang landscape or continuous over time within the rule of a single king or within the Shang dynasty. This also is seen in the fact that the center of power, the capital, was moved from place to place.

The boundaries of the Shang polity, that is, its political identity, consisted of three layers.[101] At the center was the capital at Anyang and the lands of the king. Beyond this were lands controlled by elite rulers who were allied to the Shang king. The third layer was the lands of enemies. This seems relatively straightforward, but how people conceptualized and participated in the Shang political identity varied. The lineage structure that connected the living to their ancestors meant that each group had a basic political identity built on this membership. This level of political identity could refer to different types of contexts such as a city or the royal family or networks of settlements. The political identity of "Shang" was probably most relevant to the king himself, whereas others below him were more invested in political identities centered on their lands and communities and lineages. The contribution of thinking about early politically complex polities from a networks and boundaries approach is that this framework allows researchers to see the flexibility and dynamic interactions that characterized such societies.

Themes in Politically Complex Societies

In this section we will look at several themes that are common to politically complex societies.

The Individual and the Group

Identity is a key element in understanding how societies are socially organized, and it can have implications for political organization. Identity is an expression of social roles, relationships, ideals, and classes. One simplified example of this is the well-fleshed women in paintings by Rubens from the sixteenth and seventeenth centuries. We could interpret this as an ideal form in the sense that such individuals had access to abundant food (otherwise they would have been skinny). Access to wealth and therefore abundant food was a condition to which many people aspire, so that Rubens may have been painting this ideal rather than just his notion of what was beautiful. Today, we have almost the reverse in Western societies because the ideal female form that is shown to us is quite slender, as we see in fashion shows, television commercials, magazines, and on the Internet. In their examination of identity, archaeologists and others study how the body is depicted visually in art or is associated with particular grave goods in burials.[102] Attributes include clothing and accessories, postures, modifications to bodies, and gestures, each of which helped create distinct roles for individuals and for groups within past societies. These roles are based on gender, sex, age, religion, and ethnicity.

In the Classic Maya period (see Chapter 13), for example, primary centers such as Copán in the lowlands had elite residence areas where stone sculptures of humans were placed.[103] These representations are interpreted as idealized versions of humans that certain elite families used to convey the idea of the ideal to their families and to imply that they were close to this ideal themselves. The human images were in places where guests at feasts saw them, reinforcing a concept of what was considered correct in terms of bodily representation. These sculptures portrayed young males seated cross-legged or with one leg that hung down. They were dressed and accessorized as elites and had items that linked them to various Maya gods. The central male figure was dressed differently from those who surrounded him, suggesting he represented an individual who was important in that family. Other features of the ideal included a graceful posture and attributes of beauty such as sloping foreheads.

Much of the imagery concerning the body and identity is from the context of elites. This is because elites tended to be the subject matter of art more often than were commoners in these past societies. As we will see in later chapters, the amounts of grave goods in elite burials were more abundant and more varied. Elite contexts thus provide a large data set useful in examining how the body was depicted or arranged and providing insights into the range of social identities present in politically complex societies.

Cornering the Market

One of the reasons that elites were more prominent than commoners in art and in the amounts and types of grave goods in many past societies is that elites had more access to resources. In pre-state and early state societies, one of the most common forms of wealth was surpluses from food-production economies. Depending on the region, these included domesticated wheat, maize, sorghum, millet, rice, and quinoa, tubers such as potatoes and manioc, and domesticated pigs, cattle, sheep/goats, and llamas/alpacas. However, there were other resources that also could be accumulated. We will see this with elephant ivory and gold mining for the Mapungubwe and Great Zimbabwe states in southeastern Africa (see Chapter 15). These states used ivory and gold in combination with cattle as measures of wealth.

It is one thing for people to produce a bit extra that resulted in a surplus for their household, but it is quite another for the surplus from many households to become the stockpile of just one individual/family or a small set of individuals and their families. For this transition to occur, households and their members had to agree that payment of surplus to a few was beneficial or advantageous. It also required that individuals in households think in terms of private ownership of resources rather than communally shared surpluses. How and why this shift in the concept of possession (community vs. household) happened will vary from one societal context to another. Perhaps it started with the delegation of decision-making for the community to one or a few individuals who had access to communally shared surpluses. Or maybe it began because someone in the community was a particularly valued member because of a skill set such as hunting, shamanism, pottery making, or raising cattle. Surplus resources were provided to this individual for their expertise. Over time, with knowledge sets passed down through families, such individuals and their families positioned themselves to be the "go-to" source within the community. As they received more and more surpluses from other households, they began to accumulate this wealth and to spend it in new ways that resulted in larger houses, increased exotic goods, lavish burials, feasting events, different types of clothing and accessories, and public construction efforts for ritual spaces. Once they were established as elite members of society, they could demand payments from commoners as tributes or taxes.

One of the interesting yet ironic features of this process is that by paying tributes to the elites, commoners did not always end up in a better situation, at least for some aspects of their life. An example of this is seen in the Mississippian period in the North American East (see Chapter 8).[104] At small farmsteads near Moundville, commoners paid tributes to elites using surpluses from maize agriculture and from wild resources such as deer meat. Their farmsteads, however, were not always well protected by the Moundville elites from raids by other Mississippian groups. By the end of the Early Mississippian period, in fact, many of these small farmsteads were abandoned as people moved to safer locations. Beyond that, there were health issues faced by commoners, particularly small farmstead women. Studies of their skeletons indicate that they had less access to meat than men, were shorter than expected, and may even have had less access to sufficient amounts of maize in their diet. Elite men and women at Mississippian centers such as Moundville, on the other hand, had diets with much greater amounts of meat, taller statures, and better nutritional health overall.

There are many reasons why commoners might continue to pay tribute to elites, even under life circumstances that were less than ideal. Some of these might have been the threat of military coercion, such as we will see for the Inka Empire (see Chapter 14). In many cases, however, one of the services that elites provided to commoners was participation in feasting, ritual activities, and the reinforcement of ideologies that were widely shared across regions. This is one reason that elites were able to "corner the market" when it came to surpluses/wealth.

Ideology

The belief systems that people have about the world around them are reflected in the types of rituals they performed and in motifs in art and in features of architecture. This is why we can identify a phenomenon such as the Chavín Horizon in the Andean region of South America (see Chapter 14). Its iconography—feline and raptor images—and a temple style that used a U shape with a plaza at the center were designs found over a large region. Yet within this region it was not just one society but different groups of people who shared this ideology. We have comparable examples in the world today, where people living in different modern polities are connected by shared beliefs such as Islam or Judaism or Buddhism or Christianity. Each of these modern ideological systems has its own set of motifs, and religious structures within each system have similar design features, particularly inside the places of worship.

In pre-state and early state societies, ruling elites usually played an important role in the ideology. This helped legitimize their right to rule because it directly linked the ruler to the supernatural world. This link often was used to create the notion that the ruler was divine. We will see examples of this aspect of ideology in the perceived divinity of the rulers of the Inka Empire, the Egyptian kingdom, the Mapungubwe and Great Zimbabwe states, and the Classic Maya kingdoms. How rulers were able to claim divine status varied. In the Mapungubwe and Great Zimbabwe states (see Chapter 15), for example, the king took over the ritual role of rainmaker. This ideological activity was critical in a region where rainfall was necessary for successful agriculture and cattle-raising. Success by the king in this ritual helped ensure that commoners continued to support his rule. In the Classic Maya kingdoms (see Chapter 13) and the Inka Empire (see Chapter 14), rulers traced their genealogy directly to the gods of the supernatural realms. This meant that they could intercede much more directly and presumably successfully on behalf of the peoples they ruled.[105]

Although not all rulers were considered divine, most of them established the perception that they were linked in more significant ways than commoners to the supernatural. In the case of Shang China (see Chapter 11), for example, the king used the power of his royal ancestors to intercede with the gods.[106] He also used ritual specialists called diviners who could read the cracks on oracle bones to foretell the success (or not) of planned activities such as attacking other groups. Early Dynastic Mesopotamia rulers (see Chapter 9) built temples to patron gods and goddesses, had relatives who were priests or priestesses, and used their wealth to make substantial offerings to deities.[107] Underlying all of these instances is the notion that earlier societies believed that the forces of nature were ruled by gods and goddesses who had human attributes, so that people could ask for the help of the gods/goddesses in influencing nature to create successful situations.[108] Any elite ruler who could do this consistently was therefore an individual who was powerful and who was supported by the deities of that society.

Further Reflections

Thinking About Food Production

Why should we care about the origins of food-production economies, and what does it mean for us today? As we saw earlier, domestication of plants and animals led to new ways to manage resources and to increased ability to stockpile surpluses that could be used as a form of "wealth." These surpluses "paid" for feasting, feeding people as they labored to build monuments, creating alliances between different groups, acquiring exotic goods, supplying military forces, supporting craft and religious specialists, cementing notions of private ownership of resources, and a host of other things. These are some of the building blocks upon which modern-day societies are built, even though most people today live in polities that use money rather than barter systems.

Food-production economies also give us pause to consider how we perceive the world around us. For those of us who live in the industrialized world, there is often little thought given to the diversity of foods available year-round in our stores. If I want to eat blueberries and corn on the cob in February or meat from bison or yaks, as long as I can afford the prices, I can acquire these foods relatively easily because of the countrywide and worldwide trade relationships that have been established and the proliferation of supply chains, which help create constant abundance. But this is a relatively recent phenomenon historically, which is tied partly to the types of rapid transportation we have and is not characteristic of all world regions. As recently as when I was a kid, it was not common to buy and eat most fruits out of season (one exception was apples) as they simply were not available in most stores; I even had a friend who did not know what a peach was.

Much of our recent history, and most certainly our prehistoric past, thus were times when people relied on the foods that were available each season. There were a few foods that could be stored and eaten throughout the year (for example, nuts and some seeds), but if what you were growing as crops that year failed for some reason, you were out of luck unless you had networks of others who could help out in tight times (a phenomenon that we see in various world regions even today when famines occur). It also meant there was less diversity in the diet, especially in urban settings, in which, like today, many people were far removed from being farmers.

Summary

- Hunter–gatherer–foragers were present in nearly all regions of the world, including the New World, just after 20,000 cal BC. The domestication of the dog occurred before 12,000 cal BC and may have been a process that happened independently in several places.

- During the last part of the Pleistocene ("Ice Ages"), most hunter–gatherer–foragers were highly mobile groups. There is evidence at some archaeological sites, however, that suggests longer-term camps, such as at Ohalo II in Israel and Kharaneh IV in Jordan.

- In the last part of the Pleistocene, many groups relied extensively on plant foods such as wild cereal grasses or nuts. Evidence for this diet is based on plant remains, ground stone tools to process plant foods, and sometimes stable isotope studies of human bones and teeth.

- During the Epipaleolithic period of the Middle East, long-term trends include traditional knowledge about local plant foods and animals, special rituals in which humans are buried with animals such as foxes during the Middle Epipaleolithic, aggregation sites where small, mobile groups of hunter–gatherer–foragers came together occasionally to exchange information and perhaps mates during both the Early and the Middle Epipaleolithic, and eventually small village sites in the Mediterranean forest areas of the Levant during the Late Epipaleolithic (Early Natufian phase).

- The Pre-Pottery Neolithic period in the Middle East has many examples of complex social rituals including plaster statues of humans, human skulls that have been removed from bodies and then plastered to resemble human faces, and unusual architecture such as the wall, tower, and ditch at Jericho in the West Bank, the decorated T-shape pillared rooms at Göbekli Tepe in Turkey, and the mortuary complex at Kfar HaHoresh in Israel.

- One region of the world where food production developed is the Middle East. There is a long trajectory here showing various elements that were important in the process, such as increased ritual and social complexity in hunter–gatherer–forager societies of the Epipaleolithic and the villages of the Pre-Pottery Neolithic periods. Settled life was present for hundreds, if not thousands, of years before plants and animals attained their domesticated forms (during the late PPNB).

- In the Old World, important early domesticates include wheat, barley, peas, lentils, rice, sorghum, millet, yams, cattle, sheep, goats, and pigs. There are at least eight areas within several regions (Middle East, China, Africa, New Guinea, India) where food-production economies independently began.

- In the New World, local hunter–gatherer–forager groups exploited many wild plant foods. Some of these, such as teosinte (which developed into maize), beans, squash, sunflower, chili peppers, potatoes, and quinoa, eventually became domesticated. Food-production economies arose in South America, Mesoamerica/Mexico, and the North American East. Those in South America included animals such as llama, alpaca, and guinea pigs, whereas turkeys were domesticated in Mexico and possibly in the North American Southwest.

- Many different ideas have been proposed for the origins of food-production economies. These include the "oasis" theory, in which the proximity of people, plants, and animals at oases led to detailed knowledge about their life cycles; the "readiness" theory, in which it took a long time for technologies useful in exploiting plants and animals to come together within the natural distribution of these plants and animals; and population pressure, which meant that new ways of exploiting foods had to be developed to feed increased numbers of people.

- Other ideas about the origins of food-production economies include the effects of climate change during the late Pleistocene when colder and drier conditions prevailed (Younger Dryas), which meant that people innovated ways to increase plant foods in a sparse setting; human behavioral ecology that assesses the benefits of intensifying the use of foods that are available during different seasons of the year as opposed to their costs (small seed investment); the social mechanism of feasting that drove accumulation of surplus foods by some individuals or families so that they could gain prestige by giving away food; postprocessual ideas such as manipulating nature to control it; and worldwide explanations that stress that people were not able to consistently rely on plant foods during the Pleistocene because of climatic conditions that were more hostile to plants. Only during the Holocene did conditions improve so that hunter–gatherer–foragers could focus more exclusively on some plant foods (hostile Pleistocene). One of the most recent ideas is niche construction theory, which stresses the role of traditional knowledge about plants and animals and that people will only experiment with their food resources in areas where there is a natural abundance of foods.

- Egalitarian (equal), social complexity (ranked, kin based), and political complexity (social classes, not kin based) are three terms that can be used to describe societal organization. Egalitarian and social complexity can be used to described "stateless societies" that operate using cooperative behaviors. In this book, we use the term political complexity to describe states, kingdoms, and empires.

- One example of a ranked society (social complexity) is pre-Contact Hawai'i, which had a system of elites who were chiefs (ali'i). A few decades before the arrival of Europeans, Hawai'i developed into a politically complex polity (state) with social classes.

- Many theoretical frameworks have been used to explain the origins and maintenance of politically complex polities. Among these are agency, ecodynamics, and networks and boundaries.

- Elite members of societies often used art to establish societal norms of the ideal. By identifying themselves with the ideal human body, for example, they helped create legitimacy for themselves.

- Access to considerable amounts of resources also characterized elites. This wealth was based on food-production surpluses and could include goods from trade and exchange networks. Accumulation of surpluses by elites was a result of the payment of tribute and/or taxes by commoners. Commoners must perceive benefits to themselves in the system to continue to support it.

- Ideological systems were one mechanism through which elites could claim the support of commoners. Elites defined themselves as directly connected to the supernatural realm, sometimes by claiming genealogical links to gods and goddesses. They also positioned themselves as integral to rituals that created benefits for commoners.

Endnotes

1. Revedin et al. 2010.
2. Fiedel 2005: 11; Germonpré et al. 2009: 473; Morey 2006.
3. Druzhkova et al. 2013; Germonpré et al. 2009; Skoglund et al. 2015. Note that not all researchers believe that the evidence is solid for these early instances of possible domesticated dogs; for example, see Boudadi-Maligne and Escarguel 2014 and Morey 2014. Other research on dog genetics suggests the beginning of their domestication is in southern East Asia and that they spread from there to other world regions beginning about 15,000 years ago (Wang et al. 2015). However, it is possible that dogs were domesticated in more than one place (Frantz et al. 2016).
4. Shipman 2015.
5. Olszewski 2014.
6. Olszewski 2008.
7. Olszewski and al-Nahar 2011.
8. Perkins in Kirkbride 1966.
9. Kislev et al. 1992; Nadel and Werker 1999; Weiss et al. 2008.
10. Zohar et al. 2018.
11. Maher and Macdonald 2013; Maher et al. 2012b; Richter et al. 2011, 2013; Rolston 1982.
12. Maher et al. 2001: 13–16; 2011.
13. Maher and Macdonald 2013; Richter et al. 2011, 2013.
14. Olszewski 2008.
15. Valla 1975–1977; 1991.
16. Bar-Yosef 1998.
17. Maher et al. 2012a.
18. Arranz-Otaegui et al. 2018; Olszewski 2010: 93.
19. Arranz-Otaegui et al. in press.
20. The Late Natufian village site is Nahal Ein Gev II (Grosman et al. 2016).
21. Grosman and Munro 2007; Grosman et al. 2008; Munro and Grosman 2010.
22. The remarkable organic preservation at the Early Epipaleolithic site of Ohalo II on the shores of the Sea of Galilee has yielded thousands of plant remains and ground stone with starch grains indicating grinding of wild cereals (Kislev et al. 1992; Piperno et al. 2004).
23. Bar-Yosef and Belfer-Cohen 1989; Feldman and Kislev 2007; McCorriston and Hole 1991.
24. Heun et al. 1997; Lev-Yadun et al. 2000.
25. Nesbitt 2002.
26. Albarella et al. 2006; Bradley and Magee 2006; Bruford and Townsend 2006; Luikart et al. 2006; Zeder 2006.
27. Ervynck et al. 2002.
28. This label reflects the history of archaeology in that early researchers believed that the beginning of the Neolithic period coincided with the invention of pottery. Because we now know this is not correct, labeling the earlier part of the Neolithic period required the invention of new terms such as Pre-Pottery. See also Kuijt and Goring-Morris 2002 and Simmons 2007. Some archaeologists prefer to use the term PPNC for the final PPNB period.
29. Kuijt and Mahasneh 1998: 155–157.
30. Kuijt 2000: 81.
31. Kuijt 2000: 81.
32. Kenyon 1957.
33. Barkai and Liran 2008; Bar-Yosef 1986.
34. Schmidt 2001, 2002, 2006.
35. Peters and Schmidt 2004: 185.
36. Watkins 2017.
37. Banning 2011.
38. Rollefson 1997, 1998; Rollefson and Simmons 1987.
39. Kuijt 2000: 81.
40. Bonogofsky 2001, 2004.
41. Benz 2012.
42. A good example of this is the recent reinterpretation of the "shrines" from the Pottery Neolithic phases at Çatalhöyük in Turkey, which, based on the presence of food processing and household debris, are now seen as spaces that combined daily and ritual activities (Hodder and Cessford 2004: 21–22).
43. Kuijt 2011.
44. Goring-Morris and Horwitz 2007; Goring-Morris et al. 1998.
45. Meier et al. 2016.
46. Zhang 2000; not all researchers working in China use the term Mesolithic.
47. Pei 1985.
48. Rhode et al. 2007.
49. Boaretto et al. 2009; Cohen et al. 2017; Kuzmin 2017.

50. But see Speth 2015 for use of organic containers over fires.
51. Fuller and Hildebrand 2013.
52. Rowley-Conwy 1984; Vanmontfort 2008.
53. Fritz 1990; Hart et al. 2004.
54. Moore and Dekle 2010.
55. Merrill et al. 2009.
56. See, for example, Wills 1988.
57. Austin 2006; Piperno 2011: S454.
58. Piperno 2011: S458; Zarillo et al. 2008.
59. See, for example, the articles in the 2009 "Rethinking the Origins of Agriculture" issue of *Current Anthropology* 50(5).
60. Childe 1952.
61. Braidwood 1960.
62. Binford 1968.
63. Moore and Hillman 1992.
64. See, for example, articles in Kennett and Winterhalder 2006.
65. Gremillion 2004.
66. Hayden 1990, 2009.
67. Hodder 1990.
68. Richerson et al. 2001.
69. Smith 2011; Zeder 2012.
70. Rosen and Rivera-Collazo 2012.
71. See, for example, articles in Zeder et al. 2006.
72. Bradley and Magee 2006.
73. For example, see Gremillion et al. 2014.
74. Rosen 2007; Rosen and Rivera-Collazo 2012.
75. Stanish 2017.
76. Marcus 2008: 256.
77. Marcus 2008: 253.
78. Stanish 2017.
79. Sheehan et al. 2018; Turchin et al. 2018.
80. Hommon 2013: 243, 255–256; Joffee 2018; Kirch 2010; Marcus 2008: 259; Sinopoli 2001; Trigger 2003: 43–48.
81. Stanish 2017.
82. Childe 1950.
83. I use the Hawaiian spelling, meaning that there are special apostrophes (called *okinas*) in some words that indicate glottal stops in the pronunciation of these words.

It is also common to refer to the totality of the Hawaiian Islands as Hawai'i but to the big island in this archipelago as Hawaii (without the *okina*).
84. Dye 2011: 134; Hommon 2013: 218; Kirch 2011: 22; see also Athens et al. 2014, who claim that the colonization of the Hawaiian Islands was most likely around AD 1000.
85. Fornander 1969.
86. Kahn 2015.
87. Hommon 2013: 237.
88. Kirch 2010.
89. Hommon 2013: 220.
90. Kolb and Dixon 2002.
91. Sahlins 1992: 41. Some have attributed Kamehameha I's success in part to the fact that he had access to cannons from Europeans, as well as their warships, which made traveling to the island of Kaua'i relatively easy. Kaua'i is quite distant from O'ahu, where Kamehameha I fought a successful battle in AD 1795 to conquer this island. In fact, the main *ali'i* of Kaua'i signed an agreement with Kamehameha I after the O'ahu battle to avoid conflict.
92. Hommon 2013; Kirch 2010; Kirch et al. 2015; but see Dye 2016.
93. Hommon 2013: 243–248.
94. Joffe 2018; Marcus 2008: 261–262; Sinopoli 2001.
95. Carneiro 1992; Flannery 1999; Spencer 1998.
96. Campbell 2009; Flannery 1999; Kirch 2007; Yoffee 2005.
97. For example, Turchin et al. 2018.
98. Flannery 1999: 11–15.
99. Kirch 2007.
100. Campbell 2009.
101. Campbell 2009: 837.
102. Fisher and DiPaolo Loren 2003.
103. Bachand et al. 2003: 240–242.
104. Shuler et al. 2012.
105. McAnany 2001: 141–143; Trigger 2003: 488.
106. Trigger 2003: 488–489.
107. Trigger 2003: 486–487.
108. Trigger 2003: 413.

3 On the Threshold of Political Complexity

CHAPTER 6

Prehistoric Europe North of the Mediterranean

ABOVE: Early Bronze Age Trundholm sun chariot.

Hunter–gatherer–foragers in Europe did not invest in strategies that led to food production economies. This does not mean that they did not use plant foods in intensive ways, but more simply that their use of these foods did not result in genetic changes to the plants. Aside from the dog, they had no domesticated animals. The food production way of life was instead introduced into Europe through colonization by farmers from the Middle East (who brought domesticated plants and animals with them), by transmission of ideas about this lifeway when incoming farmers encountered hunter–gatherer–forager groups, and by choices that hunter–gatherer–foragers made about engaging in food production economies. As food production became established throughout much of Europe, significant changes to peoples' lives occurred. This is seen in the types of architecture (for example, fortified villages, grave barrows, henges), social organization, violent encounters between groups, and a subsistence focus on domesticates. Many of the trends that began during the period of early food production (the Neolithic) continue into the Bronze Age. Bronze Age societies had elites with access to wealth from trade and exchange as well as agricultural produce. Male, and some female, elites are identified as warriors based on their grave goods. Some regions may have been organized as chiefdoms. During the Iron Age, a focus on fortification, warriors, and control of wealth continued, with the eventual development of possible early state-like polities. In some parts of Europe, the Roman Conquest impacted the continuation of these local developments, while in other areas (such as Ireland and Scandinavia), Iron Age lifeways endured.

Early Holocene Hunter–Gatherer–Foragers

During the Holocene, which began around 9600 cal BC with the end of the Ice Ages, climatic conditions became much warmer and forests expanded. The hunter–gatherer–foragers who lived in Europe at this time are referred to as belonging to the Mesolithic period. During the early part of the Mesolithic, England was connected to continental Europe because of lower sea levels.[1] In other words, you could walk from England to the Netherlands and Denmark. South of this Pleistocene/early Holocene land connection is the English Channel, which is a wide waterway today due to higher sea levels resulting from the melting of the Pleistocene glaciers in northern Europe.

In several regions of northern Europe, there are exceptional preservation conditions for organic materials because of peat and waterlogged contexts. In these cases, archaeologists can recover large quantities of items made of wood, antler, and bone, as well as plant food remains.

At the **Duvensee** bog in northern Germany (Figure 6.2), for example, there are a number of small Mesolithic sites with hearths dating from 8900 to 6500 cal BC.[2] Pollen information shows that this area was used when the expanding forest included many hazelnut trees. The hearths contain a bottom layer of bark that has a layer of sand on top of it. In the sand layer are burned hazelnut shells, charcoal, and stone artifacts, indicating they were roasting hazelnuts. Nuts are nutritious and have a high fat content because of their oil; they also can be easily stored. There are ground stone tools used for grinding and pounding in the processing of plant foods. Duvensee and other sites indicate that Early Mesolithic period groups in Europe were targeting high-yield plant food resources that allowed them to remain at campsites for at least a season.

One of the most studied Mesolithic period sites is **Star Carr** in England (see Figure 6.2), which dates to 9000 cal BC.[3] The site is next to a lake, with a reed swamp between dry land and the open lake waters. The 1950s excavations yielded many stone artifacts, including microliths, but also many organic materials (red deer

Duvensee a peat bog region in northern Germany with a series of Mesolithic sites showing targeted harvesting and processing of hazelnuts; the sites date between 8900 and 6500 cal BC.

Star Carr a Mesolithic site adjacent to a lake in England. It dates between 8700 and 8400 cal BC. The site had excellent organic preservation, and recovered items include red deer antler frontlets, antler points, and a wooden platform/trackway.

Timeline: Prehistoric Europe

Hunter–gatherer–forager groups existed for thousands of years alongside farming groups. Eventually, however, a food production way of life characterized most of Europe. In some places, the accumulation of surpluses led to increasingly complex forms of social and eventually political organization (Figure 6.1). We focus in this chapter primarily on developments in central and northern Europe.

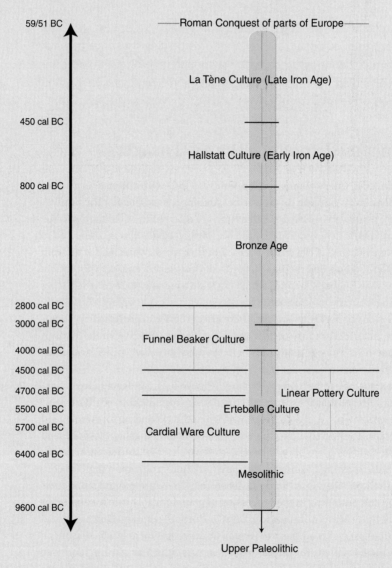

FIGURE 6.1

A timeline for prehistoric Europe north of the Mediterranean (timeline not to scale).

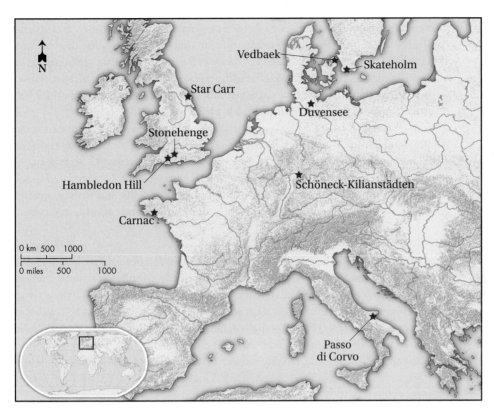

FIGURE 6.2
Map showing European Mesolithic and Neolithic sites discussed.

antler frontlets possibly used as "masks," antler tips used as points on wooden spears, animal bones) and personal ornamentations (shale beads and pendants of perforated animal teeth and amber). In the late 2000s, one dwelling structure and a wooden platform/trackway were found.[4] One of the issues, however, was that many of the artifacts were found in the reed swamp area, which led some archaeologists to suggest that this was a discard zone at the edge of the living site on dry land.[5] Other archaeologists, however, noted that during the summer months, when Star Carr was occupied, reed swamps often are dry ground. Along with the types of stone artifacts found in the reed swamp area, it seems much more likely that this was part of the living area at Star Carr rather than a waterlogged discard zone.[6] The research at Star Carr in the 2000s shows that the site was much larger than originally thought, approaching 2 hectares (5 acres). In combination with the large amount of work required to build the wooden platform and the one structure known so far, the large size of Star Carr is interpreted as indicating that many people lived at the site.

Like their counterparts in other world regions, Mesolithic period groups in Europe had well-developed exchange networks. In the Baltic Sea region, for example, hunter-gatherer-foragers transported stone raw material, ochre, amber, and seal fat between coastal and inland areas. This was facilitated using wooden dugouts and skin boats to navigate rivers and sea coasts as well as by traveling on land during the winter using wooden sleds and skis.[7] We know about these modes of transportation during the Mesolithic period because parts of these objects have been preserved. Over the course of the Mesolithic period, evidence suggests that transport and trade were increasingly controlled by specialists, which would have differentiated some people in the group from others. These people sometimes are identified on the basis of having much richer burials containing many exotic materials.[8] Cemeteries containing numerous burials became more common in the Mesolithic[9] compared to the Upper Paleolithic. This may suggest greater population density and perhaps greater control over the territories in which specific groups hunted and collected resources.

Ertebølle Culture

Ertebølle Culture a late Mesolithic hunter–gatherer–forager group (5500 to 4000 cal BC) in southern Scandinavia and northern Germany (Europe) that lived in proximity to people with food-production economies.

One of the latest of the Mesolithic hunter-gatherer-forager groups is called the **Ertebølle Culture** (5500 to 4000 cal BC).[10] They lived in southern Denmark, southern Sweden, and parts of coastal northern Germany (see Figure 6.2). To their south lived farmers (see "Linear Pottery Culture" and "Funnel Beaker Culture"). What is intriguing is that people of the Ertebølle Culture did not adopt food production but continued to hunt (deer, elk, wild boar) and collect wild plant foods and shellfish and fish (anchovy, cod, pike, herring, eels).[11] Many of their coastal sites are large and have hut structures; they also have shell middens full of discarded shellfish (oysters, mussels, clams).[12] Other sites show specialized hunting of land animals.[13]

Vedbæk an Ertebølle Culture (Mesolithic) site in Denmark (Europe). It contains graves showing gender distinctions between adult males and females in grave goods, some dog burials, evidence for violent death, and a woman buried with her newborn child placed on a swan's wing.

Two Ertebølle sites that yielded evidence of social distinctions include cemeteries. At **Vedbæk** (Denmark; see Figure 6.2) 22 individuals are buried in the cemetery.[14] Most are adults, about equally divided between males and females; there also are a few newborn infants. Red ochre was strewn across the head and hip areas of the bodies. Elderly individuals were buried with red deer antlers. Adult males had knives made of flint, while adult females had personal ornaments made of shell and animal teeth. These types of materials likely indicate differences linked to age and to gender. One burial is of three individuals—one adult male, one adult female, and one child. In addition to the gender difference in grave goods, the male has a bone point lodged in his neck, indicating that his life was not free of violence. One of the best known burials at Vedæk is of an adult female with a newborn child.[15] The female's head is on top of a cluster of snail shells and deer and wild boar teeth, which may have been sewn onto a pillow, and she has a necklace of animal teeth. The newborn child has a flint knife near its waist and was placed on a wing of a swan near the shoulder of the adult female. At the very least, this arrangement calls to mind the care and ritual that we today invest in funeral arrangements for loved ones. It might also suggest that these two people were of special status in their community or that they died tragically. One interesting feature of the Vedbæk and Skateholm (see later) cemeteries are burials of dogs. The dogs often are treated in the same way as adult male humans, that is, many have red ochre, deer antler, and stone tools, with the tools placed alongside the hip.[16]

At the cemeteries associated with settlement sites at **Skateholm** (southern Sweden: see Figure 6.2), people were interred in a variety of positions—some extended, some crouched in a seated arrangement, and some cremated (rare). They were buried individually, in double burials, and in triple burials. In some cases, parts of the skeletons are missing, perhaps because some bones were deliberately removed for ritual purposes. Wooden structures were built over at least some of the burials and subsequently burned, possibly as part of the burial ritual.[17] The position of fish remains in the graves suggests food provided for the "afterlife,"[18] and red ochre was scattered in the head and hip areas of the individuals. As at Vedbæk, grave goods were different for males and females. Males had flint knives and axes, and females had personal ornaments (animal teeth), which may have been sewn onto various items of clothing.

Sometime around 4000 cal BC, the Ertebølle Culture disappears from the archaeological record. Presumably this is because these remaining hunter–gatherer–forager groups were assimilated into a farming way of life. Studies of human genetics in prehistoric Europe, for example, indicate that over time the genetic lineages of hunter–gatherer–foragers become part of the lineages of farming populations.[19]

Skateholm an Ertebølle Culture (Mesolithic) site in Sweden (Europe). It contains graves showing a diversity of burial positions, as well as dog burials treated in the same way as human burials. Different grave goods for adult males and females indicate gender distinctions.

Early Food Production

The domesticated animals and plants present in early food production economies (Neolithic period) in Europe are not local plants or animals. They include wheat and barley, sheep, goats, cattle, and pigs, all of which were first domesticated in the Middle East. We can trace this origin in part by using genetic studies of the animals and plants, which show their Middle Eastern origin.[20] Genetic studies of farmers in the Middle East and in Europe also indicate a spread of Middle Eastern groups from Turkey and then Greece and the Balkan Peninsula into Europe.[21] The timing of the movement of domesticates and people within Europe show that they gradually spread along two major routes, one from the southeast to the west around the Mediterranean Sea, and the other from the southeast to the northwest along what is sometimes called the Danube route. What explanations might account for the movement of these farming groups? One idea is based on reproductive success in hunter–gatherer–forager groups compared to farmers.[22] Farming groups tend to have higher rates of death due to diseases (in crowded conditions) and generally poor nutrition (less diversity in food types). This would seem to be a major disadvantage compared to hunter–gatherer–foragers. The trade-off, however, is that farming populations have higher fertility rates (more children due to decreased spacing between births). So even though some children will die, having more children overall means that more of them survive to adulthood to produce their own children. This leads to population growth, less available land for farming and not enough food to feed everyone adequately, and the subsequent need for some people to move to new locations to farm.

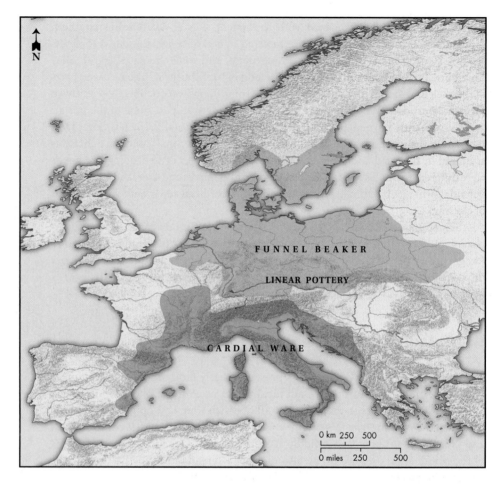

FIGURE 6.3
The areas of the Cardial Ware, Linear Pottery, and Funnel Beaker cultures (Funnel Beaker and Linear Pottery overlap to some degree).

We will look briefly at the two movements into Europe (Cardial Ware Culture[23] in the Mediterranean area and Linear Pottery Culture in the Danube route area) and then one example of a later Neolithic group (Funnel Beaker Culture) (Figure 6.3). The names of these cultures are based on the type of/or decoration on the pottery they made and used.

Cardial Ware Culture

Cardial Ware Culture Early Neolithic farming groups (6400 to 4700 cal BC) with pottery decorated by using the edges of cockle shells. They spread into Europe along the Mediterranean route by sea-faring from Greece.

The Mediterranean route of farmers into Europe was traveled by groups of people who made pottery with designs pressed into (impressed into) their pottery using cockle shells. This is called cardial or cardium ware (Figure 6.4), and they are known archaeologically as the **Cardial Ware Culture** (6400 to 4700 cal BC) (see Figure 6.3). The movement of these people along the coasts of the Mediterranean Sea was based on seafaring.[24]

This meant that they had to transport their domesticated animals (sheep and goats mainly) and seeds for domesticated plants in boats, as seen in the settlement of islands in the Mediterranean.[25] The process appears to have been one of leapfrogging from area to area along the coasts. There thus are some areas of the coasts that were "skipped over," that is, no one settled there initially, and these areas lack Neolithic archaeological sites until somewhat later.[26]

One example of a Cardial Ware Culture area is the Tavoliere Plain on the eastern side of the Italian Peninsula. Sites here have enclosure ditches, as at **Passo di Corvo** (see Figure 6.2).[27] In this case there are a series of one to three ditches around an area of about 48 hectares (119 acres). Breaks in the ditches allow entry into the enclosed space, which has 90 house compounds and water wells. Each house compound has a C-shaped ditch around it. The ditches drained water away from the house floors.

FIGURE 6.4
An example of a Cardial Ware Culture vessel.

Passo di Corvo an Early Neolithic Cardial Ware Culture site on the eastern coast of Italy.

White limestone bracelets typical of the Cardial Ware Culture in southwestern Europe are found in the Linear Pottery Culture (see next section) of northwestern Europe, indicating contact between these different groups of Neolithic migrants into Europe.[28] We know that these bracelets are Cardial Ware Culture in origin because the limestone is from southeastern France where sites of this culture are found.

Linear Pottery Culture

The route into central and eventually northwestern Europe was undertaken by Neolithic farmers that archaeologists call the **Linear Pottery Culture** (*Linearbandkeramik*; 5700 to 4500 cal BC). This name is from the designs on their pottery, which are incised lines in bands thought to be imitations of painted band designs on pottery in the Balkan Peninsula. This is the area from which Linear Pottery Culture groups initially migrated into central Europe, where they become archaeologically distinct (see Figure 6.3). Other features of the Linear Pottery Culture include longhouses built of wood, a focus on domesticated cattle, wheat and barley, stone adzes (useful in wood-working), and settlement in river floodplains with fertile soils. Some evidence suggests that these Neolithic farmers and native hunter-gatherer-forager groups may have largely avoided each other, partly because the hunter–gatherer–foragers did not live in the floodplain areas.[29]

Earlier longhouse settlements are not organized communities but represent houses built over time.[30] Sometimes these are close to older structures, but others are situated away from other houses. A typical house was about 40 meters (131 feet) long

Linear Pottery Culture Early Neolithic farming groups (5700 to 4500 cal BC) with pottery decorated with incised lines in a band. They spread into central and northwestern Europe along the Danube River and its tributaries from the Balkan Peninsula area.

and had three rows of posts to support the upper story and the roof. The longhouses are divided into three areas; some researchers believe that one area was for cattle, another was a living space, and the third was for storage. Housing cattle in part of your house might sound a bit strange to us today, but it would be a way to keep them safe from wolves and raiders at night and from the cold during the winter months. Later in time, fortified settlements of longhouses become much more common, especially in northwestern Europe.[31] These included outer ditches and wooden palisades (fences) with narrow gates. The ditches may have been up to 5 meters wide and 35 meters deep (16 feet wide and 10 feet deep) and were V-shaped, making them difficult to cross. Fortification suggests an increased need for defense (see burials, later).

Distinctions between males and females of the Linear Pottery Culture are seen in the grave goods in burials. Females had grinding slabs (also occasionally found with males), *Spondylus* shell beads and pendants, combs of bone or antler, and freshwater shell ornaments, whereas males had bracelets, buckles, and beads made of *Spondylus* shell, adzes, arrowheads, and fire-making kits.[32] *Spondylus* (spiny oyster; see Chapter 14, Figure 14.7) is a marine shell, indicating long-distance trade and exchange networks. Perhaps the most striking aspect of the Linear Pottery Culture, however, is the level of violence shown in several instances of massacres of entire communities that date to the later part of this culture; people were either left unburied or buried in mass graves.[33] One example of a mass grave is from **Schöneck-Kilianstädten** in Germany (see Figure 6.2).[34] The 26 individuals in this mass grave died from blunt force trauma to their heads or from being shot by arrows. Almost one third of them were children younger than 6. Young adult females were not present, perhaps suggesting they were taken as captives. Almost half of the individuals suffered broken legs prior to death, likely indicating torture or mutilation. Mass killings of selected individuals (non-local adult males) also occurred at other sites.[35] We might well ask why the latter part of the Linear Pottery Culture period was so violent. One potential explanation focuses on three variables: larger populations, decreased rainfall, and fewer available food resources due to lower agricultural productivity (because of less rain).[36] This meant that Linear Pottery Culture groups were not very resilient and could not easily withstand the natural and social stresses within their wider culture.

During the very late part of the Linear Pottery Culture period, there is a decline in population, and its archaeological signature disappears. It is replaced in some parts of Europe by the Funnel Beaker Culture, although it is important to remember that "replacement" does not necessarily mean replacement by different people. Instead, different ways of doing things created a changed archaeological signature for later Neolithic groups.

Funnel Beaker Culture

As with the other Neolithic cultures in Europe, the **Funnel Beaker Culture** (4100 to 2800 cal BC; see Figure 6.3) is named for the type of pottery they made. Their vessels had a rim that was outturned and flaring and a globular body (Figure 6.5).[37] Within the area of the Funnel Beaker Culture (see Figure 6.3), there were several regional

Schöneck-Kilianstädten a late Linear Pottery Culture Neolithic site in Germany (Europe) with evidence of the massacre of an entire community.

Funnel Beaker Culture Late Neolithic groups in central and northern Europe (4500 to 2800 cal BC) who made pottery that had a globular body and an out-turned flaring rim. It is often interpreted as an interaction zone rather than a single culture.

groups, leading some archaeologists to suggest that this was a large interaction zone where communities shared ideas and engaged in trade and exchange networks. For example, copper artifacts are found in Denmark, yet metalworking was not done locally.[38] Instead, metallurgy was a tradition that began in southeastern Europe, and these copper artifacts must have circulated through Europe and into the Funnel Beaker Culture area.

Funnel Beaker Culture groups had cattle, pigs, sheep, goats, and cereals. During this period there were innovations in technology. One was the introduction of the plow from the Middle East, which allowed more land to be used for farming because it is easier to break up the ground with a plow than by hand. Another was the development of wheeled vehicles, drawn by cattle. These were useful in transporting goods, such as agricultural products. Archaeological evidence includes preserved wooden parts of wheeled carts and small ceramic models of wheeled vehicles found in burials.[39] It is during the Funnel Beaker Culture period that we also see a major change in the genetics of people. The origins of this change go back into the Linear Pottery Culture period, when adults began to drink milk from their cattle (and goats in some parts of Europe). Drinking milk as an adult is difficult for most populations worldwide because of lactose (milk sugar) intolerance, which creates digestive discomfort. In the Funnel Beaker Culture area, however, the long-term practice of dairying meant that natural selection (see Chapter 2) for a gene for **lactose tolerance** occurred.[40] This is an example of the interaction between cultural practices and genetic changes in human populations.

Funnel Beaker Culture groups, and their Neolithic contemporaries in Europe (including Great Britain), began to build a variety of tombs and other constructions. Many of these had very large stones (megaliths) and/or earthen mounds. Some incorporated ditches and banks; others were first built in wood and later redone in stone. We will look next at some examples of this Neolithic tradition of building.

Neolithic Megaliths and Other Monument Building

After farming became an established way of life throughout Europe, the Neolithic societies who lived there created a landscape dotted with monuments of various types (beginning ca. 5000 cal BC). These undoubtedly held much social significance for the communities who built them and are constructions to which rituals often are attributed, particularly those we know were associated with burials. The simplest of these monuments is a **menhir**. Menhirs are single-standing megalithic stones anchored into a pit to support their upright position. Their function is not known, but they could have been territory or route markers. In some cases, menhirs are grouped

FIGURE 6.5
An example of a Funnel Beaker Culture vessel.

Lactose Tolerance most adults are not able to digest the milk sugar lactose without digestive issues. High frequencies of lactose tolerance in adults in some world populations, such as those descended from the Funnel Beaker Culture groups, shows natural selection for a gene in populations who had a cultural tradition of drinking milk.

Menhir a single standing megalithic stone, put into place by Late Neolithic farming groups in Europe. Arrangements of several menhirs can be found marking avenues, as alignments, or circles, including henges.

Carnac a series of 3,000 menhirs arranged as alignments during the Neolithic period in France (Europe).

Causewayed Enclosure a European Neolithic construction characterized by a series of concentric ditches and banks with access (causeways) across the ditches to a central open area. One interpretation is that these were ritual centers for Neolithic communities.

Hambledon Hill a Neolithic causewayed enclosure in England (Europe) that has human skulls placed at intervals in one of the ditches.

Dolmen a Neolithic tomb found in Europe. It has a few standing megalithic stones topped with a capstone.

Long Barrow a communal earthen mound tomb built in Neolithic Europe. It has wooden or stone interior corridor into which the dead were placed over an extended period of time.

Passage Grave a communal earthen mound tomb built in Neolithic Europe. It has a stone passage with one or more burial chambers at the end of the passage into which the dead were placed over an extended period of time.

together as alignments or to mark avenues. Avenues led to other Neolithic constructions such as henges, and menhirs were sometimes set along the edges of the avenues. The most famous set of alignments is at **Carnac** in France (see Figure 6.2), where the 3,000 menhirs stretch in several lines over a distance of 1.2 kilometers (¾ mile) (Figure 6.6). Menhirs also were used to build circles; these circles often were first constructed in wood.

Another type of Neolithic construction is a **causewayed enclosure**. These can be on hilltops but are also located in lower areas. They have an open, central section that is surrounded by concentric ditches and banks. Causeways (areas across the ditches and banks) allow access to the central area. The bank and ditch construction makes sense if you think about digging a ditch. If you stack the dirt from the ditch alongside it, you then have a bank. The ditches often have pottery and remains of animals in them, but they can include some parts of human bodies. One example of this is from **Hambledon Hill** in England (see Figure 6.2), where human skulls are spaced at intervals in one of the ditches.[41] These types of finds likely indicate that causewayed enclosures had a ritual function (see later).

Among the many types of megalithic constructions that served as tombs are dolmens, long barrows, and passage graves. A **dolmen** has a few upright megalithic stones with a capstone above them (Figure 6.7). A **long barrow** is a communal tomb. It has an interior wooden or megalithic stone structure forming a capped corridor covered with dirt. Its exterior appearance is as a long mound in the landscape. The dead were placed both at the end of and along the corridor. Most of the bodies are disarticulated, meaning that their bones were rearranged. This might be due to moving older burials when new ones were deposited or perhaps removing certain bones to be used in rituals elsewhere. A **passage grave** is very similar to a long barrow and also

FIGURE 6.6
Part of the Neolithic alignments at Carnac, France.

was used over an extended period of time for the burial of numerous individuals. In a passage grave, the passage is always constructed of megalithic stones that are capped with megalithic stones. It has one or more burial chambers; most of these were built off of the main burial chamber. The passage structure was covered with dirt, so that a passage grave, just like a long barrow, appears as an earthen mound in the landscape.

The Neolithic megalithic constructions that most of us are familiar with are the henge monuments, such as **Stonehenge** (see Figure 6.2; Figure 6.8). A henge is a circle of menhirs that has a bank and ditch surrounding it; this is the basic layout at Stonehenge itself. There are a couple of important things to remember about Stonehenge, however. What Stonehenge looks like today is the result of changes to it made during the Bronze Age (see later). This means that the features of Stonehenge changed over time, with many of these changes occurring during the Neolithic period. Construction at Stonehenge began about 3000 cal BC.[42] The first phase was the construction of the bank and ditch that surrounded the circular arrangement of the Aubrey Holes. Bluestones and a few cremation burials were placed in the 56 Aubrey Holes. The bluestones come from quarries in Wales[43] and weigh, on average, 3,629 to 5,543 kilograms (4 to 6 metric tons) each (read "Peopling the Past: Building Stonehenge"). Wooden posts also were present. From 2900 to 2600 cal BC, the ditch began to fill in and the bank was no longer as high. The bluestones were rearranged into an inner arc formation. After

Stonehenge a henge monument begun in the Neolithic period that underwent several changes from an initial bank and ditch surrounding cremation pits to the addition of the bluestones from Wales, the larger local sarsen stones, and an avenue.

FIGURE 6.7
An example of a dolmen in Denmark.

removing the bluestones, many of the Aubrey Holes were used for cremation burials, and wooden structures were built inside the henge. Sometime around 2620 cal BC, the sarsens (megalithic sandstones from 30 kilometers [18 miles] to the north of Stonehenge) were added. The larger sarsens have an average weight of 22,680 kilograms (23 metric tons) each. The bluestones were rearranged into two arcs, and the heelstone was positioned outside the henge. After 2470 cal BC, an avenue leading to Stonehenge was added, and the arrangement of the sarsens and bluestones that we see today (dating to the Bronze Age) was created. The ritual function of Stonehenge as a burial monument (at least as part of its use) can be seen in the 250 cremation burials of men, women, and children over the period from about 3000 to 2500 cal BC.

INTERPRETATIONS OF NEOLITHIC MEGALITHS AND OTHER MONUMENTS IN GREAT BRITAIN

The impressive monumental constructions of the Neolithic period required considerable labor efforts and organization by groups of farmers. Why they undertook these building efforts is sometimes clear; for example, one of their burial rituals was to place people from the community into shared graves (long barrows and passage graves). There are several ways that we can explain some aspects of what we see in this Neolithic landscape. These explanations are not mutually exclusive but can be used in combination. They also can include ideas such as observations of the skies (for example, equinoxes, solstices, eclipses).[48]

FIGURE 6.8
Aerial view of Stonehenge showing the henge and the ditch and bank around it.

Building Stonehenge

When we look at large monuments built by people living thousands of years ago, it is natural to wonder how they were able to accomplish these seemingly gargantuan tasks in the absence of the kinds of technologies and transport systems we have available today. Building Stonehenge is one of those instances, especially because we know that the Neolithic bluestones are from quarries in Wales 220 kilometers (137 miles) away (Figure 6.9). The Welsh origin is supported by isotope studies of bones of people in cremated burials at Stonehenge, which show that some of them lived in Wales.[44] These naturally shaped stones needed to be transported either over land or by water and land more than 220 kilometers (the straight-line distance to Stonehenge). It used to be thought that one way to transport the bluestones might be to bring them down to the sea coast and put them on rafts or suspended between two boats. These would be moved along the coastline to the mouth of the River Avon and then up that river to a place not far from Stonehenge.[45] But experiments attempting this method resulted in capsized boats. Land transport is now thought to be the way the bluestones were moved. Based on public experiments, it turns out that about 10 people are needed to pull a 1-metric ton stone on a wooden sled over a log pathway. A pace slightly better than 1.6 kilometers (1 mile) per hour can be achieved.[46] So, taking a nearly all-land route (with one river crossing) to move the bluestones might ultimately have been a relatively simple task, and one that did not require large numbers of people to accomplish.[47] The larger sarsen stones likely were transported using sleds and log roller paths.

FIGURE 6.9
The quarry for bluestones at Carn Menyn in Wales.

One explanation focuses on changes over time.[49] In the earlier part of the Neolithic in Great Britain, from 4000 to 3000 cal BC, two of the most common constructions are long barrows and causewayed enclosures. If the distribution of these two types of monuments over the landscape in Great Britain is examined, a very interesting pattern can be observed. Most long barrows each seem to be associated with a territory that includes several Neolithic habitation sites. This may suggest that all these communities within the territory shared the long barrow for disposing of the dead. Each territory is roughly the same size, perhaps indicating an egalitarian form of society. Additionally, there are clusters of long barrow territories that may be associated with one specific causewayed enclosure. The causewayed enclosures might represent ritual centers where many people from the surrounding countryside (long barrow territories) could gather for special ceremonies. The labor involved in the construction of long barrows is about 10,000 labor hours, and that for a causewayed camp is approximately 100,000 labor hours. In contrast, during the latter part of the Neolithic period in Great Britain (3000 to 2000 cal BC), long barrows and causewayed enclosures are no longer built. Instead, construction efforts are focused on large henge sites (1 million labor hours, on average); other mega-monuments such as Silbury Hill, which is 40 meters (131 feet) high and took 18 million labor hours to build; and enormous henges such as Stonehenge (30 million labor hours). The Neolithic landscape appears to now consist of much larger territories, and each territory is associated with a mega-construction. This pattern suggests larger populations and more direction needed in labor investment, which may indicate ranked society with leaders who are socially distinct from other people.

A second interpretation is based in a landscape archaeology theoretical framework (see Chapter 1). In this explanation, the focus is on the social and ritual landscape of the Neolithic period, which is said to be divided into "domains of the living" and "domains of the dead."[50] The domains of the living are characterized by structures built of wood (a perishable or temporary type of material), including those used for ritual ceremonies involving the living. On the other hand, memorials to the dead (ancestors) are built of more permanent materials (stone). If we look at the landscape around Stonehenge, we can see how this interpretation might play out. People who die at a habitation site need to be transferred from the domain of the living to that of the dead. To accomplish this, some were transported down the River Avon to a henge monument (called Bluestonehenge).[51] The dead were cremated at this henge and then transported over the avenue to Stonehenge for burial, thus completing the transition from living to dead.

Bronze Age Europe

Bronze Age a period in the Old World characterized by the manufacture of bronze artifacts. In Europe, the Bronze Age is from 3000 to 800 cal BC. Beginning and end dates differ for various regions of Europe.

The use of monuments such as Stonehenge continued into the **Bronze Age** (3000 to 800 cal BC; the Bronze Age in northwestern Europe, where Stonehenge is, begins a bit later than 3000 cal BC). The Bronze Age is named for the advent of making artifacts out of bronze, a combination of copper and tin. Metalworking actually began earlier than 4500 cal BC in southeastern Europe, with the use of copper alone. This copper metallurgy was typical in areas of southeastern Europe, but not elsewhere. Copper objects were traded into other parts of Europe, although they were rare. Bronze Age metal tools and objects initially were not common throughout Europe, because they were valuable exotics requiring access to raw materials and the specialized labor involved in metallurgy (see Chapter 15). Such artifacts, however, did serve to create further distinctions between people in societies and to help create new trade and exchange networks. By the Middle and Late Bronze Age, large quantities of metal objects were more common, and many were buried in hoards (see later).

Resource Networks, Trade, and Exchange

Most Bronze Age peoples lived in agricultural villages, some of which in Central Europe were enclosed by fencing or ditches or ramparts, suggesting possible defensive features. Villagers needed basic items such as agricultural tools and pottery, most of which could be made locally. The items that most often are discussed as resources in trade and exchange networks are copper and tin ore (the basic components of bronze), bronze artifacts, and amber (yellow- to orange- to brown-colored fossilized tree resin used for jewelry). Other trade and exchange items were gold, furs, salt, shells, textiles, silver, glass, wool, and hides.[52]

Copper ore can be found in several places in Europe, while tin ore sources are much more rare. The copper ores came from numerous mines in the Balkan Peninsula, the Carpathian Mountains and the Alps, and central and western Europe, while tin is found in a few places in western Europe (Great Britain, France) and the Mediterranean (Italy, Iberia, and Sardinia).[53] The ores were heated to very high temperatures in specially built furnaces to remove impurities. The purer ore could be shaped into ingots, which were transported from the mines to areas where the ores could be mixed and made into artifacts. There were many types of bronze artifacts; these include axes, daggers, spearheads, helmets, shields, rings, pins, bracelets, beads, and trumpets.

Gold was worked by hammering the ore into sheets, which were then cut into objects such as jewelry, handles for daggers, cups, bracelets, and axes. Given the softness of gold, items such as axes were not for use but more likely for display purposes. At the very least, as an exotic resource, access to gold artifacts suggests individuals or families that were set apart from most other people in Bronze Age societies.

There are a number of ways in which trade and exchange goods would have been moved within Europe. Some routes were over land, while others involved transport using river systems or crossing the English Channel or the Baltic Sea (from northern Europe to Scandinavia) or maritime routes from northern Europe to the Mediterranean. In the case of prestige goods, these may represent exchanges between elite individuals (especially by the late Bronze Age).[54] Other goods may have traveled as part of trading expeditions from one region to another. Overall, the control of metal

FIGURE 6.10
Bronze axes from the Driffield Hoard in Great Britain.

goods, in particular, appears to have been in the hands of elite members of societies, and this control meant that there was potential for social classes to develop.[55] Ownership of boats that could be used to transport goods would be another important factor in distinguishing elites from others.

One interesting aspect of examining the distribution of metal objects in Europe during the Bronze Age are the hundreds of hoards (buried accumulations of artifacts) that have been found (Figure 6.10). These take a variety of forms—some are deposits of copper ingots, others are broken metal artifacts, and others are combinations of tools and weapons or ornaments.[56] The scale of some of the hoards is astounding, for example, 10,000 metal objects (weighing 4,536 kilograms [5 tons]) in six hoards in Romania. Why Bronze Age people would practice this form of hoarding has been subject to a variety of interpretations.[57] In the case of hoards of broken metal objects, one idea is that they were saved to be later melted down and made into new objects, although it seems odd that no one would have retrieved these hoards to do exactly that. Other suggestions for hoarding include as a way to hide valuable items during periods of conflict or as ritual deposits. Whatever the reasons for Bronze Age hoards, one fact remains. Enormous quantities of costly metal artifacts were taken out of circulation when they were buried. This might be analogous to us taking a large portion of the gold we store in Fort Knox, burying it in some secret location, and never retrieving it.

Social Life

A number of gender studies of women and men in Bronze Age societies exist. These are based on the types and amounts of grave goods found buried with people as well as on their depictions in figurines and rock art and on rare instances of preserved clothing.[58] Much of the preserved clothes come from the Scandinavian area. These can be correlated to males or females based on biological sex identification of the skeletons. Male clothing included a cloak, leather shoes, a cap, an occasional loincloth, and a tunic. Female clothing included jackets, belts, skirts, socks, leather shoes, and hairbands/nets. The clothes were fastened with buttons and pins and decorated with various bronze items (for example, belt buckles). Metal grave goods were common in both male and female burials, particularly in the Early and Middle Bronze Age (the Late Bronze Age differs somewhat because of the widespread practice of cremation burials; see later). Although there is overlap in some types of grave goods for males and females (for example, bronze pins and ornaments as well as pottery vessels), males are uniquely associated with swords and armor (as shown also in rock art), while females had bronze diadems (forehead ornaments), necklaces, and hair spirals. One interesting observation was female graves that are extremely rich in the abundance of grave goods. Some archaeologists interpret this to mean that these individuals held status and power in the same way as males.[59] One older interpretation is that these rich female graves reflect the status of the consorts of the women,[60] that is, their graves contained valuable items because their "husbands" were wealthy and had power.

The political/social organization of the Bronze Age varied from region to region, as well as over time. In some places, societies might have been organized as "chiefdoms" (read "Further Reflections: Characterizing Social and Political Organization"). In this type of system, most people (nonelites) lived in agricultural villages or communities, some of which were fortified (see later). A few individuals (the "chiefs") had better access to prestige goods (metal artifacts and other exotics). These individuals made decisions for the populations in their areas. They also developed, over time, into a warrior elite, as seen in their grave goods. In this case, these leaders would manage conflicts with other Bronze Age groups or societies. The scale of these "chiefdoms," however, can be questioned: Are they larger and regional or smaller, local entities?

A number of changes in what people did and how their societies were organized occurred over time. In the Early Bronze Age (ca. 3000 to 1600 cal BC), for example, most settlements were agricultural villages that were not fortified. There are, however, a few exceptions, such as the site of **Bruszczewo 5** in Poland in central Europe (Figure 6.11).[61] This settlement is on a small section of land that protrudes outward toward the wetlands (lake) and is slightly elevated. The wetlands context of Bruszczewo 5 resulted in good preservation of wood. We thus know that, in addition to a ditch, this section of land was made defensible by the presence of three wooden fences (palisades) and a rampart. Inside the fortified area were houses, a production area to manufacture bronze, and a hoard of bronze artifacts. This settlement was abandoned at the end of the Early Bronze Age, possibly because of overuse of the habitat around it and erosion caused by human activities (cutting of wood leading to an open landscape more susceptible to soil loss). Social factors such as shifts in trade routes also may have contributed to its abandonment. This lasted through the Middle Bronze Age, but then a new settlement was built at the end of the Late Bronze/start of the Early Iron Age.

In the Middle Bronze Age (*ca.* 1600 to 1350 cal BC), many more fortified settlements, as well as hilltop forts, were built in central Europe. During the Late Bronze Age (1350 to 800 cal BC) these types of constructions become widespread

Bruszczewo 5 an Early Bronze Age fortified site in a wetlands (lake/moor) context in Poland (central Europe). It was abandoned during the Middle Bronze Age and reoccupied during the Late Bronze/Early Iron Age.

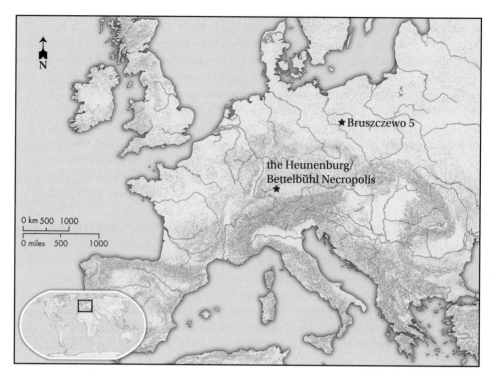

FIGURE 6.11
Bronze and Iron Age sites discussed in the text.

throughout Europe. This shift suggests that societies came into conflict with one another much more frequently over time, perhaps not surprising in a landscape that became more densely populated. Studies of the skeletons of people, in fact, indicate that they were less mobile during the Late Bronze Age compared to earlier periods.[62] This reinforces the idea of more people occupying many more places, leaving fewer options for moving elsewhere. Fortifications and defense also suggest that elite authority and power became concentrated in the hands of fewer people/ families as they established and maintained their legitimacy to control others within settlements.

Earlier we saw that one potential way to accumulate wealth (as one aspect of being an elite individual or family) was to exert control over portions of trade routes or own the boats that carried goods from place to place.[63] What is interesting is that for much of the Bronze Age, there are few indications of the wealthier individuals/ families in the size of houses or special types of houses in settlements.[64] However, exotic goods or an abundance of metal artifacts found in burial contexts do suggest such differences (read "Peopling the Past: Bronze Age Elites").

Bronze Age Elites

In the Early Bronze Age, some individuals were buried in barrows with large quantities of grave goods or with unusual grave goods. One example of this is a barrow at Irthlingborough in England.[65] A single adult male was buried in a wooden chamber covered with stone blocks and earth to form the barrow. Grave goods included an archer's stone wristguard, amber and jet jewelry, pottery, a chipped stone dagger, and the bones of as many as 185 cattle/aurochs. About 40 of the cattle may represent the remains of a feast held during the burial ritual, while additional cattle skulls were included as burial tokens. Uniquely decorated drinking cups made of amber, jet, gold, silver, and pottery are examples of exotic grave goods found in some burials identified as elites during this period.[66]

During the Middle Bronze Age, barrow burials (called tumulus burials) continued. An adult male in a tumulus burial is sometimes identified as a "chief" (read "Further Reflections: Characterizing Social and Political Organization") and as a warrior, as are younger male individuals.[67] Grave goods include bronze swords and daggers, wooden drinking cups inlaid with tin nails, and bronze ornaments, as well as wooden shields. By the Late Bronze Age, individuals in barrow graves (rather than in the urnfields) are interpreted as an "aristocratic warrior elite."[68] Grave goods consist of bronze weapons (swords, spears, axes, knives), ornaments (rings), bronze vessels (some for drinking), bronze shields, a wooden wagon, as well as bronze body armor similar to that of the Greeks (showing long-distance contacts within Europe) (Figure 6.12).

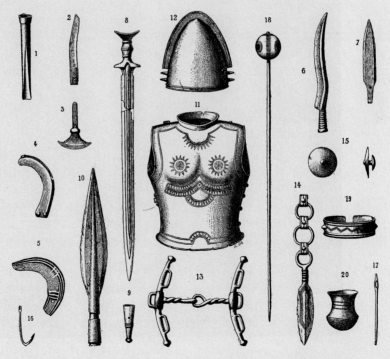

FIGURE 6.12
Examples of Late Bronze Age weapons and objects in France.

During the Late Bronze Age, burial distinctions between most people are not common in the **urnfields** (or Urnfield Culture; cemeteries containing thousands of cremation burials placed in pottery urns).[69] Urnfields began in eastern Europe and spread over time into central and western Europe. Urn burials generally have few grave goods. The sheer numbers of people buried indicate that it is most of the population rather than just a few elite individuals. The cemeteries include clusters of urns, which may suggest family groupings, just as we today tend to have family plots in cemeteries. There are, however, some burials in urnfields interpreted as elites based on the larger quantities of metal artifacts. There also are contexts that are not urnfields (read "Peopling the Past: Bronze Age Elites"). The non-urnfield contexts contain the so-called "chiefly burials," which, based on the presence of items such as weapons, helmets, and ornaments, contain individuals often described as warrior leaders.

Warfare and Violence

The abundance of metal weapons in the Bronze Age, as well as rock art scenes showing possible conflict[70] (Figure 6.13), suggests that violent acts between individuals or groups of fighters were common occurrences. This is supported by the fact that

FIGURE 6.13
Bronze Age rock art showing "battling" individuals (Tanum, Sweden).

close examination of swords shows blade-notching damage resulting from parrying slashing sword blows and resharpening of areas to correct the damage.[71] Similarly, observations of shields and helmets indicate damage sustained from being hit by spearheads, swords, axes, and spears. In some of the hoards deposited in wetlands contexts, the bronze weaponry shows unrepaired damage, perhaps suggesting that these hoards represent depositions made after conflict events (perhaps the victors offering the weapons of the defeated).

The individuals who are identified as warriors based on grave goods are usually identified as males and may have served in a variety of roles. In trade and exchange, for example, they would have protected goods traveling by boat or land routes.[72] Alternatively, they might have preyed upon others transporting these goods, much as later historic period pirates did on the high seas. Over time, individuals with fighting skills and equipment became a specialized group of people in society and were accorded higher status (as seen in the abundance of their grave goods). We saw earlier that some of these individuals likely were leaders of settlements or groups of settlements, serving as "chiefs." By the Middle to Late Bronze Age, groups of warriors were associated with a warrior leader in the fortified settlements that became common throughout much of Europe. The conflicts between these groups included raids and possibly hand-to-hand combat between leaders, but probably not warfare as most of us think of it.

Peopling the Past

Violence, Ritual, or Both in the Bronze Age?

The Bronze Age is well known for the deliberate deposition of metal artifacts and other items in river, stream, lake, and bog contexts. These occurrences are most often interpreted as ritual deposits. Another type of deposit is that of human remains, a practice that goes back in time to the Mesolithic (although the reasons for it likely differed).[75] One example comes from Late Bronze Age lakeside settlements in central Europe.[76] These communities were built on or near the shores of lakes. Fluctuations in climate meant that lake levels rose much higher at certain times and could flood the villages. Late Bronze Age peoples tried to protect themselves by building dwellings raised on stilts above the water, or house floors that could withstand being waterlogged, and even fences against advancing water. Most of this would work for temporary flooding, but when lake levels rose more permanently, such constructions would not have much effect. This is when presumably ritual offerings of children's skulls placed on the lake side near the edge of the settlements were made. The interpretation suggests that these offerings were to "gods" to avoid the flooding. Two of the children had suffered violent blows to the head, although the archaeologists suggest that they were not killed to be sacrificed for the water ritual. Rather they, and the skulls of other children, were removed sometime after death and placed around the settlements to appease the advancing floods.

Protective measures taken by communities involved building their settlements on hilltops, although this may have been partly to keep house floors away from damp valley bottom ground. It is when fences, ditches, banks, and other structures are added to these hilltop locations that the need for defense seems probable. By the Late Bronze Age, some of these hilltop locations are hill forts and settlements on lower ground also are fortified.[73] In some areas, the forts are spaced regularly along river valleys (3 to 4 kilometers [1.8 to 2.5 miles] apart) and may suggest territories controlled by each fort. If so, these territories were quite small.[74]

Iron Age Europe

Iron Age a period in Europe from about 800 to 59/51 cal BC. It is characterized by the manufacture and use of implements made of iron.

The **Iron Age** in Europe was from approximately 800 to 59/51 cal BC (when Roman influence in part of Europe began). As its name indicates, one of the main features of this period was iron metallurgy with the production and use of iron implements. Unlike bronze, which requires copper and tin to be combined, iron does not need another ore additive. As we saw earlier, copper sources in Europe are relatively widespread, but tin is not, and this helped shape the control of these ore sources, which impacted trade and exchange networks, the accumulation of wealth, and social organization. Iron metallurgy actually began prior to the Iron Age and then gradually spread throughout much of Europe. It was widespread by 800/700 cal BC.

Although early in the Iron Age wealth and iron technology tended to be concentrated at just a few places, the decline in demand for bronze and replacement of most bronze artifacts by iron helped shift the economic dynamics that characterized this phase and the Bronze Age.[77] This is because iron ore can be found in many places, and as knowledge of how to work iron spread, use of iron technology could be on a local basis rather than in only a small number of sites. Control of iron sources thus was not as profitable or as critical, although control of trade routes remained important. One social and political transformation that appears to have resulted from changes in wealth (based initially on bronze) is a shift to the eventual use of military forces to support taxation policies and land ownership. Other changes included greater numbers of people living in settlements (pre-urban centers) and an abundance of fortified sites. We will look briefly at developments in Europe using the Hallstatt (Early Iron Age) and La Tène (Late Iron Age) cultures.

Hallstatt Culture

Hallstatt Culture the early part of the Iron Age in Europe, from about 750 to 450 cal BC. It is found north of the Alps in central Europe and extends in an arc to the east and west of Italy.

The Early Iron Age includes the **Hallstatt Culture** (750 to 450 cal BC), which is found north of the Alps in central Europe but also extends in an arc-like fashion down to the Mediterranean west of Italy and into southeastern Europe east of Italy (Figure 6.14). One feature of this period is the development of large, central-place sites with dense populations.[78] Many of these are described as pre-urban[79] centers

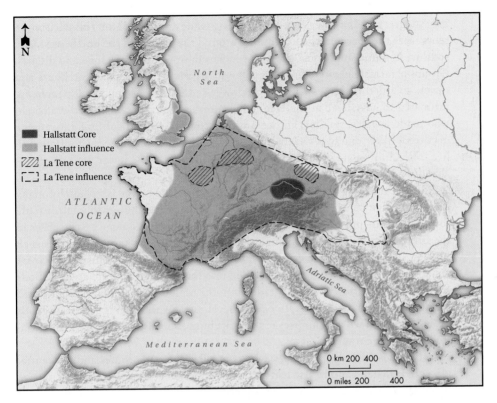

FIGURE 6.14
The core areas and extents of the Iron Age Hallstatt and La Tène Cultures.

where elites controlled surrounding regions with smaller settlements.[80] Such centers are sometimes called "princely seats."[81] They are enclosed and have a heavily fortified central area on a high area/hilltop, evidence of goods and ideas obtained from polities in the Mediterranean (Greek, Etruscan, Phoenician), and lavish burials of some people. It is important to remember, however, that these centers were not identical in layout or features, which suggests local development. In other words, the differences from one central place to another across the landscape can be interpreted as evidence that these were not all linked together as a single political unit. Those that were pre-urban contexts were not state polities, but perhaps some version of a complex chiefdom.[82]

One example of a Hallstatt Culture central place is **the Heuneburg** along the Danube River in southern Germany (see Figure 6.11).[83] Between 600 to 540/530 cal BC, the plateau hilltop at the Heuneburg had an enclosing mudbrick wall with a limestone foundation. Inside the wall were houses lined up along streets. These replaced earlier farmsteads, which were razed rather than destroyed by violence. This

(the) Heunenburg a Hallstatt Culture proto-urban center in southern Germany with evidence of trade with the Mediterranean and lavish burials of elites.

may suggest that the elites at the Heuneburg made and carried out this decision to reorganize the space. In the lower areas around the plateau to the north, west, and southwest, numerous farmsteads were enclosed by a system of banks and ditches. Groups of farmsteads were further enclosed by palisades (fences). A gatehouse and towers guarded the entrance into the lower settlement. About 5,000 people are estimated to have lived at the Heunenburg settlement. These included craftsmen who made jewelry, textiles, and ceramics. Around 540/530 cal BC, a major fire occurred, likely due to a violent encounter, and while some people continued to live in the hilltop area (which was refortified), much of the lower settlement was abandoned.

The positioning of the Heunenburg along a major river is typical of many Early Iron Age central places. These locales likely were chosen to control trade routes and thus prestige goods that were being transported (as we saw earlier in the Bronze Age). From archaeological excavation finds, we know that items such as wine (based on ceramic vessel shapes and residues), Greek pottery, and Greek and Etruscan bronze artifacts were traded into the Hallstatt Culture area.[84] Goods from northern Europe that were traded into the Mediterranean may have included metals and furs or even slaves. In one sense, Hallstatt Culture was a prestige goods economy, which we see glimpses of from the burials of elites who presumably controlled the trade routes.

The elites, including warriors, who controlled the trade routes and the central places in Hallstatt Culture also had wealth based on land ownership and control over the production of local goods.[85] Men identified as warrior "princes" had swords and wagons in their burials, among other grave goods. Hallstatt Culture barrow burials, however, show that women also were significant individuals in these societies. One example is from a barrow burial in a cemetery near the Heuneburg.[86] The cemetery is called the **Bettelbühl necropolis** (see Figure 6.11). The remaining barrow contained the lower part of a well-preserved wooden chamber with a wooden floor and dates to 583 BC based on dendrochronology (see Chapter 1). It contained a female skeleton (aged 30 to 40 years old) and a wealth of prestigious grave goods. Among the finds were gold and bronze fibulae (pins or brooches), some inset with amber, gold spheres, and beads of gold and amber; bracelets made of jet; bronze foot rings; and the remains of a decorated bronze and leather belt in her waist area. Elsewhere in the grave were decorated sheets of bronze, tusks of wild boar set into bronze sheets, fragments of textiles and fur, a pig's skeleton (possibly a food offering) with a carving knife, and glass beads. A second skeleton in one corner of the burial chamber had some simple jewelry and may have been a companion burial. There also was a bronze head fitting for a horse.

Bettelbühl Necropolis a Hallstatt Culture cemetery near the Heunenburg in Germany (Europe) which contains a barrow burial (dating to 583 BC) of an elite woman.

The pre-urban central places of the Early Iron Age did not have long life spans.[87] Although they had trade contacts with the Mediterranean area, they were peripheral to developments there, where Mediterranean city-states had begun to emerge. By 450/400 cal BC, all remaining Hallstatt central places were abandoned. The polities they represented became decentralized, a good example of how social and political developments do not always follow a linear path toward ever-increasing complexity.

La Tène Culture

In the Late Iron Age (450 to 59/51 cal BC), the **La Tène Culture** (sometimes identified as "Celtic" culture) emerged in central Europe (see Figure 6.14). Like earlier societies, much of the wealth of elites was based on agricultural products. Studies of several hillfort sites show that a greater diversity of crops were grown by La Tène Culture groups. This may suggest methods to enhance or mitigate crop output from year to year, but also may reflect growing population size.[88] The elites of La Tène Culture were large landowners whose primary concern was the accumulation of wealth and power for themselves rather than concern for commoners who worked the land.[89] These elites, who were warriors based on their grave goods, surrounded themselves with other warriors to maintain their control over land but also to conduct conquests of surrounding areas. The raids and warfare were aided by horse-drawn chariots. And, just as in earlier societies, the elites of La Tène Culture had trade and exchange networks reaching into the Mediterranean area.

The question of whether the site centers of the La Tène Culture are examples of urbanization is still debated.[90] The largest of these centers are called **oppida** (sing., oppidum) and are sometimes referred to as towns. They had defensive structures such as ramparts, usually were large settlements (25 to 50 hectares [62 to 124 acres]), were central places for trade and exchange, had ritual functions, and were sites where political and social power was concentrated.[91] One of the issues, however, is that there are other sites not described as oppida that seem to have shared some of these characteristics. These other large sites are referred to as unenclosed agglomerations.[92] Perhaps, however, the question of urbanization is not as important as questions relating to how the oppida and the unenclosed agglomerations served as places in La Tène Culture. Most oppida and unenclosed agglomerations do not seem to have had dense populations, and, in many cases, there are open spaces within these centers. Analysis of the distribution of mounds, houses, walls, and other constructions within these central places suggests that they might have been designed to shape the movement of people toward some aspects of the area, such as elite areas. One archaeological interpretation of this spatial arrangement is to see the centers as "powerscapes";[93] the open areas would have been places for people to gather for ceremonies and other activities. This is an interpretation that also resonates for many other time periods and places in the world (see, for example, Chapters 7, 8, 9, 14, and 15).

There is little question that elite individuals/families were an important feature of La Tène Culture. As noted above, some of their power was a result of their warrior status, but in all likelihood they also had to negotiate relationships with commoners so that society continued to function without major internal disruptions within communities. As warriors, they were buried with military equipment: swords, spears, shields, helmets, and, in some cases, wagons or chariots and horse

La Tène Culture the later part of the Iron Age in Europe, from approximately 450 to 59/51 cal BC, when parts of Europe were conquered by the Romans.

Oppida the plural of oppidum; large, often fortified settlements of the Late Iron Age La Tène Culture. They are sometimes described as urban centers, although not all archaeologists agree with this interpretation.

fittings.[94] By the Late La Tène Culture period, coins were minted and used in trade, and there is some suggestion that the warrior class as rulers was replaced in part by aristocratic groups of leaders who took on roles more involved in administration and trade.

When these transitions in power and control occurred in the Late La Tène Culture period, some archaeologists suggest that some of the non-Mediterranean regions in Europe were beginning to emerge as states.[95] This is because these regions had what could be called kings, who controlled large areas, as well as the coinage mentioned above, fortified oppida, and perhaps judicial systems. Whatever these possible states might have become is unknown because they were developing at the time that Roman influence in parts of Europe accelerated (59 to 51 BC). Rome's influence on many indigenous groups meant that the Roman system of political organization was imposed.

Chiefdom a category of political organization that is described as a ranked society in which rank is inherited. Elites in a chiefdom live at central places, control densely populated regions, and have greater access to prestige goods and other resources.

Further Reflections

Characterizing Social and Political Organization

One of the continuing difficulties in archaeology is deciding how to characterize the social and political organization of past societies (see Chapter 5). All were socially complex, but to what degree were they politically complex? This question arises in contexts such as the Bronze Age Europe, where some researchers describe these societies as examples of chiefdoms.[96] A **chiefdom** is a ranked society, with rank usually inherited. Other features are control of densely populated regions, social organization with a few elite individuals/ families as decision-makers for commoners, elites having access to greater wealth, and central places where the elites are housed and that coordinate all economic, social, and religious activities. One of the difficulties with saying that Bronze Age groups were chiefdoms is that most settlements are similar (that is, there are no central places), and none of the houses in them seems larger or better equipped than the others (as one would expect an elite residence to be). We do know that some individuals/ families managed to gain more access to resources, especially prestige goods, than other people. Does this mean that these "elites" were ranked, which is an expectation of the chiefdom model? Questions such as these often are hard to answer definitively because not everything is preserved in the archaeological record.

Summary

- Mesolithic hunter–gatherer–foragers lived in Europe from 9600 to 4000 cal BC. During the early part of the Mesolithic, due to lower sea levels, continental Europe was linked to Great Britain by land across the southern North Sea basin.

- Mesolithic sites in northern Europe often have good organic preservation due to waterlogged conditions or peat bogs. This allows us to gain a fuller picture of their lives and activities.

- One of the last Mesolithic groups in Europe was the Ertebølle Culture of Scandinavia. They lived just north of expanding groups of Neolithic farmers. Ertebølle Culture sites yield evidence for intensive use of shellfish in addition to hunting land and sea animals and birds. Their cemeteries show special treatment of some individuals based on their grave goods and body placements. Dogs with grave goods are buried in a manner similar to humans.

- Domesticated plants and animals were not developed locally in Europe. Instead, groups of Neolithic farmers began to spread from the Middle East, at first into southeastern Europe (Balkan Peninsula). From there, two main waves of Neolithic colonization occurred.

- Cardial Ware Culture (6400 to 4700 cal BC): these groups spread through the Mediterranean area using boats to travel along the coasts. In addition to domesticated cereals, they also had sheep and goats.

- Linear Pottery Culture (5700 to 4500 cal BC): these farmers moved into central and eventually northwestern Europe following major rivers, such as the Danube, and their tributaries. They brought with them domesticated cereals, cattle, and pigs.

- Over time, some Linear Pottery Culture groups began to fortify their villages, and there is evidence of massacres, suggesting increasing levels of violence. This archaeological culture overlaps with the Ertebølle Culture, although they did not occupy the same areas.

- Another Neolithic group that overlapped with Ertebølle Culture was the Funnel Beaker Culture (4100 to 2800 cal BC). It was during this period that agricultural innovations such as the plow and wheeled wagons were developed. The Neolithic practice of dairying (adults drinking milk) is thought to have led to natural selection for lactose tolerance (adult ability to digest milk sugar without digestive issues), a feature that persists today, especially in people from Europe.

- Neolithic groups throughout Europe are well known for their construction of monuments, sometimes incorporating megaliths (large stones). Examples of these constructions include menhirs, alignments, causewayed enclosures, henges, and tombs (dolmens, long barrows, and passage graves).

- Stonehenge is one of the best known of the henge monuments. It was redesigned several times but was first constructed during the Neolithic period. In addition to a small bank and ditch, which gradually mostly filled in, there was a series of holes (Aubrey Holes) for the placement of bluestones brought from Wales and cremation burials. When the sarsens (sandstone megaliths) were added, the blue-stones were rearranged. The layout of Stonehenge that we see today dates to the Bronze Age.

- British archaeologists have interpreted the Neolithic landscape, including monuments, in several ways. One is chronological, with changes in social practices over time—for example, the use of long barrows for group burials in the Early Neolithic but the abandonment of these structures in the Late Neolithic. Alternatively, this landscape can be perceived as landscapes of the living and of the dead, with wooden construction (e.g., houses) symbolizing the living and stone construction, such as Stonehenge, representing the dead (stone being more permanent than wood).

- During the Bronze Age (3000 to 800 cal BC), metallurgy that combined copper and tin to produce bronze artifacts was practiced. These ores and their sources became important resources in trade and exchange. Other trade items included amber, jet, salt, fur, and perhaps slaves.

- In the Early Bronze Age, most settlements are not fortified. By the Middle Bronze Age, more fortified sites, including ones on hilltops, begin to appear. This trend continues into the Late Bronze Age. Fortifications suggest increased levels of violence between communities, a pattern that may be supported by swords, daggers, shields, helmets, and other military equipment found in the burials of elite males. These elites are often called warriors. They may also have been "chiefs" controlling small "chiefdoms."

- Bronze Age elites likely controlled trade routes as their sites are evenly spaced along major river systems and they and some of their group were warriors who could protect these routes. Metals were especially important. In addition to grave goods, metal artifacts have been found in what appear to be offering deposits in wetland areas (rivers, bogs) and in hoards that can number dozens to hundreds of pieces. Many of the hoards contain broken items.

- There were many changes in Bronze Age societies over time. In addition to fortified sites, other changes include how people were buried (in barrows, in cemeteries, in urnfields). Some of these differences mark elites as opposed to commoners, others are regional, while still others are chronological. Bronze Age Europe thus was not a single unified polity but many smaller societies that developed, were independent of each other, and then disappeared.

- During the Iron Age (800 cal BC to 59/51 BC), iron metallurgy was dominant. Making iron artifacts does not require other ores, and iron ore is widespread in Europe (unlike tin ore sources in the Bronze Age). Two well-known Iron Age groups are the Hallstatt Culture and La Tène Culture.

- In the Hallstatt Culture period (750 to 450 cal BC) of the Early Iron Age, fortified sites that functioned as central places for trade and exchange and craft work were common. Elite individuals gained wealth from the control of these activities as well as from owning land and managing agricultural products. Elite males continued to be buried with military equipment and are identified as warriors, but there also are a number of richly furnished burials of elite women. This might suggest that women had important social roles in Early Iron Age societies.

- The central places of the Hallstatt Culture are sometimes described as "urban," but this is widely debated and continues to be an issue in the Late Iron Age. By the end of the Hallstatt Culture period, all of their central places were abandoned.

- Hallstatt Culture is followed by the Late Iron Age La Tène Culture (450 cal BC to 59/51 BC). Many features of this culture are similar to those of Hallstatt Culture. They include control of trade and exchange and agricultural products, land ownership, wealthy elites, male warrior leaders, and fortified central places. There are now large sites called oppida (usually fortified to some extent) and settlements identified as unenclosed agglomerations. The size and estimated population of some of these central places is sometimes argued to indicate urbanization, but not all researchers agree that La Tène had urban centers. Many of these central places, however, were not densely populated and had large open spaces that could have been used for ceremonies or other activities.

- By the late La Tène Culture period, there are indications that state-level polities may have been developing in some areas north of the Mediterranean. What these entities might ultimately have become is unknown because the Roman Empire extended its influence into parts of Europe beginning ca. 59 BC and imposed their system of political organization in these areas.

Endnotes

1. Amkreutz et al. 2018.
2. Holst 2010.
3. Clark 1954; Conneller et al. 2012; Mellars 2009: 504.
4. Conneller et al. 2012; Mellars 2009: 516.
5. Chatterton 2003: 72; Price 1989.
6. Andresen et al. 1981; Mellars 2009; Mellars and Dark 1998.
7. Whallon 2006; Zvelebil 2006: 180.
8. O'Shea and Zvelebil 1984; Spikins 2008: 184; Zvelebil 2006: 188.
9. Larsson 1989; O'Shea and Zvelebil 1984; Oshibkina 2008.
10. Sometimes called Ertebølle-Ellerbek to reflect the incorporation of the coastal sites of northern Germany (Scarre 1996).
11. Rowley-Conwy 1984.

12. Andersen 2004.

13. Richter and Noe-Nygaard 2003.

14. Albrethsen and Brinch Petersen 1976; Orme 1981.

15. Albrethsen and Brinch Petersen 1976.

16. Larsson 1990.

17. Larsson 1989, 2004.

18. Larsson 2002.

19. Pinhasi et al. 2012; Skoglund et al. 2014.

20. Ottoni et al. 2012; Troy et al. 2001; Zeder 2011.

21. Hofmanova et al. 2016; Lazaridis et al. 2016; Mathieson et al. 2015; Olalde et al. 2015.

22. Page et al. 2016.

23. This Neolithic grouping is sometimes divided into two, one being the Cardial Ware and the other Impressed Ware; alternatively, rather than being called the Cardial Ware Culture, it is called the Impressed Ware Culture.

24. Paschou et al. 2014; Zilhão 2001.

25. Atici et al. 2017.

26. Banks et al. 2013.

27. Skeates 2002. Whittle 1996: 296.

28. van Willigen 2018.

29. Vanmontfort 2008. Not everyone agrees with this perspective; for example, see Golitko and Keeley 2007.

30. Lenneis 2008.

31. Golitko and Keeley 2007.

32. John 2011; Zvelebil and Pettitt 2013.

33. Wild et al. 2004.

34. Meyer et al. 2014.

35. Meyer et al. 2018.

36. Gronenborn et al. 2014.

37. Price 2000.

38. Ottaway 1973.

39. Schovsbo 1983.

40. Berthon et al. 2018; Laland et al. 2010.

41. Mercer and Healy 2014.

42. Darvill et al. 2012; Parker Pearson et al. 2009.

43. Bevins et al. 2014; Darvill and Wainwright 2015.

44. Snoeck et al. 2018. Ten of 25 cremation burials studied are individuals most likely from Wales. These cremation burials were placed in the Aubrey Holes, which originally held bluestones.

45. John 2008.

46. Harris 2016.

47. Parker Pearson et al. 2011.

48. Meaden 2017.

49. Renfrew 1983.

50. Parker Pearson 1998.

51. Allen et al. 2016.

52. Earle et al. 2015.

53. Harding 2000: 198–201; O'Brien 2014.

54. Kristiansen 1998: 88–98.

55. Earle et al. 2015.

56. Harding 2000: 218-219, 354–356; Kristiansen 1998: 80–85.

57. Needham 2001.

58. Harding 2000: 369–376; Robb and Harris 2018; Sørensen 2013; Sosna et al. 2008.

59. Shennan, S. J. 1993 (females in this interpretation are seen as a status hierarchy separate from males); Sosna et al. 2008.

60. Shennan, S. E. 1975.

61. Kneisel 2012.

62. Macintosh et al. 2014.

63. Earle et al. 2015.

64. Harding 2000: 393–394.

65. Towers et al. 2010.

66. Needham et al. 2006; Wells 2016.

67. Kristiansen 1998: 378–384.

68. Kristiansen 1998: 384–385.

69. Kristiansen 1998: 113.

70. Another interpretation of some of these scenes is that they were ritual performances rather than depictions of actual combat (Harding 2000: 291).

71. Kristiansen 2002.

72. Earle et al. 2015; Goldhahn and Ling 2013.

73. Harding 2000: 298–299.

74. Brinker et al. 2016.

75. Gummesson et al. 2018.

76. Menotti et al. 2014.

77. Barceló et al. 2014; Kristiansen 1998: 211–218.

78. Fernández-Götz and Ralston 2017.

79. Researchers disagree as to whether the centers of Hallstatt Culture were urban; the same is true for the interpretation of Late Iron Age La Tène Culture oppida (e.g., see Kristiansen 1998: 345 as opposed to Moore 2017; Moore et al. 2015).

80. Other centers may have been primarily ceremonial, assembly, or refuge sites (Fernández-Götz and Ralston 2017: 271).

81. Fernández-Götz and Ralston 2017: 260; the actual term is *Fürstensitze*.

82. Fernández-Götz and Ralston 2017: 271.

83. Fernández-Götz and Ralston 2017: 262–264.

84. Cunliffe 2000.

85. Gosden 1985.

86. Krausse et al. 2017.

87. Fernández-Götz and Ralston 2017: 27–273.

88. Kreuz and Schäfer 2008.

89. Kristiansen 1998: 320–321.

90. Menotti et al., 2014.

91. Moore 2017.

92. Moore 2017; Moore et al. 2015.

93. Moore 2017: 289.

94. Kristiansen 1998: 340–350.

95. Scarre 2013: 428.

96. Harding 2000: 388–393.

CHAPTER 7

The North American Southwest

Above: The Ancestral Pueblo site of Keet Seel, Arizona.

The North American Southwest is the geographical region of Arizona, New Mexico, the southwest portion of Colorado, and the southeast part of Utah. In addition to early Paleoamerican groups, such as the Clovis culture, and succeeding Archaic period groups, the North American Southwest was home to several later prehistoric cultures whose archaeological remains are evidence of a diversity of cultural strategies ranging from relatively mobile lifestyles to those associated with large, settled communities and complex forms of social organization. The best known of the Southwestern cultures are the **Ancestral Pueblo** (also known as Anasazi),[1] the **Hohokam**, and the **Mogollon** (Figure 7.1). Others include the Sinagua, the Salado, the Patayan, and the Trincheras cultures. In this chapter we will focus mainly on the Ancestral Pueblo culture. They occupied northern Arizona, northwestern New Mexico, southwestern Colorado, and southeastern Utah and built settled communities, some of which are popularly called "cliff dwellings."

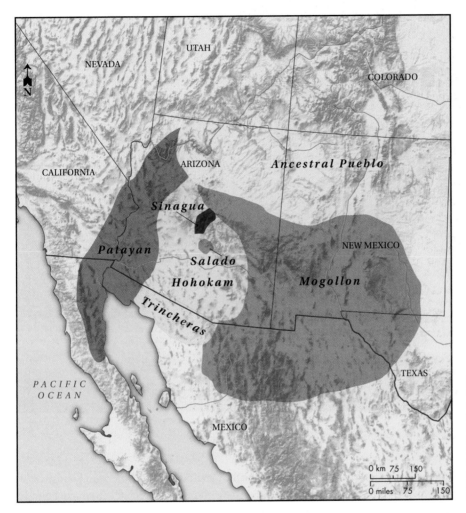

FIGURE 7.1
Prehistoric culture areas of the North American Southwest.

The descendants of the Ancestral Pueblo live today in communities such as the Hopi, Zuni, and Rio Grande pueblos, and their oral traditions and ways of life provide valuable insights into life during the Ancestral Pueblo period.

Early Food Production

Clovis and later Paleoamerican hunter–gatherer–foragers were present in the North American Southwest from 11,000 to 8000 cal BC (see Chapter 4). Beginning about 8000 cal BC, their descendants are known as Archaic period

Ancestral Pueblo an archaeological term for the Native American groups who occupied southeastern Utah, southwestern Colorado, northern Arizona, and northwestern New Mexico from 500 cal BC until just before Spanish contact in AD 1540; their descendants live in the Hopi, Zuni, and Rio Grande pueblos of Arizona and New Mexico.

Hohokam an archaeological term for the Native American groups who occupied south-central and southeastern Arizona from AD 1 until just prior to Spanish contact in AD 1540; their descendants include the Tohono O'odham and the Pima of Arizona.

Mogollon a term for the Native American groups who occupied much of central and southern New Mexico, the northern portions of the Sonoran and Chihuahuan deserts of northern Mexico, and the mountainous region of east-central Arizona from AD 100 to just before the arrival of the Spanish in AD 1540; their descendants likely moved to the Rio Grande pueblos.

FIGURE 7.2
An Archaic period site in the desert of southwestern Arizona. Note the structure often called a "sleeping circle."

hunter–gatherer–foragers (Figure 7.2; read "Timeline: North American Southwest"). They used ground stone tools to process some plant foods, probably to make flour. In addition to the hunting of wild animals and collection of wild plant foods (cactus fruits, agave, mesquite beans, wild grass seeds, local wild potatoes,[2] and pine nuts in northern areas), during the last part of the Middle Archaic period (around 2100 cal BC), people began to incorporate domesticated maize into their subsistence economies.[3] This domesticate was imported into the Hohokam region of the North American Southwest from Mesoamerica/Mexico (see Chapter 5) and then spread rapidly northward, where it was integrated into existing, relatively mobile lifeways. Because the North American Southwest is a dry region, many organic materials are preserved, including sandals and nets made out of plant fibers, split twig figurines, and rabbit skins[4].

The Late Archaic Period

Archaic period people in the North American Southwest retained a relatively mobile way of life, perhaps because they used the new domesticates in ways that allowed them to simply add these domesticates to the collection of wild foods. They could

Timeline: North American Southwest

The archaeological sequence for different pre-historic cultural regions in the North American Southwest indicates periods during which material culture, architecture, settlement patterns, and other features form relatively distinctive patterns (Figure 7.3). The dates for the divisions within the sequences often are modified with the addition of new radiocarbon, archaeomagnetic, and other dates, as well as reassessments of those dates.

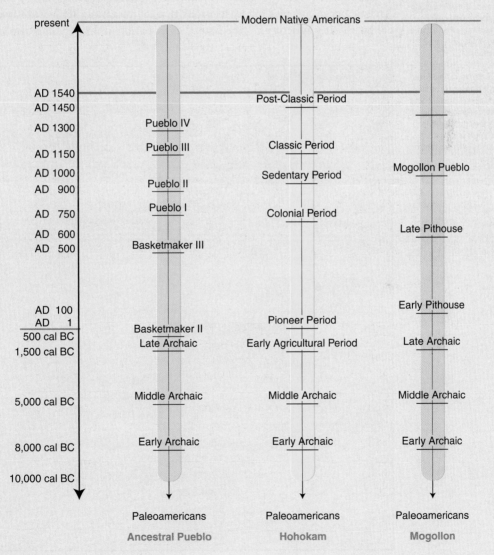

FIGURE 7.3
Timeline for the North American Southwest (red line indicates the arrival of the Spanish in the Southwest).

plant maize, for example, in damp floodplains and then leave for other places with wild resources.[5] When the maize ripened, they returned to harvest it.

Small sites, such as **Three Fir Shelter** in Arizona, in the region that later was home to the Ancestral Pueblo, have evidence for early use of maize (by 1990 cal BC[6]) (Figure 7.4). Larger sites such as **Santa Cruz Bend** (Tucson, Arizona) (see Figure 7.4), in what later would be the Hohokam region, have numerous dwellings called **pithouses**, including a very large pithouse interpreted as a communal structure (Figure 7.5). Santa Cruz Bend is representative of how some Archaic period peoples made decisions that led to a more settled lifestyle associated with early agriculture[7] (the Late Archaic period in this region is also known as

Three Fir Shelter an Archaic period site in northeast Arizona with evidence for the early use of maize by 1990 cal BC.

Santa Cruz Bend a Late Archaic period site in Tucson, Arizona, which has evidence of early maize, along with wild plants and hunting of animals. It is a small, settled village site with more than a dozen pithouse dwellings and a large, communal pithouse.

Pithouse in the North American Southwest, pithouses are usually circular to oval dwellings that have been dug into the ground, although they also can be rectangular. In most cases, poles and/or beams are used to build walls and roofing above ground.

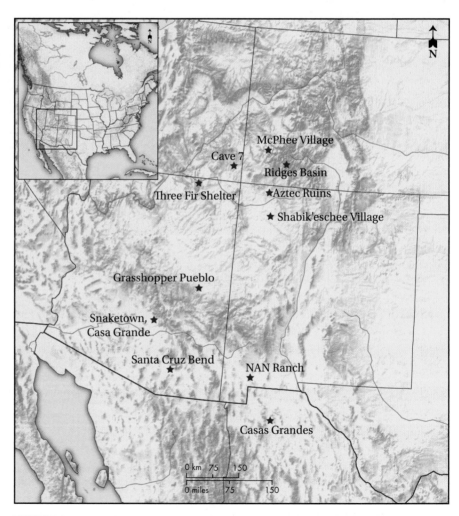

FIGURE 7.4
North American Southwest sites mentioned in the text (excluding Chaco Phenomenon sites).

FIGURE 7.5
Some of the Late Archaic (Early Agricultural Period) pithouses at the Santa Cruz Bend site in southern Arizona.

the **Early Agricultural Period**; see "Hohokam and Mogollon"). As Late Archaic period people began to rely more heavily on maize, they constructed early irrigation canals (by 1250 cal BC and possibly as early as 1750 cal BC) in what would become the Hohokam region.[8] By 1200 cal BC, domesticated squash was introduced from Mexico, and by 590 cal BC, domesticated beans from Mexico were present.[9]

One of the important features of the introduction of domesticated crops into the Archaic period North American Southwest is that it shows us that the process of integration of domesticates into existing behavioral strategies was quite variable. In southern Arizona (the eventual Hohokam region), maize became a significant part of the diet quite early. In the northern Southwest (the eventual Ancestral Pueblo region), Archaic period people used maize, but dependence on it did not occur until the succeeding Basketmaker II period (see later). Despite reliance on maize by a number of groups, all of them continued to collect wild plant foods and hunt. Using a costs and benefits human behavioral ecology viewpoint that stresses the assessment of "marginal costs," some researchers propose that the extensive variability in reliance on maize (and other domesticates) that we see across the North American Southwest reflects choices people made about the time, labor, and returns involved in foraging as opposed to farming.[10] Marginal costs is an economic term based on how much the total cost of doing something changes when you add one more unit

Early Agricultural Period a term used to describe the Late Archaic period in the area of southern Arizona that becomes the Hohokam region. This term is used in preference to Late Archaic because domesticated maize was introduced from Mesoamerica and then incorporated into mobile hunting, gathering, and foraging lifeways.

to the overall quantity. If you can collect a week's supply of pine nuts from a dense area of pinyon trees by working for one day, for example, but to add another week's supply (one unit to the overall quantity) from the remaining area that has only scattered pinyon trees takes you two or three times as long, then the marginal cost of adding this one unit is high. In most cases, hunter–gatherer–forager groups will not invest in the marginal cost of the additional unit unless there is an overriding need such as the necessity of feeding additional people. In this model, people generally will choose foraging over farming because farming requires more time and labor investment and has initially higher marginal costs. These groups, however, might grow small amounts of maize for use in rituals or as a luxury item. Other groups will develop behavioral strategies that have different combinations of foraging and farming, perhaps with greater stress on domesticates compared to wild plant foods. This type of explanation, from the theoretical perspective of human behavioral ecology is just one of many interpretations that might apply to the decisions made by Archaic and later period peoples in the North American Southwest.

The Basketmaker Phases of Ancestral Pueblo

The appearance of Ancestral Pueblo groups in northern Arizona, northwestern New Mexico, southwestern Colorado, and southeastern Utah is linked to descendants of Archaic period groups. These descendants lived during the Basketmaker period, which has two phases, Basketmaker II (500 cal BC to AD 500[11]) and Basketmaker III (AD 500 to AD 750).[12]

BASKETMAKER II

During most of Basketmaker II, people did not use or make pottery but wove baskets as containers. Extraordinary organic materials, such as fur and feather blankets and robes, woven bags, sandals, and string and cord made from cedar bark and yucca, as well as the baskets, have been preserved because of the dry climate.[13] People from the Basketmaker II period had maize agriculture, collected wild pigweed and goosefoot, and hunted deer, bison, elk, and pronghorn antelope using the atlatl and throwing sticks (to hurl darts).[14] Wild turkeys were present in some areas, usually being captured for their feathers rather than as food.[15] Floodwater farming was typical for growing maize, and many Basketmaker II sites are located near streams and washes or other areas with runoff water.[16] Other Basketmaker II groups used dry farming, which depends on rainfall. Storage facilities included slab-lined cists (rectangular "boxes") and bell-shape underground pits. Both the slab-lined cists and the bell-shape pits also were used for burials. Some occupations were in rockshelters, but there are also many pithouses and small villages of pithouses (especially in late Basketmaker II). By AD 200, there is limited use of pottery.[17]

The Basketmaker II period people living at small sites on Cedar Mesa in southeastern Utah had a diet consisting primarily of maize (80 to 90%, based on specialized studies of their bones).[18] Trash associated with these sites contains many fragments of limestone, which may have been used in stone-boiling the maize (stones are heated in a fire and then dropped into a basket with the food and water; the stones heat the water enough to cook the food). This is significant because the use of lime-stone would add lime to food made of maize and make several important nutrients in the maize easier for the body to absorb when eaten. Stone-boiling maize with lime-stone also would have the benefit of helping people avoid a nutritional disease called pellagra, which can result from diets high in maize. Once beans were introduced into the North American Southwest after 590 cal BC, the nutrients in beans compensated for the difficult-to-access nutrients in maize, and use of lime was no longer necessary when cooking maize.

A variety of coiled baskets were made by Basketmaker II period groups.[19] Similarly, sandals across the region were made using cord, bark, and yucca leaf, whereas others were made of twilled, woven tule (bulrush). Distinctions that involve different techniques of making something sometimes are assumed to represent styles or traditions that characterize different groups of people, such as these differences in coiled baskets and sandals.[20]

Basketmaker II burials can include people in multiple or individual burials.[21] One interesting burial site is **Cave 7** in southeastern Utah (see Figure 7.4).[22] It contains 96 individuals, including 39 adult males, 16 adult females, 23 infants and children, and 18 other young individuals who could not be assigned to sex. Of the adult males, 18 suffered violent deaths, which included blows to the head and arrowheads embedded into bones. This pattern is interpreted as evidence for occasional raids between Basketmaker II period groups. There is also evidence for some remarkable Basketmaker II individual burials. One is an adult male with several flutes, a stone pipe, atlatls, shell necklaces, and coils of human hair.[23] Another has a young female with shell bead necklaces, a stone pendant, a string apron, and "the entire head-skin of a 35 to 45 year old male" that was probably attached to her neck with a leather thong. This head-skin had "carefully arranged" hair and a face that "was painted with bands of green, white, red, and yellow pigment."[24] Distinctive individual burials, such as these two, often are assumed to be of individuals with a special status in society. Because both of these individuals are adults, it is likely that their status results from their achievements during life. These suggest that Basketmaker II period societies were characterized by several different social roles, probably including ritual specialists.

Cave 7 a Basketmaker II burial cave site in southeastern Utah. It contains 96 individuals of both sexes and a range of ages, including 18 adult males with signs of violence, suggesting raids between Basketmaker II groups.

BASKETMAKER III

The regional variation in pithouses and artifacts seen during Basketmaker II continues into Basketmaker III and later periods. During Basketmaker III times, the bow and arrow became a common hunting weapon, but the atlatl and throwing spear remained in use. Basketmaker III groups continued to hunt deer, pronghorn antelope, elk, bighorn sheep, and bison and also exploited rabbits.[25] In higher-elevation regions, turkeys may have been domesticated and raised (mainly for their feathers). Although they are called Basketmaker culture, pottery became important during Basketmaker III, with plain greyware jars used for cooking and storage and as water containers. Less common were painted Black-on-Grey and Black-on-White wares;

these tend to be bowls.[26] Making and using pottery vessels (compared to baskets) was an important technological innovation for several reasons. These include the security the vessels provided for storing dried maize and other seeds because mice and other rodents would not be able to chew through pottery like they might storage baskets, and food in a pottery container can be easily cooked directly over a fire.

In addition to maize and squash, which were staples of the diet during the Basketmaker phases, domesticated beans were introduced during Basketmaker III. People became much more reliant on domesticated foods, although they continued to collect wild sunflower, pigweed, goosefoot, and ricegrass. Some settlements were small, consisting of just a pithouse or two, and likely represent one or two families who located their dwellings near where they farmed. These pithouses followed a pattern of occupation for about 10 to 15 years and then often were burned and abandoned, suggesting that deterioration of the wooden posts and roofs of the pithouses made them increasingly unsafe for habitation after this relatively short period of time.[27] Other settlements were more substantial, with several pithouses, as well as one larger pithouse sometimes interpreted as a **great kiva** (a round semisubterranean structure possibly used for communal gatherings and ceremonies). Storage facilities included small antechambers attached to pithouses, exterior storage pits, and the addition of above-ground jacal (pole, stick, and mud construction) storage rooms during later Basketmaker III. The abundance of evidence for storage suggests that Basketmaker III period groups were able to accumulate food surpluses. These could be used for planting maize, beans, and squash the next year, for food during the winter months, and perhaps for ceremonies.

In Chaco Canyon and the surrounding San Juan Basin area, New Mexico, there are more than 1,000 Basketmaker III sites.[28] Most of these are small (1 to 12 pithouses), but there is one large Basketmaker III pithouse community, **Shabik'eschee Village** (Figure 7.6; see Figure 7.4).[29] This site is on the mesa top above the canyon and contains 25 excavated pithouses, one of which is a large structure interpreted as a great kiva, and more than 50 storage bins. There may be as many as 36 additional, unexcavated dwellings. The great kiva is large (95 square meters [1,022 square feet]) and had an interior bench along the wall. Detailed analysis of the Shabik'eschee Village pithouses shows that some were abandoned and burned, whereas others were abandoned and then dismantled, probably so that their beams and stone slabs could be reused for new pithouses.[30] This indicates that not all dwellings were contemporary, and recent estimates suggest that no more than 20 structures were occupied at the same time.[31] Tree-ring (dendrochronology; see Chapter 1) dates show that many structures were built around AD 550 and occupation continued until the early AD 700s (into the Pueblo I period).

The large size of Shabik'eschee Village was previously interpreted as an example of an aggregation site.[32] This idea was based on a model in which a small number of families may have lived at Shabik'eschee Village continuously, but on occasion they were joined by many other families. Evidence that was used to support this idea includes the fact that some pithouses have antechambers used for food storage, which suggests that individual families controlled these resources. The 50 or more storage

Great Kiva a large round pithouse structure used by Ancestral Pueblo groups for communal activities such as ceremonies. They are found first in the late Basketmaker III period and continue into the Pueblo periods, although they may have been used differently over time.

Shabik'eschee Village a Basketmaker III (Ancestral Pueblo) occupation in the Chaco Canyon area, New Mexico, dated to AD 550 to 700. It has 25 excavated pithouses, including a great kiva, and perhaps as many as 36 unexcavated structures. There also are more than 50 storage pits.

FIGURE 7.6
A pithouse at Basketmaker III Shabik'eschee Village (note the slab lining and the central hearth).

bins, however, were highly visible in the areas outside the pithouses and were interpreted as communal stores that belonged to a much larger set of Basketmaker III
period families. These types of storage bins were sealed containers—slab-lined and
plastered on the interior with a roof made of wicker and mud.[33] Sealing the storage
bins was a way to hinder seeds from sprouting, so that maize kernels could be stored
for years until they were needed. During years when wild food resources such as
pinyon nuts were available in large quantities, Basketmaker III period groups could
aggregate at Shabik'eschee Village, allowing them to exchange information about
the distribution of resources in the landscape, arrange marriages, and engage in other
social interactions such as storytelling and rituals. The stored maize was a backup for
years when wild resources were not as abundant.

More recently, researchers have proposed that although Shabik'eschee Village is
somewhat large given the number of pithouses, it represents simply one locale for the
entire community of Basketmaker III period families living within Chaco Canyon.[34]
In this model, Basketmaker III period families were dispersed throughout the entire
canyon area, taking advantage of available land to farm maize, as well as collect pinyon
nuts. They moved from place to place, allowing them to have maize fields in several different locales, which helped protect against crop failure in any one field. At any given
time, there would be some sites and pithouses that were occupied and others that were

vacant. Thus, the number of Basketmaker III sites and the number of pithouses reflect a strategy of shifting people across the landscape to best limit the risks of farming in an arid situation that depended on rainfall for agriculture. Rather than concentrating lots of people at fewer sites, which became typical in later periods of occupation in Chaco Canyon, the Basketmaker III pattern had many people widely distributed.

The Basketmaker III strategy that we see in Chaco Canyon is a pattern seen in several areas of the Ancestral Puebloan region. Outside the Chaco Canyon area, however, there is considerable evidence for violence among Basketmaker III period groups.[35] One suggestion is that this violence was not related to obtaining maize from other groups but instead was tied to access to areas with wild resources.[36] This is because most areas had sufficient land for farming, but locales with abundant wild game and wild foods were far fewer. Basketmaker III period groups living in Chaco Canyon, on the other hand, had lots of floodplain areas for farming and may have relied to a greater extent on maize for food than their contemporaries elsewhere in the region.

Pithouse-to-Pueblo Transition

Although people began to construct above-ground storage rooms (jacal structures) late in the Basketmaker III period, the so-called pithouse-to-pueblo transition, that is, a change from living in semisubterranean pithouses to living in masonry room above-ground dwellings, is one of the defining features of Pueblo I. This period dates from AD 750 to 900 and, during early Pueblo I, is characterized by many small sites that have a few above-ground rooms associated with a pithouse and trash area. Often these above-ground rooms were used for storage, and the pithouse was the main dwelling structure. Although the architecture of these sites differed from that found in Basketmaker III, the Pueblo I settlement system was similar in having mainly small, scattered sites housing a family or two. And, like many of the Basketmaker III sites, those of Pueblo I have evidence for abandonment after 10 to 15 years of use, with the pithouses sometimes burned and other times dismantled for roof beams that could be reused.[37] One example of this process can be seen in a series of three sites from Black Mesa, Arizona, each of which is about 0.5 kilometers (0.3 miles) from the other.[38] Each of these Pueblo I sites had a small number of above-ground rooms (ranging from three to six rooms), a pithouse, and a midden (trash) area (Figure 7.7). The above-ground rooms were for storage, whereas the pithouse was the dwelling. Tree-ring and other dates show that the pithouse at D:11:2023 was built in AD 852 and abandoned when the pithouse (with a burial on the floor) burned in AD 865. Construction of the pithouse at D:11:2025

FIGURE 7.7
The five-room unit at a Pueblo I period site (LA-11–2027) on Black Mesa in northeastern Arizona. The black marks on the slabs in the foreground unit represent burning of a storage room full of maize.

began in AD 861, and the site likely was abandoned in the early AD 870s. Nearby, at D:11:2027, the pithouse was built in AD 873 and the site abandoned in AD 885. It is tempting to think that these three sites represent the same family moving "just down the road" when it came time to abandon their existing settlement, perhaps because of insect infestations and worsening condition of the structures.

Pueblo I period people continued to make and use plain greyware pottery and painted Black-on-White ware vessels. Painted Black-on-Red ware vessels also are known and may have been traded from western to eastern areas within the Ancestral Pueblo region. Turkeys were fully domesticated, although Pueblo I period groups continued to gather wild plant foods and to hunt large and small animals. Reliance on maize, beans, and squash became greater, possibly because greater numbers of people, especially by the late Pueblo I period, began to live in larger settlements. These settlements had numerous adjoining rectangular masonry rooms arranged in blocks. The room blocks were a combination of living, storage, and activity rooms. They usually were associated with a pithouse that was used as a **kiva**, and some sites had several large pithouses that most likely were communal great kivas. These large Pueblo I settlements are known from many areas of the Ancestral Pueblo region; one example is McPhee Village, Colorado (see Figure 7.4).[39]

At **McPhee Village**, there are 20 room blocks and more than 50 pithouses, including two probable great kivas.[40] Most of the room blocks are small units with a double row of rooms made from jacal. There also are two, large U-shape masonry room blocks, which are associated with the two great kivas. The peak occupation of the village dates from AD 860 to 880. The visible differences between the jacal room blocks and the masonry U-shape room blocks suggests that there may have been social differences between the groups who occupied the two types of structures. The families who lived in the U-shape room blocks had more storage rooms and may have controlled larger amounts of privately stored foods and the ceremonies and other activities that occurred in the great kivas associated with these room blocks. Feasting would have helped establish and maintain the social status of the groups living in the U-shape room blocks.[41] The jacal room blocks and associated pithouses likely represent households composed of nuclear families (mom, dad, and the kids) and maybe a few other relatives. The U-shape room block inhabitants, however, are thought to be members of a corporate group, that is, several families who pool their resources and responsibilities, such as extended families (mom, dad, the kids, uncles, aunts, cousins, grandparents).

Architecture and burial assemblages from the **Ridges Basin** in southwestern Colorado (see Figure 7.4) suggest that at least some Pueblo I communities included several groups, each of which had its own social identity.[42] Skeletal studies of people from the Sacred Ridge Cluster and the Eastern Cluster, for example, show that they were different populations. The shapes of the pithouses in these two clusters, in addition to how they were constructed, also differed, indicating distinct cultural traditions. Additional evidence for distinct groups of people within Pueblo I communities is found in southeastern Utah. In this case, at a site in the Alkali Ridge area, distinctive pottery bowls that were not locally made have traces of cacao.[43] Cacao comes from Mesoamerica, where it

Kiva a round pithouse structure used by Ancestral Pueblo families for group activities such as storytelling, weaving, and rituals; see also Great Kiva.

McPhee Village a Pueblo I period (Ancestral Pueblo) settlement in Colorado; it includes above-ground masonry room blocks, linear jacal room blocks, and more than 50 pithouses; there are two great kivas, which are associated with the masonry room blocks.

Ridges Basin a series of spatially close Pueblo I period (Ancestral Pueblo) clusters representing a community in southwestern Colorado. Each cluster had a distinct social identity that can be seen in the types of architecture they built and in how they buried their dead.

was used by elites to make a ritual beverage (see "The Chaco Phenomenon"). Its presence in nonlocal pottery vessels at Alkali Ridge suggests that people had long-distance contacts with Mesoamerica, which makes sense given that maize itself was introduced into the North American Southwest from Mesoamerica/Mexico.

The pithouse-to-pueblo transition that occurred during the Pueblo I period reflects changes in group social structure that led in some cases to the establishment of larger corporate groups who were able to gain increased control over labor, food, and ritual and ceremony. Despite this apparent greater political influence, however, it did not extend beyond individual settlements, and most sites during Pueblo I times were small communities. In the Chaco Canyon region of New Mexico, however, the pithouse-to-pueblo transition led to an unusual and unique settlement system and social organization sometimes called the **Chaco Phenomenon**.[44]

Chaco Phenomenon an unusual set of archaeological features found in the Chaco Canyon region of New Mexico from AD 900 to 1220 (Bonito phase). It includes a population of 2,000 to 3,000 in this marginal agricultural area, great houses and small settlements, Chaocan roads, Chacoan outliers, trade with other regions of the North American Southwest and Mesoamerica, and the possible presence of elites at the great houses.

The Chaco Phenomenon

Between AD 900 and 1220 (all of Pueblo II and much of Pueblo III), numerous small settlements, the building of several multiple-room above-ground masonry structures, trade and exchange, a road system, and other aspects of life in Chaco Canyon, as well as Chacoan outliers, present a striking contrast to much of the Ancestral Pueblo in other parts of the region. This period is known locally as the Bonito Phase. Chaco Canyon today is relatively inhospitable, characterized by great dryness and little water for agriculture. As we saw earlier (Basketmaker III Shabik'eschee Village), however, Chaco Canyon had resources such as pine nuts from pinyon trees and accessible water during the past. Some of these resources were also available during the Bonito Phase, with exceptions such as the pinyon–juniper forest, which over time may have disappeared as a result of cutting for fuel.[45] The more favorable conditions during the past meant that it was possible to support large numbers of people (perhaps 2,000 to 3,000 at its peak) in Chaco Canyon and its immediately surrounding areas.[46]

People in Chaco Canyon grew maize, beans, and squash and hunted deer and rabbits. During the Bonito Phase, they developed several ways of capturing rainfall for growing crops. These included check dams, which were straight lines of rock across small water channels. When it rained, water coming down the channel was partially blocked by the rocks, allowing sediment to accumulate behind the rocks; these sediments retained moisture and were good places to plant. Chacoan people also captured rainfall coming off the mesa tops in more elaborate ways. These included the construction of dams (one is 36 meters [120 feet] long and 2 meters [7 feet] high), from which water was channeled into stone-lined canals that led to head gates where the water could be directed into ditches into gridded gardens/fields.[47] Like earlier Basketmaker III groups, many of the areas farmed were on the floodplains of the washes (intermittent streams). A recent study of the distribution of land that could be farmed based on soil conditions and water flow suggests that people living in Chaco Canyon may have had small farming plots in areas away from the floodplains.[48] Other studies indicate that, at least on some occasions, maize grown elsewhere in the San Juan Basin was imported into Chaco Canyon, perhaps to feed labor forces building some of the large structures there.[49] Because many of the largest roomblock communities were built on the floodplain below the cliffs, it also was necessary for people to construct channels to divert flood waters away from these settlements.[50]

Although there are many small roomblock sites in Chaco Canyon, during the Bonito Phase it is widely known for its "**great houses**." These are large, multiple-room blocks with several stories of rooms; there are 12 great houses in the canyon or just above on the mesa top—among them are Pueblo Bonito, Chetro Ketl, Pueblo Peñasco, Pueblo Alto, Una Vida, Kin Kletso, and Casa Chiquita (Figure 7.8). The great houses began as smaller roomblocks during the late AD 800s (late Pueblo I) with additions through the late AD 900s (Pueblo II). After a brief period with no new construction, the great houses witnessed renewed additions from AD 1020 to 1150, reaching their largest sizes. Of all the great houses, **Pueblo Bonito** is the largest and most unusual. At its peak, it had more than 350 ground-floor rooms (perhaps 650 to 700 rooms when the

Great House a large multistory building, this term is used for several of the prehistoric cultural areas in the North American Southwest. For the Ancestral Pueblo (Pueblo II times and later), it describes multiple roomblocks often built of stone, such as Pueblo Bonito in Chaco Canyon, New Mexico. In the Hohokam region, great houses were built during the Classic period and were multistory adobe structures located within compounds. Great houses also were built by Mogollon peoples.

Pueblo Bonito an Ancestral Pueblo D-shape great house in Chaco Canyon, New Mexico, that was built over the period from the late AD 800s to 1150. It had more than 350 ground-floor rooms (perhaps as many as 700 rooms total with rooms from the upper stories), 32 kivas, and 3 great kivas.

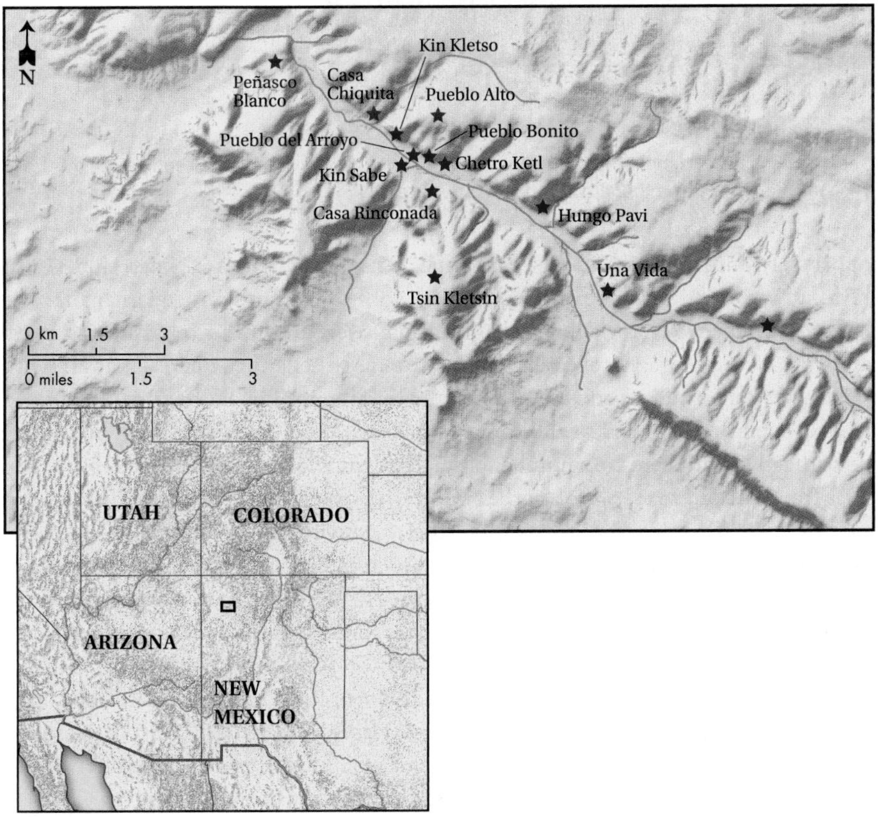

FIGURE 7.8
Great houses and Casa Rinconada in Chaco Canyon.

FIGURE 7.9

The great house at Pueblo Bonito: site overview from the canyon floor (*lower*) and part of the D-shape site from above (*upper*); round structures are kivas.

upper stories are included) for living, storage, and other activities, 32 kivas, and 3 great kivas. It was built in a D shape[51] (Figure 7.9), with the rooms arranged in an arc. The back row reached four stories in height. The rooms were arranged around an open plaza area with kivas. A straight row of single-story rooms closed the two ends of the arc, with the plaza area between it and the arc of multistory rooms. Pueblo Bonito was situated in what some archaeologists call "downtown Chaco" because several great houses are close together and there are a number of smaller roomblocks as well as roads.

The Chacoan roads were another impressive aspect of the Chaco Phenomenon (Figure 7.10). They were built straight (rather than with curves and bends), included stairways cut into rock to overcome obstacles such as cliffs, and linked places in Chaco Canyon together as well as leading in some cases to more distant areas, some of which had Chacoan outliers (see later) or contained resources that the people living in Chaco Canyon needed, such as timber for construction. There are 600 kilometers (373 miles) of known Chacoan roads, including the Great North Road and the South Road, with more segments recently discovered using LiDAR (see Chapter 1).[52] Most of the roads, however, are only a few kilometers long and link smaller settlements to great kivas and to great houses, rather than connecting Chaco Canyon and the majority of the Chacoan outliers. The road system thus was not a regional network that integrated the entire area but seems to be related to bringing people at the smaller communities to activities and ceremonies at great houses and great kivas.

About 200 **Chacoan outliers** were built outside of the Chaco Canyon area proper during the Bonito phase, and interestingly these rarely are found to the east of the canyon (see Figure 7.10). These communities had a great house and a great kiva and were surrounded by smaller roomblock settlements. One of the reasons that they are called Chacoan outliers is that their great houses were built in a way that resembles the great houses in Chaco Canyon. This included a multistory, multiple-room block that had a planned design, blocked-in kivas, enclosed plazas, walls that were core and veneer (large pieces of rock in mud mortar with a facing of nicely shaped masonry on the front and back of the wall), and banded masonry (the veneer has rows of nicely shaped rock).[53] Some of the Chacoan outliers, such as Kin Bineola, are close to Chaco Canyon, whereas others, such as Far View House in Colorado and the Bluff Great House in Utah, are 150 to 200 kilometers (90 to 125 miles) away (Figure 7.11). It is important to recognize that the similarities between Chacoan outliers and the great houses in Chaco Canyon do not necessarily mean that people in Chaco Canyon politically or socially controlled these outlying regions. Many archaeologists have pointed out that there is a great amount of diversity in construction and other features of the Chacoan outlier communities, suggesting that they may have borrowed some ideas from Chaco Canyon but were largely independent. There is, however, evidence to suggest that Chacoan people did occasionally migrate to other communities in the region.[54]

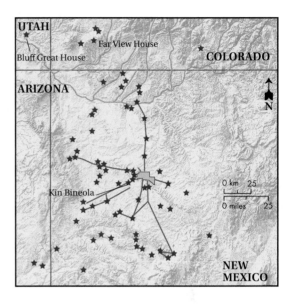

FIGURE 7.10
Major Chacoan roads (brown lines) and many of the Chacoan outliers.

Chacoan Outlier an Ancestral Pueblo community in the region outside of Chaco Canyon (New Mexico) that dates to the Pueblo II and III periods; it includes a great house built in a similar way to the great houses of Chaco Canyon, a great kiva, and several surrounding small roomblock settlements.

FIGURE 7.11
The Chacoan outlier at Kin Bineola.

Resource Networks, Trade, and Exchange

Many resources were brought into Chaco Canyon, some by Chacoan task groups but others through trade and exchange. One of the most obvious resources that Chacoan people needed was wood for posts and beams when building the great houses and great kivas and the smaller roomblock settlements. The high-quality wood (mainly ponderosa pine, but also spruce and fir) needed for construction of the great houses was not available locally; more than 240,000 imported logs were used. Prior to AD 1020, this timber came from the Zuni Mountains to the southwest of Chaco Canyon. During the heyday of great house construction after AD 1020, the main timber source area shifted to the Chuska Mountains to the west. Both source areas are 75 or more kilometers (47 miles) away.[55]

Task groups also brought pottery and special types of stone for making stone artifacts into Chaco Canyon during the Bonito phase. With several thousand people living there, wood for fuel to fire pottery would have been in high demand.[56] Trying to locally produce enough pottery for everyone living in Chaco Canyon may have been difficult. In fact, examination of pottery from great house sites in the canyon indicates that perhaps as much as 50% of Black-on-White wares and 90% of plain greywares were made outside the canyon and transported in by task groups coming from the Chuska Mountains.[57] Additionally, brown wares (from the Mogollon region) and red wares (from other parts of the Ancestral Pueblo region) were traded into the canyon.

A type of pink-to-orange translucent chert from the Narbona Pass in the Chuska Mountains to the west also was brought into Chaco Canyon. During the Bonito phase, it was 20% of the stone raw material.[58] One of the intriguing aspects of the presence of Narbona Pass chert is that although it was carried 75 kilometers (47 miles) from the mountains to the canyon, Chacoan people rarely made tools from it, and it was not found in special contexts that would suggest that it had value as status material (although it is more frequently found at the great houses than in the smaller settlements). This chert is eye-catching because of its color and transparency, and perhaps it was collected while people were in the Chuska Mountains engaged in felling trees to make posts and beams. Another type of stone brought into the canyon was obsidian, which can be identified to its source locale.[59] These studies show that during the Bonito Phase the majority of obsidian came from the Jemez Mountains in New Mexico, 100 kilometers (62 miles) east of the canyon.

Turquoise, as beads and pendants, characterized Chaco Canyon as early as Basketmaker III, but it was during the Bonito phase that turquoise was most abundant.[60] The closest turquoise source was at the prehistoric Cerillos Mines, New Mexico, 200 kilometers (125 miles) to the east of Chaco Canyon. It is not clear whether Chacoan task groups went to the mines to extract turquoise and bring it back or whether turquoise was traded into the canyon. Some turquoise in Chaco Canyon, however, was traded in from sources in southern New Mexico, Colorado, and Nevada, over distances of 300 to 500 kilometers (286 to 310 miles).[61] During the Bonito phase, there were several turquoise workshops at smaller settlements and several of the great houses (including Pueblo Bonito), suggesting part-time craft work by individuals.

Jewelry production does not appear to have been controlled by elite leaders, but turquoise was found in special contexts such as offerings made during the construction of kivas and great kivas, as well as in burials at great houses (see "Social Life").

Several other types of exotic materials arrived in Chaco Canyon through trading networks.[62] These include shell for jewelry from the Gulf of California 800 kilometers (500 miles) away, from the Pacific 900 kilometers (560 miles) distant, and from the Gulf of Mexico 1,300 kilometers (800 miles) away. There also were macaws, which were kept at Pueblo Bonito for their feathers, from northern Mexico and farther south (more than 700 kilometers [435 miles]) and copper bells from northern Mexico.[63] These goods had to be hand-carried as people traded them from settlement to settlement. Evidence also was found for the use of cacao beans in making a chocolate drink at Pueblo Bonito. Cacao beans are from central Mexico and further south into Mesoamerica, more than 2,000 kilometers (1,240 miles) away, and the use of a chocolate beverage suggests the influence of Mesoamerican rituals[64] (read "Peopling the Past: Chaco Canyon and Mesoamerican Connections"). Unusual exotic materials such as the copper bells and macaws or the cacao might represent trade goods and also objects that carried special meaning related to prestige and power. These could have been used by elite members of society to solidify their importance.

Social Life

At its height during the Bonito Phase, Chaco Canyon was a vibrant set of linked communities, with many people living in the small roomblock settlements scattered throughout the canyon and just above on the mesa tops. Fewer people lived in the great houses, despite the large number of rooms in these multistory buildings. Does this mean that the people at the great houses were elite social or political leaders who controlled economic, social, and ritual activities in Chaco Canyon, as well as at the 200 Chacoan outlier sites, some of which were hundreds of kilometers away? This question has been the focus of decades of research on the Chaco Phenomenon, and the resulting interpretations have varied greatly depending on the archaeological information available, the theoretical viewpoints applied to this information, and the more recent efforts to build interpretations that include the oral traditions and social and ritual activities as practiced by living Native American groups who are descended from the prehistoric people of Chaco Canyon (and other Ancestral Pueblo areas). Most researchers today agree that there are differences between the people who lived in the small settlements and those in the great houses in Chaco Canyon and that social organization for the scheduling of various tasks and rituals was necessary. The control over people and activities in the canyon has been debated, with some researchers suggesting that this control was not exerted by elite political leaders but rather was a power shared across many groups, with special roles given to ritual specialists for various ceremonies.[72] This perspective means that Chaco Canyon did not politically control the Chacoan outlier settlements.[73]

Previous analyses of design motifs on pottery suggested that the cylinder jars, pitchers, and bowls found at Pueblo Bonito were vessels associated with elites and

Chaco Canyon and Mesoamerican Connections

Copper bells, macaws, and certain design motifs, such as feathered serpents, in sites in Chaco Canyon have long suggested at least sporadic contacts with Mesoamerica.[65] It is the recent discovery of cacao residues in pottery vessels in the North American Southwest, however, that suggests that these contacts were long term and more intensive.[66] The cacao bean grows in the tropical areas of Mesoamerica and was widely used there by the Maya in the preparation of a chocolate beverage (see Chapter 13).[67] Initial work at Pueblo Bonito indicated that cacao residues were present in pottery vessels called cylinder jars and pitchers, while later research showed that seed jars (a pottery shape), gourd jars (a pottery shape), and mugs also were used (Figure 7.12).[68] More than 160 cylinder jars were found at Pueblo Bonito, representing about 80% of all known cylinder jars. Of these, 112 were found in one room, suggesting ritual activities associated with elite members of society who likely belonged to the same social unit. This room was deliberately burned around AD 1100, destroying the cylinder jars.[69] After this, mugs replaced both cylinder jars and pitchers as the main drinking vessel.

Additional studies have been undertaken for cylinder jars, pitchers, and bowls from elite burials at Pueblo Bonito and beakers, bowls, and mugs from elite contexts in the Hokokam area (southern Arizona). To these were added the examination of pitchers and bowls from ordinary living sites. Cacao residues were found in the majority of the elite-associated vessels but also in all of the pitchers

FIGURE 7.12
Ceramic pitchers from a room in Pueblo Bonito at Chaco Canyon; these were used for the chocolate beverage made from cacao.

and bowls used at small sites. This suggests that the ritual of making and drinking the Mesoamerican chocolate beverage was widespread in the North American Southwest.[70] It was not confined just to elites but was an activity important to commoners as well. Recent studies of residues in ceramic vessels at Pueblo Bonito and other North American Southwest sites show that people also consumed a frothed beverage made from holly (which is high in caffeine), especially in the period before AD 1200.[71] Holly could have been brought in from the coastal areas of the Gulf of Mexico (for example, Texas) or from Mesoamerica.

The consumption of the cacao and holly beverages represents trading links to Mesoamerica (and possibly to other regions) and the incorporation of aspects of Mesoamerican rituals that could be modified to fit within the Ancestral Puebloan worldview. Given that the ingredients for such beverages were not locally available, these drinks most likely were consumed only on special occasions, such as during rituals or other ceremonies.

with nonlocal peoples who moved into the canyon.[74] These same designs are found on pottery at other great houses in Chaco Canyon, as well as at Chacoan outliers and some of the small sites in the region. Isotope studies of the bones of elite individuals buried at Pueblo Bonito, however, show that they were born and grew up in Chaco Canyon or nearby. Thus, the elites (at least at Pueblo Bonito) were local products, not migrants from elsewhere (read "Further Reflections: Elite Lineage at Pueblo Bonito").

Some of the daily tasks were done by individual households, but others required coordination, for example, building and maintaining the agricultural features that captured rainfall runoff and diverted it into fields and gardens and obtaining wood for construction from the Chuska Mountains. Evidence from tree rings of the wood used in the great houses shows that most of it was harvested during the late spring and early summer each year for a few years, with the wood stored in the canyon until construction began.[75] This means that task groups from Chaco Canyon went out to the Chuska Mountains to cut trees and to prepare the wood (removing the bark and limbs and cutting it into shorter pieces) prior to bringing it back. The size of these groups did not have to be large because the work was spread out over several years. With these wood task groups away from Chaco Canyon during the time when it was necessary to prepare fields and plant them, however, other people organized as agricultural task groups would have taken on the extra work. Some researchers suggest that the wood task groups were male, whereas much of the early planting and field preparation was done by women (read "Peopling the Past: The Roles of Men and Women in Chaco Canyon").

Several types of bioarchaeological studies indicate that people who lived in the great houses had better access to food and to nonlocal resources. One measure of this is that the inhabitants of Pueblo Bonito were taller than people in the smaller settlements.[80] Taller stature is a good indicator of more and better access to food, especially high-quality food such as meat. The great houses also contain the largest quantities of exotic materials (turquoise, shell, macaws, and other items from Mexico and Mesoamerica). Additionally, there are great house burials with large quantities of grave goods, especially from Pueblo Bonito.[81] In the western part of Pueblo Bonito is a room that yielded four burials; two are female and two male. The women had textiles, feather robes, and reed mats, whereas one male had numerous stone arrowheads, arrow shafts, and a nonlocal pottery bowl (called Red Mesa), and the other male had a Red Mesa bowl, numerous shell ornaments, and a Black-on-White pitcher. In the central part of Pueblo Bonito another room has two more male burials in the lowest levels of the crypt, both with thousands of pieces of turquoise, abundant shell ornaments, and thousands of stone artifacts (read "Further Reflections: Elite Lineage at Pueblo Bonito"). Both male skeletons show evidence for violence (see later). There are also burials from the smaller settlements, some of which contain a few pieces of turquoise, indicating that access to exotic materials was not strictly limited to people living in the great houses. Although some burials indicate great investment in grave goods, researchers do not necessarily interpret

Peopling the Past

The Roles of Men and Women in Chaco Canyon

The types of tasks and activities that characterize human societies often are culturally assigned to various groups of people, with one of the most common divisions being the so-called sexual division of labor. The types of tasks that women undertake as opposed to men, of course, can vary from one society to another, and these divisions of labor are not always strictly just the work of females versus males. One activity commonly associated with women is grinding of plant foods. In the North American Southwest, this is based on ethnographic observations that women, often working in groups, were responsible for this task,[76] although we cannot necessarily assume that activity patterns we see in the present are identical to those of the past. Archaeologically, the presence of several grinding bins in the same room or area at a site suggests the presence of grinding work groups (Figure 7.13). During the Bonito phase at Chaco Canyon, sets of grinding bins were found in rooms at small village sites, as well as in rooms at the great houses. Grinding bins also were found on the roofs of kivas, in rooms next to kivas, and occasionally in kivas themselves. This suggests that grinding of maize had economic importance to Chacoan society and elements of ritual significance.[77] Maize grinding in kiva-associated contexts may have been related to the preparation of ritual meals. Social roles for females and males also can sometimes be seen in the types of grave goods buried with them; for example, males might have more ritual grave goods, whereas females have personal ornamentation[78] (see also the discussion of elites at Pueblo Bonito). One interesting observation is that males are buried with turquoise that is bluer in color, while women have a greener shade of turquoise.[79]

FIGURE 7.13
Grinding bins at an Ancestral Pueblo site (Betatakin) in Arizona.

these individuals as all-powerful political leaders buried with prestige items but rather as individuals whose roles in society led to their burial with items that symbolized those roles, some of which may have been as ritual specialists.[82]

Kivas, great kivas, and certain rooms in the great houses were associated with ritual ceremonies. These places, and the trash mounds associated with them, contain evidence for ritual discard of nonlocal materials and for feasting, as well as the preparation and drinking of a chocolate beverage (read "Peopling the Past: Chaco Canyon and Mesoamerican Connections"). One feasting example comes from the trash mound at the **Pueblo Alto** great house (see Figure 7.8).[83] The large numbers of pottery sherds from this trash mound were used to estimate how many complete vessels were broken and discarded here, an estimate of more than 150,000 vessels. Combined with the 20 household groups who lived at Pueblo Alto over 60 years, this would mean nearly 2,500 pottery vessels broken each year, a figure that is said to be far greater than what is reasonable given the small number of households. Researchers interpreted this pattern as evidence that many groups of people from across Chaco Canyon, and perhaps from other great house communities and their surrounding smaller settlements outside of Chaco Canyon, came together from time to time to participate in feasts where food and other resources were shared. Other evidence for feasting at Pueblo Alto includes abundant bones of deer and huge quantities of bones of hare and rabbit, which suggest communal hunting and the preparation of stews as feasting food, in addition to deer and maize. Other archaeologists, however, interpret the data from Pueblo Alto differently.[84] They suggest that it represents the ordinary activities of households at Pueblo Alto, as well as small feasts held just for the people living at this great house. They also note that the numbers of pottery sherds at Pueblo Alto fall within the numbers of sherds found at smaller sites and at other great houses.

Pueblo Alto an Ancestral Pueblo great house in Chaco Canyon, New Mexico, that has evidence in its trash mounds for community feasts during the Bonito Phase.

Warfare and Violence

There is evidence for violence in the Ancestral Pueblo region, especially in southwestern Colorado (Mesa Verde region).[85] The Bonito Phase in Chaco Canyon has fewer indications of violence.[86] Among the small number of examples are the two lavish male burials from the room in the central portion of Pueblo Bonito (see previous discussion).[87] Both of these individuals have head wounds, and one has cut marks on his upper leg bone. Additionally, the adult male burial from the Chetro Ketl great house has an arrowhead in his ribs.[88] Although males from Pueblo Bonito appear to have more trauma indicating violence than do females, at a nearby Chacoan outlier (Kin Bineola) many females have serious head traumas. While these individuals show signs of violent deaths, the sites in Chaco Canyon do not have fortifications or other indicators of the need for defense against other people.

The Late Bonito Phase in Chaco Canyon

Between AD 1100 and 1130 (late Pueblo II), six new great houses were added in Chaco Canyon.[89] Each of these was about 30 rooms in a block that enclosed one or more kivas. Unlike the Classic Bonito phase great houses, however, those built during the Late Bonito phase did not have enclosed plazas or associated trash mounds. People also modified some of the existing great houses, such as Pueblo Bonito, Pueblo Alto, and Chetro Ketl. Construction on the great houses in Chaco Canyon ended after AD 1130, just before the beginning of Pueblo III. Some people, however, continued to live in and use the rooms and kivas of these great houses until at least AD 1220. The lack of new additions may be related to worsening environmental conditions during which there was less rainfall to support agriculture (especially AD 1143 to 1154), thus influencing how people organized their activities.[90]

One major feature in Chaco Canyon, however, was built during this period, **Casa Rinconada** (see Figure 7.8), a great kiva measuring 19 meters (63 feet) in interior diameter, which dates to AD 1140 to 1200.[91] It has several rooms attached to it, but was not part of one of the great houses at Chaco Canyon. Instead, it is surrounded by several small roomblock settlements with kivas. Casa Rinconada has an interior bench, 2 large masonry pits that were foot drums, 34 wall niches above the bench, 4 large pits to hold posts to support roof beams, and an underground passage that leads from one set of attached rooms into the main kiva room (Figure 7.14). It is easy to imagine that during certain ceremonies this underground passage could have been used for a dramatic appearance of participants in the ceremony. The size of Casa Rinconada and its special construction features suggest that it was used as a communal structure for several smaller settlements and perhaps for everyone remaining in Chaco Canyon during the late Bonito Phase.

Casa Rinconada a great kiva built in Chaco Canyon (New Mexico) in the North American Southwest during the late Bonito phase (beginning of the Pueblo III period).

FIGURE 7.14
Underground passage leading to the spiral on the floor of the great kiva at Casa Rinconada, Chaco Canyon.

Ancestral Pueblo After the Chaco Phenomenon

The decline of the Chaco Phenomenon began about AD 1130, with the end of great house construction and the migration of people away from Chaco Canyon. As we saw above, some people continued to live here, mainly at the smaller settlements, but also occasionally using the great houses until AD 1220. The network of social integration and interactions, however, shifted away from the Chaco Canyon area to other settlements such as Aztec Ruins in New Mexico and Casas Grandes (see later) in northern Mexico.

At about the time (AD 1130) that people in Chaco Canyon stopped building and adding to the great houses there, the Ancestral Pueblo settlements called **Aztec Ruins** became an important Pueblo III center. Aztec Ruins is near the Animas River, 88 kilometers (55 miles) north of Chaco Canyon, and linked to Chaco by the Great North Road.[92] There are many great houses at Aztec Ruins, similar to the multiple great houses at Chaco Canyon, and Black-on-White pottery with styles from Aztec Ruins has been found throughout much of the northern Ancestral Pueblo region, indicating the widespread influence and exchange network of the people living there from AD 1130 to 1275. Some archaeologists, in fact, have suggested that the people at Aztec Ruins were groups who migrated north from Chaco Canyon when its great houses were largely abandoned.

Aztec Ruins an Ancestral Pueblo region in northern New Mexico with many great houses. It became an important center during the late Pueblo III period, after the abandonment of most of Chaco Canyon.

FIGURE 7.15
A keyhole kiva from a site (LA 17360) near Chaco Canyon in the AD 1200s. Note the painted bench with a light band on top of a dark band of color.

Oral Traditions and Archaeology in the North American Southwest

One of the enduring figures in Hopi oral traditions is kokopele, the so-called hunchbacked, or pack-carrying, flute player.[93] Kokopele is one of the Hopi kachina gods and is associated with fertility. Tales about kokopele discuss him handing out seeds to men, being sexually active with many young women, and using a cane (the so-called flute) to pull things to him such as young women. The antiquity of the kokopele motif is documented in the archaeological record because it is an image seen widely in rock art in the North American Southwest, as well as on some Hohokam painted pottery. At a small Ancestral Pueblo site I excavated near Chaco Canyon in New Mexico in the early 1980s, for example, we uncovered a Mesa Verde style keyhole-shape kiva that had a bench with two painted bands (see also Chapter 1). The upper band is a light color and has several different motifs. One set of these images is shown in Figure 7.16 (see also Figure 7.15). They date to the AD 1200s and are similar in design to modern kokopele figures. This may suggest that the stories told today are those known for many generations into the more remote past, with the oral traditions of living peoples providing valuable knowledge.

FIGURE 7.16
Probable kokopele figures painted on a kiva bench from a site (LA 17360) near Chaco Canyon in the AD 1200s.

Back in Chaco Canyon, the period between AD 1220 and 1300 is called the Mesa Verde Phase (late Pueblo III) because the Black-on-White decorated pottery has styles known from the Mesa Verde region of Colorado and the construction of pithouses at new small settlements in the Chaco Canyon area included keyhole-shape kivas, a design feature known from the Mesa Verde region (Figure 7.15; read "Peopling the Past: Oral Traditions and Archaeology in the American Southwest"). These types of evidence suggest that some Mesa Verde region people migrated into Chaco Canyon, where they lived for a brief period in the mid-AD 1200s.

Both Aztec Ruins and Chaco Canyon were abandoned just before and during the so-called Great Drought (AD 1276 to 1299),[94] as were many Ancestral Pueblo regions. The impact of the drought is understandable in Chaco Canyon because people living in this marginal habitat were no longer able to engage in rainfall-based farming. Aztec Ruins, on the other hand, was abandoned before the Great Drought, suggesting that other factors were at work, including the disintegration of the social bonds that had integrated people in the great houses and smaller communities there.[95] All of these groups migrated to other communities elsewhere in the North American Southwest.

Pueblo IV and Later

From AD 1300 onward, individual communities became quite large, with most people living in large roomblocks rather than in smaller settlements in areas surrounding these communities. The Pueblo IV and later pueblos had sizable plazas, rectangular kivas, and hundreds of rooms; many were multistory. One example of these communities is **Casas Grandes** (also called Paquimé) in northern Mexico, which had more than 1,100 rooms and a population of 2,500 people.[96] This settlement included a large roomblock, some portions of which were three stories, an area of ceremonial architecture (with a Mexican-style ball court and platform mounds), and many dispersed one-room structures surrounding the main roomblock. Casas Grandes is linked partly to the North American Southwest through trade and exchange because excavations there yielded evidence for scarlet macaws, shell, and copper that arrived from further south and then were traded into areas such as the Ancestral Pueblo.

Casas Grandes a large Pueblo IV settlement (also called Paquimé) in northern Mexico. It contains evidence for trade and exchange into the Ancestral Pueblo, Mogollon, and other North American Southwest regions.

The aggregation of people into large communities during Pueblo IV is the pattern seen by the Spanish when they arrived in the AD 1540s. It continues to be the architectural structure of Native American communities such as Hopi, Zuñi, Acoma, and the Rio Grande pueblos, whose traditional knowledge provides invaluable insights into earlier Ancestral Pueblo lifeways.

Hohokam and Mogollon: Contemporaries of the Ancestral Pueblo

Although the main focus of this chapter is on the Ancestral Pueblo, they were just one of several contemporary groups of peoples. Archaeological evidence indicates that there were extensive contacts between the various regions of the North American

Southwest during this period. A brief summary of two of these contemporary groups, the Hohokam of southern Arizona and the Mogollon of southwestern/central New Mexico and southeastern/central Arizona, is given here.

Hohokam

The Hohokam region stretches east from the Granite Mountains in central southwestern Arizona to the Tucson area, south to at least the border with Mexico, and north to the Phoenix area (see Figure 7.1). It encompasses a wide range of landscapes including basin and range, desert, foothills, and mountains, as well as the Gila, Salt, and Santa Cruz Rivers. These provided a wide variety of wild food resources, of which Archaic period groups made extensive use. Maize was introduced into the Hohokam region from Mesoamerica and incorporated into lifeways that included intensive use of wild amaranth, tansy mustard, agave, fruits from the saguaro cactus, and mesquite beans[97] (see Santa Cruz Bend site, discussed previously). The appearance of maize marks the beginning of the Early Agricultural Period (read "Timeline: North American Southwest"). Eventually, beans from Mesoamerica were added to the crops grown. A nonfood resource, cotton, used for making textiles, also became an important agricultural plant. Permanent villages became common in southern Arizona (Tucson Basin) at about the same time or slightly earlier than the appearance of maize in subsistence economies. Unlike the Ancestral Pueblo who built above-ground roomblocks, the Hohokam lived in single-structure dwellings dug slightly into the ground. These were grouped around open areas and people living in these groups appear to have shared cemeteries, ovens for cooking, and trash disposal locales.[98] Some archaeologists describe the Hohokam region as consisting of a core area (the Phoenix Basin) and peripheral regions (for example, the Tucson Basin and the Papagueria of southwestern Arizona). Archaeological sites, however, document that the early development of the Hohokam pattern was in the so-called peripheral areas rather than the supposed core.

Just as the Chaco Canyon area is well known for its road system and outliers, the Hohokam are identified with the construction of canal systems for irrigation agriculture (Figure 7.17). In fact, the Hohokam were the only prehistoric people in North America to construct canals on such a large scale. In the Phoenix Basin, for example, there are hundreds of kilometers of canals known from foot and aerial surveys.[99] Many of these were as much as 20 to 30 kilometers (12 to 18 miles) long, very deep, and required constant upkeep to remove accumulations of sediment deposited as water flowed through them. The extent to which people needed to be organized as labor forces to construct and maintain the canals, as well as other Hohokam building projects (see later), is one factor that has sometimes been used to argue for political and social control by Hohokam elites.[100]

Over a period of several centuries during the Pioneer, Colonial, and Sedentary periods, the Hohokam intensified and expanded their settlement and canal systems.[101] Several communities were associated with each major canal system and were situated at different points along the canal. The Hohokam used a mix of domesticated

FIGURE 7.17
A canal in the Hohokam Park of the Canals, Phoenix, Arizona.

plant foods and cactus fruits, seed grasses, and agave, in addition to hunting animals, fishing, and collecting freshwater shellfish.[102] Like the Ancestral Pueblo groups, the Hohokam were engaged in long-distance contacts that reflect journeys by Hohokam people to distant places to collect resources (marine shell from the Gulf of California) and trade with Mesoamerica and other parts of the North American Southwest.[103] Trade within the Southwest may be reflected by the movement of turquoise and obsidian, as well as artifacts made from marine shells.[104] Items entering the Hohokam area from Mesoamerica included copper bells, macaws, and pyrite mirrors, as well as the idea for the architectural structure called a ball court.

One Hohokam site with evidence for many of these features is **Snaketown** on the Gila River southeast of Phoenix (see Figure 7.4). Snaketown was occupied during the Pioneer, Colonial, and Sedentary periods.[105] More than 180 individual Hohokam pit structures (dwellings) were excavated. In addition to archaeological evidence for everyday life, such as pottery, stone artifacts, animal bones, ground stone tools, and irrigation canals, Snaketown yielded evidence for craft production. This includes the manufacture of marine shell ornaments (bracelets, rings, pendants, and etched shell). Evidence for shell ornament production was found in many houses and burials, suggesting that families or kin groups rather than full-time specialists were responsible.[106] Other items include clay human and animal figurines and stone palettes (some carved in the shape of animals), which might have been used to hold pigments or other substances. Snaketown is especially known for the two ball courts that were built and used during the Colonial and Sedentary periods. These were oval-shaped, large structures with an excavated depression that was lined on two sides

Snaketown a large Hohokam settlement in central Arizona near Phoenix. Snaketown had numerous individual pit structures occupied by families. It also had two ball courts, which are an architectural form likely introduced from Mesoamerica. Snaketown was occupied during the Pioneer, Colonial, and Sedentary periods and largely abandoned by AD 1150.

with earthen banks. Ball courts were found at numerous Hohokam sites during the Colonial and Sedentary periods and often are interpreted as arenas where a Meso-american ball game was played (there are similar structures known in Mesoamerica). One intriguing alternative interpretation is that the so-called ball courts could have been used for ceremonial rituals and dancing.[107]

It is the Classic period, between AD 1150 and 1450, however, that might be most equivalent to the Bonito Phase at Chaco Canyon. The archaeology of the Classic period is very different from that of earlier Hohokam periods.[108] Ball courts disappeared, and the construction of platform mounds (first seen on a small scale during the Sedentary period) became important. These platform mounds were large and rectangular in shape, and they likely were used for rituals and as residential space. Walls were built around them and associated structures, and burials were found within the platform mounds. The walls restricted access to the platform mounds and suggest the existence of elite social groups.[109] Other walled areas with dwellings do not have platform mounds within them, perhaps indicating nonelite groups. By the Late Classic period, some communities also had great houses built of adobe that stood a few stories high. One of the best preserved remaining great houses is **Casa Grande**, south of Phoenix (Figure 7.18; see Figure 7.4). Within the walled compound that encloses Casa Grande are several rectangular room blocks of adobe, as well as open plaza areas. Distinctions between people are apparent from where they are buried and perhaps the grave goods associated with them. Burials in platform mound compounds, for example, usually are interpreted as representing high-status individuals.[110] There is still considerable debate about the extent to which these elite members of society held influence. Some researchers argue that Hohokam Classic period elites wielded far-reaching political power, whereas other scholars suggest that elite power was restricted to their communities or perhaps just a few communities along a given canal system.[111]

After AD 1450, the archaeological signature that characterized the Hohokam region largely disappears. Their canal systems and communities were mostly abandoned. This does not mean that the Hohokam themselves disappeared. More likely, they dispersed across the region and engaged in activities and built settlements that left traces that do not mirror the Classic period occupation of this area. Their descendants most likely include the Tohono O'odham and Pima peoples.

Casa Grande a Classic period Hohokam site in Arizona. It has a great house, residential compounds, and platform mounds.

Mogollon

The archaeological record of the Mogollon is found in west-central and southwest New Mexico, southeast and mountainous central Arizona, and parts of northern Mexico (see Figure 7.1). Like both the Ancestral Pueblo and the Hohokam, the Mogollon region encompasses many different types of habitats ranging from mountains to desert, although a number of researchers characterize the Mogollon as mainly a mountain-living people. Mogollon groups adopted maize into Archaic period hunting–gathering–foraging lifestyles, with agriculture eventually becoming important as part of their subsistence system. As noted by a number of researchers, the term Mogollon has not always been accepted as a distinct cultural grouping.[112] In part, this reflects how

FIGURE 7.18
The Classic period Hohokam great house at Casa Grande, Arizona.

material culture and architecture are interpreted, with some scholars suggesting that later Mogollon developments were heavily influenced by regions such as the Ancestral Pueblo. In this chapter we use the term Mogollon to reflect a set of cultural traditions that are largely separate from those elsewhere in the North American Southwest.[113] We will look first at the Mimbres region of the Mogollon (southwest New Mexico) and then examine the Mogollon Rim region of east-central Arizona.

There are three basic time periods recognized for the Mogollon. The first of these is the Early Pithouse period, characterized by the addition of ceramic vessels.[114] As the name for the period indicates, Mogollon groups lived in pithouse dwellings, and they grew domesticated beans, maize, and squash. They also collected wild goosefoot, pigweed, and sunflower and hunted wild animals. Most of the settlements were small, some 5 or 10 dwellings, perhaps indicating that only a small number of families lived at any given site. This seems to be mirrored at some sites with numerous structures, where only a few dwellings were contemporary. It suggests that people returned to the same sites over many hundreds of years, with new pithouse dwellings built from time to time. This pattern of long-term repeated occupations of sites is sometimes called "persistent places," and it may suggest broadly held ideas about rights to the use of land by families or kin-groups.[115] Some sites also had communal structures that are identified as great kivas.[116]

Mimbres Mimbres Mogollon sites are found in southwestern New Mexico and a small portion of southeastern Arizona. They are known for their geometric designs and everyday life scenes painted on Black-on-White pottery.

NAN Ranch Site a Mogollon site in southwestern New Mexico occupied during the Pithouse and Mogollon Pueblo periods. During the Classic Mimbres phase (AD 1000 to 1130) of the Mogollon Pueblo period, Nan Ranch had three roomblocks with more than 100 rooms and a ditch and small canal system to divert water to fields and a reservoir.

During the Late Pithouse period, which began about AD 650, there are many sites with large numbers of pithouse dwellings (up to 200). The number of pithouses that appear to be lived in at the same time is 20 or 30, suggesting that these villages were a bit bigger on average than those of the Early Pithouse period.[117] Additionally, there were many smaller sites, sometimes with just one pithouse. Interactions with the Hohokam region are suggested by shell objects at some sites, particularly in the **Mimbres** region of southwestern New Mexico.[118] One example of a site with a Late Pithouse period occupation in the Mimbres region is the **NAN Ranch Site** (see Figure 7.4).[119] Excavations revealed numerous pithouses built under a later aboveground pueblo community (see later discussion). The pithouses were rectangular in shape and had plastered floors, walls, and entryways. Cultural materials found on pithouse floors include pottery vessels and ground stone tools (metates and manos). There are burials beneath pithouse floors, including infants and adults, although most people were buried outside the pithouses. Near the end of the Late Pithouse phase, there are clusters of pithouses in which the pithouses all faced an open area between them. This may have been a way for related families to claim a certain area of the site as their own space. The Late Pithouse period at NAN Ranch also had two great kivas. Both of these structures were similar in shape and design to ordinary pithouses but were considerably larger in size. They are interpreted as communal space used for ceremonies.

Beginning about AD 1000 in the Mimbres region and a few hundred years later in the mountain areas of east-central Arizona, the Mogollon began to build aboveground pueblos.[120] This represents a shift from pithouse to pueblo that is broadly analogous to the pithouse-to-pueblo transition that we saw in the Ancestral Pueblo region, although it occurred later in the Mogollon region. It is called the Mogollon Pueblo (AD 1000 to 1400). In the mountain regions, the stone roomblocks were constructed to enclose open plaza areas and contained numerous rooms; for example, in the AD 1300s, sites had from 100 to 800 rooms.[121] There is good evidence to suggest that the size of these pueblos was a result of the immigration of people from other parts of the North American Southwest.[122]

The NAN Ranch Site (see earlier) also was occupied during the Mogollon Pueblo period, which at this location dates to the Classic Mimbres phase from AD 1000 to 1130.[123] Classic Mimbres is well known for its striking Black-on-White painted ceramics, which include beautifully rendered geometric designs as well as scenes of everyday life (Figure 7.19). NAN Ranch during this period consisted of three roomblocks with more than 100 rooms (Figure 7.20). The arrangement of space is interpreted as reflecting three levels of organization. The first is nuclear families who lived in and used a small set of interconnected rooms. Burials of family members occurred beneath the floors. On the second level was the lineage or corporate group. This consisted of several related families whose households were adjacent sets of rooms (much like the Late Pithouse period clustering of dwellings around an open courtyard, discussed previously). Finally, at the third level of organization was the aggregated (many lineages/households) unit that consisted of separate roomblocks. These aggregated groupings shared the use of kivas built within each roomblock. People living at NAN Ranch depended on rainfall to grow maize, beans, and squash and also built ditch and small canal systems to direct water to fields and to a reservoir.[124] There were many Classic Mimbres phase burials found at NAN Ranch. The largest number and richest burials were from below the floor of one room (Room 29) in the south roomblock. This context yielded more than 40 burials of all ages (infants to adults), most of whom had pottery vessels, although some had other grave goods such as jewelry. Jewelry seems to mark a type of adult male status, with shell beads and bracelets and pendants of turquoise, shell, and stone found in their graves.[125] Adult females tended to have more than one pottery vessel as grave goods. About half of Classic-phase burials had a pottery vessel placed over their head, and the vessel was "killed" by punching a hole in its base. The archaeological interpretation of the Room 29 Classic period burials at NAN Ranch sees them as representing not elite individuals but perhaps special social roles in society. Shortly after AD 1130, the NAN Ranch Site was abandoned.

In the mountains (Mogollon Rim) of east-central Arizona, there were several large sites during the Mogollon Pueblo period. One of these is **Grasshopper Pueblo** (see Figure 7.4), which dates from AD 1275 to 1400.[126] In the period from AD 1300 to 1330, Grasshopper Pueblo was an aggregated community of 500 rooms distributed mainly between three large multistoried roomblocks separated by a small stream (Figure 7.21). The inhabitants of the west roomblocks were Mogollon peoples, whereas the inhabitants of the east roomblock were Ancestral Pueblo. These distinctions are based on the features of architecture, material cultural remains, and analyses of the skeletal remains from burials in the two areas of

Grasshopper Pueblo
a Mogollon Pueblo period site in the mountainous east-central part of Arizona. It was occupied between AD 1275 and 1400. At its peak between AD 1300 and 1330, it was an aggregation site with large, multistoried roomblocks with enclosed open plazas. The roomblocks to the west of the stream were occupied by Mogollon peoples, whereas those on the east side of the stream were where Ancestral Pueblo groups lived.

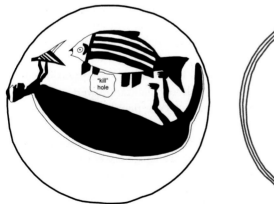 

FIGURE 7.19
Examples of Mimbres pottery designs from the interior of bowls in the Mogollon region of the North American Southwest.

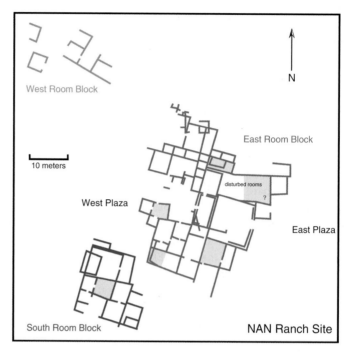

FIGURE 7.20
Plan of the existing roomblock walls at NAN Ranch (Classic Mimbres phase of the Mogollon Pueblo period). Rooms shown in yellow were identified as kivas (after Shafer 2003, Figure 6.5).

the site. The roomblocks included habitation, storage, and manufacturing rooms.[127] Manufacturing rooms contained clay, axes, and pigments that were used to make different types of artifacts. There are numerous burials, with young individuals (children and infants) and some adults buried below room floors. Most adults were buried in deep trash middens or below open plaza floors and were accompanied by personal ornaments and ceramic vessels.[128] Under one of the plazas in one of the west roomblocks (the site area with Mogollon inhabitants) were several rich burials that might represent elite members of society or people with special social roles.[129] One burial of an adult male had more than 120 stone arrowheads, more than 35 ceramic vessels, numerous bone tools (including one incised with geometric designs), carved turquoise and shell that likely were part of a covering for one of the bone tools, shell bracelets, turquoise ear ornaments, and mortars.[130] Near the end of the aggregation phase at Grasshopper Pueblo, an above-ground, rectangular great kiva was built over this large plaza area. This great kiva continued in use until AD 1400, but the nature of occupation at Grasshopper Pueblo shifted to part-time or seasonal.[131] People built smaller roomblocks of just one or a few rooms each in

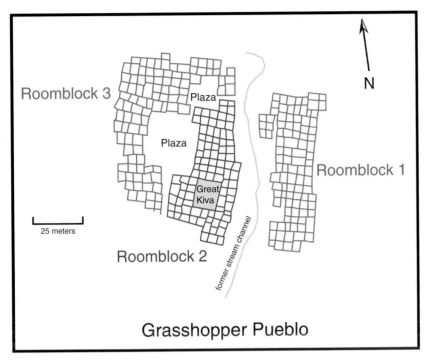

FIGURE 7.21
Plan of the Mogollon Pueblo period main roomblocks at Grasshopper Pueblo (after Longacre et al. 1982, Figure 1.2).

the area surrounding the large, multistoried roomblocks, which seem to have been partly abandoned.

By AD 1400, Mogollon pueblos were abandoned. This is a period often described as a consolidation phase, when the Mogollon and other peoples moved to regions of the North American Southwest with more dependable water sources. The dispersal of people and their relocation likely was partially because they were dependent on maize agriculture, usually using dry farming. When long-term weather conditions were good (wet and warm), people were able to farm in otherwise marginal areas. The ability to sustain large populations in marginal areas, however, was seriously impacted when environmental conditions included long periods of drier weather or drought situations.[132] The fluctuations between good times and those that were not involved a long-term process in the North American Southwest, especially between AD 860 and 1600.[133] The so-called "disappearance" of the Mogollon thus may be a result of their movement to better areas where they aggregated with other groups of people. It is widely thought that pueblos in the Hopi and Zuñi areas are some of the places to which Mogollon people relocated.

Further Reflections

Elite Lineage at Pueblo Bonito

When we identify elite individuals in various past societies, we sometimes assume that they were related to one another. Their access to power, prestige, and exotic goods in large quantities, identified by burial goods, house contents, size of houses and other special architectural features, seems like a privilege that would not be shared with non-related individuals. But can we document that our assumptions are correct? Thanks to advances in DNA analyses, there are some instances in which we can examine this question in detail. One example is people from some of the elite burials at Pueblo Bonito in Chaco Canyon.[134]

The burial crypt in Room 33 contains two male individuals with evidence of violence (see earlier), as well as 12 other later burials. Radiocarbon dating (see Chapter 1) of the bones of the skeletons and other organic materials allow us to see the sequence of events. Room 33 is one of the rooms constructed earliest at Pueblo Bonito. The richest burial is the first (late AD 800s) in Room 33, a male individual who has a lethal blow to the head. The second male with a lethal head blow also had numerous grave goods and was buried just above the first male. A wooden plank was placed above him. Additional burials of males and females were later placed above the plank. The latest burial dates to around AD 1130.

The mitochondrial DNA (see Chapter 3) of 9 of the 14 skeletons was studied. Mitochondrial DNA is passed from mothers to their male and female children and allows us to trace maternal lineages. The results of the study show that these nine individuals all belong to the same matriline (they have identical mitochondrial DNA). In one case, two of the skeletons are most likely mother and daughter, while in another, the relationship is grandmother and grandson. Leadership roles were passed down through the generations to people who shared the same female ancestry. This means that over about 330 years (the time difference between the first and last burials), people who belonged to the same matrilineage formed one of the hereditary elite groups at Pueblo Bonito, being perhaps the group that first established Pueblo Bonito. The Room 33 burial crypt is near the room with the cylinder jars used to drink the chocolate beverage beginning in the AD 900s (see earlier), possibly suggesting that these vessels belonged to this matrilineage. The pattern of social units (clans) based on matrilines is one that is also found today in many Native American groups (for example, Hopi, Zuni, and Rio Grande Pueblos).

Summary

- During the Late Archaic period, hunter–gatherer–foragers incorporated domesticated maize and squash from Mexico/Mesoamerica into their subsistence economies.

- The Ancestral Pueblo region:

  - During Basketmaker II, people grew maize using floodwater and dry farming, hunted various wild animals, and collected wild plant foods. They lived in pithouses and used baskets for stone-boiling of foods. Burials indicate there are some individuals who may have been ritual specialists.

- Pottery became widespread in Basketmaker III. As a durable container, it was more useful than baskets for storage and cooking. Basketmaker III peoples grew maize and squash and added domesticated beans from Mexico/Mesoamerica, in addition to hunting and gathering. Pithouse villages ranged in size; some villages had great kivas.

- In the Pueblo I period, people shifted from living in pithouses to above-ground masonry dwellings. Early on, there are many small sites with just a handful of above-ground rooms (habitation, storage, and activity), a pithouse (often called a kiva), and a trash area. At the end of the Pueblo I period, small roomblocks became common. These have associated pithouses, some of which are identified as great kivas. The earliest evidence for cacao, an import from Mexico/Mesoamerica, is found during Pueblo I; this bean was used to make a chocolate beverage likely used in rituals.

- The Chaco Phenomenon was centered on Chaco Canyon in the San Juan Basin in northwestern New Mexico. It occurred between AD 900 and 1220 (Pueblo II and most of Pueblo III), which is locally called the Bonito Phase.

  - Chaco Canyon had many small roomblock settlements, as well as several large roomblocks known as great houses. Another feature was the Chacoan roads, some of which connected great houses in Chaco Canyon to Chacoan outliers (great houses built in other areas of the Ancestral Pueblo region). Some of the Chacoan roads led to resource areas.

  - Connections between Chaco Canyon and Mexico/Mesoamerica included copper bells, macaws, and cacao. Other items traded into Chaco Canyon included turquoise from sources in New Mexico, Colorado, and Nevada, pottery from the Mogollon region, and shell jewelry possibly from the Hohokam region.

  - Evidence for elite members of society includes elaborate burials at Pueblo Bonito and nonlocal designs on pottery vessels associated with some of these individuals.

  - There is limited evidence for violence during the Bonito Phase.

  - During the Late Bonito Phase, several new great houses were built, as was the great kiva known as Casa Rinconada.

  - By AD 1220, the Chaco Phenomenon came to an end, although people continued to live here until AD 1300, when the canyon was finally abandoned. In this 80-year period, small sites in the so-called Mesa Verde style were built, suggesting the movement of Ancestral Pueblo people from Mesa Verde in southwestern Colorado.

  - The end of the Chaco Phenomenon is sometimes interpreted as resulting from the breakdown of social bonds and ties that linked people together.

- The Hohokam region:

  - Developments here were contemporary with those in the Ancestral Pueblo and Mogollon regions. The Hohokam are known for their extensive canal systems, which began during the Late Archaic period, allowing them to divert river water to fields to grow maize, beans, squash, and cotton.

- During the Pioneer, Colonial, and Sedentary periods, they built shallow pithouses as dwellings. Evidence for trade with Mexico/Mesoamerica included copper bells, pyrite mirrors, and macaws, but also the idea of ball courts. The Hohokam traded with other regions of the North American Southwest for turquoise, and they traveled to the Gulf of California to collect marine shell that they made into jewelry.

- The Classic period overlaps with and extends later than the Bonito Phase at Chaco Canyon. During the Classic period, the Hohokam built adobe great houses at places such as Casa Grande in Arizona, abandoned the use of ball courts, and began to construct large platform mounds. Cacao from Mexico/Mesoamerica is present at some sites.

- Around AD 1450, the Hohokam abandoned their sites and canal systems.

- The Mogollon region:

  - Mogollon groups also grew maize, beans, and squash, as well as hunted and collected wild foods. They shifted over time from living in pithouses to above-ground masonry structures, although this transition occurred later in the Mogollon region than in the Ancestral Pueblo area.

  - Pithouse villages of the Early and Late Pithouse phases could be small, just a house or two, or could be large, with up to 200 pithouses. Not all pithouses were contemporary, which reflects long-term use of sites, where some structures were abandoned or fell into disrepair and new ones were built. Some pithouse villages had great kivas.

  - The use of above-ground masonry roomblocks represents the beginning of the Mogollon Pueblo period. Room blocks could be small or large (up to about 800 rooms). Larger sites usually had more than one roomblock. At some sites, each roomblock is interpreted as representing people related to each other by lineage. At other sites, architectural styles and material remains found in each roomblock suggest that some were Mogollon peoples, whereas others were from the Ancestral Pueblo region. In both cases (lineages or different peoples), the Mogollon Pueblo sites are interpreted as aggregation sites.

  - Mogollon region sites were abandoned sometime around AD 1400.

- Abandonment in Ancestral Pueblo, Hohokam, and Mogollon regions occurred before the arrival of the Spanish and was likely caused by a combination of factors. These include prolonged and persistent drought cycles and breakdown of social bonds. Many of the people relocated to other areas of the North American Southwest. Their living descendants include Native Americans such as the Hopi, Zuñi, Rio Grande Pueblos, Tohono O'odham, Pima, and many other groups.

Endnotes

1. In the literature, the term "Anasazi" has been used for decades, and some archaeologists still use this term rather than "Ancestral Pueblo." The translation of Anasazi, however, is sometimes given as "enemy ancestor," and this is not an accurate reflection of the ancestor/descendant relationships in the Southwest because modern pueblo communities such as Zuñi, Hopi, and the Rio Grande Pueblos are the descendant populations of the prehistoric pueblo communities (see also Riggs 2005).

2. Starch grains on ground stone tools indicate the use of local potatoes (Louderback and Pavlik 2017).

3. Merrill et al. 2009.

4. Emslie et al. 1995; Geib 2000, 2004; Schwartz et al. 1958.

5. See, for example, Wills 1988.

6. Hall 2010; Merrill et al. 2009: 21020.

7. Mabry 1994; Mabry and Clark 1994.

8. Mabry 2005; Merrill et al. 2009: 21025.

9. Merrill et al. 2009: 21023 and supplemental table S3.

10. Phillips 2009.

11. Some archaeologists define the beginning of the Basketmaker at least as early as 1500 cal BC because they consider the appearance of maize agriculture a defining characteristic for the Basketmaker compared to the Archaic periods (see, for example, Matson 2006: 157–158).

12. The Pecos Conference of 1927 established a general sequence for the Ancestral Pueblo (Kidder 1927). Although this sequence included a Basketmaker I phase, there has been no definite archaeological evidence yet discovered for this phase.

13. Geib 2004; Webster and Hays-Gilpin 1994.

14. Badenhorst and Driver 2009; Coltrain et al. 2007; Matson 2006.

15. Badenhorst and Driver 2009: 1838.

16. Potter 2011.

17. Berry 1982.

18. Ellwood et al. 2013. The specialized studies of bones are done using stable carbon isotopes, which allows researchers to examine the main plant groups consumed. For example, maize is a C_4 plant and the Cedar Mesa bones show a C_4 stable carbon isotope signature.

19. Matson 2006: 153; Webster and Hays-Gilpin 1994; Tanner 1976.

20. Charles and Cole 2006; Morris and Burgh 1954; Mowrer 2006.

21 Mowrer 2006.

22. Coltrain et al. 2012.

23. Morris 1925.

24. Kidder and Guernsey 1919; Mowrer 2006: 261.

25. Badenhorst and Driver 2009.

26. Buck and Perry 1999: 481–485; Rohn 1977: 9–17; among many others.

27. Cameron 1990: 29.

28. Judge 2006: 216.

29. Roberts 1929; Wills et al. 2012; see also http://www.chacoarchive.org/cra/chaco-sites/shabikeshchee/ (accessed July 4, 2018).

30. Wills and Windes 1989: 354; Wills et al. 2102: 334.

31. Wills et al. 2012: 340.

32. Wills and Windes 1989: 358.

33. Wills and Windes 1989: 357.

34. Wills et al. 2012: 342–343.

35. Chenault and Motsinger 2000.

36. Wills et al. 2012: 344.

37. Cameron 1990.

38. Nicholas and Smiley 1984: 99–100; Olszewski 1984; Olszewski et al. 1984; Stone 1984.

39. Schachner 2010.

40. Schachner 2010.

41. Potter 1997.

42. Potter and Perry 2011.

43. Washburn et al. 2013.

44. An excellent resource for Chaco is the Chaco Research Archive, which houses written summaries, digital photographs, timelines, and other information: http://www.chacoarchive.org/cra/ (accessed July 4, 2018).

45. Samuels and Betancourt 1982; but see Wills et al. 2014, who argue that evidence for deforestation in Chaco Canyon is not as strong as claimed.

46. Mills 2002: 75; Plog et al. 2017.

47. Vivian 1991.

48. Dorshow 2012.

49. Benson et al. 2003.

50. Wills et al. 2016.

51. Chaco Research Archive: http://www.chacoarchive.org/cra/chaco-sites/pueblo-bonito/ (accessed 4 July 2018).

52. Kantner 1997; Lekson 2005. Recent discoveries of additional Chacoan road segments by using LiDAR can be found in Friedman et al. 2017.

53. Cameron 2005: 232; Mills 2002: 81.

54. Kantner 1996; Van Dyke 1999; see also Cameron 2005, who suggest that population movements between Chaco Canyon and the Mesa Verde region may help explain some of the similarities. See also *Kiva* 77(2), 2011, which is an entire issue devoted to discussions of the emulation of Chacoan styles and evidence for occasional migration of Chacoan people to other regions of the San Juan Basin.

55. Guiterman et al. 2016; but see Wills et al. 2014 for commentary on trees brought into Chaco Canyon.

56. Toll 1991.

57. Arakawa et al. 2016; Plog et al. 2017; Toll 2001.

58. Cameron 2001.

59. Duff et al. 2012.

60. Mathien 2001.

61. Hull et al. 2014.

62. Judd 1954: 305–306; Mills and Ferguson 2008: 347; Nelson 2006; Toll 2006.

63. Watson et al. 2015. These authors note that macaws were brought into Chaco Canyon as early as AD 900. In fact, most of the macaws date to the period before the major construction efforts on great houses from AD 1040 to 1110.

64. Crown and Hurst 2009.

65. Cobb et al. 1999.

66. Crown and Hurst 2009; Washburn et al. 2011.

67. See articles in McNeil 2006.

68. Crown 2018; Crown and Hurst 2009.

69. Crown 2018.

70. Washburn et al. 2011.

71. Crown et al. 2015.

72. Plog et al. 2017; Wills 2000. Some rooms at Pueblo Bonito appear to have contained ritual artifacts, such as bird wings, that could have been used in such ceremonies (Ainsworth et al. 2018).

73. Kantner 2003; Kintigh 2003.

74. Washburn 2011.

75. Windes and McKenna 2001.

76. Adams 1996.

77. Hegemon et al. 2000: 72–74.

78. Neitzel 2000.

79. Mattson 2016: 130.

80. Akins 1986; Mills 2002: 87.

81. Mathien 2001: 114–115; Mattson 2016.

82. Mills 2002: 90.

83. Potter and Ortman 2004: 179–180; Wills and Crown 2004: 156–157.

84. Plog and Watson 2012.

85. Billman et al. 2000; Kuckelman et al. 2002.

86. LeBlanc 1999: 180; Mills 2002: 95–96.

87. Harrod 2012; Harrod et al. 2012; Mathien 2001: 114.

88. LeBlanc 1999: 166.

89. Van Dyke 2004. Tankersley et al. (2017) note that a significant volcanic eruption (Sunset Crater, Arizona) in AD 1085 would have resulted in volcanic ash deposits as far away (325 kilometers [202 miles]) as Chaco Canyon. This ash would have increased the fertility of the soil, possibly aiding in greater agricultural productivity. Such productivity might be linked in part to the new great house constructions from AD 1100 to AD 1130.

90. Cook et al. 2004; Mills 2002: 75.

91. Chaco Research Archive: http://www.chacoarchive.org/cra/chaco-sites/casa-rinconada/ (accessed July 4, 2018).

92. Lekson 1997.

93. Malotki 2000.

94. Dean et al. 1994; Douglass 1929.

95. One explanation for the abandonment of much of the Four Corners region of the North American Southwest is that drought conditions forced people to be more reliant on maize (Matson 2016). If other sources of food, such as beans and turkeys, became less available, the resulting largely maize diet would have led to increased levels of disease and nutritional stress. In this situation, people would move to better watered areas, such as along the Rio Grande River in New Mexico, likely following in the footsteps of others who left the same region in the mid-AD 1100s. Additional studies (Crabtree et al. 2017) suggest that the impact that people's activities had on

their surrounding habitats created conditions where local ecologies could not rebound, and human life in those contexts was less sustainable. This also would lead to people moving away.

96. Whalen and Minnis 2000; Whalen et al. 2010: 546.
97. Roth and Freeman 2008.
98. Bayman 2001: 271.
99. Doyel 2007; Showalter 1993. A number of modern canals in the Phoenix Basin were dug into existing Hohokam canals. Many Hohokam canals were destroyed before they could be recorded as Phoenix grew in size.
100. For example, Wilcox 1991; but see Hunt et al. 2005 for an alternative view.
101. Bayman 2001: 273.
102. Masse 1991: 204–208.
103. Doyel 1991: 227–228; Mitchell and Foster 2000.
104. Fertelmes et al. 2012; Haury 1976: 277–288; Toll 1991: 83–84.
105. Haury 1976.
106. Seymour 1988.
107. Ferdon 1967.
108. Bayman 2001: 280–290.
109. Grimstead and Bayham 2010.
110. Crown and Fish 1996; Washburn et al. 2011; Wilcox 1991: 269–270.
111. Abbott et al. 2006; Hunt et al. 2005.
112. Whittlesey et al. 2010.
113. This is the position taken, for example, by Riggs 2005.
114. Whittlesey et al. 2010.
115. Schriever 2012.
116. Anyon and LeBlanc 1980.
117. Whittlesey et al. 2010.
118. Vokes and Gregory 2007.
119. Shafer 2003: 21–39.
120. Whittlesey et al. 2010.
121. Reid et al. 1996.
122. Ezzo and Price 2002.
123. Shafer 2003: 55–109.
124. Shafer 2003: 116.
125. Shafer 2003: 155–159.
126. Longacre et al. 1982; Riggs 2001.
127. Stone 2009: 81.
128. Whittlesey and Reid 2001.
129. Clark 1969; Griffin 1967.
130. A number of pieces of turquoise at Grasshopper Pueblo have been sourced to the Canyon Creek turquoise mine, which is about 27 kilometers (17 miles) south of the pueblo (Hedquist et al. 2017: Welch and Triadan 1991).
131. Riggs 2005: 255–256.
132. Benson and Berry 2009.
133. Another possibility for the abandonment of large settlements in the Ancestral Pueblo, Mogollon, and even Hohokam areas could have been the impact of diseases prevalent in large communities (Phillips et al. 2018).
134. Kennett et al. 2017.

CHAPTER 8

Eastern North America

ABOVE: The Serpent Mound (effigy mound) in Ohio; it was built either by the Adena or Fort Ancient cultures (debate continues on this issue).

In this chapter we will look at the prehistoric cultures of a portion of the North American East. This includes the region of the Mississippi River and its tributaries, such as the Ohio and Missouri rivers, part of the North American Midwest, and most of the North American Southeast. These regions were home to Paleoamerican and Early Archaic period hunter–gatherer–forager groups for several thousands of years. Unlike the North American Southwest during the Late Archaic period, cultural groups of Eastern North America domesticated native seed plants, so that this region is one example of the origins of food production. During later times, domesticated maize and beans were introduced from Mexico and became important crops. Mound building began during the Late Archaic period and continued to be a feature of later groups such as the Hopewell and Mississippian cultures (read "Timeline: Eastern North America"). We will focus mainly on the Early Mississippian period when the site of Cahokia in Illinois was politically important and had far-ranging influence throughout many parts of Eastern North America. During the later Mississippian period, the arrival of the Spanish, and later the French, brought diseases to which Native Americans had no immunity, causing huge losses of population. Some Native American groups who are descendants of earlier Mississippian culture areas include the Natchez, Apalachee, and Coosa.

Early Food Production

In the North American East/Midwest, Archaic period groups hunted deer, turkey, beaver, squirrel, ducks, and geese and fished for eels, catfish, and bass. Plant foods included hickory, chestnut, pecan, walnut, and acorns (which require additional processing to eliminate bitter tasting tannins), as well as berries, fruits, and seeds.[1] In some areas they also collected and ate shellfish. Nuts were a particularly important resource because they contain oils and fats and could be stored relatively easily for later use.

In the river basin areas of the Tennessee, Ohio, Cumberland, and middle Mississippi rivers (Figure 8.2), Middle and Late Archaic period groups invested in squashes and in seed-producing plants such as wild goosefoot, sumpweed, sunflower, maygrass, little barley, and erect knotweed, some of which underwent changes resulting in larger seeds.[2] These seeds are rich in starches and oils, and the wild plants grow well in disturbed soils that are typical of areas near longer-term base camps. They were locally domesticated and grown in gardenlike contexts, and flexibility in the growth habits of some of the plants could result in high seed yields, especially in gardens.[3] Their significance lies in the establishment of an active relationship between people and certain plants. This relationship would develop further with the introduction of domesticated maize and beans from Mexico/Mesoamerica during the Woodland period.

Although Middle and Late Archaic period peoples in Eastern North America were less dependent on food-production economies than their contemporaries in the North American Southwest who had both beans and maize from Mexico/Mesoamerica (see Chapter 7), several important social and behavioral changes occurred in the East that led to the establishment of villages, towns, long-distance trade networks, burials with exotic grave goods, and the construction of mounds, as well as the appearance of pottery late in the Late Archaic period. These developments took place among hunter–gatherer–forager groups whose abundant wild food resources made it possible for them to become settled. This contrasts with the Archaic period North American Southwest where there were fewer rivers and local habitats were more marginal and required investments in water management (for growing crops) that were not common until later phases of the Ancestral Pueblo, Hohokam, and Mogollon periods (see Chapter 7).

Other factors leading to social changes in the North American Eastern Late Archaic (and later) periods might have included the size and types of families. One study, for example, uses ethnographic data to model a potential change in family

Timeline: Eastern North America

In this timeline, Cahokia was at its height of development and power during the Early Mississippian period (Figure 8.1). Other centers such as Etowah and Moundville were important during the Late Mississippian period.

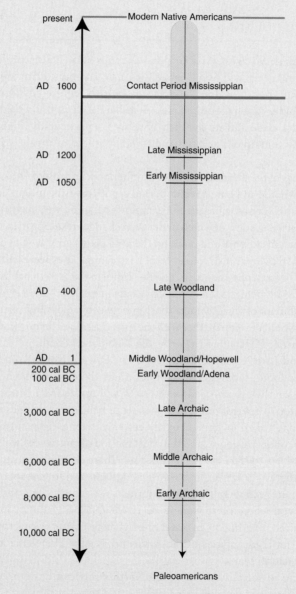

FIGURE 8.1
Timeline for the North American East (red line indicates the approximate arrival of the Spanish in the East).

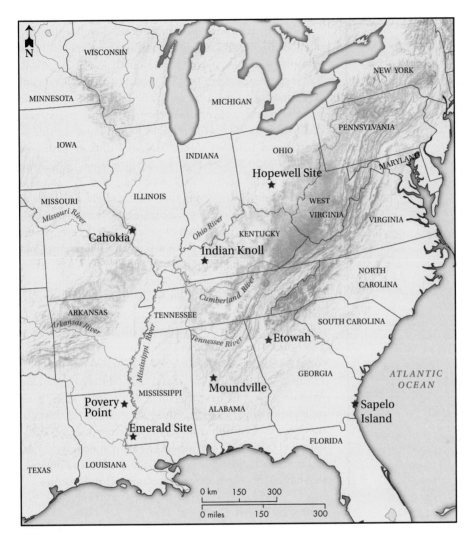

FIGURE 8.2
North American East sites mentioned in the text, including major rivers.

structure.[4] This involves adding young children as significant contributors to gathering food resources. The potential to accumulate more stored resources would have facilitated a shift to polygynous families (one mate with many spouses) for some families. Increased family size meant more people (including children) to consistently contribute to food stores and the potential for those stores to increase "wealth" disparity between different families. Sizes of houses at archaeological sites seem to support this idea. And if population size grew overall, this likely meant that people would intensify collecting and growing wild foods to meet higher levels of food demand.[5]

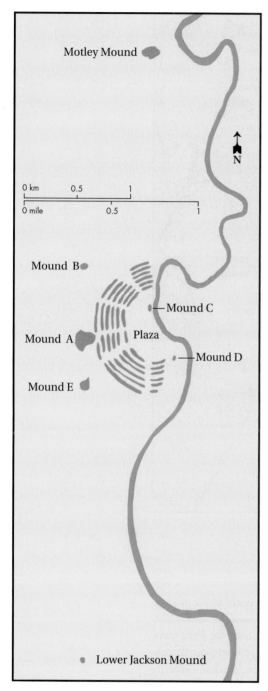

FIGURE 8.3
The Archaic period mounds at Poverty Point, Louisiana (after Sassaman 2005a).

Burials, and the types of grave goods found with them, often are used by archaeologists to assess some aspects of how past groups were organized socially. In the North American East, beginning before 3000 BC, burials with exotic types of grave goods became more frequent. These exotic materials included native copper from northern Michigan and marine shells from the Gulf of Mexico, as well as jewelry made of ground and polished stone.[6] **Indian Knoll** in Kentucky (3000 to 2500 BC; see Figure 8.2),[7] for example, has living floors, a shell midden (trash area composed of discarded shells from food), and more than 1,100 individual burials in the shell midden including adult males and females and children.[8] There is a suggestion of gender-related grave goods, with male burials having bone awls, axes, and fishhooks and female burials with nutting stones and bone beads. Certain types of hunting equipment such as parts of atlatls, as well as ritual objects, were found with both males and females. Items such as shell disk beads were buried with some individuals (mainly males). Most of the burials do not contain any grave goods, perhaps indicating differences in social status or social roles for those people buried with grave goods.

The complexity of social life during the Late Archaic period in Eastern North America is seen in its mound-building tradition.[9] These are complex earthworks that required considerable labor investment and coordination of labor. One of the best known is at Poverty Point. There also are coastal sites with large shell ring complexes that have been interpreted as monumental architecture.

Poverty Point Culture

Beginning around 1750 cal BC, Late Archaic period people at **Poverty Point**, Louisiana (see Figure 8.2), started to build a series of earth mounds, which may have had a ritual basis for their spatial organization (Figure 8.3). These include Mound A (21 meters [70 feet] tall), which has a flat area at the top.[10] Immediately to the east of Mound A are a series of six segmented, concentric ridges that form the shape of half of an octagon. Each ridge is 1.2 to 1.8 meters (4 to 6 feet) tall and is separated from the next ridge by 46 meters (150 feet). There is an open space (plaza) surrounded by the inner ridge. Six other mounds are associated with this complex. Four (Mounds B, C, D, and E) are within the main area. The Lower Jackson

Mound, however, is 2.4 kilometers (1.5 miles) south of Mound E, and the Motley Mound is 1.7 kilometers (1 mile) north of Mound C. The earthworks complex at Poverty Point covers 5 square kilometers (1.9 square miles) and involved moving 750,000 cubic meters (26,486,000 cubic feet) of sediment using digging sticks and baskets.[11] It is one of the largest earthen constructions north of Mexico.[12]

Evidence from excavations at Poverty Point[13] suggests that Late Archaic period people lived on the artificially constructed concentric ridges. Because the ridges are different with respect to access and direct sight into the open plaza area, the placement of dwellings on the ridges is sometimes interpreted as evidence for different social ranks among the people living in at Poverty Point.[14] A dwelling on the inner ridge, for example, would reflect higher rank than a dwelling on the outer ridge. The tops of the mounds appear to have been closed off to access to most people, an indication that individuals of enhanced social standing used and occupied these structures. Not everyone, however, lived at Poverty Point. There are settlements and camps for hunting, nut harvesting, and fishing up to 40 kilometers (25 miles) away that share the same types of artifacts and other features of material culture,[15] integrating them into what is sometimes called Poverty Point Culture. Trade and exchange networks brought minerals (galena, hematite, quartz crystal), stone (greenstone, basalt, soapstone), and copper into the Poverty Point Culture area. Most of these materials were locally made into objects using styles and techniques specific to Poverty Point Culture (one exception is the vessels made from soapstone, which were obtained as finished objects from regions in Alabama and Georgia).[16]

It is important to remember that settlements such as Poverty Point, and the smaller villages and task camps that were regionally associated with it, were the work of people who did not depend extensively on the use of domesticated foods. Their habitats provided an abundance of wild plant foods and animals that facilitated long-term occupations in some areas and the development of visible constructions that speak to their complex social interactions.

Shell Ring Complexes

In the coastal areas of Mississippi, Florida, Georgia, and South Carolina, Late Archaic period groups built sites that included large rings made of shellfish (oysters and clams).[17] The largest rings were 6 meters (20 feet) tall and 250 meters (820 feet) across. One early interpretation is that as shellfish debris from meals accumulated over time, people moved their dwellings on top of the rings and the interior space became an open plaza that could be used by the village. Other interpretations focus on the accumulation of the shell ring deposits as the result of feasting and of deliberate monument building. In this perspective, people with higher social status controlled access to the interiors of the rings, possibly lived on top of the rings and associated mounds, and may have been buried within the shell rings.[18] Archaeological evidence used to support this view includes larger clam sizes, more pottery, and more volume in one section of the U-shape shell rings, which may indicate the presence of people with more and better access to resources.

Indian Knoll a Late Archaic period site in Kentucky dating between 3000 and 2500 cal BC. It has a shell midden (mound) and a cemetery with more than 1,100 individual burials. Some burials have exotic materials (copper and marine shell), perhaps indicating differences in status, whereas others suggest that people were buried with probable gender-related objects (axes and fishhooks with males and nutting stones and bone beads with females).

Poverty Point a Late Archaic period site in Louisiana with complex earthworks. It dates from 1750 to 1350 cal BC and is a highly organized construction of concentric, segmented ridge mounds associated with several high mounds. There is a large open plaza area inside the inner ridge. People living on the inner ridge likely had greater social rank or standing than those living on other ridges which had no direct line of sight into the plaza. Very high-status individuals and families may have lived on the taller mounds.

One example is the **Sapelo Island Shell Ring Complex** in Georgia (see Figure 8.2).[19] This site has three shell rings, but only Ring I is built up to any extent (3 meters [10 feet] tall). Rings II and III are low and recent ground-penetrating imaging surveys, and test excavations suggest that they were habitation areas that began as discontinuous rings of separate piles of shell. Dwellings were placed just inside the shell accumulations and shared the inner open areas as communal plazas. Seasonality studies of the shells indicate that the shellfish in Rings II and III were collected during all four seasons and were deposited gradually, suggesting that at least some Archaic period people lived there year-round. The shells in Ring I, however, mainly were collected during the winter and were mostly oysters. Their accumulation was over a much shorter period of time and has been interpreted as probable evidence for feasting. Whether this means that Ring I was a deliberately constructed ritual monument, however, is more difficult to determine.

Woodland Period

Sites in the lower Mississippi Valley, such as Poverty Point, were abandoned. One reason for this change in where people lived may be the result of global climate changes on resource abundance and on flooding, which became more frequent along the major rivers and their tributaries, where many settlements were located.[20] Using a theoretical framework of agency, we can interpret the cultural responses to major flooding events as decisions made by individuals and groups as active agents in reorganizing their settlements, settlement systems, subsistence activities, and social traditions. These changes resulted in the appearance of what archaeologists call the Woodland period, which began about 1000 cal BC.

Early Woodland

With the beginning of the Woodland period, horticulture (gardens) involving locally domesticated sunflower, goosefoot, erect knotweed, and sumpweed became more important, and pottery was widespread compared to its sporadic appearance during the Late Archaic period.[21] The movement of exotic materials over great distances, through trade and exchange systems, continued during the Early Woodland period. In addition to copper from the Great Lakes region in Michigan and marine shells from the Gulf of Mexico, other materials included obsidian from Yellowstone National Park, Wyoming.[22]

During the Early Woodland period, the **Adena** tradition emerged in the central part of the Ohio Valley and surrounding areas.[23] Many of their mound complexes were burial contexts. Early burials were in sealed pits, whereas later burials for some people were in above-ground log tombs where the body would remain until the structure was needed again. Existing bodies in the log tombs would be buried elsewhere on the mound. Burials were covered by placing basket-carried earth on top of them, thus forming the mounds, and in some cases this occurred over the log tombs themselves. Over time, the mounds grew in size (up to 3 meters [10 feet] in height); most are cone shape. The log tomb burials may represent people with enhanced social status or standing because they contained exotic grave goods (bone and antler combs and beads, stone tablets with incised designs including hawks and owls, copper bracelets, shell gorgets [pendants], and stone pipes for smoking tobacco). Other burials in the mounds may be lower-status individuals because they were cremated and then their ashes were placed in the existing mounds and buried with basket-carried sediment. Adena people lived in the areas surrounding these burial mound sites. They intensified their growing of native plant foods, in some cases shifting to use of upland areas for agriculture or burning the forests to create more space for growing seed plants.[24] In some places, Adena culture and mound building continued into the Middle Woodland period.

Middle Woodland

The Middle Woodland period began about 200 cal BC and is best known for the appearance of the **Hopewell** tradition, which was centered in the Ohio River Valley in Ohio. There were several other related cultural groups including the Havana Hopewell (in the Illinois and Mississippi river valleys in Iowa, Illinois, and Missouri) and the Marksville culture (in the Lower Mississippi Valley including parts of Arkansas, Mississippi, Louisiana, and Missouri).[25] Hopewell groups still hunted as well as fished and gathered much of their food, but they also intensified their horticulture of domesticated sunflower, sumpweed, maygrass, erect knotweed, and goosefoot. This suggests larger numbers of people, either because of increases in overall population size or because of greater population densities within smaller regions.[26] Hopewell groups, however, lived in dispersed "hamlets," small sites consisting of only a few families.[27] Around AD 1, domesticated maize was introduced into Eastern North America, but its role as an agriculture crop was minor during the Middle Woodland period.[28] Many of the features seen earlier in the Archaic and Early Woodland periods, such as mound building, long-distance trade and exchange, and burial complexes, were also part of the Hopewell tradition. The social decisions that resulted in these features during the Middle Woodland period represent intensified expressions of social relationships and were widespread, shared worldviews that interconnected people over an extensive geographical region.

Hopewell an eastern North America tradition of mound building, burial complexes, and long-distance exchange networks that appears during the Middle Woodland period, starting about 200 cal BC; there are several regional groups, including the Ohio Hopewell.

HOPEWELL INTERACTION SPHERE

The interconnection of Hopewell-affiliated groups during the Middle Woodland is sometimes called the Hopewell Phenomenon or the **Hopewell Interaction Sphere** (Figure 8.4). It is important to keep in mind, however, that the features these groups shared and the interactions between them do not mean that there was a single Hopewell culture.[29] Instead, there was much cultural variation from group to group, and this variation existed even between sites that archaeologists place within the same regional tradition, such as the Ohio Hopewell.[30] When we think about the Middle Woodland period and the Hopewell, we are examining not only what these groups shared but also what made them different from each other. The Hopewell tradition was not a highly integrated and politically complex entity on the scale of early civilizations or states (see Part 4).

Hopewell Interaction Sphere a Middle Woodland "phenomenon" in which certain aspects of ritual and ceremony were shared across a wide region in eastern North America among Hopewell-affiliated groups. They also participated to varying extents in long-distance trade and exchange networks and in constructing earthen mounds used for burials and for other ceremonies.

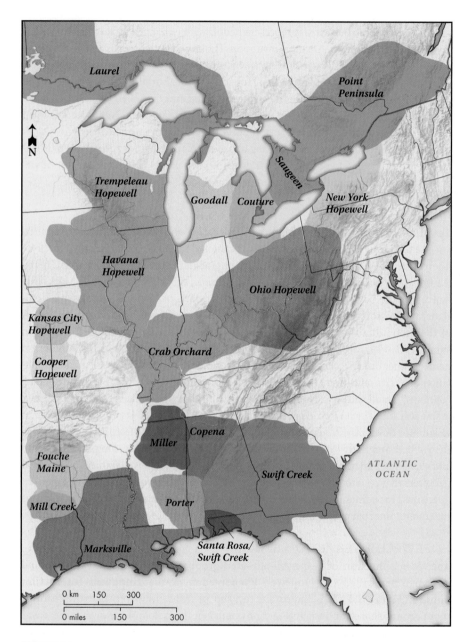

FIGURE 8.4
The Hopewell Interaction Sphere showing Hopewell period and related cultures (redrawn from Rowe 2010).

Hopewell trade and exchange systems built on those from earlier periods, but they differed in the much larger quantities of exotic materials that were transported into Hopewell areas.[31] These materials included silver and copper from the Great

FIGURE 8.5
Example of Hopewell period effigy pipe for smoking tobacco.

Lakes region, marine shell from the Gulf of Mexico and the Atlantic Ocean, obsidian from Yellowstone National Park, black bear teeth and mica from Appalachia (the central and southern portions of the Appalachian Mountain Range), and pipestone (used to carve effigy pipes; see later discussion) from Illinois and Michigan (Figure 8.5). Many of these exotic materials were recovered from burial contexts in earthen mounds, suggesting that some individuals may have held important roles in society, especially those focused on rituals and ceremonies centered on the mound complexes.

Like the Adena during the Early Woodland period, the earthen mound complexes built by Hopewell groups were not places where people settled. Instead, they lived in small dispersed communities away from these ceremonial and burial centers but occasionally came together at the mound complexes for rituals. These rituals can be thought of as ways in which people were socially integrated across the landscape (we saw the same idea for the Neolithic period in Great Britain; see Chapter 6).[32] There were several types of earthen works—burial mounds, geometric shaped mounds (circles, squares, parallel lines, and octagons), and hilltop enclosures.[33] The act of building these mounds and their use in ceremonies is thought by some researchers to reflect an emphasis on the notion of "sacred places" in the landscape.[34]

At mound complexes such as the **Hopewell Site** (Ohio) (see Figure 8.2), there were hundreds of burials, as well as ceremonial deposits.[35] Individuals often were buried with unusual grave goods and/or many items made from exotic materials, and the ceremonial deposits were filled with these goods as well. The ceremonial deposit in Altar 1 in Mound 25 at the Hopewell site, for example, contained more than 500

Hopewell Site a Middle Woodland period site in Ohio that contains earthen works including burial mounds with tens of thousands of exotic materials as grave goods and as ceremonial deposits within mounds. It is a mound complex site associated with the Hopewell tradition.

copper earspools (a type of earring), whereas Burial 7 in Mound 25 had 50 copper earspools.[36] Other offerings in burials and ceremonial deposits included platform pipes for smoking tobacco, hundreds of mica and copper cutouts (the initial stages of making shaped objects), tens of thousands of pearl and shell beads, and hundreds of arrowheads made of obsidian, as well as bone and metal beads, bear canines, perforated fox and wolf teeth, bear claws, and raccoon teeth.

Individuals buried with large quantities of unusual materials and objects in Hopewell burials in mound complexes can be interpreted as reflecting the social roles that those individuals held in life. The types of materials and objects seem to indicate individuals who were highly esteemed within the larger Hopewell community, for example, those people buried with platform pipes or hundreds to thousands of pearl and shell beads.[37] One social role may have been as a ritual specialist who acted as an intermediary between the living and the spirit world. Additionally, animal teeth or copper earspools possibly indicate membership in clans (a group of people linked by kinship and descent from particular ancestors, such as we saw at Pueblo Bonito in the North American Southwest; see Chapter 7). The Hopewell mound complexes thus represent small and large gatherings of people for lavish gift-giving ceremonies associated with burials. Rituals included feasting.[38] The individuals buried had leadership roles, but there were many people who fulfilled this social function in Hopewell society, including many ritual specialists.[39] The ceremonies that brought people together from their dispersed hamlets throughout the countryside were opportunities to honor important individuals who had died and also to create and solidify alliances, such as those made through marriages.

Late Woodland

The worldview that was shared by Hopewell-affiliated groups seems to have disappeared after AD 400 (the beginning of the Late Woodland period). This does not mean that Hopewell period people disappeared but instead reflects the fact that their social organization and how they used the landscape shifted so that their archaeological patterns became different. Some groups continued to build mounds, such as flat-top pyramids in the lower Mississippi Valley or effigy mounds in the form of birds and bears in the region from Ohio to Iowa.[40] The bow and arrow was introduced around AD 600,[41] and population increased in many areas. The growing of maize was quite important in areas such as the lower Mississippi Valley, whereas elsewhere people continued to rely more heavily on wild animals, nuts, fish, and shellfish, as well as domesticated goosefoot, sunflower, maygrass, sumpweed, and erect knotweed.[42] Storage pits dug into the ground became common, suggesting that surplus plant foods were being accumulated on a larger scale. This may be related to feasting or to hoarding activity on the part of individuals or kin groups who sought increased social control or power.

There is much variability across Eastern North America during the Late Woodland period, with some regions characterized by small hamlets, others by villages, and yet others by ceremonial complexes.[43] In the region known as the American Bottom (part of the Mississippi River floodplain near St. Louis where the Illinois and

Missouri Rivers join the Mississippi River), villages of the last 100 years of the Late Woodland period had permanent dwellings that were arranged around open courtyards.[44] In some cases, the courtyards were used to play an early version of a game in which a small carved, disk-shape piece (called a chunkey) was rolled and the teams threw special wooden poles near where the stone would eventually stop, or sometimes they attempted to stop the stone to score points. The archaeological evidence for this game is the presence of these small carved stone and clay disks at sites, as well as analogy to a game played with these types of disks by some later Native American groups. One of these Late Woodland sites was Cahokia Village.

Cahokia and the Early Mississippian Period

Around AD 1050 (the beginning of the Early Mississippian period), the large village at **Cahokia** (see Figure 8.2) underwent several transformations that resulted from decisions about the arrangement of space and of people, as well as considerations related to the planning and construction of new ritual spaces and monuments. This involved considerable negotiation between kin-based groups living at Cahokia Village, as well as with people living in smaller hamlets in nearby areas and with groups who moved into the Cahokia region.[45] The thousands of people who lived in small farming settlements that characterized much of the floodplain region near Cahokia during the Late Woodland period, for example, relocated to a vacant upland area above the floodplain. It is likely that they participated in the massive construction efforts at Cahokia, as well as in the rituals and ceremonies that were held at Cahokia. In other words, these "displaced" groups were active agents in the decisions that led to their relocation and to their continued integration into the larger Cahokia system of ideology and social politics.

Cahokia was one of three massive sites in the St. Louis region during the Early Mississippian period that seem to have formed an important center (referred to as Greater Cahokia), although the degree to which these three sites operated in combination or separately is not known. The others were the East St. Louis Site and the Mound City Site.[46] The earthen mounds of the East St. Louis and Mound City sites were mostly destroyed during the AD 1900s but included 50 truncated pyramids with temples at East St. Louis and 26 truncated pyramids and a large plaza at Mound City. The construction efforts at Cahokia itself were impressive, rivaling some of the Neolithic monuments in Europe (see Chapter 6), as well as some of the individual structures at later sites of the politically complex entities that archaeologists sometimes refer to as early states, kingdoms, and empires (see Part 4). Cahokia had a "downtown" area where the largest pyramid in North America (**Monk's Mound**), the Grand Plaza, several other large plazas, temples on tops of truncated pyramids, a Woodhenge, burial mounds, and a wooden palisade (fence) were built[47] (Figure 8.6). Surrounding this downtown area were residential neighborhoods situated around small plazas and at least 120 additional smaller truncated earthen pyramids with plazas. There also were ridge-top burial mounds that offered a view over the Greater Cahokia area.

Cahokia an Early Mississippian period site in Illinois (eastern North America). Cahokia was one of the most important political and ritual centers of the Mississippian period. Its "downtown" area contained Monk's Mound, the Great Plaza, a Woodhenge, sub-Mound 51, and a wooden palisade, as well as several other earthen mounds (such as Mound 72) and plazas. It was associated with the complexes at the East St. Louis Site and the Mound City Site.

Monk's Mound an Early Mississippian period earthen truncated pyramid at Cahokia in eastern North America; it is the largest pre-Columbian manmade construction north of Mexico.

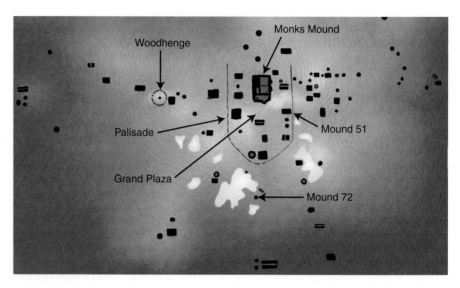

FIGURE 8.6
A map of Cahokia showing Monks Mound, the palisade, Mound 51, Mound 72, the Grand Plaza, the Woodhenge, and borrow pits (*in blue*).

The Grand Plaza at Cahokia was a deliberately constructed feature that involved leveling small hills and ridges and filling in areas with a fine sand so that a nearly level surface was created over 19 hectares (47 acres). The plaza sloped gently, allowing water to run off its surface.[48] At the same time that the Grand Plaza was under construction, Cahokians also were building the first phase of Monk's Mound to a height of 6.5 meters (21 feet). Eventually Monk's Mound became 30 meters (98 feet) tall. It had three flat, stepped terraces and covered more space at its base than the Pyramid of Cheops at Giza in Egypt.[49] Besides Monk's Mound, there were several other earthen pyramids and mounds that towered over the Grand Plaza. The earth used to construct these mounds came from nearby borrow pits (see Figure 8.6). The Woodhenge structure was a circle of wooden posts (rebuilt several times) that was used for observations of the solstices (the start of summer and winter) and equinoxes (the start of spring and fall) and also probably of special days related to the agricultural cycle.[50] This configuration of plazas, buildings, temples, dwellings, and other structures was used to great advantage in public ceremonies[51] (see "Social Life").

Cahokia and its neighboring sites of East St. Louis and Mound City formed a complex of concentrated social and ceremonial centers (read "Further Reflections: Cahokia: Paramount Chiefdom or State?"). Some of its residents were engaged in the production of crafts (pottery, stone axes, and stone hoe blades). The impressive scale of building suggests that this complex was a main regional center, what archaeologists sometimes call a central place. It was surrounded by many smaller towns (with earthen works, plazas, and residential dwellings), each of which was linked to the Cahokia complex.[52] Surrounding these smaller towns were farmsteads that seem to have been home to important families who enjoyed enhanced social roles. This is documented by the presence of exotic materials and large nonresidential structures; these individuals were linked to the small towns. There were also hamlets of people who farmed, gathered wild plant foods, and hunted. Regardless of which type of settlement they lived in, all of these people shared a common belief system (ideology) and participated to greater or lesser degrees in social and ritual ceremonies held at sites with public architecture, for example, at the plazas and the earthen pyramids. If we compare Greater Cahokia to the Chaco Phenomenon (see Chapter 7), it is clear that the Cahokian system involved construction efforts at a much greater scale and with many more people. There also was more obvious emphasis in the Cahokian system on individuals and families who managed to acquire and control surpluses of exotic materials and of food. Food surpluses resulted in part from the more favorable agricultural setting with permanent rivers and streams and their associated floodplains, as well as the abundant wild resources; neither of these situations was characteristic of the Chaco Canyon region.[53]

One key to the accumulation of food surpluses in the Cahokia region was intensive maize agriculture, which was particularly well suited to the floodplain areas to the east of Cahokia where stone hoes could be used to work the fertile soil and farmers could take advantage of new sediments laid down by floods.[54] People also continued to grow domesticated sunflower, maygrass, and sumpweed in gardens near their dwellings and to collect nuts, fruits, and freshwater mussels.[55] They hunted deer and smaller animals and fished. These domesticate and wild resources provided food for the 10,000 to 15,000 people who lived at Cahokia itself, as well as the other mound centers (East St. Louis and Mound City) and all the surrounding towns and rural farming populations.[56] What is especially striking is that these food resources supported the largest, concentrated population in North America before the nineteenth century,[57] and there were additional surpluses that could be used for social activities such as feasting. These surpluses likely would have been managed by elite individuals or families at Cahokia,[58] whose basis for power was linked to ideology and its associated rituals and ceremonies. Evidence of these elites is seen most clearly from their burials (see "Social Life").

Resource Networks, Trade, and Exchange

Many of the types of exotic materials present at Cahokia were also seen during the Archaic and Woodland periods in Eastern North America. They included copper, mica, hematite (a mineral used to create pigments), marine shells, and various types of stone raw materials that could be used to make projectile points.[59] The exchange system, however, was not necessarily an elaborate undertaking controlled by a relatively few elite people. Instead, many crafts, including certain pottery styles, ear spools, textiles, and stone hoes, were locally produced in the Cahokia region. Some items, such as stone hoes, were used by nearby farming populations but also are found in small quantities as much as 400 kilometers (250 miles) away.[60]

Crafts made on a part-time basis at hamlets or small settlements in the area around Cahokia include cloth, rope, pottery vessels, ground stone axes, and stone hoes.[61] These items also were made at Cahokia itself, often in large quantities. There, they may have been the products of smaller groups of people who specialized in certain parts of the production process. There also is abundant evidence for the manufacture of shell beads in certain areas at Cahokia, a pattern that does not seem to apply to the smaller settlements in the Cahokia region. Large quantities of craft items are sometimes found in caches or as grave goods accompanying elite burials. One of the intriguing aspects of Cahokia, however, is that its involvement in long-distance trade networks seems to be relatively slight; that is, the goods that were produced there and in the surrounding area do not seem often to have been exchanged to distant regions. In one sense, then, the greater Cahokia region might be described as largely self-sufficient (read "Peopling the Past: Resources, Trade, and Exchange at Cahokia").

Social Life

Daily activities during the Mississippian period involved decisions about scheduling of tasks as well as the division of labor. Evidence from historic and ethnohistoric records at the time of Spanish contact and later, as well as figurines and other images created by Mississippian period people at Cahokia and elsewhere throughout Eastern North America, suggest that task division was structured.[65] Men helped clear areas for agricultural fields, but women did most of the field preparation, planting, weeding, and harvesting of the crops. Women also were associated with collecting nuts and shellfish and most food-preparation tasks (grinding and cooking), as well as the manufacture of pottery, textiles, and baskets. Men did most of the hunting and fishing, as well as tasks related to building dwellings and woodworking, such as making bows and arrows and canoes. Images show women with agricultural tools and men dressed as warriors or religious leaders or as players of the game of chunkey.

The chunkey games, which had a modest beginning during the Late Woodland period (see earlier), became an important social event during the Early Mississippian period.[66] Archaeological evidence suggests that it was an event that hundreds (or thousands) of people attended at places such as Cahokia. In some ways, this is similar to modern sports events such as American football or basketball, which have thousands of in-person spectators (and millions if television or online viewing is counted). The chunkey game as played at Cahokia was a high-stakes endeavor, with gambling by the team members and others on the outcome of the game. It appears to have been under the control of the elites (chunkey stones are one of their grave goods), who may themselves have played the game, sponsored various players, or had relatives who were players. Another possibility is that there were symbolic associations with the game of chunkey that were important to elites in society.

Other large-scale social events at Cahokia included feasting, which may have been linked to the initial construction and later additions to the earthen mounds and the Great Plaza. One feasting example comes from **sub-Mound 51** next to the

Sub-Mound 51 this Early Mississippian period feature was originally a borrow pit from which sediment was removed to construct earthen works at Cahokia (North American East) and perhaps to level the Great Plaza. It was later filled in by several large debris deposition events including feasting remains.

Resources, Trade, and Exchange at Cahokia

Evidence at Cahokia, and in its surrounding region, of long-distant transport of exotic materials is abundant for its earliest phase (AD 1050 to 1100). These types of materials were found in lavish burials for elite individuals, as well as at smaller centers and in trash deposits. After AD 1100, although Cahokia continued to be a major center with elite status rulers, the quantity of exotics from great distances away was small.[62] Instead, many items were made from materials that were local. This pattern was not unique to Cahokia but was typical for other large Mississippian period centers such as Etowah in Georgia, where stone palettes were made from local sources, and the Emerald Site in Mississippi, where effigy pipes were made from nearby limestone sources.[63] On the surface, a decrease in long-distance exotics seems to reflect less elite control and/or power, which appears counterintuitive if elites remained in power at the Mississippian period centers. The shift to less long-distance exotics, however, could represent a change in how elite individuals and families maintained or established relationships within their immediate areas and with other Mississippian period centers. Producing rarer goods such as palettes (Figure 8.7) and effigy pipes locally, and thus being more "self-sufficient," could actually have increased the ability of elites to control

these items and to use them in their interactions with people from other Mississippian period centers. Evidence of these interactions, for example, can be seen in elements of Cahokia ideology that are found at Etowah and Moundville (Alabama) and in effigy pipes from limestone sources in Mississippi that are found at Moundville some 300 kilometers (186 miles) away.[64]

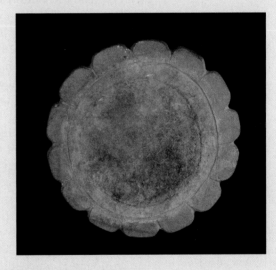

FIGURE 8.7
An example of a Mississippian period stone palette used to grind paints.

Great Plaza (see Figure 8.6). This feature was originally a borrow pit, that is, an enormous hole in the ground created by digging out sediment to use in the construction of the earthen mounds and perhaps to level the Great Plaza area.[67] It was refilled with the debris related to at least seven feasting events. There are hundreds of broken cooking vessels, and some of the seven layers of debris contain large amounts of deer bone, which was not common at sites around Cahokia. This suggests that deer were brought to Cahokia as a tribute payment to Cahokian elites and then used in the feasting events. One of the layers with deer bone had bones from swans, wild ducks, prairie chickens, and Canadian geese. Plant foods included domesticated maygrass and erect knotweed, as well as sunflower, strawberries, persimmons, grapes, hickory nuts, and squash. Interestingly, maize was not common, perhaps because it represented the main daily food and was considered too ordinary for feasting purposes. The debris from the feasting events also contained many nonfood items that probably represented the remains of some of the rituals associated with the feasts and with the construction of the mounds. The presence of large quantities of tobacco seeds, for instance, suggests the smoking of tobacco, which was a ritual act in Eastern North America.[68] Other items linked to ritual uses include projectile points made from exotic materials, pigments, painted pottery vessels, a smoking pipe, a chunkey stone, shell beads, special woods (red cedar and bald cypress), debris from making basalt axes and chert knives or adzes, and isolated human bones, some of which have cut marks and polish. Finally, roof thatch also was disposed of in the layers of sub-Mound 51, indicating that people were rebuilding structures such as temples that stood on the tops of some earthen mounds.

The activities, ceremonies, and rituals at Cahokia were directed by individuals (or families) who had elite status. They were able to access goods and labor to a degree that exceeded the reach of most families and kin-related groups. That some people were elites can be interpreted from several lines of archaeological and ethnohistoric data, including food-consumption patterns and burials (read "Peopling the Past: High-Status and Sacrificial Burials at Cahokia"). Bioarchaeological studies of human bone from burials with extraordinary grave goods in mounds and from the trash areas associated with elite dwellings show that these individuals enjoyed protein-rich diets from deer and that a number of them were migrants from elsewhere in the region.[69] In **Mound 72** (see Figure 8.6), the bones from burials of elite individuals (mainly males) show high consumption of animal protein and 45% maize in their diets. This contrasts with the burials of lower status individuals in Mound 72 whose diet was 60% maize. These lower-status people (mainly females) also show more evidence for pathologies that are linked to poor health, such as a high frequency of cavities typical of the preparation of sticky foods made from ground maize.

Mound 72 an Early Mississippian period burial mound at Cahokia, Illinois. It contains evidence for elaborate burial rituals for elite male individuals, as well as probable sacrifice burials (usually of numerous females) and offerings of exotic goods such as mica, copper, and shell beads.

Large-scale gatherings of people participated in these social and ritual activities at Cahokia, and some researchers suggest that the rituals may have been the basis for what might be called a "theater state."[78] Being able to witness and participate in ceremonies and rituals at Cahokia might have been the mechanism that brought people to this center and integrated them into a widely shared ideology. The elites who managed the dramas may have been charismatic leaders and the deaths of some of these individuals also part of the theaterlike drama, for example, the act of burying them being undertaken with the sacrifice of multiple humans found in some of the pits in Mound 72. Although it would be quite difficult to prove archaeologically, the large numbers of females possibly could have gone willingly to their deaths if Mississippian groups believed that this was an honorable or valued form of death; for example,

Peopling the Past

High-Status and Sacrificial Burials at Cahokia

Mound 72 contains 25 burial contexts with more than 270 people; most of them were killed.[70] The arrangement and features of some of these burials suggest the presence of elite members of society and the possibility that they were public rituals and ceremonies witnessed by hundreds or thousands of people.[71] One elaborate burial in Mound 72 is the Beaded Burial complex. It was originally described as an adult male placed face down and then covered with the construction of a platform in the shape of a bird that was covered with a 2-meter (6.5-foot)-long "cape" made of 20,000 shell beads. On top of the bird cape, another adult male was placed. Twelve other people were buried nearby. Recent reanalysis and new radiocarbon dates of the skeletons of the Beaded Burial complex, however, paint a very different picture.[72] The burials in this complex date between AD 991 and AD 1023,

to the beginning of Cahokia as an important center. After the construction of the earthen platform and the covering of it with thousands of beads, the body of a young female was placed so that her hips and legs were on top of the beads. Additional beads were placed over her legs. After this, the body of a young male was placed on top of the right side of the female's body. No beads were placed over the male, but beads were deposited in an arc from the young male's shoulder and face (forming the "head" of the so-called bird created by the bead deposits associated with the burial of the young female). There are an additional 10 people, some buried later and as bundle burials. Several of these also are pairs of young males and females. One burial is a child.

Some burials in Mound 72 have abundant grave goods that we associate with elites (chunkey stones,

FIGURE 8.8
Examples of chunkey stones (discoids) from burials in Mound 72 at Cahokia.

hundreds of arrows, long copper tubes that might have been poles used in the chunkey game, shell beads, and mica crystals)[73] (Figure 8.8). One mass grave has 39 face-down people who suffered violent deaths; interpretations of this suggest that some were not completely dead when they were buried (their fingers were curled into the underlying sand).[74] Most were hit on the back of the skull, 3 were decapitated, and 2 had stone arrowheads embedded in their bones. Other interments include four early pit burials from Mound 72 that contain the carefully arranged bodies of 19 to 53 young females each; these are described as sacrifices.[75] Bioarchaeological studies of strontium isotope ratios in the teeth of female skeletons from one of these pits show that they were local people; they may have been taken as captives during raids in the area around Cahokia.[76] There also is a burial of four adult males who were decapitated after death, with their hands also removed.[77] Some items in Mound 72 occurred in pits without bodies and may represent dedication offerings, such as 36,000 shell beads, several copper sheets, and a number of projectile points made from antler that were found in a single pit.

"The supporters of this state did so not because they were coerced but because they wanted to take part."[79]

Warfare and Violence

During the Early Mississippian period, when Cahokia was at its height, there is archaeological evidence for violence and guerilla-style warfare. Some researchers believe that this type of raiding was an activity done by elite males.[80] Evidence can be seen in burials from Mound 72 (discussed earlier), for example, the four adult males whose hands and heads were removed (possibly as trophy-taking). Mound 72 also contained other decapitated individuals as well as some who had arrowheads embedded in their bones. Most of the warfare raiding seems to have been limited to stealth attacks on a few individuals at a time, possibly because the use of bows and arrows facilitated this type of assault.[81]

The construction of fortifications such as wooden palisades around settlements also has been interpreted as suggesting violence and limited warfare.[82] At Cahokia, a wooden palisade of 20,000 logs that enclosed the "downtown" area was built around AD 1150. If this was a fortification, it protected only the elite dwellings and ritual areas, rather than the thousands of ordinary folks living in the many residential areas surrounding downtown. Fortified settlements, as well as evidence for increased levels of warfare, became more common after AD 1200,[83] when Cahokia's importance as a regional center was greatly diminished and other Mississippian period sites grew in size and significance. The types of palisades at these later sites suggest defense against bow-and-arrow warfare and also against fire-tipped arrows (through the use of plaster on the wooden palisades to inhibit fire).

The Mississippian After Cahokia

Around AD 1150, Cahokia and its surrounding region experienced several important changes, which culminated between AD 1200 and 1275. The local power and influence of Cahokia over areas to the north and south was reduced, and the area was
abandoned by most of its population after AD 1300.[84] One of the first inklings of these
changes was the depopulation of almost all villages and hamlets in the uplands area
in AD 1150. At Cahokia itself, the wooden palisade was built around the downtown
area. By AD 1200, although many people continued to live in hamlets scattered in the
landscape around Cahokia, most of the regional towns were no longer occupied, and
evidence for rituals and ceremonies at Cahokia suggests less public involvement. Why
this reorganization of economy, politics, and religion occurred is not entirely clear.
One factor may have been deforestation, leading to soil erosion, and impacts on maize
agricultural fields that resulted from the long-term use of wood for fuel, building, and
agricultural clearing by the many thousands of people who lived at and near Cahokia
during its peak from AD 1050 to 1200.[85] Another factor may have been two prolonged
drought periods in the AD 1200s (see Chapter 7 for similar droughts in the North
American Southwest) that affected agricultural productivity and availability of surpluses.[86] If surpluses were greatly diminished, then elites would not have the capacity
to redistribute food through feasting events. In these circumstances, ordinary folks
may have lost faith in their leaders, which ultimately resulted in their drifting away
from Cahokia as a center. Alternatively, the evidence from bioarchaeology showing
that there were many migrants into Cahokia and its surrounding area might suggest
that these people brought different ways of doing things with them when they settled
there.[87] Over time, these differences may have intensified as people came into conflict
for access to resources. Increased levels of conflict or disagreements could have led
to less participation in area-wide rituals and the eventual abandonment of Cahokia.

The Late Mississippian

The traditions seen at Cahokia did not necessarily disappear once people left. Instead,
the archaeological record includes many examples of Late Mississippian period centers elsewhere in Eastern North America, such as Moundville in Alabama and Etowah
in Georgia (Figure 8.9), which shared the ideology and construction features seen in
the Early Mississippian period. These Late Mississippian period sites had earthen
mounds with temples, elite dwellings and burials, plazas, palisades, and ditches that
surrounded centers and other settlements. One aspect of the ideology can be seen in
the **Southeastern Ceremonial Complex** (read "Peopling the Past: Symbols in the
Southeastern Ceremonial Complex"). How these Late Mississippian period centers
were organized socially and ritually varies from place to place, but all of them had elite
individuals or families who negotiated ties to their surrounding local communities.[88]

Moundville (see Figure 8.2) emerged as a regional center about AD 1200, with
the construction of 29 earthen mounds, a plaza, a palisade wall, cemeteries, and residential dwellings. Its population might have been a thousand people, who were brought

**Southeastern Ceremonial
Complex** artistic motifs that
were carved onto shell cups and
gorgets, as well as hammered
onto copper, during the Late
Mississippian period in the North
American East. Images include
males wearing costumes, snakes,
weapons, decapitations, chunkey
players, and raptors.

Moundville a Late Mississippian
period site in Alabama with 29
earthen mounds, a plaza, and a
palisade. It became a significant
center around AD 1200, but most
of its residents moved away about
AD 1250, except for elite families
and their retainers.

FIGURE 8.9
Mound C at the Late Mississippian period site of Etowah, Georgia.

together by sharing in the public works construction efforts and their accompanying rituals and ceremonies.[91] By AD 1250, only 300 elites and their retainers remained at Moundville. Most people moved away to hamlets scattered throughout the countryside. The region was still integrated, however, with elites at Moundville forging links with families at single mound settlements, who in turn drew on people living in dispersed hamlets. During this period, Moundville became a focus for death and burial rituals, and by AD 1300 the elites had elaborate sets of symbols that set them apart from others. One male elite burial, for example, had copper-covered bead bracelets on his arms and legs, copper gorgets, a necklace made of pearls, and a pendant of a human head made from amethyst. There were also stone palettes (sometimes called sun disks) that have traces of pigments on them. These palettes may have been items used in rituals.[92] All of these unusual goods would have been reserved for use by elites and would have set them apart from most other Mississippian period people in the region.

In some parts of Eastern North America, relatively rapid and large-scale depopulation of areas occurred, such as the one leading to the creation of the "Vacant Quarter" in the mid-AD 1400s.[93] This region of the lower Ohio Valley (including parts of Missouri, Illinois, Indiana, Kentucky, and Tennessee) may have been abandoned because of climate changes that affected agricultural growing seasons (as we saw in the North American Southwest as well; see Chapter 7), although Mississippian period groups in other areas of Eastern North America were not impacted to

Symbols in the Southeastern Ceremonial Complex

The Southeastern Ceremonial Complex is not a concept accepted by all scholars who work in the North American East. This is because earlier interpretations, such as influence from Mesoamerica, are no longer widely believed to be true. Additionally, using the term "complex" might imply that all Mississippian centers were integrated into one bigger social or ritual entity. As we saw earlier, this was never true. Each Mississippian period center was to a large degree independent of all other centers. At its most fundamental level, however, the Southeastern Ceremonial Complex does show us the type of imagery used in art by Mississippian people.[89] This imagery was diverse and, in some instances, particular styles appear to represent different geographical areas. The motifs were found hammered onto copper and engraved on shell cups and shell gorgets. They included male figures in costumes, weapons, combined human–animal figures, raptors, snakes, people playing chunkey, hands with an eye in the center, winged serpents, and decapitation (Figure 8.10). Some interpretations have focused on explanations such as the costumed figures representing warrior heroes or portrayals of people in myths.[90] However, given that we know these images varied in style from place to place, it is difficult to interpret their use as representing a single belief system.

FIGURE 8.10
Hand with eye and snake motifs used in the Southeastern Ceremonial Complex.

this degree. Shifts in power between different Mississippian centers could be another factor, especially because the Late Mississippian is a period of increased warfare, at least in the sense of more frequent conflicts.[94] These types of engagements were directed by elite leaders using elite warriors and male members of the general population. Although these were not standing armies, they could be quickly mobilized to attack other centers and their surrounding villages and were observed in action by the Spanish when they arrived in Southeastern North America in the mid-AD 1500s. Diseases introduced by the Spanish, such as smallpox, and by later Europeans decimated many Mississippian groups,[95] and their social organization shifted to reflect these and many other changes after Contact. Accounts written by the Spanish and other foreigners, as well as the oral traditions of descendants of the Mississippian period peoples, however, have provided archaeologists with a wealth of data that can be used to help interpret important sites such as Cahokia and Moundville.

Further Reflections

Cahokia: Paramount Chiefdom or State?

As we saw in Chapters 5 and 6, it is often difficult to decide if the social and political organization of groups of people in certain regions in the past should be described using terms such as chiefdom or state. While archaeologists have created lists of features that can be used to describe different types of political organization, such lists are not foolproof or necessarily a correct way of understanding the complexity present in prehistoric societies. In other words, the fact that Cahokia had a large population, shared ideology, community activities and rituals that involved people in the area around Cahokia, a group of elite leaders, and the capacity to undertake community planning and monumental-scale construction efforts might be interpreted by some archaeologists as an example of a paramount chiefdom (several communities integrated under a single set of leaders), while others would characterize it as a state. So, which explanation is right? This depends somewhat on which features you think might be most important. Is it

the size and density of population that elite leaders oversaw? Is it the size of the territory that appears to be controlled by leaders? Is it because leaders can coerce people to do things? These are just some of the questions that can be asked. If I had to put a label on Cahokia, I tend to support an interpretation of a paramount chiefdom. This is because I favor the idea of the impact and importance of the role of cooperative behaviors in societies, as proposed by Charles Stanish,[96] along with territory size and a few other features. Many great things can be achieved through cooperation, leading to what Stanish calls "stateless" societies (see Chapter 5). This does not mean that Cahokia was not complex socially and perhaps politically. But you need to ask if what we see at Cahokia was accomplished because people were forced into it (suggesting an absolute ruler) or instead cooperated to create this social and political milieu. One thing that we can say is that given its size, population density, and organized layout, Cahokia was certainly a city.

Summary

- During the Late Archaic period in the North American East, hunter–gatherer–forager groups domesticated local seed crops such as sunflower and maygrass.

- The Late Archaic period is known for mound-building. These large constructions were made using earth, such as at Poverty Point in Louisiana, or from the shells of shellfish food debris such as at the Sapelo Island Shellfish Ring Complex.

- Long-distance trade and exchange networks established during the Archaic period continued into the Woodland and Mississippian periods, as did mound building.

- Woodland groups such as the Adena and Hopewell cultures relied more heavily on domesticated native plants than did Archaic period groups.

- The Hopewell (Middle Woodland period) built burial mounds containing individuals with large quantities of grave goods including exotic items such as copper, mica, and quartz. These burials likely represent people with leadership roles, including ritual specialists. The presence of exotic materials was partly the result of the Hopewell Interaction Sphere, which linked many Hopewell and other groups together in trade and exchange networks.

- During the Late Woodland period, greater agricultural investment was made in the growing of maize, which had been introduced from Mexico a few centuries earlier.

- The Early Mississippian period saw the rise of Cahokia, a major social and ceremonial center. Cahokia had earthen pyramids, plazas, elaborate burials, a woodhenge, and many other features indicating its importance in the region. Surrounding Cahokia were many smaller towns with their own plazas and pyramids, as well as hamlets where farmers lived and worked.

- Centers such as Cahokia partially served as focus points for rituals such as feasting and other ceremonies and activities (such as chunkey games) that integrated people across the region. These events, as well as the building of the monuments, were likely under the control of elites and their families.

- Evidence for elites at Cahokia comes from the types and quantities of grave goods found with them, the unusual positioning (such as the young adult female and male buried in the midst of thousands of shell beads in Mound 72), burial within earthen mounds, and bioarchaeological studies of their bones showing that they had better access to higher-quality diets.

- Bioarchaeology shows that many people at Cahokia and smaller sites in the region were migrants from elsewhere in the North American East.

- By AD 1200, Cahokia and its surrounding region was mostly abandoned and other Mississippian period centers became more prominent. Why people left Cahokia is not entirely clear, although abandonment might have been related to overuse of the land for maize agriculture, droughts that affected agricultural productively, and increased conflicts.

- Late Mississippian centers, such as Moundville, also contained plazas, earthen mounds, and elaborate burials. During this period there are many examples of depopulation of areas of the North American East, possibly because of increased warfare or climatic changes that affected agricultural productivity.

- When the Spanish arrived in the AD 1500s, they encountered Mississippian period peoples. However, diseases that the Spanish and other foreigners brought from Europe decimated these Native American populations, resulting in further depopulation. Descendants of these Mississipian societies include the Coosa, Apalachee, and Natchez.

Endnotes

1. Levine 2004.
2. Goosefoot (*Chenopodium*), sunflower (*Helianthus annuus*), sumpweed, also called marsh elder (*Iva annua*), maygrass (*Phalaris*), little barley (*Hordeum pusillum*), and erect knot-weed (*Polygonum erectum*); see papers in Gremillion 2004; Mueller et al. 2017; Smith 1992; Yarnell 1978.
3. Mueller et al. 2017.
4. White 2013.
5. Zeanah 2017.
6. See, for example, Marquardt 1985.
7. Winters 1974: xviii.
8. Rothschild 1979; Webb 1946.
9. Mound-building first appeared during the Middle Archaic period, but then disappeared for 1,300 years, until it began again during the Poverty Point culture (Saunders et al. 2005: 663).
10. Ford et al. 1956: 14–19; Sassaman 2005a: 342.
11. Sassaman 2005a: 338.
12. Gibson 2007: 509.
13. Ford et al. 1956: 128.
14. Gibson 2007: 516; Sassaman 2005a: 345.
15. Gibson 2007: 515.
16. Gibson 2007: 510–513.
17. Russo 2006, 2008.
18. Russo 2008: 21.
19. Thompson and Andrus 2011.
20. Kidder 2006.
21. Mueller 2018; Sassaman 2005b.
22. Stoltman and Hughes 2004.
23. Abrams and Freter 2005.
24. Mueller 2018.
25. See, for example, papers in Charles and Buikstra 2006.
26. Some researchers argue for settled (sedentary) habitation sites (e.g., Pacheco 1996; Pacheco and Dancey 2006), whereas others (e.g., Cowan 2006) argue that Hopewell groups were mobile rather than sedentary.
27. Ruby et al. 2005; Smith 1992.
28. Bender et al. 1981; van der Merwe and Vogel 1978.
29. Carr 2005: 616–621.
30. Abrams 2009; Bolnick and Smith 2007; Coon 2009; see also papers in Charles and Buikstra 2006 and papers in Carr and Case 2005a.
31. Brose 1994; Emerson et al. 2013; Hughes et al. 1998; Stevenson et al. 2004.
32. Byers 2011.
33. Burks and Cook 2011; Lepper 1996.
34. Seeman and Branch 2006: 121.
35. More than 200 burials were found at the Hopewell Site and more than 100 at the Turner Site (Carr et al. 2005: 484).
36. Carr et al. 2005: 486–488.
37. Carr et al. 2005: 490–495.
38. Coon 2009: 56; Ruby et al. 2005: 155; Yerkes 2005: 242.
39. Carr and Case 2005b; Yerkes 2002.
40. Pauketat 2004: 8–9.
41. Bettinger and Eerkens 1999.
42. Schoeninger 2009.
43. One example of a Late Woodland mound and plaza site is the Coles Creek tradition Raffman Site in Louisiana (Kidder 2004).
44. Pauketat 2004: 60–64.
45. Pauketat 2003; Slater et al. 2014.
46. Pauketat 2004: 71.
47. Pauketat 2004: 67–95.
48. Dalan 1997; Pauketat 2004: 77.
49. Pauketat 2004: 69.
50. See the Cahokia Mounds State Historic Site website at https://cahokiamounds.org/explore/#tab-id-4 (accessed July 6, 2018).
51. In fact, Pauketat (2013) argues that constructions in Mississippian period centers and settlements were aligned to solar and lunar observations. He contends that these alignments represent the use of religion, which, in the case of Cahokia, led to pilgrimages of large numbers of people to this Mississippian center.
52. Emerson 1997b; Pauketat 2004: 96–99.
53. Cordell and Milner 1999.
54. Woods 2004: 258.
55. Fritz 2000; Kelly 1997; Yerkes 2005.
56. Pauketat 2004: 106.
57. Iseminger 1997.
58. Lulewicz and Coker 2018; White 2013.
59. Kelly 1991; Pauketat 1992: 41.
60. Muller 1999: 151–152.

61. Alt 1999; Pauketat 2004: 82–84, 100–103; Yerkes 1983.
62. Pauketat 1992: 38–39.
63. Steponaitis and Dockery 2011; Steponaitis et al. 2011.
64. Pauketat 2007; Steponaitis and Dockery 2011.
65. Emerson 1997a; Emerson et al. 2003; Thomas 2001.
66. Pauketat 2004: 63, 86.
67. Kelly 1997; Pauketat et al. 2002; Yerkes 2005.
68. Wagner 2000.
69. Ambrose et al. 2003; Kelly 1997; see also Jackson and Scott 2003 for similar nutritional data from Mississippian period Moundville in Alabama. See Slater et al. 2014 for information about migrants to Cahokia.
70. Emerson et al. 2016; Koziol 2010.
71. Pauketat 2004: 87–93; see also Fowler et al. 1999.
72. Emerson et al. 2016.
73. Fowler et al. 1999.
74. Koziol 2010: 177, 183–184, 202, 212.
75. Koziol 2010: 166–168.
76. Slater et al. 2014: 125.
77. Koziol 2010: 214.
78. Holt 2009.
79. Holt 2009: 247.
80. Milner 1999; Pauketat 2004: 156–160; the raiding type of warfare seen in the Early Mississippian period has roots in the Archaic period (for example, Mensforth 2001).
81. Milner 1999: 122.
82. Milner 1999: 118–120; Pauketat 2004: 148–149.
83. Cobb and Giles 2009; Dye 2006.
84. Pauketat 2004: 148–153; Woods 2004.
85. Woods 2004.
86. Pauketat 2004: 151–153.
87. Slater et al. 2014: 126.
88. Beck 2003.
89. Knight et al. 2001.
90. Dye 2006: 131–133; Knight et al. 2001.
91. Beck 2003: 649–654; Knight 2004: 305.
92. Moore 1905; see also Steponaitis et al. 2011 for a discussion of similar stone palettes from Etowah in Georgia.
93. Cobb and Butler 2002.
94. Dye 2006: 134–136.
95. Betts 2006.
96. Stanish 2017.

4 | Politically Complex Societies

CHAPTER 9

Early Dynastic Mesopotamia

Mesopotamia is the region situated between the Tigris and Euphrates Rivers in the Middle East and today includes Iraq and parts of southwestern Iran, northwestern Syria, and southeastern Turkey (Figure 9.1). In prehistory, cultural developments there gave rise to one of the world's earliest written languages and to the formation of politically and administratively complex entities that are called city-states. Later, empires and kingdoms become prevalent (read "Timeline: Mesopotamia"). The Mesopotamian region is considered an example of an early civilization, meaning that its origins occurred when there were few other politically complex areas developing outside of Mesopotamia (such as Egypt) (read "Further Reflections: Archaeology and Politics"). In this chapter we will examine the Neolithic and Chalcolithic foundations of Mesopotamia, especially with respect to the Early Dynastic period (Sumerian city-states). Most of these city-states and later empires and kingdoms were relatively short-lived, but the study of their social, political, and

ABOVE: Sumerian period carving of a lion hunt in Mesopotamia.

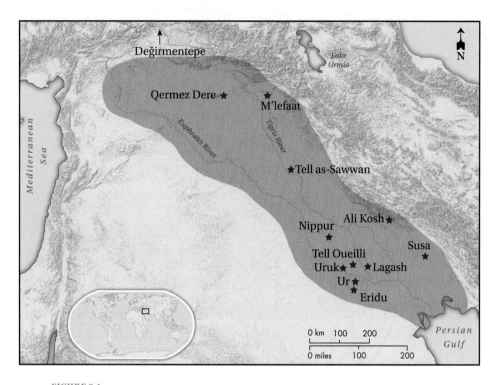

FIGURE 9.1
Map showing Mesopotamian sites mentioned in the chapter. Note that the brown area represents the greatest extent of Mesopotamia.

administrative organizations is extremely useful in understanding how they functioned and how and why these particular types of systems developed. Written records provide valuable clues about economics, religion, leadership, and many other facets of these early politically complex societies.

Early Food Production

The Middle East is one of the primary areas for the origins of food production, including cereals and legumes, as well as sheep, goat, and cattle (see Chapter 5). The domestication of cattle occurred around 7500 cal BC in marshland and forested areas along the Euphrates River in northern Syria.[2]

Pre-Pottery Neolithic

The Pre-Pottery Neolithic has many aspects of settled life, such as semipermanent to permanent villages, as well as complex rituals, but it lacks pottery vessels that are convenient for storage and cooking purposes. Archaeologists previously believed that

Timeline: Mesopotamia

The timeline for Mesopotamia is complex because of issues of early sites being buried under floodplain sediments in southern Mesopotamia and the fact that there is chronological overlap in periods depending on which part of Mesopotamia one is discussing.[1] Additionally, the several complex political entities were variously present in either southern or northern Mesopotamia or represent peoples from other regions who controlled Mesopotamia at different points in time (Figure 9.2).

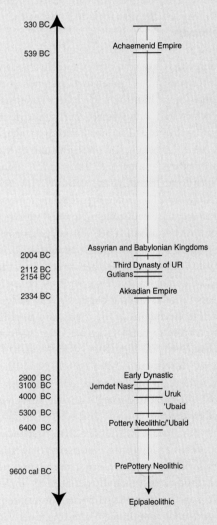

330 BC	
539 BC	Achaemenid Empire
2004 BC	Assyrian and Babylonian Kingdoms
2112 BC	Third Dynasty of UR
2154 BC	Gutians
2334 BC	Akkadian Empire
2900 BC	Early Dynastic
3100 BC	Jemdet Nasr
4000 BC	Uruk
5300 BC	'Ubaid
6400 BC	Pottery Neolithic/'Ubaid
9600 cal BC	PrePottery Neolithic
	Epipaleolithic

FIGURE 9.2

The timeline for Mesopotamia, with dates in BC for the 'Ubaid and later periods subject to revision as more evidence is collected.

domesticated plants and animals were present at Pre-Pottery Neolithic sites, but considerable research has shown that Pre-Pottery Neolithic people had a hunting and collecting economy based on wild food resources. They may have begun to bring wild cattle, goats, and sheep under closer human control, and they likely encouraged the growth of wild cereals and pulses by sowing wild seeds.[3] The Pre-Pottery Neolithic thus is similar to earlier hunter–gatherer–forager groups of the Epipaleolithic period. However, the more sedentary lifestyle of the Pre-Pottery Neolithic led to a more visible set of social interactions (including ritual behaviors) in the archaeological record. Pre-Pottery Neolithic sites include M'lefaat and Qermez Dere (in Iraq) in northern Mesopotamia.[4]

M'lefaat (see Figure 9.1), which dates to 9000 cal BC, was near a stream in a moist steppe that had small trees and shrubs. It was a small, permanent settlement with a dozen semisubterranean dwellings positioned around a clay courtyard. People living there had a hunting-and-gathering subsistence economy, with wild barley, einkorn wheat/rye, bitter vetch, lentils, and goat-grass. Among the stone artifacts were small arrowheads used for hunting gazelle. They also trapped or hunted hare, fox, and geese, partridge, and pheasant, and they fished. Ground stone tools, such as mortars, grinders, and querns (flat grinding stones), suggest that wild cereals were ground into flour. There also are woodworking tools (celts and adzes), as well as stone bowls. At **Qermez Dere** (see Figure 9.1), excavated single-room structures included nonfunctional plastered stone pillars and human skulls that appear to have been exposed for long periods of time. This suggests possible ritual or ceremonial activities in these rooms.[5] In other respects, people at Qermez Dere were engaged in the same types of tasks and hunting–gathering activities that characterized M'lefaat.

The archaeological evidence for Pre-Pottery Neolithic and earlier sites in southern Mesopotamia is lacking because many early sites are deeply buried under sediments of the floodplains of the Tigris and Euphrates rivers. Research in the nearby Deh Luran Plain region in Iran, however, yielded Pre-Pottery Neolithic sites such as **Ali Kosh** (Iran; see Figure 9.1), which dates to 7500 cal BC and is similar to sites in northern Mesopotamia.[6] Pre-Pottery Neolithic groups in southern Mesopotamia gathered wild plant foods (goosefoot, oat grass, alfalfa, einkorn wheat, and spiny milk vetch). They hunted gazelle, onager, aurochs, and wild boar, fished for carp, and collected freshwater mussels and turtles. Multiroom dwellings were constructed from slabs of natural clay (not fired), in part because wood and stone were scarce in the Mesopotamian lowlands. Houses in villages such as Ali Kosh are associated with courtyards with ovens and roasting pits. Over time during the Pre-Pottery Neolithic, wild plant foods were gradually replaced by domesticated cereals, although hunting of gazelle, aurochs, and onager became more frequent, and fishing and collecting of mussels and turtles continued. Pounding tools were present, as were stone bowls, and although these villagers did not yet make pottery, they were baking goatlike figurines in the courtyard ovens. Villagers at Ali Kosh were buried under the floors of dwellings, a ritual that may reflect maintaining links between the living and the deceased from individual families. There are few indications of differences between people

M'lefaat a Pre-Pottery Neolithic site in Iraq in northern Mesopotamia, dating to 9500 BC. It is a permanent village with evidence for the use of wild plant foods and hunting of wild animals.

Qermez Dere a small Pre-Pottery Neolithic village site in northern Iraq (northern Mesopotamia) that has evidence for use of some rooms for ritual activities. People living here hunted wild animals and used wild plant foods in the period leading up to the appearance of domesticated plants and animals.

Ali Kosh a Pre-Pottery to Pottery Neolithic site in the Deh Luran Plain of Iran, which is part of extended southern Mesopotamia. It contains evidence for early settled life based on the use of wild plants and wild animals and a later focus on domesticated plants and animals.

because most were buried with beads and pendants. Evidence for long-distance networks (perhaps trade and exchange) can be seen in the presence of turquoise, which came from northeastern Iran (near the Afghanistan border), sea shells from the Persian Gulf, obsidian from Turkey, and copper from central Iran.

Pottery Neolithic

Although sites such as Ali Kosh continued to be occupied into the Pottery Neolithic, archaeological evidence for occupation in the southern Mesopotamian lowlands is still lacking. In northern Mesopotamia, there are numerous sites that exemplify the types of settlements and social organization characteristic of this period.[7] One of these is **Tell as-Sawwan** (see Figure 9.1), dating from 6400 to 5700 cal BC,[8] which is attributed to the Samarran culture. It is an example of the expansion of farming from regions of dry farming to the alluvial plain where irrigation was necessary.[9] At Tell as-Sawwan, people used water from the Tigris River to irrigate their fields of barley, wheat, and flax. They raised domesticated cattle, sheep, and goats, hunted gazelle and onagers, collected freshwater mussels, and fished in the Tigris River. Like many earlier Pre-Pottery Neolithic sites, the Pottery Neolithic occupation of Tell as-Sawwan had small dwellings positioned around courtyards. Other features included ovens, kilns (for making pottery), and granaries (for storing cereals). A ditch was dug into the bedrock around the site, suggesting to some researchers that it may have been a defensive structure, although others believe that it was either a drainage ditch or where people obtained mud to build a simple wall around the site.[10] In one early building at Tell as-Sawwan, there were more than 125 burials, half of which are infants.[11] Most people had some grave goods (beads, pottery, or carved alabaster bowls, as well as female and animal figures), suggesting that status differences were not yet marked between people, at least as far as can be determined from burial rituals.

What is clear from the Pottery Neolithic period in northern Mesopotamia is that interaction networks (quite likely representing trade and exchange of ideas and goods) were well established by this time. This is reflected by several pottery styles. These include Samarran, Halafian, and early 'Ubaid styles. Whereas Samarran was most characteristic of northern Mesopotamia, Halafian was typical of the northern Levant, stretching from the Mediterranean Sea across northern Syria and into the very northern part of Iraq.[12] Early 'Ubaid pottery (see later), which was found in the southern Mesopotamian alluvial plain, shared a number of features with Samarran vessels.[13]

Tell as-Sawwan a Pottery Neolithic period site of the Samarran period in northern Mesopotamia, occupied from 6400 to 5700 cal BC. It represents the expansion of agricultural systems to include irrigation agriculture.

Before the Early Dynastic

The Chalcolithic period (when some tools were made of copper but people continued to use stone tools) follows the Neolithic period. The Chalcolithic includes the 'Ubaid, Uruk, and Jemdet Nasr periods. During this time, social and religious interactions and relationships, in conjunction with economic transactions, helped

Tell Oueili a site in southern Mesopotamia that has the earliest known 'Ubaid period levels. These date to 6300 to 4500 cal BC and include buildings that have long rooms with attached smaller rooms, 'Ubaid-style pottery, and an economy heavily invested in domesticated plants and animals.

'Ubaid Period during this period of the Chalcolithic in the Middle East, from 6300 to 4500 cal BC, increased interaction between southern and northern Mesopotamia is evident in the establishment of 'Ubaid colonies in Turkey. The first towns and temples appear, suggesting increasing social and political complexity.

provide impetus to increasingly complex administrative bureaucracies that provided social (and perhaps religious) control of resources, including labor.

One of the earliest sites in the southern Mesopotamian lowlands is **Tell Oueili** (see Figure 9.1), which contains occupations of the **'Ubaid period**, from 6300 to 4500 cal BC.[14] Although there are levels at this site that are below the current water table and thus cannot be excavated, its earliest 'Ubaid period level has evidence for multiroom mudbrick structures. Later occupations had dwellings with large central rooms that included roofs supported by two rows of posts, a rectangular hearth, and small platforms. These buildings are similar to Samarran architecture in the north. People living at Tell Oueili were farmers growing barley and some einkorn wheat using irrigation. They collected dates, had domesticated pigs and some domesticated cattle, and did not often hunt wild animals. Small numbers of sheep and goats were present, which may reflect the type of local habitat, which was marshy and not particularly well suited to raising goats and sheep. Some items, such as spindle whorls and beads, were made of bitumen (a naturally occurring tar or asphalt to which minerals were added), whereas others, such as sickles, were made from fired clay. The use of these types of materials reflects the fact that the southern Mesopotamian alluvial plain lacked abundant stone.

Painted pottery of the 'Ubaid style is found across much of Mesopotamia and as far north as Turkey. It also is present to the south in the Arabian Peninsula, as well as to the east in the highlands of Iran. These were locally made in each region but shared stylistic designs that suggest widespread contacts among people[15] (Figure 9.3). Most of the 'Ubaid archaeological sites were small villages characterized by self-sufficient households (each household produced or gathered the food and other materials necessary for the daily life of its extended family occupants). Some sites, however, were a bit larger and may have been early towns. These towns contained more elaborate architecture, including structures that are interpreted as temples. The appearance of temples suggests to some researchers that religion and religious specialists (such as "priests" or "priestesses") held a social role in society that allowed them to occasionally require other people to donate their labor for building temples or perhaps

FIGURE 9.3
Examples of 'Ubaid period pottery designs.

tend agricultural fields and animals that may have belonged to the temple. Other re-searchers point out that temples appear to be places where excess grain was stored, and these "banks" could be drawn on during periods of poor agricultural crop yields. It is easy to imagine how control of this system of labor and grain storage might lead to the establishment of a more permanent base of authority and power for individuals (or families) associated with the temples. The ideology of religion may have helped legitimize this authority to manage people and resources in the eyes of the other in-habitants of the town.

During the late 'Ubaid period, increased interactions between southern Meso-potamia and other regions are documented by the establishment of 'Ubaid colonies, for example, **Değirmentepe** in the Anatolian region of Turkey (see Figure 9.1).[16] This site was near sources for silver, lead, and copper, which were important metals used in exchange and the production of exotic goods. Archaeologists interpret this site as a colony because it contained the same type of architecture seen in southern Mes-opotamia, as well as abundant painted 'Ubaid pottery, seals, and sealings that were similar to those of sites from northern Mesopotamia. Seals are objects carved with distinctive pictures. They were used to make sealings (impressions) in wet clay. These sealings were a method of marking a door to a storeroom or the contents of a pottery vessel as closed/unopened. They are analogous to later historical wax seals that were placed on envelopes containing letters to indicate that the contents had not been read by anyone else. Değirmentepe also contained copper slag and smelting ovens, in-dicating the production of metal objects, which may have been taken to southern Mesopotamia or exchanged with people there.

Değirmentepe an 'Ubaid period site in Anatolia (central Turkey) that seems to represent on 'Ubaid colony with local manufacture of 'Ubaid style vessels and the use of seals and sealings with northern Mesopotamian designs. It is situ-ated near sources of silver, copper, and lead and contains evidence for the manufacture of copper objects.

The Uruk Period

As we saw earlier, a number of features that are potentially important as economic and social foundations for politically and administratively complex societies were apparent in the Mesopotamian region no later than the late 'Ubaid. It was during the succeeding **Uruk period**, however, that these features coalesced into the devel-opment of what many archaeologists consider the first cities and the first city-state.[17] Southern Mesopotamia became quite densely populated, with numerous small vil-lages, but also towns and cities. Irrigation canals facilitated large-scale agriculture, particularly of barley, and large herds of sheep and goat were raised (in the case of sheep, for their wool in making textiles). Like today, villages, towns, and cities in southern Mesopotamia were situated close to the water sources of the Tigris and Euphrates Rivers and their tributaries. In an open landscape that otherwise was rela-tively harsh because of its extremely warm summers, as population grew, people were increasingly concentrated in specific places along these waterways, rather than being spread out more evenly across the landscape. The location along waterways facili-tated movement of goods and communication between different communities using water transport.[18] At some of these population concentrations, people built their own dwellings and continued the tradition of building temples (which became larger over time), as well as large public buildings. By the late Uruk period, some of the largest

Uruk Period an important period (4000 to 3100 BC) of social and political development that resulted in the first city-states of southern Mesopotamia. It is characterized by specialized labor (scribes, bricklayers, priests, bureaucrats, etc.), tribute payments to temples, and accumulation of surplus agri-cultural products used as funding for construction projects.

and most densely populated locales were walled cities. These (and other) construction efforts required highly directed and well-organized oversight of labor, as well as the ability to feed people engaged in this construction work. The importance of increased grain surplus storage at temples was one critical variable in the rise of cities during this period.

The quantity of agricultural surpluses needed to underwrite these massive building projects, however, did not result simply from each family growing somewhat more than they needed and then contributing this to storage at temple complexes. Instead, it appears to have been an outcome of several factors.[19] Some of these were organizational and technological advances, for example, the development of blocks of long furrowed fields that were watered using irrigation canal systems. These fields produced agricultural surpluses on a scale not seen elsewhere. Estimates suggest that southern Mesopotamian irrigated agriculture outproduced rainfall agriculture in northern Mesopotamia by two or three times. These fields were furrowed using animal-drawn plows that had attached funnels that released seeds into the furrows. Once harvested, cereals were processed using another innovation, the threshing sledge, which separated cereal grain from the stalks (straw). Other factors involved effective management of different land types; for instance, prime land for large-scale irrigated agriculture yielded cereals, land with scrubby vegetation or land lying fallow was used for animal pasture, small irrigated fields were gardens and orchards, and marshlands (as well as various waterways) could be exploited for birds and fish, as well as reeds used in construction.

Uruk (Warka) the first city-state of southern Mesopotamia, which developed during the Uruk period. It had a population of 50,000 people, a complex political and bureaucratic administration, massive building projects, and sacred precincts with temples and palaces.

One of the best examples of an Uruk period city is the site of **Uruk** (also called Warka; see Figure 9.1) on an ancient course of the Euphrates River (the river channel has moved since the Uruk period).[20] Archaeologists have differing views concerning how cities such as Uruk supported themselves. Some researchers believe that goods and surplus foods entered the city as tribute payment to the temple complexes. Labor for construction and harvesting of the large block fields also would be a type of tribute payment. In this system, farmers "paid" a portion of their crops and other goods to the temples in return for social services, such as the ideology of religion. Other researchers suggest that the temple complexes were far more politically and administratively central. That is, they interpret the temple complexes as owning most of the irrigated agricultural lands. In this system, people working the land would be paid in food by the temples for their labor, whereas the temples controlled all the rest of the food surplus and storage and could use these for social, economic, and eventually military purposes. Exactly how the temple complexes came to own all the irrigated land is not clear, but presumably nontemple groups bought into the system because of perceived ideological/religious benefits. Perhaps there are parallels from more recent history and today, for example, people who donate their lands at death to religious institutions. Still other researchers stress the fact that administrative organizations were just one of several institutions present in society (kinship-based groups and communities are other types of institutions with legitimate authority and varying levels of political power) and that all of these cooperated and competed.[21]

Regardless of the exact system that provided the "funding" and the organization that supported Uruk, this city was the largest of its kind during this period, covering 100 hectares (250 acres) and perhaps populated by 50,000 people within the walled part of the city[22] (Figure 9.4). There were a variety of occupations (potters, metal workers, bricklayers, scribes, farmers, and textile makers) and different social classes (bureaucrats and temple and other elite). Most people lived in small mudbrick houses along narrow and winding streets, but some of these houses were a bit bigger, having two stories rather than one, suggesting that the occupants of the larger houses may have had access to greater amounts of resources ("wealth" in a simple sense of this term). Moreover, Uruk contained two sacred precincts, Eanna and Anu (both named after goddesses/gods). The large public buildings and temples built in this part of Uruk were 10 to 12 meters (32 to 39 feet) higher than those in the rest of the city and would have been visible to residents within the city as well as in the rural countryside surrounding Uruk. One of the earliest buildings in the Eanna precinct had a foundation of limestone blocks that had to be transported from 80 kilometers (50 miles) away; this probable temple was larger than the Parthenon in Greece.

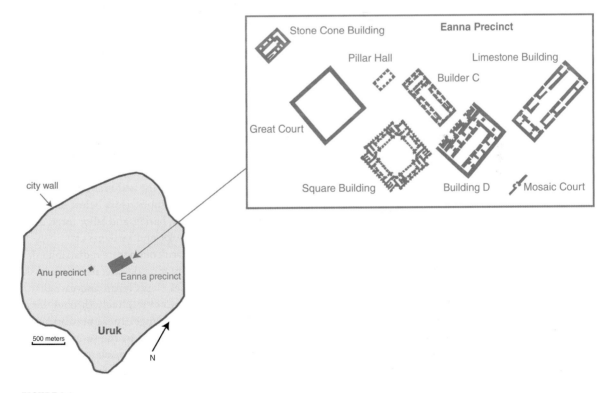

FIGURE 9.4
The city of Uruk during the Uruk period, with an inset showing some of the important buildings in the Eanna precinct.

FIGURE 9.5
The bearded male figure is
found first in the Uruk and
then in later periods.

Among the other features of the Eanna precinct were: (1) a colonnaded terrace, (2) mosaic walls (flat-top baked clay cones set into mudbrick; these cones were painted red, black, or white to form geometric designs), and (3), late in the Uruk period, large buildings referred to as palaces, as well as abundant evidence for grain storage and other administrative buildings. The Anu precinct has a series of temples, built and rebuilt in the same place over hundreds of years. Perhaps most telling is the fact that Uruk period iconography from several Uruk period sites included a male individual who was shown in a relatively standardized style. This male was a large bearded figure wearing a net skirt, with his hair pulled back into a bun, and was depicted as engaged in ritual ceremonies or as a hunter or warrior (Figure 9.5). This iconography suggests someone who was identified as a "priest-king" or other important elite authority.[23]

The administrative functions in cities such as Uruk are seen in the abundance of seals and sealings, which restricted access to stored goods to a limited number of authorized people. By the late Uruk period, early writing developed in the form of numerical counters. These counters were clay tablets used to record economic transactions involving payment in goods and quantities of stored goods. There were also hollow clay balls (called bullae) with counters within them. The use of seals, sealings, and clay tablet counters as a method to keep track of goods can be seen in the extraordinary amount of these found discarded in trash areas at Uruk. This is because they were removed to gain access to stored goods, then used as an auditing system to verify the stored contents, and finally thrown away when the goods were removed from the sealed contexts.[24] The importance of economics during the Uruk period also was reflected by 85% of all written texts being documents recording receipts and debts; they can be thought of as similar to modern bookkeepers' accounting systems. The complex role of administration in a city-state such as Uruk additionally is seen in written texts such as the "Standard Professions List." This list had a ranked hierarchy of different jobs with a "leader" at the top and various supervisors below him. The supervisors were in charge of departments such as law, barley, and labor force. Also listed were members of professions such as priests, cooks, and gardeners.[25]

Supplies and goods that came into cities such as Uruk often were redistributed.[26] The careful accounting systems show the circulation of cattle, metals, barley, fish, beer, milk products, and textiles. Semiprecious stones (lapis lazuli and carnelian), timber, silver, copper, gold, and marble, also came into cities, likely through long-distance resource networks that included trade and exchange. These networks may have been facilitated during the middle and late Uruk period by the so-called Uruk Expansion.[27] This striking phenomenon was the result of numerous large Uruk colonies that were established in northern Mesopotamia, northwestern Syria, and probably southeastern Turkey. Some researchers have suggested that these colonies reflect control of resource areas by cities (particularly Uruk) in southern Mesopotamia and exchange relationships that saw goods such as textiles and bitumen[28] exported from

Early Dynastic Period often called "Sumerian civilization," the Early Dynastic (2900 to 2350 BC) was characterized by more than a dozen city-states in southern Mesopotamia. These were largely independent of each other in terms of political control, although they shared many traditions such as cuneiform writing, a belief system oriented to the same pantheon of gods and goddesses, and similar forms of administrative, economic, religious, and political organization.

southern Mesopotamia to other areas, thus making trade one of the most important variables in the rise of politically complex societies in southern Mesopotamia.[29]
Other researchers, however, dispute this interpretation because cities such as Uruk
did not have the manpower or influence to maintain close control over such a large
geographic region.[30] It is more likely that the colonies helped negotiate with local
residents for certain valuable goods needed by the elite and others in southern Mesopotamia or were places where these materials sometimes were made into finished
products and then sent to southern Mesopotamia. In this sense, these colonies may
have been expressions of alliance-like relationships formed between southern Mesopotamia and its northern neighbors.[31]

> **City-State** a term used to de-
> scribe a political unit that includes
> an independently ruled city with
> its surrounding territory. Early
> Mesopotamia was characterized
> by city-state political organization
> during the Sumerian period.

The Uruk period is followed by the relatively short Jemdet Nasr period, for which
archaeologists have only scarce information. There were several important changes
during Jemdet Nasr, including the abandonment of
many of the Uruk colonies, the establishment of closer
links to Afghanistan, Egypt, and Iran, and the fact that
styles of architecture and pottery became distinct from
region to region.[32]

Early Dynastic Mesopotamia

During the **Early Dynastic** (I, II, and III) from 2900
to 2350 BC, southern Mesopotamia had a number of
important cities or **city-states**, rather than just one
dominant city, as seen during the Uruk period. These
city-states included Uruk, but also Ur, Lagash, Nippur,
Eridu, and Larsa (Figure 9.6; see Figure 9.1). A city-state
consisted of one or a few large urban areas surrounded
by a region of mainly uninhabited land, called a hinter-
land (read "The Big Picture: Early Dynastic Political
Organization"). Taken together, the city-states of southern Mesopotamia often are collectively called "Sumerian civilization," but in actuality, each city-state was a
more or less independent entity.[33] That is, no one city-
state was in control of all of southern Mesopotamia, but
they did all share cuneiform writing, a pantheon of gods
and goddesses, ziggurats (somewhat stepped pyramid
structures constructed at the end of the Early Dynastic
period; Figure 9.7), metalworking, and complex social
hierarchies with social classes and status differences between elites and commoners, and also between craft and
other specialists. During Early Dynastic times, many
of the rural areas around the city-states that previously

FIGURE 9.6
An aerial view of Ur, taken in 1927. The large mound near
the center is the ziggurat.

FIGURE 9.7
A drawing of the ziggurat at Ur.

contained villages were abandoned as people moved into the cities.[34] Cities such as Uruk may have housed between 55,000 to 110,000 people, as well as people who settled just outside the city walls.[35] The reasons for this population movement probably are numerous, but evidence for conflict between the city-states may have encouraged rural populations to seek safety within city walls or nearby the cities. Villagers and people living in other areas (such as southwestern Iran or upper Mesopotamia) also may have seen cities as more desirable places to live in terms of employment or access to resources,[36] just as we see today in the phenomenal growth of modern cities such as Cairo, Seoul, Mexico City, Mumbai, and Beijing, as rural and other populations move to urban areas.

The Written Word

As we saw previously, the earliest writing in Mesopotamia developed as a way of recording economic transactions and included seals, sealings, counters, bullae, and numerical tablets.[39] By the late Uruk and Jemdet Nasr periods, some clay tablets featured individual signs called ideographs that stood for ideas. These signs could be relatively realistic depictions of objects or ideas (for example, a bowl indicated a ration of food), but in other cases they were abstract depictions that did not bear any resemblance to the thing or idea that they represented. These types of signs are sometimes called protocuneiform because they were similar to cuneiform writing in the Early Dynastic and later periods. Protocuneiform did not record what the structure

The Big Picture

Early Dynastic Political Organization

The Early Dynastic period in southern Mesopotamia was characterized by two major powerful segments of society.[37] These were the royal and the religious elites. Both controlled enormous amounts of resources and directed labor to build monumental architecture such as palaces and temples. These two segments were not entirely separate because royals built temples to particular gods or goddesses and members of royal families could be ritual specialists within the temple organizations. Kings of the Early Dynastic period were associated with certain symbolic items that lent them divine legitimacy. These items included a crown, a mace, a scepter, and the throne of life.[38] Kings, however, were not divine.

Both the royal and the temple segments were organized as economic superhouseholds. As such, there were many people involved within each type of organization, for example, craft specialists, bureaucrats, armies (for royals), attached and independent laborers, and slaves. And there were other groups, such as wealthy families who maintained their own estates, city-dwellers who had assemblies of commoners to settle disputes, and rural farmers (Figure 9.8). This somewhat divided political organization was typical of each city-state, and it is easy to see how the many competing interests within and between city-states potentially could lead to instability that resulted in relatively short-lived centers of power.

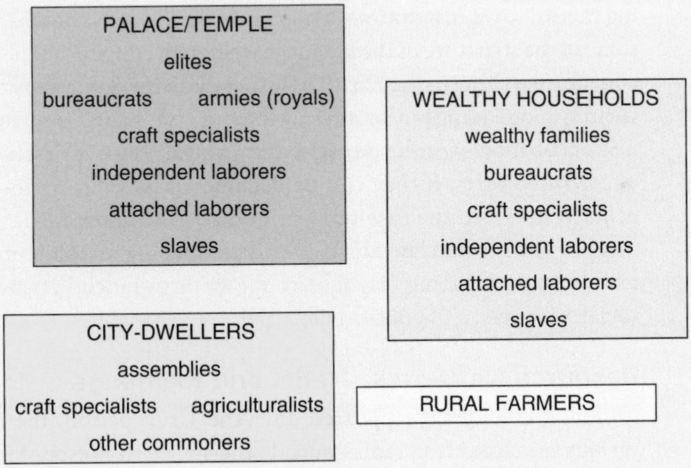

PALACE/TEMPLE
elites
bureaucrats   armies (royals)
craft specialists
independent laborers
attached laborers
slaves

WEALTHY HOUSEHOLDS
wealthy families
bureaucrats
craft specialists
independent laborers
attached laborers
slaves

CITY-DWELLERS
assemblies
craft specialists   agriculturalists
other commoners

RURAL FARMERS

FIGURE 9.8
The political structure of Early Dynastic Mesopotamia was largely organized along economic lines, regardless of secular or religious organizations.

FIGURE 9.9
A clay tablet with Sumerian cuneiform writing. It is a medical tablet.

Cuneiform a writing system developed in southern Mesopotamia during the Early Dynastic period. It was a syllabic language whose written signs are made up of combinations of lines and wedge shapes. It was used to record economic transactions, as well as inscriptions on buildings, proverbs, hymns, myths, and royal inscriptions.

of this language actually was because there were no signs that reflected the rules (syntax) of this language. Many languages today, for example, such as French, Spanish, and German, attach gender or neutrality to nouns using different forms of the article. In English, we do not have this system and we use the articles "the" or "a/an" for all our nouns. In French, on the other hand, the article "la" is used for nouns that are singular feminine and "le" for those that are singular masculine. Protocuneiform and cuneiform writing used wet clay tablets into which the signs were drawn or pressed using a reed (in the case of cuneiform). If the clay tablets then were baked, they became a permanent record.

By the beginning of the Early Dynastic, the ideographs of protocuneiform began to be written in a more abstract form using a series of wedge shapes and lines called **cuneiform** writing (Figure 9.9), and the number of individual signs was greatly reduced. Some of these cuneiform words still bore a resemblance to the original ideograph of protocuneiform, but the cuneiform words were syllabic. That is, they represented words or syllables of words rather than pictographic ideas. This shift, as well as other changes such as the inclusion of a minimal number of grammar and other syntax signs, led to the expansion of writing beyond account keeping to recording myths, royal inscriptions, recipe lists, and hymns. Because researchers can study some of the structure of the language written in cuneiform, they have determined that cuneiform writing in the Early Dynastic was in the Sumerian language. Literacy (both writing and reading) in southern Mesopotamia mainly was restricted to the specialized occupation of scribe. Most leaders (kings, priests, priestesses) were not literate.

Written texts, if they can be deciphered, offer many insights into society and belief systems. In the case of Early Dynastic Mesopotamia, although the decipherment of cuneiform clay tablets is still an ongoing research endeavor,[40] what we can read from the existing clay tablets allows us to much better understand economic, social, religious, and political life.

Resource Networks, Trade, and Exchange

Although colonies disappeared after the Uruk period, the need and demand for various resources from areas outside the southern Mesopotamian lowlands did not end. Many of the items that entered southern Mesopotamia during the Uruk and Jemdet Nasr periods also were traded or exchanged into this region during the Early Dynastic, but in much larger quantities. These included basic materials (timber and obsidian) and exotics (carnelian, lapis lazuli, gold, silver, alabaster, and shell). Many materials were brought on ships that sailed up the Tigris and Euphrates rivers from the Persian Gulf. Others came at least part of the way using donkeys as beasts of burden (especially in northern Mesopotamia).[41] The increasing demand for basic and exotic materials reflects a growth in wealthier households, but it is also a sign of the increased importance of the temple, and eventually of palace, households.

If southern Mesopotamia lacked basic items, such as stone and timber, we might wonder what resources were available there to use as goods for trade and exchange. It turns out that southern Mesopotamia's agricultural foundation provided the "raw materials" for a number of important goods. One of its assets was its fertile soil, on which large quantities of barley could be grown. Barley can be stored and used locally for various purposes, but it also can be packed into pottery vessels and traded elsewhere. Cereals were ground and made into bread, but Sumerians also used barley to make beer, which was another of their important commodities, at least within the various city-states, as their brewed beer did not keep well.[42] Perhaps one of the most significant of the southern Mesopotamian resources, however, was the wool from large herds of sheep that were pastured on fallow agricultural lands. Wool was used in making textiles, which became an extremely important commodity.[43]

The administration and organization of the production of goods, their storage, and their use or trade continued to be carefully monitored in Sumerian accounts recorded on clay tablets by scribes. This meticulous tracking of quantities of materials was enhanced by the development of standardized weights that provided an accurate measurement scale.[44] Not all exchanged goods, however, were the result of trade. Some materials were exchanged as gifts, for example, to mark the birth of royal children or religious ceremonies and/or as exchanges in establishing alliances. But how was the overall system of Sumerian production organized and managed?

SUPPLY, DEMAND, AND WEALTH

As noted earlier, during the Early Dynastic large numbers of people moved from rural into urban areas, creating densely packed populations in the cities of the city-states. The work efforts of many people continued to be organized in the context of households based on nuclear and extended families. That is, they were kin-based units that were part of the production and consumption cycle. Agricultural surpluses from the rural areas, however, declined substantially when people moved into the cities, and many households no longer had access to enough food and other goods and the temples no longer had surpluses generated by rural people giving them tribute payments. These social conditions helped create an environment that led to the development of "superhouseholds" during the Early Dynastic, or what is sometimes referred to as an *oikoi* **economy**.[45] The superhouseholds, which owned land, were typical of wealthy estates, temples, and royal palaces, and they combined the concept of kin-based households with nonkin labor (see Figure 9.8). City-dwelling lower-ranked people and their households often fell into debt, in part because they no longer had access to rural surpluses. One way to resolve this situation was to work for the elite landowners, temples, and royal palaces, all of which needed people as managers and as laborers in their agricultural fields or to herd animals and produce various crafts, including textiles.

In an *oikoi* economy, it is not the kin-based household that is the center of all economic activity, but instead the superhousehold (*oikos* is the singular form, and *oikoi* the plural form). The workforce was drawn from contracts with individuals for

Oikoi **Economy** an economy based on "superhouseholds" in which kin-based households are combined with nonkin labor. These were typical economic units during the Early Dynastic and later periods of Mesopotamia and were capable of generating large quantities of surplus textiles and crops. *Oikos* refers to a single superhousehold, whereas *oikoi* is the plural.

harvesting *oikoi* fields, public work obligations (for temples and palaces), debt-slaves (people sold into slavery to pay off debt obligations), and other slaves (female or children war captives from conflicts with other city-states). In return for their labor, workers often were paid in wool, barley, and oil, although these needed further processing to create food or textiles. Occasionally, they were paid with land that they could use themselves or rent to others, or with other types of rations such as beer, fish, meat, and cloth. The *oikoi* were headed by men and also by women, especially temple priestesses or wives and children of royal rulers. Although there were costs associated with running an *oikos*, there also were many benefits, not the least of which was its ability to amass surpluses that could be used to "fund" new ways of producing goods or agricultural products or weather a bad year for crops. These surpluses helped make the upper echelon members of the *oikoi* quite wealthy. *Oikoi* sometimes grew in size through the purchase of land and, as superhouseholds, could employ thousands of people. Because textiles were one significant type of good that was produced for trade and exchange, *oikoi* labor forces involved in making textiles (mainly women and children) sometimes were quite large. One *oikos* in the Lagash city-state, for example, employed "more than 4,000 adults and 1,800 children engaged as weavers."[46] That labor was just for textiles, rather than all the people and their labor activities that would have been typical in any given *oikos*.

Social Life

Distinctions between people in terms of the division of labor, work specialties, and social roles are apparent during the Early Dynastic, although it is important to remember that many of these societal strategies can be seen at least as early as the 'Ubaid period (read "Peopling the Past: Roles of Women and Men in Mesopotamia"). The cuneiform texts, as discussed previously, include ranked lists of professions that suggest status differences, and iconography contributes scenes showing various types of tasks, often with indications of whether these activities were mainly undertaken by men, women, children, or some combination of these groups. The development of the *oikos* economic unit further added labor and other distinctions between people, for example, a contract worker as opposed to a slave. Task or activity specialization became common, with royal rulers, religious elites, scribes, agricultural labor overseers, administrators and bureaucrats, military elite, and eventually merchants and traders. There also were many ordinary, nonelite people.

In addition to cuneiform texts, iconography, and differences in the size of residences for elite versus ordinary families, social distinctions between people also can be identified by examining burials. There were several different burial contexts, including those below house floors and in cemeteries, but also examples of people simply thrown into areas filled with trash or existing pits with no special preparations.[50] The lack of burial goods and/or types and quantities of burial goods associated with particular individuals also helps in the identification of differences between them based on religious, social, or political distinctions, as well as gender. For many people, their burials were simple in having only a few items (pottery,

Peopling the Past

Roles of Women and Men in Mesopotamia

The division of labor during the Early Dynastic often was along gender lines.[47] Manual labor in agricultural fields and the lower military ranks was done by men, as was herding of animals (Figure 9.10). Women, on the other hand, were the work force engaged in making textiles and mats, but they also herded pigs and worked in orchards. Males captured in war became slaves in the palace superhouseholds, whereas captured females became slaves in the temple superhouseholds. As we saw earlier, women were sometimes in positions of power, especially in elite households and superhouseholds,

and cuneiform tablets record a number of important male rulers of the royal dynasties of the different city-states (called the Sumerian King List).[48] Members of elite and upper-class families, including women, were administrators or priests and priestesses.[49] High-status women also were temple devotees, owned land, and participated in legal meetings. On the other hand, women from the lower classes might have had roles such as tavern managers or prostitutes, but such women were poorly treated by other members of society, to some extent because they did not have male protectors.

FIGURE 9.10
Relief of a milking scene from Tell al-Ubaid (watercolor by M. Louise Baker 1924).

beads, and, in some cases, copper pins, tools, or vessels). Children and infants were buried more often under house floors in outlying rooms or away from the burials of adults, as were adult women, whereas male adult members of those households were buried under the floors of more central rooms. Adults also frequently were buried in cemeteries, usually in simple pits with their body wrapped in a reed mat or placed in a coffin. The cemetery burials were arranged in groups, and the reopening of some of these to add later burials suggests social or kin links between the individuals. By Early Dynastic II and III times, distinctions between graves became more apparent, with some people buried without formal graves and others with large quantities of valuable or exotic items.

Royal Cemetery at Ur an Early Dynastic cemetery in Mesopotamia containing 16 elaborate burials. In addition to vast quantities of silver, gold, carnelian, and lapis lazuli jewelry, many of the graves of these socially important people contain stone, copper, gold, and silver vessels, tables, elaborately decorated chariots and the animals that drew them, and dozens of burials of retainers.

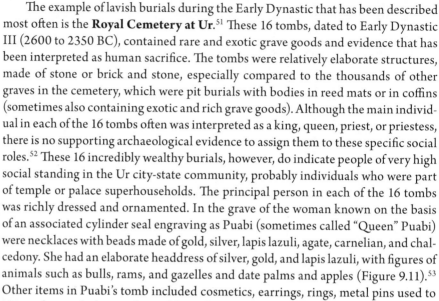

The example of lavish burials during the Early Dynastic that has been described most often is the **Royal Cemetery at Ur**.[51] These 16 tombs, dated to Early Dynastic III (2600 to 2350 BC), contained rare and exotic grave goods and evidence that has been interpreted as human sacrifice. The tombs were relatively elaborate structures, made of stone or brick and stone, especially compared to the thousands of other graves in the cemetery, which were pit burials with bodies in reed mats or in coffins (sometimes also containing exotic and rich grave goods). Although the main individual in each of the 16 tombs often was interpreted as a king, queen, priest, or priestess, there is no supporting archaeological evidence to assign them to these specific social roles.[52] These 16 incredibly wealthy burials, however, do indicate people of very high social standing in the Ur city-state community, probably individuals who were part of temple or palace superhouseholds. The principal person in each of the 16 tombs was richly dressed and ornamented. In the grave of the woman known on the basis of an associated cylinder seal engraving as Puabi (sometimes called "Queen" Puabi) were necklaces with beads made of gold, silver, lapis lazuli, agate, carnelian, and chalcedony. She had an elaborate headdress of silver, gold, and lapis lazuli, with figures of animals such as bulls, rams, and gazelles and date palms and apples (Figure 9.11).[53] Other items in Puabi's tomb included cosmetics, earrings, rings, metal pins used to fasten clothing, silver tables, a harp inset with jewels, a chariot decorated with precious stones, two wooden wagons, and vessels made from silver, gold, copper, and stone. All of this appears extremely elaborate, and Puabi's tomb also included dozens of other people (and animals), who seem to have gone to their death at the time of Puabi's burial, suggesting human sacrifice or possibly voluntary death to accompany Puabi into the afterlife.[54] Many of the other individuals in Puabi's tomb had elaborate and rich grave goods, likely indicating that their social roles were linked to hers. Some of the men were buried with copper daggers and helmets, and the women had jewelry with carnelian, gold, and lapis lazuli. One ironic twist, at least to us today, is that these incredible burials were in what was a trash dump, and rubbish continued to be thrown away in this area after the royal burials occurred.[55] We do know that past peoples in many societies disposed of their dead in trash areas, perhaps because these were easier to dig into than regular ground. Whether this is why the Royal Cemetery was placed into a trash area is difficult to know because it is possible that Sumerians had a different perspective about these associations, such as thinking of trash and the disposal of the dead in a similar way, since both are no longer of use (they do not have "life").

FIGURE 9.11

The headdress and some of the jewelry of Puabi from the Royal Cemetery at Ur.

Ritual and Religion

Burials are one type of ritual in human societies. In Early Dynastic Mesopotamia, many rituals were also associated with religion, including the fact that each city had a patron god or goddess for whom the main temples were built and modified over the generations. The city of Ur, for example, was the domain of Nanna (the moon goddess), whereas Ningirsu (the god of the plow and of thundershowers) was the patron of Lagash. Anu (the sky god) and Inanna (goddess of war and love) were associated with Uruk, and Enlil (the storm winds god) with Nippur.[56] There were also dozens of smaller temples in each city that were dedicated to gods and goddesses in the Mesopotamian pantheon other than the main patron god or goddess for the city. The linkage of forces of nature or aspects of nature with the gods and goddesses indicates that Mesopotamian religion saw these as closely connected rather than separate. Rulers and others who somehow angered the gods and goddesses would bring about crop failures or floods or losses in conflicts with other city-states. Pleasing the gods and goddesses through correct performance of rituals and temple building was a key to social, religious, and political success.

Using labor obligations to temples and palaces on the part of most community members, as well as slave labor, the construction of temples was undertaken by royal family members living in the palaces, in part because these rulers were seen as divinely connected to various gods and goddesses.[57] In a number of cases, the high priestess of a temple was a blood relative of the ruling family. Cuneiform records from periods after the Early Dynastic, for example, document the high priestess of Nanna at Ur as a sister or daughter of the city-state's ruler.[58] She held this social role for a specified amount of time and then retired, rather than serving until she died. It is likely that this method of serving the temple was similar during the Early Dynastic period. The ziggurat temples contained foundation deposits; for example, one of the temples dedicated to Inanna in Lagash had stones with inscriptions placed behind the heads of figurines made of copper that all faced to the east.[59]

Like those of the religions of today, the rituals and rites associated with Mesopotamian religion were complex and varied. Cuneiform texts contain hymns and prayers to gods and goddesses and also describe ceremonies. These included opening the eyes and mouths of statues of the gods and goddesses, dressing these statues in rich clothes and jewelry, feeding the gods and goddesses each day with dates, fish, meat, and beer, and carrying the statues in processions around cities and through the surrounding countrysides of the city-states.[60] The ideology associated with religion carried over to some extent into the ideology connected with political power (read "The Big Picture: Ideology and Art in the Early Dynastic").

Warfare and Violence

Conflict and warfare were features of Early Dynastic Mesopotamia, although these types of violence became much more organized (for example, with standing armies) in later periods.[64] Battles occurred mainly between different city-states, often over access and ownership of agricultural land, for rights to water for irrigation, and to control trade. The city-states had to contend with attacks from pastoralists who came from the Zagros Mountains to the east. These pastoral groups eventually were integrated into what became the Elamite Kingdom of southwestern Iran.[65] None of the city-states gained long-term control over the other city-states, which meant that political power across southern Mesopotamia was divided among the dozen or so different city-states. Early Dynastic Mesopotamian iconography shows men dressed

The Big Picture

Ideology and Art in the Early Dynastic

The motifs and associations of symbols in artistic representation often are important clues to the worldview of past (and present) societies. We saw previously that the image of a bearded male, dressed in a net skirt and with his hair pulled back, was a common figure in Mesopotamian art by the Uruk period (see Figure 9.5). These bearded males continued into Early Dynastic and later times, where they are interpreted as representing kings or priest-kings.[61] Early Dynastic elites also were shown in military scenes that commemorated battle victories over other city-states and, occasionally, engaged in ritual activities. The symbolic importance of these pieces of art is seen in the fact that they were taken as loot by the victors if a city-state was defeated in battle.[62] How people were depicted in art also gives us insight into social relationships and roles/statuses. For example, elite individuals such as kings usually were shown much larger than other people in a scene (Figure 9.12). Early Dynastic society associated the concept of being naked with being powerless.[63] This can be observed in military scenes where captives were naked but victors were clothed. This association may explain to some extent why elite individuals were buried with so many items of dress (clothing, headdresses, jewelry, and other accessories). They may have wanted to go into the afterlife as powerful individuals!

FIGURE 9.12
Depiction from a limestone stela from Ur of a seated king shown much larger than nonelite individuals (note also that the larger figure is holding an object).

as soldiers, wearing helmets and carrying shields, spears, axes, maces, daggers, and other lethal weapons. There also are battle scenes[66] with simple chariots, the capture of prisoners, and military formations such as the phalanx. A phalanx is a mass of heavily armed infantry organized into a rectangle that marches forward as a solid block and is able to cut through enemy lines and crush enemy soldiers underfoot.

Although the Early Dynastic period had a number of individuals who were military specialists, many of the rank-and-file fighting forces probably were drawn from labor obligations to the palaces and temples in each city-state. The "winning" side in a battle often took captives, especially women and children who could be used as slave labor. Some male captives were used as slaves, but many were killed in mass slaughter events after the battles were over, at least according to stories of various rulers and their battles that are available from cuneiform texts.[67] As many Mesopotamian researchers have noted, these types of stories seem to exaggerate these events. The control of military personnel, which was in the hands of the rulers and ruling dynasties of each city-state, was a powerful mechanism that could be used to assume greater charge of many social and economic aspects of a city-state. Control of the military, in fact, appears to have been important in increasing the political power of the ruler relative to the temples. Even in today's world, we can find many examples of countries that are ruled by individuals or families whose political power is based on control of that country's military forces.

Later Mesopotamia

Beginning in 2334 BC, under the rule of Sargon I of the city-state of Akkad, much of southern Mesopotamia was united under one ruling dynasty and is known historically as the **Akkadian Empire**. Sargon I accomplished this feat through a series of military battles with the other city-states. He also invaded parts of western Iran and Syria and as far west as Lebanon. During the Akkadian period, many of the religious traditions, social organization, and economic and administrative institutions continued in much the same way as during the Early Dynastic period, although the language of cuneiform writing became Akkadian (rather than Sumerian). Sargon and his successors also elaborated the depictions of themselves as military heroes who ruled because of their ability to successfully conquer others rather than because they were appointed by the gods and goddesses to rule (as during the Early Dynastic period). This represents a significant shift in how political authority was justified.[68] The Akkadian Empire, however, was relatively short-lived, lasting only until 2150 BC, when it was attacked by people known as the Gutians who came from highlands to the east.

The Sumerian city-state ruler of Ur, Ur-Nammu, eventually succeeded in ousting the Gutians, and it was under his rule that southern Mesopotamia was again unified in 2112 BC with the rise of the **Third Dynasty of Ur** (also known as Ur III or the Neo-Sumerian Empire). Many of the cuneiform texts of Ur III record complicated internal politics, vast economic transactions with merchants working on behalf of the

Akkadian Empire established by Sargon I from the city-state of Akkad in 2334 BC, this was the first period of unification of many of the city-states of southern Mesopotamia under one ruling dynasty and one city-state.

Third Dynasty of Ur during this period (also known as the Neo-Sumerian Empire), southern Mesopotamia was reunited under one ruler from the city of Ur. It lasted only a short time, from 2112 to 2004 BC.

state, marital alliances with competing dynasties from other city-states and regions (such northern Mesopotamia, central Iran, and eastern Iran), and land and water rights.[69] These texts also document some of the earliest laws, which are known as the Code of Ur-Nammu.[70] But unification under Ur III lasted only a short time, with the ruler of Ur (Ibbi-Sin) taken captive by the Elamites from western Iran in 2004 BC.

The later history of Mesopotamia is characterized by additional periods of competing city-states, such as Isin, Larsa, and Susa, as well as unification periods, such as the Babylonian Kingdom, which began in 1792 BC. The Babylonians used Akkadian for all official documents but Sumerian for religious texts and also are known for written laws called the Code of Hammurabi[71] (the ruler who established the Babylonian Empire). Northern Mesopotamia was home to the Assyrian Kingdom starting in 2025 BC. Groups such as the Kassites and the Elamites from the east exerted control over Mesopotamia during certain periods, as did the Assyrians from the north. Mesopotamia became part of the Achaemenid (Persian) Empire when it was conquered by Cyrus II the Great in 539 BC.

Further Reflections

Archaeology and Politics

When we examine the archaeological past, particularly those world areas where early states, kingdoms, and empires arose for the first time (such as Mesopotamia), we are confronted not only with the story of that past but also how that story is used today (see Chapter 1). To some extent, this is the appropriation of archaeology by the politics of the modern world. We might be awed by the scale of monumental construction in ancient cities or by the wealth and power that leaders of those past societies commanded. These so-called "glories" of the past lend themselves to romanticized notions about the greatness of those periods of time. This archaeological record then can be used by savvy modern leaders to legitimize themselves as modern rulers. Establishing any sort of link (even imagined ones) to that past "greatness" would be one method of creating legitimacy, because you would basically be saying that you were intimately connected to that past greatness. What is interesting about this modern approach is that this also was one of the ways that the actual leaders of those past states, kingdoms, and empires legitimized themselves! They created linkages to earlier rulers or even to gods.

Archaeology also is used politically in the modern world to create sensation and to draw attention to attempts to overthrow existing social order. One example of this is the destruction of archaeological sites by groups such as ISIS. They dynamited various Greco-Roman and Palmyrene monuments in Palmyra (Syria), claiming that these represented idolatry. But they also used some of these ancient monuments as stages for executions. Part of the rationale behind this lies in the story of Queen Zenobia of Palmyra, who ruled in the AD 200s. She is considered a national hero of the modern country of Syria. When groups such as ISIS destroy the archaeological remains of her city or use them to demonstrate their power in other ways, they are appropriating national symbols in an effort to change the fundamental basis of society.

Summary

- Early farming villages in Mesopotamia were established during the Pre-Pottery Neolithic period, although they are not found in southern Mesopotamia because they are deeply buried in floodplain sediments. By the Pottery Neolithic, some groups were using irrigation agriculture.

- The earliest known sites in southern Mesopotamia date to the 'Ubaid period. Most were small villages, but some were towns. Towns had architecture interpreted as temples, and by the late 'Ubaid period trading colonies had been established as far north as central Turkey.

- During the Uruk period, the city of Uruk became a city-state with a complex bureaucracy, social classes, secular rulers, and priestly elites. Large temple complexes were built, and many trading colonies were established in northern Mesopotamia and northwestern Syria.

- The Early Dynastic period is sometimes called Sumerian civilization. It was characterized by many competing city-states in southern Mesopotamia.

- Some of the earliest writing is Sumerian cuneiform, which often was used to record economic transactions in the *oikoi* economy that was typical of the city-states. Cuneiform writing also is a record of myths, songs, recipes, legends, and the exploits of rulers.

- Social roles and social statuses during the Early Dynastic period can be seen in artistic depictions and in burials. Men and women were shown engaged in different types of tasks such as herding (men) and weaving (women), whereas elite rulers were drawn much larger than other people. Elaborate burials with lavish grave goods, including probable human sacrifice, also mark elite individuals who had access to significant amounts of "wealth."

- Sumerian religion had a pantheon of gods and goddesses. Each city-state had one or more patron god/goddess.

- Most people owed labor obligations to rulers and to temples. This labor was used to construct monuments, work in agricultural fields, weave textiles, and fight battles.

- Early Dynastic city-states often fought battles with each other, and losers became slaves to the winners. Slaves were put to work in agriculture and weaving as well as serving other labor obligations. In addition to fighting each other, city-states also fought battles against nomadic peoples from elsewhere in the region.

- The Early Dynastic period ended when Sargon of the city-state of Akkad managed to unite all of southern Mesopotamia under his rule. This period is known as the Akkadian Empire. Later complex political entities include the Third

Dynasty of Ur and the Babylonian Kingdom. However, outsiders such as the Gutians, the Assyrians, and the Elamites controlled parts of Mesopotamia at various points in time. Eventually this region became part of the Achaemenid (Persian) Empire.

Endnotes

1. All dates shown are calendric or calibrated in the case of radiocarbon.
2. Arbuckle et al. 2016; Bradley and Magee 2006.
3. Rosen 2007: 123.
4. Kozlowski 1990, 1992, 1998; Savard et al. 2003; Watkins 1992; Watkins et al. 1989.
5. Watkins 1992: 178–179.
6. Hole 1994, 1997, 2000; Hole et al. 1969; Zeder and Hesse 2000; Zeder et al. 2006.
7. Restelli 2001.
8. Valladas et al. 1996: 383.
9. Abu es-Soof 1968; Huot 1992; Yasin 1970.
10. Blackham 1996; Forest 1983.
11. Oates 1978: 118–119; el-Wailly and es-Soof 1965.
12. Arbuckle et al. (2016) suggest that Halafan Culture was responsible for introducing domesticated cattle into northern Iraq and western Iran. These cattle were initially domesticated in areas to the west.
13. Blackham 1996.
14. Huot 1992; 1996; Valladas et al. 1996: 383.
15. Pollock 1999: 3–5; Stein 1994; Wright 1994.
16. Oates and Oates 2004: 184–185.
17. Algaze 2018; Pollock 1999: 5–6; Rothman 2004.
18. Algaze 2001, 2008.
19. Algaze 2001: 201; Liverani 2006: 15–19.
20. Algaze 2001: 203; Liverani 2006; Pollock 1999.
21. Stone and Zimansky 1995.
22. Adams 1972, 1981; Nissen 2002; articles in Rothman 2001; see also Pollock 1999 for examples of specialists at sites other than Uruk.
23. Schmandt-Besserat 2007.
24. Liverani 2006; Nissen 1986; Rothman 2004: 84–88.
25. Nissen 2001: 155–156.
26. Nissen 1986; Oates and Oates 2004: 185–187; Pollock 1999: 110–115.
27. Research in the central Zagros piedmont of Iraq now suggests that the Uruk expansion began during the early Uruk period (Vallet et al. 2017).
28. Stable isotope analyses of bitumen artifacts document that Uruk colonies and other sites to the northwest during the Middle Uruk period had large quantities of bitumen from southern Mesopotamia. The sources of bitumen and where artifacts made from them are found changes over time, showing shifts in trade relationships and the establishment of colonies (Schwartz and Hollander 2016).
29. Algaze 2001: 207–209.
30. Zagarell 1986, 1989.
31. Oates and Oates 2004: 188.
32. Pollock 1999: 6.
33. Pollock 1999.
34. Adams 1981.
35. Algaze 2018: 26–27.
36. Algaze 2018: 28.
37. Stein 2001.
38. Trigger 2003: 84.
39. Pollock 1999: 162–172; Walker 1987.
40. For specialists, there are online resources such as "The Electronic Pennsylvania Sumerian Dictionary (ePSD)," https://www.penn.museum/research/projects-researchers/babylonian-section/117-the-electronic-pennsylvania-sumerian-dictionary-epsd (accessed July 9, 2018), and "The Open Richly Annotated Cuneiform Corpus (oracc)," http://oracc.museum.upenn.edu/ (accessed July 9, 2018); both of these are databases on Sumerian and later cuneiform languages such as Akkadian.
41. Oates and Oates 2004.
42. Katz and Voigt 1986: 29. Early Dynastic beer brewing has a much more ancient heritage, with brewing beginning by at least the Uruk period.
43. Algaze 2018: 32–33.

44. Ratnagar 2003: 80.
45. Pollock 1999: 117–123; see also Zagarell 1986.
46. Pollock 1999: 123 (citing Waetzoldt, H. 1972. *Untersuchungen zur neusumerischen Textilindustrie*. Rome: Centro per le Antichità e la Storia dell'Arte del Vicino Oriente).
47. Zagarell 1986: 417.
48. Hansen 1992; Jacobsen 1939.
49. Trigger 2003: 173–174.
50. Pollock 1999: 206–214.
51. Moorey 1977; Pollock 1991; Woolley 1934.
52. Pollock 1991: 175.
53. Miller 2000; Woolley 1934: 89.
54. Baadsgaard et al. 2011; Vidale 2011.
55. Pollock 1991: 182.
56. Pollock 1999: 187.
57. Hansen 1992.
58. Moorey 1977: 37–38.
59. Hansen 1992: 208.
60. Pollock 1999: 186–187.
61. Trigger 2003: 557.
62. Pollock 1999: 184.
63. Pollock 1991: 180.
64. Gelb 1973; Trigger 2003: 244–245, 257–259.
65. Alizadeh 2010.
66. One famous set of battle and capture scenes is from the Royal Standard of Ur, a wooden object inset with semi-precious stones, ivory, and shell, which was found in one of the tombs of the Royal Cemetery at Ur (Woolley 1928: 51).
67. Gelb 1973: 73.
68. Pollock 1999: 10.
69. Algaze 2008; articles in Michalowski 2008; Sharlach 2005.
70. Kramer 1959: 52–55.
71. Although Yoffee (2005: 107, 109) has described this code not as a set of laws per se, but as political propaganda used by Hammurabi to appeal to the people of the city-states that he conquered when establishing the Babylonian Empire.

CHAPTER 10

Pharaonic State and Old Kingdom Egypt

The ancient politically and socially complex culture of Egypt is widely known to most people today because of a long-standing, worldwide public interest in the pyramids and the lavish burials of pharaohs (sometimes called kings), such as Tutankhamun. Just as in early Mesopotamia, early Egypt was home to one of the world's first written languages and is an example of an early civilization, which had some (limited) contact with Mesopotamia during the period in which both experienced the development of political complexity. One of the most striking features of Egypt is its concentration of people along the Nile River, both today and in ancient times (Figure 10.1). The Nile delta region, where the river reaches the Mediterranean Sea in the north, is and was home to dense concentrations of people, such as modern Alexandria. It is not hard to understand why people are concentrated along the Nile River. To both the west and the east of the Nile looms the inhospitable Sahara

ABOVE: Egyptian hieroglyphics.

Desert, with rare rainfall, limited water resources, and little animal life. These aspects of the landscape presented a rather different set of challenges for early Egyptians compared to those of their Mesopotamian contemporaries. In this chapter we will first briefly investigate some of the Neolithic and Predynastic background that helped set the stage for the rise of the pharaonic state and the Old Kingdom period with its pyramid-building pharaohs and then examine these politically and socially complex periods more closely. The unique landscape setting of Egypt was a factor in the longevity of its civilization, although there were several periods (called Intermediate Periods) when outsiders ruled parts of Egypt and/or Egypt was not united from north to south along the Nile River (read "Timeline: Egypt"). Just as in Mesopotamia, written texts provide a wealth of information about the lives of rulers, religion and ritual, social and economic conditions, and many other aspects of life.

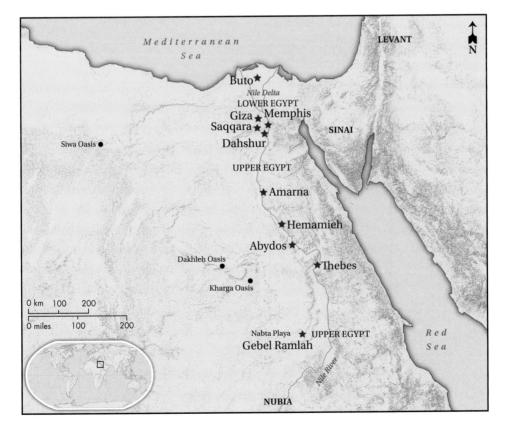

FIGURE 10.1
Location of various Egyptian sites and places.

Timeline: Egypt

The timeline for Egypt[1] shows long periods of rule by Egyptian pharaohs. These were punctuated by periods of time when non-Egyptians were able to control and rule parts of the kingdom (Figure 10.2). From 1069 BC on, Egypt mainly was ruled by outsiders.

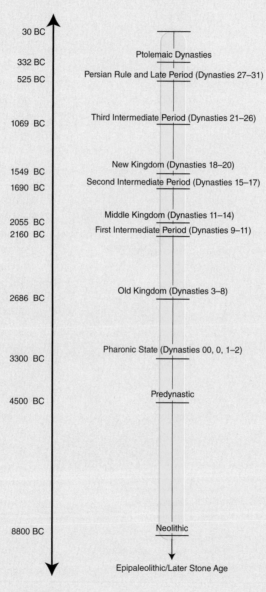

FIGURE 10.2
Timeline for Egypt.

Early Food Production

The latter part of the Later Stone Age is characterized across many parts of Africa by stone artifact assemblages that contain many microliths. Sites such as Rose Cottage Cave in southern Africa (discussed in Chapter 4) show how people organized their activities spatially within the locales where they lived. On the scale of landscapes, Later Stone Age groups made decisions that helped them lessen risks during periods of climatic and vegetation changes, such as the Last Glacial Maximum and drier periods of the Holocene, which impacted food resources.[2] Some of these strategies included innovations in technology, such as the appearance of geometric microliths (crescents, triangles, and trapezes[3]), which may signal different forms of hunting tools. Another technological strategy was to use and reuse stone artifacts by transforming flakes and blades into small cores, as we saw with Grotte des Contrebandiers in Chapter 4. Other strategies likely were social, such as exchange networks in which Later Stone Age people living in inland areas were able to obtain marine shells for personal ornamentation and some groups made ostrich eggshell beads that could be exchanged.[4]

During the early Holocene, several warm and wet climatic intervals led to increased sources of water in the form of playas (seasonal lakes) in the desert regions of Egypt.[5] During these intervals, it was possible for people to live away from the Nile River Valley, at least for brief periods of time. The resources (water and wild animals) of these playas were exploited by Later Stone Age and by Neolithic period groups of people. The Later Stone Age archaeological remains at the playas sometimes include evidence for structures interpreted as huts, suggesting a limited degree of settled life, and at other times are simply hearths and stone artifact assemblages indicating high mobility.[6] Early Neolithic period groups also occupied these playa settings. They are distinguished from the Later Stone Age groups by the presence of some pottery, abundant grinding stones, and the bones of cattle, although they also hunted wild gazelle, hartebeest, ostrich, and hare.[7]

Cattle are an intriguing aspect of the Egyptian Early Neolithic. Their presence far out in the desert at the playa wet spots might suggest that people had a close association with the management of local cattle; that is, cattle would not have been naturally present in the desert but were brought by people to the desert playas from the Nile River Valley.[8] If this was the case, then the Egyptian desert Neolithic sites are an archaeological example of pastoralism.

The Neolithic way of life in Egypt eventually included domesticated sheep, goats, pigs, and wheat and barley. None of these animals or crops has wild ancestors in Egypt, and all were brought into North Africa from the Middle East, where they were domesticated[9] (see Chapters 5 and 9). Domesticated sheep and goats may be present in the desert playas around 7000 BC, and domesticated crops (barley, emmer wheat, lentils, and peas) appear just after 5500 BC in the desert playas and along the Nile River. People living along the Nile River and in its delta area in northern Egypt also had access to a vast abundance of fish, water birds, hippopotamus, freshwater shellfish, and many wild animals, as well as the Nile flood waters that provided fertile soils for agriculture.[10]

The Nabta Playa

Nabta Playa a desert area of southern Egypt where numerous sites of the Neolithic period occur at playas (seasonal, shallow lakes).

One of the desert regions with evidence for Neolithic settlement and use is the **Nabta Playa** just west of the Nile River Valley in southern Egypt[11] (see Figure 10.1). This region has a series of wet and dry phases that alternate for several thousands of years during the early Holocene. The wet (humid) phases began about 9300 BC, and during each of these phases seasonal water was available at the playas and archaeological evidence documents Neolithic settlements. During the arid phases, the Nabta Playa region was abandoned.

The earliest Neolithic settlements date to 9000 BC and are called the el Adam phase. One of these sites (E-77–7) was quite small (10 square meters [107 square feet]) and was out on the playa sediments. It had several closely spaced burned areas interpreted as hearths as well as thousands of stone artifacts. These suggest a temporary habitation typical of mobile people who visited this locale several different times.[12] There was a limited amount of animal bone (including cattle and gazelle), one fragment of a pottery vessel, and several concentrations of ostrich eggshell. Ostrich eggs often were used as water containers, but eggshell also was made into beads; both of these types are found at E-77–7. Analysis of burned plant remains shows the presence of tamarisk (a shrub) and wild millet (a cereal grass). E-77–7, therefore, represents an early Neolithic site that was used during periods when water was available.

Slightly later in the Early Neolithic during the el Nabta/al Jerar phase, beginning about 7000 BC, the site of E-75–6 documents a more extensive type of settlement (1,200 square meters [12,916 square feet]) with several hutlike structures, bell-shape storage pits, and what are interpreted as wells, all of which were on the shores of the playa.[13] Unlike the E-77–7 situation, people at E-75–6 had longer-term access to water resources because of the wells they dug. This likely meant they could stay at this site during the dry season. The hutlike dwellings varied in size and shape and contained hearths, holes to hold pottery vessels, and post holes where tamarisk branches were bent into a frame and then probably covered with woven mats. Thousands of stone artifacts were present, as were grinding stones, ostrich eggshell beads, and pottery fragments. Animal bones included hare, gazelle, and cattle, whereas plant remains consisted of wild millets, sorghum (which possibly was cultivated at this site rather than collected as a wild resource), fruits from *Ziziphus* and caper shrubs, cattail (parts of which can be eaten), and sedges (which have tubers that are edible).[14] Although E-75–6 had dwellings, it is still likely that these represent several repeated visits to this locale on the playa shore, although visits that were for longer periods than at the earlier settlement at E-77–7.

The Early Neolithic people in the Nabta Playa region had a subsistence economy that included one possible domesticate (cattle) but also extensive use of wild resources (millet, cattail, hare, and gazelle). In some respects this is an adaptation similar to the Pre-Pottery Neolithic in the Middle East, which also had a mix of wild and domesticated resources (see Chapter 5).

By the Late Neolithic, several distinctive features of social complexity begin to appear consistently. Some of these occur in the desert playa contexts, but similar features also were typical of Late Neolithic occupations in the Nile River Valley. This should not be surprising because the groups at the desert playas likely spent some portion of each year at or near communities in the Nile Valley and may have shared in a similar ideology. At several sites in the Nabta Playa, there are large rock alignments and constructions or mounds of rocks and dirt (called tumuli) that are built over graves containing whole animals or animal parts, including domesticated cattle, sheep, and goats.[15] The parts of animals buried in the tumuli are interpreted as representing feasting, probably in the context of shrines or sacred places in the landscape. There are many reasons why such rituals might have occurred, including life celebrations, fertility rituals, and aggregations of several groups of people to arrange marriages. Some alignments of large rocks might mark lines of sight to various bright stars such as Sirius and those in Orion's "belt." All of these features (tumuli, alignments, and other rock constructions), which were situated near each other, have been interpreted as a Neolithic ceremonial center (Figure 10.3), something simple in design but perhaps analogous to Stonehenge in England (see Chapter 6).

FIGURE 10.3
One of the Neolithic ritual features at Gebel Ramlah.

Gebel Ramlah a Late Neolithic settlement in the desert Nabta Playa region of Egypt with an associated cemetery containing individuals buried with abundant grave goods. These people were pastoralists.

About 25 kilometers (15 miles) northwest of the Nabta region is the **Gebel Ramlah** (see Figure 10.1), where a Late Neolithic cemetery around 4600 BC contains burials of individuals accompanied by a wealth of grave goods.[16] Some of the cemetery pits have secondary burials, that is, people who were buried sometime after they died. This suggests that they were brought to this cemetery from elsewhere, perhaps a reasonable assumption given that they were pastoralists who moved around the landscape with their animal herds. Some of the burials are of single individuals, whereas others contain several people buried together (possibly members of the same family). Fragments of plaited plants suggest that the bodies were wrapped before burial. Grave goods include painted pottery vessels, cosmetics (red ochre and yellow and green materials) stored in cow horns along with palettes for grinding these into a powder that could be used as a paint, bracelets of shell and ivory, hundreds of limestone/shale, agate, carnelian, clay, shell, and ochre beads, pendants of animal teeth and shell, bone needles, turquoise, shaped and smoothed agate and chert pebbles, shells, a bone dagger, and stone tools such as celts and microliths. Some of these materials are evidence for long-distance exchange networks because turquoise came from the Sinai Desert in the Middle East, some shells were from the Red Sea between Egypt and the Middle East, and ivory was from sub-Saharan Africa. The burials include male and female adults, adolescents, and newborn infants, and the abundance of grave goods indicates that their pastoral lifestyle was highly successful.

Predynastic

The Gebel Ramlah cemetery grave goods contain items that were similar to the Nilotic Badarian culture of the Predynastic period, and if some of the stone structures of the Nabta Playa were astronomical in function, then researchers who argue that elements of Neolithic social life in the desert areas played a role in the later development of Egyptian politically complex societies may be correct.[17] The Predynastic period began around 4500 BC and included several cultures (Badarian, Naqada, Amratian, and Gerzean). These provide archaeological evidence for social and political changes in settlements along the Nile River that resulted in the establishment of the early dynasties of pharaonic Egypt around 3100 BC.

During the Predynastic period, agricultural communities in the Nile Valley became more common as people took advantage of the fertility of the soils and the floodwaters to grow barley, emmer wheat, and other crops. Sheep and goats, as well as cattle, could be more easily supported in this wet habitat. But people also continued to exploit many wild plant food resources, as well as wild animals. Like the desert playa Neolithic, Badarians occasionally buried animals or representations of animals. At the site of **Hemamieh** in Upper Egypt (see Figure 10.1) there were numerous pithouses. Some had hearths indicating they were dwellings, although it is not clear whether habitation was year-round or seasonal.[18] Grain storage silos

Hemamieh a Predynastic settlement and cemetery in Upper Egypt that has an early (Badarian) occupation that shares many similarities in artifacts and burials with Neolithic groups of the desert playas.

made of plaited plants also were found. Some of the Badarian painted vessels and other artifacts were similar to those found in the desert playas at Neolithic sites. The Badarian is best known for its cemeteries, which were located in the low desert. This is the region between the limestone cliffs of the high desert plateau and the irrigated farmed areas closer to the Nile River. Badarian people were buried with painted pottery, bone tools, shell from the Red Sea, grinding palettes, pottery vessels filled with ground pigments, and objects such as small clay figurines and bracelets made from ivory. There were even a few copper pins. Although distinctions between the cemetery burials that might indicate different social roles and statuses in the Badarian are not overwhelming, there is some suggestion of differences in social hierarchy when comparisons are made between burials in different sections of the cemeteries.[19]

By 3700 BC, Nile Valley settlements began to change in several ways. Among these changes was the construction of mudbrick houses (rather than pithouses), which some researchers interpret as reflecting a shift from nuclear families (pithouses) to extended families (rectangular, above-ground, adjoining houses).[20] The importance of this possible shift in how families shared and controlled space is usually thought of as indicating greater control over agricultural surpluses and more incentive to produce surpluses. This might be a mechanism that eventually led to greater social differences between individuals and families in a community, just as we have seen elsewhere (see Chapters 8 and 9). Communication between settlements along the Nile River was facilitated by water travel, just as in Mesopotamia along the Euphrates and Tigris rivers. In fact, Predynastic painted pottery often has images of boats. In some cases, population size at these mudbrick communities grew enormously, for example, at Hierakonpolis (which is south of Luxor) and Buto (which is in the delta region of northern Egypt). **Buto** was well situated to take advantage of agricultural and natural resources in the delta and also those related to trade and exchange (see Figure 10.1).[21] Its location along the Nile River and its proximity to the Mediterranean Sea meant that people at Buto had access to goods that came on river watercraft from areas to the south and also to resources that could be traded into or from the Middle East (either from land routes across the Sinai or water routes in the Mediterranean).

Buto a site in the delta region of northern Egypt with Predynastic period and later occupations. Its position at the interface of the Nile River with the delta likely was strategic for trade and exchange within Egypt and with the Middle East.

Toward the end of the Predynastic period, archaeological evidence from cemeteries begins to reflect greater differences in burials. Some of the tombs, for example, were larger and had more grave goods, with indications of elaborate burial rites.[22] Distinctions between people on this scale reflect increasing social differentiation and hierarchy, both of which are elements seen most dramatically in later politically complex societies.

Pharaonic State

Starting about 3300 BC, there were several individuals identified (by later written documents) as early pharaohs.[23] Archaeological evidence for them is relatively limited, although there are a few tombs in the Umm al-Qa'ab Royal Cemetery

FIGURE 10.4
Narmer shown wearing the two crowns of Egypt. The figure on the left has the crown of Upper Egypt, and the figure on the right has the crown of Lower Egypt (drawn from the Narmer Palette without the other associated figures and motifs).

Abydos an important settlement and cemetery complex in Upper Egypt. Royal cemeteries here contain tombs thought to be those of some of the last pharaohs of the Protodynastic period, as well as of the Pharaonic State, and Old and Middle Kingdom periods.

Narmer the last pharaoh of Dynasty 0, he is sometimes called the Scorpion King and usually is credited with unifying Egypt around 3100 BC. Narmer's Palette, an engraved stone, shows the pharaoah wearing the crown of Upper Egypt on one side and the crown of Lower Egypt on the other.

at **Abydos** in Upper Egypt (see Figure 10.1) that some researchers believe were those of the early rulers Iri-Hor and Ka.[24] The period of these early pharaohs is sometimes called the Protodynastic, or Dynasties 00 and 0.[25] One of the better known (although still enigmatic) is the last of the Dynasty 0 pharaohs, **Narmer**, who sometimes is thought to be the king called Scorpion. Narmer is usually credited with unifying Egypt around 3100 BC. In fact, an engraved stone called Narmer's Palette shows a pharaoh wearing the crown of Lower Egypt (northern Egypt) on one side and the crown of Upper Egypt (southern Egypt) on the other (Figure 10.4). There also are scenes that imply military action, suggesting that this is how Narmer unified the Nile River settlements and those of the delta region in northern Egypt. The widespread influence of Dynasty 0 is seen not only in the many sites of this period in Egypt but also from the presence of Dynasty 0 sites in the Middle East (especially the Sinai and southern Levant), where they may have been positioned to protect trade routes.[26]

The Pharaonic State began in 3100 BC with the establishment of Dynasty 1 and continued through the pharaohs of Dynasty 2. The first pharaoh of Dynasty 1 was Aha, whose tomb may be in one of the Abydos royal cemeteries. In texts from later periods, Pharaoh Aha is said to have helped establish several religious cults such as that of Sobek, the crocodile-god, in the Fayum oasis. Aha's association with particular gods and goddesses helped make his right to rule legitimate,[27] in a manner similar to the kings of Mesopotamian city-states. The association of particular Egyptian gods and goddesses with different towns and cities in Egypt was a long-standing tradition throughout most of Egypt's history. In general terms, it is somewhat similar to the Mesopotamian gods and goddesses that were patrons of particular cities in that region (see Chapter 9). Pharaohs of these early dynasties often reinforced their rule over both Lower and Upper Egypt by taking titles that reflected the names of gods and goddesses from both Lower and Upper Egypt and by building tombs for themselves and temples in both Abydos and Memphis (or its immediate area, such as Saqqara), thus identifying themselves as linked to both regions of Egypt. The Pharaoh Anedjib (Dynasty 1), for instance, called himself the "Lord of the Two Lands," whereas earlier pharaohs used titles such as "Lord of the Two Ladies," which represents Wadjet (cobra goddess) of Buto in Lower Egypt and Nekhbet (vulture goddess) of Hierakonpolis in Upper Egypt. Pharaoh Djer (Dynasty 1) is thought to have built a temple at Memphis in Lower Egypt, and his tomb is in the Umm al-Qa'ab Royal Cemetery at Abydos in Upper Egypt. Djer's tomb, like that of Puabi in Mesopotamia, had evidence not only of rich furnishings and grave goods, but also of possible human sacrifice in the form of some 76 women (interpreted as his harem) and a couple hundred other people who went with him into death.[28]

The value of the Nile River is clearly seen in its role in facilitating and maintaining unification during the early dynasties, not only because of internal trade but also because it served as a conduit for communication, including sharing and spreading elements of ideology. This ideology, in addition to cults of specific gods and goddesses in different towns, villages, and cities, can be seen in the burial of full-size wooden boats (equipped with oars and masts) at Abydos during Dynasty 1.[29] In later Old Kingdom times, such boats are called "solar boats" and reflect Egyptian belief that the soul of the deceased would travel in them just as Ra (the sun god) did. Presumably there were similar beliefs during the Pharaonic State period.

During Dynasties 1 and 2, some communities, such as **Memphis** (in Lower Egypt; see Figure 10.1), developed into densely populated and large settlements that were Egypt's first cities, but most settlements were villages and towns.[30] Memphis became the capital of the Pharaonic State during Dynasty 1, with evidence that it was an administrative center. It had workshops where goods were made for trade within Egypt and with its neighbors. Egyptians continued to build communities (using Egyptian architectural standards) in the Sinai and the southern Levant of the Middle East, presumably as trading outposts where diplomatic interchanges and alliance formations could be conducted. Trade to the south along the Nile River into Nubia (northern Sudan) was important, especially for materials such as ivory. Egyptians of this period also engaged in military skirmishes, some of which depict them vanquishing people dressed in Middle Eastern clothing. And, just as in Mesopotamia, the Pharaonic State was a complex administrative and political entity with the pharaoh at the top of the pyramid (so to speak!), then members of his family, and below them a vizier (overseer) who controlled the activities of the royal household, the treasury, and regional and local governments.[31] Palaces, just like village homes, were constructed from mudbrick, as were the above-ground parts of tombs and associated structures. These types of tombs are known as mastabas (Figure 10.5). They were rectangular in shape and had a flat top and slightly sloping sides. They are somewhat similar to the ziggurats of Mesopotamia (see Chapter 9).

Memphis an important city in Lower Egypt that became the capital during the Pharaonic State period; the central administration was located in this city.

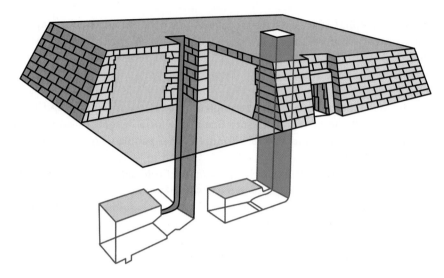

FIGURE 10.5
An example of a mudbrick mastaba, with the burial chambers located underground.

Old Kingdom Egypt

In 2686 BC, with the establishment of Dynasty 3, Egypt entered the period archaeologists and Egyptologists call the Old Kingdom, which encompasses Dynasties 3 through 8.[32] The lives of several of the pharaohs of Dynasty 3, like those of their predecessors in the Protodynastic and Pharaonic State periods, are not known in detail, although Pharaoh Djoser is recognized for his stepped pyramid tomb (see later). Most of us, however, are familiar with several of the pharaohs of Dynasty 4 because these rulers (Khufu/Cheops, Khafre/Chephren, and Menkaura/Mycerinus) had the great pyramids at Giza built as their tombs (see later). The Egyptian state during the Old Kingdom incorporated and further developed many of the social, economic, administrative, political, and ideological behaviors, organizations, and beliefs seen during Dynasties 0, 1, and 2. The pharaohs of Old Kingdom Egypt maintained control of Upper and Lower Egypt, outposts in the Sinai and southern Levant, and desert areas such as the Egyptian oases as far west as the modern Libyan border. By the time of Dynasties 7 and 8, however, political challenges from regional rulers within Egypt diminished the influence of the pharaohs, whose base of power was reduced to Lower Egypt centered at Memphis. Written records, in conjunction with archaeological data, provide a fairly substantial set of information about the Old Kingdom.

The Written Word

The early written symbols of Egypt are called hieroglyphs[33] and are pictures (ideograms) of naturally occurring things such as plants, animals, and weapons.

Over time, many of these ideograms were stylized[34] (Figure 10.6). The ideograms represented consonant sounds (rather than vowels). One unique feature of Egyptian hieroglyphs, especially when compared to Mesopotamian cuneiform (see Chapter 9), are glyphs that are "alphabetic." These were used to add grammar elements or to link particular ideograms to specific meanings. The earliest hieroglyphic writing dates to the end of the Predynastic period (about 3200 BC) and consists of one or two ideograms written in ink on pottery, seals, and small, perforated ivory pieces called labels. These were found in Tomb U-j at Abydos and have been interpreted as including the names of rulers, various types of goods, and a counting system.[35] Hieroglyphic writing became widespread in the Pharaonic State and Old Kingdom periods, with hieroglyphs usually arranged in columns that were read from right to left and from top to bottom. The names of the pharaohs were shown with the ideogram of a falcon (the god Horus), which was associated with royalty.[36] Beginning with Dynasty 4, the ideograms for the pharaoh's name were enclosed in a cartouche (an oval with a horizontal line drawn at its bottom).

In contrast to Mesopotamian cuneiform, which developed initially to record economic transactions, the role of early Egyptian hieroglyphic writing appears to have focused on telling the stories of the lives of the pharaohs and other socially important people.[37] Just as a newspaper today might include a story about a ribbon-cutting ceremony for a new public building, Egyptian texts recorded events such as pharaohs opening new irrigation canals or taking part in various

FIGURE 10.6
An example of Egyptian hieroglyphic writing.

ceremonies at palaces or cult activities associated with particular Egyptian gods and goddesses. This description of the purpose of Egyptian writing could be described as "boasting made permanent," but early texts were used for other purposes as well, such as recording economic accounts, religious mythology, magic, and various administrative tasks.[38]

Resource Networks, Trade, and Exchange

Egyptian long-distance exchange networks, as we saw above, can be traced back at least as early as the Late Neolithic and Badarian periods. The establishment of outposts in the Sinai and southern Levant during the Predynastic and of settlements in southern Egypt also facilitated long-distance trade and exchange networks that continued into the Old Kingdom period. Trade goods entered Egypt from several different regions. Copper, three types of pottery that may have contained scented resins and oils, and Lebanese cedar logs, for example, came from the Mediterranean part of the Middle East. Obsidian was likely from sources in Arabia (Middle East) or Eritrea (Horn of Africa). The semiprecious lapis lazuli (a blue-colored stone) was from Afghanistan and Iran, and ivory, panther skins, ebony, tails of giraffes, monkeys, and possibly incense were from sub-Saharan Africa.[39]

Like Mesopotamia, Old Kingdom Egypt was heavily invested in control of trade and trade routes, and some researchers have described this as a state monopoly, especially for trade with the Mediterranean Middle East.[40] This type of control was gained through military campaigns that brought regions such as Nubia (to the south) under the influence of Egypt as well as a coordinated and complex Egyptian administrative bureaucracy that oversaw trade and exchange relationships.

SUPPLY, DEMAND, AND WEALTH

Running a centralized administration with its hierarchy of bureaucrats and professions, as we saw in Mesopotamia, is no small feat. By the time of the Old Kingdom, numerous individuals held specialized jobs as scribes, military professionals, cooks and bakers, tax collectors, accountants, judiciary personnel, priests and priestesses, and craftsmen. The basis for wealth in Old Kingdom Egypt was agriculture, just as it was in Mesopotamia, with estates owned by the ruling class, by religious institutions, and by private landowners.[41] This form of wealth went directly to the owners of the estates, with one modified circumstance being that the agricultural products of private landowners were taxed. These taxes went to the central administration of the country where they could be used by the pharaoh and his family. And, the elite members of society (pharaohs and their families, as well as members of the court and other wealthy individuals and families) created a constant demand for exotic, prestigious goods that could be used to reaffirm their places in Egyptian society. The modern parallel to this is "conspicuous consumption," some of which drives our country and world economies today.

One of the most obvious displays of wealth in the Old Kingdom was the pyramids built by pharaohs of Dynasties 3 and 4. All of these were in Lower Egypt, not far from the ancient capital at Memphis, and all pyramid complexes were on the west side of the Nile River, because west represented the way into the afterlife. Building these pyramids required enormous numbers of laborers, whose jobs included quarrying the stone, shaping it, transporting it to the construction sites, and putting the large blocks in place as the structure took shape. All these individuals worked exclusively in these tasks, and their basic needs, such as food and shelter, had to be met by the Egyptian administration acting on behalf of the pharaohs. Entire villages were built to house the workers, and other individuals such as bakers and cooks spent their days making meals for the workers.[42] Some people were supervisors who oversaw different parts of the workforce, and architects controlled the details of their "blueprints" for the pyramids. The villages had breweries, fish-drying areas, cemeteries, temples, and workshops.

Although mastabas were an early style of tomb built for the burials of elites and other wealthy members of society,[43] the first pyramid constructed was built for the Pharaoh **Djoser** (3rd Dynasty) at **Saqqara** (see Figure 10.1). It was a stepped pyramid (basically a mastaba-like structure in form, but with several layers). Djoser's stepped pyramid had six terrace levels of stone blocks, with each level built smaller than the one below it, thus giving it a rough pyramid shape (Figure 10.7).

Djoser a pharaoh of Egypt's 3rd Dynasty, he is well known because of his stepped pyramid at Saqqara. This was the first type of pyramid built in Egypt.

Saqqara a necropolis on the west side of the Nile River in Egypt, it was the site of the stepped pyramid complex of the 3rd Dynasty pharaoh, Djoser.

FIGURE 10.7
The stepped pyramid of Djoser at Saqqara, Egypt.

Building the Pyramids of Egypt

The so-called Bent Pyramid at Dahshur (Figure 10.8) is thought by some researchers to be an example of miscalculating how to build a pyramid because its top portion is angled differently than its lower portion. This angling was a solution to the problem of cracks in the stone masonry resulting from the weight of overlying stone blocks.[45] Another issue that Egyptian architects faced when building pyramids at Dahshur was that the underlying bedrock was not suitable for the weight of enormous stone pyramids. When the Pharoah Khufu, for example, decided that his pyramid should be built, the solution to the bedrock problem was to move construction of stone pyramids north to the Giza area, which is underlain by solid limestone. As noted previously, the pharaohs had to establish villages for workers engaged in the construction of the pyramids, particularly because the Giza plateau was not populated to any extent at that time. The pyramid workmen numbered in the thousands and required not only careful administrative oversight but also enormous resources to house and feed everyone involved in the work. How the pyramids were built, however, is still a matter of debate. One idea is that spiral ramps that wrapped around the pyramid were constructed. These were used to move and position the stone blocks as the pyramid rose in height. An alternative idea is that stairways, levers, wedges, and slideways were used. Pyramid construction also occurred during the Middle Kingdom, although not to the scale seen at Giza,[46] possibly because their costs were too great. The last known pyramid was built at Abydos by the New Kingdom pharaoh, Ahmose I.[47]

FIGURE 10.8
The "Bent" Pyramid at Dahshur, Egypt (note the smaller pyramid in the right front of the Bent Pyramid).

His pyramid was 140 by 118 meters (460 by 387 feet) at its base and 60 meters (197 feet) tall and was inside a rectangular enclosed space that contained other buildings, building facades, and a stone chair interpreted as a throne from which the pharaoh could watch various festivities.[44] The construction of the pyramids changed during the 4th Dynasty, when Pharaoh Sneferu had pyramids built at Dahshur, southeast of Saqqara (read "Peopling the Past: Building the Pyramids of Egypt").

Pharaoh **Khufu** (Cheops), the son of Sneferu, is known by many people today because his pyramid is the largest one at **Giza** (northwest of Saqqara; see Figure 10.1). It contains nearly 2,300,000 limestone blocks, each of which weighs an average of 2.5 tons, and is more than 146 meters (480 feet) tall, with a base of 230 meters (755 feet). It also has granite blocks that weigh 25 to 80 tons each, which were rafted on the Nile River from southern Egypt to Giza, a distance of about 800 kilometers (500 miles). The entire structure was finished by adding a polished limestone facing over the blocks (this facing was taken off after AD 1300 and used to build other structures in Cairo). In addition to the interior ramp ways leading into various chambers within the pyramid, including the burial chamber, Khufu's pyramid had three associated smaller pyramids for queens and five solar boat burials. These were full-size wooden ships built to take the pharaoh on his journey into the afterlife and possibly also were the ships that brought the pharoah's mummy to his final resting place.[48] Khufu's sons, the pharaohs Khafre and Menkaura, built the other two large pyramids at Giza. Khafre also had the Sphinx sculpted. As at Saqqara, the pyramids at Giza were each part of a larger complex that included several temples. Once the pyramid was completed, all the construction debris (extra materials and ramp ways to move the stone blocks into place) had to be cleared away.[49] Such massive construction efforts were extremely costly and were supported by countrywide taxation. The pyramids legitimized the pharaoh's role in society and served as a link between the living and the world of the gods and goddesses. During the Old Kingdom, around the same time that pyramid construction became much less grandiose, Egypt's central administration became much weaker, and the 7th and 8th Dynasty pharaohs were less powerful than their predecessors.

Khufu the Egyptian name for the 4th Dynasty pharaoh who built the largest pyramid at Giza; he is also known by the Greek name of Cheops.

Giza the necropolis of the 4th Dynasty pharaohs on the west bank of the Nile River not far from the ancient capital at Memphis in Egypt, it contains the three well-known large pyramids, as well as smaller pyramids for various queens and solar boat burials.

Social Life

The nuclear family was the essential social unit for Egyptians, unlike Mesopotamia, which, in addition to the nuclear family, used the extended family and the *oikos* suprahousehold as the basis for their economy.[50] Old Kingdom Egyptians emphasized the role of individuals over their families, which is a theme seen in the personal lives of people and in the stories of the gods and goddesses. The god Seth, for example, who was the brother of the god Osiris, killed Osiris on two occasions so that he (Seth) could be the main ruler of the world.[51] Naturally, people did have ties to their families, which could be used to enhance their social standing along with any personal achievements that raised their rank in society. Both men and women used cosmetics, such as kohl (a black pigment made from grinding the mineral galena) to emphasize their eyes, and perfumes. Depictions of them in art show people wearing linen loin cloths and kiltlike skirts (men) or tight dresses (women).[52]

Like societies just about everywhere, most people lived in small or modest-size houses in villages and towns in Old Kingdom Egypt. Women seem to have held somewhat lesser status compared to their husbands, but women could inherit and sell land and material goods as well as sign legal documents, divorce their husbands, participate in court cases, and disinherit their children.[53] They were able to work outside their homes, and written records and art document women in specialist positions such as dancers and singers, weavers, musicians, administrative bureaucrats, staff for the pharaoh's wife or wives, bakers, brewers, and mortuary priestesses. Some of these "jobs" required women to be able to read and write Egyptian hieroglyphic.

People with high social ranking and roles lived in far more elaborate houses, including palaces, and in cities, rather than in smaller towns and villages. Identifying these individuals is possible partly because of their associated titles; for example, there is one title that indicates that a person was a member of the ruling class or an individual appointed to a high-ranking position within the administration[54] (read "The Big Picture: Political Organization in Old Kingdom Egypt"). Most pharaohs in Egyptian history were men, although there were eventually several female pharaohs. Male pharaohs could and did have more than one wife, as well as numerous concubines. Later pharaohs (after the Old Kingdom period) practiced incest because they married their sisters or their daughters, probably as a way to keep their divine royal blood untainted by others, but it is not known whether this type of marriage was characteristic of the Old Kingdom period.[55] Among the elite members of society, there were tasks associated with their roles, including performing rituals and attending various festivals. Many of these special occasions were times when the ruling elites used their status as gods to help ensure fertility for agriculture, the annual flooding of the Nile River (which was important for successful crop growing), and the rejuvenation of life, especially the life of the pharaoh. In the Sed festival, for example, statues of the gods and goddess were brought from all over Egypt to a special court at Saqqara. Those of Upper Egypt were in shrines along one side, whereas those of Lower Egypt were in shrines along the opposite side.[56] In the court area, markers were set up to encompass a field that was representative of Egypt. The pharaoh, who wore one or both of the crowns of Egypt, carried symbols of royal and divine authority, such as the flail. During this festival, which was usually first held when the pharaoh was in the thirtieth year of his reign and then at intervals after this, he either ran or walked between the markers to reassert his authority over both Upper and Lower Egypt and to rejuvenate his physical being by reconnecting to the gods and goddesses. Other rituals included spearing a hippopotamus, which represented the triumph of order over chaos (because a hippopotamus is a dangerous animal), and canal opening, which was important for irrigation agriculture.

The Big Picture

Political Organization in Old Kingdom Egypt

Unlike in Mesopotamia, where early control of society was to some extent shared by secular and religious elites, political control in Old Kingdom Egypt was characterized by a single ruler.[57] This was the pharaoh, who was considered divine. The motivations of the pharaoh and other elites included the accumulation of wealth. This meant controlling land and agricultural surpluses. Such surpluses were collected as taxes from Upper and Lower Egypt. They were stored and used to feed armies or laborers working on projects such as the construction of pyramids, palaces, and other elite undertakings. Surpluses also were used to make other products, such as beer from grain or linen from flax. In addition, surpluses and products made from them were used as goods in trade and exchange networks either for the "purchase" of other goods or of exotic materials such as lapis lazuli and ivory. Pharaohs were not content, however, to merely trade. They also attempted to control trade routes, which we saw previously was a consideration as early as the Predynastic period when Egyptian outposts were established in the Middle East. Managing all of these tasks required a number of different social and political positions, such as overseers, scribes, and province rulers (Figure 10.9). One of the key positions was that of vizier, an individual who oversaw all the day-to-day administration for the royal household, treasury, and regional/local governments on behalf of the pharaoh. The rulers of Egypt thus shared with Mesopotamia a structure of complex bureaucracy, although in the case of Egypt this bureaucracy was countrywide rather than limited to a single city-state.

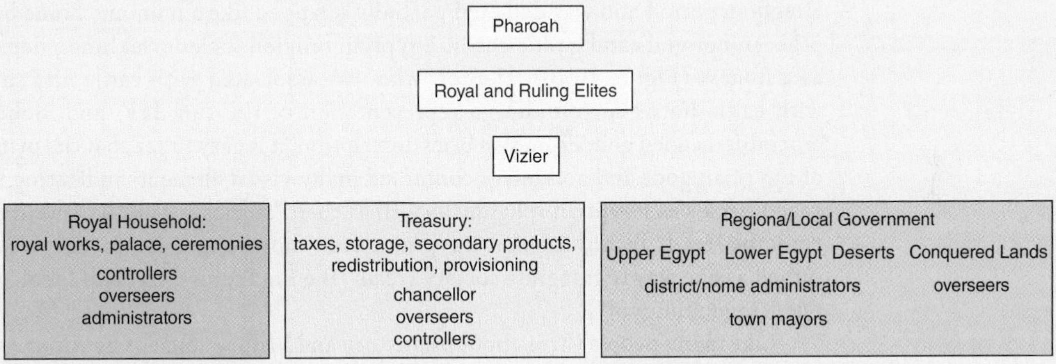

FIGURE 10.9
Political organization during the Old Kingdom (redrawn from Wilkinson 1999, Figure 4.6).

Ritual and Religion

Religion was an integral part of the Egyptian state, particularly because the pharaoh was seen as divine. As we saw above, this status was reinforced by the association of the pharaoh's name with the falcon hieroglyph that stood for Horus, who was the son of Osiris and Isis, and the ruler of Egypt's agricultural lands. Like

FIGURE 10.10
The lionness-headed
goddess, Sekhmet.

Mesopotamia, Egyptians had a pantheon of gods and goddesses, many of whom were associated with particular villages, towns, and cities, especially during the Old Kingdom period when state control of local shrines and temples was less pervasive. Most of us are familiar with the names of quite a few of the Egyptian gods and goddesses, either through articles on the Internet or in newspapers and magazines or from watching specials on TV or Hollywood blockbuster movies. These gods and goddesses each were worshipped at cult centers. That is, each had his or her own set of temples and shrines, and many were associated with specific animals.[58]

Most of the Egyptian gods and goddesses were worshipped throughout the long span of dynasties of Egypt (and quite likely long before the dynastic periods), but their roles changed over time. In some cases they were very important during some periods, but less so in others. Sometimes their features were changed as new elements were added to how they were portrayed in art. Ra, the sun god (sun disk), for example, was one of the major gods during the Old Kingdom period. He was later merged with Horus and shown as a falcon-headed man with the sun disk on his head. One of the jackal-headed gods was Anubis,[59] who was associated with death, mummification, and deciding whether a soul deserved to travel to the afterlife by weighing its measure of truth (the heart) against an ostrich feather during the Old Kingdom period. Anubis was later replaced in importance with respect to the underworld by Osiris, who was a minor god during the Old Kingdom period and was depicted partially wrapped like a mummy. Some of the other minor gods and goddesses in Egyptian religion include Sekhmet, depicted as a lioness (Figure 10.10); Hathor, who was associated with cattle and shown with cattle horns surrounding a representation of the sun disk; and, Sobek, a crocodile-headed god. From this brief description, it is easy to see that the pictures of Egyptian gods and goddesses contained many visual elements indicating their specific roles in Egyptian religion, as well as their "stories" or myths. These clues could be "read" by any ancient Egyptian, even those who were not literate, and served as one way to integrate society (read "The Big Picture: Art and Ideology in Old Kingdom Egypt").

Like many people throughout prehistory and history, ancient Egyptians were concerned with what happened to them after death and how to prepare for this event. As discussed previously, the pharaohs and other elite members of society built elaborate tombs and filled them with all sorts of goods, including food and drink, small statues of retainers and other staff to act as their servants in the afterlife, small models of bakeries and breweries, and many other things. These were symbolic of the activities needed to provide for them in the afterlife. Elites also were concerned with preserving their bodies as completely as possible, and they benefited in part from the natural climate of Egypt. This is because the dry heat of the deserts helped preserve organic materials, such as textiles, papyrus, and the bodies of people and animals. For bodies, this natural mummification no doubt was an early influence on the development of additional ways to preserve bodies

The Big Picture

Art and Ideology in Old Kingdom Egypt

The association of the secular and the religious is easily seen in Egyptian art. Gods and goddesses were sometimes shown with royal symbols such as the flail or crook or crown. When pharaohs were depicted with these items, it linked them to gods and goddesses, helped establish them as divine, and also legitimized their power over Egypt and its people.[60] Additionally, statues of pharaohs were placed in cult temples so that offerings made to gods and goddesses were also linked to the pharaoh. Egyptian art, like that of many early politically complex societies, tended to show rulers, other elites, and gods/goddesses[61] (Figure 10.11). It tells the stories of important people in society rather than of commoners. These stories, as we saw in Mesopotamia, included rulers conquering their enemies in battle and performing rituals to gods and goddesses. And, like in Mesopotamian art, the Egyptian pharaoh was depicted much larger than everyone else except for members of his family and the gods and goddesses.

FIGURE 10.11
Pharaohs and other people are frequently shown appealing to and making offerings to the gods and goddesses. In the upper scene, Shuamay and his wife are standing in front of Osiris (*seated*), Isis, and Horus, whereas in the lower scene (*center, right*), Shuamay and his wife pour libations in front of the gods and goddesses.

for the afterlife and became enshrined in the mummification processes and rituals that ancient Egyptians thought would enhance their ability to live successfully in the afterlife. To prepare for the afterlife thus often required considerable wealth, at least if an ancient Egyptian wanted to live in the style to which he or she was accustomed. This can be described as follows: "In ancient Egypt, 'not only could you take it with you'; you had to, in fact, if you really wanted to enjoy eternity."[62] Of course, many people (farmers and other laborers, for instance) were buried much more simply because they did not have the means to pay for elaborate burials and rituals.

The mummification processes included removing the organs (which contain a substantial amount of water) and drying out the body using chemical salts; poorer people had their organs removed (dissolved) by the injection of turpentine into their bodies.[63] The wealthy had their bodies made more lifelike through the use of scraps of cloth as padding in their mouths to inflate their cheeks; their bodies were packed with materials such as sand or sawdust to give them "normal" contours, and paints were used on their faces and hair. Their stomach area (which had been cut open to remove most of the organs) was sewn closed, and their bodies were covered in resin (to protect them), wrapped in linen strips, placed in a coffin, and covered with more resin. Small charms to keep evil forces away were placed either on the body before the cloth covering or in the folds of the cloth as it was wrapped around the body. All of this may sound somewhat strange to us, but if we think about how we treat the deceased today, we can see some parallels. Until relatively recently, for example, the Roman Catholic Church required people to be buried (rather than cremated) so that their souls could be reunited with their bodies after the Day of Judgment. Also until relatively recently in the United States, most bodies were washed and clothed by family members and laid out in a room at home to be viewed prior to burial. Legal requirements in the United States now mandate that bodies be prepared for burial by licensed professionals, and, in many cases, part of this preparation is draining the blood and replacing it with embalming fluid as well as preparing the body for public viewing using facial cosmetics, cheek padding, and other measures.

Warfare and Violence

The armies of Egypt in the Old Kingdom (and earlier) were not standing armies of full-time professionals. Instead, labor obligations to the state were used to draft men for fighting.[64] These were mainly farmers, who had to provide their own weapons. Military campaigns usually were led by members of the pharaoh's court or administration, although pharaohs, including Narmer, often were shown doing battle or capturing an enemy.

The use of military force within Egypt, as we saw earlier, appears to have been one factor that led to the first unification of Upper and Lower Egypt under Narmer (and was a feature in later reunifications that ended the First, Second, and Third Intermediate periods). The military also was used to consolidate Egypt's presence in the Near East (the Sinai and southern Levant) by providing protection of trade routes, and many of the battles fought may have been more along the lines of raids or skirmishes rather than full-blown campaigns to conquer territory.[65] By the 5th and 6th Dynasties, however, there is artistic evidence for Egyptian military attacks on fortified Canaanite towns in the Levant.[66] South of Egypt, in Nubia, military campaigns were used to secure territory and control trade (during the Old Kingdom, Egypt's southern border began near Aswan rather than further to the south as it is today). The Egyptians built a fort at Elephantine (an island in the Nile River near Aswan) to host a military presence at the border with Nubia and then a small fort at Buhen in Nubia.

In addition to bringing all of Egypt under one ruler, protecting trade routes, and defending borders, Egypt's military operations resulted in the capture of prisoners who were used as slave labor in agricultural fields. This is similar to Mesopotamia, where war captives, mainly women and children, were slaves used to support important economic activities (see Chapter 9). Male prisoners taken by Egyptian forces were sometimes depicted being slain by the pharaoh or as war captives in battle scenes.

After the Old Kingdom

Egypt along the Nile River was incredibly productive for agriculture and it benefited throughout its long history from the fact that it was surrounded by deserts, which protected it from invading armies, unless they came across the Sinai, by ship in the Mediterranean to Lower Egypt's delta region, or from Nubia in the south. Successive years of poor agricultural yields, likely a result of climatic fluctuations that impacted the strength of the annual Nile floods, and the internal politics of Egypt, however, occasionally weakened the central administration and the pharaoh's rule to the point where either outsiders temporarily ruled over parts of Egypt or various local Egyptian rulers (nomarchs who are analogous to governors of provinces) seized power over their regions, thus splitting Egypt into smaller polities (read "Further Reflections: Egypt's Multiple Rises and Falls").

By the time of the 6th Dynasty, competition between nomarchs and the central administration increased, and during the 7th and 8th Dynasties the power of the pharaohs declined significantly. Additionally, low water flow in the Nile may have impacted agricultural productivity, creating famines, which would have undermined the power and authority of the Old Kingdom pharaohs. It should be no surprise, then, that Egypt eventually split apart during what is called the First Intermediate Period (beginning about 2160 BC), with various rulers and dynasties claiming power but ruling only over small portions of Egypt.

Within a hundred years, however, during the 11th Dynasty, the pharaoh Mentuhotep II and the pharaohs who succeeded him managed to reunify Egypt under one rule. This began the Middle Kingdom period, which is sometimes referred to as Egypt's Classical period because of its literary works. It was a time of great prosperity, due in part to high water levels and flooding from the Nile, which enhanced agricultural productivity.[67] During the Middle Kingdom, Memphis once again became the capital, Egypt launched military campaigns (with full-time soldiers) to defend its borders and re-establish important trade routes, as well as to conquer Nubia, and, in an effort to reduce succession conflicts when a pharaoh died, the policy of co-regency was established. This meant that the pharaoh and one of his sons both ruled Egypt during the last part of the pharaoh's rule. The pharaoh's sons led military campaigns,[68] and in some cases, such as

Pharaoh Senwroset III's conquest of Nubia, the pharaoh himself led the forces. The power of the nomarchs was gradually reduced, possibly because members of their families were appointed to important positions within the central administration and thus became part of the state. The Cult of Osiris became important, with a significant center at Abydos.

All good things come to an end, and so it was with the Middle Kingdom. In the period after 1790 BC, Levantine people known as the Hyksos began to move into the delta region of Lower Egypt, where they became part of Egyptian society and gained power. They also introduced the chariot to Egypt. Around 1690 BC, the Hyksos were able to seize control of Memphis, and they established dynasties that ruled parts of Lower Egypt. This is known as the Second Intermediate Period. In Upper Egypt, an Egyptian dynasty at Thebes was in control of this region.

In 1549 BC, the Theban pharaoh Ahmose I (18th Dynasty) drove the Hyksos out of the delta area of Lower Egypt and reunified the country during what is known as the New Kingdom period. There are many pharaohs during this time whose names are widely recognized by us today because of their attempts to change Egypt's religion or the great wealth of their tombs or their military exploits. Akhenaten (also known as Amenhotep IV; 18th Dynasty), for example, built the city of Amarna and established the worship of a single god, the Aten (sun disk), at the expense of the cult of Amun-Re. By doing so, Akhenaten tried to eliminate the pantheon of gods and goddesses. He was married to Neferititi and was the father of Tutankhamun. Akhenaten's efforts to redesign Egyptian religion, however, did not outlive him. Shortly after he died, worship of the old gods and goddesses came back out into the open, his city of Amarna was destroyed, and his name was largely erased from Egyptian history until archaeology rediscovered him. His son, Pharaoh Tutankhamun (18th Dynasty) is known to everyone because his nearly unlooted tomb in the Valley of the Kings near Luxor contained foods, medicines, chariots, beds, and fabulous objects of gold, lapis lazuli, and silver, as well as his sarcophagus with his mummy. Despite his riches, CT scanning and DNA analysis show that Tutankhamun had his share of physical woes. He had a club foot and a cleft palate, suffered from Kohler's disease (in which poor blood flow was destroying his left foot), had to use a walking cane, and probably died because of a broken leg in combination with brain malaria.[69] Another well-known pharaoh of the New Kingdom was Ramesses II (19th Dynasty). He attempted to reconquer the Levant, but was ambushed by the Hittites at the Battle of Kadesh (in Syria), which ultimately ended in a draw. Back in Egypt, however, Ramesses II claimed victory. He built numerous monuments throughout Egypt, including the famous temple at Abu Simbel.

During the last dynasty of the New Kingdom, priests at Thebes became powerful and their control of this region, in combination with succession conflicts for pharaoh and poor agricultural yields resulting from climatic conditions, led to the

Third Intermediate Period beginning around 1069 BC. Egypt was briefly reunited for about 100 years but mainly was ruled by dynasties that exerted control only over small regions within Egypt. Some of the dynasties during the Third Intermediate Period were rulers from Nubia, and others were established by the Assyrians from the Levant. In 525 BC, the Achaemenid (Persian) Empire conquered Egypt and ruled as pharaohs for just over a hundred years. Egyptians regained control of their country during the Late Period but then fell again to the Achaemenid Empire. In 332 BC, Alexander the Great's Greek Empire took over rule of Egypt and the Ptolemaic dynasties were established after his death. Cleopatra VII was the last Ptolemaic ruler and the last pharaoh of Egypt, known to us today because of her liaisons with Julius Caesar and Marc Antony and her death in 30 BC, at which time Egypt became part of the Roman Empire.

Further Reflections

Egypt's Multiple Rises and Falls

One of the fascinating features of Dynastic Egyptian archaeology is that it is a record of the long-term success of complex political entities that were, for the most part, those of Egyptians. As we saw earlier, however, there were intervals when Egypt was not united under one leader or was ruled in part by foreigners. The story of the multiple rises and falls of Egyptian rule is linked to several factors. Some of these are common to many politically complex societies, for example, the use of warfare to conquer regions. The battles fought by Narmer to unify Egypt were one mechanism by which Egyptians established a single set of elites as the primary leaders during the Pharaonic State period. Later Egyptian pharaohs did the same thing after the First and Second Intermediate Periods. But warfare does not explain it all. Egyptians also held in common aspects of ideology, such as their gods and goddesses and associated rituals. If warfare was used to conquer areas in Egypt, it meant that once they were conquered, the conquered people had a common basis for buying into the new rulers because of shared ideology. Another factor mentioned earlier is that much of the Egyptian polity was situated along the Nile River with inhospitable deserts to the west and east making attacks from foreign enemies much less common compared to complex polities elsewhere (see Chapters 9, 11, 13, and 14). This helped create a certain amount of stability.

Why Egypt was not unified for its entire history, however, is a somewhat common story. It is related in part to the success of its agricultural systems, which depended on yearly flooding from the Nile River. As long as the Nile carried enough water, these floods deposited sediments and nutrients in areas that could be farmed, and agricultural productivity was high. But short-term climate changes sometimes meant that the Nile did not flood consistently for years and famines arose.[70] Added to this was the burden of taxes so that elites could build monuments and engage in other activities. For peoples who believed that their rulers were directly connected to the gods and goddesses, failures in agriculture directly reflected on those rulers and people would lose confidence in them. Coupled with this were times when the direct succession from one ruler to the next was not clear. This led to conflicts between elites and created conditions in which it was easier for some regions to break away and establish their own Egyptian rulers. It was also at times such as these that foreigners from the south (Nubia) or from the Middle East were more easily able to subdue certain parts of Egypt and establish their own rule and rulers.

Summary

- In the early Holocene, climatic conditions were wetter and there were areas of seasonal standing water (playas) in some parts of the Sahara Desert. These attracted Neolithic period groups. They hunted wild animals and used wild plant foods and eventually had domesticated animals and plant foods.

- Long-distance trade networks were a feature of the Neolithic period, as were ritual sites. Grave goods buried with people in cemeteries show that pastoralism could be a successful way of life.

- During the Predynastic period, agriculture on the floodplain of the Nile River became increasingly important. There was a shift over time from building pit-houses to constructing dwellings of mudbrick. Some towns were positioned to take advantage of trade routes, especially to the Middle East, and there is evidence for increasing social differences between people.

- Elite rulers known as pharaohs emerged during the Pharaonic State. Lavish burials associated with these individuals are found in Upper Egypt. These had a wealth of grave goods, including the first known hieroglyphic writing, and also in some cases "solar boats" and sacrificed humans.

- The pharaohs were considered divine and were associated with various Egyptian gods and goddesses. Many of them ruled both Upper and Lower Egypt and were depicted wearing the two distinctive crowns of these regions.

- Old Kingdom Egypt is well known for the construction of various pyramids, including the stepped pyramid at Saqqara, the "Bent" pyramid at Dahshur, and the pyramids of Khufu, Khafre, and Menkaure at Giza. Although pyramid building continued into later periods, it was on a much smaller scale.

- Egyptian hieroglyphic writing is an important source for understanding their religion and rituals. These included techniques thought to be useful in mummifying the bodies of elites so that they could travel into the afterlife. Written sources also describe the pantheon of gods and goddesses and their stories.

- Egypt under the Old Kingdom pharaohs was incredible wealthy, as can be seen in the massive constructions of pyramids, palaces, and towns. It required a complex bureaucracy to collect taxes in the form of agricultural surpluses, manage work forces and armies, and oversee regional, local, and town governments.

- The pharaohs fought wars to gain lands but also to control lucrative trade routes and to use captives as slaves in agricultural pursuits.

- Ancient Egypt as a complex political entity had a long history/prehistory. After the Old Kingdom, there were several periods of time when parts of Egypt were ruled by outsiders. However, some Egyptian pharaohs were able to reunite the country on several occasions, such as the establishment of the Middle Kingdom and the New Kingdom.

- The Middle Kingdom is known for its variety of literary works, as well as for being a period of incredible prosperity.

- The New Kingdom is familiar to many people because this is when Pharaoh Tutankhamun briefly ruled. He was the son of Pharaoh Akhenaten, who attempted to change the religion of Egypt to be the worship of just one god (the Aten or sun disk). Another famous New Kingdom ruler was Pharaoh Ramesses II.

- Egypt was eventually conquered by the Greek Empire and ruled by the Ptolomies. The last Ptolomaic pharaoh was Cleopatra VII, whose death in 30 BC led to Egypt falling under the rule of the Roman Empire.

Endnotes

1. Dates are shown in calendar years.
2. Mitchell 2000.
3. Barham 1989; Lubell 1974; McDonald 1991; Mercader and Brooks 2001; Mitchell 1990; Wendorf et al. 1989; Willoughby 2001, 2012. Mercader and Brooks 2001: 207–208, however, note that geometric microliths are rare in assemblages from tropical Africa.
4. Mitchell 2000: 164; Orton 2008.
5. Arz et al. 2003; Hassan 1997; Haynes 2001.
6. Briois et al. 2008; McDonald 1991; Olszewski et al. 2005: 296–300.
7. Caton-Thompson 1952; Hassan 1986; Mandel and Simmons 2001: 112–113; McDonald 2001; Warfe 2003; Wendorf et al. 2001.
8. Bradley and Magee 2006: 326; Close 1990; Gautier 2002; Wendorf et al. 1984; but see Gifford-Gonzalez and Hannotte 2011 for an alternative view.
9. Gautier 2002; McDonald 2001: 33–35; Rossignol-Strick 2002.
10. Wenke 2009: 153.
11. Wendorf et al. 1984, 2001.
12. Close and Wendorf 2001.

13. Królik and Schild 2001: 117–142.

14. Gautier 2001; Wasylikowa 2001.

15. Applegate et al. 2001; Wendorf and Królik 2001; Wendorf and Malville 2001.

16. Kobusiewicz et al. 2004.

17. See also Warfe (2003) for a discussions of possible contacts between the Dakhleh Oasis and the Nile Valley during the Neolithic and early Predynastic periods.

18. Brunton and Caton-Thompson 1928; Holmes 1988; Holmes and Friedman 1989; the pithouses probably are not Badarian, but Amratian.

19. Anderson 1992.

20. Wenke 2009: 216.

21. Midant-Reynes 2003: 109–115.

22. Midant-Reynes 2003: 191–216.

23. Wenke 2009: 240–241.

24. O'Connor 2009.

25. This seemingly odd way of numbering dynasties using zeros is the result of recently finding evidence of ruling individuals who are prior to the historically well-established pharaonic Dynasty 1 that began in 3100 BC.

26. Wenke 2009: 240.

27. Wenke 2009: 241–245.

28. Midant-Reynes 2003: 232; but see Hoffman's (1979: 275–279) account of Reisner's interpretations that suggest these individual burials around Djer's tomb are simply people who belonged to his extended household and wished to be associated with him after they died, presumably of natural causes.

29. O'Connor 1995.

30. Wenke 2009: 240–241.

31. Wilkinson 1999: 145.

32. Shaw 2000: 479–480.

33. Later forms of writing in Egypt include hieratic (simplified versions of hieroglyphs used mainly for administrative and business purposes; appears first in Dynasty 4 of the Old Kingdom) and demotic (an abbreviated, cursive form used for business, administration, and legal documents; appears first during the Third Intermediate Period) (Davis 1987).

34. Davies 1987; Ray 1986.

35. Dreyer 1992; Wilkinson 1999: 52; see also https://archive.archaeology.org/9903/newsbriefs/egypt.html (accessed July 13, 2018).

36. Wilkinson 2000: 26.

37. Trigger 2003: 587; Ray 1986: 309–310.

38. Ray 1986: 311.

39. Wenke 2009: 277; Wilkinson 1999: 158–165, 177.

40. Wilkinson 1999: 157.

41. Wenke 2009: 287.

42. Bard 2008: 169–171; Butzer et al. 2013; Hawass and Lehner 1997; Redding 2013.

43. Mastabas continued to be built during the period of pyramids as well as in later times.

44. Wenke 2009: 275–277.

45. Bárta 2005; Monnier and Puchkov 2016.

46. Grajetzki 2006: 43–50.

47. Lehner 1997.

48. O'Connor 1995: 5.

49. Bárta 1995.

50. Trigger 2003: 183.

51. Wenke 2009: 266; Osiris's wife, Isis, brought him back to life a couple of times, which is why Seth had to kill him again.

52. Wenke 2009: 319.

53. Trigger 2003: 185–186.

54. Wilkinson 1999: 185–186; the title is transliterated as "iri-p't."

55. Wenke 2009: 273.

56. Wilkinson 1999: 212–218.

57. Wilkinson 1999: 111–145.

58. Wenke 2009: 266–271; Wilkinson 2003; Wilkinson 1999: 261–320.

59. Another god associated with the jackal was Wepwawet, a more minor god than Anubis (Wilkinson 1999: 281).

60. Wilkinson 1999: 186–197.

61. Trigger 2003: 555.

62. Wenke 2009: 288.

63. Wenke 2009: 312–314.

64. Trigger 2003: 245, 252–254.
65. Wilkinson 1999: 155–157, 179–181.
66. Trigger 2003: 253.
67. Grajetzki 2006; Kemp 1983.
68. Trigger 2003: 253.
69. Hawass et al. 2010. Claims that Tutankhamun died due to a chariot accident do not seem to be supported by the evidence. His missing ribs and breastbone, for example, could have occurred during the process of mummification.
70. Macklin and Lewin 2015.

CHAPTER 11

Shang China

As is the case for Egypt, most people are aware of the magnificent discoveries and monuments of ancient China, such as the Great Wall and the army of thousands of life-size terracotta warriors and horses that were part of the massive funerary complex of the Emperor Qin Shi Huang in 210 to 209 BC. Unlike Egypt and Mesopotamia, however, the rise of complex polities in China is the story of emergence in several regions of the features of state-like organizations during the Neolithic period (read "Timeline: China"), including precursors of written symbols that may have developed into later Chinese writing. These Neolithic societies were diverse. This is reflected in the types of crop complexes they had, which in turn were related to geographical and environmental differences. Northern China, for example, was characterized by rainfall-dependent farming of millets and is particularly well known archaeologically in the Yellow (Huang He) River area, whereas the Yangtze River region was home to rice agriculture and southern China depended on root and tuber crops, such as taro, which are typical of tropical areas. In this chapter we will examine the Neolithic foundations that led to state-level societies, with a focus on the Yellow and Yangtze

ABOVE: Yangshao period pottery vessel from Banpo, China.

River areas. The fertility of these regions and the agricultural surpluses that could be generated, along with densely packed populations, helped create conditions in which cultural and social interactions led to the establishment of several competing polities and dynasties. Of these, we will concentrate mainly on the Shang period in the Yellow River region. The rich traditions of China are excellent examples of the complexities of life in earlier times because rulers commanded armies, labor, and exchange networks, and daily life for most people involved participation in ritual (including divination), religion, craftwork, farming, and a host of other tasks.

Early Food Production

Early evidence for more intensive use of food resources, including the collection of wild rice, is found during the Late Upper Paleolithic at **Yuchanyan Cave** in the Yangtze River region[1] (Figure 11.2). This focus on wild plant foods is found in what are called the Fertile Arc of China, which is a chain of different sets of mountains curving from the northeast through central China and then curving again into south China, where the terrain opens out into basins between mountains and plains[2] (see Figure 11.2). The Fertile Arc benefits from summer monsoon rainfall that falls to the east of the mountains, in the adjoining foothills. The diverse ecologies, wild cereals such as millets and rice, and the availability of water thus made the Fertile Arc an attractive place to live. It is not surprising then that we find the earliest evidence for Neolithic food production in this region.

Early Neolithic cultures (Figure 11.3), dating to 8000 BC, were sedentary villages with numerous houses (40 to 240 per site) that were spread over areas ranging from 1 to 20 hectares (2.5 to 50 acres).[3] Many were surrounded by a ditch, which is interpreted as a social boundary for each community rather than a defensive structure.[4] They had cemeteries with hundreds of individuals. There were public spaces, hearths, kilns, ash pits, ritual structures and features, ground stone tools for grinding foods, thousands of pottery vessels, chipped stone tools, animal bones, and plant remains. At some sites, excellent organic preservation means that bows and arrows, wooden canoes and oars, ladders, and matting have survived.[5] There were many Neolithic cultures, each with distinctive types of pottery, pottery designs, and other cultural materials, as well as differing emphases on plant foods and animals. We will look briefly at a few of these Neolithic societies in two of the centers of plant and animal domestication in China.

In the Yellow River region and areas to the northeast in North China, Neolithic societies used wild and domesticated foods. In many cases, the domesticated component of their diet was minor. The site of **Xinglonggou** (Xinglongwa Culture; see Figures 11.2 and 11.3) contained more than 150 dwellings.[6] Analysis of the plant and animal remains shows that these people had domesticated broomcorn and foxtail millet at 5700 BC. Other plant foods included acorns and wild grasses, and most sites had hunting of deer. There may have been some domesticated pigs, although most bones were those of wild pigs. Overall, the subsistence economy was based mainly on hunting–gathering–foraging, with a small part of the diet from domesticated plants

Yuchanyan Cave this site in northern China has evidence for the earliest known pottery at 16,350 to 13,480 cal BC and early use of rice, although it is not clear whether the rice was wild or domesticated.

Xinglonggou an early Neolithic period village site in the Yellow River region of China with evidence for domesticated broomcorn and foxtail millet and wild and domesticated pigs.

Timeline: China

Some of the complexity of the development of politically complex societies in China is shown in this timeline (Figure 11.1). Different regions of China each were home to the development of eventually competing polities.

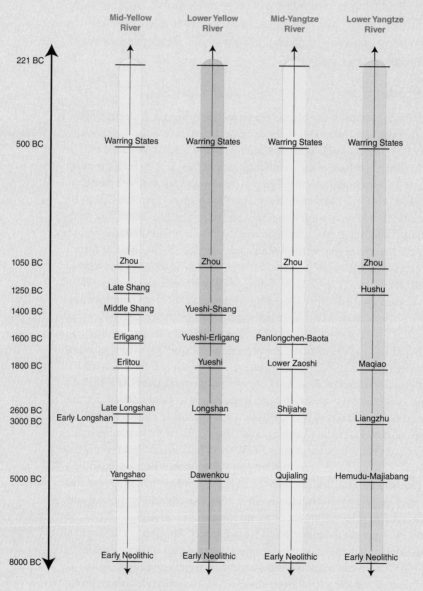

FIGURE 11.1
Timeline for the Yellow and Yangtze River areas of China.

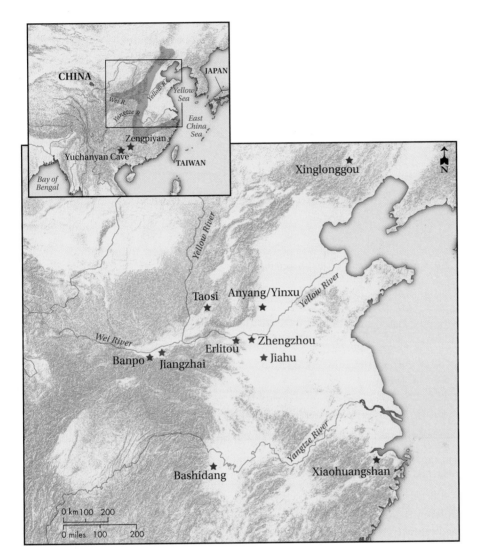

FIGURE 11.2
Map showing location of sites in China. Inset shows the "Fertile Arc" of China.

and animals. Ritual activities can be seen in the presence of small carved jade artifacts that were grave goods in some burials and also were found in houses of Xinglongwa Culture sites.[7]

In the Peiligang Culture region of the Yellow River area, most sites had evidence for dryland cultivation of domesticated millets. **Jiahu** (see Figures 11.2
and 11.3) was a large village, partly surrounded by a ditch, with at least 45 houses,
two cemeteries, and numerous pits.[8] It dates to 7000 BC. Burials suggest some

Jiahu a large Neolithic (Peiligang Culture) settlement, partly
surrounded by a ditch, in the
Yellow River area of China that
has evidence for the earliest
fermented beverage, some social
distinctions between people, and
a subsistence economy based on
domesticated and wild foods.

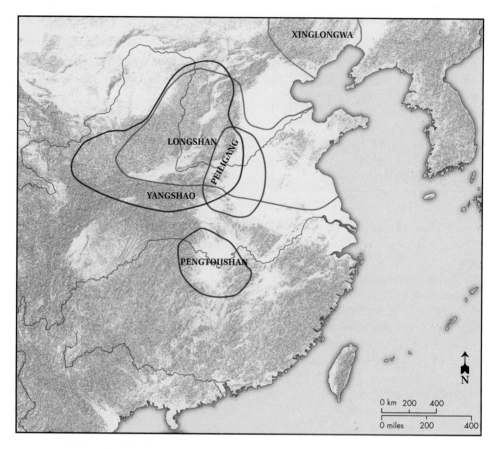

FIGURE 11.3
Map showing the Neolithic culture areas mentioned in the text.

differentiation between people based on the amount of grave goods, and the site had artifacts indicating rituals, for example, pits with dogs, bone flutes, and rattles made of tortoise shells.[9] Thousands of plant remains indicate that people at Jiahu were mainly hunter–gatherer–foragers. Among the wild plant foods are acorns, lotus roots, and soybeans. Intriguingly, the only domesticated cereal was rice, rather than the millets typically found at other Peiligang Culture sites.[10] Residues found in pottery vessels from Jiahu show that rice, as well as hawthorne fruit and honey, were used to make a fermented alcoholic beverage.[11] Dogs were domesticated, but it is not clear whether the pigs represent an early phase of domestication or were wild animals hunted by the Neolithic period residents of Jiahu. They also fished. Some graves at Jiahu yielded tortoise shells with what appear to be symbols incised on them, tempting some researchers to suggest that these signs might be an early form of Chinese writing. Most scholars, however, believe that these symbols are not Chinese writing characters but rather signs used in the practice of divination (methods used to contact the spirit world to gain answers to questions; see later).[12]

The Middle and Lower Yangtze River areas were the main region of eventual rice domestication in the Neolithic period. Pengtoushan Culture sites of the Middle Yangtze, such as **Bashidang** (see Figures 11.2 and 11.3), which dates to 6800 BC, contain materials that likely represent rituals, such as pits with polished and ornamental black stone rods, as well as numerous burials, dozens of dwellings, and ditches surrounding settlements.[13] Like the sites of North China, those of the Pengtoushan Culture have abundant evidence for the use of wild plant resources (lotus roots, peaches, plums, soybeans, acorns, and grapes), as well as fish, birds, wild water buffalo, and deer. Rice is present in limited quantities, suggesting it was not a major part of the diet, and there is some debate over whether it was domesticated. There are, however, sites elsewhere in the Yangtze River region with partially domesticated rice by 7400 BC,[14] so it may be that the rice at Bashidang was also at least a partially domesticated form. In the Lower Yangtze River region, some of the earliest Neolithic is represented by sites such as **Xiaohuangshan** (see Figure 11.2), which dates to 7000 BC.[15] This village had rectangular dwellings, burials around the edges of the site, and numerous pits thought to have been for storage for acorns and perhaps for tubers. The pottery contains impressions of rice husks used as temper for the firing process, indicating the use of this cereal, although probably harvested and cultivated as wild rice or a partially domesticated type. Dependence on domesticated rice in the diet is a feature of later Neolithic societies in this region, beginning around 4000 BC.[16]

In southern China, food-production economies during the Neolithic likely focused on tuber and root crops such as taro.[17] This is suggested by the presence of taro remains at **Zengpiyan Cave** (see Figure 11.2), dating between 10,000 and 5000 BC. Although this was a hunter–gatherer–forager site, with abundant evidence of the use of wild Asian plum, acorns, grapes, freshwater shellfish, and deer, it also had early pottery.[18] Compared to the Yangtze River area just to the north, people at sites like Zengpiyan Cave continued a relatively mobile hunter–gatherer–forager lifestyle until quite late. It is not until after 4000 BC that these hunter–gatherer–foragers adopted a more settled way of life, possibly associated with the introduction of domesticated rice from the Yangtze River area.

In all of these Early Neolithic examples, the processes leading to morphologically domesticated types of plants and animals appear to have occurred over hundreds, if not thousands, of years. Sedentary villagers exploited wild foods and likely cultivated wild plant foods early on. Over time, they became more dependent on particular species such as broomcorn and foxtail millet in North China and rice in the Yangtze River region. The same is true of their exploitation of pigs, which began with this animal being hunted but later controlled in ways that led to domesticated forms.

Bashidang a Neolithic site in the Middle Yangtze River region of China. Residents relied mainly on wild food resources but also had rice, which may have been domesticated.

Xiaohuangshan an early Neolithic period village site in the Lower Yangtze River region of China. It has evidence for the use of wild rice, as well as other wild food resources.

Zengpiyan Cave a hunter–gatherer–forager site in southern China that has evidence for the early use of taro and pottery within the context of high mobility.

Before Shang

During the later Neolithic, Chalcolithic, and Bronze Age periods, sedentary villagers in several regions became fully invested in domesticated plants and animals. At the same time, a number of intriguing features suggesting enhanced political complexity and the possible formation of the early state are apparent in the archaeological record.

Although these trends can be seen in many parts of the Yellow and Yangtze River regions, we will look most closely at only a few, including the Yangshao, Longshan, and Erlitou cultures, which were found in the Middle and Lower Yellow River area.

Yangshao Culture

Yangshao Culture a middle Neolithic period group along the middle Yellow River in China. Yangshao people used domesticated and wild food resources, and there is evidence for the beginning of social distinctions between people based on grave goods.

The **Yangshao Culture** (see Figures 11.2 and 11.3) dates between 5000 and 3000 BC and represents the Middle Neolithic period in North China. Its domesticated millet-based food-production economy included Chinese cabbage and some domesticated rice.[19] Yangshao sites had domesticated pigs, dogs, and chickens and some sheep, cattle, and goats. These Neolithic villagers continued to gather some wild plant foods and to hunt wild animals, as well as to fish and collect shellfish. There are literally thousands of Yangshao culture sites, suggesting a successful way of life that led to increased population size and density.

Banpo a large Yangshao Culture (Neolithic) village in China that is surrounded by a moat. Abstract signs incised on pottery are thought to be an example of shared symbols that may have later led to the development of writing.

One of the best known Yangshao sites is **Banpo** (see Figures 11.2 and 11.3), a large village surrounded by a ditch, a feature typical of many Neolithic sites (as discussed previously).[20] There were numerous dwellings, pits, kilns, and artifacts, including tools used in agriculture such as stone knives, hoes, and spades, as well as ground stone mortars and pestles. Decoration on the pottery included animal and fish imagery, as well as symbols that sometimes are proposed to be an early form of writing. These signs were incised in specific places on some pottery vessels and appear to be a widely shared set of symbols across the Yangshao culture region.[21] It is possible that these shared symbolic sets of signs represent an early precursor to the development of Chinese writing (see later for more on the development of writing). Banpo also had a large cemetery situated outside the village.

Jiangzhai an early Yangshao Culture Neolithic village in the Yellow River region of China. The economy was based at the household level, and some families had more access to resources, allowing them to control greater amounts of agricultural surplus.

A recent restudy of the **Jiangzhai** village (see Figures 11.2 and 11.3), which dates to the early part of the Yangshao Culture, shows that unequal access to agricultural surpluses was an integral part of Neolithic lifeways.[22] Jiangzhai was surrounded by a ditch and had an open, central plaza and two cemeteries. More than 100 dwellings surrounded the plaza, representing a village population between 300 and 400 people (Figure 11.4). Each dwelling was associated with storage pits. The village was divided into five sectors, with each sector being a cluster of dwellings that surrounded a larger structure. Researchers interpret these sectors as each representing an extended family or perhaps a lineage. Examination of the numbers of storage pits associated with houses in each sector suggests that some households were more productive (had more agricultural surplus). This may mean that low-producing households spent time in other pursuits, such as crafts like leatherworking, which they could exchange with households that had surpluses. Although Early Yangshao Culture is usually characterized as egalitarian in terms of social structure, the fact that some families could accumulate agricultural surpluses might be a forerunner to later unequal access to resources that helped create greater social divisions between individuals and families and the eventual appearance of elites.

Burials at Yangshao sites sometimes contain evidence for possible status differences between people. At the site of Xishuipo, for example, a burial of an adult male was

FIGURE 11.4
Plan view of some of the houses (*brown*) and features (*green*), such as storage pits, at Jiangzhai, China, during the Yangshao period (redrawn from Peterson and Shelach 2012, Figure 1).

accompanied by three younger people, as well as two animal mosaics.[23] These mosaics were made of shellfish and appear to represent a tiger and a dragon. Additionally, there was a smaller triangular mosaic of shellfish and two human lower leg bones (which are not from the adult male or the three other individuals). Unusual burials such as this one perhaps indicate that this person had a distinctive social role, such as a ritual specialist. Other researchers suggest that the careful arrangement of burials in Yangshao Culture cemeteries, as well as the numerous ash pits that were placed along the edges of the cemeteries, might indicate an early form of ancestor worship with sacrifices burned in the pits to the memory of the ancestors of that community buried in the cemetery.[24] Ancestor worship is well documented in later polities such as Shang (see later).

Longshan Culture

From 3000 to 1800 BC, the later Neolithic and Chalcolithic in the Middle and Lower Yellow River region included the **Longshan Culture** (see Figures 11.2 and 11.3), which was based on domesticated millet agriculture, as well as wet rice farming and the use of domesticated pigs. It was during this period that copper and

Longshan Culture a late Neolithic and Chalcolithic interaction network along the middle and lower Yellow River in China, which included standardized ways of making and decorating items such as pottery and jade. Increasing social and political complexity resulted in status differences between people, the concentration of power in the hands of fewer individuals, a settlement hierarchy with large walled settlements surrounded by smaller, unwalled sites, and evidence for warfare.

bronze metallurgy began to develop[25] and increasingly complex political entities began to emerge (in the Yellow River, the Yangtze River basin, and other parts of China).[26] Archaeologists can see evidence for this development in features such as widely shared ways of making and decorating artifacts (such as pottery and jade) that suggest far-reaching interaction networks and also in burials that show increased social differences between people in the types of grave goods that accompany them into the afterlife. Some of these people may have wielded considerable power and authority, indicating a degree of control over other members of society that did not exist in earlier times, and there are sacrificial victims in some cases. At the same time, Longshan Culture was characterized by increased numbers of people more densely packed into the landscape and a settlement system in which a few sites became quite large, whereas others nearby were smaller. This type of pattern is interpreted as reflecting a hierarchy in which some places are more important in terms of centralization of power and powerful individuals, and it has sometimes been described as a network of incipient city-states,[27] just as we saw in Mesopotamia (see Chapter 9).

The development of centralized authority at a restricted number of sites, in combination with similar processes in regions close to the area of the Longshan Culture, meant that territory sometimes was contested between different groups of people. During this period, these contests are seen in raiding between sites and in warfare within the Longshan interaction area.[28] The larger sites tended to be walled, using rammed earth to form the walls, which can be interpreted as a means of defense against raids and larger scale attacks.[29] The site of **Taosi** also had a rammed earth wall surrounding the settlement, walled enclosures within the settlement in which the houses of the higher status families were situated, evidence of craft specialization, and a possible astronomical observatory, which may have been related to high-status individuals using it to determine the agricultural calendar.[30] Evidence for conflict resulted at some sites in numerous bodies (especially boys and men) that exhibit marks of violence, such as dismembering and scalping.[31]

In addition to increasingly centralized power at larger, walled settlements, ritual also played an important role in Longshan Culture. At Taosi, for example, there are more than 1,000 tombs with evidence of social distinctions.[32] About 1% of these were large tombs with individuals of the highest rank, containing wooden coffins and hundreds of grave goods (wooden vessels, polychrome pottery, weapons, tools, jade, entire pig carcasses, and, in some cases, stone chimes and alligator skin drums). The mid-size tombs were more numerous (about 12%) and had 10 to 20 grave goods. These included some polychrome pottery, wooden vessels and some jade ornaments. Finally, the majority of the graves (87%) were small and contained only the person's body, although some of these graves had a few small objects as grave goods. Interestingly, the different-size tombs were placed in the same rows, suggesting kin-based relationships related to lineages.[33] Similar social distinctions are seen at many other sites, where the distribution of the ash pits suggests ancestor worship rituals related to the high-status individuals in the cemetery[34] (see "Yangshao Culture" for the possible

Taosi a Longshan Culture (Neolithic and Chalcolithic) walled site in China that has evidence for social differences between people in the form of separation of housing and in size of graves and types of grave goods.

beginnings of this tradition at the level of the community rather than a focus on single individuals). Another example of ritual activity is divination using **scapulimancy**.[35] This is the practice of reading or interpreting crack patterns caused by burning of animal shoulder bones (oracle bones) to predict future events. Scapulimancy became an important ritual activity in later Chinese polities (see later).

Erlitou Culture

The **Erlitou Culture** phase (1800 to 1600 BC; see Figure 11.2) in the Yellow River region was associated with what archaeologists call the Early Bronze Age,[36] and evidence suggests that the first Chinese state was beginning to emerge during this period. There was a clear hierarchy of settlements, access to and control of prestige goods (jade, turquoise, and bronze vessels) by a small group of elites, specialized craft workshops, competition perhaps resulting in some violence (such as scalping), and distinctions between people in graves and grave goods. All of these features appeared in earlier Neolithic and Chalcolithic contexts in China, but they became much more pronounced and developed in the Erlitou Culture, leading to greater political unity over a large region.

One of the best known sites is **Erlitou** (see Figure 11.2), which was an urban settlement that grew rapidly after 1900 BC, reaching 300 hectares (740 acres).[37] Within the city was a large enclosure (built on a rammed earth foundation) that was surrounded by rammed-earth walls. This was where wooden palace complexes and homes of elite families were built. The walled enclosure included craft workshops, suggesting that they were overseen and controlled by the elites.[38] Some of the elite burials were found in courtyards associated with the palace complexes. They contained white pottery vessels, shell ornaments, turquoise, bronze vessels (found only with the highest ranked elites), and jade artifacts (found only with the highest ranked elites, unlike jade in earlier times), among other grave goods.[39] One of the most striking was an adult male who had the types of grave goods just mentioned, and also a mosaic, made of 2,000 turquoise and jade pieces, in the shape of a dragon placed over his body (Figure 11.5). The dragon is an important element in Chinese mythology because it is associated with the supernatural, and we saw it also in the earlier shell mosaic example from the Yangshao Culture (discussed previously). Other burials included sacrificed victims who were bound by ropes.[40]

One way in which Erlitou and the Erlitou Culture differed from the Longshan Culture is that Erlitou appears to have been the "central place" at the top of a hierarchy of other sites. Below Erlitou in this hierarchy were secondary centers that controlled access to important resources such as kaolin (a type of clay used to make white pottery) and stone raw materials used to make items such as spades. These resources and items were sent to Erlitou from the secondary centers.[41] Associated with some of the secondary centers was the next tier in the hierarchy, smaller tertiary centers, and, below that, villages, hamlets, and outposts in resource-rich regions (copper, salt, and other commodities) beyond the Erlitou Culture area.[42] Although elites at Erlitou appear to have controlled craft workshops located at this site, these elites exchanged the exotic craft items with elites at other sites (including regional and

Scapulimancy the use of animal shoulder bones (called oracle bones), and later also turtle plastrons, in divination (predicting future events). Early scapulimancy interpreted the patterns of cracks caused by burning; later scapulimancy involved the careful preparation of animal shoulder bones and turtle plastrons by thinning them and drilling holes in them before submitting them to fire to produce crack patterns that could be interpreted.

Erlitou Culture a Bronze Age culture in north China in the Yellow River region. Some archaeologists describe it as the first state because of increased political control over this region, shared rituals, and centralized administrative functions at the main site of Erlitou.

Erlitou a large urban site in China with evidence for an elite enclosure with palace complexes, houses, and graves. It was the main center during the Erlitou Culture in the Yellow River area and held influence over a wide geographical region characterized by a hierarchy of sites.

FIGURE 11.5
A dragon mosaic from Erlitou, China.

secondary centers) rather than controlling all trade and exchange within this part of China. The elites and the various specialists in crafts and defense likely received food resources as tribute from the region over which they exerted some control, but tribute would also have included artifacts, such as the spades mentioned above, and various raw materials to use in the craft workshops.[43]

A number of the white pottery vessel types and the mostly undecorated bronze vessels and artifacts were used in ritual contexts. The white pottery types called *gui* and *he* were used for "heating liquid and pouring water over alcoholic beverages," and "*jue* vessels were probably used as drinking goblets"; all three of these types would have "facilitated ritual ceremony, most likely for ancestor worship."[44] These vessel shapes also were made from bronze later in the Erlitou Culture. The similarity in the styles of the white pottery and bronze vessels over a large geographical region suggests to some archaeologists that they represent styles from a single origin area. Their distribution thus indicates the extent of the interaction sphere during the Erlitou Culture phase, especially because the bronze ritual vessels were made only at Erlitou.[45] Beyond that, however, it also demonstrates the use of ritual and ritual objects to link people together into a more unified group[46] (somewhat like we saw with Cahokia in Chapter 8). The walled elite enclosure at Erlitou, however, suggests that most such rituals might have been seen only by other elites rather than by the commoners, at least at the main center of Erlitou. The urban city of Erlitou declined in importance by 1600 BC, as other cities, such as the nearby Yanshi and then Zhengzhou, became more prominent.[47]

Shang China

Erligang Culture a Bronze Age polity with its center at the site of Zhengzhou in the Yellow River region of China. It is sometimes referred to as early Shang and dates from 1600 to 1400 BC.

The exact relationship between Erlitou Culture and the later **Erligang Culture** (1600 to 1400 BC; see Figure 11.2), sometimes called early Shang, is not completely understood,[48] although the majority of the features of Erlitou Culture continue into

FIGURE 11.6
The taotie ("two-eye") motif from an Erligang period bronze vessel.

Erligang Culture and later Shang and other dynasties. Many of these features (such as bronze vessels used in rituals) assumed more prominent roles, and the settlement system of one main urban center at the top of a hierarchy of other sites, along with tribute payments, labor specialization, and ruling elites, became well established.

The main city of the Erligang Culture was **Zhengzhou** (see Figure 11.2; sometimes identified as the first Shang capital[49]), which was very large. Its inner rammed earth–walled city was the size of Erlitou (300 hectares [740 acres]) and contained temples and palaces, whereas an outer rammed-earth wall surrounded an area of 13 square kilometers (5 square miles), which contained this inner city as well as areas for pottery, bronze, and bone workshops, homes, and cemeteries in the area between the two concentric rammed-earth walls. Like Erlitou before it, Zhengzhou was the center for the manufacture of ritual bronze vessels, suggesting carefully monitored and controlled supervision.[50] One of the innovations during the Erligang Culture was the addition of decoration to the bronze vessels, especially a design called "two-eyed" (*taotie*), in which two eyes, a possible nose, ears and horns, and probable bodies on each side appear (Figure 11.6).[51] The Erligang interaction sphere, like Erlitou before it, included outposts in resource-rich areas, although these outposts were fortified suggesting greater military control, and the geographic extent of the Erligang Culture was much larger than that of Erlitou Culture.[52]

By 1400 BC, or the middle Shang period, and continuing through the late Shang (1250 to 1045 BC), a highly centralized state emerged in the Yellow River area of northern China and is estimated to have controlled a territory of 230,000 square kilometers (88,800 square miles).[53] Although a number of researchers describe the Shang period (and some earlier ones such as the Erlitou Culture) as states, not all scholars follow this perspective (read "The Big Picture: Political Organization in the Shang Period"). One of the most important sites was the late Shang capital city at **Anyang (Yinxu)** (Figure 11.7), which is one of several major cities that were used by the ruling dynasty during the Shang Dynasty period. Anyang was

Zhengzhou the main urban center of the Erligang Culture in the Yellow River area of northern China from 1600 to 1400 BC.

Anyang the late Shang capital city in the Yellow River region of northern China, also called Yinxu. It was home to the ruling dynasty and had rammed-earth palaces and temples, royal tombs, bronze and other workshops, residences, and large sacrificial areas.

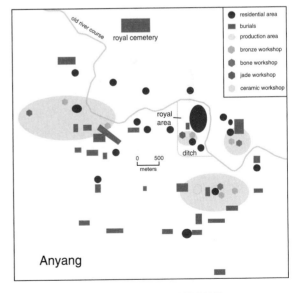

FIGURE 11.7
Plan map of some of the areas at the Shang capital of Anyang (redrawn from Campbell et al. 2011, Figure 1).

30 square kilometers (11.5 square miles) in size and, like other major cities in earlier periods, had an area of temples and palaces built of rammed earth that was surrounded by a water-filled ditch. The settlement included bronze and other workshops, residences, tombs of elite individuals with lavish grave goods, and abundant evidence for sacrifices, including humans.[54] Many of these features were much more elaborate and at a larger scale than during earlier periods (see below).

The Big Picture

Political Organization in the Shang Period

The lineage practice of ancestor worship in China was one of the fundamental bases upon which the legitimacy of the Shang kings and other elites was built. This was because the king was the living link to the dead, in this case, royal ancestors. The royal ancestors could intercede with other important powers such as earlier lords and forces of nature and ultimately with the high god, DiTi.[55] By the time of the Shang polity, kings, like the Egyptian pharaohs, ruled over a sizable amount of territory. Some of the problems they faced were maintaining order within this region and keeping all areas loyal, as well as the day-to-day running of the government. Shang kings were able to accomplish these goals because they appointed people who were kin, either by marriage or by blood.[56] This

was especially true for appointments of individuals to rule over the districts into which the Shang territory was divided. These appointments were hereditary positions that reinforced kin linkage to the king. These district officials had the title of *bo* or *hou* (Figure 11.8). Each of them had staffs of other administrators, as well as retainers, and each also was a court official. The *bo* or *hou* ruled each district, controlled the people in it, collected taxes, maintained and directed the military of the district, and oversaw work on state agricultural lands. Within each district there were smaller areas headed by local rulers living in smaller centers. These rulers were called *tian*, and they paid taxes to the *bo* or *hou* as well as raised military forces for these district rulers.

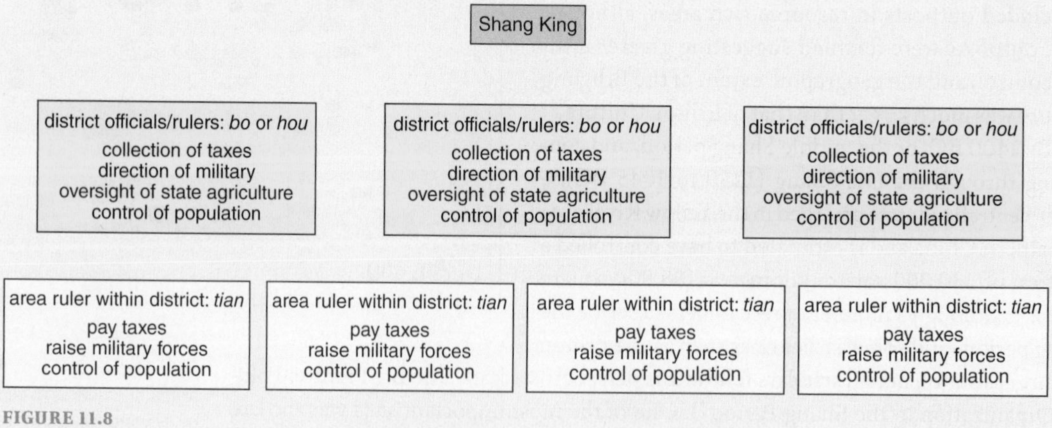

Shang King

district officials/rulers: *bo* or *hou*	district officials/rulers: *bo* or *hou*	district officials/rulers: *bo* or *hou*
collection of taxes direction of military oversight of state agriculture control of population	collection of taxes direction of military oversight of state agriculture control of population	collection of taxes direction of military oversight of state agriculture control of population

area ruler within district: *tian*	area ruler within district: *tian*	area ruler within district: *tian*	area ruler within district: *tian*
pay taxes raise military forces control of population	pay taxes raise military forces control of population	pay taxes raise military forces control of population	pay taxes raise military forces control of population

FIGURE 11.8
A simplified chart of political organization within the Shang Kingdom.

The Written Word

The origins of writing in China are still being researched. As we saw above, there are some symbols found in the Neolithic that may be early forms of writing (read "Peopling the Past: Oracle Bones, Divination, and the Origins of Writing"). The written word (some 5,000 characters), however, was definitely present by the late Shang period, where it is found in the context of scapulimancy, although inscriptions also are known from bronze and pottery vessels, as well as on jade and stone.[57] The ritual practice of divination using oracle bones and turtle plastrons (the flat inner part of the shell) was a method by which the Shang kings determined how and when to make offerings to their ancestors and asked questions about future weather (in an effort to understand whether it would affect travel and warfare), royal hunts, alliances, and warfare (Figure 11.9). The royal oracle bones thus are a record of inscriptions that are questions and answers about particular upcoming events, based on interpretations by diviners of the cracks on the oracle bones and turtle plastrons. Most such oracle bones have inscriptions that are within the realm of religion because they refer to answers about royal ancestor worship in the context of a ritual calendar (see "Ritual and Religion"). The main use of writing in Shang China thus was somewhat different from that of Mesopotamia, where it was mainly used to record economic transactions, at least in the earliest records we have (see Chapter 9), and from Egypt, where early writing mainly recorded the stories of the pharaohs' and other elite individuals' lives and occasionally economic transactions (see Chapter 10).

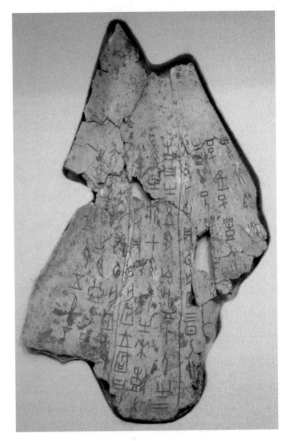

FIGURE 11.9
Chinese writing on a Shang Dynasty oracle bone.

Resource Networks, Trade, and Exchange

Political and administrative control over a relatively large region during the Shang period meant that some of the resources necessary for the craft workshops in the large cities such as Zhengzhou and Anyang could have been obtained from secondary and other cities in areas near the limits of Shang territory or from more distant places. The raw materials and partially finished goods likely represented tribute to the royal household. The production of exotic goods in the workshops often focused on ritual bronze vessels, jade artifacts, and turquoise. Tribute was moved from source areas by water along the rivers or by road because there was a relatively extensive and well-maintained road system during the Shang period.[63] Some researchers suggest that cowrie shells were used as a form of "money." Other research, however, indicates that during the Shang period, cowrie shells were more likely to be used as ornamentation,

Peopling the Past

Oracle Bones, Divination, and the Origins of Writing

In recent years there has been increased interest in examining whether the origins of Chinese writing can be traced to certain signs drawn on or incised into pottery vessels and tortoise shells during the Neolithic period. There is, however, considerable debate about these Neolithic period graphic symbols.[58] Some burials at Jiahu (see previous discussion), for example, contained incised tortoise shells (or, more rarely, incised bone). Some of these incised signs have some resemblance to Chinese characters of the Shang period, although (if they are related) they may not have had the same meaning during the Neolithic period.[59] During the slightly later Neolithic period Yangshao Culture, sites such as Banpo (see previous discussion) had numerous pottery vessels with incised signs that some researchers interpret as indicating a way to tally or count or to mark pottery rather than as characters that develop into later Chinese writing.[60] In the lower Yellow River region, however, there were Neolithic period cultures that were contemporary with the late Yangshao and the Longshan cultures. These lower Yellow River Neolithic period cultures (such as the Dawenkou) had 32 graphic symbols that appear to be widely shared throughout this region and were quite similar to several Shang written characters.[61] Beyond this, these late Neolithic graphics shared with the Shang period an association of signs with ritual contexts because they were found on ritual drinking vessels used to honor ancestors. Whether these Neolithic period signs represented the names of clans, types of ceremonies, or simply the contents of the vessels is not known. It does seem, however, that the appearance of Chinese writing by the late Shang was built at least in part on these earlier Neolithic period signs. More important, the appearance of writing in the late Shang was undoubtedly the result of a long and gradual process, with oracle bones and their inscriptions only a small part of Chinese written documents, which could have been mainly on perishable materials such as bamboo and wooden tablets.[62]

such as on trappings for horses or as personal ornaments for people, in ritual offerings, and as grave goods.[64] These shells were exotic items because they were brought into the Shang region of China through long-distance trade networks and may have been used by Shang royalty as gifts to various other elites and favored individuals.

As we saw previously, the manufacture of ritual bronze vessels was a feature not only of Shang period China but also earlier in the Erlitou Culture. These workshops required copper and tin to make bronze, although during the late Shang, the production of bronze vessels occurred not just at the main capital, Anyang, but also at other Shang cities and in regions less under the control of the Shang Dynasty.[65] Several new styles of ritual bronze vessels were added, and these artifacts likely were symbolic of religious activities and wealth and also of power and elite status. Some were inlaid with turquoise, and many had inscriptions. Bronze also was used for weapons and tools. Jade workshops were found, although compared to the earlier Neolithic period, jade was somewhat less important as a ritual and "wealth" item than the Shang ritual bronze vessels.[66] Many of the items created in the various workshops became part of an interregional network of shared cultural, symbolic, and religious ideas and activities. These artifacts may have legitimized the authority of the Shang kings (especially with regard to royal ancestral lineages), as well as cemented alliances and other political interactions with Shang cities outside the capital and in less well-controlled areas on the peripheries of Shang influence in northern China.

Recent analysis of massive bone-working workshops at Anyang suggests the manufacture of items that may have been used in trade networks.[67] Most of the animal bone was cattle, which had special significance for Shang royalty because cattle often were sacrificed in rituals (see later). Among the many items made were hairpins, awls, arrowheads, shovels, and plaques. By far the most common were hairpins and arrowheads, with estimates suggesting that the sheer quantity of these items would have far exceeded that needed by royal and elite households. Excess hairpins and arrowheads would have been valuable trade and exchange items, especially because they were made from ritually important cattle bone.

Social Life

For most people in Shang China, life was in many ways little changed from that of the earlier Neolithic period. Farmers toiled in fields tending to crops of broomcorn and foxtail millet and rice or made decisions about their domesticated pig herds. Domesticated cattle were part of the local economy. Commoners lived simply, in small households that were subject to the power of one of the senior male members of the family. Men in the family were descended from a single male ancestor, who was the object of ancestor worship.[68] There were increased labor obligations to the kings and their households, as well as other elites, particularly for the construction of rammed-earth foundations and walls for cities, palaces, and temples, as well as taking care of royal farming lands. And, there were "taxes" in the form of tributes to be paid to the Shang rulers. Like early politically complex societies elsewhere in the world, the Shang kings depended on food surpluses as one form of wealth that could be used to support or pay for other needed services, such as supplying armies with the food they needed during warfare.

Higher ranked social classes were organized similar to those of commoners (that is, along lines of male descent), although their homes were larger and their access to resources more extensive. Some specialized laborers, such as the workers in the bronze, jade, and turquoise, lived in areas of the city close to the royal households and had houses that were larger and constructed more like those of the elites.[69] Just as with Mesopotamia (see Chapter 9) and Egypt (see Chapter 10), as well as in the societies we live in today, workplaces had a variety of people in jobs at different levels of responsibility—supervisors, craftsmen, assistant craftsmen, trainees, and unskilled laborers.

Members of the elite classes, with the king as the head of the royal household, also traced their lineages to venerated male ancestors, who were the objects of ancestor worship (see "Ritual and Religion"). The king often had several wives to ensure the birth of sons who would continue the male lineage. These marriages were one way to create alliances between various parts of the Shang kingdom. The king's

wives, and other relatives of the king, helped administer political tasks such as organizing armies, leading ancestor worship rituals, and delivering messages to other
royal lineages in other parts of the Shang region.[70] Inscriptions on oracle bones document that Shang capital cities were built or maintained by kings in response to
commands received through divination, that is, on the orders of the revered royal
ancestors and gods.[71] Not only did elites live in palaces and similarly large and
expensive homes, but their tombs reflected their access to incredible amounts of
resources. Shang royal burials included the king and also sometimes some of his
consorts, spears, broadswords, arrows, axes made of bronze, large quantities of bone
arrowheads, jade artifacts including weapons, bronze ritual vessels, and numerous
sacrifices, some of which were animals (cattle and horses), but others of which were
humans (about 10,000 are estimated human sacrificial burials [many decapitated]
in the Anyang royal cemetery). Many human sacrifices were war captives, based on
inscriptions written on oracle bones.[72] Not all were sacrificed immediately, based
on isotope studies of their bones that show they were nonlocal but had a diet during
the last years of their lives that reflected living in or near Anyang.[73] As part of the
burial ceremonies, feasting rituals were held and large quantities of bronze containers were buried with the individual, for example, the tomb of Lady Hao, who was a
consort to a Shang king.[74] Hao's tomb contained 440 bronze artifacts,[75] of which
195 were ritual bronzes. Of these ritual vessels, 144 were for storing, warming, wa-
tering down, serving, and drinking wine. Other bronze vessels made in matched
sets were used to serve food, especially roasted pig or dog. These vessels were used
during the feasting ceremony at the grave and then likely washed and placed carefully in the tomb with Lady Hao. She also had a plate full of sheep and cattle legs
placed near her mouth.

Ritual and Religion

As we have seen, rituals in Shang China were tightly intertwined with power, prestige, and authority, as well as veneration of male ancestors and various gods. Some
of these included the high god, Ti, and nature gods, such as the Yellow River god,
Ho, and the Mountain god, Yueh.[76] Unlike Mesopotamia or Egypt, there were no
priests or priestesses; instead, ritual specialists (for rainmaking and summoning
spirits) and diviners helped interact with the supernatural, especially through the
use of oracle bones. Divination became highly standardized in its use of animal
shoulder bones (mainly cattle) and turtle plastrons, as well as in the preparation
of these materials prior to their use.[77] This suggests much tighter control over this
ritual during the Shang period, especially for the Shang king. Other elites, as well as
commoners, also asked questions of the supernatural using oracle bones, but these
(unlike those of the king) were not inscribed or as carefully prepared by thinning,
polishing, and drilling of holes.

Worship of ancestors involved the use of ritual bronze vessels (read "The
Big Picture: Art and Ideology in Shang China") and a yearly cycle of ritual sacrifices, with diviners setting the types and amounts of sacrifice based on reading

The Big Picture

Art and Ideology in Shang China

One of the major art forms in Shang China was bronze vessels, which were highly decorated. These vessels were used in ceremonies associated with ancestor worship, and they were linked with elites and the concept of authority.[81] There were several different shapes or forms of vessel, each of which was specific to a particular task, such as pouring wine, cooking food, or holding water that could be used in ritual cleaning. The designs on the ritual bronze vessels were mainly a limited set of animal-like forms. These included the two-eyed *taotie* (discussed previously), birdlike designs, and dragonlike motifs (Figure 11.10). Human representations were less common. One interpretation of these designs suggests that they represent references to the sacrifice of humans, the eating of various animals in ritual feasting, the journey to the afterlife, and the inhabitants of the afterlife.[82] Other researchers suggest instead that the designs were shamanistic because ritual specialists (shamans) transform themselves into animal forms.[83] Regardless of the specific interpretation, the motifs were tied to activities and ceremonies that were part of ancestor worship, particularly worship of royal ancestors by kings and other elites. As noted above, ritual bronze vessels were an important item given as gifts or in trade to elites throughout Shang territory, as well as to surrounding regions, where the bronze vessels also were used for ancestor worship rituals.

FIGURE 11.10
A Shang Dynasty ritual bronze vessel.

the oracle bones or following a standardized set of offerings.[78] Sacrificed animals included dogs, pigs, cattle, sheep, and horses, and there also were human sacrifices.[79] But not all sacrifice was necessarily in the context of ancestor worship. At Anyang, for example, there were sacrificial pits associated with the dedication of buildings. Some of these contained humans, others dogs, and still others combinations of cattle, sheep, and dogs. In another area, there were 127 sacrificial pits, most containing humans, but some with horses and chariots or dogs. Horses were introduced during the late Shang and, because they were prestigious, were associated with Shang royalty. Some sacrificial pits contained hawks, deer, fish, birds, and turtles, although wild animals were not found as frequently as domesticated animals and humans. The most common practice was to sacrifice one animal at a time, but there also were multiple sacrifices; when it came to royalty and other elites, large numbers of animals and humans were sacrificed at a single occasion.[80]

Warfare and Violence

Sacrifice of humans certainly seems to fit into the category of a type of violence, especially because such sacrifices (as noted above) were of people captured during warfare.[84] The Shang kings (just like other early rulers) used warfare for several purposes, including protection of the kingdom's borders from groups of people who were not part of Shang culture, expanding Shang territory, and keeping various parts of the kingdom under control.[85] As might be expected in a politically complex society, the Shang military was highly organized, with a variety of different ranks and tasks. Some of these were officers who oversaw command of the armies, including archers, charioteers, and the use of dogs. Other military positions included people who administered captured war goods, such as animals and plunder, those who managed the feeding of the army, and positions that saw to the repair of army equipment.[86] The Shang king and other members of royal lineages led battles. Elites each had their own private armies (3,000 to 5,000 soldiers), and a combination of these individual armies made up the bulk of the military forces when a military campaign was conducted.

The political importance of warfare to the Shang king and in Shang society is seen partly in the numerous inscriptions on oracle bones, which detail the capture of farming lands, people, and other plunder, the instability of the border regions, the capture and control of areas rich in resources such as copper and tin, and questions Shang kings asked of their royal ancestors regarding military endeavors.[87] Another goal of military campaigns was to capture non-Shang people who could be used as sacrifices to royal ancestors. The huge quantities of weapons and bronze helmets, leather shields, and trappings for chariots found in royal and other elite burials (see "Social Life") speak to the significance of warfare as part of elite life. Lady Hao herself led military campaigns that resulted in an expansion of Shang territory, although women as commanders were unusual. Lady Hao's grave goods included jade and bronze dagger-axes, as well as bronze arrowheads. Among the many battles fought by the Shang were those with the rival Western Zhou Dynasty, who were situated to the west of the Shang kingdom.

After Shang

In 1045 BC, the **Western Zhou** king, with the help of other Shang enemies, conquered the Shang and Shang lands were divided among Western Zhou royalty.[88] The Western Zhou thus benefited from capturing a successful political interaction network in which Western Zhou elite could step into roles formerly held by Shang elite. The early part of the Western Zhou period was similar to Shang China because the Western Zhou made ritual bronze vessels that were nearly identical to those of Shang and used Shang rituals including divination and ancestor worship. These may have been efforts to legitimize the rule of the Western Zhou kings. There were changes, however, such as the training of all of the men of the ruling class as warriors and the manufacture of inscribed bronze vessels as a way to celebrate battles and victories. Some later Western Zhou leaders made efforts to standardize rituals, which led to shifts away from the Shang way of performing rituals (read "Further Reflections: Consolidating the Western Zhou State Identity").[89] The Western Zhou used inscribed bronze vessels as gifts to elites that they placed in charge of various portions of their territory and as heads of vassal states, including Shang royalty, as one way to remove them from their bases of power within the former Shang kingdom.[90] These bronze vessels thus were important documents of these political relationships, as well as items that were used in feasting rituals to cement these relationships and in ancestor rituals that emulated those used by the Western Zhou king.

In 770 BC, the Western Zhou were forced to leave their main territory in the Wei River region because of the incursion of "barbarians" and possibly also because of climatic changes that impacted local agricultural productivity. They moved east, becoming the Eastern Zhou.[91] This period, however, was not politically centralized, and the Eastern Zhou were constantly fighting wars with their neighbors. One important innovation was the introduction of iron, which was used to make both tools and weapons.

Throughout the history of China, ancestor worship and divination remained significant aspects of later political states. After the Eastern Zhou, there were some periods in which many states and dynasties fought for control and others when a single dynasty managed to unite much of northern China and eventually all of what we recognize today as falling within the borders of China (read "Timeline: China"). Imperial China began in 221 BC with the Qin Dynasty and China's first emperor (although his dynasty barely outlived him). Most of us today are familiar with Qin Shi Huang because of his magnificent army of life-size terracotta people, horses, and other items, which were buried near where he planned to be interred (Figure 11.11).[92] The last of the imperial dynasties was the Qing, and the last emperor of China was overthrown in a revolutionary uprising assisted by the army in AD 1911. At that time, modern China was established.

Western Zhou the dynasty that conquered the Shang kingdom in 1045 BC; in 770 BC, it was defeated and the period called Eastern Zhou began. Eastern Zhou was not as politically integrated and was subject to many wars with neighboring states.

FIGURE 11.11
Some of the terracotta army of Emperor Qin Shi Huang. These were created as part of the funerary grave goods.

Further Reflections

Consolidating the Western Zhou State Identity

When the Western Zhou conquered the Shang state, it inherited a powerful set of networks built on ritual that characterized a large region of China. But these were Shang rituals, and the Western Zhou needed to establish itself as the dominant power among its allies. How did ancient states accomplish these types of identity changes? For the Western Zhou, there appear to have been two major periods of consolidation of ritual. The first of these dates to the early conquest era and was hastened in part because of the death of King Wu, who had defeated the Shang. His brother, the Duke of Zhou, initiated several changes in ritual to make it distinctive from Shang ritual.[93] Among

these were the incorporation of Western Zhou–style bronze vessels, a change adopted by elites in society. The new styles seen in bronze quickly became copied in ceramics by people further down the social hierarchy. Some of the changes included an emphasis on vessels used to serve food and a decrease in those used to serve wine. Some vessels were made in matched sets, and new design elements included various bird motifs. People of the lowest classes, however, did not adopt the Western Zhou style of vessels but continued to fashion their ceramic vessels using Shang designs. While this might sound rather mundane, it indicates that the early attempts to create a widespread Western Zhou identity were not completely successful.

It was during the second period of changes in ritual that consolidation of a Western Zhou identity was accomplished. This was due in part to standardizing the rituals that used bronze and ceramic vessels, and also through use of new vessel forms and decorative elements. Earlier wine vessel styles, for example, nearly disappeared, while new types were added. One of the major decorative motifs became dragon-related designs (scales, curves, waves). Elites were buried with miniature bronzes reflecting older styles and with entire sets of very heavy bronzes in the new Western Zhou styles. The new styles and presumably the manner of performing the rituals became very widespread, including in the lowest classes in society. This might be seen, therefore, as the consolidation of Western Zhou identity.

Summary

- Locally domesticated plants and animals in the Yellow and Yangtze river regions of China included pigs, water buffalo, dogs, rice, and foxtail and broomcorn millet. Neolithic period groups also relied on hunted wild animals, collection of wild plant foods, and fishing.

- The tradition of building ditches around villages began during the Neolithic period and persisted into Shang and later societies.

- Some markings on Neolithic period pottery are interpreted as early evidence for writing, but it was the practice of scapulimancy (oracle bones) that best established early Chinese writing.

- Differences between people in grave goods suggesting social role distinctions may occur in the Early Neolithic period but became established in Middle (for example, Yangshao) and Late Neolithic/Chalcolithic (Longshan) times.

- Widespread interaction networks were present by the Late Neolithic period, and there is evidence of violence/conflict.

- The Early Bronze Age (Erlitou Culture) was characterized by a central, important site and many secondary- and tertiary-level sites. The interaction sphere was widespread, extending beyond its regional boundaries, with some archaeologists arguing that it represents the first "state" in China.

- The Shang Dynasty represents the first widely accepted Chinese state. Its rulers established capital cities, and in some respects it could be considered an example of a city-state.

- Shang society was not built on a religion with priests or priestesses but instead was based on ancestor veneration.

- Shang bronze vessels were decorated with animal motifs including dragons, birds, and *taotie* (two-eyed). These vessels were used in elite ritual activities associated with ancestor worship and were an important item used as gifts and in trade to other elites.

- Like elsewhere, Shang royalty and other elites were buried with large quantities of grave goods, including ritual bronze vessels and items made of exotic materials.

- Human sacrifices, as well as those of various animals, were a common practice to honor Shang elites and ancestors and for other events such as construction of buildings.

- Shang rulers and other elites used divination (scapulimancy) to make decisions about battles, alliances, and other important life activities.

- After the Shang Dynasty, the Western Zhou Dynasty ruled part of China. Their earliest kings continued many Shang period traditions including how ritual bronze vessels were manufactured and ornamented. The Eastern Zhou were the next dynasty, and then there was a long period of contentious rule by various small Chinese states. China was unified for the first time under the Emperor Qin Shi Huang in 221 BC.

- Many dynasties followed that of Qin, with the modern country of China established in AD 1911 with the overthrow of the last emperor.

Endnotes

1. Prendergast et al. 2009.
2. Chen and Yu 2017; Ren et al. 2016.
3. Cohen 2011.
4. Shelach 2000: 401.
5. Cohen 2011: S287–S288.
6. Cohen 2011: S284–S285; Zhao 2011: S301–S302.
7. Shelach 2000: 394.
8. Cohen 2011: S281; Zhao 2011: S296–S297.
9. Liu 2004: 126–128; Zhang et al. 2004.
10. Stevens and Fuller 2017: 164.
11. McGovern et al. 2004; this ancient fermented beverage made from rice recently was recreated in a limited run: https://www.dogfish.com/brewery/beer/chateau-jiahu (accessed July 17, 2018). Residues found in pottery vessels at Mijiaya, which is west of Jiahu, indicate the local making of beer using millet and barley around 3000 BC (Wang et al. 2016).
12. Li et al. 2003: 42.
13. Cohen 2011: S285–S286.
14. Zuo et al. 2017.
15. Cohen 2011: S286–S287.
16. Stevens and Fuller 2017: 162.
17. Zhao 2011: S302–S304.
18. Lu 2010.
19. Zhao 2011: S302.
20. Yang 2004: 46–59; Zhao 2011: S302.
21. Demattè 2010: 214–215; Li et al 2003: 39.
22. Peterson and Shelach 2012.
23. Liu 2004; Yang 2004: 53.
24. Li 2000: 136–145.
25. Wangping 2000: 213.
26. Demattè 1999; Wangping 2000.
27. Demattè 1999: 140–141.
28. Wangping 2000: 199–200.
29. Demattè 1999: 123.
30. He 2018; Liu 2009: 224.
31. Demattè 1999: 137; Liu 2004: 111; Underhill 2006: 261.
32. Wangping 2000: 207–208.
33. Wangping 2000: 211.
34. Li 2000: 151–155.
35. Brunson et al. 2016; Flad 2008: 408–409.
36. Underhill 2006: 264–265.

37. Liu 2009: 225–227.

38. Liu 2003; Liu and Xu 2007: 893.

39. Liu and Xu 2007: 889.

40. Lee 2004: 180.

41. Liu et al. 2002–2004: 88–91.

42. Liu 2009: 226.

43. Lee 2004: 186.

44. Liu 2003: 19; *gui*, *he*, and *jue* are tripod vessels that have a handle; *he* also have tubelike spouts (see Figure 8 in Liu 2003: 18).

45. Liu 2003: 24.

46. Allan 2007; Underhill 2018. Interestingly, Allan (2007: 470) provides an analogy for why Erlitou and later groups may have "bought into" the ritual aspect as represented by bronze vessels. She compares it to East Asians today eating at MacDonald's, not because it is cheap or delicious but because it represents participating in American culture, which is seen as economically powerful. A similar motive may have influenced people living in the region around Erlitou, which may have been seen as ritually and politically important so that everyone wanted to "belong" to it.

47. Lee 2004: 191; Liu and Xu 2007: 892.

48. Liu 2009: 227; Liu and Xu 2007: 894–896.

49. Tang et al. 2000: 480.

50. Liu 2003: 25–29.

51. Allan 2007: 486.

52. Liu 2009: 227.

53. Trigger 2003: 108–110.

54. Campbell 2009: 828–829.

55. Campbell 2009: 826.

56. Trigger 2003: 214–216.

57. Demattè 2010: 211; Keightley 1978.

58. Boltz 1986; Demattè 2010; Keightley 2006.

59. Li et al. 2003.

60. Demattè 2010: 214–215.

61. Demattè 2010: 215–220.

62. Demattè 2010: 226.

63. Trigger 2003: 357.

64. Yung-Ti 2003.

65. Liu 2003: 29.

66. Liu 2003: 16–17.

67. Campbell et al. 2011.

68. Trigger 2003: 167–168.

69. Trigger 2003: 371.

70. Trigger 2003: 169.

71. Campbell 2009: 831.

72. Campbell 2009: 832–833; Campbell et al. 2011: 1294; Jing and Flad 2005.

73. Cheung 2018; Cheung et al. 2017.

74. Nelson 2003: 80–86.

75. Keightley in Overmyer et al. 1995: 131.

76. Keightley (Neolithic and Shang periods) in Overmyer et al. 1995: 132.

77. Flad 2008: 413.

78. Trigger 2003: 506.

79. Jing and Flad 2005.

80. Campbell 2009: 833; Jing and Flad 2005: 267.

81. Allan 2007.

82. Allan 2007: 469.

83. Trigger 2003: 556.

84. Wheatley 1971: 63.

85. Trigger 2003: 249.

86. Trigger 2003: 254–255.

87. Underhill 2006: 268–271.

88. Underhill 2006: 273–274. Evidence at Anyang for bronze vessel molds in styles found in Western Zhou elite burials suggests that the Western Zhou conquest of Anyang resulted in the destruction of its royal areas but not of the craft workshops, which shifted over into making bronze vessels for the Western Zhou (Li et al. 2018).

89. Bin and Beichen in press; Rawson in press.

90. Allan 2007: 488; Sun 2003.

91. Huang et al. 2003.

92. Portal 2007.

93. Bin and Beichen in press; Rawson in press.

CHAPTER 12

The Indus Valley

ABOVE: Harappan figurine, Indus Valley.

In the Indus River Valley of India and Pakistan, an intriguing politically complex society called the Harappan developed out of Neolithic and Chalcolithic ways of life. Although the Harappan may not have been a state, it shared many similar features with kingdoms and states such as Mesopotamia, Egypt, and China, and Harappan period groups engaged in long-distance trade relationships with at least some of these other regions. Harappan settlements were located to take advantage of the productive floodplains and water resources of the Indus and the Ghaggar–Hakra rivers, as we have seen with other politically complex societies (Egypt and Mesopotamia, for example). One key feature of the Harappan was urbanism, that is, its cities. In this regard, it can be compared to places such as Mesopotamia, China, Egypt, Mesoamerica, and South America, although the types of cities differed between early politically complex societies. Harappans had a written script, but we are not yet able to decipher it and there is considerable debate as to whether the Indus script represents written language. Significantly, the area of Harappan influence and control appears to be much larger than that of other early politically complex societies, and while there must have been individuals and families who had greater access to resources (and could be called elites), there is little evidence in Harappan burials for these groups. This region may have been unified partly through a common ideology (as were other politically complex societies), features of which can be traced through art (figurines, painted pottery vessels, and animal motifs on seals), as well as possibly through attributes of religion and architecture. From the beginnings of the Harappan until it diminished and "disappeared" is a period of about 1,500 years (read "Timeline: The Harappan"), which will be the main focus of this chapter.

Early Food Production

The Indus Valley region forms only a small part of the subcontinent of South Asia, although there is a wide variety of local ecologies with wild plant and animal resources. Research suggests that many of the main domesticated crops and animals found in the Indus Valley were introduced from the Middle East, East Asia, and Africa.[1] Recent evidence, however, suggests that some local plants were domesticated before other domesticated species from elsewhere became available. These local domesticates include native rice, millets, pulses, and sesame.[2] In addition, genetic data on cattle indicate that zebu cattle (humped cattle) are a South Asian domesticate from local wild cattle (aurochs).[3]

One of the best known sites yielding evidence for early food production in the Indus Valley region is **Mehrgarh**[4] (Figure 12.2). There were several phases of occupation, with the earliest village of multiroomed houses built from mudbrick (Figure 12.3). Among the tools were sickle blades, a type of stone tool with highly glossed edges resulting from the deposition of silica from harvesting cereals and reeds. Other items included abundant ground stone and baskets that could have been used as containers for cooking (stone-boiling) and storing foods. Pottery vessels were not present, although people understood the properties of clay because they made unfired clay figurines and containers. Some of the more than 300 burials at Mehrgarh included the sacrifice of goats, as well as baskets, beads and pendants of shell and semiprecious stones, ground stone tools, and red ochre.[5] Personal ornamentation in the burials was mainly marine shells but also included turquoise and steatite, as well as small quantities of lapis lazuli. Regional interaction networks are suggested by the presence of marine shell from the Arabian Sea for beads and bangles and the lapis lazuli, turquoise, carnelian, and steatite for beads and pendants[6] (see "Resource Networks, Trade, and Exchange"). Some of these materials came from 500 kilometers (310 miles) or more away.

As in China, early villagers in the Indus Valley relied heavily on the use of wild resources such as jujube (a small fruit), deer, pig, gazelle, goat, sheep, water buffalo,

Mehrgarh a well-documented site in the Indus Valley region of South Asia. Its deposits contain a sequence of development from Neolithic period food-producing economies through the Chalcolithic period and into the Early Harappan period.

Timeline: The Harappan

The Indus Valley region was home to a complex political entity known archaeologically as the Harappan (Figure 12.1). There do not appear to have
been single elite rulers at Harappan cities, although
cities likely were administered by a small number
of elites.

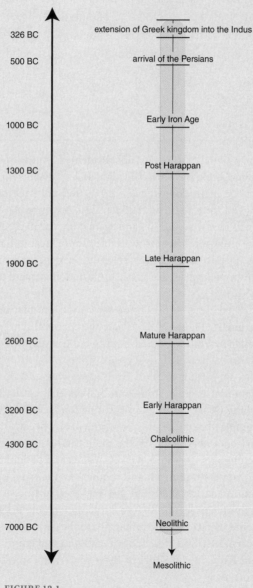

326 BC	extension of Greek kingdom into the Indus
500 BC	arrival of the Persians
1000 BC	Early Iron Age
1300 BC	Post Harappan
1900 BC	Late Harappan
2600 BC	Mature Harappan
3200 BC	Early Harappan
4300 BC	Chalcolithic
7000 BC	Neolithic
	Mesolithic

FIGURE 12.1
Timeline for the Indus Valley.

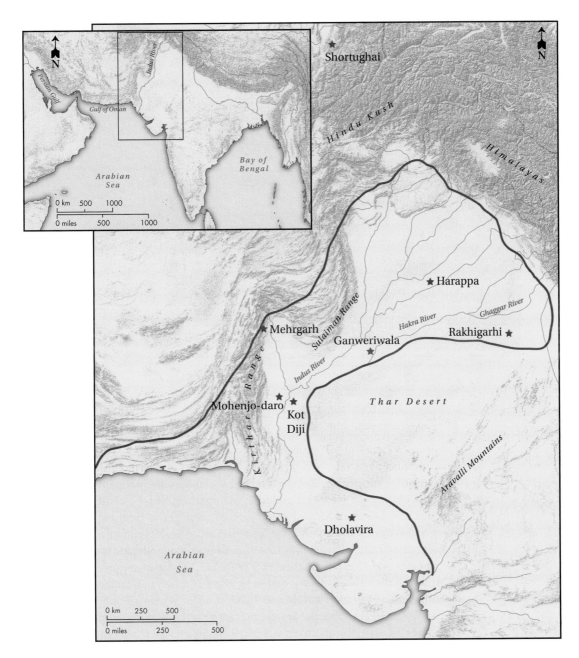

FIGURE 12.2
Indus Valley region with sites. Extent of Mature Harappan period shown with red outline (after Law 2011, Figure 2.1).

FIGURE 12.3
Houses made of mudbrick at Mehrgarh.

and onager.[7] People at Mehrgarh also used domesticated barley and wheats, which were introduced from the Middle East. In later phases of the Neolithic period, there was irrigation agriculture. Zebu cattle and sheep became increasingly important over time during the Neolithic period at Mehrgarh, with zebu cattle being locally domesticated and domesticated sheep probably brought in from the Middle East. These domesticated sheep and cattle were part of a pastoral economy, meaning that at least some of the villagers may have moved over the landscape with their herds during parts of the year. Sometime after 6000 BC, the use of cotton is documented at Mehrgarh with the discovery of cotton fibers attached to a copper bead from a Neolithic period burial of a child and an adult male.[8] Although only one bead had these fibers, several copper beads were present near the wrist of the adult. The presence of cotton may indicate that it was locally domesticated in this area of the Indus Valley region much earlier than previously thought (that is, earlier than the Mature Harappan period).

The earliest villages with food-production economies in the Indus Valley area, such as Mehrgarh, were usually small, about 2 to 3 hectares (5 to 7 acres).[9] Pottery vessels were used after 5500 BC, and some groups of people may have become full-time pastoralists. These pastoral groups are archaeologically identified based on sites with pottery but no evidence of permanent settlement, thus suggesting highly mobile people. By 4300 BC (Chalcolithic period) settlements became larger, averaging 3.5 to 6.5 hectares (8 to 16 acres), and there was a substantial increase in the number of villages. At Mehrgarh, pottery was made in ways that suggest mass production, and its painted vessels had geometric designs as well as goat/sheep, bird, and human imagery.[10] There is a partially excavated graveyard with at least 125 burials (estimates suggest more than 1,300 people might have been buried here), with nearly all people buried with their bodies aligned east–west (heads positioned to the east). Some were individual burials, whereas others were collective (several people buried together). Interestingly, compared to earlier Neolithic period burials, those of the Chalcolithic period contained few grave goods. Only 37 individuals (mainly women) had steatite, lapis lazuli, carnelian, turquoise, or shell beads, bangles, and pendants, and there are rare examples of painted pottery, baskets, stone vessels, and one copper/bronze artifact.

Many parts of the Indus Valley developed regional styles and traditions, and some groups of people began to expand to the east, across the Indus River, where they established farming and pastoral villages.

Early Harappan

The pattern of regionalism that began during the late Neolithic and Chalcolithic periods in the Indus Valley region also was a feature of the Early Harappan period (3200 to 2500 BC), where there were several groups.[11] Although these are sometimes labeled as "phases," many of them are contemporary expressions of different cultural traditions, whereas others refer to earlier and later periods within the Early Harappan. They include the Ravi, Hakra, Balakot, Amri-Nal, Kot Dijian, and Sothi-Siswal. One of the clear distinguishing features between them was in their pottery, as vessel types and decoration styles varied from one group to another. All of these people were farmer-pastoralists, like in earlier times, and the size of many of their settlements also was similar, ranging from 2.5 to 6 hectares (6 to 14 acres). There is substantial evidence, however, for other sites that were much larger (22 to 30 hectares [54 to 74 acres]), suggesting that there might be a hierarchy of sites,[12] as we saw in China and other early politically complex societies.

The site of **Harappa** (see Figure 12.2) in the Upper Indus area has deposits showing long-term continuity in occupation, starting with the Ravi phase, when the village consisted of houses, built using plastered reeds as walls, and activity areas.[13] As at Mehrgarh, people at Harappa made beads and bangles from marine shell, steatite, carnelian, and lapis lazuli, as well as terracotta (baked clay). The terracotta objects included tiny carts that indicate the presence of wheeled vehicles (Figure 12.4). Pottery included wheel-made types by the end of the Ravi phase, and a number of the vessels had signs or symbols made either before or after firing. The ones made prior to firing are called "potter's marks," and those after firing are called "graffiti"

Harappa excavations at this site in the Upper Indus Valley of South Asia document a sequence of development continuity from preurban to urban societies in the Indus Valley.

FIGURE 12.4
A wheeled cart from the site of Harappa.

(see "The Written Word"). Harappa appears to have been an important locale through which trade and exchange networks operated based on the presence of craft workshops and of raw materials that came from great distances. Lapis lazuli, for example, is from 800 kilometers (497 miles) away in what is now Afghanistan, and marine shell traveled more than 860 kilometers (534 miles).[14] In the later Kot Diji phase, the settlement at Harappa grew to 25 hectares (61 acres), and its layout was much more formal, with streets oriented either north–south or east–west. Mudbrick became the standard construction material for houses and newly built massive architecture, such as mudbrick platforms and massive walls around the two separate sections of the settlement.[15] Wheel-made pottery likely was mass-produced, and Harappa's importance in trade and exchange networks grew. Other significant developments included standardized weights (limestone cubes), for judging equivalent amounts of goods, and stamp seals.

Another example is the small Early Harappan period site of **Kot Diji** in the Lower Indus region (see Figure 12.2), which was 2.6 hectares (6.4 acres).[16] It contained an area of large mudbrick structures with stone foundations that were built on a higher part of the site called the citadel. The citadel was surrounded by a perimeter wall that had buttresses to support it, as well as bastions (structures that project out from the wall) at the wall corners. The wall was made of limestone at its base and mudbrick above the stone. The large structures within the wall included ovens, fireplaces, and a large drain, as well as pottery, all of which could be interpreted as household features. The larger size of the citadel structures and the fact that they were surrounded by a massive wall might suggest that this area of Kot Diji was where the elite families lived.

Kot Diji a small Early Harappan period site in the Lower Indus Valley (South Asia) with a higher elevation citadel that has large mudbrick buildings surrounded by a perimeter wall. On the lower ground outside the wall were smaller houses built of mudbrick.

Interestingly, this wall does not seem to have been used or rebuilt during later Mature Harappan period occupation. Some beads and bangles, as well as toys, made from ter-racotta were present in the citadel area. Below the citadel, that is, outside the mudbrick wall, were other mudbrick structures that are interpreted as houses. These also had stone foundations like the ones on the citadel but were smaller in size. One terracotta figurine of a bull was found in the Early Harappan period levels in this area of the site.

Prior to the recent excavations at Harappa, how researchers interpreted the origins of the Indus Valley politically complex society was a matter of debate.[17] Some researchers noted that several Early Harappan sites (such as Kot Diji) had evidence of extensive burning at the end of the Early Harappan period.[18] This pattern was interpreted as an indication for disruption, that is, some sort of major change marked by the setting of fires, which is not a pattern seen earlier in this region. Additionally, most Early Harappan sites appear to have been abandoned (at least for a time) at the end of the Early Harappan period, and it has been argued that most Mature Harappan period artifacts differed substantially from those of the Early Harappan period. Other researchers interpret the fires as accidental, basing this perspective on the fact that the settlements were rebuilt and that later pottery shows continuity with that of the Early Harappan period at these sites.[19] They also note that there is no evidence for the killing of large numbers of individuals, as might be expected in the context of violence or warfare. The new excavations at Harappa, in fact, show long-term continuity at this settlement, and regional surveys have expanded the number of sites known, so that the general consensus has shifted to an emphasis on continuity rather than disruption. These types of debates are part of the archaeological process of examining existing information and proposing ideas. From a processual archaeology theoretical framework (see Chapter 1), this is how scientific method works; new excavations and continuing analyses of existing collections from sites provide additional data that can be used to examine the proposed ideas, revise them, and perhaps generate new interpretations.

Earlier research suggested that among the many differences between the Early and Mature Harappan periods[20] was the fact that the Early Harappan period had little monumental architecture and little evidence (except at three sites) for city walls that would suggest a need for protection from other groups or a need to isolate or screen off the activities of elites from commoners (as we saw at Cahokia in the American East, at Mesopotamian city-states, and in China). In fact, there is no indication that social distinctions or even elite individuals and families existed, at least as far as we can tell from the types of grave goods found with Early Harappan period burials. There is now substantial evidence from the site of Harappa, however, that the beginnings of urbanism and social classes were developing during the Early Harappan period.[21] The division of space can be seen in the arrangement of houses around courtyards that were not visible to others of the community, and larger settlements eventually had public architecture such as areas for people to wash, drains that carried away spoil water, and latrines (always an important sanitation feature in a densely settled community). These sanitation features in the Early Harappan predate the appearance of similar sanitation efforts in Roman systems by at least 2,000 years.

In the last few centuries before 2600 BC, several sites (such as Harappa and Kaliban-gan) had perimeter walls and immense platforms, both of which are monumental types of architecture. Moreover, Harappa had a well-organized layout with street planning (see previous discussion). Additionally, the geographical spread of the Kot Diji phase was enormous, stretching more than 1,000 kilometers (621 miles), and Kot Diji groups had networks for trade and exchange that extended beyond the geographical spread of their culture.

The evidence for social distinctions and possibly elites comes from the presence of various ornaments made of exotic stone, as well as metal tools and painted pottery (both of which are potentially exotic and therefore valued resources), in certain houses and nearby streets.[22] There also were differences in the sizes of the houses, with the larger houses interpreted as residences for families who had greater access to resources. Finally, there were clay, ivory, bone, and copper seals. In the Early Harappan period, these usually had geometric designs or animals. Such seals (and their impressions or sealings) could have indicated ownership of the various goods that they marked, could have been used by administrators in regulating trade and exchange interactions, or could have been objects showing ideological symbols associated with rituals or ritual activities.

The Mature Harappan

During the Mature Harappan period (2500 to 1900 BC), many of the elements we examined above became common features at sites across the Indus Valley region. You might say, in fact, that the types of architecture and the layout of the sites became standardized; they represent uniformity across the Harappan region, as cities were well planned with grid-like organization (read "The Big Picture: Urbanism in the Mature Harappan"). People at these settlements began to participate in a much larger interaction sphere, which resulted in a widely shared set of ideas regarding the layout of sites, how craft goods were made and decorated, the use of standardized weights and symbol systems (writing), and the establishment of some sites as outposts for trading[23] (as we saw in Mesopotamia, Egypt, and China). Some regional differences within the Indus Valley region, however, continued, as seen in pottery styles and other features of individual settlements such as the types of large buildings constructed in each city. Population density in the region increased considerably, with double the number of sites in the Mature Harappan period compared to the Early Harappan period.[24] Research suggests a three-tier settlement hierarchy that had at the top a few major, large sites, and below them, a second tier of large settlements that may have functioned as secondary centers. At the bottom tier were the rural villages and pastoral camps.[25] Among the largest Mature Harappan period sites were the urban centers of Harappa (Upper Indus), Ganweriwala (Central Indus), Mohenjo-daro (Lower Indus), Dholavira (southeast Indus region), and Rakhigarhi (northeast Indus region) (see Figure 12.2).

Of the Indus Valley cities, **Mohenjo-daro** (see Figure 12.2) appears to have been the largest, at 250 hectares (618 acres), and probably had 20,000 to 40,000 inhabitants.[26] The city had a citadel area situated on higher ground with an immense surrounding mudbrick wall. Within the walled area were many large mudbrick buildings, including structures called a "granary" (which has a possible ramp) and the "Great Bath" (a sunken pool surrounded by a colonnade) (Figure 12.5). In the area around the citadel were several other walled districts. Each of these had an enormous mudbrick wall that surrounded large mudbrick houses, mudbrick platforms, and wide streets. The larger streets were all oriented north–south, and smaller streets ran east–west. Possibly these walled portions of the city represent the dwelling areas for different elite social classes such as merchants or large landowners. The existence of elite individuals and families also might be recognized because of the rare presence of silver and gold ornaments. Craft workshops were present in each of the walled districts and document the continued importance of exotic stone and shell goods and pottery production, as well as the manufacture of terracotta figurines (see "Ideology"), copper/bronze artifacts, seals, and beads of faience (a glaze painted onto clay prior to firing).

Harappa also had separate mudbrick-walled areas of the settlement, although there was no citadel there.[27] At its largest, this city spread out over 150 hectares

Mohenjo-daro the largest known Indus Valley city in South Asia. It has a citadel area with large mudbrick structures such as the so-called "Granary" and "Great Bath." The function of these buildings is not known, although likely they are related to administrative and political tasks.

FIGURE 12.5
The "Great Bath" at Mohenjo-Daro.

(370 acres) and likely had 25,000 to 35,000 people. Houses within the walled sections were made from fired brick and had ovens, courtyards, and areas for bathing and latrines, with waste water channeled away using drains that joined up with larger drains that ultimately dumped the waste in the area outside the perimeter mudbrick walls. Well-laid-out streets with north–south and east–west orientations continued to be a major feature, with gateways through the perimeter walls allowing access into each city area. Like Mohenjo-daro, Harappa had a large structure called a granary, although there is no archaeological evidence that indicates storage of grain, just as there is no evidence that the granary and Great Bath at Mohenjo-daro had those functions. The important point here is not the name that archaeologists gave to these structures but that the construction of these large, unusual buildings was a new feature that suggests coordinated labor and increasingly specialized and distinct activities within society. Although we may not currently know exactly what these buildings were used for, we can say that the people who used them were engaged in tasks unlike those of most other members of Harappan period society.

The cities and towns in the Indus Valley region were supported by an expansive network of relationships with rural communities in the areas around each city and town. These networks ensured the interchange of goods such as agricultural and pastoral resources, as well as wild animals and fish, and raw materials for crafts. These relationships meant that ideas could be widely shared.[28] The Mature Harappan period network has been described as one based on "central places."[29] That is, a city such as Mohenjo-daro or Harappa was a major location in the landscape that served as a place into which goods, resources, and ideas flowed in and out from both secondary centers (smaller towns) and rural villages. Additionally, central places were situated on major rivers that facilitated transportation of goods and resources. In some ways, these central places and their surrounding network of towns, villages, and pastoral camps could be called city-states. Two important differences between these Harappan city-states and others, such as in China and Mesopotamia, are that there is no archaeological evidence for warfare between the cities of the Indus Valley region and there is no indication that each city was ruled by only one set of elites. In fact, it seems that Harappan cities were politically characterized by power sharing between several higher status groups within each city.

There are some cemeteries known from the Mature Harappan period, as well as scattered burials throughout portions of sites.[30] Two of the cemeteries were in the city of Harappa. Burial within the cemeteries is usually interpreted as representing elite people from the city, particularly because these burials are far fewer than the number of people who must have lived in the city. Most of these cemetery burials had pottery vessels of various types, including plates that might suggest feasting rituals that occurred at the time of the burial. Other types of grave goods were considerably rarer, although they included shell bangles and beads of steatite, lapis lazuli, carnelian, and copper that also characterized burials during the Early Harappan period. Bangles were associated with females, as were rare copper/bronze mirrors. One interesting aspect of the Harappa cemetery burials comes from strontium isotope analyses of the bones of males and females in one of the Harappa cemeteries that suggests that females were local and males were nonlocal.[31] This may indicate that Harappans had a marriage pattern in which husbands moved into the areas/homes of their wives' families. Unlike other early politically complex societies elsewhere in the world, there is little evidence for violence or warfare in the Harappan period (no weapons in burials, no trauma from battles on skeletons).

The Written Word

The Indus script is one of the remaining undeciphered ancient written records of the world (read "Peopling the Past: Deciphering the Indus Script"). Like most written sources, it developed gradually and then became standardized (around 2600 BC).[32] The Indus script is found on artifacts from more than 60 sites, with the majority from Mohenjo-daro and Harappa. Although we cannot read the signs and symbols, we can examine the contexts in which they appear. These contexts offer clues as to how the Indus script was used during Harappan times. The script is commonly found on seals and pottery vessels but also was carved into bone, shell, ivory, steatite, and even gold, copper, silver, and bronze objects. Compared to other early written languages (such as ancient Egyptian, Sumerian, or Chinese), however, the Indus script was used for short messages. On any single artifact, the script might be just 1 to 5 signs, with the longest message consisting of 26 signs.[33] Not everyone in society would have been literate, and it is thought that the ability to read the Indus script was restricted to elite individuals, perhaps the groups who oversaw the administration and political organization of the cities. They were not royal elites but may have included wealthy landowners, religious specialists, and merchants engaged in lucrative long-distance trade networks.

When the script was written onto seals, these signs were combined with images of animals such as cattle or even what appear to be unicorns. The seals were then used to stamp goods of various sorts, and their imagery likely identified the individual sending the goods as well as transmitted some message about the goods to whoever received them. Indus script, including what are thought to be numbers, also was carved onto tablets (faience, steatite, terracotta), of which there are many identical copies that might have been used as tokens indicating receipt of goods. Inscribed pottery may have indicated what the contents of the vessel were and perhaps also the name of the owner or the place to which the vessels were sent. As such, seals, tablets, and inscribed pottery seem to be connected to economic transactions. Beyond this, there were many items of personal ornamentation and tools made of exotic materials (bronze, copper, gold, and ivory) that had small Indus script signs incised onto them. These are thought to be the names of the people to whom the tools and jewelry belonged. Finally, there also were some Indus script signs written onto more ordinary everyday objects such as beads and bangles. In this case, these messages might be ritual, such as charms for protection and good fortune.

Deciphering the Indus Script

Our ability to read ancient written scripts depends on having methods and materials useful in deciphering them. In the case of the Indus script, one challenge is the short segments that are typical of each example (usually only about five signs long), which make it difficult to examine associations of signs with each other. Another challenge is the lack of an example of a message written both in Indus script and in a known (deciphered) ancient language so that researchers can use the deciphered language to figure out the corresponding words, sounds, or ideas in the Indus script. What we do know is that the Indus script appears to have developed out of the use of potters' marks on vessels; that is, some of the symbols incised into or painted onto early pottery appear to be nearly identical to Indus script signs on later seals[34] (Figure 12.6). We also know that the script was read from right to left.[35]

FIGURE 12.6
The Indus script (*upper right*) on a Harappan seal (*colors added*).

Efforts at deciphering the Indus script often have been highly contentious.[36] Some of this debate centers on which language family contains the language used by the Harappan peoples, with some researchers suggesting Dravidian but others hotly disagreeing. Beyond that, one must figure out what aspects of written language each sign portrays. Do the signs represent a word, an idea, or a meaningful sound (called a morpheme)? One morpheme in English, for example, is "un-," which when attached to a root sound means "not," as in unknown. The fact that there are some 62 to 425 signs (or possibly more) suggests that Indus script signs include some that are words, some that are concepts, and some that are syllables (similar to Sumerian cuneiform or Mayan glyphs).[37] Nearly all Indus Valley researchers believe that the Indus script represents written language, although the pieces we have are short messages. An opposing view is extremely controversial, suggesting that Indus script is not language, but simply symbols that stand for things such as different political offices or particular families or specific ritual or agricultural activities.[38] In this viewpoint, the Harappan period region contained far too many different linguistic groups for one language to represent them all and there are only a small number of signs that are frequently used, whereas others are unique or rarely used. The signs therefore did not record speech but were nonlinguistic symbols for specific people, families, places, and aspects of ideology. There also have been efforts to use computer-assisted graphical models to examine the association of particular Indus script signs with each other to determine possible linguistic patterns. These models suggest that there is patterning in how the signs were used, perhaps indicating language rules.[39] As noted previously, some of these signs could have been people's names, counts and goods in economic transactions, and ritual words. Researchers continue to work on the fascinating puzzle of the Indus script.

Resource Networks, Trade, and Exchange

People living in the Indus Valley were engaged in long-distance exchange and trade networks from at least the time of the Neolithic period (see previous discussion). These relationships often are thought of as representing the movement of raw materials, such as shell or carnelian, and finished goods, such as beads and bangles. Such networks also resulted in the movement of domesticated plants into the Indus Valley region. Broomcorn and foxtail millet, for example, likely were introduced from China around 2500 BC, and around 2000 BC rice from China and pearl millet and sorghum from Africa arrived.[40] The extent of these trade and exchange networks appears to have grown considerably during the Mature Harappan period, resulting in what has been called the "Middle Asian Interaction Sphere,"[41] although not all researchers interpret evidence for trade with the Indus Valley as being extensive (read "The Big Picture: Trade and Exchange in the Mature Harappan").

The Big Picture

Trade and Exchange in the Mature Harappan

Most archaeologists would agree that the Mature Harappan period in the Indus Valley region was characterized by a widespread and extensive long-distance set of trade and exchange relationships. It is more difficult, however, to assess the impact of Indus Valley trade on areas outside this region. In the nearby Iranian highlands, for example, there were a small number of Indus Valley artifacts found at Helmand civilization sites, including etched carnelian beads and faience bangles.[42] Some items, however, appear to be local copies or the use of Indus Valley technologies, such as making steatite beads and shell bangles. In this sense, these trade and exchange relationships appear to be, as the authors of one study state, "sporadic trade contacts, individual trips or marriages rather than systematic, specialized forms of long-distance trade."[43]

In the Indus Valley region, however, there is abundant archaeological evidence for intensive trade and exchange networks. One example is the use of various stone raw materials at the site of Harappa[44] (Figure 12.7). These materials have been geologically traced to their sources, many of which, such as lapis lazuli, lie to the north of Harappa as well as north of the boundaries of the Indus Valley societies. Harappan period people used great quantities of some of these raw materials and likely were aware of differences in the quality of sources. Steatite, for instance, was needed in abundance and to be of good quality. To control for these features, Harappan period groups obtained steatite from near the Khyber Pass to the northwest and later also from the Aravalli Range to the southeast. Carnelian came from Gujarat to the south. In fact, during the Mature and Late Harappan periods, networks to the north and west were the most central to trade and exchange, although those to the south and east became more important for the importation of some raw materials to craft workshops. This trade and exchange even included stone for relatively mundane items such as ground stone tools, because the location of the Indus Valley cities in the river valley floodplain areas meant that good stone usually was not locally available in quantity or in quality.

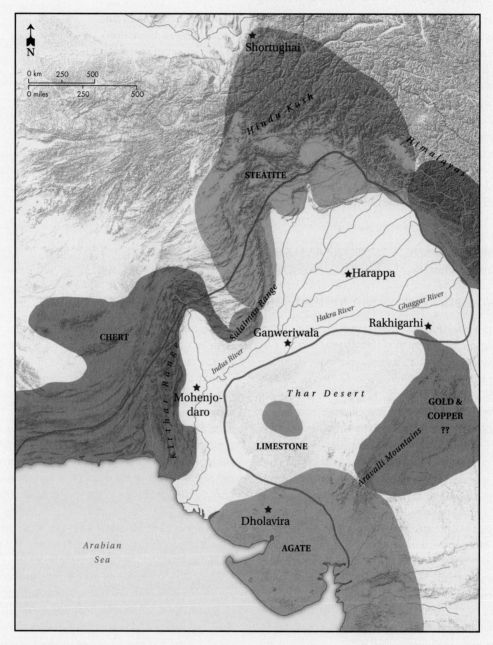

FIGURE 12.7
A proposed Indus Valley regional exchange network, mainly for stone resources (after Law 2011, Figure 13.11).
Red line indicates the extent of the Mature Harappan region.

The Middle Asian Interaction Sphere connected the Indus Valley with Mesopotamia, parts of Iran (Turan), Dilmun (thought to be Bahrain and the nearby Arabian coast), and Magan (believed to be the coastal part of Oman and the United Arab Emirates at the Strait of Hormuz as well as the Iranian side at the Strait of Hormuz)[45] (Figure 12.8). The movement of raw materials, finished goods, and domesticated crops likely was part of a maritime tradition in which rivers and the surrounding seas (Arabian Sea and the Persian Gulf) were used to transport items for trade. We know that the Indus Valley Harappan period groups had these contacts because we find artifacts such as etched carnelian beads (made in the Indus Valley) in burials in the Royal Cemetery at Ur in Mesopotamia (see Chapter 9), as well as at sites in Iran. There are also Indus Valley seals in Mesopotamia and Iran and certain pottery styles and decorations that are Harappan that are found at coastal sites in the Persian Gulf. These ceramic vessels had a pointed base and likely were storage containers for wine. Interestingly, there is far less archaeological evidence in the Indus Valley of artifacts from its trade and exchange partners. The small number of items include a few Mesopotamian-like cylinder seals, copper axes that appear to be from Iran, and pins with animal heads that look like styles from farther to the west. Most likely, Harappan period groups were importing raw materials, such as copper, which they then made into items for local use.[46] Beyond this, there is a Harappan period outpost

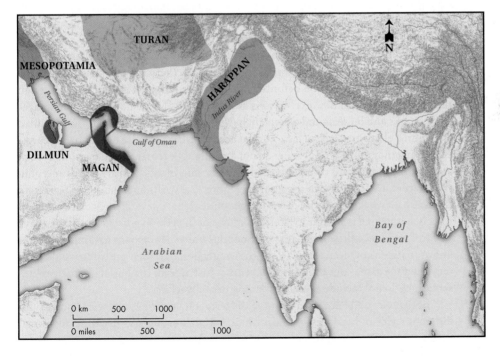

FIGURE 12.8
The Middle Asian Interaction Sphere (after Possehl 2002b, Figure 12.1).

called **Shortughai** (see Figure 12.2), which is in northern Afghanistan near a set of lapis lazuli mines. Presumably the presence of Harappan period groups there helped ensure that this semiprecious stone could be obtained and sent to craft workshops in the Indus Valley.

Workshops at the large cities such as Harappa and Mohenjo-daro were specialized for the manufacture and production of a variety of items.[47] These included pottery vessels, seals, beads, bangles, copper and bronze objects, gold and silver working, and faience artifacts. Some crafts were highly standardized, suggesting that there was administrative or political control over their production, whereas other crafts were more simply made (such as terracotta objects), probably by kin groups. One of the important features of Harappan period trade and exchange, at least within the Indus Valley, were its standardized weights. These allowed for relatively precise measurement of the quantities of goods and probably were used most often in the context of exotic materials such as semiprecious stone (carnelian and lapis lazuli) and metals (copper, bronze, gold, and silver). The Indus script on seals and pottery also may have helped merchants keep track of quantities of goods and their distribution.

Ideology

How people see the world around them and their relationships with other people and the supernatural is partially expressed in artifacts, structures, and rituals that they create and use. These are reflections of their ideas or ideology, some of which fall within the religious sphere of life, whereas other aspects might be related to political or social realms. For the Mature Harappan period of the Indus Valley region, the archaeological evidence most often used is the designs on seals and tablets, as well as certain terracotta figurines and masks. Interestingly, there were no structures in the cities and towns that can be definitely identified as religious in function, although this may change with new excavations at sites such as Mohenjo-daro.[48] The images of the masks and on seals and tablets include figures that are combinations of human and animal elements and can have curved horns.[49] Many of these figures have beards, suggesting they are male, but some do not and might be females. Other animals, such as tigers, elephants, and rhinoceros, as well as various plants, also are often present in the imagery associated with the figures (Figure 12.9). Although only one terracotta figurine has two faces, several of the images on seals have several faces on the sides of their heads, which is similar to later depictions of the Hindu god, Shiva. But we have no direct evidence that the images of the Indus Valley Harappans are linked to later known religions or, even if they were known images, that their meaning would have remained the same over thousands of years.[50] Just as with the burials, artistic representations do not include evidence for violence or warfare.

Both males and females are among the terracotta figurines and were shown with different styles of headdresses and/or hair.[51] Male headdresses usually had animal ears or horns. Female figurines appear to be far more numerous than males. Males were shown naked, whereas females had some clothing. The context in which these human figurines were found, usually rooms with only one entrance, suggests that

FIGURE 12.9
Examples of designs on Harappan period seals (*colors added*).

they might have been used in rituals associated with individual households. The ter-racotta masks often are described as having been finger puppets used in performances or associated with magic as part of the apparel worn by ritual specialists.[52] Many of these images, as well as those on the seals and tablets, with their combined human and animal features and the addition of plants and powerful animals, have been in-terpreted by researchers as indicating religious ideas that portrayed the world as a place in which nature and culture were blended together.[53] This philosophy is quite different from ideas in the Western world today, where we tend to think of nature and culture as being separate.

Beyond this, there are a small number of male figures carved in stone from Mohenjo-daro that may be representative of political or social ideology rather than the religious sphere.[54] All of these bearded males were shown seated or kneel-ing, were wearing cloaks, had a headband thought to represent a golden fillet, and likely were painted. Some had holes where jewelry, headdresses, and other items could have been attached. They are thought to be members of the elite classes, such as rulers or powerful merchants, or perhaps the ancestors of some of these elite families.

Urbanization and Its Consequences

Big-city living is, of course, different from life in small rural villages. The size of the Indus Valley cities was not large, either in absolute size or in number of people, compared to major cities today, but dense concentrations of people almost always

Urbanism in the Mature Harappan

What is truly impressive about Indus Valley cities is that they do not appear to have grown in a willy-nilly fashion as people moved to urban areas from the rural countryside. In this respect, they were unlike many of the cities of later historical periods, such as nineteenth-century London's East End, where unsanitary conditions prevailed because of the haphazard manner in which dense housing (poorly constructed and with little long-term maintenance) was added to existing city areas. Of course, Indus Valley cities were much smaller and contained fewer people in comparison. They still represented, however, relatively crowded conditions that required coordination of social relationships, mediation of disputes, and individuals or families with political clout to accomplish these tasks as well as the public construction efforts that went into building the massive mudbrick walls, drainage systems, public architecture, and streets. The large cities such as Mohenjo-daro and Harappa also had closely spaced houses, which shared walls (Figure 12.10). This is somewhat similar to modern shared walls between dwellings constructed as rowhouses, duplexes, and townhouses. Sharing walls meant being able

FIGURE 12.10
Stylized plan view of residential areas at Mohenjo-daro with North-South running streets (redrawn from Marshall 1931).

to accommodate more housing (and more people) within a neighborhood of a city.

The planning that went into the layout of the cities appears to have been based on astronomy. The north–south and east–west directions of streets and many houses were orientations gained from observations either of where the sun set and rose or perhaps from where certain stars rose each evening.[56] Aside from massive neighborhood walls, gateways, streets, latrines, and wells for drinking water, Indus Valley cities contained two-story private homes of varying sizes, much larger houses that were associated with extra rooms, and large, open, accessible courtyards that possibly were marketplaces or locales where public meetings could be held. It is easy to recognize the similarities between these Harappan cities and our own.

create conditions that require group coordination and oversight. We can see the archaeological signature of this in the fact that large cities were carefully planned in layout, with streets running north–south and east–west as well as terracotta pipe systems that carried waste water away from houses to street drains and sump pits (read "The Big Picture: Urbanism in the Mature Harappan"). Each of the large cities had several walled neighborhoods that were separated from each other by open spaces. And each of these neighborhoods seems to have had its own set of elites. The labor specialization seen in the many workshops for ceramics, bangles, and gold and silver objects also means that not everyone living in the cities was engaged in producing or obtaining food. Some city people, however, may have been farmers with fields in the fertile floodplains of the rivers and their tributaries in the Indus region, but it is likely that most foods were produced by people living in the network of smaller villages and pastoral camps that were linked to each of the major Indus Valley cities.[55]

The relationships of the smaller communities to the large cities appear to have been based on trade and exchange, with the rural areas contributing grains grown during the winter (wheat and barley) and summer (millets), as well as dates and grapes. Not all agricultural production was about food, however, because some of the plants grown, such as cotton and hemp, yielded fibers useful in making cloth.[57] Domesticated animals also were important because they were sources of meat and milk that could be traded and yielded by-products such as wool, skins, and hair. Cattle and water buffalo could be hooked up to plows and used in farming or to carts for transporting goods. Donkeys, horses, and camels also were used as beasts of burden to transport goods and foods from place to place. Other people, living in the cities and in the rural areas, focused much of their efforts on obtaining fish from the rivers of the Indus Valley region.[58] Ethnoarchaeological research indicates that modern groups in this region are able to capture large numbers of fish using different types of nets, primarily in oxbow lakes (flooded areas associated with the rivers). Study of fish bones from Harappa suggests that Mature Harappan period fishers exploited similar niches with fishing nets, where the main types of fish captured were catfish and carp. Additionally, there is some evidence suggesting that in at least a few areas of the Indus Valley region, urbanized Harappan period groups obtained various types of materials from some people who may have been hunter–gatherer–foragers.[59]

The interaction between rural and urban areas, as well as the division of people into specialized labor groups, is something that all of us can recognize in our societies today, although we are much farther removed from some types of interactions and exchanges. Although we may shop at farmers' markets and thus have relatively direct interaction with food producers, for example, most of us obtain our food (and goods) from stores, which are one set of intermediaries between actual producers and ourselves. The scale at which we operate is global rather than regional, with goods and foods arriving in our stores from many places around the world. But the consequences of urban life remain in many respects similar to that of earlier periods such as the Mature Harappan, where urban lifestyles become dependent in part on consistency in and reliability of existing trade and exchange relationships.

After the Mature Harappan

During the period known as the Late Harappan (1900 to 1300 BC), the urban phenomenon of the Indus Valley region went into decline, and, for the most part, the large cities became smaller settlements and then were abandoned as people moved north and east in this region. This suggests that the maintenance of the urban society that archaeologists call the Mature Harappan period was no longer sustainable. How sustainability is defined, however, can be debated, because some researchers have pointed to environmental and habitat changes that may have affected agricultural productivity, whereas others have focused more on political and social changes, including diminished trade and exchange networks.

Major environmental factors included the shifting of rivers in their courses and changes in seasonal flooding patterns. Farmers dependent on floodplains for their fields and deposition of new fertile soil during flooding would have been greatly affected in terms of the amounts of crops they could produce. Increased flooding, which would be damaging to crops, also appears to have impacted many smaller settlements, forcing people to relocate.[60] Additionally, drought conditions during the winter and spring became more prevalent, again affecting crops and people. Both increased flooding and drought are thought to have resulted from instability in weather patterns related to the timing and duration of monsoons,[61] which during much of the Mature Harappan period were previously described as stable.[62] However, not everyone agrees that a major environmental change resulted in the decline of the Mature Harappan. Instead, some researchers argue that decisions on the local level of the smaller rural settlements were culturally important in understanding the process of decline.[63] Basically, farmers began to grow more millets and rice, which are summer, monsoon rain–watered crops. Wheat and barley, on the other hand, are dependent on high rainfall during the winter and spring. Less winter rainfall after 2200 BC meant less wheat and barley, and millets and rice yield fewer crops per land area than do wheat and barley.[64] In combination, this meant declining agricultural surplus and likely a much reduced capacity to sustain large urban populations in addition to the people living in the towns and smaller rural settlements. Rather than an abrupt change at 1900 BC, then, the process of decline had already begun during the Mature Harappan period. The decisions about what crops to plant and when were made by the farmers, who were the people most directly affected by instability in the climate from year to year and increasingly drier conditions. In some respects, this interpretation is an example of the theoretical perspective of agency, that is, one that sees the role of individuals and groups as important in understanding change (see Chapter 1).

Abandonment of various towns and smaller settlements in the Indus Valley region during the Late Harappan period is thought to have affected trade and exchange networks (read "Further Reflections: Importance of Trade and Exchange Networks").[65] With less exotic materials (marine shell, lapis lazuli, carnelian, gold, and silver) arriving in the cities and towns, there would have been less need for specialized labor in the various workshops. Additionally, diminished access to exotics may have affected the legitimacy of the elite groups in the cities, leading ultimately to a decline in their power and importance. This likely disrupted the integration of people through shared ideology and cultural values, and archaeologically, the Late Harappan period is characterized instead by three localized regions—one in the Upper Indus, another in the Lower Indus, and the third in the southeast (Figure 12.11). Few of these Late Harappan period regions retained the Indus script, standardized weights, or stamp seals.[66] What is interesting, however, is that the number of known settlements of the Late Harappan period was actually greater than during the Mature Harappan period.[67] These late sites were smaller in size (on average, only about half as big as settlements during the Mature Harappan period), and many were concentrated in areas far from the previous urban centers such as Harappa and Mohenjo-daro.

The decline of politically complex societies such as the Mature Harappan does not mean, of course, that the Harappan people disappeared. Instead, it was their archaeological signature that did. Large urban cities such as Mohenjo-daro and Harappa were not renewed with new construction, nor were new urban centers built in other parts of the Indus Valley region until after 1200 BC.[68] These later cities did not share the same ideology and were not organized and laid out in the same way as those of the Mature Harappan period. They represented new ways of thinking about the world and how it should be organized, as well as innovations in technologies and material culture.

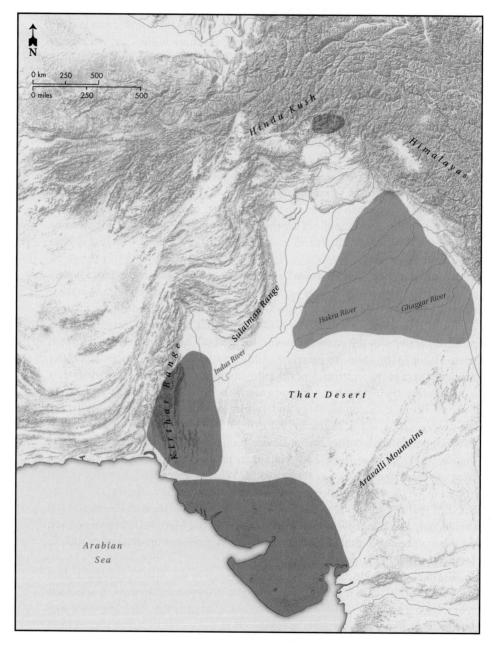

FIGURE 12.11
Regionalism during the Late Harappan period (after Law 2011, Figure 2.6D).

Further Reflections

Importance of Trade and Exchange Networks

When we examine complex societies, including politically complex entities, we are naturally interested in why they "disappear." In many cases, as with the Harappan, it is common to discuss climatic changes that may have impacted agricultural productivity, as noted earlier. Another familiar theme is social changes that result in a loss of power and authority of elites due to lack of faith in their leadership or because of the dynamics of foreign groups that migrate into the areas of these complex societies (peacefully or through raids and warfare). What is not always appreciated in considering the demise of these societies is the impact of changes in trade and exchange networks. As we saw earlier, the Harappan had extensive internal and external networks. These were due in part to a lack of suitable resources (such as good-quality stone) in the places where cities were built and to the desire for exotic materials (such as lapis lazuli). What happens if these trade and exchange networks are disrupted, either within a region or due to changes in other societies elsewhere who are the trade and exchange partners? Does this have an impact on a complex polity such as the Harappan?

If a society grows dependent on the resources that trade and exchange bring into their region, then the answer is yes. A decline, especially a rapid one, means that the commodities become scarce, making them more "expensive" and eventually perhaps not available at all. If some portion of these goods were used by elites as symbols of leadership or in rituals or in gift-giving ceremonies to cement alliances, then these social practices will be impacted, perhaps declining in importance over time. Non-elite members of society may be faced with a lack of suitable materials for making crafts or a shortage of tools used in farming, fishing, and hunting. In these circumstances, it would not be surprising to find that people reorganized their daily activities, their ritual life, and their leadership or moved to other areas with better access to resources. This would help spell the "end" of a particular complex society.

Summary

- Many domesticated plants and animals in the Indus Valley region were introduced from either the Middle East or Asia. One animal exception was zebu cattle, which were locally domesticated. New evidence shows that local rice, millets, pulses, and sesame also were domesticated in the Indus region. Early villagers also made extensive use of wild plant foods and wild animals.

- Regional networks in the Neolithic period brought exotic items, such as marine shell and lapis lazuli, into the Indus Valley area. These were used to make personal ornamentation.

- During the Early Harappan period, some sites became much larger and have evidence for public architecture such as "citadels" and public baths. Some of the houses at these sites also were much larger in size and may represent the homes of people with more access to resources. There is little evidence, however, in grave goods from burials for distinctions between elites and commoners.

- Pottery during the Early Harappan period shows evidence of several different regional styles.

- The Mature Harappan period was the height of the Indus Valley urbanism phenomenon, with several large sites housing dense populations. These cities were carefully planned and had streets running east–west and north–south. Agricultural productivity was especially high, probably partly because of relatively stable climatic conditions.

- The large cities of the Mature Harappan period were supported by trade and exchange with smaller towns and rural hamlets. Standardized weights were developed to use in these transactions. People during this time also participated in widespread trade and exchange networks with areas such as the Persian Gulf, the highlands of Iran, and Mesopotamia. This has been called the Middle Asian Interaction Sphere.

- Like complex political entities elsewhere, Harappan society included people engaged in many different types of tasks. Among these were craft specialists, farmers, fishers, ritual specialists, and elites. Larger houses in the cities had more items made of exotic materials, suggesting they were the homes of elites. Elite members of society, however, do not appear to have been kings such as were typical for places like Egypt, Mesopotamia, or China.

- Harappan groups had a written script, but it has not yet been deciphered. Symbol sets of the Indus script were generally just 1 to 5 signs long. They are found on seals, pottery, personal ornaments, and tablets. They are thought to represent words, concepts, and syllables. Some may have been economic or owners' marks, and others may have been ritual charms.

- After 1900 BC, during the Late Harappan period, the large urban cities were abandoned and settlement shifted eastward. There was increased regionalism. These changes may be related in part to instability in the monsoons, which meant that drought conditions became more frequent and people living in the Indus Valley region were unable to produce large enough quantities of food to support dense populations at urban centers. Loss of population likely affected trade and exchange networks as fewer crafts specialists might mean less demand for exotic materials. The use of the Indus script and standardized weights also declined in importance.

- Later on, the Indus Valley area was resettled, likely by descendants of earlier Harappan period groups, but their archaeological signature was different from that of the Mature Harappan period.

Endnotes

1. Bellwood 2005: 87–88; Fuller 2011; Thomas 2003.
2. Bates et al. 2017; García-Granero et al. 2016; Possehl 2002b: 24–29.
3. Bradley and Magee 2006: 325.
4. Kenoyer 1998: 37–39; Possehl 2002b: 25–28, 30–31.
5. Barthélemy de Saizieu 1994: 592–595; Kenoyer 1998: 38; Lechevallier and Quivron 1985.
6. Kenoyer 1995b, 1998: 38–39.
7. Meadow and Patel 2003: 70–71.
8. Moulherat et al. 2002.
9. Possehl 2002b: 32–36.
10. Samzun and Sellier 1985; Wright 2010: 66–69.
11. Law 2011: 42–45, and Figure 2.6a, b; Possehl 2002b: 40–46.
12. Possehl 1990: 270; Wright 2010: 80–81.
13. Kenoyer 2008: 189–191; Kenoyer and Meadow 2000.
14. Kenoyer 2008: 191.
15. Kenoyer 2008: 192–194.
16. Kenoyer 1998: 44; Khan 1965; Wright 2010: 97. Kot Diji also has later Mature Harappan levels.
17. Kenoyer 1998: 40–45; Possehl 1990, 2002b: 47–53.
18. Possehl 2002b: 49–50.
19. Kenoyer 1998: 42.
20. Possehl 1990.
21. Kenoyer 1998: 40–45, 2008: 192; Lal et al. 2003; Law 2011: 45; Wright 2010: 81.
22. Kenoyer 1998: 43–45.
23. Farooqui et al. 2013; Kenoyer 2008: 198–206; Law 2011: 45–46; Wright 2010: 106–107.
24. Possehl 1990: 270–271.
25. Wright 2010: 136–138.
26. Kenoyer 2008: 198–201; Wright 2010: 110.
27. Kenoyer 2008: 194–197; Wright 2010: 110, 115.
28. Chase et al. 2014a.
29. Wright 2010: 136–138.
30. Wright 2010: 263–269.
31. Kenoyer et al. 2013.
32. Kenoyer 1998: 69–77, 2008: 197–198; Parpola 1986.
33. Robinson 2015.
34. Kenoyer 2008: 193–194.
35. Robinson 2015.
36. Farmer et al. 2004; Lawler 2004; Parpola 1994; Patel 2010; Rao et al. 2009.
37. Robinson 2015. See http://www.user.tu-berlin.de/fuls/Homepage/indexeng.htm for a database of known Indus script signs (accessed July 19, 2018).
38. Farmer et al. 2004.
39. Rao et al. 2009.
40. Bellwood 2005: 88.
41. Possehl 2002b: 215–235, 2007.
42. Cortesi et al. 2008: 29.
43. Law 2011.
44. Good et al. 2009.
45. Possehl 2002b: 218–219; the terms Dilmun and Magan are from Mesopotamian documents, and it is not known whether they are the Sumerian names for these areas or transliterations by Sumerians of foreign names.
46. See, for example, Kenoyer and Miller 1999.
47. Kenoyer 1995a; Law 2011; Wright 2010: 182–201.
48. Wright 2010: 277.
49. Kenoyer 1998: 105–120; Wright 2010: 277–282.
50. Kenoyer 1998: 112; Wright 2010: 282.
51. Wright 2010: 285–288.
52. Kenoyer 1998: 83; Wright 2010: 285.
53. Wright 2010: 302.
54. Kenoyer 1998: 99–102.
55. Chase et al. 2014b; Wright 2010: 143.
56. Kenoyer 1998: 52–58
57. Wright 2010: 167–173.
58. Belcher 2003: 150–162; 2009.
59. Possehl 2002a.
60. Kenoyer 1998: 173; Lawler 2007.
61. Dixit et al. 2014; Dutt et al. 2018.
62. Giosan et al. 2012; Lawler 2011.
63. Madella and Fuller 2006.
64. Pokharia et al. 2014.
65. Kenoyer 1998: 174; Wright 2010: 314.
66. Kenoyer 1995a: 223–228; Law 2011: 48.
67. Madella and Fuller 2006: 1296.
68. Lawler 2008.

CHAPTER 13

Mesoamerica, the Classic Maya, and the Aztec Empire

ABOVE: Classic Maya period site of Tikal, Guatemala.

Understanding the development of the politically complex societies that archaeologists call the Classic Maya and the Aztec Empire is not simply a matter of tracing and explaining developments in their respective regions of Mesoamerica. Rather, there were several areas, ranging from the Basin of Mexico to Oaxaca to the Gulf Coast to the Maya lowlands and highlands, all of which were important (Figure 13.1). Although this chapter will focus in the most detail on the Classic Maya and the Aztec Empire, we will briefly examine these other Mesoamerican regions with a view toward the insights they provide for interactions and influences on social and political networks in this region (read "Timeline: Mesoamerica"). All of these politically complex societies were built on an agricultural foundation that included many crops that are important today, such as maize, beans, and squash, as well as chili

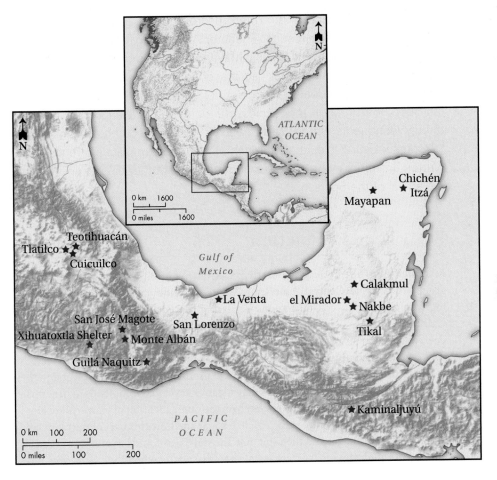

FIGURE 13.1
Map showing location of Archaic period sites and of complex polity sites for Basin of Mexico,
Valley of Oaxaca, Gulf Lowlands, and the Maya region.

peppers and avocados. Like several of the world areas we examined in
previous chapters, the Classic Maya developed a writing system based on
glyphic symbols. Many of these have been translated and are significant
historical documents for important Maya events and elite rulers, as well as
knowledge about rituals, religion, astronomy, and other aspects of life. The
Maya also had a well-developed numerical system and several types of calendars for keeping track of time. They built remarkable pyramids, temples,
palaces, and great plazas, and their elite individuals and families possessed
power and authority. Maya elites obtained control over other Maya cities
through marriage alliances and went to war against the elites of other cities,

with the archaeological and written records providing ample evidence of these battles and their results. The later Aztec Empire, although different in many respects from the Classic Maya, was built upon the foundations of complex political entities that had preceded them. They also constructed monuments and conducted wars. Control over neighboring regions was established both through their successful trade and exchange networks and through conquests. Aztec used calendars and had documents using glyphs to represent sounds such as the names of people or places. We also have written accounts by both Aztecs and the Spanish that date to shortly after the arrival of the Spanish.

Early Food Production

Like their North American counterparts, Archaic period hunter–gatherer–forager groups in Mexico/Central America inhabited a wide variety of habitats including tropical jungles, coastal regions bordering the Pacific Ocean and the gulfs of California and Mexico, highlands, mountains, and deserts. They made wide use of deer, native species of wild pigs, and rabbits, as well as birds, turtles, shellfish, and fish. Among the wild plant food resources was teosinte, the wild grass ancestor of maize ("corn"). Several parts of this plant are useful. One is its seeds, although their scarcity at early archaeological sites may mean that people initially used other parts of teosinte.[1] Some of the earliest research on the domestication of maize, for example, focused on how the teosinte stalk is rich in sugar and how this part of the plant could be chewed for the sugar and then spit out. The stalk also could be eaten as a green vegetable. Although the seeds likely were eaten seasonally when they were ripe, it also is possible to make a type of beer from the stalk, as well as from the seeds. Teosinte thus could have been used in a variety of ways[2] that for a long time de-emphasized the seeds and resulted in a relatively late appearance of the large-kernel cob that we know today.

The earliest evidence for domesticated maize and squash, about 7000 BC (beans are domesticated later, around 2500 BC), is the presence of phytoliths and starch grains on ground stone tools at Archaic period sites such as **Xihuatoxtla Shelter** in southwestern Mexico[3] (see Figure 13.1). Xihautoxtla Shelter is in the natural distribution area of teosinte, so that hunter–gatherer–forager groups living here would have been able easily to exploit teosinte. Their continued use of teosinte and eventual selection for its seeds led to genetic changes (naked seeds that stayed on the cob) resulting in domesticated maize.

Based on evidence from charcoal, phytoliths, and pollen, the technique of "slash-and-burn" agriculture was practiced in regions such as the Gulf coastal areas of southern Mexico from the region where Xihuatoxtla Shelter is located; these dates are 5300 and 5200 BC, respectively.[4] Slash-and-burn involves cutting down and

Xihuatoxtla Shelter an Archaic period site in southwestern Mexico that has phytoliths of early domesticated maize, as well as domesticated squash, about 7000 cal BC.

Timeline: Mesoamerica

Complex political entities developed in several regions in Mesoamerica (Figure 13.2). Their trajectories were interrupted by the arrival of the Spanish.

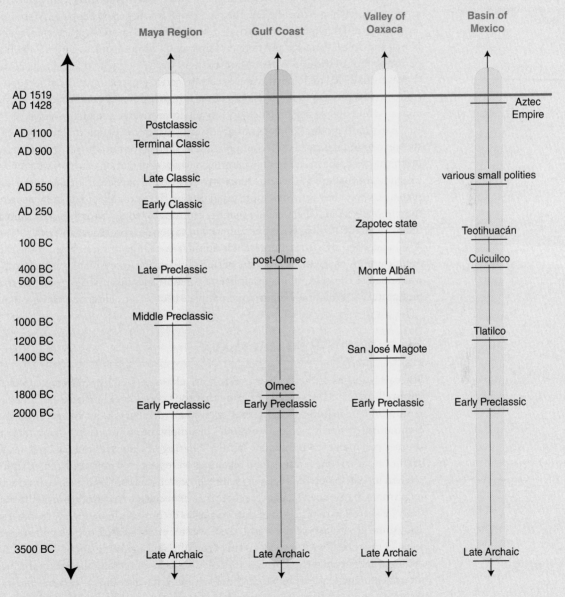

FIGURE 13.2
Timeline for various regions in Mesoamerica. Red line indicates the arrival of the Spanish.

burning vegetation, the ashes of which help fertilize the soil. Maize was planted in these now open areas within the forest. The earliest actual maize cobs were found at **Guilá Naquitz Cave** (see Figure 13.1) in highland Mexico, dating to 4200 BC.[5] Guilá Naquitz is not within the natural distribution area of teosinte, which means that people transported domesticated maize into the highland areas from places such as the area of Xihuatoxtla Shelter. The record of Archaic period people in Mesoamerica thus is similar in many ways to that of Archaic period hunter–gatherer–foragers in North and South America and to that of Epipaleolithic and/or late Upper Paleolithic period groups in the Old World. Many of them were using wild plants foods in ways that eventually led to domestication of certain cereal grasses, as well as other food resources. This process took thousands of years before domesticated versions of crops appeared and people began to heavily rely on domesticates as dietary staples.

Early food production does not necessarily mean that people had to stay at their site year-round, because they could plant and then leave until it was time to return for the harvest. The investment in planting and the expectation of a harvest, however, likely meant that groups became more strongly tied to particular locales in the landscape. Possibly they returned more often during the year and/or left a few people at the site year-round to help ensure that the crops were tended and protected from animals. Permanent villages were established in various parts of Mesoamerica between 3000 and 2000 BC. These represent a significant change in lifestyle from the more mobile groups of the earlier Archaic period. During the Late Archaic period, pottery was added to the cultural materials used by people.[6] As discussed in previous chapters, pottery has many advantages, including its use as a durable container in cooking.

Formative Mesoamerica

The early villages of the Archaic period were characterized by settlements of circular dwellings. Each was small, meaning that they could have housed a small nuclear family. Storage features were in areas open to all members of the village, suggesting community ownership of food resources or simply the willingness to share these resources outside of the immediate family.[7] Sharing of resources reduced risk for the group, because if one family's food resources were seriously impacted, other families pitched in to help out. This type of system, however, does not lend itself to producing much more than is needed, because there is an expectation that everything will potentially be shared with others, and thus surpluses do not accumulate. In Mesoamerica, as in some other parts of the world, there was an eventual shift in how villages were socially organized with respect to this type of risk. Beginning about 2000 cal BC, during what is called the Formative period, villages of rectangular structures with internal storage features replaced those with circular dwellings. This has been interpreted as a shift to private ownership of food resources by each family (because of the control over storage), and thus each family assumed the risk that used to be shared by the whole community. Because they did not have to share their resources

Guilá Naquitz Cave an Archaic period site in highland Mexico that has yielded the earliest preserved plant remains of domesticated maize and squash, dating to around 4200 cal BC.

with the entire community, there was more potential for the accumulation of surpluses. By the Middle Formative period (1000 cal BC), there was another social shift, and villages of rectangular structures became more elaborate and extended families built closely connected sets of dwellings. Having more people in a household could lead to even greater accumulations of food surpluses that could be used to support craft work and other nonfarming activities. As we saw in other regions of the world, agricultural surpluses led in some cases to increasing levels of social and political complexity. This was the situation for several regions within Mesoamerica that were interconnected by trade relationships and borrowing of ideas.[8]

The Olmec in the South Gulf Coast Lowlands

Beginning around 1800 cal BC, people living in the southern Gulf coast region of Mexico are recognized by archaeologists as groups called the **Olmec**. By 1400 cal BC, some Olmec began to modify the landscape and build a few settlements in ways that suggest the beginnings of increasingly complex social and political organization. This process is first seen at **San Lorenzo** (see Figure 13.1), where the inhabitants used a hilltop as the foundation for constructing a large, level plateau. People brought in more than 56,634 cubic meters (2 million cubic feet) of materials to create this plateau. This massive amount of labor strongly suggests planning and organization efforts led by a small group of individuals whom we might call the elites.[9] At its peak from 1400 to 1000 cal BC, San Lorenzo may have occupied 690 hectares ([1,705 acres]), and contained plazas with basalt-lined drains, public buildings, dwellings for elite families, and courtyards.[10] It had monumental art in the form of the famous Olmec heads (Figure 13.3), which are interpreted as representations of elite rulers. These and other sculptures show individuals wearing or using artifacts symbolic of power and status (for example, scepters). Sculptures include not just the large heads but also basalt stones with carved standing or seated portraits of rulers.[11] Around 900 cal BC, these sculptures and the site's architecture were deliberately destroyed, suggesting that the elite rulers were no longer viewed with the same favored status or perhaps that a competing Olmec center was able to destroy San Lorenzo.[12] The site of San Lorenzo mostly was abandoned as people moved elsewhere.

Another important Olmec center was the island of **La Venta** (see Figure 13.1), which became prominent after San Lorenzo declined. La Venta was in a swampy area without access to nearby agricultural land.[13] It was smaller (200 hectares [494 acres]) than San Lorenzo, but contained equally impressive architecture,[14] which included two large rectangular, flat-top pyramids and monumental art. There were numerous clay platforms aligned

Olmec the early socially and politically complex societies of the southern Gulf Coast of Mexico. Their main centers include San Lorenzo and La Venta, where elite rulers managed agriculture, construction labor, and trade and exchange networks. These were contemporary with several other Mesoamerican societies such as the Preclassic Maya.

San Lorenzo the first major center of the Olmec in the South Gulf Coast region of Mexico in Mesoamerica. It contains a large manmade plateau, plazas, courtyards, and large basalt sculptures of Olmec rulers. Its main period of power was between 1200 and 900 cal BC.

FIGURE 13.3
Elizabeth Ralph in 1969 with a magnetometer used to locate this Olmec head, representing an elite individual, at San Lorenzo when it was buried below ground.

La Venta an Olmec center in the South Gulf lowlands of Mexico in Mesoamerica that was important from 900 to 600 cal BC. It contains large clay platforms thought to be the foundations for elite residences, two large clay pyramids, monumental sculpted Olmec heads, and other ritual evidence suggesting it may have been a pilgrimage center.

north to south. These are interpreted as the foundations for elite dwellings but also contained evidence for craft workshops for serpentine (a green mineral that can be carved into jewelry). In addition to the enormous basalt heads of Olmec rulers and their basalt thrones, La Venta has evidence of burials and other rituals. Among the best known are the grouping of 16 small jade, serpentine, and sandstone figurines and polished stone celts (a type of axe). The celts were placed upright to form a "fence" against which one of the figures stands looking out at the other figures as they presumably enter the fenced area. Another is the so-called jaguar mosaic mask, made of pieces of serpentine, which was buried under one of the clay platforms.[15] The mosaic mask was laid out on top of tons of imported serpentine pieces. La Venta enjoyed its peak from 900 to 600 cal BC, when it is thought to perhaps have been a pilgrimage center,[16] but, like San Lorenzo, it was eventually largely abandoned. Some Olmec people reinstated the center at San Lorenzo from 600 to 400 cal BC, although on a much smaller scale.

At their peaks, both San Lorenzo and La Venta exerted influence over a much larger region around them. This certainly was the case for La Venta because of its lack of suitable agricultural lands. The food to feed the elites living at La Venta and "pay" for the construction efforts must have come from farther away in the surrounding countryside. In the case of San Lorenzo, regional archaeological surveys suggest a possible hierarchy of sites with San Lorenzo as the primary site and more than 130 villages and smaller hamlets, as well as small mound sites (perhaps secondary centers).[17] A similar settlement system is described for La Venta.[18] Agricultural products were only part of a regional network system that also saw the Olmec import serpentine, jade, and obsidian, as well as magnetite to make mirrors and all the heavy basalt for the monumental sculptures.[19] Many of these goods came from some distance away; for example, the basalt quarries for La Venta were 80 kilometers (50 miles) away, magnetite was from Oaxaca (500 kilometers [310 miles] distant), and obsidian came from 300 to 600 kilometers (186 to 372 miles) away.[20] Some Olmec art styles and goods are found in these trading regions, indicating two-way exchange of goods and ideas.[21]

The Olmec region over time was characterized by a series of relatively small political entities that some archaeologists call chiefdoms.[22] In this sense, the Olmec were similar to developments such as various European regions in the Bronze and Iron Ages and Mississippian Cahokia in the North American East (see Chapters 6 and 8). The Olmec region was not alone in Mesoamerica in being characterized by these types of socially and politically complex societies.

Early and Middle Preclassic Maya

Like the Olmec, evidence for more permanent and larger settlements in the Maya region is more frequent after 1600 to 1500 cal BC[23] (see Figure 13.1). Traditionally, archaeologists often speak of the Maya in terms of the highlands and lowlands. The highlands are the mountainous portions of Guatemala and Chiapas in

Mexico, whereas the lowlands region encompasses part of the southern Gulf coast and the Yucatan Peninsula in Mexico, Belize, El Salvador, and the lower elevations of Guatemala. Early Preclassic period farmers in the Maya area began to focus more intensively on the growing of maize and eventually were engaged in long-distance trade and exchange networks. Their villages grew in size and population, and there is evidence that suggests that some individuals or families had greater access to exotic resources. In some parts of the Maya Lowlands, farmers developed canal systems for their fields, not as a way to bring water to crops but to drain it away because of increasingly swampy conditions that occurred when the water table rose.[24] There are not many known Early and Middle Preclassic Maya sites, possibly because they are deeply buried by floodplain sediments along rivers or are in unexcavated areas at the bottom of sites with extensive later period occupations. Many of the trends in increasing population density at villages, involvement in trade and exchange networks, access to exotic goods, and expansion of the agricultural base that developed over the course of the Early Preclassic period (1600 to 1000 cal BC) became more common during the Middle Preclassic period (1000 to 350 cal BC).

By the Middle Preclassic period, the Maya in both the lowlands and the highlands lived in settlements that were linked to primary centers where elite individuals and families dwelled. Their social–political organization, like that of the Olmec, was that of chiefdoms. Primary centers were linked to rural settlements and communities within relatively small regions. The elite classes were able to direct the labor forces needed for massive construction projects, including plaza and pyramid complexes.[25] Unlike their Olmec counterparts (except perhaps for the destruction of San Lorenzo), the Maya chiefdoms may have engaged in raiding and violence, which we can see archaeologically in the destruction or burning of buildings at some Maya sites.[26]

Several Maya primary centers became important in the Middle Preclassic period. One of these was **Nakbe** in the lowlands (see Figure 13.1), which around 1000 cal BC was a settlement of relatively simple dwellings constructed of pole and thatch.[27] Within 200 years, people began to build platforms made of stone covered with plaster. These stood about half a meter (1.6 feet) high and eventually 2 meters (6.5 feet) high[28] and were associated with dense deposits of household refuse (middens). Eventually, even larger and taller terraced platforms (up to 18 meters [59 feet] high) were built, representing monumental construction that would have had structures on top of them. These monuments were associated with plazas and may have been ritual in function. Nakbe had a ball court (see "Maya Ritual and Religion"), an elevated stone causeway (road) that ran from one platform complex to another within the site, a large plaza with a pyramid on the west side and three structures on top of a long platform on the east side, and sculpted stone altars and stelae (singular, **stela**).[29] Nakbe might have been 50 hectares (123 acres), which was quite a bit smaller than the Olmec centers at San Lorenzo and La Venta. Its size possibly was constrained by the fact that the lowlands region had several contemporary primary centers[30] (unlike the Olmec situation, which seems to have had only one primary center at a time).

Nakbe a Maya Lowlands center in Mesoamerica that began during the Middle Preclassic period. It eventually had monumental architecture including a ball court, stone platforms, and a plaza associated with a pyramid and a platform with three structures, as well as stelae and altars.

Stela a standing carved stone. In this book it is used to describe monuments in Mesoamerica showing important Maya rulers, gods, or goddesses, and often Maya glyphic writing as well.

Kaminaljuyú a Maya highlands center in Mesoamerica that began to develop into a politically complex society during the Middle Preclassic period. During the late Preclassic and Classic periods, it became one of the largest urban areas and most important of the Maya highlands sites.

Zapotec a state-level politically complex society that emerged in the Valley of Oaxaca about 20 cal BC during the Late Formative period. Its capital was Monte Albán.

San José Mogote a significant political center in the Valley of Oaxaca, Mexico, that developed initially during the same period as the Olmec and Early and Middle Preclassic Maya. San José Mogote was involved in long-distance trade networks with other Mesoamerican regions and had public architecture that included stairways and terraces built of stone and a town divided into different sections with different craft specialties.

Monte Albán the main center in the Valley of Oaxaca in Mesoamerica after 500 cal BC. It was a population center and large town with a perimeter wall and important ceremonial structures, which became the hub of the Zapotec state beginning in 30 to 20 cal BC.

In the Maya highlands, **Kaminaljuyú** (see Figure 13.1) began to develop during the Middle Preclassic period.[31] The settlement overall is somewhat difficult to reconstruct because it was not built of stone but of adobe bricks, and much of it has eroded over time or been impacted by modern construction. There were adobe platforms and mounds for temples and dwellings for the elites. These platforms and mounds were associated with plazas, just as at Nakbe and other Maya sites in the highlands and the lowlands. Carved stone altars and stelae were placed in front of important structures. The elites living at Kaminaljuyú were able to direct large numbers of laborers to build these monuments as well as several large canals with secondary canals radiating off them that supplied water for irrigation agriculture in nearby fields. Kaminaljuyú had contacts with nearby Pacific coast settlements, where socially and politically complex centers also were developing.[32]

The Valley of Oaxaca

The Valley of Oaxaca is a highlands region in Mexico where **Zapotec** politically complex society emerged. By 1400 cal BC, there were a number of small sites scattered throughout the valley, including **San José Mogote** (see Figure 13.1).[33] This site grew in size over time and eventually had four residential areas that were involved in the production of different crafts. People in one neighborhood made mirrors from magnetite, whereas in another neighborhood they made marine shell ornaments. Different residential areas obtained stone raw materials (obsidian and chert) from different regions. These distinctions seem to be carried over into designs such as the "fire-serpent" and the "were-jaguar" on their pottery vessels (Figure 13.4). Within each neighborhood, there were burials with jade that suggest that some individuals may have enjoyed higher status. The dwellings for elites and public structures were relocated to the acropolis area of San José Mogote, where they could be better defended. While San José Mogote was the most important center in the northern part of the Valley of Oaxaca, its settlement hierarchy included tiers of smaller villages, some of which also had public buildings and probably elite families.

San José Mogote remained the most important community until 500 cal BC, when it was burned and many of its people moved to **Monte Albán** on the top of a mountain (Figure 13.5; see also Figure 13.1) or to el Palenque.[34] Monte Albán became one of the main centers in the Valley of Oaxaca and was densely populated, with the settlement expanding from 324 hectares (800 acres) to 442 hectares (1,092 acres).[35] Construction of monumental architecture included a defensive wall that stretched more than 3 kilometers (2 miles) and a platform mound that had an important carved

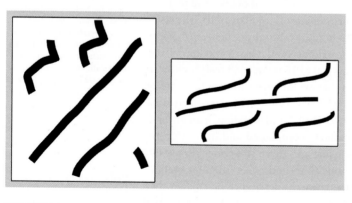

FIGURE 13.4
Examples of the fire-serpent Olmec design found at at San José Magote, Valley of Oaxaca (after Marcus 1989: 171).

FIGURE 13.5
The plaza area with monumental architecture at Monte Albán, Valley of Oaxaca.

gallery showing 300 slain captives that indicated violence between different centers in the valley.[36] There were temples, palaces, and tombs for elite rulers.[37] The political (and religious?) power of Monte Albán's rulers continued to be challenged by at least one other important center in the valley, Tilcajete (near San José Mogote and el Palenque), until Monte Albán successfully attacked and burned it around 30 to 20 cal BC, during the Late Formative period. This event helped consolidate the territorial power of the elite rulers at Monte Albán, who managed to conquer all of the Valley of Oaxaca and who controlled a settlement hierarchy of secondary and tertiary centers as well as villages. Monte Albán became the capital of what archaeologists recognize as the Zapotec state-level polity.

The Basin of Mexico

The Basin of Mexico is another highland region in Mesoamerica important to our understanding of the rise of politically complex societies in this region of the world. By 1500 cal BC (Early Formative period), possible evidence for interaction with the Olmec area is seen in pottery types called "hollow dolls" (figurines with chubby bodies and a "baby face," often shown wearing a "helmet" similar to those on the monumental Olmec heads at San Lorenzo) and design motifs that include jaguar paws. Some researchers, however, argue that many of the motifs seen in the Basin of Mexico were not indicators of interaction with specific regions but rather pan-Mesoamerican images.[38] The possible Olmec-style pottery was found among the grave goods at **Tlatilco** (see Figure 13.1), as were many figurines that showed local elements of daily life.[39] There also were pottery styles that were similar to those seen at San José Mogote in the Valley of Oaxaca.[40] In addition to dwellings, Tlatilco had low clay platforms that may have been the foundations for elevated ritual structures. Over time, more and more villages in the Basin of Mexico had items suggestive of some Olmec contact, but around 950 cal BC (just before the fall of San Lorenzo), these Olmec traits disappeared. This may suggest a disruption in trade and exchange relationships with the Olmec area but may also indicate that the growing local populations in the Basin of Mexico began to emphasize indigenous cultural features.

Tlatilco an Early Formative period site in the Basin of Mexico. Archaeological materials include pottery designs and forms that show contact with the Olmec region of Mesoamerica, as well as burials that suggest social ranking of people.

FIGURE 13.6
Aerial view of the Pyramid of the Moon area at Teotihuacan.

Cuicuilco a Middle to Late Formative period ceremonial center and town in the Basin of Mexico. It went into decline around the same time that Teotihuacán became an important center in this area.

Teotihuacán one of the most important centers in the Basin of Mexico after 150 cal BC. At its height during the Early Classic period, Teotihuacán was a large, planned city with a ceremonial precinct (Pyramids of the Sun and Moon, Street of the Dead, elite residences and other temples) and outlying areas of dwellings, temples, plazas, and markets.

By the latter part of the Middle Formative period, the ceremonial center at **Cuicuilco** (see Figure 13.1), on Lake Texcoco's southern shore, emerged as a major center. During this period, there were adobe platforms built that soon were superceded by large stone-built platforms.[41] By 400 cal BC (Late Formative period), Cuicuilco possibly had 20,000 people living in a town covering 20 hectares (50 acres) that also had a large round pyramid (20 meters [65 feet] high). The town was laid out on a grid system, with large dwellings (probably for elite families) and avenues.[42] By AD 150, Cuicuilco went into a slow decline, losing much of its population, and its ceremonial structures were no longer maintained.[43] Eventually, the town was covered by lava from a nearby volcanic eruption (AD 245 to 315).

At about the same time that Cuicuilco was an important city, the center at **Teotihuacán** (see Figure 13.1) also became prominent in the Basin of Mexico (Figure 13.6). This city, as at Cuicuilco, was laid out on a grid system and had a central ceremonial precinct that is well known for the Pyramids of the Sun (built in the first or second centuries AD) and Moon,[44] the so-called Street of the Dead, and the Citadel Complex, along with numerous elite residences and smaller temples. In areas surrounding this central precinct, there were plazas, other temples, markets, streets, palaces, reservoirs, apartment complexes, and slums.[45] Teotihuacán reached its peak (150,000 people in a city covering 20 square kilometers [8 square miles]) in AD 350 to 550 during the subsequent Early Classic period of Mesoamerica, when the city had extensive trade and exchange relationships with many parts of this region and alliances and other less friendly interactions with the Early Classic period lowlands Maya (see later). The city was burned in the late AD 500s.

Late Preclassic Maya

The Late Preclassic (Late Formative) period (beginning 400 cal BC) in the Maya area was a time of several emerging, powerful primary centers that some archaeologists describe as early states.[46] Each of these was characterized by a hereditary ruling dynasty that coordinated and controlled the massive construction efforts and trade and exchange networks, warfare, and aspects of religion. These elite individuals were buried in royal tombs, which sometimes included elaborate grave goods. Violence from raiding or perhaps warfare is seen in mass burials of males who died violent deaths (butchered bodies and healed fractures) at some sites.[47] An ever-increasing population meant that food production also had to increase, and to accomplish this the Maya used a wide diversity of agricultural strategies including raised fields, canals, terraces, field draining, slash and burn, and tree crops. As we saw previously, many of these features were present by the Middle Preclassic period but became more common throughout the Maya region during the Late Preclassic period. Two key innovations of the Late Preclassic period were the first appearance of a writing system, which used Maya glyphs, and the calendric system[48] (more on these later).

In the Maya highlands, the primary center at Kaminaljuyú reached its peak during the Late Preclassic period.[49] It contained 200 platforms made of adobe that were the foundations for structures built of perishable thatch and wood. At this time, Kaminaljuyú was 4 square kilometers (1.5 square miles) in size. There were carved stone monuments that showed the rulers, sometimes surrounded by captured people who were bound and kneeling. One reason that this highlands primary center was important was its control over jade and obsidian that were widely sought by other primary center rulers in the Maya lowlands and elsewhere in Mesoamerica. The elite rulers of Kaminaljuyú were buried in some splendor, with hundreds of pottery vessels and exotic items such as jade. The Maya highlands, however, declined in political importance after the Late Preclassic period, when developments in the Maya lowlands supplanted the highlands region.

One of the prominent centers in the Maya lowlands during the earlier part of the Late Preclassic period was **El Mirador** (Figure 13.7; see Figure 13.1), which is

El Mirador an important center during the Late Preclassic period in the Maya lowlands of Mesoamerica. Its monumental architecture, including the El Tigre pyramid, is significantly more massive than that at later Maya sites such as Tikal.

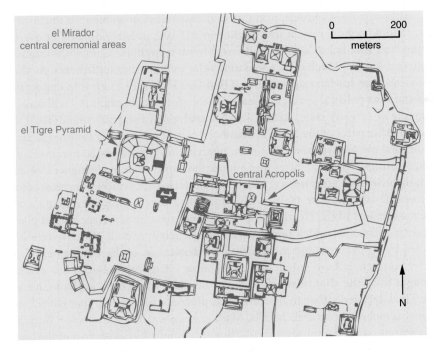

FIGURE 13.7
A stylized plan map of the central ceremonial areas at El Mirador, Guatemala. The area outlined in red shows one of several examples of the triadic architectural form here.

in the same region as Nakbe (see previous discussion) and connected to Nakbe by a causeway (road).[50] In fact, El Mirador was linked by causeways to many sites in the Mirador Basin, suggesting its pre-eminent position in the settlement hierarchy. The scale of monumental building at El Mirador was impressive and dwarfed that seen in later centers such as Tikal (see later). One of the pyramids at El Mirador, the El Tigre pyramid, for example, is 55 meters (180 feet) high and covers 19,600 square meters (210,973 square feet).[51] As some researchers have noted, El Tigre pyramid would have covered the entire Northern Acropolis at Tikal, as well all of the Temples I and II and Great Plaza areas. El Tigre pyramid was not the only monument at El Mirador. Others included the Central Acropolis, which had a large palace-like structure where elite individuals lived, and there were platforms on top of which temples were erected.[52] One of the features seen at El Mirador (and other Late Preclassic sites), which continued into the later Classic period, was an arrangement of monuments in what is called a triadic architectural form.[53] This consisted of one main structure that often was built on a platform. To the sides of this main structure were two smaller constructions that faced inward onto an open space between the three buildings. The monuments, including their stairways, had facades with carved or plaster-molded and painted ideological motifs important in Maya mythology. They included masks, birds, serpents, the sky, the sun, and the earth.[54]

Although El Mirador appears to have controlled or influenced much of its surrounding region, it went into decline in AD 100, possibly because of overuse of the land that led to erosion and fewer trees, as well as issues with obtaining sufficient water.[55] Much of its population relocated to other settlements. At about the same time, lowland sites such as **Tikal** (see Figure 13.1) grew in importance and status as political centers. Some archaeologists would say that Tikal was one example of an early state. Recent LiDAR analysis of the area around Tikal and several other parts of the Maya lowlands, in fact, revealed an extensive system of additional causeways, house mounds, quarries, fortresses, walls, pyramids, and other features.[56] This indicates that population density was much higher than previously believed. Excavations at Tikal itself show that elite rulers were present long before AD 100, because their lavishly furnished royal tombs were found under the monuments of the North Acropolis.[57] These royal tombs were burials placed under platforms on which temples were constructed, and all of these were later buried by renovations and monumental constructions of the Classic period. As many researchers have noted, one of the most intriguing is Burial 85, which is thought to be the elite ruler acknowledged in later Maya texts as the founder of the Tikal dynasty, although his burial was preceded by several other elites.[58] His name, as recorded centuries later by Maya scribes, was Yax Ehb Xook.[59] Burial 85 was a stone-vaulted tomb that, in addition to a bundle burial of most of the bones of an adult male (except his head and some leg bones), contained a jade mask with inlaid shell and coral for the teeth and eyes, enormous pottery vessels, three vessels from Kaminaljuyú in the Maya highlands, a stingray spine, a jade bead, and a

Tikal a Maya lowlands center in Mesoamerica that became important after AD 100. Tikal has abundant evidence for monumental construction (Northern Acropolis, Temple I, Great Plaza) beginning in the Late Preclassic and continuing into the Classic period, when Tikal became one of the most important of several competing state-like polities.

marine shell pendant. The mask was probably sewn to the bundle to represent the missing head and had a special motif interpreted as a royal "crown," which in the later Classic period is recognized as a symbol for rulership (Figure 13.8). As mentioned previously, Tikal had its share of monumental architecture in the Northern Acropolis, the Great Plaza, and Temple I. For reasons that are not yet understood, Tikal was one of the few lowland Maya primary centers that flourished in the last centuries of the Late Preclassic period. Tikal and its rulers became increasingly important as the Classic Maya period began.

FIGURE 13.8
Jade burial mask from Tikal, Guatemala.

The Lowland Classic Maya

As we have seen, politically complex societies became common in many regions of Mesoamerica by the Late Formative period. Within the Maya area, most archaeologists would agree that the two earliest state-level examples were Tikal and **Calakmul** (see Figure 13.1), both of which were in the southern part of the Maya lowlands.[60] These two states became especially important during the Classic period. Both had ruling dynasties, an administrative hierarchy that included surrounding towns and rural areas, control over large labor forces who could be used to build monumental architecture and for conducting wars against other communities, an established religion and its associated ideology, and control over extensive trade and exchange networks, monumental art, and writing, calendrics, and astronomy. Tikal and Calakmul did suffer declines in their importance and power, some of which is evident from the written record. Over time, a number of other Maya cities also became states, although not all were equally powerful or at their peaks at the same moment in time. Our ability to translate Maya inscriptions has led to a much more detailed understanding of these events and of the rulers of the various Maya cities.

Calakmul a Classic period lowlands Maya city in Mesoamerica that was the main state rival to the state centered at Tikal. Calakmul had an extensive monumental elite and religious center characterized by palaces, temples, pyramids, and avenues, and its ruling dynasty established a wide network of alliances with other Maya cities.

The Maya Written Word

The Maya writing system was used for 1,700 years (beginning by AD 1) and was based on glyphs that represented words (logographic) and sounds (phonetic), as well as dots, bars, and a shell symbol for numbers used in calendars and mathematics[61] (Figure 13.9). Like many early writing systems, Maya glyphs were used to record the details and stories of the lives of the rulers of the various Maya states. These stories included their birth and death, when they came to power, their marriages and other alliances with ruling families from other cities, and their success (or failure) in warfare. The Maya also wrote about their gods, goddesses, and religious rituals. Maya rulers traced their genealogical relationship back to mythological figures such as the Hero Twins, and when they

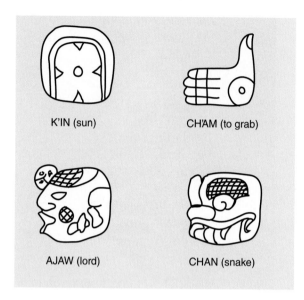

K'IN (sun)

CH'AM (to grab)

AJAW (lord)

CHAN (snake)

FIGURE 13.9
Examples of Maya logogram glyphs with the Maya syllable and translation. Some syllables could be expressed using one of several different glyphs.

FIGURE 13.10
A *Spondylus princeps* shell (spiny oyster). These were cut into pieces to make beads.

came to power, they changed their names to include an association with a specific god,[62] thus emphasizing their legitimacy. Some Maya texts also record special types of economic transactions, mainly those of tribute being paid to royal elites. Tribute items included cacao beans (to make a highly valued chocolate beverage; see also Chapter 7), textiles, certain types of marine shells (*Spondylus*/spiny oyster; Figure 13.10), and green feathers for ritual paraphernalia.[63] In contrast, some of the writing present on specific objects (such as pottery vessels) simply indicated the owner of the object. The Maya scribes, who were specialists likely enjoying relatively high status, wrote on a variety of mediums, from pottery vessels to tomb walls to carved stone monuments and stelae to sheets of bark paper (called a codex). Because bark paper is a perishable material that does not survive well, and due to the Spanish burning of Maya writings, we have few examples of codices.[64] Learning to write meant attending a "school" and practicing making the glyphs. Practice texts on sculpture have been found.[65]

The development of a variety of calendars also was an achievement of the Maya, and their recording of the lives of rulers and other events was contextualized with calendar dates, similar to how we record events today using current calendar systems such as the Gregorian calendar (which came into use in AD 1582) for many parts of the world including the United States, or the Islamic calendar, based on the Prophet Mohammed's move from Mecca to Medina and on lunar phases. The Maya used their observations of the sun, moon, and planets, as well as their mathematical system, to establish the count cycle for their calendars. In their counting system, a dot represented 1, a bar was 5, and the shell glyph stood for zero. Creating a symbol to represent the concept of zero was independently invented only three times, and the Maya were the earliest to do so.[66] Maya calendars were used in part to predict and prophesy certain celestial events, and the ability to do so successfully was one way to legitimize rulers and religion. Many calendars were used by the Maya. One was the 260-day cycle in the Sacred Almanac. Another was the Solar Year, which was a 365-day cycle, with 18 months of 20 days and an additional 5-day period, somewhat different from how we organize our solar year today. And there was the Long Count (Figure 13.11), which was a cycle of 5,128 years that began in the year 3114 BC and ended on December 21, 2012 (in our calendar system).[67] The end of the long count did not mean that the Maya were predicting the end of the world, as popular Hollywood movies have recently implied. Rather, the long count would start again once the cycle was completed. The earliest recorded date known from the Maya region is on Tikal Stela 29 and corresponds to our calendar date of AD 292, whereas the last known Long Count date is from Monument 101 at the Terminal Classic period highlands site of Toniná (Mexico) and corresponds to our calendar date of AD 909.[68]

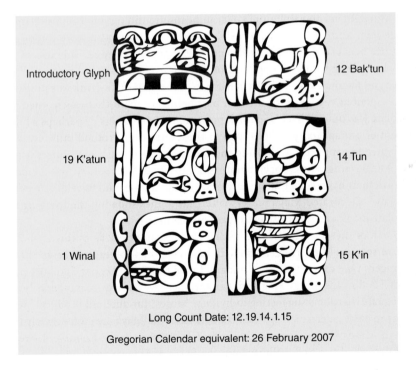

Introductory Glyph

12 Bak'tun

19 K'atun

14 Tun

1 Winal

15 K'in

Long Count Date: 12.19.14.1.15

Gregorian Calendar equivalent: 26 February 2007

FIGURE 13.11

A stylized Maya Long Count calendar date and its equivalent in our calendar system. It represents the amount of time that has passed since August 13, 3114 BC. Numbers are the dots and bars to the left of each glyph. The units in the long count represent 144,000 days or about 400 years (one bak'tun), 7,200 days or about 20 years (one k'atun), 360 days (one tun), 20 days (one winal), and single days (k'in) (Martin 2012: 24). As noted in the text, this long count cycle ended on December 21, 2012, and a new long count cycle began.

Maya Resource Networks, Trade, and Exchange

The highlands and lowlands regions of the Maya area of Mesoamerica contained a variety of resources that could be used for the production of everyday items, as well as exotic materials that held higher value and were used in special ritual and elite contexts and for trade with other parts of Mesoamerica. Local households were the basic producers and consumers of maize and ramon nuts and a variety of pottery vessels for cooking, eating, and storage of foods.[69] Beyond this, households obtained basalt and obsidian and made ground stone for processing foods. Salt was another basic product used by individual households and traded throughout the Mesoamerican region, as well as into the North American Southwest (see Chapter 7). Maya society included full-time laborers involved in workshops for the manufacture of specialized goods, such as obsidian blades at Kaminaljuyú.[70] Among the rare exotic products were jade carvings, paper made of bark, pyrite mirrors, feather headdresses, and coral and shell items. The Maya also had other natural resources that held great significance within their religious and political system. These included cacao beans, jaguar pelts, stingray spines, and shark teeth (see "Maya Ritual and Religion"). Cacao beans are interesting because they were a trade item and eventually a form of "money," but they also were important in Maya life because they were made into a chocolate beverage. This use of cacao beans has a long history going back into the Early Formative period in both the Olmec and Pacific Coast regions of Mexico.[71] The chocolate drink was prepared in special spouted vessels, with the best part being the foam that was frothed as the chocolate was poured back and forth between the containers[72] (perhaps a bit reminiscent of our specialty coffees such as those including frothed milk/cream like café latte and cappuccino). During the Classic period, Maya elite rulers used the chocolate beverage as part of elaborate feasting rituals they held to mark important events in their lives, such as marriage or winning a battle, and to celebrate political alliances.[73] Decorated Maya pottery often has scenes showing the frothing of the chocolate drink and its presence at feasting events.

Some of these products were traded in the market plazas of towns and cities and overseen by Maya rulers, who may have collected "taxes" on the goods being exchanged. One example of such a market is in the East Plaza at Tikal, where several of Tikal's causeways came together and there was a large rectangular building with equal-size rooms suggesting individual "stores" for different products, perhaps similar to our modern mall stores. Products from the Maya area were widely traded through Mesoamerica. During the Early Classic period, for example, there were well-established ties to Teotihuacán in the Basin of Mexico with evidence of Maya people in this highlands Mexican city.[74] Trade and exchange was not one way, because some products made at Teotihuacán were brought into the Maya region, such as obsidian blades and cylinder tripod pottery vessels.[75] Many of the Maya cities were ideally situated to control land routes for north–south trade between Central America and Mexico or east–west trade between the Pacific and Gulf of Mexico, and this may have been one factor in their rise to power during the Classic period.[76]

Maya Social Life

The Maya were characterized by social hierarchies that included elite rulers and their families, scribes, religious practitioners, estate managers, warriors, ordinary people who were farmers and part-time craft manufacturers, and slaves/war captives.[77] Most of the lower classes lived in simple houses constructed of poles and thatch, which were built on small platforms of earth or rubble that elevated the houses slightly above ground level. These nonelite households were situated away from the center of the cities and towns. Even within the community of commoners, however, there were status distinctions related to social prestige gained from performing rituals and differences in wealth and access to resources.[78] This is seen in a few exotic items such as jade and *Spondylus* shells that were found in nonelite burials. In some respects, our modern city and town neighborhoods are similar in reflecting these smaller distinctions in social prestige and status, such as the condition/upkeep of one's house and yard or the types of jewelry worn (costume jewelry as opposed to silver, gold, and precious and semiprecious stones).

The elite classes, of course, had much greater access to resources, power, and prestige. They had a wider diversity of foods in their diet, and by the Late Classic period, elites ate more meat than did commoners.[79] Their clothing, accessories, and skull shape also set them apart from nonelites.[80] As babies, their foreheads were flattened by tying a board to the forehead while bone growth was still occurring. This was considered a mark of beauty. Elite Maya had their incisors (front teeth) notched and sometimes inlaid with jade. And they wore more highly decorated clothing, especially the kings, whose clothing included feathers sewn onto cotton cloth, headdresses made of quetzal bird feathers, jade masks as chest plaques, bracelets, necklaces, earrings, and lip ornaments of jade, coral, and shell, as well as jaguar pelts. In death, Maya elites had sumptuous goods and tombs. At Tikal, for example, the probable burial (Burial 10) of the ruler Yax Nuun Ahiin I (sometimes called "Curl Snout" based on the appearance of the glyph for his name) included numerous decorated pottery vessels, a headless crocodile, five turtle shells of varying sizes, a jade ornament, a musical instrument, and the bodies of nine sacrificed humans.[81] The decorations on the pottery show many design elements that look like those from Mexico, which, along with other information, suggest the influence of Teotihuacán (more on this in "Maya Warfare and Violence"). Such lavish burials were typical of the major Classic Maya cities. At Tikal's rival, Calakmul, for instance, the probable burial (Tomb 4) of the ruler Yuknoom Yich'aak K'ahk' (sometimes called "Claw of Fire" based on his name glyph) was below a massive structure and included decorated pottery vessels, ornaments made of jade, *Spondylus* shells, bone, and mother of pearl, and a mosaic mask of jade; the body of this individual was covered with the skin of a jaguar as well as textiles. The scale of elite burials also can be seen in the North Acropolis at Tikal, where each king was buried during the Classic period. This required remodeling existing temples and building new ones until the complex of temples, many built one over another, finally grew so large that after AD 734, the kings scattered their burial temples throughout the city.[82]

Elites controlled and/or could organize the labor forces needed for the construction of pyramids, temples, palaces, plazas, and causeways that characterized the central portions of cities where these elite families lived and performed rituals. Their residences tended to be built of stone, which was a more expensive type of construction, and were much larger than the dwellings of the lower classes. The central position of elite dwellings in the cities and towns indicated their higher status. And the dwellings of the elite rulers were veritable palaces placed on high masonry platforms so that they towered above associated plazas and the surrounding area. The complexity of the administration of these cities and the larger state-level polities that they represented was partly reflected in the number of different titles that individuals were given.[83] The king was usually referred to as "lord" or "divine lord," and there were sublord titles for the rulers in the secondary and tertiary centers associated with cities such as Tikal (read "The Big Picture: Political Organization in the Classic Maya"). Other titles indicated the specialized occupations of individuals, such as "stonecutter," "scribe," and "he who worships."

The Maya kings and their families held power in part because they claimed kinship or lineage descent from Maya deities.[86] Just as important, their power also came from their ability to be successful rulers, such as conquering other cities and capturing their kings or establishing favorable alliances through marriages with competing royal families.[87] It meant (as it often does today) that their reigns needed to be ones in which economic conditions for everyone were good or excellent. This helped ensure that ordinary people (who produced much of the agricultural surpluses) "bought into" the system and supported it, a process that was helped along by the kings being sponsors of shared religious rituals and events, such as ball court games (see later).

Maya Ritual and Religion

We know many details of Maya religion because of the decipherment of Maya texts and inscriptions and from early Spanish accounts. Their religious system and its creation myth (called the Popol Vuh) was a worldview that did not distinguish between the supernatural and nonsupernatural.[88] The Maya believed that all things (animate and inanimate) possessed a sacred power. In humans, this power was associated with the elements of the heart, blood, and breath. The underworld was a particularly dangerous place. Entrances to it were represented by caves where some of the dead were buried but also by proxy in that some of the Maya temple doorways were used by priests and elite rulers to symbolically enter a "cave" (the temple platform) and speak with underworld gods. Their beliefs were based in part on the notion of rebirth; for example, the sun setting every day was a type of death when it went down into the underworld, but it was reborn when it rose the next day. The Maya believed that their kings also underwent this rebirth process, when after their death they were transformed into gods and became stars in the night sky.

The Maya pantheon of gods and goddesses included deities that possessed many different features and qualities based on aspects such as color, direction, age, sex, and "invisible" attributes, which makes identification of all the Maya gods and goddesses a bit difficult. But some are relatively well known, such as Chaak (the storm and rain god often shown with reptile features), Kimi (the death god, shown as a skeleton or bloated body), Hun Hunapu (the maize god and father of the Hero Twins), and Itzamnaaj (the main

The Big Picture

Political Organization in the Classic Maya

During the Classic period Maya, political structure was organized at least partially along economic lines based on the concept of the extended family[84] (Figure 13.12). This was similar in some respects to the situation in Mesopotamia (see Chapter 9). For Maya royalty, it meant that royal courts, whose members were palace residents, administered the tasks necessary to produce, control, and use agricultural surpluses, to trade exotic and more common materials, and to make craft items, especially prestige goods such as jade ornaments. Not everyone in the royal court was related because its membership included not just the king and his family, but also priests, guards, advisors, servants, various retainers, and craft specialists. Of special importance were items of exotic materials that were made in craft workshops controlled by the royal court. These prestige goods represented the status and legitimacy of the king, as did the fact that the kings were priests and thus had control of some types of esoteric knowledge. Moreover, the Maya king and his royal court held large banquets where they displayed their wealth and consumed large amounts of food and beverages, including the frothed chocolate drink.[85] These feasts were held on occasions such as important dates in the calendar cycles, ball games, and events in their personal lives. Such feasting ceremonies also could be used to establish alliances with other Maya cities to establish control over much larger areas within the Maya region.

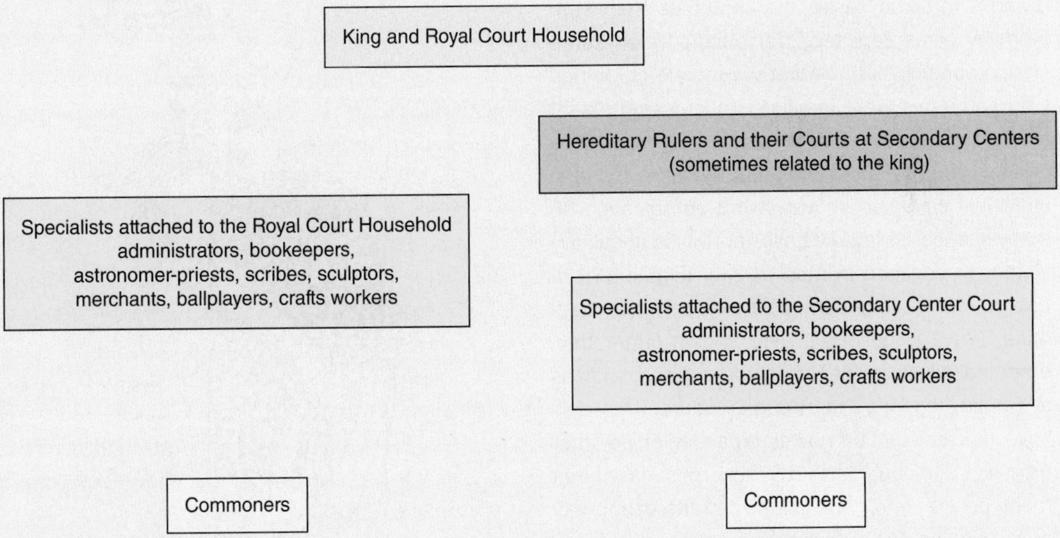

King and Royal Court Household

Hereditary Rulers and their Courts at Secondary Centers
(sometimes related to the king)

Specialists attached to the Royal Court Household
administrators, bookeepers,
astronomer-priests, scribes, sculptors,
merchants, ballplayers, crafts workers

Specialists attached to the Secondary Center Court
administrators, bookeepers,
astronomer-priests, scribes, sculptors,
merchants, ballplayers, crafts workers

Commoners

Commoners

FIGURE 13.12
Maya political organization along the lines of household economies.

god who ruled over all major opposing forces such as day and night and life and death; he was sometimes depicted as a two-headed serpent). As in the Mesopotamian region (see Chapter 9), each Maya city was associated with certain specific gods; for example, Calakmul had the deer–serpent deity. The close relationship of the Maya kings to the deities is seen in some of the rituals and activities in which the kings engaged during public ceremonies. A king, for example, impersonated a god by dressing in a costume that represented that god and then performed rituals or dances (read "The Big Picture: Art and Ideology in the Classic Maya"), likely in the plazas, where the ritual was watched by thousands of people.[89] These ceremonies involved offerings to the gods, and the most powerful type of offering was the sacred power in humans. The offering of blood occurred when the Maya engaged in bloodletting by piercing various parts of their bodies with stingray spines or obsidian blades[90] and when they sacrificed humans (often war captives).

The Big Picture

Art and Ideology in the Classic Maya

Maya kings used limited access to ritual areas of public architecture and imagery in art to establish their special role in society and their access to the divine.[91] In some cases, the costumes that were worn by elites depicted in art incorporated some clothing and/or features that were male combined with some that were female.[92] This may represent a mixed gender that was associated with the Maya creator gods.[93] If so, it lent great power to the elite individual who was shown in this combination. In many scenes, a Maya king was portrayed in military victory or engaged in ritual activity (Figure 13.13). Like rulers in many early politically complex societies, Maya kings often were shown larger than other individuals in scenes. In some cases, such as at Copan, the king was the only figure. This may have indicated that his power depended on no other mortals,[94] although obviously there must have been many people who were involved in the day-to-day tasks of ruling. To emphasize their right to rule, kings also were drawn or sculpted into dynasty lists of rulers that suggested that the links between rulers through time were continuous. These dynasty lists could include connections to various Maya gods.

FIGURE 13.13
Stylized image of a Maya king dressed in a jaguar costume for a ritual.

Among the many Maya ceremonies was the elite ritual version of the ball game held in a public ball court, which was an architectural feature found in most Maya cities and towns. The two teams wore padded clothing on their heads and waists and played with a basketball-size rubber ball that could not be hit with their feet or hands.[95] In this special ball game, captured warriors were one team of players, whereas the victorious warriors were the other team. Of course, the captured warriors always lost the game and then were sacrificed as a result. This ritual was tied into the fact that the mythology associated with the Hero Twins deities had them playing and winning a ball game against death gods and sacrificing those death gods when the Hero Twins won. Probably, fortunately, a less ritualized version of the ball game also was played in which the stakes were not quite so high. That is, the losing team simply lost their clothing and other items to members of the winning team and to the audience.

Maya Warfare and Violence

The Maya lowlands region, as well as Mesoamerica in general, has abundant evidence that violence and warfare were long-standing features of the interactions between the various political entities.[96] During the Classic period in the Maya lowlands, this aspect of society is seen in the rivalry between the Tikal and Calakmul states.[97] These two cities did not always war directly against one another but used other less powerful Maya cities, to which Tikal and Calakmul were allied, as proxies. These proxies would attack the economic, political, and military capabilities of either Tikal or Calakmul by attempting to conquer other allies of those two major states.

There are many types of archaeological finds that document Maya warfare. Many of the cities, for example, had fortifications. At Tikal there was a large (4 meters [13 feet] wide and 3 meters [10 feet] deep) ditch with a steep outer embankment that stretched 24.6 kilometers (15 miles) as it encircled much of the area around Tikal except to the south.[98] The width of the ditch and its placement behind the embankment meant an attacking army could not cross it without a bridge (although because it was not finished in the south, this opened up other possibilities for attack). And, interestingly, it protected a much larger region around Tikal than just the central areas of the city where the elites resided. This pattern differed from that in many other Maya cities that seem only to have had fortifications for the central parts of the cities.[99] Another line of evidence is the deliberate destruction of palaces and temples, as well as mass burials, including the remains of children, women, and men at Tikal that are interpreted as the deliberate slaying of elite families.[100]

If we look at the Tikal state more closely, we can see how violence and warfare during the Classic period impacted the fortunes of Maya rulers and states, both large (as at Tikal and Calakmul) and smaller (other Maya cities such as Piedras Negras, Caracol, Toniná, and Quirigua). The history of Tikal as a major center began, as we saw earlier, during the Late Preclassic period when a number of rulers were successively buried there, and the "official" founder of the Tikal dynasty was

Maya designs   Mexican designs

FIGURE 13.14
Mexican motifs are found
along with Maya motifs in
Maya contexts, indicating
long-distance relationships
between these two regions
of Mesoamerica.

recognized by later Maya rulers as Yax Ehb Xook. By the beginning of the Classic period, about AD 250, Tikal had a well-established dynastic succession of rulers who asserted links back to deities as part of their claim to legitimacy. Early Tikal kings such as Chak Tok Ich'aak I (also called "Great Misty Claw" based on his name glyph) were shown trampling enemies underfoot,[101] a common motif for victory in battles. Because of its long-distance trade network and possibly also marriage alliances, Tikal had contact with Teotihuacán in the Valley of Mexico. The influence of Teotihuacán is seen in various Mexican design elements in the architecture built at Tikal. Teotihuacán's influence, however, became prominent beginning on January 16, AD 378, when Chak Tok Ich'aak I died at the same time that an individual called Sihyaj K'ahk' (or "Fire Born") arrived. This event is interpreted as a military conquest of Tikal by Teotihuacán, which established a new, possibly foreign, ruling dynasty at Tikal under Yax Nuun Ahiin I ("Curl Snout") in AD 379. It was also when stelae that dated prior to AD 378[102] were destroyed (thus "erasing" Tikal's earlier history). Recent isotopic study of the bones of Yax Nuun Ahiin I, however, do not show that he was from central Mexico, although an individual from a different royal burial may be foreign.[103] There are, however, decorated pottery vessels and carved monuments that show various individuals in Mexican styles of clothing, including Yax Nuun Ahiin I himself, at Tikal and at other Maya lowlands cities (Figure 13.14).

The fortunes of Tikal waxed and waned for decades after the establishment of this new dynasty. In AD 562, Tikal was defeated by one of the Maya cities associated with the Snake Kingdom, which was politically controlled by Tikal's major rival, the city of Calakmul under the ruler "Sky Witness."[104] Interestingly, this is the same period during which Teotihuacán declined, which may have been a factor in the losses suffered by Tikal and its rulers. Tikal's defeat once again resulted in the destruction of its rulers' monuments, and its ruling dynasty was likely replaced. Moreover, it was subject to the power of Calakmul and its alliance of Maya cities. From AD 657 to 679, Tikal occasionally fought battles with cities allied to Calakmul, sometimes winning and at other times losing.[105] Under the Tikal ruler Jasaw Chan K'awil I, in AD 695, Tikal captured Yuknoom Yich'aak K'ahk ("Jaguar Paw"), the ruler of Calakmul, and killed him. From that point on, Tikal regained some of its former importance and then returned to much of its Early Classic period prominence under the ruler Yik'in Chan K'awiil I from AD 734 to 746 and some of his successors (read "Peopling the Past: Maya Politics and Warfare"). Beginning in AD 794, however, Tikal's long history as a powerful state declined, and by AD 869, its ruling dynasty and political, social, and economic control over a relatively large region were gone.[106]

Peopling the Past

Maya Politics and Warfare

Maya cities can be described as primary centers that served as the ritual and political focus for the regions around them.[107] Like the city-states of Mesopotamia, however, each of the regions controlled by a primary center probably was not large. Warfare between these cities could be to gain territory and also to capture elite rulers who could be sacrificed during important ritual activities[108] (Figure 13.15). Capture and sacrifice of conquered kings would have been one way to gain prestige, reaffirm legitimacy, and reinforce loyalty of commoners. One interesting feature of Maya warfare is that Maya kings do not seem to have maintained standing armies, as did early politically complex societies elsewhere in the world.[109] This would have greatly reduced costs and presumably taxes on commoners. Instead, Maya elites served as the "core" army who gathered commoners together to fight when need required it. The two partial exceptions to this pattern appear to be Tikal and Calakmul, both of which created extensive networks of allies that they controlled. In this sense, both of these primary centers could be described as much larger regional polities, and it is one of the reasons that both are sometimes called states.

FIGURE 13.15
An image of a captive on incised bone from a burial at Tikal.

After the Classic Maya

Archaeologists traditionally mark the end of the Classic Maya period in the year AD 900, and as noted previously, the last stela with a carved date corresponds to AD 909. The "disappearance" of the Classic Maya states means that the complex political entities that characterized the lowlands Maya during the Classic period first underwent reorganization and then abandonment, and there was a shift of political power to the northern part of the Maya lowlands (the Yucatan Peninsula) and eventually to the Maya highlands. The factors that brought about the end of the Classic period were the result of a combination of several processes that together disrupted what had been a relatively successful long-term set of strategies.[110] Among these factors, the most frequently mentioned are the effects of increasing warfare between the cities, prolonged droughts that impacted agricultural yields in at least some parts of the Maya lowlands, unstable political alliances that resulted from conquests of subordinate cities, and a shift on the part of the commoners from support of the elites to a "loss of faith" in their leadership abilities and the ideologies that the elites promoted.[111] These types of processes are not so difficult to understand, and we can see analogous events in the modern world, such as the recent "Arab Spring" that has overthrown or modified the political structures of several countries across North Africa and the Middle East.

Terminal Classic and Postclassic Maya

The period from AD 900 to 1100 is known as the Terminal Classic, whereas the Postclassic period is from AD 1100 to 1524. During the Terminal Classic, the northern lowlands became politically important, as can be seen in the rise of the city of **Chichén Itzá** (see Figure 13.1) on the Yucatan Peninsula. This Maya capital was situated to take advantage of connections to trade and exchange networks tied into sea coast routes, and part of its success was related to a different type of political system and religious ideology than that which characterized the Classic Maya period, as well as its ability to conquer and control some of its neighboring cities.[112] The Chichén Itzá state gained its wealth from trade, including basic but important everyday goods such as salt and exotic items such as gold from Mexico and Panama. The importance of Chichén Itzá also is seen in the fact that it was the largest Maya city known, with the most ball courts (including the largest ever built), as well as important temples such as the Castillo and the Caracol, and the colonnaded Temple of the Warriors (colonnades were a Mexican architectural design feature incorporated into these Terminal Classic Maya buildings). Unlike other Maya cities, even during the Terminal Classic period, Chichén Itzá did not celebrate the deeds and events of individual elite rulers but seems instead to have had a political structure that involved a combination of several elites including dynastic rulers and military, religious, and merchant "power brokers." The sociocultural framework at Chichén Itzá has been described by some researchers as cosmopolitan, meaning that it represented ideologies that were more than local Maya traditions. These included its use of the feathered serpent deity (called K'uk'ulkan in the Maya area and Quetzalcoatl in Mexico) as its major religious figure (Figure 13.16).

During the Postclassic period, Chichén Itzá lost its political, economic, religious, and social power. Some of this loss resulted from a military conquest by the city of **Mayapan** (see Figure 13.1), which became the main capital in the Yucatan region for 250 years.[113] As a city, Mayapan was smaller than Chichén Itzá, but this worked to its advantage because it was easier to fortify and protect during battles, which became more frequent during the Postclassic period. Like Chichén Itzá, Mayapan's power was built on its control of commerce and its strategy of forcing subordinate elite rulers of allied cities and towns to live in Mayapan where they could be controlled by Mayapan's ruling dynasty.[114] The Mayapan state was defeated in AD 1441, and

Chichén Itzá a Terminal Classic period city that was a state-level political entity in the Maya lowlands of Mesoamerica. Its power was built on commerce, and it had strong ties to the Mexican region. Rather than being ruled by a single king, its political structure was based on several elites from royal dynasties, the military, merchants, and religious practitioners.

Mayapan a Postclassic period city and state in the Maya lowlands of Mesoamerica. It became powerful after defeating Chichén Itzá and was characterized by its control of lucrative trade.

FIGURE 13.16
The serpent deity at the base of a pyramid at Chichén Itzá in the Maya lowlands.

after this, there were a series of short-lived states. The Maya highlands during the Postclassic period were also subject to many military conflicts and had a number of small competing states, including the K'iche Maya.[115]

The Aztec Empire

During the Postclassic period in Mesoamerica, in addition to the Postclassic Maya, there were other important polities that existed. One of these was the **Aztec Empire** (AD 1428 to 1519; Figure 13.17). Various Aztlan groups began migrating into the Valley of Mexico in central Mexico sometime around AD 1200.[116] As migrants, they established their own settlements in an area that was already populated. These settlements grew rapidly and soon became towns and cities. Cities had ceremonial precincts characterized by twin-stair pyramids, an Aztec feature. The Aztlan migrants are thought either to have spoken Nahuatl (the Aztec language at the time of Spanish arrival) or to have adopted Nahuatl soon after their migrations into the Valley of Mexico. The cities grew into city states between which there were conflicts, just as we saw with the city states of the Classic Maya period.

Aztec Empire a late politically complex entity (AD 1428 to 1519) that was centered in the Valley of Mexico, where today's Mexico City is built. It consisted of what is known as the Triple Alliance and was defeated by the Spanish in AD 1521.

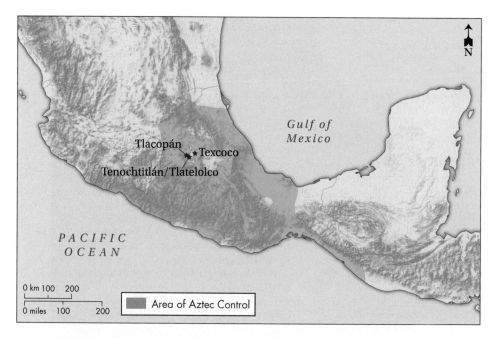

FIGURE 13.17
The Aztec Empire at its greatest extent, just prior to the arrival of the Spanish.

Mexica an Aztlan group that migrated into the Valley of Mexico in AD 1250. They established the city of Tenochtitlán (the eventual Aztec Empire capital) and became one of the most important groups in the Aztec Empire.

Tenochtitlán the Aztec Empire capital (now under/in Mexico City) in the Valley of Mexico. It was established in AD 1325 by the Aztlan group known as the Mexica.

One of the later (AD 1250) migrant Aztlan groups was the **Mexica**. The Mexica were valued as outstanding warriors and were used in armies by some of the existing city-states in their battles against others. Their relations with one of the city-states, however, soured when, according to mythological oral stories, they killed and flayed a princess sent to them to be worshipped as a goddess.[117] They were driven out of their homes and eventually settled on an island in a swampy area, which they chose based on an omen saying they should look for the place where an eagle was perched on a cactus. This locale became the city of **Tenochtitlán** (see Figure 13.17), which later was the capital of the Aztec Empire.

While Tenochtitlán was growing in size and population (AD 1325 to 1428), two city-states in the Valley of Mexico were rapidly expanding.[118] These were led by the Aztlan groups of the Tepanecs and the Acolhua. The Mexica allied themselves with the Tepanecs, becoming their subjects. Because of the outstanding warrior abilities of the Mexica, they were able to help the Tepanecs conquer ever increasing parts of the Valley of Mexico. During this process, the Mexica and their city of Tenochtitlán became politically important, to the point where they decided they needed a king as a ruler. To accomplish this, they created a marriage alliance with a royal dynasty at one of the city-states. This city-state (Culhuacan) had a royal dynasty that traced its roots to the Toltecs, an earlier city-state whose dynasties and warrior abilities were highly regarded by Aztlan groups. The Mexica thus quickly established a royal ruler for themselves, one with excellent legitimacy because of the possible link to the earlier Toltec dynasties.

In AD 1426, the powerful ruler of the Tepanec polity died. This resulted in battles for succession, which led to the establishment of the **Triple Alliance** in AD 1428, which was the foundation for the Aztec Empire.

Triple Alliance the basis of the Aztec Empire, it consisted of alliances between three city-states (Tenochtitlán, Texcoco, and Tlacopan). Eventually the Mexica of Tenochtitlan dominated the alliance.

The Triple Alliance

The Triple Alliance consisted of the city-states of Tenochtitlán, Texcoco, and Tlacopan (see Figure 13.17). It was a political agreement that combined military and economic efforts, much like alliances do today. If one was attacked, others came to their defense. Taxes from subjugated areas were divided up between the three members of the alliance. Marriages between ruling dynasties were arranged to cement relationships, with Aztec male royalty having several wives, and thus networks of relations across the Valley of Mexico, as well as with dynasties from other regions. The successes of the Triple Alliance meant that many people in the Valley of Mexico saw Tenochtitlán as a desirable place to live, and the population of the city grew as more people migrated there. Its rulers also had many major successes in conquering other city-states. One resulting outcome was that the Mexica became the dominant force in the Triple Alliance by AD 1502.

During the early years of the Triple Alliance, much effort was spent on consolidating power and control of the Valley of Mexico.[119] The next targets for conquest were regions outside the valley. In AD 1440, Motecuhzoma I ("Montezuma" I) became the ruler of the Aztec Empire. It was this ruler who established tight control over the Valley of Mexico. He accomplished this by making Mexica individuals the tax collectors and replacing the kings of some city-states with rulers whom the Mexica could easily control. His successors, including some of his sons and grandsons, continued to conquer and reconquer various regions, thus continually expanding the size of the Aztec Empire, which was second in size only to the Inka Empire of South America (see Chapter 14). In AD 1502, Motecuhzoma II came to the throne. He reorganized the government by staffing it with members of the Mexica nobles and is said to have ruled using terror rather than cooperation as a mechanism. Motecuhzoma II is the ruler encountered by the Spanish in AD 1519 (see later).

Aztec Trade and Exchange Networks

The Aztec system of trade and exchange was very well developed. They had a series of established markets that were organized within a hierarchy. This meant that most villages and small towns had markets that were open from time to time, while the larger city-state markets tended to be open every five days, and the **Tlatelolco** market (in the twin city to the capital city of Tenochtitlán; Figure 13.18) was open daily.[120] There was an enormous diversity of goods and foods in such large markets, with the stalls of the vendors organized by street. Each street/market area had only one type of commodity, much as we might (on a much smaller scale) think about how goods are arranged by aisles in modern grocery or department stores. A few of the

Tlatelolco the largest market in the Aztec Empire; it was in the twin city to the capital city of Tenochtitlán and was open on a daily basis.

FIGURE 13.18
A portion of Aztec Tlateloco (in Mexico City) where the city-state market was held.

Pochteca an Aztec merchant class that traveled internationally and within the Aztec Empire. They served as spies and traveled armed as warriors through the lands of enemies to set up trade and exchange relationships.

market places specialized in certain commodities such as slaves or dogs, or jewelry, while most others had a wide range of goods.[121]

Given the level of complexity of the market hierarchy and the scale of the market system in the Aztec Empire,[122] it is not surprising to find that one class of people who were quite important were the merchants. Many of these individuals operated on a regional system within the empire. The group of merchants we know the most about and who held the highest status below Aztec nobility were the **pochteca**.[123] These were merchants who operated internationally, that is, organizing trade and exchange expeditions to regions outside the Aztec Empire, as well as within the empire. They also served as spies because of their wide travels. *Pochteca* individuals traveled armed as warriors and were known to take captives and to battle with enemies when their routes took them through the lands of enemies of the empire.

While some of the economics of the Aztec market system were trading one type of commodity for another, the Aztec also used two types of goods as "money."[124] These were cotton textiles[125] and cacao beans (see earlier in the Classic Maya for the cacao beans beverage; wealthy Aztecs also used the beans for this beverage). The Aztecs established prices to be paid for certain items, for example, an egg from a turkey cost 3 cacao beans (based on a price list from early in the Spanish Colonial period). Cotton cloaks, which were made of different qualities of cotton and in several standard sizes, were used to purchase more expensive items, such as gold jewelry.

Aztec Social Life

Despite the fact that the Aztec Empire had a well-developed commercial system in its markets and some merchants became quite wealthy, social life was regulated by social classes.[126] In a manner similar to the Inka Empire (see Chapter 14), Aztec society used clothing as one means of distinguishing people of different social classes, ranks, and ethnicities.[127] For the most part, it was not possible to move from one social class into another. The one exception was in the military, where a warrior could achieve a noble title. This title was passed to their offspring. Otherwise, to be a member of the nobility (elites) in Aztec society, one had to be born into that social class. Such status thus was hereditary. Aztec nobility were wealthy, just as elites in most societies are. Their wealth was based on controlling taxes, land, and labor. Commoner families had to provide labor to the nobility, as did slaves. Being a slave in the Aztec Empire came about due to punishment or debt rather than birth into a hereditary social class. Children born to slaves were free individuals.

There were three types of noble residences: palaces on raised platforms that were used for residence and for administration, mansions, and pleasure palaces, including vast gardens for which laws decreed the right of the garden owners to grow certain plants.[128] The size of the palaces of the nobility depended on their rank within this hereditary social class. The higher the rank, the larger the palaces. Access to items indicating wealth also depended on a noble's rank. The highest rank within the nobility was the title of "great speakers" (*huey tlatoque*; we often substitute the term "emperor" when we discuss the Aztecs). Marriages were to other nobles, sometimes with a lower-ranked male noble marrying the daughter of a higher-ranked noble. Like elsewhere, Aztec nobility had a system of ritual exchanges and gift giving that helped cement their relationships.

Much of what we know about Aztec society comes from documentary sources. These are writings by the Aztecs and their descendants, Spanish accounts of the Aztecs, and detailed drawings of people in various art mediums.

Aztec Religion and Ritual

Aztec nobility maintained their position through ideology, ritual, and religion. An example of this is instilling the idea that everyone's destiny is decided by the gods.[129] Sentiments such as this help uphold "the way things are" and discourage people from attempting to change the existing social order. If we examine any of the major religions in the world today, for example, we see the power of ideas, such as that a person's deeds in life determine if they go to "heaven" or not.

Templo Mayor the major pyramid in the ceremonial precinct at the Aztec capital of Tenochtitlán. It had two temples at its top, one to the god Huitzilopochtli and the other to the god Tlaloc.

The Aztecs had a pantheon of gods and goddesses, some of which were borrowed from earlier Mesoamerican societies such as Teotihuacán (see earlier).[130] Priests had full-time duties to the temples for each of the gods, including performing rituals (such as bloodletting), managing temple economies, caretaking, teaching priesthood initiates, and keeping sacred books (priests were literate).[131] Two of the important Aztec gods were the Mexica god Huitzilopochtli (associated with sacrifice, warfare, death, and blood; Figure 13.19) and the central Mexico god Tlaloc (linked to fertility in agriculture, rain, and moisture).[132] Temples to these two gods were on top of the **Templo Mayor** pyramid in the ceremonial precinct at Tenochtitlán (the remains of which are mostly buried under

FIGURE 13.19
A stylized depiction of the Aztec (Mexica) god of war, Huitzilopochtli.

FIGURE 13.20
Part of the Aztec Templo Mayor (in Mexico City), showing an altar with carvings of skulls.

modern Mexico City; Figure 13.20). This precinct also had a ball court and temples to other Aztec gods, as well as a temple where the gods of conquered peoples were kept.[133] One interesting feature of the ceremonial area at Tenochtitlán was that it was walled.[134] This meant that while perhaps hundreds of people might be able to witness ceremonies there, massive numbers of people could not. In other city-states under Aztec rule, ceremonial precincts were not walled, thereby giving access to everyone.

Due to the worship of gods such as Huitzilopochtli, the themes of blood, war, and sacrifice were prominent in Aztec religion. One ritual was bloodletting, which priests performed on themselves. But just about everyone in Aztec society performed bloodletting on occasion, usually as a way to ask the gods for fertility (agricultural or human).[135] The type of ritual that many people today associate with the Aztec Empire, however, is heart and human sacrifice. The human sacrifices were most often captive warriors, and it was a great honor to be chosen to represent one of the gods to be sacrificed. Why were gods sacrificed? This practice simply repeated what the gods themselves had done (that is, they sacrificed themselves) in the myths associated with Aztec religion. One version of the ritual had the heart cut out of the living sacrificial victim at the top of the pyramid stairs, the body sent rolling down afterwards and then decapitated, and the head placed on a pole. Various other body parts were taken as trophies. Some accounts also mention cannibalism of some sacrificial victims, but this practice may be exaggerated in Spanish writings (there are no eyewitness accounts).[136]

While human sacrifices were common in many Mesoamerican polities, the Aztec Empire used this ritual far more often. It was, on the one hand, a way to appease the gods and presumably bring the sacrificers closer to the gods.[137] On the other hand, there were political benefits. If the Aztec performed such rituals when they had rulers from other city-states as guests, this sent a message about the power of the Aztec Empire. It also sent a message to the commoners, one that discouraged uprisings against the nobility.

Aztec Warfare and Violence

The Aztec Empire was centered on the Mexica city-state of Tenochtitlán but, as we saw above, included two other city-states in its Triple Alliance. Each of these city-states conquered others, creating a system of dominant and subordinate cities. Subordinate cities paid tribute to the nobility and rulers (including the emperor) of the Triple Alliance cities. Some of the warfare conducted by the Aztec Empire thus was concerned with gaining additional sources of tribute (more cities, towns, and villages), as well as with enforcing tribute payments from subordinates who might be refusing.[138] Other reasons included harm done to the Aztec *pochteca* spies or ambassadors by other polities, or that the Aztecs felt that they had been insulted.

Although the Aztec conquered other areas, they did not have a military philosophy of leaving Aztec warriors to guard those places, nor did they often fortify locales (although fortifications were present along some borders, such as with the Tarascans to the west).[139] These fortified sites often were on hilltops and without warriors unless a war was on-going at the time. One reason why warriors were not left in conquered areas or full-time in border fortified sites is that the Aztec did not have a standing army. Armies were raised from the nobility and commoners only when warfare was anticipated.

In addition to wars fought to subdue conquered areas that decided to no longer pay tribute or to avenge harm to Aztec merchants or ambassadors, the Aztecs also fought wars of attrition (slow destruction).[140] In one case, attrition was relatively rapid in that the Aztec army would kill any and all of the opposing army during battles and would then proceed to destroy their cities. In the other case, attrition was much slower because the goal was to capture warriors who could be used as sacrifices; this was called a "flower war." While a number of warriors died on the battlefield, it was not a complete slaughter. Interestingly, the flower wars were prearranged for specific dates and places, rather than being surprise attacks.

Although the Aztec Empire was quite successful overall in many of its warfare encounters, they did not always win. Despite the fact that they fought on many occasions with the Tarascans to the west, for example, the Aztec never conquered them. Given that the Aztec Empire did not have standing armies and its tribute-paying conquered polities were not always happy to submit to Aztec rule, there were chinks in the armor of the Aztec Empire that could be successfully exploited by its enemies.

Arrival of the Spanish

It is difficult to know what ultimately would have happened politically in the Maya and Aztec regions of Mesoamerica. Would a single city or state ultimately have controlled the lowlands or even both the lowlands and the highlands in the Maya area? Or is it more likely that the pattern of competing smaller states would have continued? Would the Aztec Empire have expanded even further? The reason we cannot answer these questions is because of the disruption to Mesoamerican polities caused by the arrival of the Spanish in the Aztec region in AD 1519 and in the Maya area in AD 1524. In military campaigns prior to these dates, the Spanish allied themselves with various local groups and managed to defeat the Aztec Empire in the Basin of Mexico in AD 1521.[141] By AD 1524, the Spanish, in combination with Mexican warriors, defeated the highlands Maya states, and then from AD 1527 to 1546, the Spanish and their allies managed to subjugate nearly all of the Maya lowlands.[142] The Spanish in these expeditions were few in number; after all, it was only small groups of them who made the journey across the Atlantic to the New World. But they managed to use the enemies of various Mesoamerican polities as their allies in conquering these states, and they had superior killing power both in the technologies they brought (guns and gunpowder) and in the effects of Old World diseases such as smallpox, to which Mesoamerican people had no natural immunity. The documentation of Maya and Aztec life, including their religious ceremonies and other customs, by the Spanish are valuable historical records that can be used to better understand the archaeological record. However, the Spanish accounts are not unbiased, and their descriptions of many Maya and Aztec customs as "barbaric" must be tempered by the fact that the Spanish had a different cultural perspective and were on a mission to bring Catholicism to "pagans." In addition, the Spanish were extremely brutal in their treatment of subjugated Maya and Aztec elites and commoners. In some cases, we can gain a different perspective about the Aztec and Maya through the accounts provided by native and mestizo (mixed ancestry) sources (read "Further Reflections: Historical Documents, the Maya, and the Aztecs").

Further Reflections

Historical Documents, the Maya, and the Aztecs

There is an old saying that history is written by the conquerors. This has many implications for understanding the past. The Spanish, for example, not only wrote about the empires and people they conquered in the Americas, they also destroyed native documents such as many of the Maya codices. By doing so, they eliminated some of the sources of information about Maya ways of life and views of the world around them. It also means that anyone who reads the Spanish accounts of the Maya is seeing the Maya filtered through Spanish biases and perspectives about life. This also is true for Spanish descriptions of the Aztecs.

Fortunately, we still have access to native accounts of their societies that help mitigate what the Spanish wrote. In the case of the Maya, these are from the surviving codices, writings on stone monuments, and oral traditions of descendant communities. For the Aztec, there are native descriptions of preconquest and conquest period lifeways, as well as oral traditions. One example of a discrepancy between Spanish and native beliefs is how the actions of the Aztec ruler Motecuhzoma II are interpreted. In the writings of Hernán Cortés (who is credited with conquering the Aztec), Motecuhzoma II voluntarily hands over the Aztec Empire to the king in Spain.[143] He is thus seen as "weak." In the context of the belief systems of the Aztec, however, Motecuhzoma II actively turns over his empire because he believes that Cortés is a legitimate representative of the true ruler of Tenochtitlán. This belief was based on the story of the Toltecs, from whom the Aztecs claimed descent. When the Toltec empire fell, its people dispersed but were led by a ruler who left and later returned. When he returned, his people no longer accepted his rule, so he left again. When the Spanish came into the Aztec Empire, Motecuhzoma II interpreted this as the return of the Toltec lord (represented by Cortés). In Motecuhzoma II's native perspective, he was expected to relinquish his rule to that of the true ruler. Was Motecuhzoma II therefore "weak"?

Summary

- The agricultural foundation of Mesoamerica was maize, squash, and beans, all of which were domesticated during the Archaic period.

- Private control or "ownership" of agricultural surpluses appears to be present just after 2000 cal BC.

- Mesoamerica was characterized by several regions where early politically complex entities developed over time. These included the Gulf Coast lowlands, the Valley of Oaxaca, the Basin of Mexico, and the Maya lowlands and highlands. Contact between these regions is seen in their trade and exchange networks.

- Groups known as the Olmec lived in the Gulf Coast lowlands. They built monumental architecture and monumental stone sculptures of elite rulers. No single Olmec city politically controlled the entire region; instead, the pattern was for one city at a time to be the most important center. These included San Lorenzo and La Venta.

- During the Early and Middle Preclassic periods, several Maya cities in the highlands and lowlands gained prominence. Like the Olmec, the Maya cities had monumental architecture and certain cities were centers associated with a hierarchy of smaller centers and rural villages.

- Evidence for elite individuals and families is found at sites in the Valley of Oaxaca. Initially there were several important centers in different parts of the valley. Beginning about 500 cal BC, power shifted to Monte Albán, which consolidated its control over the valley in 30 to 20 cal BC. This became the Zapotec state.

- In the Basin of Mexico, similar processes were underway, with large cities, monumental architecture, and long-distance trade and exchange. One important city was Teotihuacán, which grew in size and reputation beginning in AD 100. Teotihuacán may have played a role in conquering or influencing some Maya ruling dynasties during the Early Classic period.

- During the Late Preclassic period, Maya cities in the highlands and lowlands continued to be important centers. However, the highlands region declined by the Early Classic period. Instead, cities in the lowlands, such as Tikal and Calakmul, emerged as state-level polities. No single city, however, ever controlled the entire Maya region.

- Classic period lowlands Maya cities were primary centers associated with secondary centers and smaller towns, villages, and rural settlements. Each city had monumental architecture including temples, palaces, plazas, causeways, and pyramids.

- The Maya developed a writing system using glyphs. Researchers have been able to decipher this script, which was used to record the lives and exploits of Maya rulers, describe religious stories of the gods and goddesses, and create several types of calendars.

- Like their predecessors and contemporaries, Maya cities were engaged in long-distance trade networks that brought jade, feathers, obsidian, basalt, salt, marine shells, and other resources to craft workshops and markets.

- Maya kings were considered divine and genealogically linked to the gods. As elite members of society, they had access to exotic goods, better and more varied foods, and surpluses that could be used to "fund" monumental constructions, crafts, and the military. Their elite status also can be seen in their burials, which had lavish grave goods. Kings were buried under temples.

- As a society, the Maya were characterized by considerable amounts of warfare and violence. These were efforts to conquer other Maya cities and allies of competing primary centers. War captives were sacrificed, and the stelae recording their rulers' lives in the conquered cities were destroyed.

- Beginning about AD 900, the Classic Maya "disappear," as does their writing system, but other cities in the Maya lowlands rose to prominence. These cities, such as Chichén Itzá and Mayapan, were based on the wealth created by trade and exchange networks. They also engaged in warfare with various lowlands cities, including each other.

- Migrants to the Valley of Mexico in the AD 1200s included Aztlan groups, one of which was the Mexica. The Mexica were fierce warriors and soon established alliances with other groups based their facility to win battles.

- After the Mexica's activities soured their relationships with some of the Valley of Mexico polities, they relocated to a swampy area where they built what would become their capital, Tenochtitlán.

- In AD 1428, Tenochtitlán allied itself with the city-states of Texcoco and Tlacopan. This became the Triple Alliance and was the foundation for what became the Aztec Empire when Tenochtitlán assumed prominence in the alliance.

- The economic basis of the Aztec Empire was not only its agricultural products but also its extensive market system used both within the empire and with polities outside of the Valley of Mexico. The *pochteca* were high-status merchants who traveled internally and internationally and acted as spies for the empire.

- Aztec society was highly stratified, and, for the most part, there was no upper mobility (you remained in the social class into which you were born). Elites in Aztec society controlled vast wealth accumulated from their estates and from taxes and tribute payments. They oversaw the monumental construction resulting in pyramids, temples, plaza areas, and other architecture in the cities.

- Aztec religion and ritual, like other Mesoamerican polities, had a pantheon of gods and goddesses. Everyone from elites to commoners practiced bloodletting as one ritual. Major rituals involved the sacrifice of humans (often capture warriors).

- The Aztec Empire engaged in many periods of warfare with their neighbors. In some cases, this led to an expansion of the boundaries of the empire. They were not always successful, however, as they were never able to conquer the Tarascans who lived to the west of the empire.

- The ultimate trajectory for the Maya and Aztec polities will never be known because their indigenous development was interrupted by the arrival of the Spanish in AD 1519 to 1524 and the subjugation of these regions by the Spanish between AD 1521 and 1546.

Endnotes

1. Webster 2011.
2. But see Piperno et al. 2009: 5023, who argue that the types of maize phytoliths found indicate use of maize kernels at Archaic period sites such as Xihuatoxtla Shelter in southwestern Mexico, rather than teosinte stalks or seeds.
3. Ranere et al. 2009; Piperno et al. 2009.
4. Kennett et al. 2010; Piperno et al. 2007; Pohl et al. 2007.
5. Benz 2001; Piperno and Flannery 2001.
6. Adams 2005: 45; Brush 1965.
7. Flannery 2002.
8. Flannery and Marcus 2000: 30; Rosenswig et al. 2015.
9. Adams 2005: 54; Coe and Diehl 1980b: 147–149.
10. Adams 2005: 60–61; Coe and Diehl 1980a: 50–126; not everyone agrees that San Lorenzo was as large as 690 hectares; for example, Spencer and Redmond 2004: 185 suggest a size of 150 hectares, and Flannery et al. 2005: 11222 also raise questions about the large size estimate for San Lorenzo.
11. Harer 2009: 34.
12. Flannery and Marcus 2000: 4; Marcus 2004.
13. Adams 2005: 65–71.
14. Gillespie and Volk 2014: fly-over video clips of Complex A at La Venta can be found at: http://dx.doi.org/10.1016/j.daach.2014.06.001 (accessed July 20, 2018).
15. Lowe 1989: 56.
16. Rust and Sharer 1988.
17. Symonds 2000.
18. Rust and Sharer 1988.
19. Flannery and Marcus 2000: 3; Hirth et al. 2013; Joyce and Henderson 2001: 20.
20. Hirth et al. 2013.
21. Flannery et al. 2005: 11221–11222; Love 2007: 288.
22. Flannery and Marcus 2000.
23. Adams 2005: 87–90; Love 2007; Marcus 2003; Rosenswig 2006.
24. Pohl et al. 1996: 366.
25. Inomata et al. 2013.
26. Marcus 2003: 80.
27. Sharer 2009: 51.
28. Hansen 1998: 56–63.
29. Estrada-Belli 2011: 52; Hansen 1998: 74–75; Marcus 2003:
30. Hansen 2005: 57.
31. Kidder et al. 1977; Valdés and Wright 2004.
32. Bove 2005; Love 2007: 290–291.
33. Marcus 1989; 2004: 361–363.
34. Recent excavations at el Palenque, near San José Mogote, show that the earliest palace in the Valley of Oaxaca was built here in 300 to 100 BC (Redmond and Spencer 2017). The temple area at el Palenque was destroyed in 100 BC to AD 200, as was the palace.
35. Marcus 2008: 260–261; Spencer and Redmond 2004: 175–184.
36. Marcus and Flannery 1996.
37. Redmond and Spencer 2006; although the earliest known temple is from the Maya site of El Palenque at 300 cal BC (Redmond and Spencer 2017).
38. Flannery and Marcus 2000: 29.
39. Adams 2005: 83–84.
40. Flannery and Marcus 2000: 14.
41. Adams 2005: 114–115; Heizer and Bennyhoff 1958.

42. Adams 2005: 247.

43. Carballo 2016; Plunket and Uruñuela 2010.

44. Sugiyama et al. 2013. Ritual caches are associated with the construction of the Pyramids of the Sun and the Moon at Teotihuacan. These contain sacrificed humans, animals, and symbolic artifacts. Based on stable isotope studies of the animal bones, many wild species were held in captivity and fed on maize prior to being sacrificed (Sugiyama et al. 2015). Others had bone pathologies from being tethered. The wild animals include golden eagles, wolves, puma, and jaguars.

45. Adams 2005: 219–222; Spencer and Redmond 204: 191–193.

46. For example, Estrada-Belli 2011: 54–66; Sharer 2005: 51–59. See also the entire issue of *Expedition* 54(1) from 2012 for public-oriented articles on the Maya.

47. Marcus 2003: 81–82.

48. Sharer 2009: 52.

49. Sharer 2009: 53–54.

50. Marcus 2003: 82.

51. Hansen 1998: 76–77.

52. Spencer and Redmond 2004: 188–189.

53. Hansen 1998: 77–81; Sharer 2005: 57.

54. Estrada-Belli 2001: 84–110; Hansen 1998: 81–82; Marcus 2003: 85.

55. Estrada-Belli 2011: 64–65; Hansen et al. 2008.

56. https://news.nationalgeographic.com/2018/02/maya-laser-lidar-guatemala-pacunam/ (accessed July 21, 2018).

57. Coe 1990.

58. Coe and McGinn 1963; Estrada-Belli 2011: 56; Martin 2003.

59. Martin and Grube 2008: 26; Sharer 2005: 65.

60. Marcus 2003: 87–94; Sharer 2005: 63.

61. Houston 2000: 142; Sharer 2005: 228–232; see also the dictionary for Maya glyphs available at http://www.famsi.org/mayawriting/calvin/index.html (accessed July 20, 2018).

62. Houston 2000: 164; Sharer 2005: 239.

63. Baron 2018; Houston 2000: 173; Thornton and Emery 2016..

64. Bower 2016.

65. Houston 2000: 154.

66. Sharer 2009: 228.

67. Sharer 2009: 242–244.

68. Sharer 2009: xvii–xix.

69. Sharer 2009: 144–155.

70. Anderson and Hirth 2009.

71. Powis et al. 2007.

72. Hurst et al. 2002.

73. Reents-Buder 2006.

74. Taube 2003.

75. Smyth 2008.

76. See Pyburn 2008 for a discussion of consumption of trade commodities by both elites and lower classes.

77. Sharer 2009: 168–169, 179–181.

78. Blackmore 2011.

79. Somerville et al. 2013.

80. Sharer 2009: 173–176.

81. Martin and Grube 2008: 32–33, 110–111.

82. Martin and Grube 2008: 43.

83. Marcus 2003: 102.

84. Feinman 2001: 161–164; Lucero 1999: 231–240; Rice 2009.

85. Rice 2009.

86. Sharer 2009: 194–199.

87. Gillespie and Joyce 1997: 198–206.

88. Sharer 2009: 206–209, 211–216.

89. Grube 1992; Houston and Stuart 1996.

90. Haines et al. 2008.

91. Sanchez 2005.

92. Baudez 2000.

93. Joyce 1996: 182–185.

94. Sanchez 2005.

95. Sharer 2009: 176–177.

96. Carleton et al. 2017.

97. Houston 2000: 171.

98. Puleston and Callender 1967; Webster et al. 2007.

99. Webster 2000: 73; although see Golden et al. 2008 and Zorich (2011) for evidence of stone walls and nearby fortified settlements used to defend state territory boundaries for Piedras Negras and Yaxchilan in Guatemala. It also is possible that more fortification features will be found once LiDAR is used more extensively in the Maya region (see web link in Endnote 56).

100. Webster 2000: 75–76.

101. Marcus 2003: 90; Martin and Grube 2008: 28–33.

102. Sharer 2009: 67.

103. Wright 2012: 349.
104. Martin and Grube 2008: 38–40; Sharer 2005: 71.
105. Martin and Grube 2008: 42–50.
106. Sharer 2009: 79.
107. Webster 2000: 86.
108. Lucero 1999: 243.
109. Webster 2000: 106–111.
110. Masson 2012.
111. Dahlin 2002; Hoggarth et al. 2017; Inomata et al. 2017; Kennett and Beach 2013; Marcus 2003: 104–106; Peterson and Haug 2005; Rice 2007; Webster 2002. See Carleton et al. 2014 for an alternative view regarding the effects of droughts on the Classic Maya.
112. Sharer 2009: 100–106.
113. Sharer 2009: 112–116.
114. The internal politics of Mayapan were not without conflict, as seen in a mass grave with burned and butchered individuals (probably elites) that dates to the period between AD 1302 and 1400 (Paris et al. 2017).
115. Sharer 2009: 122–124.
116. Beekman and Christensen 2003; Smith 2012: 38.
117. Van Tuerenhout 2005: 68.
118. Smith 2012: 46–49.
119. Smith 2012: 49–59.
120. Van Tuerenhout 2005: 85–87.
121. Smith 2012:109-114.
122. Smith 2010.
123. Smith 2012: 114-116.
124. Smith 2012: 116–119.
125. Baron 2018.
126. Smith 2012: 134–135.
127. Nichols and Evans 2009.
128. Evans 2004.
129. Smith 2012: 150.
130. Nichols 2016.
131. Smith 2012: 215–219.
132. Smith 2012: 201–205.
133. Smith 2012: 225–232.
134. Sanders 2008.
135. Graulich 2000; Smith 2010: 219–225.
136. Isaac 2005.
137. Graulich 2000.
138. Van Tuerenhout 2005: 158–160.
139. Hassig 1988; Van Tuerenhout 2005: 168–170.
140. Hassig 1988: 225; Van Tuerenhout 2005: 170–172.
141. Adams 2005: 388.
142. Sharer 2009: 127–129.
143. Oudijk and Castañeda de la Paz 2017.

CHAPTER 14

Andean South America and the Inka Empire

ABOVE: Inka emperor's estate at Machu Picchu, Peru.

The Andes Mountains region, consisting of parts of modern Peru and Bolivia, as well as parts of Chile, Argentina, and Ecuador, was under the control of the Inka Empire, which is one example of a chronologically late politically complex polity. The appearance of this empire did not occur in a vacuum. Rather, the Inka (also spelled Inca) were preceded by a long prehistory of other powerful and politically complex entities, such as the Wari and Tiwanaku empires, as well as the Moché states and the earlier Chavín Horizon, which is known for its widely shared artistic motifs (read "Timeline: The Andean Region"). In this chapter we will briefly examine a number of the early societies that characterized the Andean region and some of the Peruvian coast, as well as their agricultural foundations. In the coastal areas of Peru and Ecuador, as well as the Andean highlands, there were a number of different wild plants and animals that eventually became domesticates. Some, such as cotton, were economically important because they were used to make textiles. Maize appeared relatively early in South America, being introduced from the Mesoamerican region (see Chapter 13). It was an important food crop and was used to make a beverage that was key in ritual feasting. The Inka Empire emerged from this background to become one of the most significant polities of South America. Unlike several of the other politically complex societies that we examined in previous chapters, however, the Inka and their predecessors left no record using written symbols. Instead, there was a knotted cord system used as a device to keep track of economic and administrative information and quite possibly narratives that were sent as letters (see "The Nonwritten Record"). Early Spanish accounts also provide some insights. For all its magnificence and power, the Inka Empire was relatively short lived, lasting less than 100 years. It was overcome by a series of events, some of which were associated with the arrival of the Spanish.

Early Food Production

South American Archaic period groups had a highly diverse set of landscape habitats, with Pacific and Atlantic coastal regions, tropical forests and jungles, deserts, and massive mountains such as the Andes. People living in these areas positioned their settlements to take advantage of different zones—the coast, loma (fog oases), and mountains.[1] The abundance of resources from these ecological zones helped create a situation in which people might have been able to live year-round. One example is **Site 80** in coastal Ecuador[2] (Figure 14.2). Near this site were mangrove swamps, lagoons, salt marshes, the sea coast, and rivers, all of which yielded important food resources including crabs, clams, oysters, and mussels, as well as sea catfish, sharks, and sea bass. People here hunted rabbits, deer, squirrels, and peccary (a type of wild pig).

    These Archaic period groups lived during what are archaeologically called the Early and Middle Preceramic periods. Their subsistence economy was based on the use of wild food resources, as well as squash and maize, by 6000 to 4800 cal BC.[3] In the Andean highlands, Archaic period hunter–gatherer–foragers in the Early and Middle Preceramic periods focused one of their economic strategies on camelids (the vicuña and guanaco). Archaeological research has documented a long-term shift in the hunting and use of these animals, a shift that led to the domesticated forms, the llama (from the guanaco) and alpaca (from the vicuña). In the period from 9000 to 7500 cal BC, bones of camelids comprise 50% of the faunal assemblage at sites.[4] From 7500 to 3300 cal BC, camelid bones reach 70%, and by the Late Preceramic period (3300 to 1000 cal BC), they comprise 85 to 100% of the assemblages. This indicates that people intensified their strategies for hunting and for capturing and controlling these animals. This control was likely a form of protected herding; there

Site 80 an Archaic period site in coastal Ecuador in South America, where hunter–gatherer–forager groups exploited both marine and land food resources. They also had small gardens where they grew domesticated maize and squash.

Timeline: The Andean Region

As noted in the text, the Inka Empire was the successor to a number of earlier, important polities (Figure 14.1).

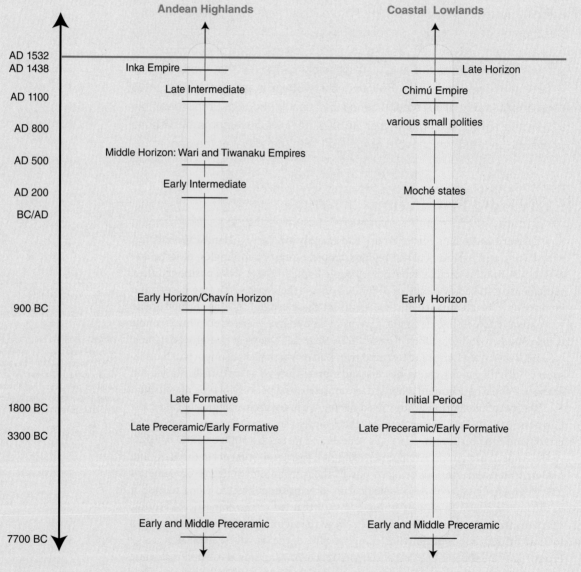

Andean Highlands   **Coastal Lowlands**

	Andean Highlands	Coastal Lowlands
AD 1532		
AD 1438	Inka Empire	Late Horizon
AD 1100	Late Intermediate	Chimú Empire
AD 800		various small polities
AD 500	Middle Horizon: Wari and Tiwanaku Empires	
AD 200	Early Intermediate	Moché states
BC/AD		
900 BC	Early Horizon/Chavín Horizon	Early Horizon
1800 BC	Late Formative	Initial Period
3300 BC	Late Preceramic/Early Formative	Late Preceramic/Early Formative
7700 BC	Early and Middle Preceramic	Early and Middle Preceramic

FIGURE 14.1
Timeline for Andean and Pacific coastal South America. Red line indicates arrival of the Spanish.

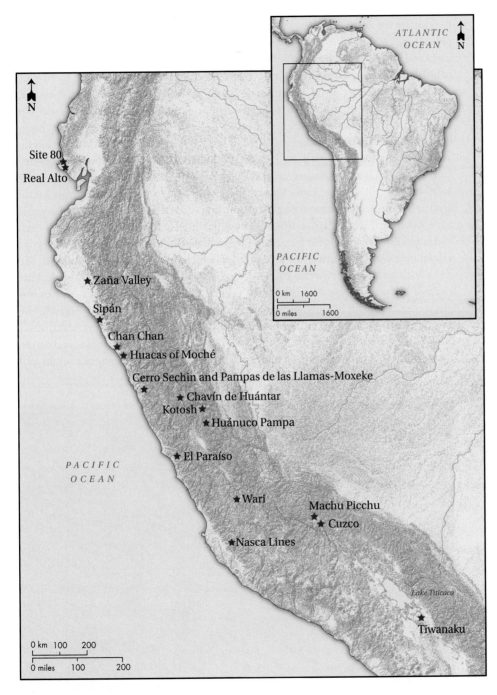

N

ATLANTIC
OCEAN

PACIFIC
OCEAN

0 km   1600
0 miles   1600

N

Site 80
Real Alto

Zaña Valley

Sipán

Chan Chan
★ Huacas of Moché

Cerro Sechin and Pampas de las Llamas-Moxeke
★ Chavín de Huántar
Kotosh ★
★ Huánuco Pampa

★ El Paraíso

PACIFIC
OCEAN

★ Wari

Machu Picchu
★
★ Cuzco

★ Nasca Lines

Lake Titicaca

★ Tiwanaku

0 km 100   200
0 miles   100   200

FIGURE 14.2
South American sites mentioned in the text.

is evidence for corrals at some sites. The domesticated forms (llama and alpaca) are present by 2200 to 1000 cal BC. Llama and alpaca were important not only for their meat and hair for weaving into clothing but also because they became the main beast of burden for transporting heavy loads over long distances (see "Resource Networks, Trade, and Exchange") and were used in rituals in several South American societies.

Management of animals that led in some cases to domesticated forms was not the only food-production strategy of hunter–gatherer–foragers in the Andean highlands. In some areas they were actively engaged in low levels of food production involving plants such as squash by 8500 cal BC, peanuts, manioc, and quinoa (grain) by 6700 cal BC, and potatoes around 5000 cal BC; they were growing cotton by 4300 cal BC.[5] Sites in the **Zaña Valley** (see Figure 14.2) and its tributaries in northern Peru are especially interesting for examining these strategies.[6] These settlements have dwellings, small garden areas, storage facilities, stone-lined mounds of dirt, and small ditches/canals for irrigating garden plots (Figure 14.3). Some of the crops grown here were not native to the highlands, which means that people living in the Zaña Valley and its tributaries had wide-reaching exchange or social networks that enabled them to import and then grow several of these plants. Peanuts, for example, were likely from the lowland areas of Bolivia/Argentina/Paraguay/Brazil to the east, whereas squash and cotton might have been obtained from the coastal areas of Peru/Ecuador. The groups in the Zaña Valley, however, were hunter–gatherer–foragers, although because they had garden plots, some archaeologists might call

Zaña Valley a region in the Andes Mountains in Peru in South America. Archaic period sites here have evidence for hunter–gatherer–forager groups who grew cotton, coca, and peanuts and who had begun to invest in the building of small, village-like settlements.

FIGURE 14.3
An unexcavated house structure from a Preceramic period site in the Zaña Valley, Peru.

them horticulturalists (gardeners). This term suggests somewhat less overall time spent in crop production than is typically assumed for people we identify in the archaeological record as agriculturalists. However, the agricultural cycle involved in gardening (including management of canals), along with rituals and ceremonies at a Zaña Valley site with mounds,[7] indicates that these groups were developing social strategies that eventually led to differences in status and social roles between people and neighboring groups.

Late Preceramic Period

The interval from 3300 to 1800 cal BC is the Late Preceramic period (also called the Cotton Preceramic or Early Formative period). In the coastal regions of Ecuador and Peru, villagers at **Real Alto** and other Ecuadoran settlements (see Figure 14.2) during the **Valdiva period** had maize. Their diet also included arrowroot, jack beans, squash, manioc, and chili peppers.[8] Among the nonedible domesticated plants was cotton, which could be made into textiles for clothing as well as other types of cloth. By 2800 cal BC, a number of these Valdiva period coastal sites, including Real Alto, became ritual or ceremonial centers with large mounds, plazas, evidence for feasting, and trash areas.[9] There were large and small dwellings for the people who lived at Real Alto, suggesting that there were differences in status or social roles. Extensive use of maize by Late Preceramic groups in the Norte Chico area of central coastal Peru also has been documented.[10]

By 2000 cal BC, there were a number of coastal and near coastal sites with monumental construction. The inland site of **El Paraíso** (see Figure 14.2) in Peru had a stone-built series of structures that formed a U shape with a plaza in the center.[11] These structures and plaza covered 58 hectares (143 acres). Smaller structures also were present. Some of the rooms in these buildings had floors painted red, grinding stones with red pigment on them, colorful bird feathers (including evidence for bird pens), and net bags containing rocks, figurines, and tree branches. The range of materials recovered from the rooms suggests activities related to rituals, although there also was abundant evidence for everyday activities. El Paraíso was inhabited for several hundred years based on subsistence resources gathered from nearby marshlands, lomas, the sea, and the growing of some crops such as maize to a limited degree.[12] Its monumental construction suggests that groups there were engaged in increasingly complex social relationships. Although there are other sites in this region with U-shape ceremonial areas, indicating a widely shared set of traditions, these Late Preceramic period coastal and inland groups do not appear to have been a single political unit.

In the Andean highlands, Late Preceramic period groups were growing chili peppers, quinoa, arrowroot, manioc, squash, jack beans, and maize, as well as potatoes and cotton.[13] In addition to herding strategies centered on camelids, they domesticated guinea pigs, which were raised for food.[14] Like their contemporaries in the coastal and lowland inlands, many of the Andean highland societies were constructing monumental architecture. One of the best known examples is that of the **Kotosh Religious Tradition**. This is named after the site of **Kotosh** (see Figure 14.2)

Real Alto a Late Preceramic site in coastal Ecuador (South America) with evidence for maize, squash, and manioc agriculture. Cotton also was grown.

Valdiva Period an interval during the Late Preceramic period in coastal Ecuador (South America). Some sites have evidence for ritual or ceremonial constructions (mounds and plazas).

El Paraíso a Late Preceramic period site situated inland from the coastal region in Peru in South America. It has a large U-shape architectural layout interpreted as a ceremonial complex. The central portion of the U-shape area was a large plaza.

Kotosh Religious Tradition a shared set of architectural features and images (for example, a serpent painted on a staircase leading into a temple) in the Andean highlands of South America, which are interpreted as a widely shared set of religious beliefs.

Kotosh a Late Preceramic site in the Andean highlands of Peru in South America. It has 100 temples, many of which were built on top of each other.

FIGURE 14.4
The crossed hands from a temple at Kotosh, Peru.

Casma Valley a Peruvian coastal valley system (South America) with several large sites during the Initial Period. These sites have U-shape architecture, pyramids, plazas, residential areas, and military theme images.

Pampas de las Llamas-Moxeke an Initial Period site in the Casma Valley of Peru (South America). It had pyramids, plazas, administrative buildings, and a residential area.

in Peru, which had mounds and a series of superimposed temples.[15] There were as many as 100 of these temples just at Kotosh. The Temple of the Crossed Hands there was a relatively small structure (81 square meters [872 square feet] high by 2 meters [6.5 feet] high), but it had typical Kotosh artistic and architectural motifs. These included a white serpent that was painted on the stairway leading to the temple, a red painted plastered entrance, interior wall niches, a central, circular fire pit in the floor, and a pair of hands sculpted out of clay that were positioned just below a large wall niche (Figure 14.4). These types of architectural details are found at other highland sites and support the idea of a shared religious or ritual tradition that differed from what people were doing at the coastal and near coastal sites.

Initial Period

The Initial period began about 1800 cal BC and was a time during which sites became much larger, with even greater investments in construction of monuments and increasingly complex relationships between sites.[16] Although some archaeologists suggest that some of the first states emerged during this period, not everyone agrees. There were widely shared architectural traditions and motifs, but it is difficult to find evidence that suggests that only one or two sites were controlling larger regions. In the Peruvian coastal and near coastal areas, for instance, there were a number of important sites in the **Casma Valley**, including Cerro Sechin and Pampa de las Llamas-Moxeke (see Figure 14.2). These had large U-shape structures that included stone- and adobe-built terraced pyramids, as well as large plazas and residential buildings. At Cerro Sechin there was a series of carved basalt scenes around the pyramid wall. These show military themes, such as decapitation of captives, severed arms and legs, and victorious warriors, which might reflect mythological events. This interpretation results from the fact that there were no defensive walls indicating potential for conflicts at the Casma Valley sites.[17] At **Pampa de las Llamas-Moxeke**, the orientations of two enormous pyramid/platform mounds, plazas, more than 100 buildings (interpreted as administrative), and a large residential area suggest a planned layout[18] (Figure 14.5). One of the pyramid mounds had an ornamented band about 10 meters (32 feet) above the ground, where it would have been easily seen by people. The ornamentation included geometric designs, as well as enormous heads and clay sculptures of individuals, some of whom held two-headed snakes with forked tongues. These may have been important motifs related to rituals and other ceremonial activities.

The architectural style that used U-shape monuments also was typical in areas of the Andean highlands, including at Chavín de Huántar (see "Early Horizon") in the Central Highlands.[19] Farther south in the highlands, in the Lake Titicaca Basin region, other societies also were constructing monuments and administrative buildings. These included large sunken courts, stone-built temples, and buildings constructed on

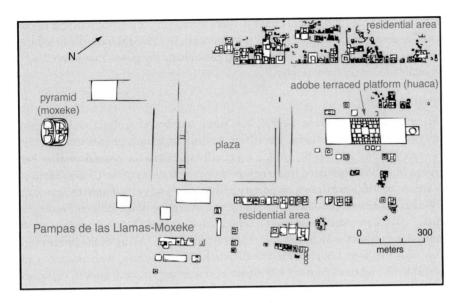

FIGURE 14.5
A stylized plan view of the settlement layout at Pampas de las Llamas-Moxeke in the Casma Valley, Peru (after Pozorski and Pozorski 1993, Figure 2).

top of platforms.[20] There is some suggestion that over time the ceremonies held in the sunken courts may have shifted from being open to most of the people at these sites to being more restricted. Restricting access to rituals may indicate that there were social distinctions between people at these sites and the development of groups or individuals who may have held a more "elite-like" social/political role.

Before the Inka

Archaeological evidence indicates that many areas within the coastal and highlands areas were engaged in large-scale monument building that required planning and organization of labor by the Late Preceramic period. Some of these architectural styles were shared between neighboring sites (and sometimes more widely between coast and highlands), and the same can occasionally be said for some of the artistic motifs, as with the Kotosh Religious Tradition. The coastal and near coastal sites with monument building, such as those in the Casma Valley, however, went into decline after 900 to 600 cal BC. In the highlands region, on the other hand, the period after 900 cal BC witnessed an intensification of monument building and artistic motifs. This is seen in the widely shared ideology of the Chavín Horizon during the Early Horizon period and then the increasingly complex political and social structures of the Moché states in the Early Intermediate period, followed by the development of the state-level polities of Wari and Tiwanaku during the Middle Horizon period. During the following Late Intermediate period, there were many small states in this region, as well as the Chimú Empire on the Peruvian coast. In the highlands, the Late Intermediate period was when the Inka begin to consolidate the power that would lead to the establishment of their empire.

Early Horizon

During the Early Horizon period, the most widely recognized archaeological entity is the **Chavín Horizon**, a northern Andean highlands phenomenon in Peru between 900 and 200 cal BC, which eventually spread to the coastal areas of Peru (Figure 14.6). Widely shared imagery was one of the features of the Chavín Horizon. Its artistic motifs were drawn on pottery and painted and carved onto temple walls, as well as made into pendants. This imagery is evocative of the different ecological areas—coasts, tropical forests, and mountains—that these South American societies lived in and with which they had trade relationships.[21] Many of the images were of animals that were not native to the Chavín highlands region, such as jaguars and crocodile-like figures (Figure 14.7). There also were eagles, bats, snakes, crabs, and fish. One of the most important images was the jaguar/feline, which was seen in depictions that were combinations of jaguars/felines and people, and also as the so-called "fanged deity" that had snakes as hair. Because Chavín Horizon imagery was found at many sites in the highlands and in the Peruvian coastal area, a number of archaeologists interpret this as a shared ideology or religion, which acted as an integrative mechanism that facilitated peoples' willingness to contribute labor to construct monuments and participate in rituals and ceremonies, including feasting.

One of the major sites of the Chavín Horizon is the highlands site of **Chavín de Huántar** (see Figure 14.2), which is described as a ceremonial center.[22] It had monumental architecture in the form of sunken courts (plazas), platform mounds, and large terraced platforms. These were arranged in two U-shape complexes, showing continuity with earlier architectural traditions in this region (see previous discussion). The Old Temple there was built of large stone blocks and had an interior filled with dirt and rocks, into which underground rooms, canals, ventilation shafts, and passages were constructed. One of the rooms, known as the Lanzón Galley, had a large granite rock with a carved fanged deity. The construction of these monuments may have occurred in the context of feasting (a tradition known throughout the Andean region), where rituals associated with the sharing of food involved labor exchanged for feasting.[23] Such feasts would have been organized by elite members of society. These individuals perhaps held religious social roles, because evidence for status differences between groups of people was found in the distribution of exotic goods and in burial structures and associated grave goods.[24] In the ceremonial areas of the site, exotic items included mirrors made of anthracite (hard coal) and marine shells such as *Spondylus* (see Chapter 13, Figure 13.10) and *Strombus* (Figure 14.8).[25] The *Strombus* shells were used as "trumpets."[26] People living at Chavín de Huántar (perhaps as many as 3,000) also engaged in the manufacture of textiles. In other parts of the Chavín region, crafts included the working of gold, copper, and silver.

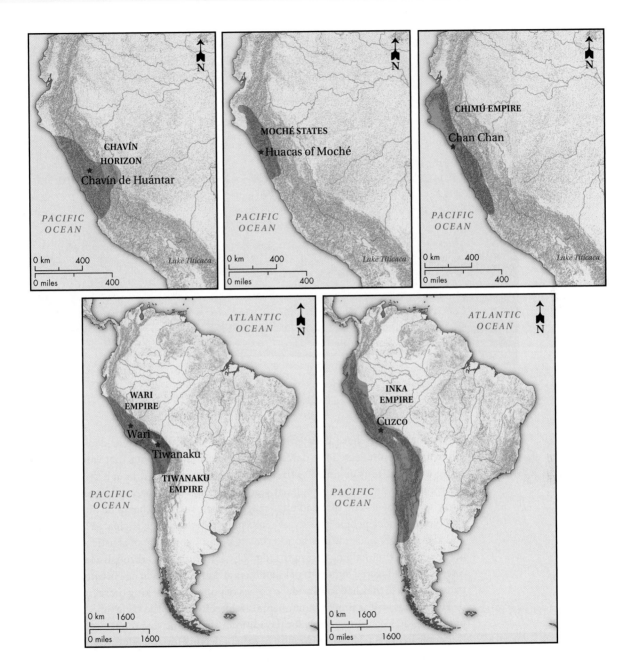

FIGURE 14.6

The greatest extents of the Chavín Horizon, Moché states, and Wari, Tiwanaku, Chimú, and Inka empires. The top three images encompass mainly the area of modern Peru with portions of surrounding countries.

FIGURE 14.7
The "smiling god" from Chavín de Huántar, Peru.

Archaeologists have debated the degree to which the shared ideology of the Chavín Horizon reflected the development of social mechanisms that would characterize it as politically complex, with regard to being a state.[27] Although these types of interpretations are not yet completely resolved, many researchers do characterize the Chavín Horizon as one that had pilgrimage centers, such as Chavín de Huántar.[28] In this type of model, people who traveled to a pilgrimage center participated in its rituals and also brought back to their homes the ideas and knowledge of artistic motifs seen at the centers, thus helping spread the ideology (or a form of it) through a large region. Sites that were located hundreds of kilometers away from Chavín de Huántar show this pattern because they had locally made copies of pottery mimicking those from Chavín de Huántar, as well as similar monumental architecture.[29] At the same time, these more peripheral sites continued many local traditions, suggesting that they were not "ruled" by people living at Chavín de Huántar or other Chavín Horizon pilgrimage centers.

Early Intermediate Period/Early Middle Horizon

Nasca Lines enormous figures (geometrics, animals, fish, lines, birds, spiders, other lines) created on the desert plateau surface by the Nasca Culture (100 BC to AD 700) in the coastal area of southern Peru.

In the southern Peruvian coastal area, figures created by removing rocks on the ground or brushing aside small surface stones to expose lighter-colored underlying sediment in enormous patterns on the desert plateau was the work of the Nasca Culture (100 BC to AD 700).[30] These figures (geoglyphs) are the **Nasca lines** (see

Figure 14.2), and they are in a minimum area of 360 hectares (900 acres). They include many triangles, trapezoids, lines (some are paths), and figures such as a monkey (which is not native to this region), a spider, birds, plants, fish, and lizards (Figure 14.9). Although early speculation thought that these figures could only be seen from above (that is, as if you were in a plane), this is not true; the figures are at least partially visible just standing on the ground with them or if you are on nearby low hills or other elevated spots. One recent interpretation suggests that at least some of the Nasca lines were meant to be walked by single individuals as part of a possible spiritual experience.[31] This would mean that being able to see the entire figure at one time was not necessary; instead you would experience it as you walked it.

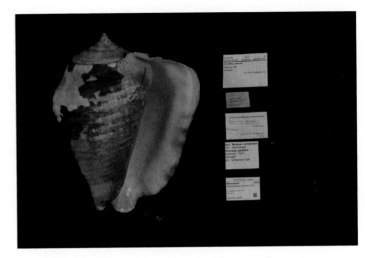

FIGURE 14.8
An example of a Strombus shell.

FIGURE 14.9
Aerial view of the figure of a spider created as one of the Nasca Lines.

In the period from AD 100 to 800, the northern coastal region of Peru was inhabited by the Moché (see Figure 14.6). As with many socially and politically complex groups in earlier prehistory, both in South America and elsewhere in the New and Old Worlds, archaeologists are divided in their interpretations of the Moché. Were they a society organized as a single state that controlled a relatively large portion of what is now Peru, or were they two or more states unified in part by a common ideology and artifact styles?[32] Recent research on the Moché suggests that at their peak (during the early part of the Middle Horizon period), they were divided into a southern **Moché state** and either a series of valley-based states in the north or possibly a single late northern state.[33] These southern and northern polities were separated by a stretch of coastal desert.

Archaeologically, the Moché were initially identified on the basis of their distinctive pottery vessels, many of which were decorated with naturalistic scenes such as people visiting elites and burying their dead, animals and gods, and sculpted depictions of people shown performing various sexual acts.[34] The coastal and near-coastal locations of the Moché centers meant that they had access to several important trade resources, such as *Spondylus* shells, feathers of tropical forest birds, gold ore (from rivers), which they used to manufacture ornaments for elites and artifacts used in rituals, and copper ore, which they fashioned into various artifacts and which is an ore used in making bronze items.[35] The Moché produced large quantities of *chicha*, which is a beer made from maize.[36] The use of *chicha* in ceremonies was important in many Andean societies (see later). Craft production may have been overseen by elite members of society. Because Moché centers and villages were situated in the coastal river valleys leading from the Andes Mountains to the ocean, they developed highly productive agriculture based on extensive use of canal irrigation, which began during the Late Preceramic period but was expanded and improved by the Moché. Crops grown include most of those discussed above—cotton, quinoa, manioc, maize, potatoes, and peanuts. The Moché also had llamas, guinea pigs, ducks, and dogs.

Each of the river valleys along the northern Peruvian coast had at least one large Moché center with monumental architecture. In the Moché Valley itself, the main center was the **Huacas of Moché** (see Figure 14.2). Each center had two adobe terraced platforms (called huacas) that formed pyramids (built of thousands of adobe bricks), cemeteries, residences, craft workshops, plazas, and streets.[37] The large adobe platform/pyramids were rebuilt several times, just as we have seen in other examples of monumental architecture of politically complex societies such as the Maya in Mesoamerica (see Chapter 13). To gain access to the tops of the platforms, ramps were built. Structures on the platforms included rooms, corridors, and patios and are interpreted as public buildings, temples, and possibly palaces that elites used for religious, political/administrative, and residential purposes. One activity that occurred on these restricted access pyramids was human sacrifice, which may be related to the frequent theme of warfare and captives in Moché iconography[38] (Figure 14.10). The study of the bones of Moché victims indicates that they were sacrificed by having their throats cut and/or suffered tremendous head blows. Some show evidence of torture

Moché States states situated in the northern coastal area of Peru in South America. There was a southern Moché state and either a series of valley-based northern states or perhaps a single northern state during the early Middle Horizon period.

Huacas of Moché this site was the Moché center in the Moché Valley of Peru in South America during the Early Intermediate period when the Moché states were present. It has two large terraced pyramids with ramps leading to the top, plazas, residences, craft workshops, and cemeteries.

FIGURE 14.10
Design from a Moché vessel with Moché warriors parading with their captives (shown naked).

and flaying. That there were elite individuals who ruled the individual Moché centers is known from a small number of burials, such as those at **Sipán** (see Figure 14.2) in the Lambayeque Valley in the northern Moché region. One of the Sipán burials is identified as the "Lord of Sipán" or the "Warrior-Priest."[39] This individual was buried within one of the adobe pyramids and dressed in a costume representing a supernatural deity. He had rich grave goods including copper sandals, bracelets with turquoise beads, nose and ear ornaments made of gold, war clubs, cotton textiles, spears, hundreds of ceramic vessels, a couple of llamas and a dog, and ornaments made of feathers, as well as the bodies of five sacrificed individuals (two men and three women).

Because there were several Moché polities, understanding their collapse is not a matter of identifying one or two major reasons that would explain the collapse over the entire region. A number of researchers instead have discussed different variables in the contexts of the various river valley systems found in the Moché region, a discussion that is ongoing because of new data that constantly emerge from archaeological work there.[40] Among the ideas are "mega El Niño events" that created local environmental disasters (torrential rains), particularly with regard to agricultural productivity, social stressors such as struggles for power between religious and civil elites at Moché centers, and perhaps the fact that people including elites "lost faith" in their ideological systems and abandoned them. The upshot is that by AD 800 (in the early part of the Middle Horizon period), the Moché polities significantly declined in power and authority.

Middle Horizon

In the highlands region during the Middle Horizon period, there were two Andean empires that were contemporary with each other and partly contemporary with the Moché states of the coastal area. These were the Wari Empire in the central highlands and the Tiwanaku Empire in the southern highlands (see Figure 14.6).

Sipán this early Middle Horizon period Moché center in the northern part of the Moché states region of coastal Peru (South America) yielded a rich burial of an individual identified as the "Lord of Sipan."

WARI EMPIRE

Wari Empire a Middle Horizon period complex political entity situated in the central Andean highlands of Peru (South America). It controlled an area about 1,300 kilometers (807 miles) long north–south, and its iconography has links to the earlier Chavín Horizon.

From AD 600 to 1000, the central highlands were home to the **Wari Empire** (see Figure 14.6). At its peak, it extended more than 1,300 kilometers (807 miles) north–south, as well as 100 to 400 kilometers (62 to 248 miles) east–west, including some areas on the coast.[41] As we saw previously with other societies, the Wari Empire had an iconography that was used to legitimize elites in their political and religious roles. One of these images was a human wearing an ornate headdress and holding a staff in each hand.[42] This depiction is similar to an image seen as early as the Chavín Horizon and might suggest long-lived traditions in terms of powerful deities. This should not be so strange to us today because we can see similar phenomena in many of the modern world's long-lived religions, such as the images of the Christian cross or the Hindu Shiva deity. Other Wari images show military figures (some of whom wore human trophy heads), warriors with weapons, and captives.[43]

Wari the capital of the Wari Empire in the Andean highlands of South America during the Middle Horizon period. It has a central stone-walled section with restricted access points. This is thought to be an area only for elite members of society.

The capital of the Wari Empire was **Wari** (see Figure 14.2), a large city covering 15 square kilometers (5.8 square miles).[44] There were many residences in this urban area, which also had a walled stone central area covering 200 hectares (495 acres). The population was at least 10,000 people and perhaps as many as 70,000.[45] The walled enclosure had few entrances and no windows, suggesting that it was built to keep most people out. This was a different philosophy compared to that of earlier and contemporary Andean centers that included more open architectural space (plazas and sunken courts) and seem to have served as the focus of pilgrimages during which many people could participate in rituals and other ceremonies.[46] This arrangement of a central area with restricted entry was typical of all the Wari centers.[47]

The site of Wari was in a productive agricultural area, although elites living there would have had to import food from surrounding areas to support the large population in this capital, including feeding the labor force that constructed the monumental architecture.[48] Elite individuals and families would have overseen these labor forces, as well as craft production, administration of trade and exchange networks, and other bureaucratic tasks, not just at Wari itself but also at the many administrative centers spread throughout the region that fell under the control and influence of the Wari Empire. The types of prestige items were those which we have seen elsewhere in the Andes, such as turquoise, *Spondylus* and *Strombus* shells, gold, silver, and copper artifacts, and finely decorated ceramic vessels—these items were found primarily in elite residences and in temple/religious contexts. The control of trade and exchange, in addition to control of agricultural surpluses, was one mechanism by which elites amassed large quantities of "wealth" that were used to underwrite construction efforts and influence people at other sites to become more fully integrated into a single polity. Some researchers have suggested that the Wari Empire strategically placed administrative centers in more peripheral areas to eventually take over the trade routes, thereby increasing the wealth available to the empire. Of course, not all such interactions were peaceful, and there is skeletal evidence indicating violent encounters, although these were not necessarily the result of warfare. They could, for example, represent raiding or ritual fights between elites.[49] Human remains from at least one Wari administrative center indicate that some of the people buried in ritual contexts were not locals. These ritual contexts also included human trophy heads, some of which were nonlocal people. The capture of these individuals (including women and children) and their sacrifice and/or transformation into trophy heads were probably the results of raiding activities carried out to obtain captives.

TIWANAKU EMPIRE

One of the major polities that bordered the Wari Empire was the **Tiwanaku Empire** (AD 600 to 1000) of the southern-central Andean highlands (southern Peru, Bolivia, and northern Chile), centered near Lake Titicaca (see Figure 14.6).[50] It had a capital city integrated with other large urban centers, as well as smaller towns, villages, and hamlets.[51] One of the major ways that the Tiwanaku Empire differed from the Wari Empire, as well as the later Inka Empire, was that the Tiwanaku Empire was not a large, contiguous territory. Rather, in regions away from Lake Titicaca, the Tiwanaku Empire established colonies in the southern-central Andean highlands and exerted control over strategic areas. The colonies could be hundreds of kilometers away from the central region around Lake Titicaca, and interestingly, the routes between the Lake Titicaca region and the colonies do not appear to have been militarily controlled or administratively maintained by the ruling elites of the empire. The colonies were established by immigrants from the empire's core region near Lake Titicaca, which we know archaeologically because they brought with them their own traditions of how to build houses, as well as their artifacts and clothing styles.[52] The colonies were positioned to take advantage of a variety of ecological zones that were rich in resources. These included agricultural potential (llama herding, potatoes, and quinoa at higher elevations; maize in lower locations; fish from Lake Titicaca[53]) and sources of exotic materials (obsidian, lapis lazuli, gold, copper, and marine shells). Trade and exchange networks thus were important features of the Tiwanaku Empire, with material goods traveling along with some religious motifs (felines and winged llamas, and the same deity holding two staffs that was part of the Wari Empire iconography). These were painted on artifacts or carved in stone.[54] Archaeological evidence also suggests that the Tiwanaku Empire consisted of many diverse ethnic groups who were linked by ideology but who were not absorbed into a single state-level polity. Instead, each of these groups maintained their own identities, and some of them immigrated to the capital city near Lake Titicaca, which created additional economic and social relationships between the capital and peoples' home regions.[55]

The capital of the Tiwanaku Empire was the large urban city of **Tiwanaku** in Bolivia (see Figure 14.2), just south of Lake Titicaca. It was a planned city (covering 4 to 6 square kilometers [1.5 to 2.3 square miles]) with palaces, temples, sunken courts, pyramids, administrative buildings, stone enclosures, streets, and residences scattered over a wide region around the city.[56] The total population of the Tiwanaku Valley may have been as many as 60,000 people. Among the monumental structures at Tiwanaku were the Akapana Pyramid, which was 18 meters (60 feet) high but never finished entirely, and the Pumapunka Temple Complex, another unfinished

Tiwanaku Empire a Middle Horizon period politically complex polity in the southern central Andean highlands of South America. The territory it controlled was not contiguous but consisted of a central region near Lake Titicaca and colonies in more remote areas. The colonies controlled strategic resource regions.

Tiwanaku the capital city of the Tiwanaku Empire in South America in the Middle Horizon period, it was situated near Lake Titicaca in the Andean highlands. The city had large ceremonial complexes (unfinished) with temples and pyramids, where large-scale feasting rituals took place.

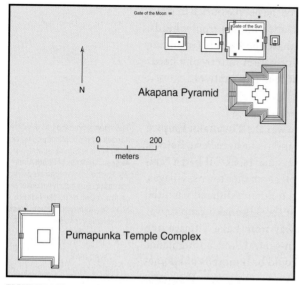

FIGURE 14.11

Plan view of the Akapana and Pumapunka complexes at Tiwanaku. Blue rectangles indicate stone monoliths and statues.

structure that had a four-tiered platform with a sunken court and ramps leading to the top of the platform (Figure 14.11). Although unfinished, both structures were used for ceremonies and rituals including feasting and, like other ritual structures there, were built to align with astronomical phenomena and with natural features of the landscape such as sacred mountain peaks.

The Akapana Pyramid complex included several rich burials that might represent religious specialists. It also had sacrificed llamas, 23 human burials (some of which might represent sacrifices of captives), and deliberately broken ceramic vessels.[57] It has been suggested that these ritual complexes at Tiwanaku were designed in part to overwhelm visitors with the impressiveness of the architecture and the entrance into the central areas of the complexes. This was one way to create an experience that participants and observers in large public ceremonies would remember vividly.[58] Although there must have been elite individuals and families who organized and oversaw the construction and rebuilding of the monuments, as well as the administration of trade and exchange with the empire's colonies, there is little evidence of these elites from burial contexts.[59] Studies of the residences in cities such as Tiwanaku, however, show that people lived in distinct and bounded neighborhoods, with household architectural features as well as associated material goods (including items that were used to partake of hallucinogens) indicating differences in social statuses between the residential compounds.[60] The higher-status residences tended to be closer to the ceremonial monuments.

The elite rulers at Tiwanaku after AD 800 began to exert greater control over trade and exchange networks, although the Tiwanaku Empire still did not incorporate all of the lands between the central region at Lake Titicaca and its colonies elsewhere in the region.[61] By AD 1000, in combination with environmental changes that affected agricultural productivity in some areas, the many socially distinct groups that were part of the empire's politically decentralized structure began to "opt out" of the increasingly heavy political and administrative oversight of the elites at Tiwanaku. These factions established their own political centers and the Tiwanaku Empire came to an end.

LATE INTERMEDIATE PERIOD

After the demise of the Wari and Tiwanaku Empires, there were many small states and political centers in the highlands and the lowlands during what is known as the Late Intermediate period. One of these polities, situated in the northern coastal region of Peru, was the **Chimú Empire**, from AD 1370 to 1470[62] (see Figure 14.6). The capital was **Chan Chan** (Figure 14.12; see Figure 14.2), in the Moché Valley (the same region where one of the earlier Moché states was established). The empire included a number of ethnically distinct groups, but, unlike the Tiwanaku Empire, that of Chimú represented a single unified administration. The empire was ruled by a succession of kings who lived at Chan Chan and who held the empire together through alliances and military strength as well as trade and exchange relationships.[63] The architecture at Chan Chan included monumental pyramids, U-shape structures, and palace compounds called *ciudadelas* as well as residences for elites of lower status than the king and his family and residences for craft workers and commoners. Kings

FIGURE 14.12
Aerial view of Chan Chan, Peru.

were buried in their palace compounds in elaborate tombs that included human sacrifices, but other members of the Chimú Empire were buried according to their social class in large cemeteries, most of which were associated with specific city neighborhoods.[64] Some archaeologists suggest that the U-shape buildings at Chan Chan, which were located within the *ciudadelas*, were part of the administrative bureaucracy because these buildings had features that suggest they were storage facilities for various goods. Researchers frequently comment on the scale of monument building and the need for labor organization and logistics that likely were provided by elite members of earlier societies. It is worth bearing in mind, however, that although the structures being built were impressive, our perceptions of the efforts required might be somewhat misleading. A recent study of one of the *ciudadelas* at Chan Chan, for example, indicates that it could have been built by just 250 laborers over a period of six years.[65] Coordinating 250 people (and probably feeding them) would require organization and scheduling, but this is actually a small number of laborers considering that the population of Chan Chan is thought to have been around 30,000.

In the Andean highlands during the Late Intermediate period, polities such as Tiwanaku and Wari became highly fragmented, and there were many independent groups of people who competed with one another. This can be seen in the types of settlements, now mostly villages and hamlets, along with fortified hilltop locations.[66] Over time, some of these groups began to consolidate and to expend more effort in building larger, fortified sites that included residences and cemeteries, as well as pasture land for camelids. Another change during the Late Intermediate period was in how graves were constructed. Rather than continuing to be below ground, they were built of stone in visibly prominent locations, perhaps as territorial markers, and they contained dozens to hundreds of people in each funerary structure (called a *chullpa*).

Among the many small groups in the Andean highlands were the Inka, who lived in the region of the Cuzco Basin. Beginning in AD 1000, there were a number of fortified hilltop sites and small villages, and by AD 1300, there were several secondary centers linked to the urban capital at Cuzco.[67] At a number of the administrative centers, there were temples and evidence for high-status elites who owned estates. The archaeological signature of the Inka during the Late Intermediate period suggests that they were a small, centralized state-level polity who came into conflict with a number of their neighbors. But, as we will see below, in AD 1438, the Inka began to expand in ways that led to the establishment of an empire.

The Inka Empire

The Inka Empire (also known as **Tawantinsuyu**; see Figure 14.6), dates from AD 1438 to 1533 and developed from a small, state-level polity in the Cuzco Basin of the Andean highlands.[68] Its history and traditions were recorded in written form by the Spanish, who copied down information provided by the Inka about themselves and their empire.[69] These written documents are a valuable resource, but archaeologists also examine the material remains of the Inka to verify and/or revise the stories that the Inka told about themselves and how these have been interpreted by later generations of researchers. The rise of the empire occurred relatively rapidly, but only after Inka power had been consolidated within the Cuzco Basin. This power was partially achieved through marriage alliances with neighboring regions and with non-Inka groups,[70] a political strategy that was typical in many regions of the world where early states developed (see China, Mesopotamia, and Mesoamerica, for example). As the power of the Inka and their ruler increased, so did their control over agricultural and craft production, as well as administrative functions and economic networks and labor, including the ability to engage in raids and warfare.

The capital of the empire was **Cuzco** (see Figure 14.2). According to historical sources, at the beginning of the empire period, Cuzco was redesigned by the king Pachakuti and built to include features of the sacred landscape. This architectural layout gave Cuzco its status as the center of the world.[71] It had two main streets, with several crosscutting streets, in the central ("downtown") part of the city (Figure 14.13). There were two large plaza areas for ceremonies, as well as palaces and religious buildings, such as the Temple of the Sun, and the ritual and fortress compound

Cuzco the capital city of the Inka Empire in the Andean highlands of South America. The Inka considered it the center of the world. It had impressive temple, pyramid, fortress, and plaza areas and incorporated significant sacred places in the landscape.

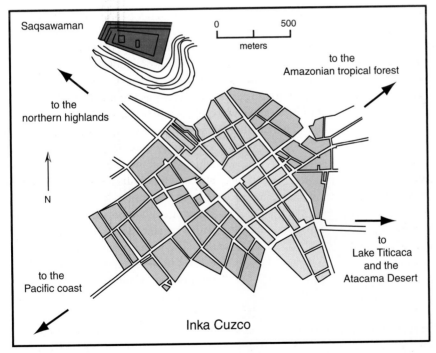

FIGURE 14.13
Plan map of Inka Cuzco (after D'Altroy 2002, Figure 6.2). Areas are upper Cuzco (*yellow*), lower Cuzco (*green*), some of the surrounding residential neighborhoods (*blue*), and the fortress/religious complex of Saqsawaman (*red*).

called Saqsawaman[72] (see "Social Life" and "Ritual and Religion"). In the areas around the central district of Cuzco were the residences for other royal families and numerous shrines, as well as agricultural fields, and canal systems to water the fields. Members of the elite ruling class owned vast estates in the countryside.

At its height, the Inka Empire controlled 4,300 kilometers (2,672 miles) of territory that included highland and coastal regions[73] (see Figure 14.6). Its direct administration, however, appears to have varied. In some highland areas, the Inka moved/displaced entire populations and built large administrative or pilgrimage centers, whereas in other highland regions, as well as the coastal areas, the Inka seem to have exerted indirect control or at least had a reduced presence (smaller administrative centers, fewer store houses, and some road improvements).[74] The Inka Empire, however, was the largest state-level polity in the Americas prior to the arrival of the Spanish.

The Nonwritten or Written (?) Word

As many scholars have noted, one of the somewhat unusual features of the Inka Empire was that it did not develop a system of writing with characters. We saw in previous chapters that writing systems were key elements for other early state-level polities. They were used for keeping track of economic transactions and recording the mythologies that underlay the religious and ritual foundations of state religions, as well as telling the stories of important rulers and their life events. For the Inka, many of these aspects of life were parts of oral traditions passed down through the generations, stories depicted in images painted onto wood or woven into textiles, or even perhaps motifs on pottery.[75] The Inka, however, did have an ingenious method of keeping track of information using a system of knots as a recall device.[76] This knotted record was called the **khipu**, and it was quite complex (Figure 14.14). It consisted of different types of knots that had different meanings, as well as spacing of the knots, and also of differently twisted cords (on which the knots were made) that were attached to a primary cord, and different colors of cords/knots. The colors comprised literally hundreds of shades, each with a specific meaning in a specific context. The potential number of combinations of these features was huge, and thus the number of meanings that could be conveyed also was enormous. Moreover, reading the *khipu* meant that a person had to have a set of specialized knowledge about particular *khipu*, and these individuals can be thought of as having specialized roles similar to those of scribes in contexts with writing systems.

Khipu a recording system used by the Inka during the period of the Inka Empire in South America. It was a complex set of twisted and knotted strings of different colors that was used to keep track of material goods, agricultural products, and taxes owed and paid. It likely also records stories using a logosyllabic system.

FIGURE 14.14
An example of a khipu.

The Inka used the *khipu* to keep track of many accounting-like sets of data. These included detailed census records for each region of the Inka Empire, the amount of tribute that each area/family group owed to the empire, the contents of store rooms and warehouses, and the number and types of animals in herds. The *khipu* could be used to keep track of calendar events and possibly in some instances were records of calendars.[77] *Khipu* also appear to have been devices to help with remembering verses and other things that did not have a numerical origin.[78] Additionally, recent studies of some *khipu* show that they have at least 95 different symbols.[79] This means that these symbols could be part of a logosyllabic writing system (words, phrases, or sound represented by symbols) and have the potential to be deciphered. Some of the symbols appear to be lineage names, while others may record stories about events. One of the difficulties is that Inka *khipu* were made of animal hair, which keeps the original dye colors well, but due to preservation (and other) issues, many of these have not survived. *Khipu* made of cotton are generally post-Inka Empire and do not retain original dye colors very well.

Resource Networks, Trade, and Exchange

Running an empire requires a massive amount of goods that can be used to underwrite the daily lives of the ruling elites and their families, and also military endeavors, labor forces for construction of monuments, administration, and religious and political rituals. The Inka rulers, like those of other early politically complex societies, established tight control over trade and exchange, as well as the raw material resources needed to manufacture different types of goods. Inka control was so extensive that they discouraged trade with regions beyond the borders of the empire, although a few items, such as *Spondylus* shell, which were important in rituals, had to be obtained from other areas.[80] To control precious metal resources, the Inka expanded their empire to add areas in Bolivia and Chile that were rich in ores. They also brought skilled craftspeople to Cuzco and had them work for elite families or state institutions. These crafts included metallurgy, weaving, and pottery, and the styles of the master craftspeople were copied by government-run craft workshops at other administrative centers within the empire.[81] Full-time specialists were supported by exemptions from certain types of taxes (such as requirements to donate labor time to construct monuments or maintain road systems), as well as having their food provided by the government. In Cuzco and its surrounding area, as in other parts of the empire, exacting counts and management of which resources and goods were entering and leaving the city or town were made, and certain types of luxury items required proof that the government had authorized the travel and types of goods being transported.[82]

For the most part, the Inka Empire can be described as being self-sufficient. Agricultural produce and llama and alpaca herds provided food and clothes for its inhabitants (cotton and wool woven into clothing), and virtually all of the resources to make other types of goods were found within the borders of the empire.[83] Inka royalty owned enormous flocks of llamas and alpacas. These were used for transporting goods from place to place within the Inka Empire and also for rituals, as well as for transport and food for the military.[84] Inka elites closely monitored the supplies of gold, silver, copper, intricately woven cloth, decorated pottery, the numbers of herd animals, and the taxes placed on goods such as agricultural produce and wool from the herds of commoners. Some of these highly specialized or luxury goods were used as gifts to other royalty, to cement alliances with non-Inka peoples within the empire, or as rewards to highly skilled specialists. Goods belonging to the state or the religious institutions were placed in government or temple storehouses that were built within each part of the empire.[85] This meant that each area of the empire had a mirror image system for the collection of resources and the products made from them, their storage, and their distribution as needed for feeding the military, specialists, or laborers, or for use in rituals. The storehouses were built along the Inka roads, where they could be easily accessed, or next to government farms. The Inka road system, in fact, was an integral part of how the Inka rulers and other royalty maintained communication throughout the empire (read "Peopling the Past: The Inka Road System"), and all the main towns that the road system connected were places that were built first by the Inka.[86] That is, there is no archaeological evidence at these locales for settlements earlier than the Inka Empire period.

Peopling the Past

The Inka Road System

The road system built by the Inka was an impressive network that rebuilt older, existing routes between cities and towns, as well as established new routes.[87] There were 30,000 kilometers (18,600 miles) of roads, which consisted of two major north–south routes with many other smaller ones that ran east–west from the highlands to coasts, thus creating links between the north–south routes (Figure 14.15). There also were smaller roads going into the lowlands to the east of the Inka Empire. As with road systems in the modern world, the Inka roads included some major "highways" and lots of smaller, less elaborately constructed roads. The Inka also built hanging bridges over ravines to cross difficult terrain. The major Inka roads were well paved and well drained, and sometimes there were several parallel roads, perhaps a bit like having frontage roads alongside a modern highway today. Transport of goods using llamas in caravans was one type of road use, whereas others included movement of military forces, relay runners carrying messages from place to place, and officials visiting different parts of the empire. The roads were associated with storehouses at smaller centers and at various types of way stations.[88] Most of these goods stayed in the local regions, whereas people, such as the military, traveling along the roads could use foods and other items from the storehouses as they passed through those regions. The road system also brought marine shells, gold, silver, and bird feathers from their source areas into Cuzco, where the royal elites could control their use. Road segments, especially those far away from the main Inka centers, could be used by local traffic as a way to build up the network of local crafts, as these roads served as convenient (already built) ways to move local goods from place to place within a small region and possibly as places where one could set up roadside stands.[89]

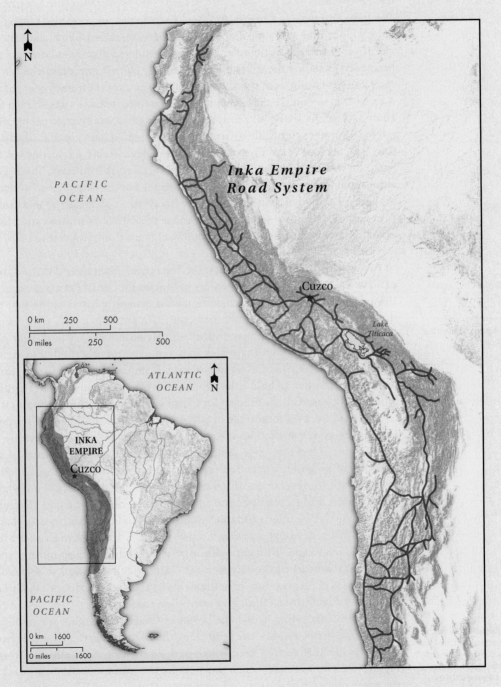

FIGURE 14.15
The road system of the Inka Empire (after Jenkins 2001, Figure 1).

Social Life

The Inka Empire was a highly stratified society and was organized along kinship lines.[90] Elites were at the top and were themselves stratified. The highest status individual, for example, was the ruler, who was considered divine, and then members of his family, including the wives of the Inka king.[91] Other important elites below the ruler and his family were people who could claim descent from earlier rulers. This is a situation not unlike the remnants of monarchies in today's world, such as in the United Kingdom. In the Inka Empire, high status also was given to people who were not royal but were ethnically Inka and to other honored individuals (called "Inkas by privilege" because of their service to the state). Beyond this, distinctions were made based on wealth, military prominence, and social roles in society. There were also elites appointed by the Inka in the various regions of the empire, who oversaw local production and other matters (read "The Big Picture: Political Organization in the Inka Empire"). Commoners included various specialists, as we saw earlier for crafts, as well as farmers, herders, and weavers. The organization of the commoners' villages was kin based.[92]

As wealthy members of society, the Inka royal elites owned vast estates. One of these was the worldwide-known site of **Machu Picchu** in Peru (see Figure 14.2). It was owned by the ruler Pachakuti, who is generally listed as the first ruler in the Inka kings' list.[94] This estate had two main areas, one with terraces and the other with a central plaza surrounded by finely built masonry buildings. Many of these were dwellings, but there also were temples and other religious structures. These estates were used for residence away from the capital at Cuzco, for royals to visit one another, to hold rituals for former rulers, as a means to safeguard and build wealth based on the land and resources contained within an estate, and even for the dead because mummies of rulers were kept at the estates. The capital of Cuzco, however, was the hub of social, administrative, and religious life for the Inka Empire. Its central area contained residences for elite members of society, administration buildings, and religious complexes.[95] Inka elite were required to live at Cuzco for several months each year, and non-Inka rulers of outlying areas in the empire had to send one son to Cuzco to learn the language (Quechua) of the Inka, as well as to learn Inka customs and rituals. The architectural arrangement of Cuzco, as noted previously, was based on incorporating various features of a sacred landscape. With elite, administrative, and religious buildings and compounds at the heart of the city, central Cuzco was structured to serve those of Inka ethnicity.[96] It was only in settlements in the areas surrounding Cuzco that nonelites and non-Inka ethnicities were allowed to live.

What is interesting is that the layout of Cuzco, although it was replicated to some extent in towns and cities built along the Inka road system, was not necessarily always identical in who used which parts of the city. At **Huánuco Pampa** (see Figure 14.2), for example, which was built by the Inka as an administrative city to the north of Cuzco, some researchers suggest that the central area, which is a large plaza surrounded by buildings with many doors, was for the use of commoners,

Machu Picchu this site was part of the estate of the Inka ruler, Pachakuti, in the Andean highlands of South America. It was used as a royal residence away from the capital at Cuzco.

Huánuco Pampa an administrative city built to the north of the Inka capital at Cuzco in the Andean highlands of South America. Huánuco Pampa has a large central plaza where feasting rituals appear to have occurred.

The Big Picture

Political Organization in the Inka Empire

The Inka system of political organization included several ranks of royal elites at the top of the hierarchy, followed by nonroyal elites who managed smaller regions and their peoples[93] (Figure 14.16). The royal elites, as might be expected, were in charge of the overall government of the kingdom and its administration, as well as being the heads of the various provinces. Within each of the provinces, there were several administrative levels. Below the governor, who was royal elite, the next highest offices were staffed by non-Inka individuals, who held these as hereditary positions. Each of these non-Inka elite within a province was in charge of a certain number of families. The Inka broke these down into units of 10,000, 5,000, 1,000, 500, and 100 families. Supervision below the level of 100 families was the task of nonhereditary commoner officeholders who were organized with respect to the number of families they oversaw. The 100 families at this level of organization were divided into small units of 50 families and then 10 families. One goal of this system was to ensure that people paid their taxes and performed their labor obligations to the kingdom and remained loyal subjects.

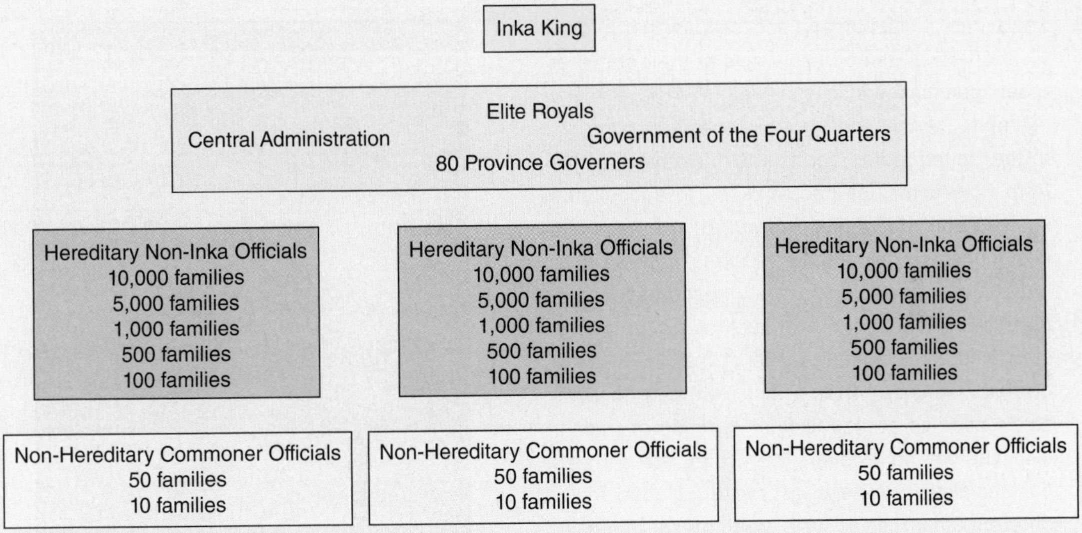

FIGURE 14.16
A simplified view of the political organization of the Inka Empire.

whereas members of local elites had compounds to the east of the plaza.[97] This meant that important ceremonies were held for the general public in the central part of town. These ceremonies included giving gifts to commoners and feasting. Such feasts involved the consumption of large quantities of *chicha* (maize beer) as well as eating camelid meat.[98] Archaeological evidence for feasting comes from pottery jars used to store *chicha* and maize kernels to make more beer, as well as pottery plates and cooking facilities in the buildings that surrounded the central plaza. One of the large structures on the north side of the large central plaza at Huánuco Pampa appears to have been where a special class of women wove cloth and brewed the beer. These feasting and religious ceremonies helped to socially and politically integrate the diverse ethnic groups that were part of the Inka Empire. The elites had their own compounds where they also held rituals that were attended by a much more select group of people. Peoples' rank and social roles in society were designated visibly in a variety of ways, including the clothing they wore (read "The Big Picture: Art and Ideology in the Inka Empire").

The Big Picture

Art and Ideology in the Inka Empire

The types of clothing and accessories that people wear often can be representative of their status or other identities within societies. We have many examples of this today within specific countries. In the United States, for example, clothing ranges from how homeless people dress to subcultures such as Goths to wealthy individuals in Armani and designer shoes. In comparable terms, the Inka ruler wore large earspools and fancy headdresses, carried royal symbols of power such as a scepter and staff, and wore clothing made of the finest grade of cloth[99] (Figure 14.17). Other royal and nonroyal elites also had access to finer qualities of materials, whereas commoners were dressed in much coarser clothing. The Inka Empire included many different ethnicities as well, which meant that each group of people had distinctive clothing and hairstyles that marked them as members of a specific group of people within the empire. Ethnic groups, however, had little choice in dressing "ethnically." This was because the Inka king and his administration required people to dress ethnically, possibly as a means of keeping them looking distinctive and easier to manipulate when some groups were

FIGURE 14.17
Inka tunic for royalty from ca. AD 1550.

moved to areas where they were not native inhabitants.[100] In many respects, this was a quite different philosophy than what we see today, when people dress ethnically because they want to maintain and honor their heritages.

Ritual and Religion

The Inka religious system was based on a number of beliefs. Their state religion included several gods, with the Sun god (Inti) given the most prominence. Inka rulers claimed direct descent from him, and it was often a member of the royal family who served as the High Priest of the Sun.[101] The Sun god's wife was the Moon, also worshipped by the Inka, and another important member of the pantheon was the Thunder god. Not only did these gods have major temples and religious complexes built to them in Cuzco and all the towns and cities of the empire, as well as vast farmlands and storehouses that were part of their holdings, but the Inka built pilgrimage centers to the Sun and Moon gods on islands in Lake Titicaca in the highlands between Bolivia and Peru.[102] These centers reaffirmed the Inka creation myth that their origins were at Lake Titicaca.[103] These areas of Lake Titicaca, however, were religiously important also to non-Inka people who lived in the region, so that the use and expansion of the religious structures there helped the Inka integrate at least some of the non-Inka ethnicities into Inka religious beliefs.[104] This should not be surprising to us because we have many historical examples of this process, for example, the incorporation of pagan ritual days into Christianity, such as pagan harvest festivals/festivals for the dead becoming part of All Hallow's Eve (which we know more generically as Halloween).

Beyond the major gods, the Inka viewed many landscape places as sacred, as did non-Inka peoples who lived within the boundaries of the empire. The sacred spots included mountaintops, springs and other water sources, caves, trees, stones, and fields, as well as palaces, temples, and tombs. Their sacredness was partly the result of Inka belief in spirits, generally ancestors, who inhabited or came from these places. Shrines were established at these spots.[105] Within a given region, such as the area where Cuzco was situated, hundreds of these shrines were linked together by "lines" that originated at the Sun Temple in central Cuzco. Each of these lines and the shrines on them was the responsibility of a particular social group, who conducted ceremonies at each shrine according to a ritual cycle based on dates in the solar and lunar calendars.[106] Beyond this, the Inka preserved the mummies of royal rulers, whom they venerated as part of an ancestor cult. These mummies owned estates and acted just as they would have in life; that is, they "consumed" food and beverages and visited other mummies.[107]

The rituals that the Inka carried out at temples and shrines varied quite a bit. Most of us have read about or seen photos of the sacrificed children, sometimes found in frozen condition on mountaintops.[108] These types of sacrifices, however, were relatively rare, even for the Inka, who performed the sacrifice of children only for important events such as the beginning of a war campaign or when a new ruler came to power.[109] Of course, the numbers of children sacrificed on a given occasion might have amounted to hundreds, if Spanish accounts are accurate (although there is little archaeological evidence to support large numbers of children being sacrificed at a single occasion). Sacrifice of adult humans was more common, and for especially important events, the number of sacrifices might be in the thousands.[110] The Inka ritual calendar had yearly ceremonies related to puberty rites for Inka boys who were members of the elite royal families, purification of a city from disease, and the beginning of the cultivation season.[111] The start of plowing was an enormously elaborate festival undertaking because it lasted for eight or nine days, involved all royalty including the Inka ruler, as well as royal mummies that were brought out for the occasion, and all the religious specialists and other residents of Cuzco. Vast quantities of meat and *chicha*, as well as other items, were sacrificed to ensure a successful season. A few months later, the time for the sowing of maize (a state crop) also was marked by rituals.[112]

Warfare and Violence

The ideological and political center of the Inka Empire was at the capital of Cuzco in the Andean highlands. It was from the Valley of Cuzco that the Inka began to expand by incorporating allies and by military campaigns against non-Inka groups. Inka warfare had a long tradition, extending back in time to the Late Intermediate period after the end of the Tiwanaku and Wari Empires,[113] with their initial expansion occurring in the period from AD 1000 to 1200. One aspect of Inka success in their early campaigns actually had more do to with a type of diplomacy rather than pitched battles between military forces. An Inka military force would send a messenger to the area they intended to annex or conquer. This messenger offered enticements to local rulers such as the retention of their power and lands, as well as gifts, and allowed for local communities to keep many of their resources if they surrendered to the Inka. Some non-Inka groups accepted and thus avoided conflict and Inka retaliation. If the Inka were forced to do battle and won, then their defeated enemies could expect a variety of penalties ranging from deportation from their homes and communities to capture and sacrifice in Inka ritual ceremonies.[114]

Inka military forces were based on labor that males owed to the state, in a sense, a type of military draft. Most of these men during the period of their military service were provided with food and clothing from the Inka storehouses. They were trained and organized into military units, which during periods of warfare were led by elite individuals from their region because there were so many different languages spoken in the empire that it was necessary to have someone who spoke the language of the conscripts in each of the military units. Inka elites, including the sons of the Inka ruler, were themselves trained in the arts of warfare and served as leaders of some of the military units.[115] As time passed, the Inka developed some full-time military specialists and soldiers, rather than relying only on conscripts who owed labor to the state. This meant that the Inka Empire could more successfully field armies for longer periods of time and create loyal forces to man the outposts along the edges of the Inka Empire or to put down the many small rebellions and conflicts that occurred within the empire.

After the Inka

The Inka Empire did not disappear immediately with the arrival of the Spanish, who first made contact with the Inka prince, Atawallpa, late in AD 1532.[116] However, Francisco Pizarro soon captured Atawallpa using Spanish weapons, armor, and horses, as well as the layout of Inka cities, which allowed the Spanish to hide and attack

Further Reflections

Challenges to the State/Empire

We have seen in several chapters (including this one) dealing with complex political entities, such as empires and states, that many types of challenges arise to their continued existence. Most of the time, these challenges consist of a combination of variables such as climate change, loss of faith in leaders, arrival of outside groups, declining agricultural productivity, and alliances of enemies. By and large, most earlier states and empires eventually were unable to deal successfully with these challenges and most were either taken over by other groups or disappeared into the mists of time. Given the long temporal span that archaeology provides about past societies, we might ask ourselves if the modern nation-states of today could face similar fates. Our recent history certainly tells us that empires fall, for example, the Ottoman and the Austro-Hungarian Empires during World War I, and that political realignments occur, for instance, the breakup of the former Soviet Union.

Although there is currently considerable debate about human-caused climate change and its potential impact on planet Earth, much of the scientific community has accepted the reality of this challenge. The impact of worldwide habitat changes is most likely an enormous issue with which human societies will need to deal, and it has potential for realigning how we organize ourselves politically and socially, perhaps to the detriment of existing nation-states. We know, for example, that vertebrate species currently are going extinct at an astonishing rate, some 1,000 times faster than the normal process of extinction of species.[117] This trend began in the AD 1800s, with the Industrial Revolution. There is a 25% decline in population of vertebrate species every 10 years. Many researchers, in fact, believe that we are at the beginning of the sixth mass extinction event during which 75% or more of all living things on planet Earth will go extinct in the next 240 to 540 years.[118] It is very difficult to see how these processes will not have an effect on humans. If resources and habitats that we depend on are no longer available or available only to a limited extent, how might this play out in the long run? Will there be mass migrations of people to better habitats? Will some people decide to overthrow existing governments? These are only some of the many questions we could ask.

relatively easily. During Atawallpa's captivity, the Spanish gained important information about rivalries within the Inka royalty and the existence of non-Inka groups within the empire who were willing to fight to overthrow Inka rule. The Spanish execution of Atawallpa set off a chain event leading to Spanish (allied with non-Inka groups) battles with Inka forces, which, by and large, the Spanish and their allies won. Late in AD 1533, the Spanish and their allies captured Cuzco, installed the prince Manqo Inka on the throne, and then briefly co-ruled the empire with this Inka noble. However, the Spanish and their allies continued to fight battles with Inka armies, some of whom laid siege to Cuzco, including those led by Manqo Inka, who had escaped. The Inkas were able to continue their rule for several decades in regions to the east of Cuzco, but this area finally was subjugated by the Spanish and their allies in AD 1572. With the Spanish execution of the last Inka ruler in the Fall of AD 1572, the Inka Empire came to an end (read "Further Reflections: Challenges to the State/Empire").

Summary

- South American groups had subsistence economies that used domesticates by the Early/Middle Preceramic (Archaic) periods. These included native plants such as potatoes, peanuts, cotton, manioc, and quinoa, with maize and squash introduced from Mesoamerica. Domesticated animals eventually included llama, alpaca, and guinea pig.

- By the Late Preceramic period, a number of sites in the Pacific coastal areas of Ecuador and Peru had monumental architecture. This same trend occurred in the Andean highlands. Many of the features of these sites in both regions suggest ceremonial or ritual uses.

- During the Initial Period, sites in the coastal and highlands regions became much larger. Some features, such as U-shape architectural layouts for sites, likely indicate long-term continuity with earlier traditions. There is no evidence, however, that any one site or area exerted political control over large territories.

- Large pilgrimage sites that had the same sets of artistic motifs, such as jaguars, crocodiles, snakes, and eagles, were found in the northern Andes and the coastal areas during the Early Horizon period. Exotic goods in burials suggest social differences between individuals. These sites were part of the Chavín Horizon and appear to document a widely shared religious system rather than a political entity such as a state or kingdom.

- In the coastal region of southern Peru, the Nasca lines were constructed by exposing the lighter-colored sediment under the rock-strewn desert. These enormous geoglyphs included geometric designs, animals, fish, and birds, among other images. They may have been part of a ritual landscape that was walked by Nasca Culture peoples.

- The early part of the Middle Horizon period (sometimes called the Early Intermediate period) was characterized by the Moché in the coastal region. The southern part of this area appears to have been a state, whereas the northern coastal area may have been a set of smaller political entities. The Moché polities engaged in relatively frequent raiding of or warfare with each other, which was depicted in their imagery. Elite rulers were buried with lavish grave goods and sacrificed humans.

- The Middle Horizon saw the rise of two contemporary complex political systems in the Andean highlands, the Wari and the Tiwanaku Empires.

- The Wari Empire was located in the central Andean highlands and positioned itself to control lucrative trade routes. Wari iconography included an individual wearing a headdress and holding staffs. This image was similar to one from the earlier Chavín Horizon. The Wari were involved in raiding and warfare, with a number of instances known of sacrificed humans and human trophy heads.

- The Tiwanaku Empire was located in the southern-central Andean highlands and shared a border with the Wari Empire. It was centered in the area of Lake Titicaca. Unlike many other empires both contemporary and later, the Tiwanaku Empire was unusual because it was not a contiguous region. Rather, the Tiwanaku Empire strategy was to establish colonies far outside its borders. These colonies controlled strategic resources. Massive ceremonial complexes for public ceremonies were built at the capital (Tiwanaku), although they were never completely finished.

- During the succeeding Late Intermediate period, the coastal region was the home of the Chimú Empire. In the Andean highlands, there were no comparable political entities. Instead, there were many groups, including the Inka, who competed against one another.

- The Inka Empire emerged during the Late Horizon period in the Andean highlands. Before the arrival of the Spanish, it was the largest state-level polity anywhere in the Americas.

- Unlike a number of other early politically complex entities, the Inka did not have a written language. Instead, they used a system of knotted strings called the *khipu* as a memory device to keep track of information. Much of this was devoted to accounting records, but new evidence suggests that the system, in some cases, may be a logosyllabic record that includes stories.

- The Inka were excellent managers, which can be seen in the vast network of storehouses and the road systems that they built throughout the empire. They also controlled the trade and exchange networks within the empire and with regions outside its boundaries.

- Inka society was based on kinship and was highly stratified. The king, who was considered divine, enjoyed the highest rank, with members of his family and other royal elites involved in the government and administration of the empire. There also were non-Inka elites who held hereditary offices in the provinces within the empire and commoners who staffed nonhereditary offices in the administration and control of agricultural products, crafts, and taxes.

- The Inka, like many other South American groups, believed in the sacredness of the landscape. Their architecture, religious structures, and ideology reflected these features of their religious system.

- Archaeology provides much evidence about the Inka and their empire; however, we also have access to information about them from the records that the Spanish made. These not only describe what the Spanish saw and interpreted (which can include biases) but also include accounts given by the Inka to the Spanish.

- Whether the Inka Empire would have continued long term or whether other South American polities would have eventually succeeded the Inka are questions for which we will never know the answers. This is because the arrival of the Spanish and their subjugation of South American polities was a game-changer.

Endnotes

1. Scheinsohn 2004: 350.
2. Stothert et al. 2003.
3. Aceituno and Loaiza 2018; King et al. 2018; Piperno 2011: S458; Zarillo et al. 2008.
4. Mengoni Goñalons and Yacobaccio 2006.
5. Dillehay et al. 2007; Pearsall 2008: 110; Rumold and Aldenderfer 2016. Recent genetic work indicates that domesticated potatoes are from a wild species found in northern Peru (Spooner et al. 2005).
6. Dillehay et al. 1989; 2007.
7. Dillehay et al. 2010 suggest that mounds were used in a ritual that produced lime in a nearby area. Lime can be mixed with salt and ash and then chewed with coca leaves. Chewing of coca leaves, however, was not related to public ceremonies. Instead, people likely chewed this combination of coca and lime/ash/salt because it releases a stimulant and also can act as a medicine.
8. Pearsall et al. 2007; Perry et al. 2007; Piperno 2011: S458–S461.
9. Pearsall et al. 2004: 424; Raymond 2003: 49–54.
10. Haas et al. 2013.
11. Quilter 1985.
12. Caramanica et al. 2018.
13. Bruno 2006; Langlie et al. 2011; Perry et al. 2007.
14. Wing 1986.
15. Burger 1992; Burger and Salazar-Burger 1980.
16. Stanish 2001b: 48–51.
17. Burger 1992: 78.
18. Burger 1992:82–83; Pozorski and Pozorski 1994.
19. Stanish 2001b: 49–50.
20. Beck 2004.
21. Burger 1992.
22. Burger 1992; Contreras 2009.
23. Chicoine 2001: 434.
24. Burger 1992: 165–227; Burger and Matos Mendieta 2002: 172.
25. Vaughn 2006: 320.
26. Rick and Lubman 2002.
27. Stanish 2001b: 52.
28. Burger 1992; Rick 2005; Vaughn 2006: 317–321.
29. Burger and Matos Mendieta 2002.
30. Ruggles and Saunders 2012. There are some figures also from the earlier Paracas Culture.
31. Ruggles and Saunders 2012.
32. Chapdelaine 2011; Quilter 2002.
33. But see Quilter and Koons 2012 for an alternative view.
34. Quilter 2002: 164–166; Weismantel 2004.
35. Quilter 2002: 156–157; Vaughn 2006: 330–332.
36. Curry 2010; Quilter 2002: 176.
37. Chapdelaine 2011: 199.
38. Quilter 2002: 167–168; Sutter and Cortez 2005; Swenson 2003: 268–272; 2012; Toyne et al. 2014.
39. Alva 1988; Alva and Donnan 1993; Donnan 2001.
40. Chapdelaine 2011: 210–211.
41. Schreiber 2001: 85; for a recent study of Wari female elites at a coastal site, see Knudson et al. 2017.
42. Schreiber 2001: 92.
43. Tung and Knudson 2011: 259.
44. Stanish 2001b: 54.
45. Jennings and Craig 2001: 480.
46. Schreiber 2001: 92; it should be noted, however, that analysis of architecture at Wari centers suggests that the core areas were initially more open and became restricted in access over time (Nash and Williams 2005).
47. Jennings and Craig 2001: 481–482.
48. Jennings and Craig 2001: 480–481; Vaughn 2006: 324.
49. Tung 2007; Tung and Knudson 2008, 2011.
50. Stanish 2001b: 53–54.
51. Janusek 2004: 151.
52. Stanish et al 2010: 528.
53. Capriles et al. 2014.
54. Albarracin-Jordan 1996; Janusek 2006: 481; Stanish 2001b: 54; Stanish et al. 2010; Vaughn 2006: 328–329.
55. Janusek 2002: 52–53.
56. Stanish 2001b: 53–54; Vranich 2006.
57. Janusek 2004: 154.
58. Janusek 2006; Vranich 2006.
59. Stanish 2001b: 60.
60. Janusek 2002, 2004: 147.
61. Janusek 2004: 165–167; Williams 2002.
62. The Chimú were present as a polity beginning about AD 900, but not united as an empire until AD 1370.

63. Topic 2003: 248–251.

64. Moore 2004: 113–118.

65. Smailes 2011.

66. Arkush 2010: 34–38; Bongers et al. 2012; D'Altroy 2002: 55–61.

67. Covey 2003.

68. Covey 2003: 336–343.

69. Stanish 2001a: 214–215.

70. Covey 2003: 348.

71. D'Altroy 2002: 109–111.

72. D'Altroy 2002: 115–140.

73. Stanish 2001a: 213.

74. Stanish 2001a: 230–233.

75. Bray 2000.

76. D'Altroy 2002: 15–19.

77. Urton 2001.

78. Ascher 2005: 110.

79. Hyland 2017.

80. Sepulveda et al. 2019; Trigger 2003: 352.

81. Trigger 2003: 370–371.

82. Trigger 2003: 352.

83. Covey 2011.

84. D'Altroy 2002: 278–279.

85. D'Altroy 2002: 280–285.

86. Morris 2008: 301; Stanish 2001a: 227.

87. D'Altroy 2002: 242–246.

88. Jenkins 2001.

89. Garrido 2016.

90. Covey 2015.

91. Covey 2006: 192–194; D'Altroy 2002: 181.

92. Covey 2006: 178.

93. Trigger 2003: 212–214.

94. Covey 2006: 185; D'Altroy 2002: 137–138.

95. D'Altroy 2002: 117–125.

96. Trigger 2003: 136–137.

97. Morris 2008.

98. Feasting was an important ritual throughout the empire. Similar evidence can be found at many Inka cities and towns, for example, at Tiwanaku during the period of Inka rule (Knudson et al. 2012).

99. Moore 2004: 100–101.

100. Trigger 2003: 143.

101. D'Altroy 2002: 145–150.

102. Stanish 2001a: 226.

103. D'Altroy 2002: 144.

104. Jennings 2003: 116.

105. Bongers et al. 2012; Moore 2004: 96.

106. D'Altroy 2002: 155–167; Moore 2004.

107. Covey 2003: 351–352; D'Altroy 2002: 141; Moore 2004: 112.

108. Reinhard 1998; 2016; but see Andrushko et al. (2011) for an example of child sacrifice at a town and Besom (2010) for an example of child sacrifice used as a method to link peripheral regions to the empire.

109. D'Altroy 2002: 172–174; Eeckhout and Owens 2008: 391–392.

110. D'Altroy 2002: 172.

111. D'Altroy 2002: 154–155.

112. Doutriaux 2001: 94–95.

113. Andrushko and Torres 2011; Arkush 2008, 2009; Covey 2003: 338–339, 345–346; D'Altroy 2002: 206–207.

114. D'Altroy 2002: 229.

115. Trigger 2003: 246–247, 251–252.

116. D'Altroy 2002: 311–320.

117. Li et al. 2016.

118. Barnosky et al. 2011.

CHAPTER 15

Mapungubwe and Great Zimbabwe in Africa

There were a number of important politically complex societies on the African continent. Some were early developments, such as in Egypt (see Chapter 10), whereas others were later in time, including kingdoms in West Africa, the highland region of Ethiopia, and the coast and highlands of East Africa. In this chapter we will focus on the late politically complex entities of southeastern Africa, known as the Mapungubwe and Zimbabwe cultures. The archaeological sites of these cultures are in the modern countries of Zimbabwe, Botswana, South Africa, and KwaZulu-Natal (an eastern province in South Africa). By the time that the Mapungubwe and Zimbabwe cultures are recognizable archaeologically (read "Timeline: Southeast Africa"), Africa had experienced a long history of food-production economies, including cattle pastoralism. It also witnessed the development and expansion of metallurgy and extensive trade and exchange networks that linked highland areas to the

ABOVE: Interior of the Great Enclosure at Great Zimbabwe, Zimbabwe

coasts and sea routes used for trade to other parts of the east African coast and places more distant, such as the Indo-Pacific region (for example, India). The Mapungubwe and Zimbabwe cultures depended on the "wealth" represented by cattle herds, and both cultures mined gold that was made into status items. Other important luxury goods included ivory, copper, and glass beads. Like the Inka (see Chapter 14), the people of the Mapungubwe and Zimbabwe cultures did not leave a written record of their societies. There are, however, Portuguese accounts of slightly later (and presumably similar) southeastern African highland kingdoms that are used to potentially describe some of the features of Mapungubwe and Zimbabwe societies. Some researchers also use oral histories from modern Shona-speaking groups, who are the descendants of these earlier cultures, as a guide to interpreting some features at archaeological sites.

Food Production

The domesticated plants and animals used by African groups included those introduced from other parts of the world and some that were indigenous to Africa. Cattle herded by pastoral groups in eastern and southeastern Africa were a genetic combination of native cattle and zebu cattle from India that were introduced from the sea trade routes along the coasts of eastern Africa, whereas sheep and goat were from the Middle East, and chickens were brought from Asia.[1] In contrast, many of the important plant food crops were African in origin. These included cereals such as bulrush millet, finger millet, teff, and sorghum.[2] Although many of these domesticates were present by 4000 to 3000 cal BC in north-central Africa and the northern parts of East Africa, domesticates and the social changes they represented in terms of how people organized their lifeways were relatively late in arriving in southeastern Africa.

Many Later Stone Age hunter–gatherer–foragers, however, did not adopt these new subsistence strategies. Instead, some groups continued to rely on wild foods into the present day, whereas others chose only some parts of the domestication "package" of features.[3] The types of features chosen vary from group to group but can include adoption of pottery or one of the domesticated plants or animals or some combination of these. Such adoptions were integrated into a hunting–gathering–foraging lifeway that persisted for hundreds or thousands of years.

The spread of food-production economies in Africa has been the focus of much research. This dispersal appears to be tied to the migration of speakers of Bantu languages from west-central Africa to the southeast and then east[4] (read "Further Reflections: The Bantu Expansion") They are recognized archaeologically as a complex characterized by farming, pastoralism, iron metallurgy, pottery, and settled villages that appeared in the region around Lake Victoria (which is between Uganda, Kenya,

Timeline: Southeast Africa

The African continent was home to several complex political entities. Southeastern African developments are shown here (Figure 15.1).

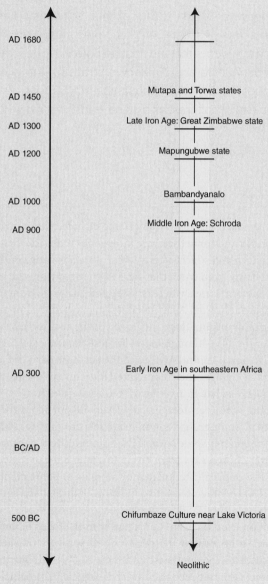

FIGURE 15.1
A timeline for southeastern Africa.

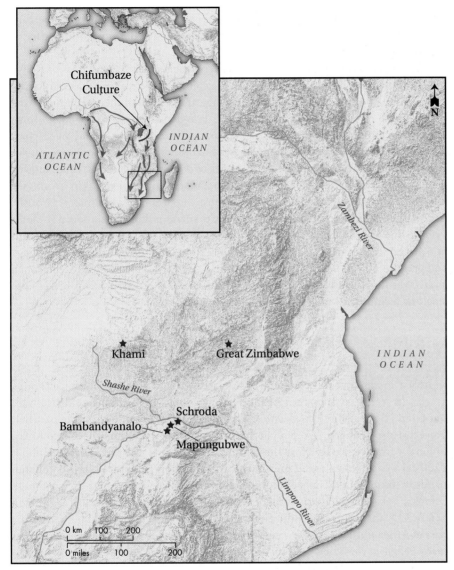

FIGURE 15.2
Southeastern Africa showing sites. Green arrows in inset show directions of the Bantu expansion.

and Tanzania) about 500 cal BC. From there, various aspects of this complex (some-times referred to as the **Chifumbaze complex**[5] or, more generically, as the Early Iron Age) were carried south to other parts of Africa as several waves of Bantu speakers moved into regions where people were still hunter–gatherer–foragers (Figure 15.2). In many cases, hunter–gatherer–foragers did not readily or rapidly adopt the features and lifeways of the Chifumbaze. This may not be surprising in a context in which the

Chifumbaze complex a term used by some archaeologists to indicate the Early Iron Age Bantu-speaking groups whose migrations from central Africa spread iron metallurgy, farming, and herding ways of life to eastern and southern Africa.

initial numbers of Iron Age people involved in population movements were perhaps small, so that two different ways of life could be sustained in the same area, at least for some time.

By AD 200, some of these Bantu speakers reached the coastal areas of Kenya and Tanzania, and by AD 300, this Iron Age complex reached southeastern Africa. Although there is not much direct archaeological evidence of their plant foods, the remains that are found indicate that these Iron Age peoples were growing bulrush millet, finger millet, sorghum, cowpeas, squash, and beans.[6] Cattle (and sheep/goat) pastoralism was an important component of Chifumbaze economic strategies, but they also hunted wild animals. Similar mixes of domesticated animals and hunting were characteristic of other early food-production economies, such as in China (see Chapter 11). In southeastern Africa, the most important herd animal was cattle, and villages often were laid out with the houses surrounding a cattle corral (called a **kraal**).[7] The significance of this central corral is seen by the fact that it was used also as a place to bury important men and women from the village. And the knowledge and practice of iron metallurgy was key in the production of domestic items (such as arrowheads and knives) and for ritual artifacts (see later), especially when the ore smelting techniques were extended to copper and gold.

Kraal a walled, circular enclosure to hold livestock, usually situated at the center of a settlement or village in southeastern/southern Africa.

Metallurgy

In Africa, metallurgy was commonly associated with the working of iron, although as we will see, in southeastern Africa, making copper and working gold also were important. Because the knowledge of how to smelt iron ore to recover the part that is useable is specialized, it is thought that iron metallurgy was introduced into Africa originally from regions such as the Middle East, where it was first developed about 1200 cal BC.[8] As mentioned previously, iron metallurgy appeared in sub-Saharan Africa in the vicinity of Lake Victoria around 500 cal BC as part of the Chifumbaze complex, but archaeological evidence for metallurgy in southeastern Africa is limited before AD 500. This reflects the fact that Early Iron Age groups did not reach this part of Africa until the first few centuries AD and probably also that there were not many people in these new communities migrating into the area who had the specialized knowledge needed to smelt iron as well as copper.[9]

Metallurgy involves a number of processes.[10] First, the ore is mined from its source. Then the metal is extracted (smelted and smithed) from the ore. Finally, the metal is forged (made into practical, ornamental, and ritual artifacts). The actual smelting requires a detailed understanding of the interplay of temperature (produced by charcoal firing), furnace construction (usually of clay), and air (injected into the furnace by operating bellows connected to pipes). The amount of heat needed to smelt is considerable because temperatures in the furnace must reach at least 1100°C (2012°F). The melted iron (called the iron bloom) then is separated from the slag (waste materials), which requires a second heating cycle, this time to

900°C (1652°F), and then hammering (called smithing). Some of the items made from iron included arrowheads, spearheads, hoes, beads, bars and rods, wire, bangles, rings, and pendants.

Specialists in metallurgy in later African societies were men, and archaeologists believe that this also was true in earlier periods. Working with metals was limited to a small number of men with the requisite knowledge and was highly ritualized because it was associated with the idea of reproduction.[11] The smiths had to observe certain ritual prohibitions, such as not having sex when they were working the metal, to keep themselves ritually pure.[12] In addition, the location of the furnace(s) and the activities involved in smelting, smithing, and forging were kept separate from the rest of the community by situating them somewhere outside the village. The degree to which this pattern also was true of the Early Iron Age has been debated by archaeologists, especially because some evidence points to inclusion of smelting and smithing in villages rather than separation of these activities.[13] This separation of activities, however, may have been the situation by the Middle Iron Age around AD 900. Control over metallurgy had implications for the development of political power and status differences that access to wealth (in the form of iron, copper, bronze, or gold artifacts) often accompanied.

The Rise of Mapungubwe and Great Zimbabwe

By the end of the Early Iron Age, southeastern Africa was characterized by numerous villages with farming, pastoralism, and metallurgy. Many of these village societies were engaged in moderately extensive trade networks that stretched from the highland plateaus to the coast of what is now Mozambique. Because of their social role, male leaders (often called chiefs) of these villages were individuals with greater access to cattle, metal items, exotic goods for trade such as elephant ivory, and land for farming. Access to resources by chiefs came about because of payments made to chiefs for tribute, for settling disputes, and from the greater amounts of bride-price that they received when their daughters married.[14] Chiefs also could exert a certain amount of control over activities in villages. Combined with their greater wealth, this meant that chiefs were important socially and politically. Additionally, village life by the Middle Iron Age (AD 900) spread to many areas that were not occupied previously by societies engaged in food-production economies, and population density in the region grew.[15] Some of these villages, because of their locations, were better positioned to take advantage of various natural resources, and their leaders became increasingly more powerful as their influence extended beyond the confines of their immediate village. We will look briefly at several of the important archeological sites involved in documenting the social and political changes from village-based social organization to state-level society and then examine in more detail some themes that characterized these groups, such as trade and exchange networks, social life, religion and ritual, and oral traditions.

Schroda a Middle Iron Age large village established by Zhizo groups in the Shashe–Limpopo area of southeastern Africa. It is sometimes described as a capital for what would later become the Mapungubwe state.

Zhizo a Middle Iron Age group of Bantu-speaking peoples who built the early regionally important center (sometimes called a capital) at Schroda in the Shashe–Limpopo region of southeastern Africa.

One early example of this Middle Iron Age process is seen at the site of **Schroda** in the basin of the Shashe–Limpopo Rivers confluence (see Figure 15.2). Schroda sometimes is identified as the first capital of what later became the Mapungubwe state and was 12 hectares (30 acres) in size.[16] This large village was established by the **Zhizo** people. They brought cattle herding and agriculture from southern Zimbabwe into this area just south of the Limpopo River for the first time. In addition to houses, Schroda had storage bins for grain and a *kraal* for animals. Interestingly, it appears that it was not access to new farming land that led the Zhizo groups here, because rainfall was not abundant in this region, but rather the fact that the area had numerous elephants. Elephants would be rather destructive to farming, especially if farms were located close to the water sources that elephants used. In fact, studies of the settlement pattern of Zhizo villages show that villages were not in places where soil conditions would be most favorable for farming. The attraction of numerous elephants was their ivory tusks, because ivory was a valuable trade item[17] (see "Resource Networks, Trade, and Exchange"). By establishing a village at Schroda, this Zhizo group was able to control an important commodity. Archaeological evidence for this includes abundant debris from working ivory in one part of the village. Other trade items included numerous glass beads, not only at Schroda but throughout the Zhizo settlement area in the Shashe–Limpopo region. There were also caches of clay figurines of both humans and animals that were recovered near the cattle *kraal* at Schroda, indicating probable ritual activities.[18]

Leopard's Kopje cluster Bantu-speaking Iron Age groups who established a regional center first at Bambandyanalo and then at Mapungubwe, which became the political capital of a state-level polity that exerted control over some 30,000 square kilometers (11,583 square miles) of the plateau region in southeastern Africa.

Bambandyanalo a capital established by Leopard's Kopje groups in the Shashe–Limpopo area of southeastern Africa. It controlled a lucrative trade in ivory and abundant imported glass beads are found here and at other sites in the region.

Central Cattle Pattern a village layout in southeastern Africa where a centrally placed *kraal* (corral) is surrounded by the houses of the chief and his family members. The *kraal* area is used for cattle and also as a court where disputes can be heard and settled.

After about a hundred years, around AD 1000, Zhizo groups were replaced by people of the **Leopard's Kopje cluster**, based on the disappearance of Zhizo-style pottery and the appearance of that of Leopard's Kopje.[19] A new capital was established at **Bambandyanalo** (also known as K2; see Figure 15.2), which is 6 kilometers (3.7 miles) to the southwest of Schroda. Bambandyanalo was much larger than Schroda, with 1,500 people (compared to 300 to 500 at Schroda).[20] From AD 1000 to 1220, the people of Bambandyanalo raised cattle, which were a major form of wealth, and continued to hunt elephants for their ivory tusks. Archaeological evidence ranging from chips of ivory to complete tusks indicates that the ivory was worked into luxury and trade items, such as bracelets and knife handles. Ivory items were traded to the coastal region (just as they were earlier at Schroda), as were copper artifacts, which also were made at Bambandyanalo. These perhaps were exchanged for glass beads, which show up in large quantities at Leopard's Kopje settlements in this plateau region. There is evidence showing that some people at Bambandyanalo made glass beads using some of the trade glass beads as the source material. The layout of the town initially had a central *kraal* surrounded by houses. This type of village or town plan is known as the **Central Cattle Pattern**, in which the chief's residence was on the western site of the *kraal*, whereas the other members of his family lived in the other houses around the central *kraal*[21] (Figure 15.3). The central *kraal* also was the area where the chief's court was held to settle disputes, which could be thought of in terms analogous to our system in which the Supreme Court is the final decision-maker. At Bambandyanalo, the central *kraal* was large (30 meters [98 feet] in diameter) and seems to have been used only occasionally to hold cattle. Later, the *kraal* was covered over by trash deposits, and although the court continued to be held in this area, it was no longer associated with cattle.[22] Ordinary people lived in small settlements in the countryside around Bambandyanalo.[23] Each settlement was laid out in the Central Cattle Pattern, so that their local courts continued to be associated with cattle and the central *kraal*. The separation of *kraal* from court at Bambandyanalo accompanied other changes that perhaps indicated a consolidation of political power and wealth by the chief and his family. Accumulation of extraordinary wealth, including eventual ownership of all cattle, was brought about in part because of the trade networks, but also because a pattern of increased rainfall after AD 1000 meant that farming was much more successful and large surpluses of grains (finger millet, sorghum, and pearl millet) could be stored. To help ensure successful agriculture, rainmaking ceremonies were held on top of high hills with steep sides. Associated archaeological materials include sorghum, which was used to make beer, and pottery vessels in which beer was made and drunk.[24] The concentration of power in the hands of the chief at Bambandyanalo seems to indicate that the more elite members of Leopard's Kopje society were becoming increasingly distinct from other people. Around AD 1220, Bambandyanalo was abandoned when the elites and other people moved to a nearby area next to the hill at Mapungubwe in the area of the confluence of the Shashe and Limpopo rivers.

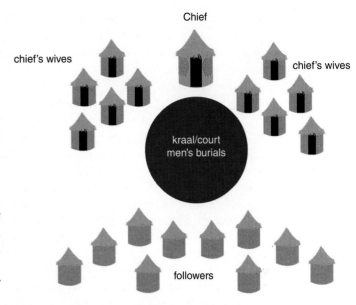

FIGURE 15.3
A schematic view of the Central Cattle Pattern (after Huffman 2000).

Mapungubwe became the capital of what is described as the Mapungubwe state[25] (see Figure 15.2). It was sparsely occupied before the move from Bambandyanalo but became densely inhabited (5,000 people), although only for a short time (80 years). Mapungubwe also is recognized as the first archaeological evidence of **Zimbabwe Pattern** (Zimbabwe Culture), in which stone-walled structures were built for elite members of society as well as for marking the center of the town. Some researchers suggest that there were ideological meanings accompanying this layout[26] (see later for discussion). As we saw earlier, Shroda and Bambandyanalo contained evidence that status differences existed between wealthier chiefs and the rest of society. By the time of Mapungubwe, these distinctions became even more marked, with the elite ruler now living in near seclusion from everyone else, whereas other members of his family dealt with day-to-day political and legal matters. The separation of the ruler is clearly seen archaeologically because his stone-walled residence (palace) and a rainmaking ceremony area were built on top of the hill, and royal graves were located there[27] (Figure 15.4). Gaining access to the top of the steep hill was restricted

Mapungubwe the capital of the Mapungubwe state in the Shashe–Limpopo area of southeastern Africa during the Middle Iron Age. It controlled the ivory trade, as well as trade and exchange in cattle and other goods. The Zimbabwe Pattern was first established here.

Zimbabwe Pattern also called Zimbabwe Culture, it consists of stone-walled structures built for elites with the ruler's residence secluded on top of a relatively inaccessible hill and the rest of the royalty houses built immediately adjacent to the base of the hill. Commoners lived in daga (clay) huts farther away from the hill.

FIGURE 15.4
Aerial view of the hilltop at Mapungubwe where the king lived and conducted rainmaking rituals.

to four paths, and few people other than members of the royal family and their staffs, ritual specialists, important visitors, and soldiers to guard the paths used them. The stone-walled residences for other elite members of society were situated at the base of the hill, thus surrounding the king. This area also held the court for commoners. To the east of the hill was where the commoners lived in thatch-roofed houses built of *daga* (a mix of dung and mud to form walls). Trade continued to be an important avenue to accumulating wealth and included cattle, iron, copper, and grains within the region where Mapungubwe was located, whereas trade with the coastal sea routes consisted of ivory (as we saw in earlier periods) and the addition of gold items. As before, Asian glass beads were traded inland from the coasts. Around AD 1290 to 1300, Mapungubwe was abandoned, possibly because of climatic changes that made agriculture in this area unsustainable.[28] We will examine some of the details of life at Mapungubwe later.

The next state-level political system in southeastern Africa was centered at **Great Zimbabwe** (Figure 15.5; see Figure 15.2), which was 300 kilometers (186 miles) north of Mapungubwe.[29] The people who built and lived at this capital, however, were not from Mapungubwe,[30] although some archaeologists have suggested that members of the Mapungubwe dynasty were established at Great Zimbabwe to provide local control over trade resources, when Great Zimbabwe was not yet politically important.[31] This might explain why the Zimbabwe Pattern for site layout

Great Zimbabwe the capital city of the Great Zimbabwe state in the plateau region of southeastern Africa. It controlled a vast trade and exchange network in gold, cattle, iron, ivory, and copper. Great Zimbabwe was organized using the Zimbabwe Pattern.

FIGURE 15.5
Aerial view of the Great Enclosure at Great Zimbabwe; stone ruins in front of the Great Enclosure are part of the Valley Complex.

and distinction between ruling elites and commoners was used for construction there. Alternatively, this spatial arrangement might have been one shared by several different groups of people in competing polities in this region of Africa.[32] There were small archaeological deposits representing rainmaking ceremonies on the hill at Great Zimbabwe relatively early, but it was after AD 1290 that Great Zimbabwe became a large town (720 hectares [1,780 acres]) of perhaps 18,000 people.[33] Like Mapungubwe, Great Zimbabwe was characterized by the contrast between areas of stone-walled structures and those with simple *daga* huts.[34] The ruler (king) lived on top of the hill in the Hill Complex. This had several stone-walled enclosures where he and other members of the royal family resided. In the area below the hill was a court and a massive stone-walled structure called the Great Enclosure, which had three entrances and a number of interesting internal features including platforms, towers, and internal walls (see discussion later). Both the Great Enclosure and the Hill Complex were set off from the rest of the valley by a perimeter wall. Outside this perimeter wall were the houses of commoners, as well as other stone-walled enclosures. These would have been the residences of other elites, with stone-walling keeping them separate from commoners. Smaller sites in the region also had features of stone-walled construction, indicating their links to the capital at Great Zimbabwe, as well as social and political status differences (on a smaller scale) within each of these outlying communities. Like its predecessors, at least some of the political might of Great Zimbabwe was a result of its importance in regional and international trade networks.

Resource Networks, Trade, and Exchange

The plateau region of southeastern Africa where sites such as Schroda, Bambandyanalo, Mapungubwe, and Great Zimbabwe were situated is a region that had a number of important resources. In some cases, these resources were basic features such as soil fertility of floodplains and adequate rainfall for successful farming that permitted the accumulation of crop surpluses. As we saw in previous chapters, surpluses were a form of wealth because they can be used to "fund" construction or other efforts. In southeastern Africa they also were used as tribute payments to village chiefs and eventually to royalty at Mapungubwe and Great Zimbabwe. The same was true with respect to raising cattle. Much of this region lies at an elevation above the distribution of the tsetse fly, which causes debilitating disease and death to cattle.[35] Thus, cattle herds were both healthy and large in much of the region of the southeastern African state-level polities. Cattle were a more secure form of wealth than crops, which could suffer large declines from droughts and loss of soil fertility.[36] In addition, cattle were owned by men who could trade them for other resources or loan them to others (analogous to taking a loan from a bank today). Village chiefs and eventually elite rulers and their families owned vast herds of cattle and thus a considerable proportion of the available wealth in these societies.

In addition to crops and cattle, as well as iron and copper objects, which could be used as trade resources within this region, one of the early resources present there that was used for external trade, as we saw earlier, was ivory.[37] Along with raising cattle and doing some limited farming, the people of Schroda hunted elephants, worked their tusks into various items, and then traded these to Swahili traders, who took them to the towns on the sea routes along the Mozambique coast. International trade in ivory continued to be important for the people at Bambandyanalo and Mapungubwe and then declined somewhat during the period when Great Zimbabwe was the political center, when gold became an important commodity. This may have resulted partly from the fact that there were more gold ore resources in the area near Great Zimbabwe than in the region of Schroda, Bambandyanalo, and Mapungubwe. International demand for gold helped drive this process, and gold and artifacts made from it became one of the crafts of the plateau region.[38] Mining and smelting of gold, as well as support for iron and copper metallurgy, and the manufacture of ivory items in the plateau region were paid for by some of the cattle wealth of the royal families at Mapungubwe and Great Zimbabwe.[39] The plateau region also likely provided skins from wild animals such as leopards as part of this international trade relationship. In return, the highland region received glass beads from Asia, which were found in enormous quantities at the town and city centers of Schroda, Bambandyanalo, Mapungubwe, and Great Zimbabwe (read "The Big Picture: Trade and Exchange in the Shashe–Limpopo and Plateau Region"). The elites at Mapungubwe and Great Zimbabwe also received glazed ceramics from China.[40]

The Big Picture

Trade and Exchange in the Shashe–Limpopo and Plateau Region

International trade was an important source of wealth and political power for elites in earlier large village networks such as that represented by Schroda and Bambandyanalo and in the later state-level polities represented by Mapungubwe and Great Zimbabwe.[41] One of the most easily identified imports into the Shashe–Limpopo and Plateau area are glass beads.[42] These appeared in large quantities around AD 1000 and included Indo-Pacific beads that were probably from India or possibly Southeast Asia. The origin area for some types of beads, such as those of translucent turquoise to blue–green colors, is not known. Others may have come from bead-making centers in the Middle East. As imports, glass beads were a type of exotic good, and one example of their use comes from an elite burial on Mapungubwe Hill. This individual was associated with large quantities of beads that likely were sewn onto clothing. The importance of glass beads also is seen in the fact that some of them were used locally to make Garden Roller beads (Figure 15.6). At sites such as Bambandyanalo, pottery molds into which these Garden Roller beads fit were found. This indicates that Leopard's Kopje groups were melting down the blue–green to turquoise-colored imported beads to create a new type of bead that perhaps was a prestige item in the Shashe–Limpopo and Plateau areas.

FIGURE 15.6
Small trade glass beads (left, bottom) next to Garden Roller glass beads (right and top) from Mapungubwe.

Social Life

As we saw previously, most settlements and villages in the Iron Age in southeastern Africa were laid out in a specific manner, which some archaeologists call the Central Cattle Pattern.[43] This layout created areas that were linked to men and others that were for women. In the men's area at the center of the settlement were *kraals* for cattle, storage bins for grains, the court to settle disputes, and graves of high-ranking men. Iron metallurgy also could be undertaken in this central area of the settlement. Away from the central area were the dwellings for wives (one male could have more than one wife), along with their kitchens and graves. In many of these settlements and villages, there were particular individuals who were the leaders or chiefs responsible for political and social decisions; their position was hereditary. Such chiefs had greater access to resources (including exotic items), lived in larger huts, had more wives, and owned more cattle than other people. The spatial arrangement of the Central Cattle Pattern also incorporated differences between people in the settlement, with higher ranked individuals living in dwellings closer to that of the chief. In one sense, however, all the people living in these Central Cattle Pattern settlements were commoners, although chiefs and their families had a slightly elevated status. The village at Schroda, although its chief controlled internal and external trade to a much greater extent than other Zhizo settlement chiefs, was essentially an example of the Central Cattle Pattern on a larger scale.

When the Leopard's Kopje people established Bambandyanalo as the regional center ("capital") that controlled trade and whose chiefs made the important legal and political decisions for the village and the surrounding region, they also initially used the Central Cattle Pattern for the layout of the settlement. However, as discussed above, this central portion of the site now was reserved for the chief and his family, including his many wives, whereas everyone else lived in settlements farther out. This suggests a subtle shift toward greater separation of higher-status individuals and families from the rest of the community. This separation eventually included moving the cattle away from the center of the settlement, as the *kraal* areas became covered over by refuse or were used exclusively as a commoners' court for settling disputes. Burials found in the area where women had their houses were of females and children, as might be expected in a settlement layout that separated women's from men's areas of activity.[44]

The distinctions between higher- and lower-status individuals accelerated once the capital shifted to Mapungubwe. Although most people continued to live in settlements organized along the lines of the Central Cattle Pattern model, the elite ruler and his immediate family were completely separated from commoners. This type of settlement organization is known, as mentioned previously, as the Zimbabwe Pattern. The ruler lived on top of the rainmaking hill, and both he and the rest of the nobility had stone-walled residences, whereas commoners lived in *daga* huts in areas that were physically separated from the royalty.[45] Archaeological evidence from the hilltop location clearly shows the types of materials that indicated high status/high rank. The structures were stone-walled and large.[46] There was a western hut complex

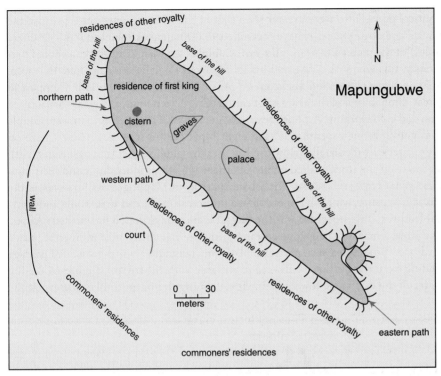

FIGURE 15.7
Plan map of Mapungubwe (after Huffman 2008, Figure 12).

on the hill where the first king lived, as well as a palace and rainmaking area toward the middle part of the hill where the second king lived (Figure 15.7). Additionally, a royal cemetery was located between the palace and the wives' residences. It contained 23 graves, of which 3 were especially luxurious.[47] The grave goods associated with one probable male included gold plating, wire, and tacks, part of a staff, a gold rhinoceros, large amounts of glass beads, and several clay vessels (the "Original Gold Grave"). Another male burial had a gold scepter, gold rhinoceros, gold beads and clay bowls (the "Sceptre Skeleton"). The third burial is thought to be a female (the "Gold Grave"); she was buried with more than 26,000 glass beads, 12,000 gold beads, more than 100 gold bangles, and pottery vessels. The king's status became sacred,[48] at least in part because he allied himself directly with the important ritual of rainmaking (see later). The king would have ruled from Mapungubwe partly by establishing alliances with various settlements through marriage, and some of his wives would have lived in those communities rather than at Mapungubwe. Some estimates of the extent of Mapungubwe's regional influence suggest an area of 30,000 square kilometers (11,600 square miles).[49]

Great Zimbabwe continued, and perhaps expanded, the social class separation and settlement layout of the Zimbabwe Pattern. Its regional influence and political power also were greater than that of the Mapungubwe state because the Great Zimbabwe state may have controlled 90,000 square kilometers (34,750 square miles) of the plateau region.[50] The Hill Complex at Great Zimbabwe, as noted previously, was where the king and his family lived in elaborate *daga* huts that were built inside stone-walled enclosures.[51] As at Mapungubwe, the Hill Complex at Great Zimbabwe had ritual areas for rainmaking ceremonies, as well as furnaces for iron and gold working. Among the luxury items found in this elite area were double iron gongs, bronze spearheads, and eight birds carved from soapstone (more on these later). Immediately below the hill was the public court (not associated with a *kraal*) and the stone-walled homes of other high-status individuals and their families. What really sets Great Zimbabwe apart from Mapungubwe, however, is the Great Enclosure, which had more than a million stone blocks in its walls and internal features. This structure was the largest stone construction in southern Africa. The Great Enclosure had three entrances, an internal enclosure, two interior stone towers in the southeastern part, two platform areas, and an internal walled passage leading from the northern entrance to the area with the towers (Figure 15.8). The larger of the two stone towers had a dentelle (angular or tooth-like) pattern at the

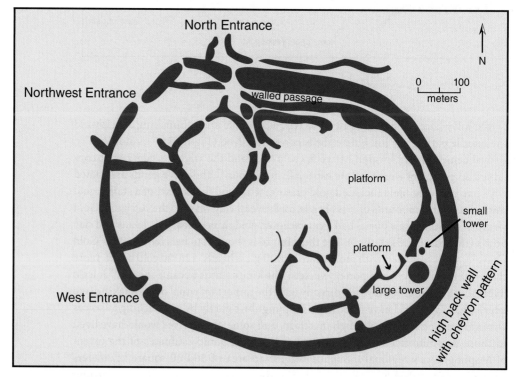

FIGURE 15.8
Plan map of the Great Enclosure at Great Zimbabwe (after Chirikure and Pikirayi 2008, Figure 6; Huffman 1984, Figure 2).

top, possibly suggesting crocodile teeth.[52] An exterior chevron decorative motif was placed at the top of the southeastern part of the enclosure wall.[53] Immediately adjacent to and north of the Great Enclosure were a series of living and storage areas that were interconnected, including the Renders Ruin. Excavations in the Renders Ruin yielded abundant evidence for access to exotic and status items, including finger rings and a box made of copper, iron objects (gongs, a spoon, bangles, hoes, axes, and a lamp holder), bronze spearheads, gold beads, marine shells, and thousands of glass beads.[54] There are at least a couple of different interpretations for the Great Enclosure. One of these is that it was used in part for initiation ceremonies for young boys and girls and that its northern entrance connected it to the residential area (including the Renders Ruin) for royal wives of the king.[55] An alternative view suggests that the Great Enclosure was a residential area for the king, in a sequence that saw the first royal residence in the Hill Complex, and then a later move to the valley floor and the Great Enclosure.[56] These types of contrasting interpretations, as we have seen in previous chapters, are a vital feature of archaeological debate because they provide new examinations of existing and new data sets from various fields of inquiry (discussed in more detail later).

Ritual and Religion

For people living in southeastern Africa, adequate rainfall in this somewhat dry region would have been important for farming, as well as for the growth of wild grasses on which cattle could graze. To help ensure that it would rain, the Leopard's Kopje groups developed a set of rainfall ceremonies conducted by specialists who kept this knowledge secret. The archaeological study of these rituals uses data from excavations as well as information from ethnographic studies (modern or historic observations). During the period that Bambandyanalo was occupied, rainmaking ceremonies likely were conducted by rainmaker specialists (who were men). Initially, these rainmakers appear to have been hunter–gatherer–foragers rather than the Leopard's Kopje farmers/herders.[57] These hunter–gatherer–foragers were recognized as the people who were the first in the region and may have been seen as especially connected to place and to nature. The hunter–gatherer–foragers thus might be thought of as having greater power to affect natural events such as rainfall. The hilltops where the rainmaking rituals were conducted were at some distance from the villages in the river valleys where the farmers lived. Over time, the Leopard's Kopje farmers at Bambandyanalo as well as other sites took over the rainmaking rituals. Some farmers became specialists and conducted ceremonies in special places behind their houses, whereas other people in the community, including the chief, assisted by spreading "rain medicine" on farm lands and by burning cattle dung to create smoke that would bring rain clouds.[58] If drought conditions occurred, then the rainmaker went to special hilltops that were relatively inaccessible but had natural depressions that held water. There the specialist built temporary storage bins for grain and made beer to be used as an offering to the ancestors for their help in bringing rain. The pottery vessels that held the beer were left on the hill after the ceremony, and the grain bins were destroyed. As we saw previously, during the period that Mapungubwe was occupied, elite rulers built their residences on top of the rainmaking hill, and eventually the ruler became the rainmaker, a tradition that carried over to Great Zimbabwe.[59]

The Big Picture

Art and Ideology at Great Zimbabwe

The seven birds carved from soapstone found at Great Zimbabwe were unique and are used today as one of the symbols of the modern country of Zimbabwe. Each bird was a raptor, probably an eagle. Instead of having talons, most were depicted with human toes/fingers, and most had humanlike legs.[61] Additionally, each bird was distinguished from the others because each had individual features. One, for example, had human lips instead of a beak, and each had a different symbol carved onto the pillar on which it sat[62] (Figure 15.9). The uniqueness of the soapstone birds and

their placement in the hilltop Eastern Enclosure at Great Zimbabwe has suggested to some archaeologists that the birds might symbolize a combination of human and nonhuman and also represent earlier elite rulers. The rationale for this interpretation is that the rulers at Great Zimbabwe had these soapstone bird images carved to legitimize their right to rule and their connections to earlier rulers and to the spirit world. This would help establish their credentials as divine and as integral to the rainmaking rituals that called upon ancestors to intercede.

FIGURE 15.9
Stylized drawings of some of the soapstone birds from Great Zimbabwe (after Walton 1955, Figure 2). Distinctive markings are shown in red; note also the humanlike toe/finger feet on some of the examples.

When elite rulers took over the role as rainmaker, this established a pattern in which the ancestors of the rulers were the most powerful and the links between these ancestors and the ruler helped create conditions under which the ruler became a sacred person. Rulers often have a set of symbols that are associated with them, just as we saw in previous chapters. For the elite rulers of Mapungubwe and Great Zimbabwe, ideology connected them to powerful creatures such as crocodiles.[60] One of the reasons for this association is that crocodiles are linked to water and thus, more broadly, to rainfall. Others include characteristics such as being dangerous and not afraid of enemies, which were traits that a ruler should have. It has been argued that some designs on pottery as early as Mapungubwe were those that represented the crocodile. These included deep pits punched into the clay, which could represent the skin pits of a crocodile and the dentelle pattern found in stonework such as at the palace and Great Enclosure tower at Great Zimbabwe. One of the most intriguing symbols, however, was the soapstone birds found at Great Zimbabwe (read "The Big Picture: Art and Ideology at Great Zimbabwe").

Oral Traditions

To build interpretations of past societies, archaeologists normally have only the evidence of the archaeological record for a particular time and place. On rare occasions, they can draw on historical documents (such as the Spanish accounts of the Inka; see Chapter 14) to aid in understanding some of the features of sites, the cultural materials from them, and the social, political, and religious activities and organizations of those past societies. The rarest type of information is obtained from the oral traditions of living people who are the descendants of those who created that archaeological record (for example, North American Southwest Native Americans; see Chapter 7). In the case of the early southeastern African politically complex societies discussed earlier, some archaeologists have argued that the oral traditions of modern Shona speakers and related Venda speakers, as well as the conceptual ways in which they organize their living spaces, can be used to interpret the ideological world view of the peoples who lived at Mapungubwe and Great Zimbabwe, as well as the Iron Age groups using the Central Cattle Pattern for their settlement layout.[63] These oral traditions can be supplemented with information recorded by the Portuguese about slightly later southeastern African states. At the heart of this type of archaeological interpretation is the link between today and the past. The fact that types of Leopard's Kopje pottery were used relatively recently by Shona speakers perhaps suggests that the earlier Iron Age Leopard's Kopje groups spoke a type of Shona.[64]

This approach can described as an example of cognitive archaeology (see Chapter 1). In this perspective, most of the spatial arrangement of features in individual structures, as well as an entire site, had ideological meanings. These meanings are said to be related to life forces and status[65] and included divisions such as male/female, public/private, and old/young, which are divisions known from Shona oral traditions and ethnography. One example is seen in the interpretation of the Great Enclosure at Great Zimbabwe as a place where initiation ceremonies for young women were carried out.[66] With respect to male/female separation, researchers note that the northern entrance of this structure is accessed only from the area where the king's wives lived, whereas the western entrance led to the men's court at the base of the hill where the ruler lived. Once inside the Great Enclosure, the northern (female) entrance was connected to a stone-walled passageway that had vertical grooves that were associated with women (based on their presence in other women's areas of Great Zimbabwe) and that led to the area with the two stone towers. On the other hand, the western (male) entrance put one immediately into a large open space that once had two tall standing stones that were associated with men (based on similar monoliths in the king's palace) and where one could gain access to the two stone towers by walking to the southeastern part of the Great Enclosure. The concepts of public and private are seen by the entrances being on the north/west, which would be considered the "front" and thus public, whereas the two stone towers and associated features are found directly opposite in the southeast part of the enclosure (which also had a much higher exterior wall), meaning that this portion represented the "back" of the structure and thus the area that was private.

The notion that the Great Enclosure was used for initiation rituals incorporates these ideas of male/female and public/private, but also the concept of old/young. It is based on modern Venda traditions for initiating young women that include lessons on manners, sex, and proper behavior. In the private (or sacred) area of the Great

The Role of Oral History and Historical Documents

Early Shona speakers were clearly responsible for the Mapungubwe and Great Zimbabwe states. The extent to which the oral traditions of living Shona speakers and existing historical documents can be used to interpret these early societies, however, has been much debated. As described in the text, some archaeologists use these sources to recreate social perceptions and societal organization of the people who lived at sites such as Great Zimbabwe. Other researchers argue that the archaeological record and historic documents suggest an alternative interpretation of the stone-walled features on the hilltop and in the valley below.[67] They propose that the Western Enclosure on the hilltop, as well as the Great Enclosure in the valley, were the residences of different

kings who ruled at this site. They support their argument with radiocarbon dates from these structures, as well as architectural details of construction and artifacts indicating the presence of both men and women in these structures. In this interpretation, the first ruler built and lived with his wives in the Western Enclosure on the hilltop. His successor built and lived with his wives in the Great Enclosure in the valley below. The period of rulers living in the Great Enclosure coincides with the height of Great Zimbabwe's regional power. During the period of Great Zimbabwe's decline, its rulers moved to other stone-walled enclosures in other parts of the valley floor (Figure 15.10). The hilltop area remained an important sacred spot, especially for rainmaking rituals.

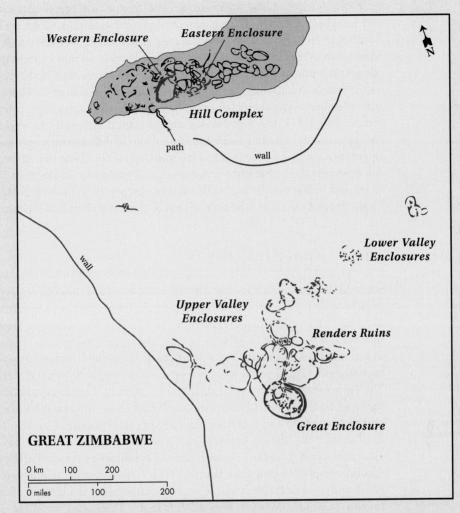

FIGURE 15.10
Plan map of Great Zimbabwe (after Chirikure and Pikirayi 2008, Figure 2; Huffman 1981, Figure 7). In the Hilltop Complex, the black outlined objects are large boulders that were incorporated into the stone-walled structures (shown in red). In the valley, the red outlined structures are stone-walled enclosures.

Enclosure with its two stone towers, there were a number of cultural materials and artistic motifs that may suggest these types of initiation ceremonies. The larger of the stone towers, for example, is on the west side (the same as the western public entrance for males) and has a dentelle (crocodile/male) design at the top, whereas the smaller tower is to the north. The tall tower is interpreted as representing the concept of old male (who is wise) and the smaller tower as old female (who represents unity and who is the teacher). A double chevron pattern (representing snakes, which are symbols of fertility) in front of the two towers is seen as associated with the notion of young male, whereas the black-and-white design (interpreted as a zebra pattern that mirrors the sexual union of a couple) in front of the two towers is identified as representing young female. Additionally, a large *daga* platform in this area of the Great Enclosure yielded numerous figurines (abstract, human, animal), suggesting a ritual function for the platform. Taken together, the archaeological materials, the observations of Venda practices regarding initiation rituals, and oral traditions in general are used to propose a young women's initiation function for the Great Enclosure. However, not everyone agrees that historical sources, oral traditions, and modern practices of living descendants can be used in this way to interpret these earlier Iron Age societies (read "Peopling the Past: The Role of Oral History and Historical Documents").

After Great Zimbabwe

Torwa state state to the southwest of Great Zimbabwe in southeastern Africa that was a powerful political entity after the decline of Great Zimbabwe. Its capital was at Khami in what is now the modern country of Zimbabwe.

Mutapa state a complex political entity to the north of Great Zimbabwe, near the Zambezi River. It may have been established by people from Great Zimbabwe and was the state encountered and described by the Portuguese.

From AD 1420 to 1450, the capital at Great Zimbabwe declined in importance, possibly because trade routes to the coast shifted to more northerly rivers, such as the Zambezi.[68] This meant that the ruler at Great Zimbabwe no longer had much control over the lucrative trade in gold, ivory, iron, and other commodities. Without access to this wealth, their importance and influence diminished. Instead, other regions of southeastern Africa became more powerful, including the Torwa and Mutapa states. The **Torwa state** had its capital at Khami (in modern Zimbabwe) and was situated to the southwest of Great Zimbabwe (see Figure 15.2). The **Mutapa state** was to the north (closer to the Zambezi River) and possibly was established by elites from Great Zimbabwe.[69] The Mutapa state was encountered by the Portuguese, who were interested in the gold from the interior regions of southeastern Africa. Portuguese negotiators attempted to gain more control of this trade by going directly to the Mutapa court, and some of the Portuguese wrote descriptions of the settlements and political and social situations that they encountered.[70] These are some of the documents sometimes used as a baseline to describe and interpret the features of the earlier states controlled by elites at Mapungubwe and Great Zimbabwe.

Further Reflections

The Bantu Expansion

The importance of the Bantu expansion, which occurred very rapidly (over about 3,000 years) and is supported by genetic data, cannot be overstated.[71]

It was groups of Bantu language speakers who brought food-production economies and metallurgy for the first time to much of southern Africa (see Figure 15.2), being early influences on what would become the social and political trajectories that resulted in the Mapungubwe and Zimbabwe kingdoms, among others. Bantu speakers themselves also established politically complex polities such as the Zulu kingdom in southern Africa. But how did the Bantu expansion occur, and why was it so successful?

The homeland region for the Bantu languages is known to be in central-western Africa, what is today the Nigeria–Cameroon border region. They were groups of people who lived in the savanna (grasslands) habitat, where they could farm relatively easily. They began to migrate around 3000 BC, but it was when the rainforest shrank a bit in size, due to climatic changes around 2000 BC, that they were able to initially expand.[72] This occurred because, although some Bantu groups did eventually expand into the rainforest, their initial preference was for savannah habitats. With the shrinkage of the rainforest, people could move into areas along the edges of the rainforest. A second major climatic event around 500 BC, which altered the pattern of monsoons, resulted in the opening up of some of the central portions of the rainforest, thus creating a savannah "corridor" that could be used to migrate to the southeast and eventually both to the east and further south.[73] The new seasonal rainfall patterns also were conducive to growing cereals. It was during this period that Bantu speakers were able to rapidly migrate elsewhere, taking their food-production and metallurgy ways of life to other parts of Africa. They were entering regions that had only hunter–gatherer–forager groups whose uses of the landscape likely did not conflict (at least initially) with those of the incoming Bantu-speaking groups.

Summary

- Food-production economies were introduced into southeastern Africa by Bantu-speaking groups during the Early Iron Age. Cattle pastoralism was one important feature of domestication economies there, along with growing millets and sorghum.

- Metallurgy during the Iron Age included iron, gold, and copper. The knowledge needed to work iron was extensive, and specialists in this craft appear to have been men. Ironworking required certain ritual practices and often was done in areas away from villages.

- In southeastern Africa, by the end of the Early Iron Age, many villages had a central cattle *kraal* with houses around it. These villages were led by chiefs, who exerted some control over trade and exchange networks, including elephant ivory.

- During the Middle Iron Age, in the Shashe–Limpopo rivers area, Zhizo groups established much larger villages. They appear to have settled here because of access to large herds of elephants and thus to ivory.

- About a hundred years later, Leopard's Kopje groups moved into the Shashe–Limpopo region and established a capital at Bambandyanalo that was characterized by the Central Cattle Pattern. This pattern consisted of a *kraal* with the chief's house to the west and the houses of the chief's family surrounding the rest of the *kraal*. The *kraal* area was used to hold court to settle various disputes.

- Large quantities of imported glass beads at Leopard's Kopje sites suggest extensive trade and exchange networks beyond the Shashe–Limpopo region.

- The next capital was nearby at Mapungubwe, which is sometimes described as the Mapungubwe state. A new settlement layout called the Zimbabwe Pattern was established. This was marked by the construction of stone-walled residences for elite rulers, who usually built their residence on a hilltop, which was associated with rainmaking rituals. The king lived in near seclusion from most people.

- The state centered at Great Zimbabwe was the successor to the Mapungubwe state. It also controlled lucrative trade and exchange in ivory, cattle, gold, and imported glass beads. Stone-walled residences for the king were constructed on the hilltop. There also was a large stone-walled construction called the Great Enclosure in the valley below. Interpretations of the function of the Great Enclosure are debated, with some researchers believing that it was a residence for the king and his wives but others arguing that it served a role in initiation ceremonies for young women and men.

- Rainmaking was a significant and important ritual activity and was conducted on relatively inaccessible hilltops. It was one of the functions taken over by elite rulers who used it to legitimize their rule. It relied on appealing to ancestors to intercede to bring rain. As the king was a rainmaker, his rule likely was partially dependent on his success.

- Reconstruction of the past lifeways of the people of the Mapungubwe and Great Zimbabwe states relies on several sources of information. The archaeological record is one of these, but researchers also use oral traditions of Shona speakers, who are the descendants of those earlier groups, and historical documents written by foreign visitors to the region.

- These historical documents describe similar states in southeastern Africa, but ones that came after Great Zimbabwe. Among them were the Torwa and Mutapa states. The Mutapa were encountered by the Portuguese.

Endnotes

1. Hanotte et al. 2002.
2. Marshall and Hildebrand 2002; Neumann et al. 2012.
3. Lane et al. 2007.
4. Bostoen et al. 2015; Grollemund et al. 2015.
5. Phillipson 2005: 249, Footnote 2.
6. Phillipson 2005: 258.
7. Huffman 1993, 2001.
8. Phillipson 2005: 214–216.
9. Chirikure 2007: 89–90.
10. Miller 2002.
11. Calabrese 2000: 109.
12. Childs and Killick 1993: 327.
13. Chirikure 2007: 90–93.
14. Huffman 2005: 10; Pikirayi 2001: 85–88.
15. Kim and Kusimba 2008: 137.
16. Huffman 2005: 10; Phillipson 2005: 256–257.

17. Huffman 2009: 42.
18. Huffman 2005: 11; Pikirayi 2001: 89.
19. Huffman 2009: 42; Zhizo groups seem to have abandoned the Shashe–Limpopo basin and moved into what is now eastern Botswana, where they established a ranked society that coexisted with that of the Shashe–Limpopo area (Pikirayi 2001: 97).
20. Huffman 2005: 10, 17.
21. Huffman 2009: 42–43.
22. Huffman 2000: 20.
23. Huffman 2005: 24–25.
24. Huffman 2005: 27.
25. Huffman 2015.
26. Huffman 2000: 21, 2009: 39; Phillipson 2005: 298.
27. Huffman 2005: 34–37; Kim and Kusimba 2008: 140–141.
28. Huffman 2009: 51.
29. Huffman 2005: 55.
30. See Chirikure et al. 2013 for a discussion of the archaeological and dating evidence suggesting several temporally overlapping state-level polities and for data concerning the establishment of Great Zimbabwe by peoples different from those at Mapungubwe.
31. Huffman 2010a: 8.
32. Chirikure et al. 2013.
33. Phillipson 2005: 300.
34. Kim and Kusimba 2008: 144; Pikirayi 2001: 131–140.
35. Garlake 1978: 484–486.
36. Pikirayi 2001: 112.
37. Pikirayi 2001: 91.
38. Miller 2002: 1127; Miller et al. 2000: 95–96.
39. Kim and Kusimba 2008: 141, 143.
40. Huffman 2005: 53.
41. Kusimba 2008: 243.
42. Wood 2000.
43. Huffman 1993; 2009: 38–39.
44. Huffman 2005: 19.
45. Huffman 2009: 39.
46. Huffman 2005: 38, 42–44; 2009: 43–45.
47. Steyn 2007.
48. Huffman 2010a: 6–7.
49. Huffman 2009: 44.
50. Huffman 2010a: 8.
51. Pikirayi 2001: 134–138.
52. Huffman 1984: 256.
53. Chirikure and Pikirayi 2008: 987.
54. Huffman 1981: 136.
55. Huffman 1981, 1984, 2010b.
56. Chirikure and Pikirayi 2008, 2011.
57. Schoeman 2006: 162.
58. Huffman 2009: 40–41.
59. .Huffman 2009: 41, 46; Schoeman 2006: 163–164.
60. Huffman 2009: 51–53.
61. Huffman 2009: 52–53.
62. Walton 1955.
63. Huffman 1981, 1984, 2009: 39–40.
64. Huffman 2005: 17.
65. Huffman 1981: 131.
66. Huffman 1984.
67. Beach 1998; Chirikure and Pikirayi 2008.
68. Pikirayi 2001: 150–153.
69. Huffman 2010a: 2.
70. Pikirayi 2001: 170–192.
71. Bostoen et al. 2015; Grollemund et al. 2015.
72. Grollemund et al. 2015.
73. Bostoen et al. 2015.

5 | Epilogue

Epilogue

One of the great advantages of the archaeological record is its capacity to provide data used to examine and interpret change over time. These data are from time spans that exceed the lifetime of any one individual as well as generations of people. Although archaeology documents the lives of named and unnamed elite members of socially and politically complex societies, as we have seen in previous chapters, it also is the story of the multitude of nonelites who were the most numerous members of those past groups. Beyond that, archaeology is a record of the diversity of cultural and social responses of humans to the world around them, including to other people, as well as their behavioral strategies. We focused in many chapters on examining those strategies that led to the development of politically complex entities in different parts of the world. It is important to remember, however, that those trajectories represent only part of the vast spectrum of societal organizations that characterize humans past and present. Not every group that engaged in food production, for example, became a kingdom, a state, or an empire. Some people remained hunter–gatherer–foragers despite exposure

ABOVE: Petroglyphs at Kaunolu on the island of Lana'i, Hawai'i.

to neighboring food-producing groups. These non–politically complex peoples are not "exceptions to the rule" because there is no one rule. This is because the types of decisions that people made were from a large array of choices available to them at any one moment. These choices varied over time and were influenced by many factors. Some of these choices related to the natural productivity of the landscape where people lived. Others were influenced by environment or climate. Still others hinged on people's social relationships within their groups and with neighbors, as well as their ideological values including rituals and religion. Ultimately, all this resulted in many different trajectories, each of which had its own specific archaeological record.[1]

All Good Things Come to an End

There are many research questions and interpretations concerning the origins of politically complex societies and how they functioned socially, politically, and economically. There also is equal interest in understanding why they ultimately were not successful. In some of the examples in previous chapters, the end came about as a result of a combination of internal issues and newly arrived foreigners. This was the case for the Inka and Aztec empires with the coming of the Spanish (see Chapters 13 and 14). And, although they were not state polities, Late Mississippian period groups in the North American East also were significantly impacted by the arrival of the Spanish (see Chapter 8). Studying the disappearance of early polities is relatively complex because there were many factors at work. These include the social perception by commoners and competing elites of the success of the society and its ruler, environmental variables such as persistent droughts or increased flooding, shifts in demand by outsiders for exotic and other goods, overuse of the landscape for food production resulting in decreased soil fertility and decreased surpluses, and the costs—in terms of labor, tribute, and other taxes—of supporting the system.[2] It is unlikely that any single explanation is sufficient, although literature on the disappearance of past politically complex societies often gives that impression.[3] Even the terminology that we use, such as "collapse" or "disappearance," is difficult. By using the term "good" in the title to this section, for example, I have potentially biased your understanding of these early politically complex polities. For whom were these polities good? Presumably, their elite rulers thought of them as good because they could accomplish various objectives. But other elite segments of those societies and the commoners who made up the majority of the population were not benefited to the same degree as an elite ruler. Did they see their society as good for them?

In most cases, when early politically complex polities ended, there continued to be people living in the region. What they were doing and how they were organized socially and in terms of their settlement patterns changed, resulting in the disappearance of the archaeological signature (types of monumental buildings, site hierarchies, centers/capitals, and other features) of that polity. This is a reflection of the lack of support of those commoners for that political system, as well as possibly decreased participation in its rituals and ideology. It also can reflect the movement of people into nearby regions and other political systems, which may have shared similar ideology. The social perception of commoners about the society they lived in is likely significant in helping to understand these behavioral shifts.[4] This perception occurred in a context where ecology, population density, agricultural surpluses, and life were intertwined with ideology and ritual. Imagine, for example, that you are the king of Mapungubwe (see Chapter 15). Adequate rainfall is essential for food production and you are the chief rainmaking ritual specialist. In fact, your status as divine partially results from the fact that your dynasty moved its residence to the top of the rainmaking hill and was successful in its rainmaking activities that ended a prolonged drought around AD 1250.[5] But recently, your rainmaking rituals are not successful and lower average temperatures also are affecting food production. Additionally, your trade and exchange relationships are challenged by elites living at Great Zimbabwe to the north. There are fewer imports of glass beads and other materials partly because your trade partners became interested in gold and your city is not as close to gold sources as is Great Zimbabwe. This combination led to your people thinking you no longer held a favorable status with respect to the supernatural powers that you appeal to in rainmaking and other rituals. A loss of supernatural favor means that people blamed you for decreased agricultural productivity and they lost faith in your rule. Eventually, you are challenged internally by other elites, and people begin to move away to places where conditions are more favorable for their success. The Mapungubwe state comes to an end.

Each politically complex society must be examined archaeologically from the standpoint of its sustainability in the contexts of the various factors that had the potential to prolong or to shorten its existence. People's agency was one of these, as was climatic change, innovations, the effects of changes in resource networks, conflicts with neighbors near and far, and the demands of the state on its people.

Lessons from the Past?

We have seen throughout this book that archaeology provides a long-term perspective on change. The processes involved in change that archaeologists study concern social/cultural and natural, as well as biological, variables. As some societies became increasingly complex both socially and politically, their sustainability was an issue for the many generations of people who participated in them, although any one generation may not have been aware of the long-term outcomes of their activities. One feature of many (but not all) early polities, for example, was the process of urbanism.[6] More people moved to urban landscapes (cities) over time, which had the potential of creating problems such as overcrowding and fewer rural farmers to grow the food needed to feed everyone. These types of problems in cities resonate to greater or lesser degrees with us today. One of the fascinating lessons from archaeology in this context is that many ancient urban contexts were sustainable, with cities that lasted for hundreds or even thousands of years.

The cities of the Classic Maya (see Chapter 13) are one example of sustainability because many of them had life spans of around 1,000 years.[7] Part of the reason for their longevity was that they were relatively low-density urban landscapes. Maya cities had central areas with monumental pyramids, palaces, administrative buildings, and elite residences. Beyond this core area, the residential areas of other people were spread out so that there were open areas between buildings and between concentrations of residences (neighborhoods) that surrounded secondary centers and their ceremonial complexes. Some of these open areas were used as gardens, others had agricultural terraces, and others were large fields. This meant that the people in the cities grew a substantial proportion of their own food, rather than having to rely on rural farmers. As archaeologists have noted, Tikal had a city longevity that was more than three times that of Washington, D.C.[8] Examining the details of the archaeology of ancient sustainable cities might yield information that we can use today as modern cities are planned and replanned. Other lessons from the past might operate on smaller scales, for example, the success of Native Hawaiians who are re-establishing/rebuilding fishponds and agricultural terrace systems used in pre-Contact Hawai'i[9] (Figure E.1). This is sustainable agriculture that reconnects Native Hawaiians to traditional lifeways.

There are a multitude of stories from the archaeological record. Because of factors such as incomplete preservation, lack of written records, and ancient and modern destruction from rebuilding on the same spot and from looting, we often have only partial pictures of our past. But the one thing that archaeology does demonstrate is that humanity's story is one of dynamism because behavioral decisions made by individuals and groups about relationships with the landscape and with each other altered social, and political, organization. This was as true of hunter–gatherer–forager societies as it was of politically complex polities. The vast sweep and diversity of past societies is a hallmark signature of humans.

FIGURE E.1
Native Hawaiians have been reintroducing traditional methods of subsistence, including reconstructing fishponds (top: on the island of Moloka'i) and re-establishing kalo fields using ancient terraces (bottom: in Waipi'o Valley on the island of Hawaii).

Summary

- The "disappearance" of past politically complex societies was the consequence of a combination of factors that differed from one region to another. In some cases it resulted from the arrival of foreigners, such as the Spanish, in conjunction with internal stresses and regional enemies. In other instances, climatic change, loss of confidence in elite rulers, and people relocating to more favorable locations combined to create a situation in which people no longer participated in/supported the system, and its archaeological signature ended.

- The past societies studied by archaeologists yield information that can be useful today. One example is sustainable agriculture in urban landscapes.

- Humanity's story is ultimately about the dynamic nature and flexibility of human societies.

Endnotes

1. Middleton 2012; Tainter 2006.
2. Middleton 2012; Tainter 2006.
3. See, for example, Diamond 2005.
4. Middleton 2012.
5. Huffman 2008: 2043.
6. See Flad 2018 and Jennings and Earle 2016 for alternative perspectives on urbanism and its meaning for polities.
7. Isendahl and Smith 2013: 135–138. See also Beach et al. 2015, who discuss the "Mayacene," that is, cumulative positive and negative impacts that the Maya had on the landscape.
8. Isendahl and Smith 2013: 142.
9. Olszewski 2000.

Glossary

Absolute Dating: methods of obtaining calendar dates for archaeological sites or fossil finds, including dendrochronology, radiocarbon dating, thermoluminescence, optically stimulated luminescence, and potassium–argon dating.

Abydos: an important settlement and cemetery complex in Upper Egypt. Royal cemeteries here contain tombs thought to be those of some of the last pharaohs of the Protodynastic period, as well as of the Pharaonic State, and Old and Middle Kingdom periods.

Acheulian: flaked stone tool tradition characterized by bifaces such as handaxes. It first appears in Africa 1.7 million years ago, but not in East Asia until 800,000 years ago and in Europe until 500,000 years ago.

Adena: an archaeological mound-building tradition that first appears during the Early Woodland period in eastern North America, about 1000 cal BC. The conical mounds contain burials that accumulated over many years, with the size of the mounds growing as basket-carried earth was added to cover new burials in the same place.

Agency: a theoretical perspective that discusses the role of the individual in shaping change in cultures and societies.

Ahupua'a: a division of land in the Hawaiian Islands that includes coastal and inland areas. Each *ahupua'a* was controlled by an *ali'i* (chief) and was essentially self-sufficient in terms of resources.

'Ain Ghazal: a large Pre-Pottery Neolithic B village site in Jordan. It has two caches of plaster statues of humans and also plastered human skulls, figurines, beads, and enormous quantities of artifacts reflecting everyday life.

'Ain Mallaha: a Late Epipaleolithic (Natufian period) site in Israel. It dates between about 13,000 and 9600 cal BC and is an example of a small village in the Mediterranean forest region of the Levant.

Akkadian Empire: established by Sargon I from the city-state of Akkad in 2334 BC, this was the first period of unification of many of the city-states of southern Mesopotamia under one ruling dynasty and one city-state.

Ali Kosh: a Pre-Pottery to Pottery Neolithic site in the Deh Luran Plain of Iran, which is part of extended southern Mesopotamia. It contains evidence for early settled life based on the use of wild plants and wild animals and a later focus on domesticated plants and animals.

Altamira: a painted cave site in Spain with Magdalenian Upper Paleolithic images including the famous Hall of the Bison.

Ancestral Pueblo: an archaeological term for the Native American groups who occupied southeastern Utah, southwestern Colorado, northern Arizona, and northwestern New Mexico from 500 cal BC until just before Spanish contact in AD 1540; their descendants live in the Hopi, Zuni, and Rio Grande pueblos of Arizona and New Mexico.

Anyang: the late Shang capital city in the Yellow River region of northern China, also called Yinxu. It was home to the ruling dynasty and had rammed-earth palaces and temples, royal tombs, bronze and other workshops, residences, and large sacrificial areas.

Apollo 11 Cave: a Later Stone Age site in Namibia in Africa, it contains the oldest known African rock art at 30,000 to 28,000 cal BC.

Archaeomagnetism: an absolute dating method that uses variation in the position of the Earth's magnetic pole over time. The orientation of the iron particles in a feature such as a clay-lined hearth align to the magnetic north pole when heated. This orientation is compared to a magnetic north pole sequence to determine an age for the firing of the feature. This technique can be used for sites that are younger than 10,000 years old.

Archaeometallurgy: this archaeological specialty concerns the study of how metals were produced and used in the past.

Ardipithecus ramidus: a fossil hominin from 4.4 million years ago in East Africa, this species has some skeletal features indicating a trend toward bipedalism, but also apelike features such as long arms and monkeylike features in its grasping foot.

Assimilation Model: it uses a combination of the fossil and mtDNA evidence indicating a mainly African origin for modern humans in combination with nuclear DNA evidence showing that modern humans interbred with sister lineages such as the Neandertals and Denisovans.

Aurignacian: an Early Upper Paleolithic archaeological culture, dating between 43,000 and 33,000 cal BC and associated with modern humans. It is found in Europe and has the earliest evidence for art and musical instruments in this part of the world.

Australopithecus afarensis: a fossil hominin dating between 3.7 and 3 million years ago in East Africa. It was a habitual biped but retained long arms and curved finger bones that are apelike traits. There is some evidence indicating sexual dimorphism.

Australopithecus africanus: a fossil hominin known from South Africa in the interval between 3.3 and 2.5 million years ago. Although it was a habitual biped, there are some features of the big toe and knee that suggest these areas of the skeleton were still somewhat apelike. Like other gracile australopiths, it also had long arms and curved finger bones, indicating that it spent at least some of its time in the trees.

Australopithecus sediba: a fossil from South Africa dating between 1.95 and 1.78 million years ago. It has some typical australopith features such as long arms and curved finger bones, as well as a small brain size. However, its skeleton also shows features that are more like those of the genus *Homo*, such as smaller molars, lack of flaring cheek bones, and its bipedal structure.

Australopiths: a generic term for the subtribe taxonomic category of Australopithecina; it includes genera such as *Sahelanthropus, Ardipithecus, Australopithecus,* and *Paranthropus.*

Aztec Empire: a late politically complex entity (AD 1428 to 1519) that was centered in the Valley of Mexico, where today's Mexico City is built. It consisted of what is known as the Triple Alliance and was defeated by the Spanish in AD 1521.

Aztec Ruins: an Ancestral Pueblo region in northern New Mexico with many great houses. It became an important center during the late Pueblo III period, after the abandonment of most of Chaco Canyon.

Bambandyanalo: a capital established by Leopard's Kopje groups in the Shashe–Limpopo area of southeastern Africa. It controlled a lucrative trade in ivory and abundant imported glass beads are found here and at other sites in the region.

Banpo: a large Yangshao Culture (Neolithic) village in China that is surrounded by a moat. Abstract signs incised on pottery are thought to be an example of shared symbols that may have later led to the development of writing.

Basal Ganglia: a subcortical structure in the brain responsible for motor control and sequencing; it is important in the production of human speech sounds.

Bashidang: a Neolithic site in the Middle Yangtze River region of China. Residents relied mainly on wild food resources but also had rice, which may have been domesticated.

Basicranial Flexion: a series of measurements along the base of the skull that have been interpreted as indirect evidence for the length of the pharynx and thus for whether various hominin species were capable of producing human speech sounds.

Beringia: a land bridge that connected Siberia to Alaska during the Pleistocene; when sea levels rose after the Pleistocene, this land bridge was submerged, and the area today is the waterway called the Bering Strait.

Bettelbühl Necropolis: a Hallstatt Culture cemetery near the Heunenburg in Germany (Europe) which contains a barrow burial (dating to 583 BC) of an elite woman.

Bioarchaeology: specialists in this discipline examine human bones to identify features of individuals and populations. These include health, age, sex, habitual activities, height, diet, and nutrition.

Bipedal: the use of the lower limbs (legs) to move around when walking or running.

Blackwater Draw Locality 1: a Paleoamerican Clovis kill and butchery site found near the town of Clovis in New Mexico. This is the source for the name of the Clovis culture and the Clovis point.

Blombos Cave: a Middle Stone Age archaeological site in South Africa with evidence for symbolic behaviors around 100,000 years ago.

Bluefish Caves: a site in Alaska that dates to 22,000 cal BC. It is the earliest site in the Americas and documents the movement of people from Siberia across the Beringian land bridge to the Americas.

Boxgrove: a coastal region in England with several sites dating to 500,000 years ago and later. It is the earliest area in northern Europe with the Acheulian tradition. Bifaces are associated with butchery of animal carcasses and rare hominin fossils are identified as *Homo heidelbergensis*.

Bronze Age: a period in the Old World characterized by the manufacture of bronze artifacts. In Europe, the Bronze Age is from 3000 to 800 cal BC. Beginning and end dates differ for various regions of Europe.

Bruszczewo 5: an Early Bronze Age fortified site in a wetlands (lake/moor) context in Poland (central Europe). It was abandoned during the Middle Bronze Age and reoccupied during the Late Bronze/Early Iron Age.

Buang Merabak: an early archaeological site in Sahul (Bismarck Archipelago, Pacific region); it has a shell midden and possibly shows the exploitation of bats (42,000 cal BC).

Buto: a site in the delta region of northern Egypt with Predynastic period and later occupations. Its position at the interface of the Nile River with the delta likely was strategic for trade and exchange within Egypt and with the Middle East.

Cahokia: an Early Mississippian period site in Illinois (eastern North America). Cahokia was one of the most important political and ritual centers of the Mississippian period. Its "downtown" area contained Monk's Mound, the Great Plaza, a Woodhenge, sub-Mound 51, and a wooden palisade, as well as several other earthen mounds (such as Mound 72) and plazas. It was associated with the complexes at the East St. Louis Site and the Mound City Site.

Calakmul: a Classic period lowlands Maya city in Mesoamerica that was the main state rival to the state centered at Tikal. Calakmul had an extensive monumental elite and religious center characterized by palaces, temples, pyramids, and avenues, and its ruling dynasty established a wide network of alliances with other Maya cities.

Cardial Ware Culture: Early Neolithic farming groups (6400 to 4700 cal BC) with pottery decorated by using the edges of cockle shells. They spread into Europe along the Mediterranean route by sea-faring from Greece.

Carnac: a series of 3,000 menhirs arranged as alignments during the Neolithic period in France (Europe).

Cartesian Coordinate System: a three-dimensional grid system in which horizontal axes (x and y) are combined with a vertical axis (z) to calculate the position of any given point. Each axis is perpendicular to the others. At archaeological sites, the x grid axis often corresponds to north–south and the y grid axis represents east–west. The z-grid axis is the elevation of each point.

Casa Grande: a Classic period Hohokam site in Arizona. It has a great house, residential compounds, and platform mounds.

Casa Rinconada: a great kiva built in Chaco Canyon (New Mexico) in the North American Southwest during the late Bonito phase (beginning of the Pueblo III period).

Casas Grandes: a large Pueblo IV settlement (also called Paquimé) in northern Mexico. It contains evidence for trade and exchange into the Ancestral Pueblo, Mogollon, and other North American Southwest regions.

Casma Valley: a Peruvian coastal valley system (South America) with several large sites during the Initial Period. These sites have U-shape architecture, pyramids, plazas, residential areas, and military theme images.

Causewayed Enclosure: a European Neolithic construction characterized by a series of concentric ditches and banks with access (causeways) across the ditches to a central open area. One interpretation is that these were ritual centers for Neolithic communities.

Cave 7: a Basketmaker II burial cave site in southeastern Utah. It contains 96 individuals of both sexes and a range of ages, including 18 adult males with signs of violence, suggesting raids between Basketmaker II groups.

Caverna da Pedra Pintado: a Paleoamerican site in the Amazon region of Brazil. It documents the wide range of foods that Paleoamericans ate and also contains the earliest cave art known in South America.

Central Cattle Pattern: a village layout in southeastern Africa where a centrally placed *kraal* (corral) is surrounded by the houses of the chief and his family members. The *kraal* area is used for cattle and also as a court where disputes can be heard and settled.

Chacoan Outlier: an Ancestral Pueblo community in the region outside of Chaco Canyon (New Mexico) that dates to the Pueblo II and III periods; it includes a great house built in a similar way to the great houses of Chaco Canyon, a great kiva, and several surrounding small roomblock settlements.

Chaco Phenomenon: an unusual set of archaeological features found in the Chaco Canyon region of New Mexico from AD 900 to 1220 (Bonito phase). It includes a population of 2,000 to 3,000 in this marginal agricultural area, great houses and small settlements, Chaocan roads, Chacoan outliers, trade with other regions of the North American Southwest and Mesoamerica, and the possible presence of elites at the great houses.

Chan Chan: the capital of the Chimú Empire in the northern coastal region of Peru (South America) during the Late Intermediate period. The kings ruled from this administrative and ceremonial center, which controlled trade and exchange routes. The city had U-shape architecture, large pyramids, and palace compounds for royal elites.

Chatelperronian: an Early Upper Paleolithic tradition made by Neandertals in France (western Europe); it contains evidence for bone tools and personal ornamentation at sites such as Grotte du Renne.

Chauvet Cave: an Upper Paleolithic painted cave in France (western Europe) with the oldest known Aurignacian drawings at 35,000 cal BC; it also has art from later Upper Paleolithic periods.

Chavín de Huántar: this site in the northern Andean highlands of South America represents one of the best known of the Chavín Horizon pilgrimage centers. Its architecture includes U-shape complexes with sunken courts/plazas, large terraced platforms, and platform mounds.

Chavín Horizon: a widely shared set of imagery found in the northern Andean highlands and the Pacific coastal region of South America during the Early Horizon period. Examples of images are jaguars/felines, snakes, crocodiles, eagles, bats, and crabs. It is interpreted as a representing a probable religious tradition.

Chichén Itzá: a Terminal Classic period city that was a state-level political entity in the Maya lowlands of Mesoamerica. Its power was built on commerce, and it had strong ties to the Mexican region. Rather than being ruled by a single king, its political structure was based on several elites from royal dynasties, the military, merchants, and religious practitioners.

Chiefdom: a category of political organization that is described as a ranked society in which rank is inherited. Elites in a chiefdom live at central places, control densely populated regions, and have greater access to prestige goods and other resources.

Chifumbaze Complex: a term used by some archaeologists to indicate the Early Iron Age Bantu-speaking groups whose migrations from central Africa spread iron metallurgy, farming, and herding ways of life to eastern and southern Africa.

Chimpanzee-Human Last Common Ancestor: the last common ancestor for panins (chimpanzees and bonobos) and hominins (humans and their ancestors), which likely lived sometime between 6.3 and 5.4 million years ago.

Chimú Empire: a complex political entity during the Late Intermediate period. It was situated in the northern coastal region of Peru (South America) and ruled by a dynasty of kings.

City-State: a term used to describe a political unit that includes an independently ruled city with its surrounding territory. Early Mesopotamia was characterized by city-state political organization during the Sumerian period.

Clovis: an early Paleoamerican culture in the Americas, dating between 11,300 and 10,850 cal BC; they made a distinctive, bifacially flaked stone spear point called a Clovis point and are associated with kill and butchery sites of mammoth and other now-extinct animals.

Control of Nature through Its Manipulation: a postprocessual explanation for the origins of food-production. It postulates that people attempted to control wild resources through rituals, food storage, and food processing technologies. This led to domestication as the wild resources were transformed into controlled resources.

Cuicuilco: a Middle to Late Formative period ceremonial center and town in the Basin of Mexico. It went into decline around the same time that Teotihuacán became an important center in this area.

Cultural Resource Management (CRM): archaeologists who work in the field of CRM have projects that are based on recovering data about areas that will be impacted by new construction or otherwise potentially destroyed. Federal or state-owned lands, as well as federally funded projects, are subject to a number of laws, regulations, and reporting requirements.

Cuneiform: a writing system developed in southern Mesopotamia during the Early Dynastic period. It was a syllabic language whose written signs are made up of combinations of lines and wedge shapes. It was used to record economic transactions, as well as inscriptions on buildings, proverbs, hymns, myths, and royal inscriptions.

Cuzco: the capital city of the Inka Empire in the Andean highlands of South America. The Inka considered it the center of the world. It had impressive temple, pyramid, fortress, and plaza areas and incorporated significant sacred places in the landscape.

Darwinian Archaeology (evolutionary archaeology): a theoretical perspective that interprets changes in cultures over time as the result of evolutionary processes, such as natural selection, known from biological evolution.

Datum: a reference point on the ground with known spatial coordinates, sometimes calculated as Easting (x) and Northing (y), as well as elevation (z). One or more datums are established at archaeological sites and used to set up site grids and for precision location measurement of artifacts, animal bones, structures, features, and samples found during excavation at a site, as well as for archaeological survey.

Değirmentepe: an 'Ubaid period site in Anatolia (central Turkey) that seems to represent on 'Ubaid colony with local manufacture of 'Ubaid style vessels and the use of seals and sealings with northern Mesopotamian designs. It is situated near sources of silver, copper, and lead and contains evidence for the manufacture of copper objects.

Dendrochronology: an absolute dating method that provides calendar year dates based on the analysis of tree-ring sequences of thicker and thinner annual growth rings; used in parts of Europe and in the American Southwest, but only extends back in time some 8,700 to 12,000 years.

Denisova Cave: genetic analysis of fossil hominin bones found at this Siberian site in Russia indicates that this population is distantly related to Neandertals. The Denisovans interbred with later modern humans because about 4 to 6% of their genes are present in the gene pool of some Pacific region populations.

Dhra': a Pre-Pottery Neolithic A site in Jordan. It was a small village with circular stone-walled dwellings that used mudbrick in the construction of the upper portions of each structure.

Diepkloof Rock Shelter: a Middle Stone Age archaeological site in South Africa with evidence of art in the form of engraved geometric patterns on ostrich egg shell containers that date to 60,000 years ago.

Dietz Site: a series of Clovis Paleoamerican camp locales in Oregon. They are situated near a travel route between several different resource areas and contain artifacts made from various stone raw materials found in different parts of this region.

Djoser: a pharaoh of Egypt's 3rd Dynasty, he is well known because of his stepped pyramid at Saqqara. This was the first type of pyramid built in Egypt.

Dmanisi: a 1.7-million-year-old site in the Republic of Georgia that contains fossils of early *Homo erectus*, animal bones, and choppers and flakes. It is one of the earliest sites known outside of Africa.

Dolmen: a Neolithic tomb found in Europe. It has a few standing megalithic stones topped with a capstone.

Dolní Věstonice: an Eastern Gravettian (Mid-Upper Paleolithic) set of sites in the Czech Republic in Central Europe, dating between 30,000 and 27,000 cal BC. It contains evidence for early experiments in firing claylike sediment (making ceramics) and exceptional burials.

Domestication: changes over time in the features of wild plants and animals that made these species more attractive to humans for a variety of reasons. These were genetic changes that were "selected" because of human manipulation.

Duvensee: a peat bog region in northern Germany with a series of Mesolithic sites showing targeted harvesting and processing of hazelnuts; the sites date between 8900 and 6500 cal BC.

Early Agricultural Period: a term used to describe the Late Archaic period in the area of southern Arizona that becomes the Hohokam region. This term is used in preference to Late Archaic because domesticated maize was introduced from Mesoamerica and then incorporated into mobile hunting, gathering, and foraging lifeways.

Early Dynastic Period: often called "Sumerian civilization," the Early Dynastic (2900 to 2350 BC) was characterized by more than a dozen city-states in southern Mesopotamia. These were largely independent of each other in terms of political control, although they shared many traditions such as cuneiform writing, a belief system oriented to the same pantheon of gods and goddesses, and similar forms of administrative, economic, religious, and political organization.

Ecodynamics: a theoretical framework that combines social behaviors and natural landscape factors (soil fertility, rainfall, etc.) to understand the processes that led to the development of politically complex societies.

Ecological Archaeology: a theoretical perspective developed in the 1930s to interpret long-term cultural changes in how people responded socially, economically, and technologically to local ecology and changes in local ecology.

El Bajio: a Clovis Paleoamerican area in Sonora in Mexico. This region contains a quarry for stone raw materials, camp sites, and knapping locales where people made stone artifacts.

El Mirador: an important center during the Late Preclassic period in the Maya lowlands of

Mesoamerica. Its monumental architecture, including the El Tigre pyramid, is significantly more massive than that at later Maya sites such as Tikal.

El Paraíso: a Late Preceramic period site situated inland from the coastal region in Peru in South America. It has a large U-shape architectural layout interpreted as a ceremonial complex. The central portion of the U-shape area was a large plaza.

Enkapune ya Muto: this site in Kenya is one of the oldest Later Stone Age sites in Africa and contains ostrich egg shell beads dating to 40,000 years ago (the dates are on materials that are not calibrated).

Epi-Gravettian: a Late Upper Paleolithic archaeological culture found in eastern and parts of central Europe from 20,000 to 10,000 cal BC; during this period people recolonized northerly parts of Europe and Siberia.

Epipaleolithic: an archaeological term most often used to refer to hunter–gatherer–forager groups living in the Middle East in the interval between 23,000 and 9,600 cal BC.

Erligang Culture: a Bronze Age polity with its center at the site of Zhengzhou in the Yellow River region of China. It is sometimes referred to as early Shang and dates from 1600 to 1400 BC.

Erlitou: a large urban site in China with evidence for an elite enclosure with palace complexes, houses, and graves. It was the main center during the Erlitou Culture in the Yellow River area and held influence over a wide geographical region characterized by a hierarchy of sites.

Erlitou Culture: a Bronze Age culture in north China in the Yellow River region. Some archaeologists describe it as the first state because of increased political control over this region, shared rituals, and centralized administrative functions at the main site of Erlitou.

Ertebølle Culture: a late Mesolithic hunter–gatherer–forager group (5500 to 4000 cal BC) in southern Scandinavia and northern Germany (Europe) that lived in proximity to people with food-production economies.

Ethnoarchaeology: a discipline that uses the study of the behaviors of living people to better understand past patterns in the use of cultural materials, site organization, and settlement systems.

Ethnography: a subfield of cultural anthropology in which living people are studied using firsthand observation.

Fauna: terrestrial and marine animals, birds, fish, reptiles and amphibians, as well as shellfish and microfauna.

Feasting Model: feasting is a strategy that allows the sharing of food resources and brings prestige to those who host the feasts. It is one possible explanation for the origins of food-production because it hypothesizes that increasing the abundance of certain foods (to be used in feasting rituals) through their manipulation resulted in domestication.

Fertile Crescent: a geographical region in the Middle East characterized by the association of Mediterranean forest, wild cereals, and wild sheep and goats. It was a feature used in the readiness theory to explain the origins of food-production.

FLK 22 Site: an important Early Stone Age archaeological and hominin fossil site in Tanzania (Africa), which produced remains of *Paranthropus* and *Homo habilis* as well as a well-preserved animal bone assemblage and Oldowan stone artifacts.

Folsom: a Paleoamerican culture that follows Clovis culture. Folsom dates between 10,800 and 9,800 cal BC. It is characterized by the hunting of extinct bison and is found mainly in the Plains and southern Rocky Mountains in the United States.

Folsom Site: a Paleoamerican kill/butchery site of the Folsom culture in New Mexico; it is associated with the hunting of extinct bison.

Foramen Magnum: the opening in the skull where the spinal column joins the head. The position of the foramen magnum can be used to determine whether a fossil species was a biped or a quadruped.

FOXP2: the human form of this gene regulates the growth and development of the basal ganglia, a brain structure important in motor control and sequencing for bipedalism and for spoken language.

Funnel Beaker Culture: Late Neolithic groups in central and northern Europe (4500 to 2800 cal BC) who made pottery that had a globular body and an out-turned flaring rim. It is often interpreted as an interaction zone rather than a single culture.

Gebel Ramlah: a Late Neolithic settlement in the desert Nabta Playa region of Egypt with an associated cemetery containing individuals buried with abundant grave goods. These people were pastoralists.

Gender Archaeology: a theoretical perspective that examines the roles of women, men, and other genders, as well as their relationships, in prehistory.

Gene Flow: an evolutionary process in which interbreeding between neighboring populations allows genes from one population to enter the gene pool of another population; over geographical space, this transmission of genes from one group to another maintains similarity in the genetic structure of populations that are widely separated from one another.

Genus: a taxonomic category that includes all similar species that share a common ancestry.

Geoarchaeology: specialty in which geological analyses are used to aid in the interpretation of archaeological sites, such as the role of natural processes in how site layers form and of the formation of landscapes.

Geochemistry: specialty in which researchers study the chemical composition of artifacts and bones as well as participate in laboratory analyses to determine the absolute age of sites.

Giza: the necropolis of the 4th Dynasty pharaohs on the west bank of the Nile River not far from the ancient capital at Memphis in Egypt, it contains the three well-known large pyramids, as well as smaller pyramids for various queens and solar boat burials.

Göbekli Tepe: an unusual Pre-Pottery Neolithic A and B site in Turkey. It has structures that incorporate large T-shape pillars. Many of the T-shape pillars are decorated with motifs such as snakes, aurochs, gazelle, felines, and other images. It has been interpreted as a ritual center with each structure being a temple.

Gran Dolina at Atapuerca: a Lower Paleolithic archaeological site in Spain (western Europe) with deposits containing choppers and flakes dating as early as 1 million years ago; fossil hominins (*Homo erectus*) are found here 800,000 years ago with evidence for cannibalism.

Grasshopper Pueblo: a Mogollon period site in the mountainous east-central part of Arizona. It was occupied between AD 1275 and 1400. At its peak between AD 1300 and 1330, it was an aggregation site with large, multistoried roomblocks with enclosed open plazas. The roomblocks to the west of the stream were occupied by Mogollon peoples, whereas those on the east side of the stream were where Ancestral Pueblo groups lived.

Gravettian/Eastern Gravettian: archaeological cultures of the Mid-Upper Paleolithic, dating between 30,000 and 20,000 cal BC and associated with abundant "Venus" figurines, experiments with firing claylike sediments, and some unusual burials; Gravettian is found in western Europe and Eastern Gravettian in central and eastern Europe.

Great House: a large multistory building, this term is used for several of the prehistoric cultural areas in the North American Southwest. For the Ancestral Pueblo (Pueblo II times and later), it describes multiple roomblocks often built of stone, such as Pueblo Bonito in Chaco Canyon, New Mexico. In the Hohokam region, great houses were built during the Classic period and were multistory adobe structures located within compounds. Great houses also were built by Mogollon peoples.

Great Kiva: a large round pithouse structure used by Ancestral Pueblo groups for communal activities such as ceremonies. They are found first in the late Basketmaker III period and continue into the Pueblo periods, although they may have been used differently over time.

Great Zimbabwe: the capital city of the Great Zimbabwe state in the plateau region of southeastern Africa. It controlled a vast trade and exchange network in gold, cattle, iron, ivory, and copper. Great Zimbabwe was organized using the Zimbabwe Pattern.

Grotte des Contrebandiers: a site in Morocco with its upper deposits dating to the Later Stone Age where the study of scaled pieces in the flaked stone artifact assemblage suggests that they were used as cores and thus represent an intensive use of stone raw materials that is similar to recycling.

Grotte du Renne: a French (western Europe) Middle Paleolithic site with evidence for Neandertal bone tools and personal ornamentation.

Guilá Naquitz Cave: an Archaic period site in highland Mexico that has yielded the earliest preserved plant remains of domesticated maize and squash, dating to around 4200 cal BC.

Guitarrero Cave: a site in the Andes in northern Peru in South America. Its earliest occupation dates to the Paleoamerican period when people used the cave for short-term visits.

Hallstatt Culture: the early part of the Iron Age in Europe, from about 750 to 450 cal BC. It is found north of the Alps in central Europe and extends in an arc to the east and west of Italy.

Hambledon Hill: a Neolithic causewayed enclosure in England (Europe) that has human skulls placed at intervals in one of the ditches.

Harappa: excavations at this site in the Upper Indus Valley of South Asia document a sequence of development continuity from preurban to urban societies in the Indus Valley.

Hemamieh: a Predynastic settlement and cemetery in Upper Egypt that has an early (Badarian) occupation that shares many similarities in artifacts and burials with Neolithic groups of the desert playas.

Herto: a site in Ethiopia (Africa) that yielded skeletally modern human (*Homo sapiens*) fossils dating to 160,000 years ago.

(the) Heunenburg: a Hallstatt Culture proto-urban center in southern Germany with evidence of trade with the Mediterranean and lavish burials of elites.

Hillazon Tachtit: a Late Natufian phase site of the Late Epipaleolithic period in the Levantine Middle East where evidence for an elaborate burial ritual associated with an elderly woman from a hunter–gatherer–forager group was found.

Hohle Fels Cave: dating to more than 33,000 cal BC, this Aurignacian (Early Upper Paleolithic) site in Germany (Central Europe) contains the oldest known female figurine ("Venus" figurine) and the oldest known musical instruments (ivory and bird bone flutes).

Hohokam: an archaeological term for the Native American groups who occupied south-central and southeastern Arizona from AD 1 until just prior to Spanish contact in AD 1540; their descendants include the Tohono O'odham and the Pima of Arizona.

Hominin: the generic term for the tribe taxonomic category of Hominini; it includes humans and their ancestors.

Hominoidea: the superfamily taxonomic category that includes gibbons, orangutans, gorillas, common chimpanzees/bonobos, and modern humans and their ancestors.

Homo erectus: the earliest hominin in genus *Homo* that is essentially skeletally modern from the neck down; *H. erectus* appears in Africa 1.9 million years ago. They migrate out of Africa around 1.7 million years ago to the Middle East, parts of Europe, Southeast Asia, and East Asia.

Homo floresiensis: hominins from the island of Flores in Indonesia (Southeast Asia) who lived between 100,000 and 60,000 years ago. Their small stature and small brain size, along with other primitive skeletal features, suggest that they are an isolated population descended from either *Homo erectus* or earlier australopith-like hominins. They overlap in time with *Homo sapiens*.

Homo habilis: the slightly larger brain size of this fossil species from East Africa led Louis Leakey to place it in the genus *Homo* rather than that of *Australopithecus*. It has some apelike features such as long arms and curved finger bones.

Homo heidelbergensis: a later member of genus *Homo* that appears in Africa 800,000 years ago or slightly earlier; they migrate out of Africa and into the Middle East and Europe carrying Acheulian biface technology with them.

Homo neanderthalensis: hominins living in Western Eurasia (Europe, Middle East, Central Asia) between 300,000 and 39,000 years ago. Although they have a distinctive set of skeletal features suggesting they are a lineage separate from modern humans, recent nuclear DNA studies indicate that Neandertals interbred with modern humans.

Homo sapiens: the genus and species name for skeletally modern humans, who first appeared in Africa 315,000 years ago. People living today are members of *Homo sapiens*.

Hopewell: an eastern North America tradition of mound building, burial complexes, and long-distance exchange networks that appears during the Middle Woodland period, starting about 200 cal BC; there are several regional groups, including the Ohio Hopewell.

Hopewell Interaction Sphere: a Middle Woodland "phenomenon" in which certain aspects of ritual and ceremony were shared across a wide region in eastern North America among Hopewell-affiliated groups. They also participated to varying extents in long-distance trade and exchange networks and in constructing earthen mounds used for burials and for other ceremonies.

Hopewell Site: a Middle Woodland period site in Ohio that contains earthen works including burial mounds with tens of thousands of exotic materials as grave goods and as ceremonial deposits within mounds. It is a mound complex site associated with the Hopewell tradition.

Hostile Pleistocene Theory: an explanation for the world-wide origins of food-production in the Holocene. It attributes this transition to the fact that climatic conditions during the Pleistocene were not conducive to dependable reliance on plant foods. With less extreme climatic fluctuations in the Holocene, hunter-gatherer-forager groups could manipulate plant foods more successfully, resulting in their abundance and domestication.

Huacas of Moché: this site was the Moché center in the Moché Valley of Peru in South America during the Early Intermediate period when the Moché states were present. It has two large terraced pyramids with ramps leading to the top, plazas, residences, craft workshops, and cemeteries.

Huánuco Pampa: an administrative city built to the north of the Inka capital at Cuzco in the Andean highlands of South America. Huánuco Pampa has a large central plaza where feasting rituals appear to have occurred.

Human Behavioral Ecology: a set of theoretical models, based in ecology, that uses human decisions about resources (including food) and resource use to examine diversity in cultures across geographic space and through time.

Ice-Free Corridor: a term mainly used to indicate the passageway between the Cordilleran and Laurentide glaciers that covered Canada during the Pleistocene; it is widely thought to be a route used during the peopling of the Americas after 11,500 cal BC.

Indian Knoll: a Late Archaic period site in Kentucky dating between 3000 and 2500 cal BC. It has a shell midden (mound) and a cemetery with more than 1,100 individual burials. Some burials have exotic materials (copper and marine shell), perhaps indicating differences in status, whereas others suggest that people were buried with probable gender-related objects (axes and fishhooks with males and nutting stones and bone beads with females).

Indigenous Archaeology: this discipline relies on consultation and collaboration of archaeologists with native communities. It seeks to incorporate traditional knowledge, such as oral histories, values, and concerns of native groups about places in the landscape to better understand the past. Native communities are active participants in interpretation.

Iron Age: a period in Europe from about 800 to 59/51 cal BC. It is characterized by the manufacture and use of implements made of iron.

Jebel Irhoud: the earliest site to yield fossils of early modern humans, at 315,000 years ago. It is in Morocco (northwest Africa).

Jericho: a large site in the West Bank in the Levantine Middle East, it has many different periods of occupation. During the Pre-Pottery Neolithic A, it was a moderate-size village of circular dwellings that were associated with a monumental stone wall, stone tower, and external ditch. These monumental features are unique for this time period.

Jiahu: a large Neolithic (Peiligang Culture) settlement, partly surrounded by a ditch, in the Yellow River area of China that has evidence for the earliest fermented beverage, some social distinctions between people, and a subsistence economy based on domesticated and wild foods.

Jiangzhai: an early Yangshao Culture Neolithic village in the Yellow River region of China. The economy was based at the household level, and some families had more access to resources, allowing them to control greater amounts of agricultural surplus.

Kaminaljuyú: a Maya highlands center in Mesoamerica that began to develop into a politically complex society during the Middle Preclassic period. During the late Preclassic and Classic periods, it became one of the largest urban areas and most important of the Maya highlands sites.

Kfar HaHoresh: a Pre-Pottery Neolithic B site in Israel in the Middle East. It was a mortuary complex with evidence for burials, plastered skulls, skull removal, feasting, and lime production to make plaster for the burial areas.

Kharaneh IV: a large aggregation site in the Azraq Basin area of eastern Jordan (Levantine Middle East). It was occupied during the Early and the Middle Epipaleolithic and yielded evidence for long-distance exchange for marine shells, dwelling structures, hearths, burials, and the hunting of gazelle and aurochs.

Khipu: a recording system used by the Inka during the period of the Inka Empire in South America. It was a complex set of twisted and knotted strings of different colors that was used to keep track of material goods, agricultural products, and taxes owed and paid. It likely also records stories using a logo-syllabic system.

Khufu: the Egyptian name for the 4th Dynasty pharaoh who built the largest pyramid at Giza; he is also known by the Greek name of Cheops.

Kiva: a round pithouse structure used by Ancestral Pueblo families for group activities such as storytelling, weaving, and rituals; see also Great Kiva.

Kot Diji: a small Early Harappan period site in the Lower Indus Valley (South Asia) with a higher elevation citadel that has large mudbrick buildings surrounded by a perimeter wall. On the lower ground outside the wall were smaller houses built of mudbrick.

Kotosh: a Late Preceramic site in the Andean highlands of Peru in South America. It has 100 temples, many of which were built on top of each other.

"Kotosh Religious Tradition": a shared set of architectural features and images (for example, a serpent painted on a staircase leading into a temple) in the Andean highlands of South America, which are interpreted as a widely shared set of religious beliefs.

Kraal: a walled, circular enclosure to hold livestock, usually situated at the center of a settlement or village in southeastern/southern Africa.

Lactose Tolerance: most adults are not able to digest the milk sugar lactose without digestive issues. High frequencies of lactose tolerance in adults in some world populations, such as those descended from the Funnel Beaker Culture groups, shows natural selection for a gene in populations who had a cultural tradition of drinking milk.

Laetoli: a site in Tanzania that yielded *Australopithecus afarensis* fossils as well as a trail of fossilized footprints attributed to *Australopithecus afarensis*.

Landscape Archaeology: a theoretical perspective that uses features of the natural landscape in combination with the placement of archaeological sites and the cultural materials at those sites to better understand potential cultural meanings, symbolism, and ritual in past societies.

Larynx: the "voice box;" an organ in the throat that uses puffs of air to vibrate and produce sounds.

Lascaux: a well-known Late Upper Paleolithic cave art site in France (western Europe); most of the hundreds of images date to the Magdalenian period.

La Tène Culture: the later part of the Iron Age in Europe, from approximately 450 to 59/51 cal BC, when parts of Europe were conquered by the Romans.

Later Stone Age: the time period in Africa beginning before 50,000 cal BC; it is characterized by modern humans with modern human behaviors including abundant evidence for symbolism.

La Venta: an Olmec center in the South Gulf lowlands of Mexico in Mesoamerica that was important from 900 to 600 cal BC. It contains large clay platforms thought to be the foundations for elite residences, two large clay pyramids, monumental sculpted Olmec heads, and other ritual evidence suggesting it may have been a pilgrimage center.

Leopard's Kopje Cluster: Bantu-speaking Iron Age groups who established a regional center first at Bambandyanalo and then at Mapungubwe, which became the political capital of a state-level polity that exerted control over some 30,000 square kilometers (11,583 square miles) of the plateau region in southeastern Africa.

Levallois: a special way of knapping a core so that it is shaped in a way that allows the removal of a thin, well-shaped flake. These are known as Levallois flakes and Levallois points and are found in both Middle Stone Age and Middle Paleolithic stone artifact traditions.

Liang Bua Cave: an archaeological site on the island of Flores in Indonesia (Southeast Asia) that yielded the remains of *Homo floresiensis*. It also contains animal bones such as the dwarfed, elephant-like, extinct *Stegodon*.

Linear Pottery Culture: Early Neolithic farming groups (5700 to 4500 cal BC) with pottery decorated with incised lines in a band. They spread into central and northwestern Europe along the Danube River and its tributaries from the Balkan Peninsula area.

Lomekwian: is the earliest known stone tool industry. It dates to 3.3 million years ago and is found in East Africa. The stone artifacts include cores, flakes, anvils, and percussors.

Long Barrow: a communal earthen mound tomb built in Neolithic Europe. It has wooden or stone interior corridor into which the dead were placed over an extended period of time.

Longshan Culture: a late Neolithic and Chalcolithic interaction network along the middle and lower Yellow River in China, which included standardized ways of making and decorating items such as pottery and jade. Increasing social and political complexity resulted in status differences between people, the concentration of power in the hands of fewer individuals, a settlement hierarchy with large walled settlements surrounded by smaller, unwalled sites, and evidence for warfare.

Machu Picchu: this site was part of the estate of the Inka ruler, Pachakuti, in the Andean highlands of South America. It was used as a royal residence away from the capital at Cuzco.

Macrobotanical Remains: plant remains that are sometimes recovered from archaeological sites. They can include seeds and wood charcoal and are useful in reconstructing plant use (including plant foods) by earlier people, as well as aspects of local environments.

Madjebebe: the earliest site in Australia at 65,000 years ago. It documents the early colonization of the Australian part of Sahul.

Magdalenian: a Late Upper Paleolithic archaeological culture found in Western and Central Europe from 15,000 to 9,000 cal BC; the majority of Paleolithic cave art and portable art (figurines, etc.) were made during this period.

"Mammoth Steppe": a vast dry grasslands set of habitats that characterized the entire region from western Europe to Alaska during the Upper Paleolithic; it supported animal herds such as horses, bison, and mammoth, as well as unusual combinations of plants and animals that are not found together today.

Mapungubwe: the capital of the Mapungubwe state in the Shashe–Limpopo area of southeastern Africa during the Middle Iron Age. It controlled the ivory trade, as well as trade and exchange in cattle and other goods. The Zimbabwe Pattern was first established here.

Mayapan: a Postclassic period city and state in the Maya lowlands of Mesoamerica. It became powerful after defeating Chichén Itzá and was characterized by its control of lucrative trade.

McPhee Village: a Pueblo I period (Ancestral Pueblo) settlement in Colorado; it includes aboveground masonry room blocks, linear jacal room blocks, and more than 50 pithouses; there are two great kivas, which are associated with the masonry room blocks.

Megadont: term often used to describe the enormous premolar and molar teeth of species of *Paranthropus*.

Mehrgarh: a well-documented site in the Indus Valley region of South Asia. Its deposits contain a sequence of development from Neolithic period food-producing economies through the Chalcolithic period and into the Early Harappan period.

Memphis: an important city in Lower Egypt that became the capital during the Pharaonic State period; the central administration was located in this city.

Menhir: a single standing megalithic stone, put into place by Late Neolithic farming groups in Europe. Arrangements of several menhirs can be found marking avenues, as alignments, or circles, including henges.

Mesolithic: an archaeological term used in some parts of the Old World, such as Europe and Asia, to describe late hunter–gatherer–forager groups. The chronology associated with this term varies from region to region. For example, in Europe, the Mesolithic is found between 9600 and 5000 cal BC.

Mexica: an Aztlan group that migrated into the Valley of Mexico in AD 1250. They established the city of Tenochtitlán (the eventual Aztec Empire capital) and became one of the most important groups in the Aztec Empire.

Mezhirich: an Epi-Gravettian (Late Upper Paleolithic) site in Ukraine (eastern Europe) that is a winter base camp; it contains four substantial dwellings built of mammoth bones and tusks, large storage pits, and hearths.

Microfauna: this term refers to small animals such as mice, moles, and snails; these small animals are sensitive to changes in local temperature and moisture and thus are valuable indicators of paleoenvironments.

Middle Paleolithic: a term used for the period between 250,000 and 39,000 years ago in Western Eurasia. The European Middle Paleolithic is associated with Neandertals.

Middle Stone Age: a term for the period between 300,000 to 50,000 years ago in Africa. The Middle Stone Age has evidence for personal ornamentation, art, bone tools, and different types of stone points, as well as the incorporation of shellfish in the diet at coastal sites.

Mimbres: Mimbres Mogollon sites are found in southwestern New Mexico and a small portion of southeastern Arizona. They are known for their geometric designs and everyday life scenes painted on Black-on-White pottery.

Miocene: a geological epoch from about 23 to 5 million years ago. The first hominins appear in Africa during the late Miocene.

Mitochondrial DNA: a type of DNA located outside the nucleus in a cell; it is passed down from mothers to their children and represents maternal lineages. It is useful in examining the relationship of Neandertals to modern humans as well as human migration events in prehistory.

M'lefaat: a Pre-Pottery Neolithic site in Iraq in northern Mesopotamia, dating to 9500 BC. It is a permanent village with evidence for the use of wild plant foods and hunting of wild animals.

Moché States: states situated in the northern coastal area of Peru in South America. There was a southern Moché state and either a series of valley-based northern states or perhaps a single northern state during the early Middle Horizon period.

Mogollon: a term for the Native American groups who occupied much of central and southern New Mexico, the northern portions of the Sonoran and Chihuahuan deserts of northern Mexico, and the mountainous region of east-central Arizona from AD 100 to just before the arrival of the Spanish in AD 1540; their descendants likely moved to the Rio Grande pueblos.

Mohenjo-daro: the largest known Indus Valley city in South Asia. It has a citadel area with large mud-brick structures such as the so-called "Granary" and "Great Bath." The function of these buildings is not known, although likely they are related to administrative and political tasks.

Monk's Mound: an Early Mississippian period earthen truncated pyramid at Cahokia in eastern North America; it is the largest pre-Columbian manmade construction north of Mexico.

Monte Albán: the main center in the Valley of Oaxaca in Mesoamerica after 500 cal BC. It was a population center and large town with a perimeter wall and important ceremonial structures, which became the hub of the Zapotec state beginning in 30 to 20 cal BC.

Monte Verde: a Paleoamerican site in Chile in South America that is one of the earliest sites in the Americas south of the Cordillaran and Laurentide glaciers covering Canada. It dates to 12,600 cal BC and suggests that some groups followed a coastal route from the Alaskan part of Beringia.

Mosaic Evolution: represents a situation in which natural selection acts at different rates of change on various parts of the body. One example in the hominins is the combination of habitual bipedalism with ape-like long arms and curved finger bones. In this case, natural selection acted earlier on structural changes leading to bipedalism than it did on structural changes to the modern form of the arm and hand.

Mound 72: an Early Mississippian period burial mound at Cahokia, Illinois. It contains evidence for elaborate burial rituals for elite male individuals, as well as probable sacrifice burials (usually of numerous females) and offerings of exotic goods such as mica, copper, and shell beads.

Moundville: a Late Mississippian period site in Alabama with 29 earthen mounds, a plaza, and a palisade. It became a significant center around AD 1200, but most of its residents moved away about AD 1250, except for elite families and their retainers.

Mutapa State: a complex political entity to the north of Great Zimbabwe, near the Zambezi River. It may have been established by people from Great Zimbabwe and was the state encountered and described by the Portuguese.

Multidisciplinary Approach: to interpret the cultural materials and natural features of archaeological sites, site taphonomy, and landscapes, archaeologists collaborate with specialists within archaeology (phytolith researchers, zooarchaeologists, archaeometallurgists, and geoarchaeologists), as well as specialists from other disciplines (architects, materials conservators, geochemists, ethnographers, and chronology laboratories).

Multiregionalism Model: an interpretive model for the origins of modern humans, it is based on the evolutionary process of gene flow and hypothesizes that modern humans everywhere in the Old World evolved locally from archaic hominins because gene flow kept all populations similar enough to interbreed successfully.

Mutation: changes in genetic material found in genes; most of these are disadvantageous and are subject to negative selection so that they are quickly removed from the gene pool of a population. A few mutations are advantageous and are subject to positive selection, for example, a mutation in one brain gene that led to more neurons that expanded the size of the neocortex and of cognitive abilities in the hominins.

Nabta Playa: a desert area of southern Egypt where numerous sites of the Neolithic period occur at playas (seasonal, shallow lakes).

Nakbe: a Maya Lowlands center in Mesoamerica that began during the Middle Preclassic period. It eventually had monumental architecture including a ball court, stone platforms, and a plaza associated with a pyramid and a platform with three structures, as well as stelae and altars.

NAN Ranch Site: a Mogollon site in southwestern New Mexico occupied during the Pithouse and Mogollon Pueblo periods. During the Classic Mimbres phase (AD 1000 to 1130) of the Mogollon Pueblo period, Nan Ranch had three roomblocks with more than 100 rooms and a ditch and small canal system to divert water to fields and a reservoir.

Narmer: the last pharaoh of Dynasty 0, he is sometimes called the Scorpion King and usually is credited with unifying Egypt around 3100 BC. Narmer's Palette, an engraved stone, shows the pharaoah wearing the crown of Upper Egypt on one side and the crown of Lower Egypt on the other.

Nasca Lines: enormous figures (geometrics, animals, fish, lines, birds, spiders, other lines) created on the desert plateau surface by the Nasca Culture (100 BC to AD 700) in the coastal area of southern Peru.

Natufian: an alternative name for the Late Epipaleolithic period in the Levantine Middle East, dating between 13,000 and 9600 cal BC. During the Early Natufian, which coincided with the climatic optimum, several small village sites were established in the Mediterranean forest area. A return to colder and drier conditions during the Late Natufian corresponds to a return to higher mobility by hunter–gatherer–foragers.

Natural Selection: refers to a major principle of evolution (sometimes called Darwinian evolution) that is based on the individuals who are best adapted to an environment, having the best chance of surviving to reproduce and pass their genes along to the next generation. This process leads to gradual evolutionary change over time, such as the shift from quadrupedalism to bipedalism in the hominins.

Networks and Boundaries: a theoretical framework that examines how networks of power and authority are developed and maintained in complex political societies. These networks integrate with how people create boundaries for their community and political identities.

Niche Construction Theory: the idea that humans actively change or manipulate features of the landscape around them and resources in those landscapes in ways that build a niche or habitat in which they can be successful over long periods of time. It incorporates evolutionary ideas from biology and applies them to humans.

Nonhoning Chewing: is characterized by small, nonprojecting canine teeth and no gap in the tooth row, a feature of hominins. This contrasts with apes, where the large projecting upper canines have a sharp edge that hones (rubs) against a sharp edge on the lower premolar behind the canine. Apes use these naturally sharpened teeth to slice through food before they chew it.

"Oasis" Theory: an early idea for the origins of food-production. It assumed this transition was the result of hunter-gatherer-foragers observing features of plants and animals while living at well-watered places. This knowledge was then used to manipulate the animals and plants.

Ohalo II: an Early Epipaleolithic site on the shore of the Sea of Galilee in Israel (Levantine Middle East). It contains thousands of well-preserved organic remains such as wild cereal grasses. This demonstrates early and intensive use of a plant food that became one of the major domesticates some 10,000 or so years later.

***Oikoi* Economy:** an economy based on "super-households" in which kin-based households are combined with nonkin labor. These were typical economic units during the Early Dynastic and later periods of Mesopotamia and were capable of generating large quantities of surplus textiles and crops. *Oikos* refers to a single superhousehold, whereas *oikoi* is the plural.

Oldowan: these stone tools appear 2.6 million years ago in eastern Africa. The most common types are choppers, flakes, hammerstones, and scrapers.

Olmec: the early socially and politically complex societies of the southern Gulf Coast of Mexico. Their main centers include San Lorenzo and La Venta, where elite rulers managed agriculture, construction labor, and trade and exchange networks. These were contemporary with several other Mesoamerican societies such as the Preclassic Maya.

Olorgesailie Basin: an area in Kenya in East Africa, it contains many important archaeological sites with Acheulian bifaces.

Omo Kibish: a site in Ethiopia (Africa) that yielded fossils of early *Homo sapiens* (skeletally modern humans) dating to 195,000 years ago.

Oppida: the plural of oppidum; large, often fortified settlements of the Late Iron Age La Tène Culture. They are sometimes described as urban centers, although not all archaeologists agree with this interpretation.

Optically Stimulated Luminescence Dating: an absolute dating technique in which quartz or feldspar grains are extracted from sediment samples from sites and subjected to laboratory treatment that releases light trapped in these grains. The emitted light, which accumulated from ionizing radiation in the sediment, is measured and used in calculating the last time the grains were exposed to sunlight. The accumulated light represents the period of time since the grains were buried.

O. V. Clary Site: a later Paleoamerican site in Nebraska. It was a winter habitation with activities such as hide working, food processing (of bison), and possibly hide clothing manufacture.

Paleoamerican: a term used by some archaeologists to describe the earliest people in the Americas (other archaeologists use the term Paleoindian); their descendants are the Native Americans/First Nations of North, Central, and South America.

Paleoanthropology: the study of human cultural and biological evolution by archaeologists and biological anthropologists; this term is commonly applied to biological anthropologists studying early hominin fossils.

Paleoenvironment: the types of environments and habitats characteristic of regions during the past; these developed because of changes in climate, as well as human manipulation of vegetation and animal communities.

Paleomagnetism: this type of absolute dating technique uses reversals in the magnetic pole of the earth; that is, at some points in time the South Pole was the magnetic pole, whereas at other times, such as today, the North Pole is the magnetic pole. The alignment of magnetic particles in rock can be measured to examine where the magnetic pole was at the time that the layer was deposited. This technique is useful for sites dating to 780,000 years ago and older.

Palynology: specialty that focuses on the study of plant pollen to better understand past environments, human impact on environments, human diet, and climate change.

Pampas de las Llamas-Moxeke: an Initial Period site in the Casma Valley of Peru (South America). It had pyramids, plazas, administrative buildings, and a residential area.

Panin: a generic term for the tribe taxonomic category of Panini; it includes the common chimpanzee (*Pan troglodytes*) and the bonobo (*Pan paniscus*).

Paranthropus: genus name for the robust australopith species found in South and East Africa. These groups have extremely large premolar and molar teeth and massive chewing muscles. Males have a sagittal crest to which chewing muscles attach. These features indicate a low-nutrition diet requiring them to eat most of the day. They are a side branch to the lineage leading to modern humans.

Passage Grave: a communal earthen mound tomb built in Neolithic Europe. It has a stone passage with one or more burial chambers at the end of the passage into which the dead were placed over an extended period of time.

Passo di Corvo: an Early Neolithic Cardial Ware Culture site on the eastern coast of Italy.

Pharynx: the part of the throat above the larynx (voice box); in modern humans, the pharynx is long and this aids in the production of the variety of sounds found in modern languages.

Phytoliths: microscopic plant parts composed of silica or calcium oxalate that have shapes and sizes specific to particular plants; they usually preserve well and can lend insight into plant use, plant foods, and local environments at archaeological sites.

Pinnacle Point 13B: a Middle Stone Age archaeological site in South Africa with some of the earliest evidence for potentially modern human behaviors (use of red ochre and diet expansion to include shellfish), dating to 164,000 years ago.

Pithouse: in the North American Southwest, pithouses are usually circular to oval dwellings that have been dug into the ground, although they also can be rectangular. In most cases, poles and/or beams are used to build walls and roofing above ground.

Pleistocene: a geological epoch (sometimes called the Ice Ages) beginning 2.6 million years ago and lasting until 10,000 years ago; the first stone tools appear just before the beginning of the Pleistocene.

Pochteca: an Aztec merchant class that traveled internationally and within the Aztec Empire. They served as spies and traveled armed as warriors through the lands of enemies to set up trade and exchange relationships.

Political Complexity: a term used to describe societies for which social classes have replaced kin groups in societal organization. Politically complex societies can be kingdom, state, or empire polities. They usually have one or a few ruling elites, although one exception may have been the Indus Valley in South Asia.

Population Pressure: an early idea for the origins of food-production, it assumed that population growth drove the need for people to begin to experiment with plants and animals in ways that led to their domestication.

Postprocessual Archaeology: a theoretical perspective that emphasizes the study of particular cultures and their histories, especially the role of ideology and the actions of individuals; it does not stress the use of scientific method.

Potassium–Argon Dating: a radiometric dating technique that provides absolute dates based on the half-life decay rate of the radioactive isotope ^{40}K (potassium) into the nonradioactive isotope ^{40}Ar (argon); used in dating inorganic materials such as lava flows or tuff beds in the period from 100,000 years ago to hundreds of millions of years ago.

Poverty Point: a Late Archaic period site in Louisiana with complex earthworks. It dates from 1750 to 1350 cal BC and is a highly organized construction of concentric, segmented ridge mounds associated with several high mounds. There is a large open plaza area inside the inner ridge. People living on the inner ridge likely had greater social rank or standing than those living on other ridges which had no direct line of sight into the plaza. Very high-status individuals and families may have lived on the taller mounds.

Pre-Pottery Neolithic: the earliest part of the Neolithic period in the Levantine region of the Middle East, dating between 9600 and 6250 cal BC.

Numerous small and large villages with evidence for complex ritual activities are present. People of the PPN relied heavily on the cultivation of wild plants and the hunting of wild animals, and their economic strategies eventually led to genetic changes characteristic of domestication.

Processual Archaeology: a theoretical perspective that uses social, economic, and environmental dynamics to interpret cultural changes over time; it is based on the use of scientific methodology.

Pueblo Alto: an Ancestral Pueblo great house in Chaco Canyon, New Mexico, that has evidence in its trash mounds for community feasts during the Bonito Phase.

Pueblo Bonito: an Ancestral Pueblo D-shape great house in Chaco Canyon, New Mexico, that was built over the period from the late AD 800s to 1150. It had more than 350 ground-floor rooms (perhaps as many as 700 rooms total with rooms from the upper stories), 32 kivas, and 3 great kivas.

Qermez Dere: a small Pre-Pottery Neolithic village site in northern Iraq (northern Mesopotamia) that has evidence for use of some rooms for ritual activities. People living here hunted wild animals and used wild plant foods in the period leading up to the appearance of domesticated plants and animals.

Quadrupedalism: the use of all four limbs to move around.

Quebrada Jaguay: a Paleoamerican site in Peru (South America) that dates to 12,000 cal BC. It contains evidence for the use of maritime resources such as shellfish and fish, rather than an exclusive focus on hunting extinct forms of land mammals.

Quebrada Santa Julia: a Paleoamerican site in Chile (South America) that is associated with the bones of extinct horse and fluted spear points. It dates to 11,000 cal BC and represents Paleoamerican traditions that are not Clovis.

Quebrada Tacahuay: a later Paleoamerican site in coastal Peru (South America). People here continued to focus on maritime resources, especially seabirds and fish.

Radiocarbon Dating: an absolute dating method that uses the decay rate of the radioactive isotope carbon-14 (^{14}C) to calculate the age of organic materials found at archaeological sites. It can be used to date materials from the past 50,000 years. Because of fluctuations in the amount of ^{14}C in the earth's atmosphere over time, radiocarbon dates must be calibrated (adjusted) to obtain the actual date of a sample.

Radiometric Techniques: dating techniques that use the principle of a known rate of decay of specific radioactive isotopes into stable isotopes over time; examples include radiocarbon dating and potassium–argon dating.

Readiness Theory: an early idea for how food-production arose. It hypothesized a long and gradual transition to food-production that occurred in the Fertile Crescent in the Middle East. This allowed time for technologies such as ground stone to develop and be applied to grinding cereals in an optimal habitat.

Real Alto: a Late Preceramic site in coastal Ecuador (South America) with evidence for maize, squash, and manioc agriculture. Cotton also was grown.

Recent Single Origin: an interpretive model for the origins of modern humans, based on the idea that modern humans originated only on the continent of Africa and spread from there to other world regions; it hypothesizes that modern humans replaced more archaic hominins living in regions outside Africa.

Relative Dating: dating techniques that provide a sequence of "older" and "younger" rather than calendar dates; examples include stratigraphy and seriation.

Remote Sensing: uses technology such as satellite images, ground-penetrating radar, and LiDAR (light detection and ranging) to aid in the location of archaeological sites and buried or vegetation covered features of sites.

Ridges Basin: a series of spatially close Pueblo I period (Ancestral Pueblo) clusters representing a community in southwestern Colorado. Each cluster had a distinct social identity that can be seen in the types of architecture they built and in how they buried their dead.

Rose Cottage Cave: a site in South Africa with Middle and Later Stone Age deposits. It has several spatially separated activity areas.

Royal Cemetery at Ur: an Early Dynastic cemetery in Mesopotamia containing 16 elaborate burials. In addition to vast quantities of silver, gold, carnelian, and lapis lazuli jewelry, many of the graves of these socially important people contain stone, copper, gold, and silver vessels, tables, elaborately decorated chariots and the animals that drew them, and dozens of burials of retainers.

Sagittal Crest: a ridge of bone from the front to the back along the top of the skull; one set of chewing muscles attaches to this crest in species of *Paranthropus*, as well as in male gorillas.

Sahelanthropus tchadensis: a fossil from Central Africa in the period between 7 and 6 million years ago. It is usually described as a hominin, but some researchers argue against this classification, suggesting that maybe it represents a group related to the chimpanzee-human last common ancestor.

Sahul: the merged land masses of Australia and New Guinea (Pacific region) during the Pleistocene; they were connected to each other by land exposed due to lower sea levels.

Sangiran: a site on Java in Indonesia (Southeast Asia), it contains the remains of *Homo erectus* from 1.6 million years ago.

San José Mogote: a significant political center in the Valley of Oaxaca, Mexico, that developed initially during the same period as the Olmec and Early and Middle Preclassic Maya. San José Mogote was involved in long-distance trade networks with other Mesoamerican regions and had public architecture that included stairways and terraces built of stone

and a town divided into different sections with different craft specialties.

San Lorenzo: the first major center of the Olmec in the South Gulf Coast region of Mexico in Mesoamerica. It contains a large manmade plateau, plazas, courtyards, and large basalt sculptures of Olmec rulers. Its main period of power was between 1200 and 900 cal BC.

Santa Cruz Bend: a Late Archaic period site in Tucson, Arizona, which has evidence of early maize, along with wild plants and hunting of animals. It is a small, settled village site with more than a dozen pithouse dwellings and a large, communal pithouse.

Sapelo Island Shell Ring Complex: a Late Archaic period site in Georgia, it has evidence for three shell rings. Rings II and III are low and appear to be habitation areas where dwellings were placed inside the ring and shared the open plaza area there. Ring I is more substantial and seasonality evidence suggests that parts of it may have been rapidly deposited, perhaps indicating ritual feasting events.

Saqqara: a necropolis on the west side of the Nile River in Egypt, it was the site of the stepped pyramid complex of the 3rd Dynasty pharaoh, Djoser.

Scapulimancy: the use of animal shoulder bones (called oracle bones), and later also turtle plastrons, in divination (predicting future events). Early scapulimancy interpreted the patterns of cracks caused by burning; later scapulimancy involved the careful preparation of animal shoulder bones and turtle plastrons by thinning them and drilling holes in them before submitting them to fire to produce crack patterns that could be interpreted.

Schaefer Mammoth Site: a site in Wisconsin (United States) with dates between 12,800 and 12,200 cal BC; it predates the opening of the "ice-free corridor" and suggests that hunter–gatherers may have entered the Americas south of the glaciers using a coast-hopping route down the western coasts along Alaska and Canada and then spread east and south.

Schöneck-Kilianstädten: a late Linear Pottery Culture Neolithic site in Germany (Europe) with evidence of the massacre of an entire community.

Schöningen: an archaeological site of *Homo heidelbergensis* in Germany, dating to 337,000 years ago, with several wooden spears associated with horse bones.

Schroda: a Middle Iron Age large village established by Zhizo groups in the Shashe–Limpopo area of southeastern Africa. It is sometimes described as a capital for what would later become the Mapungubwe state.

Scientific Method: the process of gathering information (through observation or experimentation) and using this information to create and test hypotheses (ideas); testing hypotheses allows new information to be added and facilitates corrections that need to be made to the hypotheses.

Seriation: a relative dating method in which the frequency of artifact types or styles is used to construct a chronology of "older than" or "younger than" based on the popularity of types or styles over time.

Sexual Dimorphism: differences between males and females, such as (on average) greater weight and height and more visible body hair in males, as well as differences in sex organs.

Shabik'eschee Village: a Basketmaker III (Ancestral Pueblo) occupation in the Chaco Canyon area, New Mexico, dated to AD 550 to 700. It has 25 excavated pithouses, including a great kiva, and perhaps as many as 36 unexcavated structures. There also are more than 50 storage pits.

Shawnee–Minisink Site: a Clovis Paleoamerican habitation site in Pennsylvania. It yielded fish and plant remains, suggesting that Clovis diets were much broader than focusing on large animals such as mammoth and mastodon.

Shortugai: a Mature Harappan period trading outpost in northern Afghanistan. It is located near mines for semiprecious lapis lazuli, and people here presumably helped in exporting this stone raw material to craft workshops in the Indus Valley (South Asia).

Shubayqa 1: an Early Natufian (Late Epipaleolithic) period site in the Middle East (Jordan). It has the remains of the world's oldest bread at 12,650 cal BC.

Sipán: this early Middle Horizon period Moché center in the northern part of the Moché states region of coastal Peru (South America) yielded a rich burial of an individual identified as the "Lord of Sipan."

Site 80: an Archaic period site in coastal Ecuador in South America, where hunter–gatherer–forager groups exploited both marine and land food resources. They also had small gardens where they grew domesticated maize and squash.

Site Taphonomy: the natural and cultural processes that affect archaeological sites. Natural processes include the actions of animals who might consume animal bones left at a site, the effects of rain and sun on exposed archaeological materials, and erosion. Cultural processes include pit digging by later occupants at a site, reuse of stone artifacts left at a site, and modern-day looting.

Skateholm: an Ertebølle Culture (Mesolithic) site in Sweden (Europe). It contains graves showing a diversity of burial positions, as well as dog burials treated in the same way as human burials. Different grave goods for adult males and females indicate gender distinctions.

Sloth Hole: a Clovis Paleoamerican kill site in Florida in the United States. It dates to 11,050 cal BC and yielded more than 30 ivory points.

Small Seed Investment: an origins of food-production idea based on ecological habitats in eastern North America. It notes that heavy use of edible small seeds is a seasonal activity that does not conflict with the gathering of other food resources. Manipulation of these small seed producing plants leads to the domestication of some of them.

Snaketown: a large Hohokam settlement in central Arizona near Phoenix. Snaketown had numerous individual pit structures occupied by families. It also had two ball courts, which are an architectural form likely introduced from Mesoamerica. Snaketown was occupied during the Pioneer, Colonial, and Sedentary periods and largely abandoned by AD 1150.

Social Complexity: a term often used to describe societies that are no longer egalitarian in social structure. There are status and rank differences between people, although relationships usually are still based on kin groups.

Southeastern Ceremonial Complex: artistic motifs that were carved onto shell cups and gorgets, as well as hammered onto copper, during the Late Mississippian period in the North American East. Images include males wearing costumes, snakes, weapons, decapitations, chunkey players, and raptors.

Species: a taxonomic category generally based on the biological species concept in which interbreeding natural populations are reproductively isolated from other populations.

Spit: a term used by some archaeologists to describe an excavation unit that has an arbitrarily assigned specific depth and size; it is especially useful if natural or cultural layers are not easily seen in the stratigraphy.

Star Carr: a Mesolithic site adjacent to a lake in England. It dates between 8700 and 8400 cal BC. The site had excellent organic preservation, and recovered items include red deer antler frontlets, antler points, and a wooden platform/trackway.

Stela: a standing carved stone. In this book it is used to describe monuments in Mesoamerica showing important Maya rulers, gods, or goddesses, and often Maya glyphic writing as well.

Stonehenge: a henge monument begun in the Neolithic period that underwent several changes from an initial bank and ditch surrounding cremation pits to the addition of the bluestones from Wales, the larger local sarsen stones, and an avenue.

Stratigraphy: the layers or levels at an archaeological site. These can be defined as natural (geological) or cultural and can be used as a relative dating technique in which cultural materials found in deeper levels or layers are older than those in overlying levels or layers.

Sub-Mound 51: this Early Mississippian period feature was originally a borrow pit from which sediment was removed to construct earthen works at Cahokia (North American East) and perhaps to level the Great Plaza. It was later filled in by several large debris deposition events including feasting remains.

Sunda: the merged land masses of many of the Southeast Asia islands (such as those of Indonesia) and mainland Southeast Asia during the Pleistocene; they were connected to each other by land exposed because of lower sea levels.

Sungir: an Eastern Gravettian (Mid-Upper Paleolithic) site in Russia (eastern Europe) with several spectacular burials including the double child burial that contained mammoth ivory spears, thousands of mammoth ivory beads, red ochre, ivory pendants, pierced arctic fox teeth, and ivory discs.

Taosi: a Longshan Culture (Neolithic and Chalcolithic) walled site in China that has evidence for social differences between people in the form of separation of housing and in size of graves and types of grave goods.

Taung: a site in South Africa that yielded the first fossil recognized as a human ancestor (in 1925); led to the naming of *Australopithecus africanus* and to the recognition that human ancestors are African in origin.

Tawantinsuyu: the Inka name for their empire in South America. It translates as "land of the four quarters."

Taxonomy: a classification system that divides animal and plant groups into categories based on their evolutionary relationships, for example, modern humans/our ancestors and common chimpanzees/bonobos are members of the same subfamily (Homininae) but are different tribes (Panini for common chimpanzees/bonobos and Hominini for modern humans/our ancestors) within that subfamily.

Tell Oueili: a site in southern Mesopotamia that has the earliest known 'Ubaid period levels. These date to 6300 to 4500 cal BC and include buildings that have long rooms with attached smaller rooms, 'Ubaid-style pottery, and an economy heavily invested in domesticated plants and animals.

Tell as-Sawwan: a Pottery Neolithic period site of the Samarran period in northern Mesopotamia, occupied from 6400 to 5700 cal BC. It represents the expansion of agricultural systems to include irrigation agriculture.

Templo Mayor: the major pyramid in the ceremonial precinct at the Aztec capital of Tenochtitlán. It had two temples at its top, one to the god Huitzilopochtli and the other to the god Tlaloc.

Tenochtitlán: the Aztec Empire capital (now under/in Mexico City) in the Valley of Mexico. It was established in AD 1325 by the Aztlan group known as the Mexica.

Teotihuacán: one of the most important centers in the Basin of Mexico after 150 cal BC. At its height during the Early Classic period, Teotihuacán was a large, planned city with a ceremonial precinct (Pyramids of the Sun and Moon, Street of the Dead, elite residences and other temples) and outlying areas of dwellings, temples, plazas, and markets.

Thermoluminescence Dating: an absolute dating technique that uses the principle of when a stone tool or a piece of pottery was last exposed to heating. Heating releases trapped electrons (light) and sets the clock to zero. After the heating event, ionizing radiation in the sediment of a site bombards the stone artifact or ceramic and electrons begin to accumulate in those pieces. In the laboratory, the electrons can be released as light and measured and then used to calculate when in time that piece was last heated.

Third Dynasty of Ur: during this period (also known as the Neo-Sumerian Empire), southern Mesopotamia was reunited under one ruler from the city of Ur. It lasted only a short time, from 2112 to 2004 BC.

Three Fir Shelter: an Archaic period site in northeast Arizona with evidence for the early use of maize by 1990 cal BC.

Tikal: a Maya lowlands center in Mesoamerica that became important after AD 100. Tikal has abundant evidence for monumental construction (Northern Acropolis, Temple I, Great Plaza) beginning in the Late Preclassic and continuing into the Classic period, when Tikal became one of the most important of several competing state-like polities.

Tiwanaku: the capital city of the Tiwanaku Empire in South America in the Middle Horizon period, it was situated near Lake Titicaca in the Andean highlands. The city had large ceremonial complexes (unfinished) with temples and pyramids, where large-scale feasting rituals took place.

Tiwanaku Empire: a Middle Horizon period politically complex polity in the southern central Andean highlands of South America. The territory it controlled was not contiguous but consisted of a central region near Lake Titicaca and colonies in more remote areas. The colonies controlled strategic resource regions.

Tlatelolco: the largest market in the Aztec Empire; it was in the twin city to the capital city of Tenochtitlan and was open on a daily basis.

Tlatilco: an Early Formative period site in the Basin of Mexico. Archaeological materials include pottery designs and forms that show contact with the Olmec region of Mesoamerica, as well as burials that suggest social ranking of people.

Torwa State: state to the southwest of Great Zimbabwe in southeastern Africa that was a powerful political entity after the decline of Great Zimbabwe. Its capital was at Khami in what is now the modern country of Zimbabwe.

Total Station: equipment that combines a theodolite (which measures vertical and horizontal angles) with an electronic distance meter (EDM). The EDM uses a laser beam to measure the distance from the total station to an object or point (where a prism is placed). The angles and distance are used to calculate *x*, *y*, and *z* coordinates (Cartesian coordinates) for each point.

Triple Alliance: the basis of the Aztec Empire, it consisted of alliances between three city-states (Tenochtitlan, Texcoco, and Tlacopan). Eventually the Mexica of Tenochtitlán dominated the alliance.

'Ubaid Period: during this period of the Chalcolithic in the Middle East, from 6300 to 4500 cal BC, increased interaction between southern and northern Mesopotamia is evident in the establishment of 'Ubaid colonies in Turkey. The first towns and temples appear, suggesting increasing social and political complexity.

'Ubeidiya: dating to 1.5 million years ago, this site in Israel in the Levantine Middle East is early evidence for the movement of *Homo erectus* out of Africa.

Upper Paleolithic: an archaeological term widely used in the Old World (except for sub-Saharan Africa) to represent the period from 45,000 to 9700 cal BC. In Europe, all of the Upper Paleolithic cultures, except for the Chatelperronian, are associated with modern humans.

Urnfields: European Late Bronze Age cemeteries where thousands of people were buried in pottery urns after being cremated.

Uruk (Warka): the first city-state of southern Mesopotamia, which developed during the Uruk period. It had a population of 50,000 people, a complex political and bureaucratic administration, massive building projects, and sacred precincts with temples and palaces.

Uruk Period: an important period (4000 to 3100 BC) of social and political development that resulted in the first city-states of southern Mesopotamia. It is characterized by specialized labor (scribes, bricklayers, priests, bureaucrats, etc.), tribute payments to temples, and accumulation of surplus agricultural products used as funding for construction projects.

UTM Coordinates: Universal Transverse Mercator (UTM) coordinates are Easting and Northing numbers that are based on a system of metric grid cells that divide the world. Each Easting and Northing set of coordinates provides an extremely specific geographical location.

Uyun al-Hammam: a Middle Epipaleolithic site in Jordan (Levantine Middle East). It contains a cemetery in which several humans are buried with parts of animals such as tortoise shells, goat horns and deer antler, and foxes. This indicates that human–animal symbolic associations were part of hunter–gatherer–forager societies long before the appearance of settled communities.

Valdiva Period: an interval during the Late Preceramic period in coastal Ecuador (South America). Some sites have evidence for ritual or ceremonial constructions (mounds and plazas).

Vedbæk: an Ertebølle Culture (Mesolithic) site in Denmark (Europe). It contains graves showing gender distinctions between adult males and females in grave goods, some dog burials, evidence for violent death, and a woman buried with her newborn child placed on a swan's wing.

"Venus" Figurines: these female carvings are found throughout Europe during the Gravettian/Eastern Gravettian period of the Upper Paleolithic; the earliest known "Venus," however, is from the Aurignacian period at Hohle Fels in Germany.

Vilakuav: one of the earliest archaeological sites in New Guinea (Pacific region), documenting the colonization of this part of Sahul at least as early as 47,000 cal BC.

Wadi Madamagh: a small rockshelter site in the Petra region of Jordan (Levantine Middle East). It has cultural materials of the Early Epipaleolithic period and an emphasis on the hunting of wild goats, which were common in the rugged terrain in which the site is situated.

Wally's Beach: a Paleoamerican site south of the Cordilleran and Laurentide glaciers covering Canada. It dates to 11,300 cal BC and represents occupation occurring before the ice-free corridor opened completely.

Wari: the capital of the Wari Empire in the Andean highlands of South America during the Middle Horizon period. It has a central stone-walled section with restricted access points. This is thought to be an area only for elite members of society.

Wari: Empire a Middle Horizon period complex political entity situated in the central Andean highlands of Peru (South America). It controlled an area about 1,300 kilometers (807 miles) long north–south, and its iconography has links to the earlier Chavín Horizon.

Western Zhou: the dynasty that conquered the Shang kingdom in 1045 BC; in 770 BC, it was defeated and the period called Eastern Zhou began. Eastern Zhou was not as politically integrated and was subject to many wars with neighboring states.

Xiaohuangshan: an early Neolithic period village site in the Lower Yangtze River region of China. It has evidence for the use of wild rice, as well as other wild food resources.

Xihuatoxtla Shelter: an Archaic period site in southwestern Mexico that has phytoliths of early domesticated maize, as well as domesticated squash, about 7000 cal BC.

Xinglonggou: an early Neolithic period village site in the Yellow River region of China with evidence for domesticated broomcorn and foxtail millet and wild and domesticated pigs.

Yangshao Culture: a middle Neolithic period group along the middle Yellow River in China. Yangshao people used domesticated and wild food resources, and there is evidence for the beginning of social distinctions between people based on grave goods.

Younger Dryas Theory: the rapid cooling and aridity of this late glacial period was used as an explanation for the origins of food production. It assumes that as climate worsened, hunter-gatherer-forager groups began to manipulate plants and animals to assure their availability and abundance.

Yuchanyan Cave: this site in northern China has evidence for the earliest known pottery at 16,350 to 13,480 cal BC and early use of rice, although it is not clear whether the rice is wild or domesticated.

Zaña Valley: a region in the Andes Mountains in Peru in South America. Archaic period sites here have evidence for hunter–gatherer–forager groups who grew cotton, coca, and peanuts and who had begun to invest in the building of small, village-like settlements.

Zapotec: a state-level politically complex society that emerged in the Valley of Oaxaca about 20 cal BC during the Late Formative period. Its capital was Monte Albán.

Zengpiyan Cave: a hunter–gatherer–forager site in southern China that has evidence for the early use of taro and pottery within the context of high mobility.

Zhengzhou: the main urban center of the Erligang Culture in the Yellow River area of northern China from 1600 to 1400 BC.

Zhizo: a Middle Iron Age group of Bantu-speaking peoples who built the early regionally important center (sometimes called a capital) at Schroda in the Shashe–Limpopo region of southeastern Africa.

Zhoukoudian: a *Homo erectus* site in China dating to 750,000 to 410,000 years ago; it has chopper/chopping tools similar to the Oldowan.

Zimbabwe Pattern: also called Zimbabwe Culture, it consists of stone-walled structures built for elites with the ruler's residence secluded on top of a relatively inaccessible hill and the rest of the royalty houses built immediately adjacent to the base of the hill. Commoners lived in daga (clay) huts farther away from the hill.

Zooarchaeology: the study of animal bones found at archaeological sites. Zooarchaeologists identify the types of animals and their uses to gain information about human behaviors.

References

Abbate, E., and M. Sagri. 2012. Early to Middle Pleistocene *Homo* Dispersals from Africa to Eurasia: Geological, Climatic and Environmental Constraints. *Quaternary International* 267: 3–19.

Abbott, D. R., S. E. Ingram, and B. G. Kober. 2006. Hohokam Exchange and Early Classic Period Organization in Central Arizona: Focal Villages or Linear Communities? *Journal of Field Archaeology* 31(3): 285–305.

Abrams, E. M. 2009. Hopewell Archaeology: A View from the Northern Woodlands. *Journal of Archaeological Research* 17(2): 169–204.

Abrams, E. M., and A. C. Freter. 2005. *Emergence of Moundbuilders: Archaeology of Tribal Societies in Southeastern Ohio.* Athens, OH: Ohio University Press.

Abu es-Soof, B. 1968. Tell Es-Sawwan: Excavations of the Fourth Season (Spring 1967) Interim Report. *Sumer* 24: 3–16.

Aceituno, F. J., and N. Loaiza. 2018. The Origins and Development of Plant Food Production and Farming in Columbian Tropical Forests. *Journal of Anthropological Archaeology* 49: 161–172.

Achilli, A., U. A. Perego, H. Lancioni, A. Olivieri, F. Gandini, B. H. Kashani, V. Battaglia, V. Grugni, N. Angerhofer, M. P. Rogers, R. J. Herrera, S. R. Woodward, D. Labuda, D. G. Smith, J. S. Cybulski, O. Semino, R. S. Malhi, and A. Torroni. 2013. Reconciling Migration Models to the Americas with the Variation of North American Native Mitogenomes. *Proceedings of the National Academy of Sciences USA* 110: 14308–14313.

Adams, J. L. 1996. The People behind the Rocks. *Archaeology in Tucson Newsletter of the Center for Desert Archaeology* 10(4): 1–4 (The Center for Desert Archaeology is now hSouthwest Archaeology).

Adams, R. E. W. 2005. *Prehistoric Mesoamerica,* 3rd ed. Norman, OK: University of Oklahoma Press.

Adams, R. McC. 1972. Patterns of Urbanization in Early Southern Mesopotamia. In *Man, Settlement and Urbanism,* P. G. Ucko, R. Tringham, and G. Dimbleby (eds.), pp. 735–749. London: Duckworth.

Adams, R. McC. 1981. *Heartland of Cities.* Chicago: Aldine.

Aiello, L. C. 2010. Five Years of *Homo floresiensis. American Journal of Physical Anthropology* 142: 167–179.

Aiello, L. C., and P. Wheeler. 2003. Neanderthal Thermoregulation and the Glacial Climate. In *Neanderthals and Modern Humans in the European Landscape of the Last Glaciation: Archaeological Results of the Stage 3 Project,* T. H. van Andel and W. Davies (eds.), pp. 147–166. Cambridge, UK: McDonald Institute for Archaeological Research.

Ainsworth, C. S., P. L. Crown, E. L. Jones, and S. E. Franklin. 2018. Ritual Depostion of Avifauna in the Northern Burial Cluster at Pueblo Bonito, Chaco Canyon. *Kiva* 84(1): 110–135.

Akins, N. J. 1986. *A Biocultural Approach to Human Burials from Chaco Canyon, New Mexico.* Vol. 9. Branch of Cultural Research, US Department of the Interior, National Park Service.

Albarella, U., K. Dobney, and P. Rowley-Conwy. 2006. The Domestication of the Pig (*Sus scrofa*): New Challenges and Approaches. In *Documenting Domestication: New Genetic and Archaeological Paradigms,* M. A. Zeder, D. G. Bradley, E. Emshwiller, and B. D. Smith (eds.), pp. 209–227. Los Angeles: University of California Press.

Albarracin-Jordan, J. 1996. Tiwanaku Settlement System: The Integration of Nested Hierarchies in the Lower Tiwanaku Valley. *Latin American Antiquity* 7(3): 183–210.

Albrethsen, S., and E. Brinch Petersen. 1976. Excavation of a Mesolithic Cemetery at Vedbaek, Denmark. *Acta Archaeologica* 47: 1–28.

Algaze, G. 2001. Initial Social Complexity in Southwestern Asia: The Mesopotamian Advantage. *Current Anthropology* 42(2): 199–233.

Algaze, G. 2008. *Ancient Mesopotamia at the Dawn of Civilization: The Evolution of an Urban Landscape.* Chicago: University of Chicago Press.

Algaze, G. 2018. Entropic Cities: The Paradox of Urbanism in Ancient Mesopotamia. *Current Anthropology* 59(1): 23–54.

Allen, M. J., B. Chan, R. Cleal, C. French, P. Marshall, J. Pollard, R. Pullen, C. Richards, C. Ruggles, D. Robinson,

J. Rylatt, J. Thomas, K. Welham, and M. P. Pearson. 2016. Stonehenge's Avenue and 'Bluestonehenge.' *Antiquity* 90: 991–1008.

Allan, S. 2007. Erlitou and the Formation of Chinese Civilization: Toward a New Paradigm. *Journal of Asian Studies* 66(2): 461–496.

Alizadeh, A. 2010. The Rise of the Highland Elamite State in Southwestern Iran. *Current Anthropology* 51(3): 353–383.

Alt, S. M. 1999. Spindle Whorls and Fiber Production at Early Cahokian Settlements. *Southeastern Archaeology* 18: 124–133.

Alva, W. 1988. Discovering the New World's Richest Unlooted Tomb. *National Geographic Magazine* 147: 510–548.

Alva, W., and C. Donnan. 1993. *Royal Tombs of Sipán.* Los Angeles: Fowler Museum of Cultural History, University of California–Los Angeles.

Ambrose, S. H. 1998. Chronology of the Later Stone Age and Food Production in East Africa. *Journal of Archaeological Science* 25: 377–392.

Ambrose, S. H., J. E. Buikstra, and H. W. Krueger. 2003. Status and Gender Differences in Diet at Mound 72, Cahokia, Revealed by Isotopic Analysis of Bone. *Journal of Anthropological Archaeology* 22: 217–226.

Amick, D. S. 2017. Evolving Views on the Pleistocene Colonization of North America. *Quaternary International* 431: 125–151.

Amirkhanov, H., and S. Lev. 2008. New Finds of Art Objects From the Upper Palaeolithic Site of Zaraysk, Russia. *Antiquity* 82: 862–870.

Amkreutz, L., A. Verpoorte, A. Waters-Rist, M. Niekus, V. van Heekeren, A. van der Merwe, H. van der Plicht, J. Glimmerveen, D. Stapert, and L. Johansen. 2018. What Lies Beneath . . . Late Glacial Human Occupation of the Submerged North Sea Landscape. *Antiquity* 92: 22–37.

Amorim, C. E. G., K. Nunes, D. Meyer, D. Comas, M. C. Bortolini, F. M. Salzano, and T. Hünemeier. 2017. Genetic Signature of Natural Selection in First Americans. *Proceedings of the National Academy of Sciences USA* 114: 2195–2199.

Andersen, S. H. 2004. Danish Shell Middens Reviewed. In *Mesolithic Scotland and Its Neighbours*, A. Saville (ed.), pp. 393–411. Edinburgh: Society of Antiquaries for Scotland.

Anderson, D. G., and J. C. Gilliam. 2000. Paleoindian Colonization of the Americas: Implications from an Examination of Physiography, Demography, and Artifact Distribution. *American Antiquity* 65(1): 43–66.

Anderson, J. H., and K. G. Hirth. 2009. Obsidian Blade Production for Craft Consumption at Kaminaljuyu. *Ancient Mesoamerica* 20(1): 163–172.

Anderson, W. 1992. Badarian Burials: Evidence of Social inequality in Middle Egypt during the Predynastic Era. *Journal of the American Research Center in Egypt* 29: 51–66.

Andresen, J. M., B. F. Byrd, M. D. Elson, R. H. McGuire, R. G. Mendoza, E. Staski, and J. P. White. 1981. The Deer Hunters: Star Carr Reconsidered. *World Archaeology* 13: 31–46.

Andrushko, V. A., M. R. Buzon, A. M. Gibaja, G. F. McEwan, A. Simonetti, and R. A. Creaser. 2011. Investigating a Child Sacrifice Event from the Inca Heartland. *Journal of Archaeological Science* 38: 323–333.

Andrushko, V. A., and E. C. Torres. 2011. Skeletal Evidence for Inca Warfare from the Cuzco Region of Peru. *American Journal of Physical Anthropology* 146: 361–372.

Anikovich, M. V., A. A. Sinitsyn, J. F. Hoffecker, V. T. Holliday, V. V. Popov, S. N. Lisitsyn, S. L. Forman, G. M. Levkovskaya, G. A. Pospelova, I. E. Kuz'mina, N. D. Burova, P. Goldberg, R. I. Macphail, B. Giaccio, and N. D. Praslov. 2007. Early Upper Paleolithic in Eastern Europe and Implications for the Dispersal of Modern Humans. *Science* 315: 223–226.

Anschuetz, K. F., R. H. Wilshusen, and C. I. Scheick. 2001. An Archaeology of Landscapes: Perspectives and Directions. *Journal of Archaeological Research* 9(2): 157–211.

Antiquities Act Centennial Section (various authors). 2006. *The SAA Archaeological Record* 6(4): 34–50.

Antón, S. C., and C. C. Swisher III. 2004. Early Dispersals of *Homo* from Africa. *Annual Review of Anthropology* 33: 271–296.

Anyon, R., and S. A. LeBlanc. 1980. The Architectural Evolution of Mogollon-Mimbres Communal Structures. *Kiva* 45(3): 253–277.

Applegate, A., A. Gautier, and S. Duncan. 2001. The North Tumuli of the Nabta Late Neolithic Ceremonial Complex. In *Holocene Settlement of the Egyptian Sahara.* Vol. 1: *The Archaeology of Nabta Playa*, F. Wendorf, R. Schild, and Associates, pp. 468–488. New York: Kluwer Academic/Plenum.

Arakawa, F., D. Gonzales, N, McMillan, and M. Murphy. 2016. Evaluation of Trade and Interaction Between

Chaco Canyon and Chaco Outlier Sites in the American Southwest by Investigating Trachybasalt Temper in Pottery Sherds. *Journal of Archaeological Science: Reports* 6: 115–124.

Arbuckle, B. S., M. D. Price, H. Hongo, and B. Öksüz. 2016. Documenting the Initial Appearance of Domestic Cattle in the Eastern Fertile Crescent (Northern Iraq and Western Iran). *Journal of Archaeological Science* 72: 1–9.

Argue, D., C. P. Groves, M. S. Y. Lee, and W. L. Jungers. 2017. The Affinities of *Homo floresiensis* Based on Phylogenetic Analyses of Cranial, Dental, and Postcranial Characters. *Journal of Human Evolution* 107: 107–133.

Arkush, E. 2008. War, Chronology, and Causality in the Titicaca Basin. *Latin American Antiquity* 19(4): 339–373.

Arkush, E. 2009. Warfare, Space, and Identity in the South-Central Andes: Constraints and Choices. In *Warfare in Cultural Context: Practice, Agency, and the Archaeology of Violence,* A. E. Nielsen and W. H. Walker (eds.), pp. 190–217. Tucson: University of Arizona Press.

Arkush, E. 2010. Hilltop Forts and the History Channel: A View from the Late Prehispanic Andes. *The SAA Archaeological Record* 10(4): 33–39.

Arnold, B. 1991. The Deposed Princess of Vix: The Need for an Engendered European Prehistory. In *The Archaeology of Gender,* D. Walde and N. D. Willows (eds.), pp. 366–374. Calgary, Canada: Archaeological Association.

Arranz-Otaegui, A., L. González Carretero, M. N. Ramsey, D. Q. Fuller, and T. Richter. 2018. Archaeobotanical Evidence Reveals the Origins of Bread 14,400 Years Ago in Northeastern Jordan. *Proceedings of the National Academy of Sciences USA* 115: 7925–7930

Arranz-Otaegui, A., L. González Carretero, J. Roe, and T. Richter. 2018. "Founder Crops" v. Wild Plants: Assessing the Plant-Based Diet of the Last Hunter-Gatherers in Southwest Asia. *Quaternary Science Reviews* 186: 263–283.

Arz, H. W., J. Lamy, P. Patzold, P. J. Miller, and M. Prins. 2003. Mediterranean Moisture Source for an Early Holocene Humid Period in the Northern Red Sea. *Science* 300: 118–121.

Ascher, M. 2005. How Can Spin, Ply, and Knot Direction Contribute to Understanding the Quipu Code? *Latin American Antiquity* 16(1): 99–111.

Ashmore, W., and A. B. Knapp. 1999. *Archaeologies of Landscape: Contemporary Perspectives.* Malden, MA: Blackwell.

Athens, J. S., T. M. Reith, and T. S. Dye. 2014. A Paleoenvironmental and Archaeological Model-Based Age Estimate for the Colonization of Hawai'i. *American Antiquity* 79(1): 144–155.

Atici, L, S. E. Pilaar Birch, and B. Erdoğu. 2017. Spread of Domestic Animals Across Neolithic Western Anatolia: New Zooarchaeological Evidence from Uğurlu Höyük, the Island of Gökçeada, Turkey. *PLoS One* 12: e0186519.

Austin, D. F. 2006. Fox-Tail Millets (Setaria: Poaceae)—Abandoned Food in Two Hemispheres. *Economic Botany* 60(2): 143–158.

Baadsgaard, A., J. Monge, S. Cox, and R. L. Zettler. 2011. Human Sacrifice and Intentional Corpse Preservation in the Royal Cemetery of Ur. *Antiquity* 85: 27–42.

Bachand, H., R. A. Joyce, and J. A. Hendon. 2003. Bodies Moving in Space: Ancient Mesoamerican Human Sculpture and Embodiment. *Cambridge Archaeological Journal* 13(2): 238–247.

Backwell, L. R., and F. d'Errico. 2001. Evidence of Termite Foraging by Swartkrans Early Hominids. *Proceedings of the National Academy of Sciences USA* 98(4): 1358–1363.

Badenhorst, S., and J. C. Driver. 2009. Faunal Changes in Farming Communities from Basketmaker II to Pueblo III (A.D. 1–1300) in the San Juan Basin of the American Southwest. *Journal of Archaeological Science* 36(9): 1832–1841.

Balme, J., and K. Morse. 2006. Shell Beads and Social Behaviour in Pleistocene Australia. *Antiquity* 80: 799–811.

Banks, W. E., N. Antunes, S. Rigaud, and F. d'Errico. 2013. Ecological Constraints on the First Prehistoric Farmers in Europe. *Journal of Archaeological Science* 40: 2746–2753.

Banning, E. B. 2011. So Fair a House: Göbekli Tepe and the Identification of Temples in the Pre-Pottery Neolithic of the Near East. *Current Anthropology* 52(5): 619–660.

Barceló, J. A., G. Capuzzo, and I. Bogdanović. 2014. Modeling Expansive Phenomena in Early Complex Societies: The Transition from Bronze Iron Age in Prehistoric Europe. *Journal of Archaeological Method and Theory* 21: 486–510.

Bard, K. A. 2008. Royal Cities and Cult Centers, Administrative Towns, and Workmen's Settlements in

Ancient Egypt. In *The Ancient City. New Perspectives on Urbanism in the Old and New World*, J. Marcus and J. A. Sabloff (eds.), pp. 165–182. Santa Fe, NM: School for Advanced Research Press.

Barham, L. S. 1989. A Preliminary Report on the Later Stone Age Artefacts from Siphiso Shelter in Swaziland. *South African Archaeological Bulletin* 44: 33–43.

Barkai, R., and R. Liran. 2008. Midsummer Sunset at Neolithic Jericho. *Time and Mind: The Journal of Archaeology, Consiousness and Culture* 1(3): 273–284.

Barnosky, A. D., N. Matzke, S. Tomiya, G. O. U. Wogan, B. Swartz, T. B. Quental, C. Marshall, J. L. McGuire, E. L. Lindsey, K. C. Maguire, B. Mersey, and E. A. Ferrer. 2011. Has the Earth's Sixth Mass Extinction Already Arrived? *Nature* 471: 51–57.

Baron, J. P. 2018. Ancient Monetization: The Case of Classic Maya Textiles. *Journal of Anthropological Archaeology* 49: 100–113.

Bárta, M. 1995. Location of the Old Kingdom Pyramids of Egypt. *Cambridge Archaeological Journal* 15(2): 177–191.

Barthélemy de Saizieu, B. 1994. Éléments de géometrie préhistorique à partir des parures funéraires du Néolithique ancient de Mehrgarh (Balouchistan Pakistanais). *L'Anthropologie* 98(4): 589–624.

Barton, R. N. E., Bouzouggar, J., Collcutt, S. N., Gale, R., Higham, T. F. G., Humphrey, L. T., Parfitt, S., Rhodes, E., Stringer, C. B., and Malek, F. 2005. The Late Upper Palaeolithic Occupation of the Moroccan Northwest Maghreb during the Last Glacial Maximum. *African Archaeological Review* 22(2): 77–100.

Barton, C. M., G. A. Clark, and A. E. Cohen. 1994. Art as Information: Explaining Upper Palaeolithic Art in Western Europe. *World Archaeology* 26(2): 185–207.

Bar-Yosef, O. 1986. The Walls of Jericho: An Alternative Interpretation. *Current Anthropology* 27: 157–162.

Bar-Yosef, O. 1998. The Natufian Culture in the Levant, Threshold to the Origins of Agriculture. *Evolutionary Anthropology* 6(5): 159–177.

Bar-Yosef, O., and A. Belfer-Cohen. 1989. The Origins of Sedentism and Farming Communities in the Levant. *Journal of World Prehistory* 3: 447–498.

Bar-Yosef, O., M. Eren, J. Yuan, D. J. Cohen, and Y. Li. 2011. Were Bamboo Tools Made in Prehistoric Southeast Asia? An Experimental View from South China. *Quaternary International* 269: 9–21.

Bar-Yosef, O., and N. Goren-Inbar. 1993. *The Lithic Assemblages of 'Ubeidiya, a Lower Paleolithic Site in the Jordan Valley.* Jerusalem: The Institute of Archaeology, Hebrew University.

Bar-Yosef, O., B. Vandermeersch, B. Arensburg, A. Belfer-Cohen, P. Goldberg, H. Laville, L. Meignen, Y. Rak, J. D. Speth, E. Tchernov, A.-M. Tillier, and S. Weiner. 1992. The Excavations in Kebara Cave, Mount Carmel. *Current Anthropology* 33: 497–550.

Bates, J., C. A. Petrie, and R. N. Singh. 2017. Approaching Rice Domestication in South Asia: New Evidence from Indus Settlements in Northern India. *Journal of Archaeological Science* 78: 193–201.

Baudez, C.-F. 2000. The Maya King's Body, Mirror of the Universe. *RES: Anthropology and Aesthetics* 38: 134–143.

Bayman, J. M. 2001. The Hohokam of Southwest North America. *Journal of World Prehistory* 15(3): 257–311.

Beach, D. 1998. Cognitive Archaeology and Imaginary History at Great Zimbabwe. *Current Anthropology* 39(1): 47–72.

Beach, T., S. Luzzadder-Beach, D. Cook, N. Dunning, D. J. Kennett, S. Krause, R. Terry, D. Trein, and F. Valdez. 2015. Ancient Maya Impacts on the Earth's Surface: An Early Anthropocene Analog? *Quaternary Science Reviews* 124: 1–30.

Bearzi, M., and C. Stanford. 2010. A Bigger, Better Brain. *American Scientist* 98(5): 402–409.

Beck, R. A., Jr. 2003. Consolidation and Hierarchy: Chiefdom Variability in the Mississippian Southeast. *American Antiquity* 68(4): 641–661.

Beck, R. A., Jr. 2004. Architecture and Polity in the Formative Lake Titicaca Basin, Bolivia. *Latin American Antiquity* 15(3): 323–343.

Beekman, C. S., and A. F. Christensen. 2003. Controlling for Doubt and Uncertainty Through Multiple Lines of Evidence: A New Look at the Mesoamerican Nahua Migrations. *Journal of Archaeological Method and Theory* 10(2): 111–164.

Belcher, W. R. 2003. Fish Exploitation of the Indus Valley Tradition. In *Indus Ethnobiology: New Perspectives from the Field*, S. A. Weber and W. R. Belcher (eds.), pp. 95–174. New York: Lexington Books.

Belcher, W. R. 2009. Understanding Ancient Fishing and Butchery Strategies of the Indus Valley Civilization. *The SAA Archaeological Record* 9(5): 10–14.

Bellwood, P. 2005. *First Farmers: The Origins of Agricultural Societies*. Oxford: Blackwell.

Belmaker, M., E. Tchernov, S. Condemi, and O. Bar-Yosef. 2002. New Evidence of Hominid Presence in the Lower Pleistocene of the Southern Levant. *Journal of Human Evolution* 43: 43–56.

Benazzi, S., K. Douka, C. Fornai, C. G. Bauer, O. Kullmer, J. Svoboda, I. Pap, F. Mallegni, P. Bayle, M. Coquerelle, S. Condemi, A. Ronchitelli, K. Harvati, and G. W. Weber. 2011. Early Dispersal of Modern Humans in Europe and Implications for Neandertal Behaviour. Nature 479: 525–528.

Bender, M. M., D. A. Baerreis, and R. L. Steventon. 1981. Further Light on Carbon Isotopes and Hopewell Agriculture. *American Antiquity* 46: 346–353.

Benson, L. V., and M. S. Berry. 2009. Climate Change and Cultural Response in the Prehistoric American Southwest. *Kiva* 75(1): 87–117.

Benson, L., L. Cordell, K. Vincent, H. Taylor, J. Stein, G. L. Farmer, and K. Futa. 2003. Ancient Maize from Chacoan Great Houses: Where Was It Grown? *Proceedings of the National Academy of Sciences USA* 100: 13111–13115.

Benz, B. F. 2001. Archaeological Evidence of Teosinte Domestication from Guilá Naquitz, Oaxaca. *Proceedings of the National Academy of Sciences USA* 98: 2104–2106.

Benz, M. 2012. "Poor Little Babies"—Creation of History Through Death at the Transition from Foraging to Farming. In *Beyond Elites. Alternatives to Hierarchial Systems in Modelling Social Formations*, T. L. Kienlin and A. Zimmermann (eds.), pp. 169–182. Bonn, Germany: Verlag Dr. Rudolf Habelt GMBH.

Berger, L. R., D. J. de Ruiter, S. E. Churchill, P. Schmid, K. J. Carlson, P. H. G. M. Dirks, and J. M. Kibii. 2010. *Australopithecus sediba*: A New Species of Homo-like Australopith from South Africa. *Science* 328: 195–204.

Berger, L. R., and P. Tobias. 1996. A Chimpanzee-like Tibia from Sterkfontein, South Africa and Its Implications for the Interpretation of Bipedalism in *Australopithecus africanus. Journal of Human Evolution* 30: 343–348.

Berger, T. D., and E. Trinkaus. 1995. Patterns of Trauma Among the Neandertals. *Journal of Archaeological Science* 22: 841–852.

Bermúdez de Castro, J. M., J. L. Arsuaga, E. Carbonell, A. Rosas, I. Martínez, and M. Mosquera. 1997. A Hominid from the Lower Pleistocene of Atapuerca, Spain: Possible Ancestor to Neandertals and Modern Humans. *Science* 276: 1392–1395.

Bermúdez de Castro, J. M., M. Martinón-Torres, R. Blasco, J. Rosell, and E. Carbonell. 2013. Continuity or Discontinuity in the European Early Pleistocene Human Settlement: The Atapuerca Evidence. *Quaternary Science Reviews* 76: 53–65.

Berry, M. S. 1982. *Time, Space, and Transition in Anasazi Prehistory*. Salt Lake City: University of Utah Press.

Berthon, R., L. Kovačiková, A. Tresset, and M. Balasse. 2018. Integration of Linearbandkeramik Cattle Husbandry in the Forested Landscape of the Mid-Holocene Climate Optimum: Seasonal-Scale Investigations in Bohemia. *Journal of Anthropological Archaeology* 51: 16–27.

Besom, T. 2010. Inka Sacrifice and the Mummy of Salinas Grandes. *Latin American Antiquity* 21(4): 399–422.

Bettinger, R. L., and J. Eerkens. 1999. Point Typologies, Cultural Transmission, and the Spread of Bow-and-Arrow Technology in the Prehistoric Great Basin. *American Antiquity* 64: 231–242.

Betts, C. M. 2006. Pots and Pox: The Identification of Protohistoric Epidemics in the Upper Mississippi Valley. *American Antiquity* 71(2): 233–259.

Bevins, R. E., R. A. Ixer, and N. J. G. Pearce. 2014. Carn Goedog Is the Likely Major Source of Stonehenge Doleritic Bluestones: Evidence Based on Compatible Element Geochemistry and Principle Components Analysis. *Journal of Archaeological Science* 42: 179–193.

Bicho, N., A. F. Carvalho, C. González-Sainz, J. L. Sanchidrián, V. Villaverde, and L. G. Straus. 2007. The Upper Paleolithic Rock Art of Iberia. *Journal of Archaeological Method and Theory* 14(1): 81–151.

Billman, B. R., P. M. Lambert, and B. L. Leonard. 2000. Cannibalism, Warfare, and Drought in the Mesa Verde Region during the Twelfth Century AD. *American Antiquity* 65(1): 145–178.

Bin, C., and B. Chen. in press. Ritual Changes and Social Transition in the Western Zhou Period (ca. 1050–771 BCE). *Archaeological Research in Asia*.

Binford, L. R. 1968. Post-Pleistocene Adaptations. In *New Perspectives in Archaeology,* S. R. Binford and L. R. Binford (eds.), pp. 313–342. Chicago: Aldine.

Binford, L. 1988. Fact and Fiction about the *Zinjanthropus* Floor: Data, Arguments, and Interpretations. *Current Anthropology* 19(1): 123–135.

Binford, L. R. 2001. Constructing Frames of Reference. An Analytical Method for Archaeological Theory Building Using Hunter–Gatherer and Environmental Data Sets. Los Angeles: University of California Press.

Binford, L. R., and C. K. Ho. 1985. Taphonomy at a Distance: Zhoukoudian, "The Cave Home of Beijing Man." *Current Anthropology* 26(4): 413–442.

Binford, L. R., and N. M. Stone. 1986. Zhoukoudian: A Closer Look. *Current Anthropology* 27(5): 453–475.

Bird, M. I., R. J. Beaman, S. A. Condie, A. Cooper, S. Ulm, and P. Veth. 2018. Palaeogeography and Voyage Modeling Indicates Early Human Colonization of Australia was Likely from Timor-Roti. *Quaternary Science Reviews* 191: 431–439.

Blackham, M. 1996. Further Investigations as to the Relationship of Samarran and Ubaid Ceramic Assemblages. *Iraq* 58: 1–15.

Blackmore, C. 2011. Ritual among the Masses: Deconstructing Identity and Class in an Ancient Maya Neighborhood. *Latin American Antiquity* 22(2): 159–177.

Blasco, R., J. Rosell, A. Rufà, A. Sánchez Marco, and C. Finlayson. 2016. Pigeons and Choughs, a Usual Resource for the Neanderthals in Gibraltar. *Quaternary International* 421: 62–77.

Blumenshine, R. J., J. A. Carvallo, and S. D. Capaldo. 1994. Competition for Carcasses and Early Hominind Behavioral Ecology: A Case Study and Conceptual Framework. *Journal of Human Evolution* 27: 197–213.

Blumenshine, R. J., I. G. Stanistreet, J. K. Njau, M. K. Bamford, F. T. Masao, R. M. Albert, H. Stollhofen, P. Andrews, K. A. Prassack, L. J. McHenry, Y. Fernández-Jalvo, E. L. Camilli, and J. I. Ebert. 2012a. Environments and Hominin Activities across the FLK Peninsula during *Zinjanthropus* Times (1.84 Ma), Olduvai Gorge, Tanzania. *Journal of Human Evolution* 63: 364–383.

Blumenshine, R. J., F. T. Masao, H. Stollhofen, I. G. Stanistreet, M. K. Bamford, R. M. Albert, J. K. Njau, and K. A. Prassack. 2012b. Landscape Distribution of Oldowan Stone Artifact Assemblages across the Fault Compartments of the Eastern Olduvai Lake Basin during Early Lowermost Bed II Times. *Journal of Human Evolution* 63: 384–394.

Boaz, N. T., R. L. Ciochon, Q. Xu, and J. Liu. 2004. Mapping and Taphonomic Analysis of the *Homo erectus* Loci at Locality 1 Zhoukoudian, China. *Journal of Human Evolution* 46(5): 519–549.

Bocherens, H., D. G. Drucker, D. Billiou, M. Patou-Mathis, and B. Vandermeersch. 2005. Isotopic Evidence for Diet and Subsistence Pattern of the Saint Césaire I Neanderthal: Review and Use of a Multi-Source Mixing Model. *Journal of Human Evolution* 49(1): 71–87.

Boe, L.-J., J.-L. Heim, K. Honda, and S. Maeda. 2002. The Potential Neanderthal Vowel Space Was as Large as That of Modern Humans. *Journal of Phonetics* 30: 465–484.

Boesch, C. 1994. Cooperative Hunting in Wild Chimpanzees. *Animal Behavior* 48: 653–667.

Boaretto, E., X. Wu, J. Yuan, O. Bar-Yosef, V. Chu, Y. Pan, K. Liu, D. Cohen, T. Jiao, S. Li, H. Gu, P. Goldberg, and S. Weiner. 2009. Radiocarbon Dating of Charcoal and Bone Collagen Associated with Early Pottery at Yuchanyan Cave, Hunan Province, China. *Proceedings of the National Academy of Sciences USA* 106: 9595–9600.

Bolnick, D. A., and D G. Smith. 2007. Migration and Social Structure among the Hopewell: Evidence from Ancient DNA. *American Antiquity* 72(4): 627–644.

Boltz, W. G. 1986. Early Chinese Writing. *World Archaeology* 17(3): 420–436.

Bongers, J., E. Arkush, and M. Harrower. 2012. Landscapes of Death: GIS-Based Analyses of Chullpas in the Western Lake Titicaca Basin. *Journal of Archaeological Science* 39: 1687–1693.

Bonjean, D., Y. Vanbrabant, G. Abrams, S. Pirson, C. Burlet, K. Di Modica, M. Otte, J. Vander Auwera, M. Golitko, R. McMillan, and E. Goemaere. 2015. A New Cambrian Black Pigment Used during the Late Middle Palaeolithic Discovered at Scladina Cave (Ardenne, Belgium). *Journal of Archaeological Science* 55: 253–265.

Bonogofsky, M. 2001. Cranial Modeling and Neolithic Bone Modification at 'Ain Ghazal: New Interpretations. *Paléorient* 27(2): 141–146.

Bonogofsky, M. 2004. Including Women and Children: Neolithic Modeled Skulls from Jordan, Israel, Syria and Turkey. *Near Eastern Archaeology* 67(2): 118–119.

Bordes, F., and J. Lafille. 1962. Découverte d'un squelette d'enfant moustérien dans le gisement du Roc-de-Marsal, commune de Campagne-du-Bugue (Dordogne). *Comptes Rendus de l'Academie des Sciences* 524: 714–715.

Bostoen, K., B. Clist, C. Doumenge, R. Grollemund, J.-M. Hombert, J. K. Muluwa, and J. Maley. 2015. Middle to Late Holocene Paleoclimatic Change and the Early Bantu Expansion in the Rain Forests of Western Central Africa. *Current Anthropology* 56(3): 354–384.

Boudadi-Maligne, M., and G. Escarguel. 2014. A Bio-Metric Re-Evaluation of Recent Claims for Early Upper Palaeolithic Wolf Domestication in Eurasia. *Journal of Archaeological Science* 45: 80–89.

Bourgeon, L., A. Burke, and T. Higham. 2017. Earliest Human Presence in North America Dated to the Last Glacial Maximum: New Radiocarbon Dates from Bluefish Caves, Canada. *PLoS One* 12(1): e0169486.

Bousman, C. B. 2005. Coping with Risk: Later Stone Age Technological Strategies at Blydefontein Rock Shelter, South Africa. *Journal of Anthropological Archaeology* 24: 193–226.

Bouzouggar, J., Barton, R. N. E., Blockley, S., Bronk-Ramsey, C., Collcutt, S. N., Gale, R., Higham, T. F. G., Humphrey, L. T., Parfitt, S., Turner, E., and Ward, S. 2008. Reevaluating the Age of the Iberomaurusian in Morocco. *African Archaeological Review* 25: 3–19.

Bove, F. J. 2005. The Dichotomy of Formative Complex Societies in Pacific Guatemala: Local Developments vs. External Relationships. In *New Perspectives on Formative Mesoamercian Cultures*, T. Powis (ed.), pp. 95–110. British Archaeological Reports International Series 1377. Oxford: Archaeopress.

Bower, J. 2016. The Mayan Written Word: History, Controversy, and Library Connections. *International Journal of the Book* 14(3): 15–25.

Boyle, K. V. 2000. Reconstructing Middle Palaeolithic Subsistence Strategies in the South of France. *International Journal of Osteoarchaeology* 10: 336–356.

Bradley, D. G., and D. A. Magee. 2006. Genetics and the Origins of Domestic Cattle. In *Documenting Domestication: New Genetic and Archaeological Paradigms*, M. A. Zeder, D. G. Bradley, E. Emshwiller, and B. D. Smith (eds.), pp. 317–328. Los Angeles: University of California Press.

Braidwood, R. J. 1960. The Agricultural Revolution. *Scientific American* 203: 130–141.

Bray, T. L. 2000. Inca Iconography: The Art of Empire in the Andes. *RES: Anthropology and Aesthetics* 38: 168–178.

Breuil, H. 1952. *Four Hundred Centuries of Cave Art* (in translation). Montignac: Centre d'Études et de Documentation Préhistoriques.

Brinker, U., A. Schramm, D. Jantzen, J. Piek, K. Hauenstein, and J. Orschiedt. 2016. The Bronze Age Battlefield in the Tollense Valley, Northeast Germany—Combat Marks on Human Bones as Evidence of Early Warrior Societies in Northern Middle Europe? In *Late Prehistory and Protohistory: Bronze Age and Iron Age. The Emergence of Warrior Societies and Its Economic, Social and Environmental Consequences*, F. Coimbra and D. Delfino (eds.), pp. 39–56. Proceedings of the XVII UISPP World Congress Volume 9 / Session A3c. Oxford: Archaeopress.

Briois, F., B. Midant-Reynes, and M. Wuttmann. 2008. *Le gisement épipaléolithique de ML1 à 'Ayn-Manâwir, Oasis de Kharga*. Cairo: Institut française d'archéologie orientale.

Brose, D. S. 1994. Trade and Exchange in the Midwestern United States. In *Prehistoric Exchange Systems in North America*, T. G. Baugh and J. E. Ericson (eds.), pp. 215–240. New York: Plenum Press.

Brown, P., T. Sutikna, M. J. Morwood, R. P. Soejono, Jatmiko, E. W. Saptomo, and R. A. Due. 2004. A New Small-Bodied Hominin from the Late Pleistocene of Flores, Indonesia. *Nature* 431: 1055–1061.

Bruford, M. W., and S. J. Townsend. 2006. Mitochondrial DNA Diversity in Modern Sheep. In *Documenting Domestication: New Genetic and Archaeological Paradigms*, M. A. Zeder, D. G. Bradley, E. Emshwiller, and B. D. Smith (eds.), pp. 306–316. Los Angeles: University of California Press.

Brumm, A., G. D. van den Bergh, M. Storey, I. Kurniawan, B. V. Alloway, R. Setiawan, E. Setiyabudi, R. Grün, M. W. Moore, D. Yurnaldi, M. R. Puspaningrum, U. P. Wibowo, H. Insani, I. Sutisna, J. A. Westgate, N. J. G. Pearce, M. Duval, H. J. M. Meijer, F. Aziz, T. Sutikna, S. van der Kaars, S. Flude, and M. J. Morwood. 2016. Age and Context of the Oldest Known Hominin Fossils from Flores. *Nature* 534: 249–253.

Brunet, M., F. Guy, D. Pilbeam, H.MacKaye, A. Likius, D. Ahounta, A. Beauvilains, C. Blondel, H. Bocherens, J.-R. Boisserie, L. de Bonis, Y. Coppens, J. Dejax, C. Denys, P.Duringer, V.Eisenmann, G.Fanone, P.Fronty, D.Geraads, T.Lehmann, F.Lihoeau, A.Louchart, A.Mahamat, G.Merceron, G. Mouchelin, O. Otero, P. Campomanes, M. Ponce de Leon, J.-C. Rage, M. Sapanet, M. Schuster, J. Sudre, P. Tassy, X. Valentin, P. Vignaud, L. Viriot, A. Zazzo, and C. Zollikofer. 2002. A New Hominid from the Upper Miocene of Chad, Central Africa. *Nature* 418: 145–151.

Bruno, M. C. 2006. A Morphological Approach to Documenting the Domestication of Chenopodium in the Andes. In *Documenting Domestication: New Genetic and Archaeological Paradigms*, M. A. Zeder, D. G. Bradley, E. Emshwiller, and B. D. Smith (eds.), pp. 32–45. Los Angeles: University of California Press.

Brunson, K., X. Zhao, N. He, X. Dai, A. Rodrigues, and D. Yang. 2016. New Insights into the Origins of Oracle Bone Divination: Ancient DNA from Late Neolithic Chinese Bovines. *Journal of Archaeological Science* 74: 35–44.

Brunton, G., and G. Caton-Thompson. 1928. *The Badarian Civilization*. London: The British School of Archaeology in Egypt.

Brush, C. F. 1965. Pox Pottery: Earliest Identified Mexican Ceramic. *Science* 149:194–195.

Buck, L. T., and C. B. Stringer. 2014. Having the Stomach for It: A Contribution to Neanderthal Diets? *Quaternary Science Reviews* 96: 161–167.

Buck, P. E., and L. Perry. 1999. A Late Basketmaker III Storage and Habitation Site Near Hurricane, Utah. *Kiva* 64(4): 471–494.

Bueno, L., J. Feathers, and P. De Blasis. 2013. The Formation Process of a Paleoindian Open-Air Site in Central Brazil: Integrating Lithic Analysis, Radiocarbon and Luminescence Dating. *Journal of Archaeological Science* 40: 190–203.

Bulbeck, D. 2007. Where River Meets Sea. *Current Anthropology* 48(2): 315–321.

Bunn, H. T. 2007. Meat Made Us Human. In *Evolution of the Human Diet. The Known, the Unknown, and the Unknowable*, P. S. Unger (ed.), pp. 191–211. New York: Oxford University Press.

Bunn, H. T., and E. M. Kroll. 1986. Systematic Butchery by Plio-Pleistocene Hominids at Olduvai Gorge, Tanzania. *Current Anthropology* 27: 431–452.

Burger, R. L. 1992. *Chavin and the Origins of the Andean Civilzation*. New York: Thames and Hudson.

Burger, R. L., and R. Matos Mendieta. 2002. Atalla: A Center on the Periphery of the Chavín Horizon. *Latin American Antiquity* 13(2): 153–177.

Burger, R. L., and L. Salazar-Burger. 1980. Ritual and Religion at Huaricoto. *Archaeology* 33: 26–32.

Burke, A. 2004. The Ecology of Neanderthals: Preface. *International Journal of Osteoarchaeology* 14: 155–161.

Burke, H., C. Smith, and L. Z. Zimmerman. 2008. *The Archaeologist's Field Handbook: North American Edition*. Lanham, MD: Altamira Press.

Burks, J., and R. A. Cook. 2011. Beyond Squier and Davis: Rediscovering Ohio's Earthworks Using Geophysical Remote Sensing. *American Antiquity* 76(4): 667–689.

Butzer, K. W., E. Butzer, and S. Love. 2013. Urban Geoarchaeology and Environmental History at the Lost City of the Pyramids, Giza: Synthesis and Review. *Journal of Archaeological Science* 40(8): 3340—3366.

Byers, A. M. 2011. *Sacred Games, Death, and Renewal in the Ancient Eastern Woodlands. The Ohio Hopewell System of Cult Solidarity Heterarchies*. New York: Altamira Press.

Byers, D. A., and A. Ugan. 2005. Should We Expect Large Game Specialization in the Late Pleistocene? An Optimal Foraging Perspective on Early Paleoindian Prey Choice. *Journal of Archaeological Science* 32: 1624–1640.

Cachola-Abad, K. 2013. Cultural Resource Management Challenges in Hawai'i. *The SAA Archaeological Record* 13(1): 33–34.

Calabrese, J. A. 2000. Metals, Ideology and Power: The Manufacture and Control of Materialised Ideology in the Area of the Limpopo-Shashe Confluence, c. AD 900 to 1300. In *African Naissance: The Limpopo Valley 1000 Years Ago*, M. Lesley and T. M. Maggs (eds.), pp. 100–111. South African Archaeological Society Goodwin Series 8. Vlaeberg, South Africa: South African Archaeological Society.

Cameron, C. M. 1990. Pit Structure Abandonment in the Four Corners Region of the American Southwest: Late Basketmaker III and Pueblo I Periods. *Journal of Field Archaeology* 17(1): 27–37.

Cameron, C. M. 2001. Pink Chert, Projectile Points, and the Chacoan Regional System. *American Antiquity* 66(1): 79–101.

Cameron, C. M. 2005. Exploring Archaeological Cultures in the Northern Southwest: What Were Chaco and Mesa Verde? *Kiva* 70(3): 227–253.

Campbell, R. B. 2009. Toward a Networks and Boundaries Approach to Early Complex Polities: The Late Shang Case. *Current Anthropology* 50(6): 821–848.

Campbell, R. B., Z. Li, Y. He, and Y. Jing. 2011. Consumption, Exchange, and Production at the Great Settlement Shang: Bone-Working at Tiesanlu Anyang. *Antiquity* 85: 1279–1297.

Camps, G. 1974. *Le civilisations préhistoriques de l'Afrique du nord et du Sahara*. Paris: C.N.R.S.

Cann, R., M. Stoneking, and A. Wilson. 1987. Mitochondrial DNA and Human Evolution. *Nature* 325 31–36.

Cannon, M. D., and D. J. Meltzer. 2004. Paleoindian Foraging: Examining the Faunal Evidence for Large Mammal

Specialization and Regional Variability in Prey Choice. *Quaternary Science Reviews* 23: 1955–1987.

Cannon, M. D., and D. J. Meltzer. 2008. Explaining Variability in Early Paleoindian Foraging. *Quaternary International* 191: 5–17.

Capriles, J. M., K. M. Moore, A. I. Domic, and C. A. Hastorf. 2014. Fishing and Environmental Change during the Emergence of Social Complexity in the Lake Titicaca Basin. *Journal of Anthropological Archaeology* 34: 66–77.

Caramelli, D., C. Lalueza-Fox, C. Vernesi, M. Lari, A. Casoli, F. Mallegni, B. Chiarelli, I. Dupanloup, J. Bertranpetit, G. Barbujani, and G. Bertorelle. 2003. Evidence for a Genetic Discontinuity between Neandertals and 24,000-Year-Old Anatomically Modern Europeans. *Proceedings of the National Academy of Sciences USA* 100(11): 6593–6597.

Caramanica, A., J. Quilter, L. Huaman, F. Villanueva, and C. R. Morales. 2018. Micro-Remains, ENSO, and Environmental Reconstruction of el Paraíso, Peru, a Late Preceramic Site. *Journal of Archaeological Science: Reports* 17: 667–677.

Caraballo, D. M. 2016. *Urbanization and Religion in Ancient Central Mexico.* New York: Oxford University Press.

Carbonell, E., I. Cáceres, M. Lozano, P. Saladié, J. Rosell, C. Lorenzo, J. Vallverdú, R. Huguet, A. Canals, and J. M. Bermúdez de Castro. 2010. Cultural Cannibalism as a Paleoeconomic System in the European Lower Pleistocene. *Current Anthropology* 51(4): 539–549.

Carbonell, E., M. Esteban, A. M. Nájera, M. Mosquera, X P. Rodríguez, A. Ollé, R. Sala, and J. M. Vergès. 1999. The Pleistocene Site of Gran Dolina, Sierra de Atapuerca, Spain: A History of the Archaeological Investigations. *Journal of Human Evolution* 37: 313–324.

Carleton, W. C., D. Campbell, and M. Collard. 2014. A Reassessment of the Impact of Drought Cycles on the Classic Maya. *Quaternary Science Reviews* 105: 151–161.

Carleton, W. C., D. Campbell, and M. Collard. 2017. Increasing Temperature Exacerbated Classic Maya Conflict Over the Long Term. *Quaternary Science Reviews* 163: 209–218.

Carneiro, R. L. 1992. Point Counterpoint: Ecology and Ideology in the Development of New World Civilizations. In *Ideology and Pre-Columbian Civilizations,* A. A. Demarest and G. W. Conrad (eds.), pp. 175–203. Santa Fe, NM: School of American Research Press.

Carr, C. 2005. Rethinking Interregional Hopewellian "Interaction." In *Gathering Hopewell: Society, Ritual, and Ritual Interaction,* C. Carr and D. T. Case (eds.), pp. 575–623. New York: Springer.

Carr, C., and D. T. Case (eds.). 2005a. *Gathering Hopewell: Society, Ritual, and Ritual Interaction.* New York: Springer.

Carr, C., and D. T. Case. 2005b. The Nature of Leadership in Ohio Hopewellian Societies: Role Segregation and the Transformation from Shamanism. In *Gathering Hopewell: Society, Ritual, and Ritual Interaction,* C. Carr and D. T. Case (eds.), pp. 177–237. New York: Springer.

Carr, C., B. J. Goldstein, and J. D. Weets. 2005. Estimating the Sizes and Social Compositions of Mortuary-Related Gatherings at Scioto Hopewell Earthwork-Mound Sites. In *Gathering Hopewell: Society, Ritual, and Ritual Interaction,* C. Carr and D. T. Case (eds.), pp. 480–532. New York: Springer.

Carter, W. E., R. L. Shrestha, and J. C. Fernandez-Diaz. 2016. Archaeology from the Air. *American Scientist* 104(1): 28–35.

Castellanoa, S., G. Parraa, F. A. Sánchez-Quinto, F. Racimo, M. Kuhlwilma, M. Kircher, S. Sawyer, Q. Fu, A. Heinze, B. Nickel, J. Dabney, M. Siebauer, L. White, H. A. Burbano, G. Renaud, U. Stenzel, C. Lalueza-Fox, M,. de la Rasilla, A. Rosas, P. Rudan, D. Brajković, Ž. Kucan, I. Gušic, M. V. Shunkov, A. P. Derevianko, B. Viola, M. Meyer, J. Kelso, A. M. Andrés, and S. Pääbo. 2014. Patterns of Coding Variation in the Complete Exomes of Three Neandertals. *Proceedings of the National Academy of Sciences USA* 111: 6666–6671.

Castelli, A. 2010. Ibex Images from Magdalenian Culture. *PaleoAnthropology* 2010: 123–157.

Caton-Thompson, G. 1952. *Kharga Oasis in Prehistory.* London: Athlone Press.

Cattelain, P. 1997. Hunting during the Upper Paleolithic: Bow, Spearthrower, or Both? In *Projectile Technology,* H. Knecht (ed.), pp. 213–240. New York: Plenum Press.

Cerling, T. E., J. Quade, S. H. Ambrose, and N. E. Sikes. 1991. Fossil Soils, Grasses and Carbon Isotopes from Fort Ternan, Kenya: Grassland or Woodland. *Journal of Human Evolution* 21: 295–306.

Cerling, T. E., N. E. Levin, J. Quade, J. C. Wynn, D. L. Fox, J. D. Kingston, R. G. Klein, and F. H. Brown. 2010. Comment on the Paleoenvironment of *Ardipithecus ramidus. Science* 328: 1105-d.

Cerling, T. E., E, Mbua, F. Kiera, F. K. Manthi, F. E. Grine, M. G. Leakey, M. Sponheimer, and K. T. Uno. 2011. Diet of *Paranthropus boisei* in the Early Pleistocene of East Africa. *Proceedings of the National Academy of Sciences USA* 108: 9337–9341.

Chapdelaine, C. 2011. Recent Advances in Moche Archaeology. *Journal of Archaeological Research* 19: 191–231.

Charles, D. K., and J. E. Buikstra (eds.). 2006. *Recreating Hopewell.* Gainesville: University Press of Florida.

Chase, A. F., D. Z. Chase, C. T. Fisher, S. J. Leisz, and J. F. Weishampel. 2012. Geospatial Revolution and Remote Sensing LiDAR in Mesoamerican Archaeology. *Proceedings of the National Academy of Sciences USA* 109: 12916–12921.

Chase, B., P. Ajithprasad, S. V. Rajesh, A. Patel, and B. Sharma. 2014a. Materializing Harappan Identities: Unity and Diversity in the Borderlands of the Indus Civilization. *Journal of Anthropological Archaeology* 35: 63–78.

Chase, B., D. Meiggs, P. Ajithprasad, and P. A. Slater. 2014b. Pastoral Land-Use of the Indus Civilization in Gujarat: Faunal Analyses and Biogenic Isotopes at Bagasra. *Journal of Archaeological Science* 50: 1–15.

Chase, P. G. 1990. Tool-Making Tools and Middle Paleolithic Behavior. *Current Anthropology* 31(4): 443–447.

Chase, P. G., and H. L. Dibble. 1987. Middle Paleolithic Symbolism: A Review of Current Evidence and Interpretation. *Journal of Anthropological Archaeology* 6: 263–296.

Chatters, J. C., D. J. Kennett, Y. Asmerom, B. M. Kemp, V. Polyak, A. N. Blank, P. A. Beddows, E. Reinhardt, J. Arroyo-Cabrales, D. A. Bolnick, R. S. Malhi, B. J. Culleton, P. L. Erreguerena, D. Rissolo, S. Morell-Hart, and T. W. Stafford Jr. 2014. Late Pleistocene Human Skeleton and mtDNA Link Paleoamericans and Modern Native Americans. *Science* 344: 750–754.

Chatterton, R. 2003. Star Carr Reanalyzed. In *Peopling the Mesolithic in a Northern Environment,* L. Bevan and J. Moore (eds.), pp. 81–86. British Archaeological Reports International Series 1157. Oxford: Archaeopress.

Chauvet, J. M., E. B. Deschamps, and C. Hillaire. 1996. *Dawn of Art: The Chauvet Cave: The Oldest Known Painting in the World.* New York: Abrams.

Chen, S.-q. and P.-L. Yu. 2017. Variations in the Upper Paleolithic Adaptations of North China: A Review of the Evidence and Implications for the Onset of Food Production. *Archaeological Research in Asia* 9: 1–12.

Chenault, M. L., and T. N. Motsinger. 2000. Colonization, Warfare, and Regional Competition: Recent Research into the Basketmaker III Period in the Mesa Verde Region. In *Foundations of Anasazi Culture: The Basketmaker-Pueblo Transition,* P. F. Reed (ed.), pp. 45–68. Salt Lake City: University of Utah Press.

Cheung, C. 2018. The Chinese History That Is Written in Bone. *American Scientist* 106(3): 133–134.

Cheung, C., Z. Jing, J. Tang, D. A. Weston, and M. P. Richards. 2017. Diets, Social Roles, and Geographical Origins of Sacrificial Victims at the Royal Cemetery at Yinxu, Shang China: New Evidence from Stable Carbon, Nitrogen, and Sulfer isotope Analysis. *Journal of Anthropological Archaeology* 48: 28–45.

Chicoine, D. 2011. Feasting Landscapes and Political Economy at the Early Horizon Center of Huambacho, Nepeña Valley, Peru. *Journal of Anthropological Archaeology* 30: 432–453.

Childe, V. G. 1950. The Urban Revolution. *Town Planning Review* 21: 3–17.

Childe, V. G. 1952. *New Light on the Most Ancient East,* 4th ed. London: Routledge and Kegan Paul.

Childs, S. T., and D. Killick. 1993. Indigenous African Metallurgy: Nature and Culture. *Annual Review of Anthropology* 22: 317–337.

Chimpanzee Sequencing and Analysis Consortium. 2005. Initial Sequence of the Chimpanzee Genome and Comparison with the Human Genome. *Nature* 437: 69–87.

Chirikure, S. 2007. Metals in Society: Iron Production and Its Position in Iron Age Communities of Southern Africa. *Journal of Social Archaeology* 7: 72–100.

Chirikure, S., M. Manyanga, I. Pikirayi, and M. Pollard. 2013. New Pathways of Social Complexity in Southern Africa. *African Archaeological Review* 30: 339–366.

Chirikure, S., and I. Pikirayi. 2008. Inside and Outside the Dry Stone Walls: Revisiting the Material Culture of Great Zimbabwe. *Antiquity* 82: 976–993.

Chirikure, S., and I. Pikirayi. 2011. Debating Great Zimbabwe. *Azania: Archaeological Research in Africa* 46(2): 221–231.

Clark, G. A. 1969. A Preliminary Analysis of Burial Clusters at the Grasshopper Site, East-Central Arizona. *Kiva* 35: 57–86.

Clark, J. G. D. 1954. *Excavations at Star Carr.* Cambridge, UK: Cambridge University Press.

Clark, J., J. X. Mitrovica, and J. Alder. 2014. Coastal Paleogeography of the California–Oregon–Washington and Bering Sea Continental Shelves during the Latest Pleistocene and Holocene: Implications for the Archaeological Record. *Journal of Archaeological Science* 52: 12–23.

Clark, P. U., A. S. Dyke, J. D. Shakun, A. E. Carlson, J. Clark, B. Wohlfarth, J. X. Mitrovica, S. W. Hostetler, and A. M. McCabe. 2009. The Last Glacial Maximum. *Science* 325: 710–714.

Clarke, R., and P. Tobias. 1995. Sterkfontein Member 2 Foot Bones of the Oldest South African Hominind. *Science* 269: 521–524.

Clarkson, C., Z. Jacobs, B. Marwick, R. Fullagar, L. Wallis, M. Smith, R. G. Roberts, E. Hayes, K. Lowe, X. Carah, S. A. Florin, J. McNeil, D. Cox, L. J. Arnold, Q. Hua, J. Huntley, H. E. A. Brand, T. Manne, A. Fairbairn, J. Shulmeister, L. Lyle, M. Salinas, M. Page, K. Connell, G. Park, K. Norman, T. Murphy, and C. Pardoe. 2017. Human Occupation of Northern Australia by 65,000 Years Ago. *Nature* 547: 306–310.

Close, A. E. 1990. Living on the Edge: Neolithic Herders in the Eastern Sahara. *Antiquity* 64: 79–96.

Close, A. E., and F. Wendorf. 2001. Site E-77-7 Revisited: The Early Neolithic of El Adam Type at El Gebal El Beid Playa. In *Holocene Settlement of the Egyptian Sahara. Vol. 1: The Archaeology of Nabta Playa*, F. Wendorf, R. Schild, and Associates, pp. 57–70. New York: Kluwer Academic/Plenum.

Cobb, C. R., and B. M. Butler. 2002. The Vacant Quarter Revisited: Late Mississippian Abandonment of the Lower Ohio Valley. *American Antiquity* 67(4): 625–641.

Cobb, C. R., and B. Giles. 2009. War Is Shell: The Ideology and Embodiment of Mississippian Conflict. In *Warfare in Cultural Context: Practice, Agency, and the Archaeology of Violence*, A. E. Nielsen and W. H. Walker (eds.), pp. 84–108. Tucson: University of Arizona Press.

Cobb, C. R., J. Maymon, and R. H. McGuire. 1999. Feathered, Horned, and Antlered Serpents: Mesoamerican Connections with the Southwest and Southeast. In *Great Towns and Regional Polities in the Prehistoric American Southwest and Southeast*, J. Neitzel (ed.), pp. 165–181. Albuquerque: University of New Mexico Press.

Coe, M. D., and R. A. Diehl. 1980a. *In the Land of the Olmec. Vol. 1: The Archaeology of San Lorenzo Tenochtitlán*. Austin: University of Texas Press.

Coe, M. D., and R. A. Diehl. 1980b. *In the Land of the Olmec. Vol. 2: The People of the River*. Austin: University of Texas Press.

Coe, W. R. 1990. *Excavations in the Great Plaza, North Terrace, and Acropolis of Tikal*. Philadelphia: University of Pennsylvania Museum of Archaeology and Anthropology Monograph 61.

Coe, W. R., and J. J. McGinn. 1963. Tikal: The North Acropolis and and Early Tomb. *Expedition* 5(2): 25–32.

Cohen, D. J. 2011. The Beginnings of Agriculture in China. A Multiregional View. *Current Anthropology* 52(Suppl. 4): S273–S293.

Cohen D. J., O. Bar-Yosef, X. Wu, I. Patania, and P. Goldberg. 2017. The Emergence of Pottery in China: Recent Dating of Two Early Pottery Cave Sites in South China. *Quaternary International* 441: 36–48.

Collard, M., B. Buchanan, M. J. Hamilton, and M. J. O'Brien. 2010. Spatiotemporal Dynamics of the Clovis-Folsom Transition. *Journal of Archaeological Science* 37: 2513–2519.

Coltrain, J. B., J. C. Janetski, and S. W. Carlyle. 2007. The Stable- and Radio-Isotope Chemistry of Western Basketmaker Burials: Implications for Early Puebloan Diets and Origins. *American Antiquity* 72(2): 301–321.

Coltrain, J. B., J. C. Janetski, and M. D. Lewis. 2012. A Re-Assessment of Basketmaker II Cave 7: Massacre Site or Cemetery Context. *Journal of Archaeological Science* 39: 2220–2230.

Colwell-Chanthaphonh, C., and T. J. Ferguson (eds.). 2007. *Collaboration in Archaeological Practice: Engaging Descendant Communites*. Walnut Creek, CA: Altamira Press.

Conard, N. J. 2009. A Female Figurine from the Basal Aurignacian of Hohle Fels Cave in Southwestern Germany. *Nature* 459: 248–252.

Conard, N. J., M. Malina, and S. C. Münzel. 2009. New Flutes Document the Earliest Musical Tradition in Southwestern Germany. *Nature* 460: 737–740.

Conneller, C., N. Milner, B. Taylor, and M. Taylor. 2012. Substantial Settlement in the European Early Mesolithic: New Research at Star Carr. *Antiquity* 86: 1004–1020.

Conkey, M. 1984. To Find Ourselves: Art and Social Geography of Prehistoric Hunter Gatherers. In *Past and Present in Hunter Gatherer Studies*, C. Schrire (ed.), pp. 253–276. New York: Academic Press.

Conkey, M. 1985. Ritual Communication, Social Elaboration, and the Variable Trajectories of Paleolithic Material Culture. In *Prehistoric Hunter–Gatherers: The Emergence of Cultural Complexity,* T. D. Price and J. Brown (eds.), pp. 299–323. New York: Academic Press.

Contreras, D. A. 2009. Reconstructing Landscape at Chavín de Huántar, Perú: A GIS-Based Approach. *Journal of Archaeological Science* 36: 1006–1017.

Cook, E. R., C. Woodhouse, C. M. Eakin, D. M., Meko, and D. W. Stahle. 2004. Long-Term Aridity Changes in the Western United States. *Science* 306: 1015–1018.

Coon, M. S. 2009. Variation in Ohio Hopewell Political Economies. *American Antiquity* 74(1): 49–76.

Cordell, L. S., and G. R. Milner. 1999. The Organization of Late Precolumbian Societies in the Southwest and Southeast. In *Great Towns and Regional Polities in the Prehistoric American Southwest and Southeast,* J. E. Neitzel (ed.), pp. 109–113. Albuquerque: University of New Mexico Press.

Cortés-Sánchez, M., A. Morales-Muñiz, M. D. Simón-Vallejo, M. C. Lozano-Francisco, J. L. Vera-Peláez, C. Finlayson, J. Rodríguez-Vidal, A. Delgado-Huertas, F. J. Jiménez-Espejo, F. Martínez-Ruiz, M. Aranzazu Martínez-Aguirre, A. J. Pascual-Granged, M. M. Bergadà-Zapata, J. F. Gibaja-Bao, J. A. Riquelme-Cantal, J. A. López-Sáez, M. Rodrigo-Gámiz, S. Sakai, S. Sugisaki, G. Finlayson, D. A. Fa, and N. F. Bicho. 2011. Earliest Known Use of Marine Resources by Neanderthals. *PLoS One* 6(9): e24026.

Cortesi, E., M. Tosi, A. Lazzari, and M. Vidale. 2008. Cultural Relationships beyond the Iranian Plateau: The Helmand Civilization, Baluchistan and the Indus Valley in the 3rd Millennium BCE. *Paléorient* 34(2): 5–35.

Covey, R. A. 2003. A Processual Study of Inka State Formation. *Journal of Anthropological Archaeology* 22: 333–357.

Covey, R. A. 2006. Chronology, Succession, and Sovereignty: The Politics of Inka Historiography and Its Modern Interpretation. *Comparative Studies in Society and History* 48(1): 169–199.

Covey, R. A. 2011. Landscapes and Languages of Power in the Inca Imperial Heartland (Cuzco, Peru). *The SAA Archaeological Record* 11(4): 29–32.

Covey, R. A. 2015. Kinship and the Inca Imperial Core: Multiscalar Archaeological Patterns in the Sacred Valley (Cuzco, Peru). *Journal of Anthropological Archaeology* 40: 183–195.

Cowan, F. L. 2006. A Mobile Hopewell? Questioning Assumptions of Ohio Hopewell Sedentism. In *Recreating Hopewell,* D. K. Charles and J. E. Buikstra (eds.), pp. 26–49. Gainesville: University Press of Florida.

Cowgill, L. W., M. B. Mednikva, A. P. Buzhilova, and E. Trinkaus. 2015. The Sunghir 3 Upper Paleolithic Juvenile: Pathology versus Persistence in the Paleolithic. *International Journal of Osteoarchaeology* 25: 176–187.

Crabtree, S. A., L. J. S. Vaughn, and N. T. Crabtree. 2017. Reconstructing Ancestral Pueblo Food Webs in the Southwestern United States. *Journal of Archaeological Science* 81: 116–127.

Crown, P. L. (ed.). 2000. *Women and Men in the Prehispanic Southwest.* Santa Fe, NM: School of American Research Press.

Crown, P. L. 2018. Drinking Performance and Politics in Pueblo Bonito, Chaco Canyon. *American Antiquity* 83(3): 387–406.

Crown, P. A., and S. K. Fish. 1996. Gender and Status in the Hohokam Pre-Classic to Classic Transition. *American Anthropologist* 98(4): 803–817.

Crown, P. A., J. Gu, W. J. Hurst, T. J. Ward, A. D. Bravenec, S. Ali, L. Kebert, M. Berch, E. Redman, P. D. Lyons, J. Merewether, D. A. Phillips, L. S. Reed, and K. Woodson. 2015. Ritual Drinks in the Pre-Hispanic US Southwest and Mexican Northwest. *Proceedings of the National Academy of Science USA* 112: 11436–11442.

Crown, P. A., and W. J. Hurst. 2009. Evidence of Cacao Use in the Prehispanic American Southwest. *Proceedings of the National Academy of Science USA* 106(7): 2110–2113.

Cunliffe, B. 2000. Brittany and the Atlantic Rim in the Later First Millennium BC. *Oxford Journal of Archaeology* 19(4): 367–386.

Curry, A. 2010. Trophy Skulls and Beer. *Archaeology* 63(1): 38–43.

Dahlin, B. H. 2002. Clinate Change and the End of the Classic Period in Yucatan. *Ancient Mesoamerica* 13: 327–340.

Dalan, R. 1997. The Construction of Mississippian Cahokia. In *Cahokia: Domination and Ideology in the Mississippian World,* T. R. Pauketat and T. E. Emerson (eds.), pp. 89–102. Lincoln: University of Nebraska Press.

D'Altroy, T. N. 2002. *The Incas.* Malden, MA: Blackwell.

Dart, R. 1925. *Australopithecus africanus*: The Man-Ape of South Africa. *Nature* 2884(115): 195–199.

Darvill, T., and G. Wainwright. 2015. Beyond Stonehenge: Carn Menyn Quarry and the Origin and Date of Bluestone Extraction in the Preseli Hills of South-West Wales. *Antiquity* 88: 1099–1114.

Darvill, T., P. Marshall, M. Parker Pearson, and G. Wainwright. 2012. Stonehenge Remodelled. *Antiquity* 1021–1040.

Darwin, C. 1981. *The Descent of Man, and Selection in Relation to Sex*. Princeton, NJ: Princeton University Press (first published in 1871).

David, B., J.-M. Geneste, F. Petchey, J.-J. Delannoy, B. Barker, and M. Eccleston. 2013. How Old Are Australia's Pictographs? A Review of Rock Art Dating. *Journal of Archaeological Science* 40: 3–10.

Davidson, I. 2010. The Colonization of Australia and Its Adjacent Islands and the Evolution of Modern Cognition. *Current Anthropology* 51(Supplement 1): S177–S189.

Davies, R., and P. Gollop. 2003. The Human Presence in Europe during the Last Glacial Period II: Climate Tolerance and Climate Preferences of Mid- and Late Glacial Hominids. In *Neanderthals and Modern Humans in the European Landscape during the Last Glaciation*, T. H. van Andel and W. Davies (eds.), pp. 131–146. Cambridge, UK: McDonald Institute for Archaeological Research.

Davies, R., and S. Underdown. 2006. The Neanderthals: A Social Synthesis. *Cambridge Archaeological Journal* 16(2): 145–164.

Davies, W. V. 1987. *Egyptian Hieroglyphs*. Los Angeles: University of California Press and The British Museum.

Dean, J. S., W. H. Doelle, and J. D. Orcutt. 1994. Adaptive Stress, Environment, and Demography. In *Themes in Southwest Prehistory*, G. J. Gumerman (ed.), pp. 53–86. Santa Fe, NM: School of American Research Press.

deFrance, S. D., D. K. Keefer, J. B. Richardson, and A. Umire Alvarez. 2001. Late Paleo-Indian Coastal Foragers: Specialized Extractive Behavior at Quebrada Tacahuay, Peru. *Latin American Antiquity* 12(4): 413–426.

DeMarrais, E., and T. Earle. 2017. Collective Action Theory and the Dynamics of Complex Societies. *Annual Review of Anthropology* 46: 183–201.

Demattè, P. 1999. Longshan Era Urbanism: The Role of Cities in Predynastic China. *Asian Perspectives* 38(2): 119–153.

Demattè, P. 2010. The Origins of Chinese Writing: The Neolithic Evidence. *Cambridge Archaeological Journal* 20(2): 211–228.

Dembo, M., N. J. Matzke, A. Ø. Mooers, and M. Collard. 2015. Bayesian Analysis of a Morphological Supermatrix Sheds Light on Controversial Fossil Hominin Relationships. *Proceedings of the Royal Society B* 282: 20150943.

d'Errico, F., L. Backwell, P. Villa, I. Degano, J. J. Lucejko, M. K. Bamford, T. F. G. Higham, M. P. Colombini, and P. B. Beaumont. 2012. Early Evidence of San Material Culture Represented by Organic Artifacts from Border Cave, South Africa. *Proceedings of the National Academy of Sciences USA* 109: 13214–13219.

d'Errico, F., C. Henshilwood, M. Vanhaeren, and K. van Niekerk. 2005. *Nassarius kraussianus* Shell Beads from Blombos Cave: Evidence for Symbolic Behaviour in the Middle Stone Age. *Journal of Human Evolution* 48: 3–24.

d'Errico, F., R. García Moreno, and R. F. Rifkin. 2012. Technological, Elemental and Colorimetric Analysis of an Engraved Ochre Fragment from the Middle Stone Age Levels of Klasies River Mouth Cave 1, South Africa. *Journal of Archaeological Science* 39(4): 942–952.

d'Errico, F., and M. Vanhaeren. 2007. Evolution or Revolution? New Evidence for the Origin of Symbolic Behaviour in and out of Africa. In *Rethinking the Human Revolution*, P. Mellars, K. Boyle, O. Bar-Yosef, and C. Stringer (eds.), pp. 275–286. Cambridge, UK: McDonald Institute for Archaeological Research.

d'Errico, F., M. Vanhaeren, N. Barton, A. Bouzouggar, H. Mienis, D. Richter, J.-J. Hublin, S. P. McPherron, and P. Lozouet. 2009. Additional Evidence on the Use of Personal Ornaments in the Middle Paleolithic of North Africa. *Proceedings of the National Academy of Sciences USA* 106(38): 16051–16056.

Dennell, R. 2016. Life without the Movius Line: The Structure of the East and Southeast Asian Early Palaeolithic. *Quaternary International* 400: 14–22.

de Saint Pierre, M. 2017. Antiquity of mtDNA Lineage D1g from the Southern Cone of South America Supports Pre-Clovis Migration. *Quaternary International* 444: 19–25.

Dewar, G., D. Halkett, T. Hart, J. Orton, and J. Sealy. 2006. Implications of a Mass Kill Site of Springbok (*Antidorcas marsupialis*) in South Africa: Hunting Practices, Gender

Relations, and Sharing in the Later Stone Age. *Journal of Archaeological Science* 33: 1266–1275.

Devès, M., D. Sturdy, N. Godet, G. C. P. King, and G. N. Bailey. 2014. Hominin Reactions to Herbivore Distribution in the Lower Palaeolithic of the Southern Levant. *Quaternary Science Reviews* 96: 140–160.

Diamond, J. 2001. Australia's Last Giants. *Nature* 411: 755–757.

Diamond, J. D. 2005. *Collapse: How Societies Choose to Fail or Succeed*. New York: Viking.

Dibble, H. L., A. Abdolahzadeh, V. Aldeias, P. Goldberg, S. P. McPherron, and D. M. Sandgathe. 2017. How Did Hominins Adapt to Ice Age Europe without Fire? *Current Anthropology* 58(supplement S16): S278–S287.

Dibble, H. L., V. Aldeias, P. Goldberg, S. P. McPherron, D. Sandgathe, and T. E. Steele. 2015. A Critical Look at Evidence from La Chapelle-aux-Saints Supporting an Intentional Neandertal Burial. *Journal of Archaeological Science* 53: 649–657.

Dibble, H. L., F. Berna, P. Goldberg, S. P. McPherron, S. Mentzer, L. Niven, D. Richter, D. Sandgathe, I. Théry-Parisot, and A. Turq. 2009. A Preliminary Report on Pech de l'Azé IV, Layer 8 (Middle Paleolithic, France). *PaleoAnthropology* 2009: 182–219.

Dibble, H. L., and S. P. McPherron. 2006. The Missing Mousterian. *Current Anthropology* 47(5): 777–803.

Dillehay, T. D., P. J. Netherly, and J. Rossen. 1989. Middle Preceramic Public and Residential Sites on the Forested Slopes of the Western Andes, Northern Peru. *American Antiquity* 54: 733–759.

Dillehay, T. D., J. Rossen, T. C. Andres, and D. E. Williams. 2007. Preceramic Adoption of Peanut, Squash, and Cotton in Northern Peru. *Science* 316: 1890–1893.

Dillehay, T. D., J. Rossen, P. J. Netherly, and A. Karathanasis. 2010. Early Holocene Coca Production in Northern Peru. *Antiquity* 84: 939–953.

Diogo, R., J. L. Molnar, and B. Wood. 2017. Bonobo Anatomy Reveals Stasis and Mosaicism in Chimpanzee Evolution, and Supports Bonobos as the Most Appropriate Extant Model for the Common Ancestor of Chimpazees and Humans. *Scientific Reports* 7: 608.

Dixit, Y., D. A. Hodell, and C. A. Paige. 2014. Abrupt Weakening of the Summer Monsoon in Northwest India ~4100 Years Ago. *Geology* 42: 339–342.

Dixon, E. J. 2001. Human Colonization of the Americas: Timing, Technology and Process. *Quaternary Science Reviews* 20: 277–299.

Dobres, M. A., and J. E. Robb. 2000. Agency in Archaeology: Paradigm or Platitude? In *Agency in Archaeology*, M. A. Dobres and J. E. Robb (eds.), pp. 3–17. London: Routledge.

Domínguez-Rodrigo, M. 2002. Hunting and Scavenging by Early Humans: The State of the Debate. *Journal of World Prehistory* 16(1): 1–54.

Dongoske, K., M. Aldenderfer, and K. Doehner. 2000. *Working Together: Native Americans and Archaeologists*. Washington, DC: SAA Press.

Donnan, C. B. 2001. Moche Burials Uncovered. *National Geographic Magazine* 199: 58–73.

Dornan, J. 2002. Agency and Archaeology: Past, Present, and Future Directions. *Journal of Archeological Method and Theory* 17: 303–329.

Dorshow, W. B. 2012. Modeling Agricultural Potential in Chaco Canyon during the Bonito Phase: A Predictive Geospatial Approach. *Journal of Archaeological Science* 39: 2098–2115.

Dortch, J., M. Cupper, R. Grün, B. Harpley, K. Lee, and J. Field. 2016. The Timing and Cause of Megafauna Mass Deaths at Lancefield Swamp, South-Eastern Australia. *Quaternary Science Reviews* 145: 161–182.

Douglass, A. E. 1929. The Secret of the Southwest Solved by Talkative Tree Rings. *National Geographic* 56: 737–770.

Douglass, A. E. 1941. Crossdating in Dendrochronology. *Journal of Forestry* 39(10): 825–831.

Doutriaux, M. 2001. Power, Ideology, and Ritual: The Practice of Agriculture in the Inca Empire. *Kroeber Anthropological Society Papers* 85: 91–108.

Doyel, D. E. 1991. Hohokam Exchange and Interaction. In *Chaco & Hohokam: Prehistoric Regional Systems in the American Southwest*, P. L. Crown and W. J. Judge (eds.), pp. 225–252. Santa Fe, NM: School of American Research Press.

Doyel, D. E. 2007. Irrigation, Production, and Power in Phoenix Basin Hohokam Society. In *The Hohokam Millennium*, S. K. Fish and P. R. Fish (eds.), pp. 82–89. Santa Fe, NM: School for Advanced Research Press.

Dreyer, G. 1992. Recent Discoveries at Abydos Cemetery U. In *The Nile Delta in Transition: 4th–3rd Millennium B.C.*, E. C. M van den Brink (ed.), pp. 293–299. Tel Aviv: van den Brink.

Druzhkova, A. S., O. Thalmann, V. A. Trifonov, J. A. Leonard, N. V. Vorobieva, N. D. Ovodov, A. S. Graphodatsky, and R. K. Wayne. 2013. Ancient DNA Analysis Affirms the Canid from Altai as a Primitive Dog. *PLoS One* 3(3): e57754.

Duff, A. I., J. M. Moss, T. C. Windes, J. Kantner, and M. S. Shackley. 2012. Patterning in Procurement of Obsidian in Chaco Canyon and in Chaco-Era Communities in New Mexico as Revealed by X-Ray Fluorescence. *Journal of Archaeological Science* 39: 2995–3007.

Dunnell, R. 1980. Evolutionary Theory and Archaeology. *Advances in Archaeological Method and Theory* 3: 35–99.

Dutt, S., A. K. Gupta, B. Wünnemann, and D. Yan. 2018. A Long Arid Interlude in the Indian Summer Monsoon during ~4,350 to 3,450 Cal, Yr BP Contemporaneous to Displacement of the Indus Valley Civilization. *Quaternary International* 482: 83–92.

Dye, D. H. 2006. The Transformation of Mississippian Warfare: Four Case Studies from the Mid-South. In *The Archaeology of Warfare: Prehistories of Raiding and Conquest*, E. N. Arkush and M. W. Allen (eds.), pp. 101–147. Gainesville: University Press of Florida.

Dye, T. S. 2011. A Model-Based Age Estimate for Polynesian Colonization of Hawai'i. *Archaeology in Oceania* 46: 130–138.

Dye, T. S. 2016. Long-Term Rhythms in the Development of Hawaiian Social Stratification. *Journal of Archaeological Science* 71: 1–9.

Earle, T., J. Ling, C. Uhnér, Z. Stos-Gale, and L. Melheim. 2015. The Political Economy and Metal Trade in Bronze Age Europe: Understanding Regional Variability in Terms of Comparative Advantages and Articulations. *European Journal of Archaeology* 18(4): 633–657.

Eastham, A. 1989. Cova Negra and Gorham's Cave: Evidence of the Place of Birds in Mousterian Communities. In *The Walking Larder*, J. Clutton-Brock (ed.), pp. 350–357. Boston: Unwin Hyman.

Eeckhout, P., and L. S. Owens. 2008. Human Sacrifice at Pachacamac. *Latin American Antiquity* 19(4): 375–398.

Eckhardt, R. B., M. Henneberg, A. S. Weller, and K. J. Hsü. 2014. Rare Event in Earth History Include the LB1 Human Skeleton from Flores, Indonesia, as a Developmental Singularity, not a Unique Taxon. 2014. *Proceedings of the National Academy of Sciences USA* 111: 11961–11966.

Ellwood, E. C., M. P. Scott, W. D. Lipe, R. G. Matson, and J. G. Jones. 2013. Stone-Boiling Maize with Limestone: Experimental Results and Implications for Nutrition among SE Utah Preceramic Groups. *Journal of Archaeological Science* 40: 35–44.

Emerson, T. E. 1997a. Cahokian Elite Ideology and the Mississippian Cosmos. In *Cahokia: Domination and Ideology in the Mississippian World*, T. R. Pauketat and T. Emerson (eds.), pp. 190–228. Lincoln: University of Nebraska Press.

Emerson, T. E. 1997b. Reflections from the Countryside on Cahokian Hegemony. In *Cahokia: Domination and Ideology in the Mississippian World*, T. R. Pauketat and T. Emerson (eds.), pp. 167–189. Lincoln: University of Nebraska Press.

Emerson, T. E., K. B. Farnsworth, S. U. Wisseman, and R. E. Hughes. 2013. The Allure of the Exotic: Reexamining the Use of Local and Distant Pipestone Quarries in Ohio Hopewell Pipe Caches. *American Antiquity* 78(1): 48–67.

Emerson, T. E., K. M. Hedman, E. A. Hargrave, D. E. Cobb, and A. R. Thompson. 2016. Paradigms Lost: Reconfiguring Cahokia's Mound 72 Beaded Burial. *American Antiquity* 81(3): 405–425.

Emerson, T. E., R. E. Hughes, M. R. Hynes, and S. U. Wisseman. 2003. The Sourcing and Interpretation of Cahokia-Style Figurines in the Trans-Mississippi South and Southeast. *American Antiquity* 68: 287–313.

Emslie, S. D., J. I. Mead, and L. Coats. 1995. Split-Twig Figurines in Grand Canyon, Arizona: New Discoveries and Interpretations. *Kiva* 61(2): 145–173.

Enard, W., M. Przeworski, S. E. Fischer, C. S. L. Lai, V. Wiebe, T. Kitano, A. P. Monaco, and S. Pääbo. 2002. Molecular Evolution of FOXP2, a Gene Involved in Speech and Language. *Nature* 418: 869–872.

Erem, M. I., R. J. Patten, M. J. O'Brien, and D. J. Meltzer. 2013. Refuting the Technological Cornerstone of the Ice-Age Atlantic Crossing Hypothesis. *Journal of Archaeological Science* 40: 2934–2941.

Erlandson, J. M., and T. J. Braje. 2015. Coasting Out of Africa: The Potential of Mangrove Forests and Marine Habitats to Facilitate Human Coastal Expansion via the Southern Route. *Quaternary International* 382: 31–41.

Ervynck, A., K. Dobney, H. Hongo, and R. Meadow. 2002. Born Free!: New Evidence for the Status of Pigs from Cayönü Tepesi, Eastern Anatolia. *Paléorient* 27(2): 47–73.

Estévez, J. 2004. Vanishing Carnivores: What Can the Disappearance of Large Carnivores Tell Us about the Neanderthal World? *International Journal of Osteoarchaeology* 14: 190–200.

Estrada-Belli, F. 2011. The First Maya Civilization. Ritual and Power before the Classic Period. New York: Routledge.

Evans, S. T. 2004. Aztec Palaces and Other Elite Residential Architecture. In *Palaces of the Ancient New World*,

S.T. Evans and J. Pillsbury (eds.), pp. 7–58. Washington, DC: Dumbarton Oaks Research Library and Collection.

Expedition 54(1) (all articles). 2012. Special Issue: Maya 2012: Lords of Time.

Ezzo, J. A., and T. D. Price. 2002. Migration, Regional Reorganization, and Spatial Group Composition at Grasshopper Pueblo, Arizona. *Journal of Archaeological Science* 29: 447–520.

Fagundes, N. J. R., A. Tagliani-Ribeiro, R. Rubicz, L. Tarskaia, M. H. Crawford, F. M. Salzano, and S. L. Bonatto. 2018. How Strong Was the Bottleneck Associated to the Peopling of the Americas? New Insights from Multilocus Sequence Data. *Genetics and Molecular Biology* 41 (1, Suppl.): 206–214.

Farmer, S., R. Sproat, and M. Witzel. 2004. The Collapse of the Indus-Script Thesis: The Myth of a Literate Harappan Civilization. *Electronic Journal of Vedic Studies* 11(2): 19–57.

Farooqui, A., A. S. Gaur, and V. Prasad. 2013. Climate, Vegetation and Ecology during Harappan Period: Excavations at Kanjetar and Kaj, Mid-Saurashtra Coast, Gujarat. *Journal of Archaeological Science* 40(6): 2631–2647.

Ferguson, C. W., and D. A. Graybill. 1983. Dendrochronology of Bristlecone Pine: A Progress Report. *Radiocarbon* 25(2): 287–288.

Feinman, G. M. 2001. Mesoamerican Political Complexity: The Corporate-Network Distribution. In *From Leaders to Rulers,* J. Haas (ed.), pp. 151–175. New York: Kluwer Acadmic/Plenum.

Feldman, M., and M. E. Kislev. 2007. Domestication of Emmer Wheat and Evolution of Free-Threshing Tetraploid Wheat. *Israel Journal of Plant Sciences* 55(3–4): 207–221.

Ferdon, E. N., Jr. 1967. The Hohokam "Ball Court": An Alternative View of Its Function. *Kiva* 33(1): 11–14 [reprinted in 2009: *Kiva* 75(2): 165–178].

Ferguson, C. W., and D. A. Graybill. 1983. Dendrochronology of Bristlecone Pine: A Progress Report. *Radiocarbon* 25(2): 287–288.

Fernández-Götz, M., and I. Rankin. 2017. The Complexity and Fragility of Early Iron Age Urbanism in West-Central Temperate Europe. *Journal of World Prehistory* 30: 259–279.

Ferring, R., O. Oms, J. Agustí, F. Berna, M. Nioradze, T. Sheila, M. Tappen, A. Vekua, D. Zhvania, and D. Lordkipanidze. 2011. Earliest Human Occupations at Dmanisi (Georgian Caucasus) Dated to 1.85–1.78 Ma. *Proceedings of the National Academy of Sciences USA* 108(26): 10432–10436.

Fertelmes, C. M., D. R. Abbott, and M. S. Shackley. 2012. Obsidian Source Characterization at Las Colinas: Shifting Exchange Patterns during the Hohokam Sedentary-Classic Transition. *Kiva* 77(3): 281–312.

Fiedel, S. J. 2005. Man's Best Friend—Mammoth's Worst Enemy? A Speculative Essay on the Role of Dogs in Paleoindian Colonization and Megafaunal Extinction. *World Archaeology* 37: 11–25.

Field, J. S., and M. M. Lahr. 2005. Assessment of the Southern Dispersal: GIS-Based Analyses of Potential Routes at Oxygen Isotope Stage 4. *Journal of World Prehistory* 19(1): 1–45.

Fisher, G., and D. DiPaolo Loren. 2003. Introduction. Special Section: Embodying Identity in Archaeology. *Cambridge Archaeological Journal* 13(2): 225–230.

Fitzhugh, B., V. L. Butler, K. M. Bovy, and M. A. Etnier. 2019. Human Ecodynamics: A Perpective for the Study of Long-Term Change in Socioecological Systems. *Journal of Archaeological Science: Reports* 23: 1077–1094.

Flad, R. K. 2008. Divination and Power. A Multiregional View of the Development of Oracle Bone Divination in Early China. *Current Anthropology* 49(3): 403–437.

Flad, R. K. 2018. Urbanism as Technology in Early China. *Archaeological Research in Asia* 14: 121–134.

Flannery, K. V. 1968. Archeological Systems Theory and Early Mesoamerica. In *Anthropological Archeology in the Americas,* B. J. Meggars (ed.), pp. 67–87. Washington, DC: Anthropological Society of Washington.

Flannery, K. V. 1999. Process and Agency in Early State Formation. *Cambridge Archaeological Journal* 9(1): 3–21.

Flannery, K. V. 2002. The Origins of the Village Revisited: From Nuclear to Extended Households. *American Antiquity* 67(3): 417–433.

Flannery, K. V., A. K. Balkansky, G. M. Feinman, D. C. Grove, J. Marcus, E. M. Redmond, R. G. Reynolds, R. J. Sharer, C. S. Spencer, and J. Yeager. 2005. Implications of New Petrographic Analysis for the Olmec "Mother Culture" Model. *Proceedings of the National Academy of Sciences USA* 102: 11219–11223.

Flannery, K. V., and J. Marcus. 2000. Formative Mexican Chiefdoms and the Myth of the "Mother Culture." *Journal of Anthropological Archaeology* 19: 1–37.

Florio, M., T. Namba, S. Pääbo, M. Hiller, and W. B. Huttner. 2016. A Single Splice Site Mutation in

Human-Specific *ARHGAP11B* Causes Basal Progenitor Amplification. *Science Advances* 2: e1601941.

Foley, R. 2002. Adaptive Radiations and Dispersals in Hominin Evolutionary Ecology. *Evolutionary Anthropology* Supplement 1: 32–37.

Ford, J. A., C. H. Webb, J. B. Bird, and M. Beckman. 1956. Poverty Point, a Late Archaic Site in Louisiana. *Anthropological Papers of the American Museum of Natural History* 46(1): 5–136.

Forest, J. D. 1983. Aux origines de l'architecture obeidienne, les plans de type Samarra. *Akkadica* 34: 1–47.

Formicola, V. 2007. From the Sunghir Children to the Romito Dwarf: Aspects of the Upper Paleolithic Funerary Landscape. *Current Anthropology* 48(3): 446–453.

Formicola, V., and A. P. Buzhilova. 2004. Double Child Burial from Sunghir (Russia): Pathology and Inferences for Upper Paleolithic Funerary Practices. *American Journal of Physical Anthropology* 124: 189–198.

Formicola, V., A. Pontrandolfi, and J. Svoboda. 2001. The Upper Paleolithic Triple Burial of Dolní Věstonice: Pathology and Funerary Behavior. *American Journal of Physical Anthropology* 115: 372–379.

Fornander, A. 1969. An Account of the Polynesian Race, Its Origins and Migrations, and the Ancient History of the Hawaiian People to the Times of Kamehameha, 3 vols. Rutland, VT: Tuttle [first published in 1878–1885].

Forum. 2010. *American Antiquity* 75(2): 211–238 (various authors).

Fowler, M. L., J. C. Rose, B. Vander Leest, and S. R. Ahler. 1999. *Mound 72 Area: Dedicated and Sacred Space in Early Cahokia.* Springfield: Illinois State Museum Report of Investigations No. 54.

Frantz, L. A. F., V. E. Mullin, M. Pionnier-Capitan, O. Lebrasseur, M. Ollivier, A. Perri, A. Linderholm, V. Mattiangeli, M. D. Teasdale, E. A. Dimopoulos, A. Tresset, M. Duffraisse, F. McCormick, L. Bartosiewicz, E. Gál, É. A. Nyerges, M. V. Sablin, S. Bréhard, M. Mashkour, A. Bălăşescu, B. Gillet, S. Hughes, O. Chassaing, C. Hitte, J.-D. Vigne, K. Dobney, C. Hänni, D. G. Bradley, and Greger Larson. 2016. Genomic and Archaeological Evidence Suggests a Dual Origin of Domestic Dogs. *Science* 352: 1228–1231.

Friedman, R. A., A. Sofaer, and R. S. Weiner. 2017. Remote Sensing of Chaco Roads Revisited. Lidar Documentation of the Great North Road, Pueblo Alto Landscape, and Aztec Airport Mesa Road. *Advances in Archaeological Practice* 5(4): 365–381.

Friedrich, M., S. Remmele, B. Kromer, J. Hofmann, M. Spurk, K. F. Kaiser, C. Orcel, and M. Küppers. 2004. The 12,460-Year Hohenheim Oak and Pine Tree-Ring Chronology from Central Europe—A Unique Annual Record for Radiocarbon Calibration and Paleoenvironment Reconstructions. *Radiocarbon* 46: 1111–1122.

Fritz, G. J. 1990. Multiple Pathways to Farming in Precontact Eastern North America. *Journal of World Prehistory* 4: 387–435.

Fritz, G. J. 2000. Native Farming Systems and Ecosystems in the Mississippi River Valley. In *Imperfect Balance: Landscape Transformations in the Precolumbian Americas,* D. L. Lentz (ed.), pp. 225–250. New York: Columbia University Press.

Fuller, D. Q. 2011. Finding Plant Domestication in the Indian Subcontinent. *Current Anthropology* 52 (Suppl. 4): S347–S362.

Fuller, D. Q., and E. Hildebrand. 2013. Domesticating Plants in Africa. In *Oxford Handbook of African Archaeology,* P. Mitchell and P. J. Lane (eds.), pp. 506–526. Oxford: Oxford University Press.

Gabunia, L., S. C. Antón, D. Lordkipanidze, A. Vekua, A. Justus, and C. C. Swisher III. 2001. Dmanisi and Dispersal. *Evolutionary Anthropology* 10: 158–170.

Gaines, E. P., G. Sanchez, and V. T. Holliday. 2009. Paleoindian Archaeology in Northern and Central Sonora, Mexico. A Review and Update. *Kiva* 74(3): 305–335.

Garcea, E. A. A. 2010. The Lower and Upper Later Stone Age of North Africa. In *South-eastern Mediterranean Peoples between 130,000 and 10,000 years ago,* E. A. A. Garcea (ed.), pp. 54–65. Oakville, CT: Oxbow Books.

García-Granero, J. J., C. Lancelotti, M. Madella, and P. Ajithprasad. 2016. Millets and Herders. The Origins of Plant Cultivation in Semiarid North Gujarat (India). *Current Anthropology* 57(2): 149–173.

Gargett, R. H. 1989. Grave Shortcomings: The Evidence for Neanderthal Burial. *Current Anthropology* 30(2): 157–190.

Gargett, R. H. 1999. Middle Palaeolithic Burial Is Not a Dead Issue: The View from Qafzeh, Saint-Césaire, Kebara, Amud, and Dederiyeh. *Journal of Human Evolution* 37: 27–90.

Garlake, P. S. 1978. Pastoralism and Zimbabwe. *Journal of African History* 19(4): 479–493.

Garrido, F. 2016. Rethinking Imperial Infrastructure: A Bottom-Up Perspective on the Inca Road. *Journal of Anthropological Archaeology* 43: 94–109.

Gaudzinski, S. 2004. Subsistence Patterns of Early Pleistocene Hominids in the Levant—Taphonomic Evidence from the 'Ubeidiya Formation (Israel). *Journal of Archaeological Science* 31(1): 65–75.

Gautier, A. 2001. The Early to Late Neolithic Archeofaunas from Nabta and Bir Kiseiba. In *Holocene Settlement of the Egyptian Sahara*. Vol. 1: *The Archaeology of Nabta Playa*, F. Wendorf, R. Schild, and Associates, pp. 609–635. New York: Kluwer Academic/Plenum.

Gautier, A. 2002. The Evidence for the Earliest Livestock in North Africa: Or Adventures with Large Bovids, Ovicaprids, Dogs and Pigs. In *Droughts, Food and Culture. Ecological Change and Food Security in Africa's Later Prehistory*, F. A. Hassan (ed.), pp. 195–207. New York: Kluwer Academic/Plenum.

Gebo, D. L., and G. T. Schwartz. 2006. Foot Bones from Omo: Implications for Hominid Evolution. *American Journal of Physical Anthropology* 129(4): 499–511.

Geib, P. R. 2000. Sandal Types and Archaic Prehistory on the Colorado Plateau. *American Antiquity* 65(3): 509–524.

Geib, P. R. 2004. AMS Dating of a Basketmaker II Hunter's Bag (Cache 1) from Sand Dune Cave, Utah. *Kiva* 69(3): 271–282.

Gelb, I. J. 1973. Prisoners of War in Early Mesopotamia. *Journal of Near Eastern Studies* 32(1/2): 70–98.

Geller, P. L. 2009. Identity and Difference: Complicating Gender in Archaeology. *Annual Review of Anthropology* 38: 65–81.

Germonpré, M., M. V. Sablin, R. E. Stevens, R. E. M. Hedges, M. Hofreiter, M. Stiller, and V. R. Després. 2009. Fossil Dogs and Wolves from Palaeolithic Sites in Belgium, the Ukraine and Russia: Osteometry, Ancient DNA and Stable Isotopes. *Journal of Archaeological Science* 36: 473–490.

Gheyle, W., B. Stichelbaut, T. Saey, N. Note, H. Van den Berghe, V. Van Eetvelde, M. Van Meirvenne, and J. Bourgeois. 2018. Scratching the Surface of War. Airborne Lasar Scans of the Great War Conflict Landscape in Flanders (Begium). *Applied Geography* 90: 55–68.

Gibbard, P. L., M. J. Head, M. J. C. Walker, and the Subcommission on Quaternary Stratigraphy 2010. Formal Ratification of the Quaternary System/Period and the Pleistocene Series/Epoch with a Base at 2.58 Ma. *Journal of Quaternary Sciences* 25: 96–102.

Gibson, J. L. 2007. "Formed from the Earth at That Place": The Material Side of Community at Poverty Point. *American Antiquity* 72(3): 509–523.

Gifford-Gonzalez, D., and O. Hannotte. 2011. Domesticating Animals in Africa: Implications of Genetic and Archaeological Findings. *Journal of World Prehistory* 24: 1–23.

Gillespie, S. D., and R. A. Joyce. 1997. Gendered Goods: The Symbolism of Maya Hierarchical Exchange Relations. In *Women in Prehistory: North America and Mesoamerica*, C. Claassen and R. A. Joyce (eds.), pp. 189–207. Philadelphia: University of Pennsylvania Press.

Gillespie, S. D., and M. Volk. 2014. A 3D Model of Complex A, La Venta, Mexico. *Digital Applications in Archaeology and Cultural Heritage* 1(3–4): 72–81.

Gilligan, I. 2007. Neanderthal Extinction and Modern Human Behaviour: The Role of Climate Change and Clothing. *World Archaeology* 39(4): 499–514.

Gingerich, J. A. M. 2011. Down to Seeds and Stones: A New Look at the Subsistence Remains from Shawnee–Minisink. *American Antiquity* 76(1): 127–144.

Giosan, L., P. D. Clift, M. G. Macklin, D. Q. Fuller, S. Constantinescu, J. A. Durcan, T. Stevens, G. A. T. Duller, A. R. Tabrez, K. Gangal, R. Adhikari, A. Alizai, F. Filip, S. VanLaningham, and J. P. M. Syvitski. 2012. Fluvial Landscapes of the Harappan Civilization. *Proceedings of the National Academy of Sciences USA* 109: E1688–E1694.

Gladkikh, M. I., N. L. Kornietz, and O. Soffer. 1984. Mammoth Bone Dwellings on the Russian Plain. *Scientific American* (November): 164–175.

Goebel, T. 1999. Pleistocene Human Colonization of Siberia and Peopling of the Americas: An Ecological Approach. *Evolutionary Anthropology* 8: 208–227.

Goebel, T., M. R. Waters, and D. O'Rourke. 2008. The Late Pleistocene Dispersal of Modern Humans in the Americas. *Science* 319: 1497–1502.

Goldberg, P., S. Weiner, O. Bar-Yosef, Q. Xu, and J. Liu. 2001. Site Formation Processes at Zhoukoudian, China. *Journal of Human Evolution* 41(5): 483–530.

Golden, C., A. K. Scherer, A. R. Muñoz, and R. Vasquez. 2008. Piedras Negras and Yaxchilan: Divergent Political Trajectories in Adjacent Maya Polities. *Latin American Antiquity* 19(3): 249–274.

Goldhahn, J., and J. Ling. 2013. Bronze Age Rock Art in Northern Europe: Contexts and Interpretations. In *The*

Oxford Handbook of European Bronze Age, H. Fokkens and A. Harding (eds.), pp. 270–290. Oxford: Oxford University Press.

Golitko, M., and L.H. Keeley. 2007. Beating Ploughshares Back into Swords: Warfare in the Linearbandkeramik. *Antiquity* 81: 332–342.

Golovanova, L. V., V. B. Doronichev, N. E. Cleghorn, M. A. Koulkova, T. V. Sapelko, and M. S. Shackley. 2010. Significance of Ecological Factors in the Middle to Upper Paleolithic Transition. *Current Anthropology* 51(5): 655–691.

Gonzalez, S., D. Huddart, I. Israde-Alcántara, G. Domínguez-Vázquez, J. Bischoff, and N. Felstead. 2015. Paleoindian Sites from the Basin of Mexico: Evidence from Stratigraphy, Tephrochronology and Dating. *Quaternary International* 363: 4–19.

Good, I. L., J. M. Kenoyer, and R. H. Meadow. 2009. New Evidence for Early Silk in the Indus Civilization. *Archaeometry* 51(3): 457–466.

Goring-Morris, N., and L. K. Horwitz. 2007. Funerals and Feasts during the Pre-Pottery Neolithic B of the Near East. *Antiquity* 81: 1–17.

Goring-Morris, N., R. Burns, A. Davidzon, V. Eshed, Y. Goren, I. Hershkovitz, S. Kangas, and J. Kelecevic. 1998. The 1997 Season of Excavations at the Mortuary Site of Kfar Hahoresh, Galilee, Israel. *Neo-Lithics* 3/98: 1–4.

Gosden, C. 1985. Gifts and Kin in Early Iron Age Europe. *Man* 20: 475–493.

Gradstein, F. M., J.G. Ogg, and A. G. Smith (eds.). 2004. *A Geologic Time Scale 2004.* New York: Cambridge University Press.

Graf, K. E., and I. Buvit. 2017. Human Dispersal from Siberia to Beringia. Assessing a Beringian Standstill in Light of the Archaeological Evidence. *Current Anthropology* 58 (Suppl. 17): S583–S603.

Grajetzki, W. 2006. *The Middle Kingdom of Ancient Egypt: History, Archaeology and Society.* London: Duckworth.

Graulich, M. 2000. Aztec Sacrifice as Expiation. *History of Religions* 39(4): 352–371.

Grayson, D. K. 2007. Deciphering North American Pleistocene Extinctions. *Journal of Archaeological Research* 63(2): 185–213.

Grayson, D. K., and D. J. Meltzer. 2015. Revisiting Paleoindian Exploitation of Extinct North American Mammals. *Quaternary International* 56: 177–193.

Green, R. E., J. Krause, A. W. Briggs, T. Maricic, U. Stenzel, M. Kircher, N. Patterson, H. Li, W. Zhai, M. His-Yang Fritz, N. F. Hansen, E. Y. Durand, A.-S. Malaspinas, J. D. Jensen, T. Marques-Bonet, C. Alkan, K. Prüfer, M. Meyer, H. A. Burbano, J. M. Good, R. Schultz, A. Aximu-Petri, A. Butthof, B. Höber, B. Höffner, M. Siegemund, A. Weihmann, C. Nusbaum, E. S. Lander, C. Russ, N. Novod, J. Affourtit, M. Egholm, C. Verna, P. Rudan, D. Brajkovic, Z. Kucan, I. Gušic, V. B. Doronichev, L. V. Golovanova, C. Lalueza-Fox, M. de la Rasilla, J. Fortea, A. Rosas, R. W. Schmitz, P. L. F. Johnson, E. E. Eichler, D. Falush, E. Birney, J. C. Mullikin, M. Slatkin, R. Nielsen, J. Kelso, M. Lachmann, D. Reich, and S. Pääbo. 2010. A Draft Sequence of the Neandertal Genome. *Science* 328: 710–722.

Gremillion, K. J. 2004. Seed Processing and the Origins of Food Production in Eastern North America. *American Antiquity* 69(2): 215–233.

Gremillion, K. J., L. Barton, and D. R. Piperno. 2014. Particularism and the Retreat from Theory in the Archaeology of Agricultural Origins. *Proceedings of the National Academy of Sciences USA* 111(17): 6171–6177.

Grier, C., and L. Shaver. 2008. Working Together: The Role of Archaeologists and First Nations in Sorting out Some Very Old Problems in British Columbia, Canada. *The SAA Archaeological Record* 8(1): 33–35.

Griffin, P. B. 1967. A High Status Burial from Grasshopper Ruin, Arizona. *Kiva* 33: 37–53 [reprinted in *Kiva* 76(2): 223–237].

Grimstead, D. N., and F. E. Bayham. 2010. Evolutionary Ecology, Elite Feasting, and the Hohokam: A Case Study from a Southern Arizona Platform Mound. *American Antiquity* 75(4): 841–864.

Grollemund, R., S. Branford, K. Bostoen, A. Meade, C. Venditti, and M. Pagel. 2015. Bantu Expansion Shows that Habitat Alters the Route and Pace of Human Dispersals. *Proceedings of the National Academy of Sciences USA* 112: 13296–13301.

Gronenborn, D., H.-C. Strien, S. Dietrich, and F. Sirocko. 2014. "Adaptive Cycles" and Climate Fluctuations: A Case Study from Linear Pottery Culture in Western Central Europe. *Journal of Archaeological Science* 51: 73–83.

Grootes, P. M., and M. Stuiver 1997. Oxygen 18/16 Variability in Greenland Snow and Ice with 10^{-3}- to 10^5-Year Time Resolution. *Journal of Geophysical Research* 192: 26455–26470.

Grosman, L., and N. D. Munro. 2007. The Sacred and the Mundane: Domestic Activities at a Late Natufian Burial Site in the Levant. *Before Farming* 2007/4 Article 4: 1–14.

Grosman, L., N. D. Munro, I. Abadi, E. Boaretto, D. Shaham, A. Belfer-Cohen, and O. Bar-Yosef. 2016. Nahal Ein Gev II, a Late Natufian Community at the Sea of Galilee. *PLoS One* 11: e0146647.

Grosman, L., N. D. Munro, and A. Belfer-Cohen. 2008. A 12,000-year-old Shaman Burial from the Southern Levant (Israel). *Proceedings of the National Academy of Sciences USA* 105: 17665–17669.

Groube, L., J. Chappell, J. Muke, and D. Price. 1986. A 40,000 Year-Old Human Occupation Site at Huon Peninsula, Papua New Guinea. *Nature* 324: 453–455.

Grube, N. 1992. Classic Maya Dance: Evidence from Hieroglyphs and Iconography. *Ancient Mesoamerica* 3: 201–218.

Guiterman, C. H., T. W. Swetnam, and J. S. Dean. 2016. Eleventh-Century Shift in Timber Procurement Areas for the Great Houses of Chaco Canyon. *Proceedings of the National Academy of Sciences USA* 113: 1186–1190.

Gummesson, S., F. Hallgren, and A. Kjellström. 2018. Keep Your Head High: Skulls on Stakes and Cranial Trauma in Mesolithic Sweden. *Antiquity* 92: 74–90.

Guthrie, R. D. 2001. Origin and Causes of the Mammoth Steppe: A Story of Cloud Cover, Woolly Mammoth Tooth Pits, Buckles, and Inside-Out Beringia. *Quaternary Science Reviews* 20: 549–574.

Guthrie, R. D. 2006. New Carbon Dates Link Climatic Change with Human Colonization and Pleistocene Extinctions. *Nature* 441: 207–209.

Guthrie, R. D., and T. Van Kolfschoten. 2000. Neither Warm and Moist, nor Cold and Arid: The Ecology of the Mid Upper Palaeolithic. In *Hunters of the Golden Age: The Mid Upper Palaeolithic of Eurasia 30,000—20,000 BP*, W. Roebroeks, M. Mussi, J. Svoboda, and K. Fennema (eds.), pp. 13–20. Leiden, The Netherlands: University of Leiden.

Haas, J., W. Creamer, L. H. Mesía, D. Goldstein, K. Reinhard, and C. V. Rodríguez. 2013. Evidence for Maize (*Zea mays*) in the Late Archaic (3000–1800 B.C.) in the Norte Chico Region of Peru. *Proceedings of the National Academy of Sciences USA* 110(13): 4945–4949.

Haile-Selassie, Y., B. Z. Saylor, A. Deino, N. E. Levin, M. Arlene, and B. M. Latimer. 2012. A New Hominin Foot from Ethiopia Shows Multiple Pliocene Bipedal Adaptations. *Nature* 483: 565–570.

Haines, H. R., P. W. Willink, and D. Maxwell. 2008. Stingray Spine Use and Maya Bloodletting Rituals: A Cautionary Tale. *Latin American Antiquity* 19(1): 83–98.

Halverson, J. 1987. Art for Art's Sake in the Paleolithic. *Current Anthropology* 28(1): 63–89.

Hamm, G., Mitchell, P., Arnold, L. J., Prideaux, G. J., Questiaux, D., Spooner, N. A., Levchenko, V. A., Foley, E. C., Worthy, T. H., Stephenson, B., and Coulthard, V. 2016. Cultural Innovation and Megafauna Interaction in the Early Settlement of Arid Australia. *Nature* 539: 280–283.

Hanotte, O., D. G. Bradley, J. W. Ochieng, Y. Verjee, E. W. Hill, and J. E. O. Rege. 2002. African Pastoralism: Genetic Imprints of Origins and Migrations. *Science* 296: 336–339.

Hansen, D. P. 1992. Royal Building at Sumerian Lagash in the Early Dynastic Period. *The Biblical Archaeologist* 55(4): 206–211.

Hansen, R. 1998. Continuity and Disjunction: The Preclassic Antecedents of Classic Maya Architecture. In *Function and Meaning in Classic Maya Architecture*, S. D. Houston (ed.), pp. 49–122. Washington, DC: Dumbarton Oaks.

Hansen, R. D. 2005. Perspectives on Olmec-Maya Interaction in the Middle Formative Period. In *New Perspectives on Formative Mesoamercian Cultures*, T. Powis (ed.), pp. 51–72. British Archaeological Reports International Series 1377. Oxford: Archaeopress.

Hansen, R. D., W. K. Howell, and S. P. Guenter. 2008. Forgotten Structures, Haunted Houses, and Occupied Hearts: Ancient Perspectives and Contemporary Interpretations of Abandoned Sites and Buildings in the Mirador Basin, Guatemala. In *Ruins of the Past: The Use and Perception of Abandoned Structures in the Maya Lowlands*, T. W. Stanton and A. Mignoni (eds.), pp. 25–64. Boulder: University Press of Colorado.

Harcourt-Smith, W. E. H., and L. C. Aiello. 2004. Fossils, Feet and the Evolution of Human Bipedal Locomotion. *Journal of Anatomy* 204: 403–416.

Harcourt-Smith, W. E. H., Z. Throckmorton, K. A. Congdon, B. Zipfel, A. S. Deane, M. S. M. Drapeau, S. E. Churchill, L. R. Berger, and J. M. DeSilva. 2015. The Foot of *Homo naledi*. *Nature Communications* 6: 8432.

Harding, A. F. 2000. *European Societies in the Bronze Age*. New York: Cambridge University Press.

Harmand, S., J. E. Lewis, C. S. Feibel, C. J. Lepre, S. Prat, A. Lenoble, X. Boës, R. L. Quinn, M. Brenet, A. Arroyo, N. Taylor, S. Clément, G. Daver, J.-P. Brugal, L. Leakey,

R. A. Mortlock, J. D. Wright, S. Lokorodi, C. Kirwa, D. V. Kent, and H. Roche. 2015. 3.3–Million–Year–Old Stone Tools from Lomekwi 3, West Turkana, Kenya. *Nature* 521: 310–315.

Harris, B. 2016. Profile: Moving Stonehenge. *Public Archaeology* 15: 148–156.

Harris, E. C. 1989. *Principles of Archaeological Stratigraphy*, 2nd ed. New York: Academic Press.

Harrison, T. 2010. Apes among the Tangled Branches of Human Origins. *Science* 327: 532–534.

Harrod, R. P. 2012. Centers of Control: Revealing Elites among the Ancestral Pueblo during the "Chaco Phenomenon." *International Journal of Paleopathology* 2 (2–3): 123–135.

Harrod, R. P., D. L. Martin, and S. W. Carlyle. 2012. Taphonomy after the Fact: Violence and Ritual in Room 33 at Chaco and Room 178 at Aztec. *Landscapes of Violence* 2(2): Article 5.

Hart, J. P., R. A. Daniels, and C. J. Sheviak. 2004. Do *Curcurbita pepo* Gourds Float Fishnets? *American Antiquity* 69(1): 141–148.

Hartley, L. 1953. *The Go-Between*. London: Hamilton.

Harvati, K., S. R. Frost, and K. P. McNulty. 2004. Neanderthal Taxonomy Reconsidered: Implications of 3D Primate Models of Intra- and Interspecific Differences. *Proceedings of the National Academy of Sciences USA* 101(5): 1147–1152.

Hassan, F. A. 1986. Holocene Lakes and Prehistoric Settlements of the Western Fayum. *Journal of Archaeological Science* 13: 483–501.

Hassan, F. A. 1997. Holocene Paleoclimates of Africa. *African Archaeological Review* 14: 213–230.

Hassig, R. 1988. *Aztec Warfare. Imperial Expansion and Political Control*. Norman: University of Oklahoma Press.

Haury, E. W. 1976. *The Hohokam: Desert Farmers & Craftsmen*. Snaketown, 1964–1965. Tucson, University of Arizona Press.

Hawass, Z., Y. Z. Gad, S. Ismail, R. Khairat, D. Fathalla, N. Hasan, A. Ahmed, H. Elleithy, M. Ball, F. Gaballah, S. Wasef, M. Fateen, H. Amer, P. Gostner, A. Selim, A. Zink, and C. M. Pusch. 2010. Ancestry and Pathology in King Tutankhamun's Family. *Journal of the American Medical Association* 303(7): 638–647.

Hawass, Z., and M. Lehner. 1997. Builders of the Pyramids: Excavations at Giza Yield the Settlements and Workshops of Three Generations of Laborers. *Archaeology* 50(1): 31–38.

Hawks, J. 2012. Longer Time Scale for Human Evolution. *Proceedings of the National Academy of Sciences USA* 109: 15531–15532.

Hayden, B. 1990. Nimrods, Piscators, Pluckers, and Planters: The Emergence of Food Production. *Journal of Anthropological Archaeology* 9: 31–69.

Hayden, B. 2009. The Proof Is in the Pudding: Feasting and the Origins of Domestication. *Current Anthropology* 50(5): 597–601.

Haynes, C. V., Jr. 2001. Geochronology and Climate Change of the Pleistocene–Holocene Transition in the Darb el Arba'in Desert, Eastern Sahara. *Geoarchaeology* 16(1): 119–141.

Haynes, G. 2002. *Early Settlement of North America: The Clovis Era*. New York: Cambridge University Press.

Hays, J. D., J. Imbrie, and N. J. Shackleton. 1976. Variations in Earth's Orbit: Pacemaker of the Ice Ages. *Science* 194: 1121–1132.

He, N. 2018. Taosi: An Archaeological Example of Urbanization as a Political Center in Prehistoric China. *Archaeological Research in Asia* 14: 20–32.

Hedquist, S. L., A. M. Thibodeau, J. R. Welch, and D. J. Killick. 2017. Canyon Creek Revisited: New Investigations of a Late Prehispanic Turquoise Mine, Arizona, USA. *Journal of Archaeological Science* 87: 44–58.

Hegemon, M. 2003. Setting Theoretical Egos Aside: Issues and Theory in North American Archaeology. *American Antiquity* 68(2): 213–243.

Hegemon, M., S. G. Ortman, and J. L. Mobley-Tanaka. 2000. Women, Men, and the Organization of Space. In *Women and Men in the Prehispanic Southwest*, P. L. Crown (ed.), pp. 43–90. Santa Fe, NM: School of American Research Press.

Heintzman, P. D., D. Froeseb, J. W. Ives, A. E. R. Soares, G. D. Zazula, B. Letts, T. D. Andrews, J. C. Driver, E. Hall, P. G. Hare, C. N. Jass, G. MacKay, J. R. Southon, M. Stiller, R. Woywitka, M. A. Suchard, and B. Shapiro. 2016. Bison Phylogeography Constrains Dispersal and Viability of the Ice Free Corridor in Western Canada. *Proceedings of the National Academy of Sciences USA* 113: 8057–8063.

Heizer, R., and J. Bennyhoff. 1958. Archaeological Investigations at Cuicuilco, Mexico, 1956. *Science* 127: 232–233.

Helvenston, P., and P. Bahn. 2003. Testing the "Three Stages of Trance" Model. *Cambridge Archaeological Journal* 13(2): 213–224.

Hemmings, C. A. 2005. An Update on Recent Work at Sloth Hole (8JE121), Aucilla River, Jefferson County, Florida. *Current Research in the Pleistocene* 22: 47–49.

Henneberg, M., R. B. Eckhardt, S. Chavanaves, and K. J. Hsü. 2014. Evolved Developmental Homeostasis Disturbed in LB1 from Flores, Indonesia, Denotes Down Syndrome and Not Diagnostic Traits of the Invalid Species *Homo floresiensis. Proceedings of the National Academy of Sciences USA* 111: 11967–11972.

Henry, A. G., A. S. Brooks, and D. R. Piperno. 2010. Microfossils in Calculus Demonstrate Consumption of Plants and Cooked Foods in Neanderthal Diets (Shanidar III, Iraq; Spy I and II, Belgium). *Proceedings of the National Academy of Sciences USA* 108(2): 486–491.

Henshilwood, C. S. 2007. Fully Symbolic Sapiens Behaviour: Innovation in the Middle Stone Age at Blombos Cave, South Africa. In *Rethinking the Human Revolution. New Behavioural and Biological Perspectives on the Origin and Dispersal of Modern Humans,* P. Mellars, K. Boyle, O. Bar-Yosef, and C. Stringer (eds.), pp. 123–132. Cambridge, UK: McDonald Institute for Archaeological Research.

Henshilwood, C. S., F. d'Errico, K. L. Van Niekerk, Y. Coquinot, Z. Jacobs, S.-E. Lauritzen, M. Menu, and R. García-Moreno. 2011. A 100,000-Year-Old Ochre Processing Workshop at Blombos Cave, South Africa. *Science* 334: 219–222.

Henshilwood, C. S., F. d'Errico, and F. Watts. 2009. Engraved Ochres from the Middle Stone Age Levels at Blombos Cave, South Africa. *Journal of Human Evolution* 57: 27–47.

Henshilwood, C. S., and C. W. Marean. 2003. The Origin of Modern Human Behavior. Critique of the Models and Their Test Implications. *Current Anthropology* 44(5): 627–651.

Henshilwood, C. S., J. C. Sealy, R. Yates, K. Cruz-Uribe, P. Goldberg, F. E. Grine, R. G. Klein, C. Poggenpoel, K. van Niekerk, and I. Watts. 2001. Blombos Cave, Southern Cape, South Africa: Preliminary Report on the 1992–1999 Excavations of the Middle Stone Age Levels. *Journal of Archaeological Science* 28: 421–448.

Hester, T., H. Shafer, and K. L. Feder. 2008. *Field Methods in Archaeology,* 7th ed. Walnut Creek, CA: Left Coast Press.

Heun, M., R. Schäfer-Pregl, D. Klawan, R. Castagna, M. Accerbi, B. Borghi, and F. Salamini. 1997. Site Einkorn Wheat Domestication Identified by DNA Fingerprinting. *Science* 278: 1312–1314.

Higham, T., T. Compton, C. Stringer, R. Jacobi, B. Shapiro, E. Trinkaus, B. Chandler, F. Gröning, C. Collins, S. Hillson, P. O'Higgins, C. FitzGerald, and M. Fagan. 2011. The Earliest Evidence for Anatomically Modern Humans in Northwestern Europe. *Nature* 479: 521–524.

Higham, T., K. Douka, R. Wood, C. Bronk Ramsey, F. Brock, L. Basell, M. Camps, A. Arrizabalga, J. Baena, C. Barroso-Ruíz, C. Bergman, C. Boitard, P. Boscato, M. Caparrós, N. J. Conard, C. Draily, A. Froment, B. Galván, P. Gambassini, A. Garcia-Moreno, S. Grimaldi, P. Haesaerts, B. Holt, M.-J. Iriate-Chiapusso, A. Jelinek, J. F. Jordá-Pardo, J.-M. Maíllo-Fernández, A. Marom, J. Maroto, M. Menéndez, L. Metz, E. Morin, E. Moroni, F. Negrino, E. Panagopoulou, M. Peresani, S. Pirson, M. de la Rasilla, J. Riel-Salvatore, A. Ronchitelli, D. Santamaria, P. Semal, L. Slimak, J. Soler, N. Soler, A. Villaluenga, R. Pinhasi, and R. Jacobi. 2014. The Timing and Spatiotemporal Patterning of Neanderthal Disappearance. *Nature* 512: 306–309.

Hill, M. E., Jr. 2008. Variation in Paleoindian Faunal Use on the Great Plains and Rocky Mountains of North America. *Quaternary International* 191: 34–52.

Hill, M. G., D. J. Rapson, T. J. Loebel, and D. W. May. 2011. Site Structure and Activity Organization at a Late Paleoindian Base Camp in Western Nebraska. *American Antiquity* 76(4): 752–772.

Hillson, S. W., R. G. Franciscus, T. W. Holliday, and E. Trinkaus. 2005. The Ages at Death. In *Early Modern Human Evolution in Central Europe: The People of Dolní Věstonice and Pavlov,* E. Trinkaus and J. Svoboda (eds.), pp. 31–45. New York: Oxford University Press.

Hirth, K., A. Cyphers, R. Cobean, J. De León, and M. D. Glascock. 2013. Early Olmec Obsidian Trade and Economic Organization at San Lorenzo. *Journal of Archaeological Science* 40(6): 2784–2798.

Hockett, B. 2012. The Consequences of Middle Paleolithic Diets on Pregnant Neanderthal Women. *Quaternary International* 264: 78–82.

Hodder, I. 1990. The Domestication of Europe: Structure and Contingency in Neolithic Societies. Cambridge, MA: Blackwell.

Hodder, I. (ed.). 1991. The Meanings of Things: Material Culture and Symbolic Expression. New York: Routledge.

Hodder, I. (ed.). 2001. *Archaeological Theory Today.* Malden, MA: Blackwell.

Hodder, I., and C. Cessford. 2004. Daily Practice and Social Memory at Çatalhöyük. *American Antiquity* 69(1): 17–40.

Hodgson, D. 2006. Altered States of Consciousness and Palaeoart: An Alternative Neurovisual Explanation. *Cambridge Archaeological Journal* 16(1): 27–37.

Hoffecker, J. F. 2002. *Desolate Landscapes: Ice-Age Settlement in Eastern Europe.* New Brunswick, NJ: Rutgers University Press.

Hoffecker, J. F. 2005. Innovation and Technological Knowledge in the Upper Paleolithic of Northern Eurasia. *Evolutionary Anthropology* 14: 186–198.

Hoffecker, J. F., S. A. Elias, and D. H. O'Rourke. 2014. Out of Beringia? *Science* 343: 979–980.

Hoffecker, J. F., V. T. Holliday, M. V. Anikovich, A. A. Sinitsyn, V. V. Popov, S. N. Lisitsyn, G. M. Lekovskaya, G. A. Pospelova, S. L. Forman, and B. Giaccio. 2008. From the Bay of Naples to the River Don: The Campanian Ignimbrite Eruption and the Middle to Upper Paleolithic Transition in Eastern Europe. *Journal of Human Evolution* 55: 858–870.

Hoffecker, J. F., I. E. Kuz'mina, E. V. Syromyanikova, M. V. Anikovich, A. A. Sinitsyn, V. V. Popov, and V. T. Holliday. 2010. Evidence for Kill–Butchery Events of Early Upper Paleolithic Age at Kostenki, Russia. *Journal of Archaeological Science* 37: 1073–1089.

Hoffman, M. A. 1979. *Egypt before the Pharaohs. The Prehistoric Foundations of Egyptian Civilization.* Austin: University of Texas Press.

Hoffmann, D. L., D. E. Angelucci, V. Villaverde, J. Zapata, and J. Zilhão. 2018. Symbolic Use of Marine Shells and Mineral Pigments by Iberian Neandertals 115,000 Years Ago. 2018a. *Science Advances* 4: eaar5255.

Hoffmann, D. L., C. D. Standish, M. García-Diez, P. B. Pettitt, J. A. Milton, J. Zilhão, J. J. Alcolea-González, P. Cantalejo-Duarte, H. Collado, R. de Balbín, M. Lorblanchet, J. Ramos-Muñoz, G.-Ch. Weniger, and A. W. G. Pike. 2018b. U-Th Dating of Carbonate Crusts Reveals Neandertal Origin of Iberian Cave Art. *Science* 359: 912–915.

Hofmanova, Z., S. Kreutzera, G. Hellenthal, C. Sell, Y. Diekmann, D. Díez-del-Molino, L. van Dorp, S. López, A. Kousathanas, V. Link, K. Kirsanow, L.M. Cassidy, R. Martiniano, M. Strobel, A. Scheu, K. Kotsakis, P. Halstead, S. Triantaphyllou, N. Kyparissi-Apostolika, D. Urem-Kotsou, C. Ziota, F. Adaktylou, S. Gopalan, D.M. Bobo, L. Winkelbach, J. Blöcher, M. Unterländer, C. Leuenberger, Ç. Çilingiroğlu, B. Horejs, F. Gerritsen, S.J. Shennan, D.G. Bradley, M. Currat, K.R. Veeramah, D. Wegmann, M.G. Thomas, C. Papageorgopoulou, and J. Burger. 2016. Early Farmers from Across Europe Directly Descended from Neolithic Aegeans. *Proceedings of the National Academy of Sciences USA* 113: 6886–6891.

Hoggarth, J. A., M. Restall, J. W. Wood, and D. J. Kennett. 2017. Drought and Its Demographic Effects in the Maya Lowlands. *Current Anthropology* 58(1): 82–113.

Hole, F. 1994. Interregional Aspects of the Khuzestan Aceramic—Early Pottery Neolithic Sequence (Synthesis Contribution). In *Neolithic Chipped Stone Industries of the Fertile Crescent,* H.-G. Gebel and S. K. Kozlowski (eds.), pp. 101–116. Studies in Early Near Eastern Production, Subsistence, and Environment 1. Berlin: *ex oriente.*

Hole, F. 1997. *Studies in the Archaeological History of the Deh Luran Plain: The Excavation of Chagha Sefid.* Memoires of the Museum of Anthropology No. 9. Ann Arbor: Museum of Anthropology, University of Michigan.

Hole, F. 2000. New Radiocarbon Dates for Ali Kosh, Iran. *Neo-Lithics* 1/00: 13.

Hole, F., K. V. Flannery, and J. A. Neely (eds.). 1969. *Prehistory and Human Ecology of the Deh Luran Plain, an Early Village Sequence from Khuzistan, Iran.* Memoirs of the Museum of Anthropology 1. Ann Arbor: University of Michigan Press.

Holliday, T. 1997. Postcranial Evidence of Cold Adaptation in European Neandertals. *American Journal of Physical Anthropology* 104(2): 245–258.

Holliday, V. T., and D. Killick. 2013. An Early Paleoindian Bead from the Mockingbird Gap Site, New Mexico. *Current Anthropology* 54(1): 85–95.

Holmes, D. L. 1988. The Predynastic Lithic Industries of Badari, Middle Egypt: New Perspectives and Inter-Regional Relations. *World Archaeology* 20(1): 70–86.

Holmes, D. L., and R. F. Friedman. 1989. The Badari Region Revisted. *Nyame Akuma* 31: 15–19.

Holst, D. 2010. Hazelnut Economy of Early Holocene Hunter-Gatherers: A Case Study from Duvensee, Northern Germany. *Journal of Archaeological Science* 37: 2871–2880.

Holt, J. Z. 2009. Rethinking the Ramey State: Was Cahokia the Center of a Theater State? *American Antiquity* 74(2): 231–254.

Hommon, R. J. 2013. *The Ancient Hawaiian State. Origins of a Political Society.* New York: Oxfod University Press.

Houston, S. D. 2000. Into the Minds of Ancients: Advances in Maya Glyph Studies. *Journal of World Prehistory* 14(2): 121–201.

Houston, S. D., and D. Stuart. 1996. Of Gods, Glyphs, and Kings: Divinity and Rulership among the Classic Maya. *Antiquity* 70: 289–312.

Huot, J.-L. 1992. The First Farmers at Oueili. *The Biblical Archaeologist* 55(4): 188–195.

Huot, J.-L. (ed.). 1996. *Oueili. Travaux de 1987 et 1989.* Paris: Éditions Recherche sur les Civilisations.

Hovers, E., S. Ilani, O. Bar-Yosef, and B. Vandermeersch. 2003. An Early Case of Color Symbolism. Ochre Use by Modern Humans in Qafzeh Cave. *Current Anthropology* 44(4): 491–522.

Huang, C. C., S. Zhao, J. Pang, Q. Zhou, S. Chen, P. Li, L. Mao, and M. Ding. 2003. Climatic Aridity and the Relocations of the Zhou Culture in the Southern Loess Plateau of China. *Climatic Change* 61(3): 361–378.

Hublin, J.-J., A. Ben-Ncer, S. E. Bailey, S. E. Freidline, S. Neubauer, M. M. Skinner, I. Bergmann, A. Le Cabec, S. Benazzi, K. Harvati, and P. Gunz. 2017. New Fossils from Jebel Irhoud, Morocco and the Pan-African Origin of *Homo sapiens*. *Nature* 546: 289–292.

Huffman, O. F., J De Vos, A. W. Berkhout, and F. Azia. 2010. Provenience Reassessment of the 1931–1933 Ngandong *Homo erectus* (Java), Confirmation of the Bone-Bed Origin Reported by the Discoverers. *Paleo-Anthropology* 2010: 1–60.

Huffman, T. N. 1981. Snakes and Birds: Expressive Space at Great Zimbabwe. *African Studies* 40: 131–150.

Huffman, T. N. 1984. Where You Are the Girls Gather to Play: The Great Enclosure at Great Zimbabwe. In *Frontiers: Southern African Archaeology Today,* M. Hall, G. Avery, D. M. Avery, M. L. Wilson, and A. J. R. Humphreys (eds.), pp. 252–265. Oxford: British Archeological Reports International Series 207.

Huffman, T. N. 1993. Broederstroom and the Central Cattle Pattern. *South African Journal of Science* 89: 220–226.

Huffman, T. N. 2000. Mapungubwe and the Origins of the Zimbabwe Culture. In *African Naissance: The Limpopo Valley 1000 Years Ago,* M. Lesley and T. M. Maggs (eds.), pp. 14–29. South African Archaeological Society Goodwin Series 8.

Huffman, T. N. 2001. The Central Cattle Pattern and Interpreting the Past. *Southern African Humanities* 13: 19–35.

Huffman, T. 2005. *Mapungubwe: Ancient African Civilization on the Limpopo.* Johannesburg: Wits University Press.

Huffman, T. N. 2008. Climate Change during the Iron Age in the Shashe–Limpopo Basin, Southern Africa. *Journal of Archaeological Science* 35: 2032–2047.

Huffman, T. 2009. Mapungubwe and Great Zimbabwe: The Origin and Spread of Social Complexity. *Journal of Anthropological Archaeology* 28: 37–54.

Huffman, T. 2010a. State Formation in Southern Africa: A Reply to Kim and Kusimba. *African Archaeological Review* 27: 1–11.

Huffman, T. 2010b. Revisiting Great Zimbabwe. *Azania: Archaeological Research in Africa* 45(3): 321–328.

Huffman, T. 2015. Social Complexity in Southern Africa. *African Archaeological Review* 32(1): 71–91.

Hughes, R. E., T. E. Berres, D. M. Moore, and K. B. Farnsworth. 1998. Revision of Hopewellian Trading Patterns in Midwestern North America Based on Mineralogical Sourcing. *Geoarchaeology* 13(7): 709–729.

Hull, S., M. Fayek, F. J. Mathien, and H. Roberts. 2014. Turquoise Trade of the Ancestral Puebloan: Chaco and Beyond. *Journal of Archaeological Science* 45: 187–195.

Humphreys, A. J. B. 2007. Behavioural Ecology and Hunter–Gatherers: From the Kalahari to the Later Stone Age. *South African Archaeological Bulletin* 62: 98–103.

Hunt, R. C., D. Guillet, D. R. Abbott, J. Bayman, P. Fish, S. Fish, K. Kintigh, and J. A. Neeley. 2005. Plausible Ethnographic Analogies for the Social Organization of Hohokam Canal Irrigation. *American Antiquity* 70(3): 433–456.

Hurst, W. J., S. M. Tarka Jr., T. G. Powis, F. Valdez Jr., and T. R. Hester. 2002. Cacao Usage by the Earliest Maya Civilization. *Nature* 418: 289–290.

Hyland, S. 2017. Writing with Twisted Cords. The Inscriptive Capacity of Andean Khipus. *Current Anthropology* 58(3): 412–419.

Ingman, M., H. Kaessmann, S. Pääbo, and U. Gyllensten 2000. Mitochondrial Genome Variation and the Origin of Modern Humans. *Nature* 408: 708–713.

Ingmanson, E. J. 1998. Comment on Craig Stanford's "The Social Behavior of Chimpanzees and Bonobos: Empirical Evidence and Shifting Assumptions." *Current Anthropology* 39(4): 409–410.

Inomata, T., D. Triadan, K. Aoyama, V. Castillo, and H. Yonenobu. 2013. Early Ceremonial Constructions at Ceibal, Guatemala, and the Origins of Lowland Maya Civilization. *Science* 340: 467–471.

Inomata, T., D. Triadan, J. MacLellan, M. Burham, K. Aoyama, J. M. Palomo, H. Yonenobu, F. Pinzón, and H. Nasu. 2017. High-Precision Radiocarbon Dating of Political Collapse and Dynastic Origins at the Maya Site of Ceibal, Guatamala. *Proccedings of the National Academy of Sciences USA* 114: 1293–1298.

Isaac, B. L. 2005. Aztec Cannabilism. Nahua versus Spanish and Mestizo Accounts in the Valley of Mexico. *Ancient Mesoamerica* 16: 1–10.

Isaac, G. L. 1977. *Olorgesailie. Archaeological Studies of a Middle Pleistocene Lake Basin in Kenya.* Chicago: University of Chicago Press.

Isaac, G. L. 1978. The Food-Sharing Behavior of Protohuman Hominids. *Scientific American* 238: 90–108.

Isaac, G. L. 1983. Bones in Contention: Competing Explanations for the Juxtaposition of Early Pleistocene Artifacts and Faunal Remains. In *Animals and Archaeology,* Volume 1: *Hunters and Their Prey,* J. Clutton-Brock and C. Grigson (eds.), pp. 3–19. Oxford: British Archaeological Reports International Series 163.

Isbell, L. A., and T. P. Young. 1996. The Evolution of Bipedalism in Hominids and Reduced Group Size in Chimpanzees: Alternative Responses to Decreasing Resource Availability. *Journal of Human Evolution* 30: 389–397.

Iseminger, W. R. 1997. Culture and Environment in the American Bottom: The Rise and Fall of Cahokia Mounds. In *Common Fields: An Environmental History of St. Louis,* A. Hurley (ed.), pp. 38–57. St. Louis: Missouri Historical Society Press.

Isendahl, C., and M. E. Smith. 2013. Sustainable Agrarian Urbanism: The Low-Density Cities of the Mayas and Aztecs. *Cities* 31: 132–143.

Jackson, D., C. Méndez, R. Seguel, A. Maldonado, and G. Vargas. 2007. Initial Occupation of the Pacific Coast of Chile during Late Pleistocene Times. *Current Anthropology* 48(5): 725–731.

Jackson, L. J. 1995. A Clovis Point from South Coastal Chile. *Current Research in the Pleistocene* 12: 21–23.

Jackson, H. E., and S. L. Scott. 2003. Patterns of Elite Faunal Utilization at Moundville, Alabama. *American Antiquity* 68(3): 552–572.

Jacobsen, T. 1939. *The Sumerian King List.* Assyriological Studies No. 11, The Oriental Institute of the University of Chicago. Chicago: University of Chicago Press.

Janusek, J. W. 2002. Out of Many, One: Style and Social Boundaries in Tiwanaku. *Latin American Antiquity* 31(1): 35–61.

Janusek, J. W. 2004. Tiwanaku and Its Precursors: Recent Research and Emerging Perspectives. *Journal of Archaeological Research* 12(2): 121–183.

Janusek, J. W. 2006. The Changing "Nature" of Tiwanaku Religion and the Rise of an Andean State. *World Archaeology* 38(3): 469–492.

Jatmiko. 2001. New Discoveries of Paleolithic Tools in Some Paleolithic Sites in Indonesia. In *Sangiran: Man, Culture, and Environment in Pleistocene Times*, T. Simanjuntak, B. Prasetyo, and R. Handini (eds.), pp. 171–184. Jakarta: Yayasan Obor Indonesia.

Jenkins, D. 2001. A Network Analysis of Inka Roads, Administrative Centers, and Storage Facilities. *Ethnohistory* 48(4): 655–687.

Jennbert, K. 2011. Ertebølle Pottery in Southern Sweden—A Question of Handicraft, Networks and Creolisation in a Period of Neolithisation. *Bericht der Römisch-Germanischen Kommission* 2008(89): 89–110.

Jennings, J. 2003. The Fragility of Imperialist Ideology and the End of Local Traditions, an Inca Example. *Cambridge Archaeological Journal* 13(1): 107–120.

Jennings, J., and N. Craig. 2001. Politywide Analysis and Imperial Political Economy: The Relationship between Valley Political Complexity and Administrative Centers in the Wari Empire of the Central Andes. *Journal of Anthropological Archaeology* 20: 479–502.

Jennings, J., and T. Earle. 2016. Urbanization, State Formation, and Cooperation. A Reappraisal. *Current Anthropology* 57(4): 474–493.

Jennings, T. A. 2012. Clovis, Folsom, and Midland Components at the Debra L. Friedkin Site, Texas: Context, Chronology, and Assemblages. *Journal of Archaeological Science* 39: 3239–3247.

Jennings, T. A. 2013. The Hogeye Clovis Cache, Texas: Quantifying Lithic Reduction Sequences. *Journal of Archaeological Science* 40: 649–658.

Jing, Y., and R. Flad. 2005. New Zooarchaeological Evidence for Changes in Shang Dynasty Animal Sacrifice. *Journal of Anthropological Archaeology* 24: 252–270.

Joffe, A. H. 2018. Defining the State. In *Enemies and Friends of the State. Ancient Prophecy in Context*, C. A. Rollston 9ed.), pp. 3–23. University Park, PA: Eisenbrauns.

Johanson, D. C., and T. D. White. 1979. A Systematic Assessment of Early African Hominids. *Science* 203: 321–330.

John, B. 2008. The Bluestone Enigma: Stonehenge, Preseli and the Ice Age. Newport, UK: Greencroft Books.

John, J. 2011. Status of *Spondylus* Artifacts within the LBK Grave Goods. In *Spondylus in Prehistory: New Data and Approaches. Contributions to the Archaeology of Shell Technologies*, F. Ifantidis and M. Nikolaidou (eds.), pp. 39–45. British Archaeological Reports International Series 2216. Oxford: Oxbow Books.

Johnson, C. N., J. Alroy, N. J. Beeton, M. I. Bird, B. W. Brook, A. Cooper, R. Gillespie, S. Herrando-Pérez, Z. Jacobs, G. H. Miller, G. J. Prideaux, R. G. Roberts, M. Rodríguez-Rey, F. Saltré, C. S. M. Turney, and C. J. A. Bradshaw. 2016. What Caused Extinction of the Pleistocene Megafauna of Sahul? *Proceedings of the Royal Society B* 283: 20152399.

Jolly, C. 1970. The Seed-Eaters: A New Model of Hominid Differentiation Based on a Baboon Analogy. *Man* 5(1): 5–26.

Jones, P. R. 1981. Experimental Implement Manufacture and Use; A Case Study from Olduvai Gorge, Tanzania. *Philosophical Transactions of the Royal Society of London B* 292: 189–195.

Joyce, D. J. 2006. Chronology and New Research on the Schaefer Mammoth (?*Mammuthus primigenius*) Site, Kenosha County, Wisconsin, USA. *Quaternary International* 144–143: 44–57.

Joyce, R. A. 1996. The Construction of Gender in Classic Maya Monuments. In *Gender and Archaeology*, R. P. Wright (ed.), pp. 167–195. Philadelphia: University of Pennsylvania Press.

Joyce, R. A., and J. S. Henderson. 2001. Beginnings of Village Life in Eastern Mesoamerica. *Latin American Antiquity* 12(1): 5–23.

Judd, N. M. 1954. *The Material Culture of Pueblo Bonito*. Washington, DC: Smithsonian Miscellaneous Collections No. 124.

Judge, W. J. 2006. Chaco Canyon-San Juan Basin. In *Dynamics of Southwest Prehistory*, L. S. Cordell and G. J. Gummerman (eds.), pp. 209–261. Tuscaloosa: University of Alabama Press.

Jungers, W. L., W. E. H. Harcourt-Smith, R. E. Wunderlich, M. W. Tocheri, S. G. Larson, T. Sutikna, R. A. Due, and M. J. Morwood. 2009. The Foot of *Homo floresiensis*. *Nature* 459: 81–84.

Kahn, J. G. 2015. Identifying Residences of Ritual Practitioners in the Archaeological Record as a Proxy for Social Complexity. *Journal of Anthropological Archaeology* 40: 59–81.

Kantner, J. 1996. Political Competition among the Chaco Anasazi of the American Southwest. *Journal of Anthropological Archaeology* 15: 41–105.

Kantner, J. 1997. Ancient Roads, Modern Mapping. Evaluating Chaco Anasazi Roadways Using GIS Technology. *Expedition* 39(3): 49–61.

Kantner, J. 2003. Rethinking Chaco as a System. *Kiva* 69(2): 207–227.

Katz, S. H., and M. M. Voigt. 1986. Bread and Beer: The Early Use of Cereals in the Human Diet. *Expedition* 28(2): 23–34.

Keefer, D. K., S. D. deFrance, M. E. Moseley, J. B. Richardson III, D. R. Satterlee, and A. Day-Lewis. 1998. Early Maritime Economy and El Niño Events at Quebrada Tacahuay, Peru. *Science* 281: 1833–1835.

Keightley, D. N. 1978. Sources of Shang History: The Oracle-Bone Inscriptions of Bronze Age China. Los Angeles: University of California Press.

Keightley, D. N. 2006. Marks and Labels: Early Writing in Neolithic and Shang China. In *Archaeology of Asia*, M. T. Stark (ed.), pp. 177–201. Oxford: Blackwell.

Kelly, J. E. 1991. Cahokia and Its Role as a Gateway Center in Interregional Exchange. In *Cahokia and Its Hinterlands: Middle Mississippian Cultures of the Midwest*, T. E. Emerson and R. B. lewis (eds.), pp. 61–80. Urbana: University of Illinois Press.

Kelly, L. S. 1997. Patterns of Faunal Exploitation at Cahokia. In *Cahokia: Domination and Ideology in the Mississippian World*, T. R. Pauketat and T. E. Emerson (eds.), pp. 69–88. Lincoln: University of Nebraska Press.

Kemp, B. J. 1983. Old Kingdom, Middle Kingdom and Second Intermediate Period c. 2686–1552 B.C. In *Ancient Egypt: A Social History*, B. Trigger, B. J. Kemp, D. O'Connor, and A. Llyod (eds.), pp. 71–174. Cambridge, UK: Cambridge University Press.

Kennett, D. J., and T. P. Beach. 2013. Archaeological and Environmental Lessons for the Anthropocene from the Classic Maya Collapse. *Anthropocene* 4: 88–100.

Kennett, D. J., D. R. Piperno, J. G. Jones, H. Neff, B. Voorhies, M. K. Walsh, and B. J. Culleton. 2010.

Pre-Pottery Farmers on the Pacific Coast of Southern Mexico. *Journal of Archaeological Science* 37: 3401–3411.

Kennett, D. J., S. Plog, R. J. George, B. J. Culleton, A. S. Watson, P. Skoglund, N. Rohland, S. Mallick, K. Stewardson, L. Kistler, S. A. LeBlanc, P. M. Whiteley, D. Reich, and G. H. Perry. 2017. Archaeogenomic Evidence Reveals Prehistoric Matrlineal Dynasty. *Nature Communications* 8: 14115.

Kennett, D. J., and B. Voorhies. 1996. Oxygen Isotope Analysis of Archaeological Shells to Detect Seasonal Use of Wetlands on the Southern Pacific Coast of Mexico. *Journal of Archaeological Science* 23: 689–704.

Kennett, D. J., and B. Winterhalder (eds.). 2006. *Behavioral Ecology and the Transition to Agriculture*. Los Angeles: University of California Press.

Kenoyer, J. M. 1995a. Interaction Systems, Specialized Crafts and Culture Change: The Indus Valley Tradition and the Indo-Gangetic Tradition in South Asia. In *The Indo-Aryans of Ancient South Asia: Language, Material Culture and Ethnicity*, G. Erdosy (ed.), pp. 213–257. New York: Walter de Gruyter.

Kenoyer, J. M. 1995b. Shell Trade and Shell Working during the Neolithic and the Early Chalcolithic at Mehrgarh, Pakistan. In *Mehrgarh: Field Reports 1974–1985 from Neolithic Times to the Indus Civilization*, C. Jarrige, J. F. Jarrige, R. H. Meadow, and G. Quivron (eds.), pp. 566–582. Karachi, Pakistan: Department of Culture and Tourism, Government of Sindh.

Kenoyer, J. M. 1998. *Ancient Cities of the Indus Valley Civilization*. New York: Oxford University Press.

Kenoyer, J. M. 2008. Indus Urbanism: New Perspectives on Its Origin and Character. In *The Ancient City: New Perspectives on Urbanism in the Old and New World*, J. Marcus and J. A. Sabloff (eds.), pp. 183–208. Santa Fe, NM: School for Advanced Research Press.

Kenoyer, J. M., and R. H. Meadow. 2000. The Ravi Phase: A New Cultural Manifestation at Harappa. In *South Asian Archaeology 1997*, M. Taddei and G. De Marco (eds.), pp. 55–76. Naples: Istituto Universitario Orientale.

Kenoyer, J. M., and H. M.-L. Miller. 1999. Metal Technologies of the Indus Valley Tradition in Pakistan and Western India. In *The Emergence and Development of Metallurgy*, V. C. Piggot (ed.), pp. 107–151. Philadelphia: University Museum Publications.

Kenoyer, J. M., T. D. Price, and J. H. Burton. 2013. A New Approach to Tracking Connections between the Indus Valley and Mesopotamia: Initial Results of Strontium Isotope Analyses from Harappa and Ur. *Journal of Archaeological Science* 40: 2286–2297.

Kenyon, K. 1957. *Digging Up Jericho*. London: Benn.

Khan, F. A. 1965. Excavations at Kot Diji. *Pakistan Archaeology* 2: 11–85.

Kidder, A. V. 1927. Southwestern Archaeological Conference. *Science* 66: 489–491.

Kidder, A. V., and S. J. Guernsey. 1919. *Archaeological Exploration in Northeastern Arizona*. Bureau of American Ethnology 65. Washington DC: Smithsonian Institution.

Kidder, A. V., J. D. Jennings, and E. M. Shook. 1977. *Excavations at Kaminaljuyu, Guatemala*. University Park: Pennsylvania State University [original publication: 1946, Carnegie Institution of Washington Monograph Series No. 561.]

Kidder, T. R. 2004. Plazas as Architecture: An Example from the Raffman Site, Northeast Louisiana. *American Antiquity* 69(3): 514–532.

Kidder, T. R. 2006. Climate Change and the Archaic to Woodland Transition (3000–2500 cal B.P.) in the Mississippi River Basin. *American Antiquity* 71(2): 195–231.

Kilby, J. D., and B. B. Huckell. 2014. Clovis Caches: Current Perspectives and Future Directions. In *Clovis Caches: Recent Discoveries and New Research*, B. B. Huckell and J. D. Kilby (eds.), pp. 257–272. Albuquerque: University of New Mexico Press.

Kim, N., and C. Kusimba. 2008. Pathways to Social Complexity and State Formation in the Southern Zambizian Region. *African Archaeological Review* 25: 131–152.

Kimbel, W. H., C. A. Lockwood, C. V. Ward, M. G. Leakey, Y. Rak, and D. C. Johanson. 2006. Was *Australopithecus anamensis* Ancestral to *A. afarensis*? A Case of Anagenesis in the Hominin Fossil Record. *Journal of Human Evolution* 51: 134–152.

King, C. L., A. R. Millard, D. R. Gröcke, V. G. Standen, B. T. Arriaza, and S. E. Halcrow. 2018. Marine Resource Reliance in the Human Populations of the Atacama Desert, Northern Chile—A View from Prehistory. *Quaternary Science Reviews* 182: 163–174.

Kintigh, K. W. 2003. Coming to Terms with the Chaco World. *Kiva* 69(2): 93–116.

Kirch, P. V. 2007. Hawaii as a Model System for Human Ecodynamics. *American Anthropologist* 109(1): 8–26.

Kirch, P. V. 2010. *How Chiefs Became Kings: Divine Kingship and the Rise of Archaic States in Ancient Hawai'i.* Los Angeles: University of California Press.

Kirch, P. V. 2011. When Did the Polynesians Settle Hawai'i? A Review of 150 Years of Scholarly Inquiry and a Tentative Answer. *Hawaiian Archaeology* 12: 1–26.

Kirch, P. V., R. Mertz-Kraus, and W. D. Sharp. 2015. Precise Chronology of Polynesian Temple Construction and Use for Southeastern Maui, Hawaiian Islands Determined by ^{230}Th Dating of Corals. *Journal of Archaeological Science* 53: 166–177.

Kirkbride, D. 1966. Five Seasons at the Pre-Pottery Neolithic Village of Beidha in Jordan. *Palestine Exploration Quarterly* 98(1): 8–72.

Kislev, M. E., D. Nadel, and I. Carmi. 1992. Epipalaeolithic (19,000 BP) Cereal and Fruit Diet at Ohalo II, Sea of Galilee, Israel. *Review of Palaeobotany and Palynology* 73: 161–166.

Klein, R. G. 2009. *The Human Career: Human Biological and Cultural Origins,* 3rd ed. Chicago: University of Chicago Press.

Klein, R. G. 2008. Out of Africa and the Evolution of Human Behavior. *Evolutionary Anthropology* 17: 267–281.

Klieger, P. C., D. I. Olszewski, and T. A. Yardley. 1998. A Cultural Landscape of the Sites 2010 and 2137 Region. In *Activities and Settlement in an Upper Valley. Data Recovery and Monitoring Archaeology in North Hālawa Valley, O'ahu,* L. L. Hartzell, S. A. Lebo, H. A. Lennstrom, S. P. McPherron, and D. I. Olszewski (report organizers). Report on file, Hawaii State Historic Preservation District and Bishop Museum. Honolulu, Hawai'i.

Klima, B. 1988. A Triple Burial from the Upper Paleolithic of Dolní Věstonice, Czechoslovakia. *Journal of Human Evolution* 16: 831–835.

Kneisel, J. 2012. The Problem of Middle Bronze Age Inception in Northeast Europe or: Did the Únětice Society Collapse? In *Collapse or Continuity? Environment and Development of Bronze Age Human Landscapes,* J. Kneisel, W. Kirleis, M. Dal Corso, N. Taylor, and V. Tiedtke (eds.), pp. 209–234. Bonn: Verlag Dr. Rudolf Habelt GmbH.

Knell, E. J., and M. E. Hill Jr. 2012. Linking Bones and Stones: Regional Variation in Late Paleoindian Cody Complex Landuse and Foraging Strategies. *American Antiquity* 77(1): 40–70.

Knight, V. J., Jr. 2004. Characterizing Elite Midden Deposits at Moundsville. *American Antiquity* 69(2): 304–321.

Knight, V. J., Jr., J. A. Brown, and G. E. Lankford. 2001. On the Subject Matter of the Southeastern Ceremonial Complex Art. *Southeastern Archaeology* 20(2): 129–141.

Knudson, K. J., K. R. Gardella, and J. Yaeger. 2012. Provisioning Inca Feasts at Tiwanaku, Bolivia: The Geographical Origins of Camelids in the Pumapunku Complex. *Journal of Archaeological Science* 39: 479–491.

Knudson, D. J., M. Giersz, W. Więckowski, and W. Tomczyk. 2017. Reconstructing the Lives of Wari Elites: Paleomobility and Paleodiet at the Archaeological Site of Castillo de Huarmey, Peru. *Journal of Archaeological Science: Reports* 13: 249–264.

Kobusiewicz, M., J. Kabaciński, R. Schild, J. D. Irish, and F. Wendorf. 2004. Discovery of the First Neolithic Cemetery in Egypt's Western Desert. *Antiquity* 78: 566–578.

Kolb, M. J., and B. Dixon. 2002. Landscapes of War: Rules and Conventions of Conflict in Ancient Hawai'i (and Elsewhere). *American Antiquity* 67(3): 514–534.

Kopp, G. H., C. Roos, T. M. Butynski, D. E. Wildman, A. N. Alagaili, L. F. Groeneveld, and D. Zitnner. 2014. Out of Africa, But How and When? The Case of Hamadryas Baboons (*Papio hamadryas*). *Journal of Human Evolution* 76: 154–164.

Kornfield, M., and M. L. Larson. 2008. Bonebeds and Other Myths: Paleoindian to Archaic Transition on North American Great Plains and Rocky Mountains. *Quaternary International* 191: 18–33.

Koziol, K. 2010. *Violence, Symbols, and the Archaeological Record: A Case Study of Cahokia's Mound 72.* Ph.D. thesis. Fayetteville: University of Arkansas.

Kozlowski, S. K. (ed.). 1990. *Nemrik 9. Pre-Pottery Neolithic Site in Iraq (General Report-Seasons 1985–1986).* Warsaw: Wydawnictwa Uniwersytetu Warszawskiego.

Kozlowski, S. K. (ed.). 1992. *Nemrik 9. Pre-Pottery Neolithic Site in Iraq. Vol. 2: House No 1/1A/1B.* Warsaw: Wydawnictwa Uniwersytetu Warszawskiego.

Kozlowski, S. K. 1998. M'lefaat: Early Neolithic Site in Northern Irak. *Cahiers de l'Euphrate* 8: 179–273.

Kramer, P. A., and A. D. Sylvester. 2009. Bipedal Form and Locomotor Function: Understanding the Effects of Size and Shape on Velocity and Energetics. *PaleoAnthropology* 2009: 238–251.

Kramer, S. N. 1959. *History Begins at Sumer.* Garden City, NY: Doubleday.

Krause, J., Q. Fu, J. M. Good, B. Viola, M. V. Shunkov, A. P. Derevianko, and S. Pääbo. 2010. The Complete

Mitochondrial DNA Genome of an Unknown Hominin from Southern Siberia. *Nature* 464:894–897.

Krause-Kyora, B., C. Makarewicz, A. Evin, L. Girdland Flink, K. Dobney, G. Larson, S. Hartz, S. Schreiber, C. von Carnap-Bornheim, N. von Wurmb-Schwark, and A. Nebel. 2013. Use of Domesticated Pigs by Mesolithic Hunter-Gatherers in Northwestern Europe. *Nature Communications* 4: 2348.

Kreuz, A., and E. Schäfer. 2008. Archaeobotanical Consideration of the Development of Pre-Roman Iron Age Crop Growing in the Region of Hesse, Germany, and the Question of Agricultural Production and Consumption at Hillfort Sites and Open Settlements. *Vegetation History and Archaeobotany* 17(Suppl. 1): S159–S179.

Krings, M., A. Stone, R. W. Schmitz, H. Krainitzki, and S. Pääbo. 1997. Neandertal DNA Sequences and the Origin of Modern Humans. *Cell* 90: 19–30.

Krings, M., C. Capelli, F. Tschentscher, H. Geisert, S. Meyer, A. von Haeseler, K. Grossschmidt, G. Possnert, M. Paunovic, and S. Pääbo. 2000. A View of Neandertal Genetic Diversity. *Nature Genetics* 26: 144–146.

Kristiansen, K. 1998. *Europe before History.* New York: Cambridge University Press.

Kristiansen, K. 2002. The Tale of the Sword—Swords and Swordfighters in Bronze Age Europe. *Oxford Journal of Archaeology* 21(4): 319–332.

Kroeber, A. L., and C. Kluckhohn. 1952. *Culture: A Critical Review of Concepts and Definitions.* Cambridge, MA: The Museum.

Królik, H., and R. Schild. 2001. Site E-75–6: An El Nabta and Al Jerar Village. In *Holocene Settlement of the Egyptian Sahara.* Vol. 1: *The Archaeology of Nabta Playa,* F. Wendorf, R. Schild, and Associates, pp. 111–146. New York: Kluwer Academic/Plenum.

Kuckelman, K. A., R. R. Lightfoot, and D. L. Martin. 2002. The Bioarchaeology and Taphonomy of Violence at Castle Rock and Sand Canyon Pueblos, Southwestern Colorado. *American Antiquity* 67(3): 486–513.

Kuijt, I. 2000. People and Space in Early Agricultural Villages: Exploring Daily Lives, Community Size, and Architecture in the Late Pre-Pottery Neolithic. *Journal of Anthropological Archaeology* 19: 75–102.

Kuijt, I. 2011. Home Is Where We Keep Our Food: The Origins of Agriculture and Late Pre-Pottery Neolithic Food Storage. *Paléorient* 37(1): 137–152.

Kuijt, I., and A. N. Goring-Morris. 2002. Foraging, Farming, and Social Complexity in the Pre-Pottery Neolithic of the Southern Levant: A Review and Synthesis. *Journal of World Prehistory* 16: 361–440.

Kuijt, I., and H. Mahasneh. 1998. Dhra': An Early Neolithic Village in the Southern Jordan Valley. *Journal of Field Archaeology* 25: 153–161.

Kusimba, C. 2008. Early African Cities: Their Role in the Shaping of Urban and Rural Interaction Spheres. In *The Ancient City. New Perspectives on Urbanism in the Old and New World,* J. Marcus and J. A. Sabloff (eds.), pp. 229–246. Santa Fe, NM: School for Advanced Research Press.

Kuzmin, Y. V. 2017. The Origins of Pottery in East Asia and Its Neighboring Regions: An Analysis Based on Radiocarbon Data. *Quaternary International* 441: 29–35.

Lahr, M. M., and R. Foley. 1994. Multiple Dispersals and Modern Human Origins. *Evolutionary Anthropology* 3: 48–60.

Lai, S. J., S. E. Fisher, J. A. Hurst, F. Vargha-Khadem, and A. P. Monaco. 2001. A Fork-Head Domain Gene Is Mutated in a Severe Speech and Language Disorder. *Nature* 413: 519–523.

Laitman, J. T., and R. C. Heimbuch. 1982. The Basicranium of Plio-Pleistocene Hominids as an Indicator of Their Upper Respiratory Systems. *American Journal of Physical Anthropology* 59: 323–344.

Lal, B. B., B. K. Tharpar, J. P. Joshi, and M. Bala (eds.). 2003. *Excavations at Kalibangan: The Early Harappans (1960–1969).* New Delhi: Memoirs of the Archaeological Survey of India No. 98.

Laland, K.N., J. Odling-Smee, and S. Myles. 2010. How Culture Shaped the Human Genome: Bringing Genetics and the Human Sciences Together. *Nature Reviews Genetics* 11: 137–148.

Lalueza, C., A. Pérez-Pérez, and D. Turbón. 1996. Dietary Inferences through Buccal Microwear Analysis of Middle and Upper Pleistocene Human Fossils. *American Journal of Physical Anthropology* 100: 367–387.

Lalueza-Fox C., J. Krause, D. Caramelli, G. Catalano, L. Milani, M. L. Sampietro, F. Calafell, C. Martínez-Maza, M. Bastir, A. García-Tabernero, M. de la Rasilla, J. Fortea, S. Pääbo, J. Bertranpetit, and A. Russo. 2006. Mitochondrial DNA of an Iberian Neandertal Suggests a Population Affinity with Other European Neandertals. *Current Biology* 16: 629–630.

Lane, P., C. Ashley, O. Seitsonen, P. Harvey, S. Mire, and F. Odede. 2007. The Transition to Farming in East Africa: New Faunal and Dating Evidence from Wadh Lang'o and Usenge, Kenya. *Antiquity* 81: 62–81.

Langergraber, K. E., K. Prüfer, C. Rowney, C. Boesch, C. Crockford, K. Fawcett, E. Inoue, M. Inoue-Muruyama, J. C. Mitani, M. N. Muller, M. M. Robbins, G. Schubert, T. S. Stoinski, B. Viola, D. Watts, R. M. Wittig, R. W. Wrangham, K. Zuberbühler, S. Pääbo, and L. Vigilant. 2012. Generation Times in Wild Chimpanzees and Gorillas Suggest Earlier Divergence Times in Great Ape and Human Evolution. *Proceedings of the National Academy of Sciences USA* 109: 15716–15721.

Langlie, B. S., C. A. Hastorf, M. C. Bruno, M. Berman, R. M. Bonzani, and W. Castellón Condarco. 2011. Diversity in Andean Chenopodium Domestication: Describing a New Morphological Type from La Barca, Bolivia 1300–1250 B.C. *Journal of Ethnobiology* 31(1): 72–88.

Larson, S. G., W. L. Jungers, M. J. Morwood, T. Sutikna, Jatmiko, E. W. Saptomo, R. A. Due, and T. Djubiantono. 2007. *Homo floresiensis* and the Evolution of the Hominin Shoulder. *Journal of Human Evolution* 53: 718–731.

Larsson, L. 1989. Late Mesolithic Settlements and Cemeteries at Skateholm, Southern Sweden. In *The Mesolithic in Europe*, C. Bonsall (ed.), pp. 367–378. Edinburgh: John Donald.

Larsson, L. 1990. Dogs in Fraction, Symbols in Action. In *Contributions to the Mesolithic in Europe*, B. Vermeersch and P. van Peer (eds.), pp. 153–160, Leuven, The Netherlands: Leuven University Press.

Larsson, L. 2002. Food for the Living, Food for the Dead. *Before Farming: The Archaeology and Anthropology of Hunter-Gatherers* 2002 (3–4): 1-11.

Larsson, L. 2004. The Mesolithic period in Southern Scandinavia, With Special Reference to Burials and Cemeteries. In *Mesolithic Scotland and Its Neighbours*, A. Saville (ed.), pp. 371–392. Edinburgh: Society of Antiquaries for Scotland.

Law, R. W. 2011. *Inter-Regional Interaction and Urbanism in the Ancient Indus Valley: A Geological Provenience Study of Harappa's Rock and Mineral Assemblage*. Occasional Paper 11: Linguistics, Archaeology and the Human Past. Kyoto: Indus Project, Research Institute for Humanity and Nature.

Lawler, A. 2004. The Indus Script—Write or Wrong? *Science* 306: 2026–2029.

Lawler, A. 2007. Climate Spurred Later Indus Decline. *Science* 316: 978–979.

Lawler, A. 2008. Indus Collapse: The End of the Beginning of an Asian Culure? *Science* 320: 1281–1283.

Lawler, A. 2011. In Indus Times, the River Didn't Run through It. *Science* 332: 23.

Lazaridis, I., D. Nadel, G. Rollefson, D. C. Merrett, N. Rohland, S. Mallick, D. Fernandes, M. Novak, B. Gamarra, K. Sirak, S. Connell, K. Stewardson, E. Harney, Q. Fu, G. Gonzalez-Fortes, E.R. Jones, S. Alpaslan Roodenberg, G. Lengyel, F. Bocquentin, B. Gasparian, J.M. Monge, M. Gregg, V. Eshed, A.-S. Mizrahi, C. Meiklejohn, F. Gerritsen, L. Bejenaru, M. Blüher, A. Campbell, G. Cavalleri, D. Comas, P. Froguel, E. Gilbert, S.M. Kerr, P. Kovacs, J. Krause, D. McGettigan, M. Merrigan, D.A. Merriwether, S. O'Reilly, M.B. Richards, O. Semino, M. Shamoon-Pour, G. Stefanescu, M. Stumvoll, A. Tönjes, A. Torroni, J.F. Wilson, L. Yengo, N.A. Hovhannisyan, N. Patterson, R. Pinhasi, and D. Reich. 2016. Genomic Insights into the Origin of Farming in the Ancient Near East. *Nature* 536: 419–424.

Lechevallier, M., and G. Quivron. 1985. Results of the Recent Excavations at the Neolithic Site of Mehrgarh, Pakistan. In *South Asian Archaeology 1983*, Vol. 1, J. Schotsman and M. Taddei (eds.), pp. 67–90. Naples: Istituto Universitario Orientale Dipartimento di Studi Asiatici Series Minor XXIII.

Leakey. L. S. B., P. Tobias, and J. Napier. 1964. A New Species of the Genus *Homo* from Olduvai Gorge. *Nature* 202: 7–9.

Leakey, M. 1967. Preliminary Survey of the Cultural Material from Beds I and II, Olduvai Gorge, Tanzania. In *Background to Evolution in Africa*, W. W. Bishop and J. D. Clark (eds.), pp. 417–446. Chicago: Chicago University Press.

Leakey, M. 1971. *Olduvai Gorge*, Vol. 3. *Excavations in Bed I and II, 1960–1963*. Cambridge, UK: Cambridge University Press.

Leavesley, M., and J. Allen. 1998. Dates, Disturbance and Artefact Distributions: Another Analysis of Buang Merabak, a Pleistocene Site on New Ireland, New Guinea. *Archaeology in Oceania* 3(2): 63–82.

Leavesley, M. G., M. I. Bird, L. K. Fifield, P. A. Hausladen, G. M. Santos, and M. L. di Tada. 2002. Buang Merabak: Early Evidence for Human Occupation in the Bismarck Archipelago, Papua New Guinea. *Australian Archaeology* 54: 55–57.

LeBlanc, S. A. 1999. *Prehistoric Warfare in the American Southwest.* Salt Lake City: University of Utah Press.

Lee, Y. K. 2004. Control Strategies and Polity Competition in the Lower Yi-Luo Valley, North China. *Journal of Anthropological Archaeology* 23: 172–195.

Lehner, M. 1997. *The Complete Pyramids.* New York: Thames and Hudson.

Lekson, S. H. 1997. Rewriting Southwestern Prehistory. *Archaeology* 50(1): 52–55.

Lekson, S. H. 2005. Cacho and Paquimé: Complexity, History, Landscape. In *North American Archaeology*, T. R. Pauketat and D. D. Loren (eds.), pp. 235–272. Malden, MA: Blackwell.

Lell, J. T., M. D. Brown, T. G. Schurr, R. I. Sukernik, Y. B. Starikovskaya, A. Torroni, L. G. Moore, G. M. Troup, and D. C. Wallace. 1997. Y Chromosome Polymorphisms in Native American and Siberian Populations: Identification of Native American Y Chromosome Haplotypes. *Human Genetics* 100: 536–543.

Lenneis, E. 2008. Perspectives on the Beginnings of the Earliest LBK in East-Central Europe. In *Living Well Together? Settlement and Materiality in the Neolithic of South-East and Central Europe*, D. Bailey, A. Whittle, and D. Hofmann (eds.), pp. 164-178. Oxford: Oxbow Books.

Leonard, R. D. 2001. Evolutionary Archaeology. In *Archaeological Theory Today*, I. Hodder (ed.), pp. 65–97. Cambridge, MA: Polity Press.

Leonard, W. R., and M. L. Robertson. 1997. Rethinking the Energetics of Bipedality. *Current Anthropology* 38(2): 304–309.

Lepper, B. T. 1996. The Newark Earthworks and the Geometric Encousres of the Scioto Valley: Connections and Conjectures. In *In a View from the Core: A Synthesis of Ohio Hopewell Archaeology*, P. J. Pacheco (ed.), pp. 224–241. Columbus: The Ohio Archaeological Council.

Lesnek, A. J., J. P. Briner, C. Lindqvist, J. F. Baichtal, and T. H. Heaton. 2018. Deglaciation of the Pacific Coastal Corridor Directly Preceded the Human Colonization of the Americas. *Science Advances* 4: eaar5040.

Lev, E., M. E. Kislev, and O. Bar-Yosef. 2005. Mousterian Vegetal Food in Kebara Cave, Mt. Carmel. *Journal of Archaeological Science* 32: 475–484.

Levine, M. A. 2004. The Clauson Site: Late Archaic Settlement and Subsistence in the Uplands of Central New York. *Archaeology of Eastern North America* 32: 161–181.

Lev-Yadun, S., A. Gopher, and S. Abbo. 2000. The Cradle of Agriculture. *Science* 288: 1602–1603.

Lewis-Williams, J. D. 1983. *The Rock Art of Southern Africa.* New York: Cambridge University Press.

Lewis-Williams, J. D., and T. A. Dowson. 1988. The Signs of All Times: Entoptic Phenomena in Upper Paleolithic Art. *Current Anthropology* 29(2): 201–246.

Lewis-Williams, J. D., and D. G. Pearce. 2004. Southern African San Rock Painting as Social Intervention: A Study of Rain-Control Images. *African Archaeological Review* 21(4): 199–218.

Li, H., J. Xiang-Yu, G. Dai, Z. Gu, C. Ming, Z. Yang, O. A. Ryder, W.-H. Li, Y.-X. Fu, and Y.-P. Zhang. 2016. Large Number of Vertebrates Began Rapid Populaton Decline in the Late 19th Century. *Proceedings of the National Academy of Sciences USA* 113: 14079–14084.

Li, L. 2000. Ancestor Worship: An Archaeological Investigation of Ritual Activities in Neolithic North China. *Journal of East Asian Archaeology* 2 (1–2): 129–164.

Li, X., G. Harbottle, J. Zhang, and C. Want. 2003. The Earliest Writing? Sign Use in the Seventh Millennium BC at Jiahu, Henan Province, China. *Antiquity* 77: 31–44.

Li, Y.-t., Z. Yue, and Y. He. 2018. Annihilation or Decline: The Fall of Anyang as an Urban Center. *Archaeological Research in Asia* 14: 97–105.

Lieberman, D. E., and R. C. McCarthy. 1999. The Ontogeny of Cranial Base Angulation in Humans and Chimpanzees and Its Implications for Reconstructing Pharyngeal Dimensions. *Journal of Human Evolution* 36: 487–517.

Lieberman, P. 1991. *Uniquely Human: The Evolution of Speech, Thought, and Selfless Behavior.* Cambridge, MA: Harvard University Press.

Lieberman, P. 2007. The Evolution of Human Speech. Its Anatomical and Neural Bases. *Current Anthropology* 48(1): 39–66.

Liu, L. 2003. "The Product of Minds as Well as of Hands": Production of Prestige Goods in the Neolithic and Early State Periods in China. *Asian Perspectives* 42(1): 1–40.

Liu, L. 2004. *The Chinese Neolithic: Trajectories to Early States.* New York: Cambridge University Press.

Liu, L. 2009. State Emergence in Early China. *Annual Review of Anthropology* 38: 217–232.

Liu, L., X. Chen, Y. K. Lee, H. Wright, and A. Rosen. 2002–2004. Settlement Patterns and Development of Social

Complexity in the Yiluo Region, North China. *Journal of Field Archaeology* 29: 75–100.

Liu, L., and H. Xu. 2007. Rethinking Erlitou: Legend, History and Chinese Archaeology. *Antiquity* 81: 886–901.

Liverani, M. 2006. *Uruk: The First City.* London: Equinox.

Lohse, J. C., J. Awe., C. Griffith, R. M. Rosenswig, and F. Valdez, Jr. 2006. Preceramic Occupations in Belize: Updating the Paleoindian and Archaic Record. *Latin American Antiquity* 17(2): 209–226.

Lombard, M. 2005. Evidence of Hunting and Hafting during the Middle Stone Age at Sibudu Cave, KwaZulu-Natal, South Africa: A Multianalytical Approach. *Journal of Human Evolution* 48: 279–300.

Lombard, M. 2007. The Gripping Nature of Ochre: The Association of Ochre with Howiesons Poort Adhesives and Later Stone Age Mastics from South Africa. *Journal of Human Evolution* 53: 406–419.

Longacre, W. A., S. J. Holbrook, and M. W. Graves (eds.). 1982. *Multidisciplinary Research at Grasshopper Pueblo, Arizona.* Tucson: University of Arizona Press.

Lordkipanidze, D., M. S. Ponce de León, A. Margvelashvili, Y. Rak, G. P. Rightmire, A. Vekua, and C. P. E. Zollikofer. 2013. A Complete Skull from Dmanisi, Georgia, and the Evolutionary Biology of Early *Homo. Science* 342: 326–331.

Louderback, L. A., and B. M. Pavlik. 2017. Starch Granule Evidence for the Earliest Potato Use in North America. *Proceedings of the National Academy of Sciences USA* 114: 7606–7610.

Love, M. 2007. Recent Research in the Southern Highlands and Pacific Coast of Mesoamerica. *Journal of Archaeological Research* 15: 275–328.

Lovejoy, C. O. 1981. The Origin of Man. *Science* 211: 341–350.

Lovejoy, C. O., G. Suwa, S. W. Thompson, J. H. Matthews, and T. D. White. 2009. The Great Divides: *Ardipithecus ramidus* Reveals the Postcrania of Our Last Common Ancestors with African Apes. *Science* 326: 100–106.

Lowe, G. W. 1989. The Heartland Olmec: Evolution of Material Culture. In *Regional Perspectives on the Olmec*, R. J. Sharer and D. C. Grove (eds.), pp. 33–67. New York: Cambridge University Press.

Liu, W., M. Martinón-Torres, Y.-j. Cai, S. Xing, H.-w. Tong, S.-w. Pei, M. J. Sier, X.-h. Wu, L. E. Edwards, H. Cheng, Y.-y. Li, W.-y. Yang, J. M. Bermudez de Castro, and W.-j. Wu. 2015. The Earliest Unequivocally Modern Humans in Southern China. *Nature* 526, 696–699.

Lu, D., H. Lou, K. Yuan, X. Wang, Y. Wang, C. Zhang, Y. Lu, X. Yang, L. Deng, Y. Zhou, Q. Feng, Y. Hu, Q. Ding, Y. Yang, S. Li, L. Jin, Y. Guan, B. Su, L. Kang, and S. Xu. 2016. Ancestral Origins and Genetic History of Tibetan Highlanders. *American Journal of Human Genetics* 99: 580–594.

Lu, T. L.-D. 2010. Early Pottery in South China. *Asian Perspectives* 49(1): 1–42.

Lubell, D. 1974. *The Fakhurian. A Late Paleolithic Industry from Upper Egypt.* Cairo: The Geological Survey of Egypt.

Lubell, D. 2001. Late Pleistocene–Early Holocene Maghreb. In *The Encyclopedia of Prehistory, Volume 1: Africa*, P. N. Peregrine and M. Ember (eds.), pp. 129–149. New York: Plenum Press.

Lucero, L. J. 1999. Classic Lowland Maya Political Organization: A Review. *Journal of World Prehistory* 13(2): 211–263.

Luikart, G., H. Fernández, M. Mashkour, P. R. England, and P. Taberlet. 2006. Origins and Diffusion of Domestic Goats Inferred from DNA Markers: Example Analyses of mtDNA, Y Chromosome, and Microsatellites. In *Documenting Domestication: New Genetic and Archaeological Paradigms*, M. A. Zeder, D. G. Bradley, E. Emshwiller, and B. D. Smith (eds.), pp. 294–305. Los Angeles: University of California Press.

Lulewicz, J., and A. B. Coker. 2018. The Structure of the Mississippian World: A Social Network Approach to the Organization of Sociopolitical Interactions. *Journal of Anthropological Archaeology* 50: 113–127.

Lynch, T. F., R Gillespie, J. A. J. Gowlett, and R. E. M. Hedges. 1985. Chronology of Guitarrero Cave, Peru. *Science* 229: 864–867.

Lynch, T. F., and K. A. R. Kennedy. 1970. Early Human Cultural and Skeletal Remains from Guitarrero Cave, Northern Peru. *Science* 169: 1307–1309.

Mabry, J. 1994. Discovery of an Early "Big House" at Vacas Muertas. *Archaeology in Tucson Newsletter of the Center for Desert Archaeology* 8(3): 6–7 (The Center for Desert Archaeology is now Archaeology Southwest).

Mabry, J. 2005. Changing Knowledge and Ideas about the First Farmers in Southeastern Arizona. In *The Late Archaic across the Borderlands: From Foraging to Farming*, B. J. Vierra (ed.), pp. 41–85. Austin: University of Texas Press.

Mabry, J., and J. J. Clark. 1994. Early Village Life on the Santa Cruz River. *Archaeology in Tucson Newsletter of the*

Center for Desert Archaeology 8(1): 1–5 (The Center for Desert Archaeology is now Southwest Archaeology).

Macaulay, V., C. Hill, A. Achilli, C. Rengo, D. Clarke, W. Meehan, J. Blackburn, O. Semino, R. Scozzari, F. Cruciani, A. Taha, N. K. Saari, J. M. Raja, P. Ismail, Z. Zainuddin, W. Goodwin, D. Bulbeck, H.-J. Bandelt, S. Oppenheimer, A. Torroni, and M. Richards. 2005. Single, Rapid Coastal Settlement of Asia Revealed by Analysis of Complete Human Mitochondria Genomes. *Science* 308: 1034–1036.

Machin, A. J., R. T. Hosfield, and S. J. Mithen. 2007. Why Are Some Handaxes Symmetrical? Testing the Influence of Handaxe Morphology on Butchery Effectiveness. *Journal of Archaeological Science* 34(6): 883–893.

Macintosh, A. A., R. Pinhasi, and J. T. Stock. 2014. Lower Limb Skeletal Biomechanics Track Long-Term Decline in Mobility Across ~6150 Years of Agriculture in Central Europe. *Journal of Archaeological Science* 52: 376–390.

MacDonald, K. 2018. Fire-Free Hominin Strategies for Coping with Cool Winter Temperatures in North-Western Europe from Before 800,000 to 400,000 Years Ago. *PaleoAnthropology* 2018: 7–26.

MacLarnon, A., and G. Hewitt. 2004. Increased Breathing Control: Another Factor in the Evolution of Human Language. *Evolutionary Anthropology* 13: 181–197.

Macklin, M. G., and J. Lewin. 2015. The Rivers of Civilization. *Quaternary Science Reviews* 114: 228–244.

Madella, M., and D. Q. Fuller. 2006. Palaeoecology and the Harappan Civilisation of South Asia: A Reconsideration. *Quaternary Science Reviews* 25: 1283–1301.

Madella, M., M. K. Jones, P. Goldberg, Y. Goren, and E. Hovers. 2002. The Exploitation of Plant Resources by Neanderthals in Amud Cave (Israel): The Evidence from Phytolith Studies. *Journal of Archaeological Science* 29: 703–719.

Maher, L., M. Lohr, M. Betts, C. Parslow, and E. B. Banning. 2001. Middle Epipalaeolithic Sites in the Wadi Ziqlab, Northern Jordan. *Paléorient* 27(1): 5–19.

Maher, L., and D. Macdonald. 2013. Assessing Typo-Technological Variability in Epipalaeolithic Assemblages: Preliminary Results from Two Case Studies from the Southern Levant. In *Stone Tools in Transition: From Hunter-Gatherers to Farming Societies in the Near East, 7th Conference on PPN Chipped and Ground Stone Industries of the Fertile Crescent*, F. Borrell, J. J.Ibáñez,

and M. Molist (eds.), pp. 29–44. Barcelona: Autonomous University of Barcelona.

Maher, L., T. Richter, D. Macdonald, M. D. Jones, L. Martin, and J. T. Stock. 2012b. Twenty Thousand-Year-Old Huts at a Hunter-Gatherer Settlement in Eastern Jordan. *PLoS ONE* 7(2): e31447.

Maher, L., T. Richter, and J. T. Stock. 2012a. The Pre-Natufian Epipaleolithic: Long-Term Behavioral Trends in the Levant. *Evolutionary Anthropology* 21: 69–81.

Maher, L., J. T. Stock, S. Finney, J. J. N. Heywood, P. T. Miracle, and E. B. Banning. 2011. A Unique Human-Fox Burial from a Pre-Natufian Cemetery in the Levant (Jordan). *PLoS ONE* 6(1): e15815.

Majkić, A., S. Evans, V. Stepanchuk, A. Tsvelykh, and F. d'Errico. 2017. A Decorated Raven Bone from the Zaskalnaya VI (Kolosovskaya) Neanderthal Site, Crimea. *PLoS One* 12(3): e0173435.

Maloney, T., S. O'Connor, R. Wood, K. Aplin, and J. Balme. 2018. Carpenters Gap: A 47,000 Year Old Record of Indigenous Adaption and Innovation. *Quaternary Science Reviews* 191: 204–228.

Malotki, E. 2000. *Kokopelli. The Making of an Icon*. Lincoln: University of Nebraska Press.

Mandel, R. D., and A. H. Simmons. 2001. Prehistoric Occupation of Late Quaternary Landscapes Near Kharga Oasis, Western Desert of Egypt. *Geoarchaeology* 16(1): 95–117.

Marcus, J. 1989. Zapotec Chiefdoms and the Nature of Formative Religions. In *Regional Perspectives on the Olmec*, R. J. Sharer and D. C. Grove (eds.), pp. 148–197. Santa Fe, NM: School of American Research Press.

Marcus, J. 2003. Recent Advances in Maya Archaeology. *Journal of Archaeological Research* 11: 71–148.

Marcus, J. 2004. Primary and Secondary State Formation in Southern Mesoamerica. In *Understanding Early Classic Copan*, E. E. Bell, M. A. Canuto, and R. J. Sharer (eds.), pp. 357–373. Philadelphia: University of Pennsylvania Museum of Archaeology and Anthropology Publications.

Marcus, J. 2008. The Archaeological Evidence for Social Evolution. *Annual Review of Anthropology* 37: 251–266.

Marcus, J., and K.V. Flannery. 1996. *Zapotec Civilization: How Urban Society Evolved in Mexico's Oaxaca Valley*. London: Thames and Hudson.

Marean, C. W., and Z. Assefa. 1999. Zooarchaeological Evidence for the Faunal Exploitation Behavior of

Neandertals and Early Modern Humans. *Evolutionary Anthropology* 8: 22–37.

Marean, C. W., M. Bar-Matthews, J. Bernatchez, E. Fisher, P. Goldberg, A. I. R. Herries, Z. Jacobs, A. Jeradino, P. Karkanas, T. Minichillo, P. J. Nilssen, E. Thompson, I. Watts, and H. M. Williams. 2007. Early Human Use of Marine Resources and Pigment in South Africa during the Middle Pleistocene. *Nature* 449: 905–908.

Marquardt, W. H. 1985. Complexity and Scale in the Study of Fisher–Gatherer–Hunters: An Example from the Eastern United States. In *Prehistoric Hunter-Gatherers: The Emergence of Social Complexity*, T. D. Price and J. A. Brown (eds.), pp. 59–98. New York: Academic Press.

Marshall, J. 1931. *Mohenjo-daro and the Indus Civilization*. London: A. Probsthain.

Marshall, F., and E. Hildebrand. 2002. Cattle before Crops: The Beginnings of Food Production in Africa. *Journal of World Prehistory* 16(2): 99–143.

Martin, P. S. 2005. Twilight of the Mammoths: Ice Age Extinctions and the Rewilding of North America. Berkeley: University of California Press.

Martin, S. 2003. In Line of the Founder: A View of Dynastic Politics at Tikal. In *Tikal: Dynasties, Foreigners, and Affairs of State*, J. A. Sabloff (ed.), pp. 3–45. Sante Fe, NM: School of American Research Press.

Martin, S. 2012. Maya Calendars: An Overview. *Expedition* 54(1): 24–25.

Martin, S., and N. Grube. 2008. *Chronicle of the Maya Kings and Queens*, 2nd ed. London: Thames & Hudson.

Martínez, G., M. A. Gutiérrez, P. G. Messineo, C. A. Kaufmann, and D. J. Rafuse. 2016. Subsistence Strategies in Argentina during the Late Pleistocene and Early Holocene. *Quaternary Science Reviews* 144: 51–65.

Marzke, M. W. 1997. Precision Grips, Hand Morphology, and Tools. *American Journal of Physical Anthropology* 102: 91–110.

Masse, W. B. 1991. The Quest for Subsistence Sufficiency and Civilization in the Sonoran Desert. In *Chaco & Hohokam: Prehistoric Regional Systems in the American Southwest*, P. L. Crown and W. J. Judge (eds.), pp. 195–223. Santa Fe, NM: School of American Research Press.

Masson, M. A. 2012. Maya Collapse Cycles. *Proceedings of the National Academy of Sciences USA* 109(45): 18237–18238.

Mathien, J. 2001. The Organization of Turquoise Production and Consumption by the Prehistoric Chacoans. *American Antiquity* 66(1): 103–118.

Mathieson, I., I. Lazaridis, N. Rohland, S. Mallick, N. Patterson, S. Alpansan Roodenberg, E. Harney, K. Stewardson, D. Fernandes, M. Novak, K. Sirak, C. Gamba, E.R. Jones, B. Llamas, S. Dryomov, J. Pickrell, J.L. Arsuaga, J.M. Bermúdez de Castro, E. Carbonell, F. Gerritsen, A. Khokhlov, P. Kuznetsov, M. Lozano, H. Meller, O. Mochalov, V. Moiseyev, M.A. Rojo Guerra, J. Roodenberg, J.M. Vergès, J. Krause, A. Cooper, K.W. Alt, D. Brown, D. Anthony, C. Lalueza-Fox, W. Haak, R. Pinhasi, and David Reich. 2015. Genome-Wide Patterns of Selection in 230 Ancient Eurasians. *Nature* 528: 499–503.

Matson, R. G. 2006. What Is Basketmaker II? *Kiva* 72(2): 149–165.

Matson, R. G. 2016. The Nutritional Context of the Pueblo III Depopulation of the Northern San Juan: Too Much Maize? *Journal of Archaeological Science: Reports* 5, 622–631.

Mattson, H. V. 2016. Ornaments as Socially Valuable Objects: Jewelry and Identity in the Chaco and Post-Chaco Worlds. *Journal of Anthropological Archaeology* 42: 122–139.

McAnany, P. A. 2001. Cosmology and the Institutionalization of Hierarchy in the Maya Region. In *From Leaders to Rulers*, J. Haas (ed.), pp. 125–148. New York: Kluwer Academic/Plenum.

McBrearty, S. 2007. Down with the Revolution. In *Rethinking the Human Revolution. New Behavioural and Biological Perspectives on the Origin and Dispersal of Modern Humans*, P. Mellars, K. Boyle, O. Bar-Yosef, and C. Stringer (eds.), pp. 133–151. Cambridge, UK: McDonald Institute for Archaeological Research.

McBrearty, S., and A. S. Brooks. 2000. The Revolution That Wasn't: A New Interpretation of the Origin of Modern Human Behavior. *Journal of Human Evolution* 39: 453–563.

McCorriston, J., and F. Hole. 1991. The Ecology of Seasonal Stress and the Origins of Agriculture in the Near East. *American Anthropologist* 93: 46–69.

McDermott, L. 1996. Self-Representation in Upper Paleolithic Female Figurines. *Current Anthropology* 37: 227–276.

McDonald, M. M. A. 1991. Technological Organization and Sedentism in the Epipaleolithic of Dakhleh Oasis, Egypt. *African Archaeological Review* 9:81–109.

McDonald, M. M. A. 2001. The Late Prehistoric Radiocarbon Chronology for Dakhleh Oasis within the Wider Environmental and Cultural Setting of the Egyptian Western

Desert. In *The Oasis Papers 1: The Proceedings of the First Conference of the Dakhleh Oasis Project,* C. A. Marlow and A. J. Mills, eds., pp. 26–42. Oxford: Oxbow Books.

McDougall, I., F. Brown, and J. Fleagle. 2005. Stratigraphic Placement and Age of Modern Humans from Kibish, Ethiopia. *Nature* 433: 733–736.

McGhee, R. 2008. Aboriginalism and the Problems of Indigenous Archaeology. *American Antiquity* 73(4): 579–597.

McGhee, R. 2010. Of Strawmen, Herrings, and Frustrated Expectations. *American Antiquity* 75(2): 239–243.

McGovern, P. E., J. Zhang, J. Tang, Z. Zhang, G. R. Hall, R. A. Moreau, A. Nuñez, E. D. Butrym, M. P. Richards, C-S. Wang, G. Cheng, Z. Zhao, and C. Wang. 2004. *Proceedings of the National Academy of Sciences USA* 101: 17593–17598.

McGrew, W. C., P. J. Baldwin, L. F. Marchant, J. D. Pruetz, S. E. Scott, and C. E. G. Tutin. 2003. Ethnoarchaeology and Elementary Technology of Unhabituated Wild Chimpanzees at Assirik, Senegal. *PaleoAnthropology* 2003 (05.02): 1–20.

McHenry, H., and L. Berger. 1998. Body Proportions in *Australopithecus afarensis* and A. *africanus* and the Origin of the Genus *Homo. Journal of Human Evolution* 35: 1–22.

McNeil, C. (ed.). 2006. *Chocolate in Mesoamerica: A Cultural History of Cacao.* Gainesville: University Press of Florida.

MacNeish, R. S., and M. W. Eubanks. 2000. Comparative Analysis of the Río Balsas and Tehuacán Models for the Origins of Maize. *Latin American Antiquity* 11(1): 3–20.

McPherron, S. P. 1999. Ovate and Pointed Handaxe Assemblages: Two Points Make a Line. *Préhistoire Européenne* 14: 9–32.

McPherron, S. P., and H. L. Dibble. 2001. *Using Computers in Archaeology. A Practical Guide.* New York: McGraw-Hill Mayfield.

Meadon, G. T. 2017. Stonehenge and Avebury: Megalithic Shadow Casting at the Solstices at Sunrise. *Journal of Lithic Studies* 4(4): 39–66.

Meadow, R. H., and A. K. Patel. 2003. Perhistoric Pastoralism in Northwestern South Asia from the Neolithic through the Harappan Period. In *Indus Ethnobiology: New Perspectives from the Field,* S. A. Weber and W. R. Belcher (eds.), pp. 65–93. New York: Lexington Books.

Meier, J. S., A. N. Goring-Morris, and N. D. Munro. 2016. Provisioning the Ritual Neolithic Site of Kfar HaHoresh, Israel at the Dawn of Animal Management. *PloS One* 11: e0166573.

Mellars, P. 2005. The Impossible Coincidence: A Singe-Species Model for the Origins of Modern Human Behavior. *Evolutionary Anthropology* 14: 12–27.

Mellars, P. 2009. Moonshine over Star Carr: Post-Processualism, Mesolithic Myths and Archaeological Realities. *Antiquity* 83: 502–517.

Mellars, P., K. Boyle, O. Bar-Yosef, and C. Stringer. 2007. *Rethinking the Human Revolution. New Behavioural and Biological Perspectives on the Origin and Dispersal of Modern Humans.* Cambridge, UK: McDonald Institute for Archaeological Research.

Mellars, P., and P. Dark. 1998. *Star Carr in Context: New Archaeological and Palaeoecological Investigations at the Early Mesolithic Site of Star Carr, North Yorkshire.* Cambridge, UK: McDonald Institute for Archaeological Research.

Mengoni Goñalons, G. L., and H. D. Yacobaccio. 2006. The Domestication of South American Camelids: A View from the South-Central Andes. In *Documenting Domestication: New Genetic and Archaeological Paradigms,* M. A. Zeder, D. G. Bradley, E. Emshwiller, and B. D. Smith (eds.), pp. 228–244. Los Angeles: University of California Press.

Menotti, F., B. Jennings, and H. Gollnisch-Moos. 2014. "Gifts for the Gods": Lake-Dwellers' Macabre Remedies against Floods in the Central European Bronze Age. *Antiquity* 88: 456–469.

Mensforth, R. P. 2001. Warfare and Trophy Taking in the Archaic Period. In *Archaic Transitions in Ohio and Kentucky Prehistory,* O. H. Prufer, S. E. Pedde, and R. S. Meindl (eds.), pp. 110–138. Kent, OH: Kent State University Press.

Mercader, J., and A. S. Brooks. 2001. Across Forests and Savannas: Later Stone Age Assemblages from Ituri and Semliki, Democratic Republic of Congo. *Journal of Anthropological Research* 57(2): 197–217.

Mercer, R., and F. Healy. 2014. Hambledon Hill, Dorset, England: Excavation and Survey of a Neolithic Monument Complex and Its Surrounding Landscape. London: English Heritage Publishing.

Mercier, N., H. Valladas, O. Bar-Yosef, B. Vandermeersch, C. Stringer, and J. L. Joron. 1993. Thermoluminescence Date for the Mousterian Burial Site of Es-Skhul, Mt. Carmel. *Journal of Archaeological Science* 20(2): 169–174.

Merrill, W. L., R. J. Hard, J. B. Mabry, G. J. Fritz, K. R. Adams, J. R. Roney, and A. C. MacWilliams. 2009. The Diffusion of Maize to the Southwestern United States and Its Impact. *Proceedings of the National Academy of Science USA* 106(50): 21019–21026.

Meskell, L. 1999. *Archaeologies of Social Life: Age, Sex, Class etc. in Ancient Egypt.* Malden, MA: Blackwell.

Meyer, C., C. Knipper, N. Nickllisch, A. Münster, V. Dresely, H. Meller, and K.W. Alt. 2018. Early Neolithic Executions Indicated by Clustered Cranial Trauma in the Mass Grave of Halberstadt. *Nature Communications* 9: 2472.

Meyer, C., C. Lohr, D. Gronenborn, and K.W. Alt. 2014. The Massacre Mass Grave of Schöneck-Kilianstädten Reveals New Insights into Collective Violence in Early Neolithic Central Europe. *Proceedings of the National Academy of Sciences USA* 112: 11217–11222.

Michalowski, P. (ed.). 2008. *On the Third Dynasty of Ur. Studies in Honor of Marcel Sigrist.* Boston: American Schools of Oriental Research.

Michel, V., H. Valladas, G. Shen, W. Wang, J.-x. Zhao, C.-C. Shen, P. Valensi, and C. J. Bae. 2016. The Earliest Modern *Homo sapiens* in China? *Journal of Human Evolution* 101: 101–104.

Midant-Reynes, B. 2003. *Aux origines de l'Égypte. Du Néolithique à l'émergence de l'État.* Paris: Fayard.

Middleton, G. D. 2012. Nothing Lasts Forever: Environmental Discourses on the Collapse of Past Societies. *Journal of Archaeological Research* 20: 257–307.

Miller, D. 2002. Smelter and Smith: Iron Age Metal Fabrication Technology in Southern Africa. *Journal of Archaeological Science* 29: 1083–1131.

Miller, D., N. Desai, and J. Lee-Thorp. 2000. Indigenous Gold Mining in Southern Africa: A Review. In *African Naissance: The Limpopo Valley 1000 Years Ago*, M. Lesley and T. M. Maggs (eds.), pp. 91–99. South African Archaeological Society Goodwin Series 8.

Miller, G., J. Magee, M. Smith, N. Spooner, A. Baynes, S. Lehman, M. Fogel, H. Johnston, D. Williams, P. Clark, C. Florian, R. Holst, and S. DeVogel. 2016. Human Predation Contributed to the Extinction of the Australian Megafaunal Bird *Genyornis newtoni* ~47 ka. *Nature Communications* 7: 10496.

Miller, N. F. 2000. Plant Forms in Jewelry from the Royal Cemetery at Ur. *Iraq* 62: 149–155.

Mills, B. J. 2002. Recent Research on Chaco: Changing Views on Economy, Ritual, and Society. *Journal of Archaeological Research* 10(1): 65–117.

Mills, B. J., and T. J. Ferguson. 2008. Animate Objects: Shell Trumpets and Ritual Networks in the Greater Southwest. *Journal of Archaeological Method and Theory* 15: 338–361.

Milner, G. R. 1999. Warfare in Prehistoric and Early Historic Eastern North America. *Journal of Archaeological Research* 7(2): 105–151.

Mitchell, D. R., and M. S. Foster. 2000. Hohokam Shell Middens along the Sea of Cortez, Puerto Peñasco, Sonora, Mexico. *Journal of Field Archaeology* 27(1): 27–41.

Milton, K. 2000. A Hypothesis to Explain the Role of Meat-Eating in Human Evolution. *Evolutionary Anthropology* 8: 11–21.

Mitchell, P. J. 1990. Preliminary Report of the Later Stone Age Sequence from Tloutle Rock Shelter, Western Lesotho. *South African Archaeological Bulletin* 45: 100–105.

Mitchell, P. J. 2000. The Organization of Later Stone Age Lithic Technology in the Caledon Valley, Southern Africa. *African Archaeological Review* 17(3): 141–176.

Monjeau, J. A., B. Araujo, G. Abramson, M. N. Kuperman, M. F. Laguna, and J. L. Lanata. 2017. The Controversy Space on Quaternary Megafaunal Extinctions. *Quaternary International* 431: 194–204.

Monnier, F., and A. Puchkov. 2016. The Construction Phases of the Bent Pyramid at Dahshur. A Reassessment. *Équipe Égypte Nilotique et Méditerranéenne* 9: 15–26.

Moore, A. M. T., and G. C. Hillman. 1992. The Pleistocene to Holocene Transition and Human Economy in Southwest Asia: The Impact of the Younger Dryas. *American Antiquity* 57(3): 482–494.

Moore, C. B. 1905. Certain Aboriginal Remains of the Black Warrior River. *Journal of the Academy of Natural Sciences of Philadelphia* 13: 124–244.

Moore, C. R., and V. G. Dekle. 2010. Hickory Nuts, Bulk Processing and the Advent of Early Horticultural Economies in Eastern North America. *World Archaeology* 42(4): 595–608.

Moore, J. D. 2004. The Social Basis of Sacred Spaces in the Prehispanic Andes: Ritual Landscapes of the Dead in Chimú and Inka Societies. *Journal of Archaeological Method and Theory* 11(1): 83–124.

Moore, T. 2017. Alternatives to Urbanism? Reconsidering *Oppida* and the Urban Question in Late Iron Age Europe. *Journal of World Prehistory* 30: 281–300.

Moore, T., A. Braun, J. Creighton, L. Cripps, P. Haupt, I. Klenner, P. Nouvel, C. Ponroy, and M. Schönfelder. 2015. Oppida, Agglomerations, and Suburbia: The Bibracte Environs and New Perspectives on Late Iron Age Urbanism in Central-Eastern France. *European Journal of Archaeology* 16(3): 491–517.

Moorey, P. R. S. 1977. What Do We Know About the People Buried in the Royal Cemetery? *Expedition* 20(1): 24–40.

Morey, D. F. 2006. Burying Key Evidence: The Social Bond between Dogs and People. *Journal of Archaeological Science* 33: 158–175.

Morey, D. F. 2014. In Search of Paleolithic Dogs: A Quest with Mixed Results. *Journal of Archaeological Science* 52: 300–307.

Morris, C. 2008. Links in the Chain of Inka Cities: Communication, Alliance, and the Cultural Production of Status, Value, and Power. In *The Ancient City: New Perspectives on Urbanism in the Old and New World*, J. Marcus and J. A. Sabloff (eds.), pp. 299–319. Santa Fe, NM: School for Advanced Research Press.

Morris, E. 1925. Exploring in the Canyon of Death. *National Geographic* XLVIII(3): 263–300.

Morris, E., and R. F. Burgh. 1954. *Basketmaker II Sites Near Durango, Colorado*. Washington DC: Carnegie Institution Publication No. 604.

Morrow, J. E., and T. A. Morrow. 1999. Geographic Variation in Fluted Projectile Points: A Hemispheric Perspective. *American Antiquity* 64(2): 215–231.

Morwood, M. J., P. Brown, Jatmiko, T. Sutikna, E. W. Saptomo, K. E. Westaway, R. A. Due, R. G. Roberts, T. Maeda, S. Wasisto, and T. Djubiantono. 2005. Further Evidence for Small-Bodied Hominins from the Late Pleistocene of Flores, Indonesia. *Nature* 437: 1012–1017.

Moulherat, C., M. Tengberg, J,-F. Haquet, and B. Mille. 2002. First Evidence of Cotton at Neolithic Mehrgarh, Pakistan: Analysis of Mineralized Fibres from a Copper Bead. *Journal of Archaeological Science* 29: 1393–1401.

Mowrer, K. 2006. Basketmaker II Mortuary Practices: Social Differentiation and Regional Variation. *Kiva* 72(2): 259–281.

Mueller, N. G. 2018. The Earliest Occurrence of a Newly Described Domesticate in Eastern North America: Adena/Hopewell Communities and Agricultural Innovation. *Journal of Anthropological Archaeology* 49: 39–50.

Mueller, N. G., G. J. Fritz, P. Patton, S. Carmody, and E. T. Horton. 2017. Growing the Lost Crops of Eastern North America's Original Agricultural System. *Nature Plants* 3: 17092.

Muller, J. 1999. Southeastern Interaction and Integration. In *Great Towns and Regional Polities in the Prehistoric American Southwest and Southeast*, J. E. Neitzel (ed.), pp. 143–158. Albuquerque: University of New Mexico Press.

Mulvaney, J., and J. Kamminga. 1999. *Prehistory of Australia*. Sydney: Allen and Unwin.

Munro, N. D., and L. Grosman. 2010. Early Evidence (*ca.* 12,000 B.P.) for Feasting at a Burial Cave in Israel. *Proceedings of the National Academy of Sciences USA* 107: 15362–15366.

Mussi, M., J. Cinq-Mrs, and P. Bolduc. 2000. Echoes from the Mammoth Steppe: The Case of the Balzi Rossi. In *Hunters of the Golden Age: The Mid Upper Palaeolithic of Eurasia 30,000—20,000 BP*, W. Roebroeks, M. Mussi, J. Svoboda, and K. Fennema (eds.), pp. 105–124. Leiden, The Netherlands: University of Leiden.

Nadel, D., and E. Werker. 1999. The Oldest Ever Brush Hut Plant Remains from Ohalo II, Jordan Valley, Israel. *Antiquity* 73: 755–764.

Nagle, N., M. van Oven, S. Wilcox, S. van Holst Pellekaan, C. Tyler-Smith, Y. Xue, K. N. Ballantyne, L. Wilcox, L. Papac, K. Cooke, R. A. H. van Oorschot, P. McAllister, L. Williams, M. Kayser, R. J. Mitchell, and The Genographic Consortium. 2017. Aboriginal Australian Mitochondrial Genome Variation—An Increased Understanding of Population Antiquity and Diversity. *Scientific Reports* 7: 43041.

Nami, H. G. 2007. Research in the Middle Negro River Basin (Uruguay) and the Paleoindian Occupation of the Southern Cone. *Current Anthropology* 48(1): 164–174.

Nash, D. J., and P. R. Williams. 2005. Architecture and Power on the Wari-Tiwanaku Frontier. *Archaeological Papers of the American Anthropological Association* 14: 151–174.

Needham, S. 2001. When Expediency Broaches Ritual Intention: The Flow of Metal Between Systemic and Buried Domains. *Journal of the Royal Anthropological Institute* 7 (n.s.): 275–298.

Needham, S., K. Parfitt, and G. Varndell (eds.). 2006. *The Ringlemere Cup: Precious Cups and the Beginning of the Channel Bronze Age*. London: British Museum Research Publication 163.

Neitzel, J. E. 2000. Gender Hierarchies. A Comparative Analysis of Mortuary Data. In *Women and Men in the Prehispanic Southwest*, P. L. Crown (ed.), pp. 137–168. Santa Fe, NM: School of American Research Press.

Nelson, B. A. 2006. Mesoamerican Objects and Symbols in Chaco Canyon Contexts. In *The Archaeology of Chaco Canyon, an Eleventh Century Pueblo Regional Center*, S. H. Lekson (ed.), pp. 339–371. Santa Fe, NM: School of American Research Press.

Nelson, S. M. 2001. Diversity of Upper Paleolithic "Venus" Figurines and Archaeological Mythology. In *Gender in Cross-Cultural Perspective*, 3rd edition, C. B. Brettell and C. F. Sargent (eds.), pp. 82–89. Upper Saddle River, NJ: Prentice Hall.

Nelson, S. M. 2003. Feasting the Ancestors in Early China. In *The Archaeology and Politics of Food and Feasting in Early States and Empires*, T. L. Bray (ed.), pp. 65–89. New York: Kluwer Academic/Plenum.

Nesbitt, M. 2002. When and Where Did Domesticated Cereals First Occur in Southwest Asia? In *The Dawn of Farming in the Near East*, R. T. J. Cappers and S. Bottema (eds.), pp. 113–132. Studies in Near Eastern Production, Subsistence, and Environment 6. Berlin: *ex oriente*.

Neumann, K., K. Bostoen, A. Höhn, S. Kahlheber, A. Ngomanda, and B. Tchiengué. 2012. First Farmers in the Central African Rainforest: A View from Southern Cameroon. *Quaternary International* 249: 53–62.

Nicholas, G. P. 2008. Native Peoples and Archaeology. In *Encyclopedia of Archaeology*, D. M. Pearsall (ed.), pp. 1660–1669. New York: Elsevier/Academic Press.

Nichols, D. L. 2016. Teotihuacan. *Journal of Archaeological Research* 24(1): 1–74.

Nichols, D. L., and S. T. Evans. 2009. Aztec Studies. *Ancient Mesoamerica* 20: 265–270.

Nichols, D. L., and F. E. Smiley. 1984. A Summary of Prehistoric Research on Northern Black Mesa. In E*xcavations on Black Mesa, 1982, A Descriptive Report*, D. L. Nichols and F. E. Smiley (eds.), pp. 89–107. Carbondale: Southern Illinois University at Carbondale Center for Archaeological Investigations Research Paper No. 39.

Nissen, H. 1986. The Archaic Texts from Uruk. *World Archaeology* 17(3): 317–334.

Nissen, H. 2001. Cultural and Political Networks in the Ancient Near East during the Fourth and Third Millennium BC. In *Uruk Mesopotamia and Its Neighbors: Cross-Cultural Interactions in the Era of State Formation*, M. S. Rothman (ed.), pp. 149–180. Santa Fe, NM: School of American Research Press.

Nissen, H. 2002. Uruk: Key Site of the Period and Key Site of the Problem. In *Artefacts of Complexity: Tracking the Uruk in the Near East*, N. Postgate (ed.), pp. 1–16. Wiltshire, UK: British School of Archaeology in Iraq.

Oates, J. 1978. Religion and Ritual in Sixth-Millennium B.C. Mesopotamia. *World Archaeology* 10(2): 117–124.

Oates, J., and D. Oates. 2004. The Role of Exchange Relations in the Origins of Mesopotamian Civilization. In *Explaining Social Change: Studies in Honour of Colin Renfrew*, J. Cherry, C. Scarre, and S. Shennan (eds.), pp. 177–192. Cambridge, UK: McDonald Institute for Archaeological Research.

Needham, S. 2001. When Expediency Broaches Ritual Intention: The Flow of Metal Between Systemic and Buried Domains. *Journal of the Royal Anthropological Institute* 7 (n.s.): 275–298.

Needham, S., K. Parfitt, and G. Varndell (eds.). 2006. *The Ringlemere Cup: Precious Cups and the Beginning of the Channel Bronze Age*. London: British Museum Research Publication 163.

O'Connell, J. F., and J. Allen. 2015. The Process, Biotic Impact, and Global Implications of the Human Colonization of Sahul About 47,000 Years Ag0. *Journal of Archaeological Science* 56: 73–84.

O'Connor, D. 1995. The Earliest Egyptian Boat Graves. *Egyptian Archaeology* 6: 3–7.

O'Connor, D. 2009. *Abydos: Egypt's First Pharoahs and the Cult of Osiris*. Cairo: American University in Cairo Press.

O'Connor, S. 2007. New Evidence from East Timor Contributes to Our Understanding of Earliest Modern Human Colonization East of the Sunda Shelf. *Antiquity* 81: 523–535.

Olalde, I., H. Schroeder, M. Sandoval-Velasco, L. Vinner, I. Lobón, O. Ramirez, S. Civit, P. García Borja, D. C. Salazar-García, S. Talamo, J. M. Fullola, F. X. Oms, M. Pedro, P. Martínez, M. Sanz, J. Daura, J. Zilhão, T. Marquès-Bonet, M. T. P. Gilbert, and C. Lalueza-Fox. 2015. A Common Genetic Origin for Early Farmers from Mediterranean Cardial and Central European

LBK Cultures. *Molecular Biology and Evolution* 32 (12): 3132–3142.

Olley, J. M., R. G. Roberts, H. Yoshida, and J. M. Bowler. 2006. Single-Grain Optical Dating of Grave-Infill Associated with Human Burials at Lake Mungo, Australia. *Quaternary Science Reviews* 25: 2469–2474.

Olsen, S. L. 1989. Solutré: A Theoretical Approach to the Reconstruction of Upper Paleolithic Hunting Strategies. *Journal of Human Evolution* 18: 295–327.

Olszewski, D. I. 1984. Arizona D:11:2023. In *Excavations on Black Mesa, 1982, A Descriptive Report,* D. L. Nichols and F. E. Smiley (eds.), pp. 183–192. Carbondale: Southern Illinois University at Carbondale Center for Archaeological Investigations Research Paper No. 39.

Olszewski, D. I. (ed.). 2000. *The Mahele and Later in Waipi'o Valley, Hawai'i.* Native Hawaiian Culture and Arts Program. Research report on file, Library and Archives, Bishop Museum, Honolulu; Hamilton Library, University of Hawai'i-Manoa, Honolulu.

Olszewski, D. I. 2008. The Palaeolithic Period, Including the Epipalaeolithic. In *Jordan: An Archaeological Reader,* R. Adams (ed.), pp. 35–69. Oakville, CT: Equinox.

Olszewski, D. I. 2010. On the Margins: Early Natufian in the Wadi al-Hasa Region, Jordan. *Eurasian Prehistory* 7(1): 85–97.

Olszewski, D. I. 2014. Middle East: Epipalaeolithic. In *Encyclopedia of Global Archaeology,* C. Shen and Z. Jacobs (section eds.), C. Smith (ed.), pp. 4922–4929. New York: Springer.

Olszewski, D. I., H. L. Dibble, U. A. Schurmans, S. P. McPherron, and J. R. Smith. 2005. High Desert Paleolithic Survey at Abydos, Egypt. *Journal of Field Archaeology* 30: 283–303.

Olszewski, D. I., and M. al-Nahar. 2011. New Excavations at Wadi Madamagh, Petra Region. *Neo-Lithics* 2/11: 5–10.

Olszewski, D. I., U. A. Schurmans, and B. A. Schmidt. 2011. The Epipaleolithic (Iberomaurusian) from Grotte des Contrebandiers, Morocco. *African Archaeological Review* 28: 97–123.

Olszewski, D. I., M. C. Trachte, and R. M. Kohl. 1984. Arizona D:11:2027. In *Excavations on Black Mesa, 1982, A Descriptive Report,* D. L. Nichols and F. E. Smiley (eds.), pp. 209–222. Carbondale: Southern Illinois University at Carbondale Center for Archaeological Investigations Research Paper No. 39.

Ono, R., S. Soegondho, and M. Yoneda. 2009. Changing Marine Exploitation during Late Pleistocene in Northern Wallacea: Shell Remains from Leang Sarru Rockshelter in Talaud Islands. *Asian Perspectives* 48(2): 318–341.

Ørme, B. 1981. Anthropology for Archaeologists: An Introduction. London: Duckworth.

Orton, J. 2008. Later Stone Age Ostrich Eggshell Bead Manufacture in the Northern Cape, South Africa. *Journal of Archaeological Science* 35: 1765–1775.

O'Shea, J., and M. Zvelebil. 1984. Oleneostrovki Mogilnik: Reconstructing the Social and Economic Organization of Prehistoric Foragers in Northern Russia. *Journal of Anthropological Archaeology* 3(1): 1–40.

Oshibkina, S. V. 2008. Mesolithic Burial Grounds and Burial Complexes in the Forest Zone of Eastern Europe. *Anthropology & Archaeology of Eurasia* 46(4): 46–70.

Ottaway, B. 1973. Earliest Copper Ornaments in Northern Europe. *Proceedings of the Prehistoric Society* 39: 294–331.

Ottoni, C., L. Girdland Flink, A. Evin, C. Geörg, B. De Cupere, W. Van Neer, L. Bartosiewicz, A. Linderholm, R. Barnett, J. Peters, R. Decorte, M. Waelkens, N. Vanderheyden, F.-X. Ricaut, C. Çakırlar, Ö. Çevik, A.R. Hoelzel, M. Mashkour, A.F. Mohaseb Karimlu, S. Sheikhi Seno, J. Daujat, F. Brock, R. Pinhasi, H. Hongo, M. Perez-Enciso, M. Rasmussen, L. Frantz, H.-J. Megens, R. Crooijmans, M. Groenen, B. Arbuckle, N. Benecke, U. Strand Vidarsdottir, J. Burger, T. Cucchi, K. Dobney, and G. Larson. 2012. Pig Domestication and Human-Mediated Dispersal in Western Eurasia Revealed through Ancient DNA and Geometric Morphometrics. *Molecular Biology and Evolution* 30(4): 824–832.

Oudijk, M. R. and M. Castañeda de la Paz. 2017. Nahua Thought and the Conquest. In *The Oxford Handbook of the Aztecs,* D. L. Nichols and E. Rodríguez-Alegría (eds.). New York: Oxford University Press. http://www.oxfordhandbooks.com/view/10.1093/oxfordhb/9780199341962.001.0001/oxfordhb-9780199341962-e-6.

Ovchinnikov, I. V., A. Götherström, G. P. Romanova, V. M. Kharitonov, K. Lidén, and W. Goodwin. 2000. Molecular Analysis of Neanderthal DNA from the Northern Caucasus. *Nature* 404: 490–493.

Overmyer, D. L., D. N. Keightley, E. L. Shaughnessy, C A. Cook, and D. Harper. 1995. Introduction. *Journal of Asian Studies* 54(1): 124–160.

Pacheco, P. J. 1996. Ohio Hopewell Regional Settlement Patterns. In *A View from the Core: A Synthesis of Ohio*

Hopewell Archaeology, P. J. Pacheco (ed.), pp. 16–35. Columbus: The Ohio Archaeological Council.

Pacheco, P. J., and W. S. Dancey. 2006. Integrating Mortuary and Settlement Data on Ohio Hopewell Society. In *Recreating Hopewell*, D. K. Charles and J. E. Buikstra (eds.), pp. 3–25. Gainesville: University Press of Florida.

Pagani, L., D. J. Lawson, E. Jagoda, A. Mörseburg, A. Eriksson, M. Mitt, F. Clemente, G. Hudjashov, M. DeGiorgio, L. Saag, J. D. Wall, A. Cardona, R. Mägi, M. A. Wilson Sayres, S. Kaewert, C. Inchley, C. L. Scheib, M. Järve, M. Karmin, G. S. Jacobs, T. Antao, F. Mircea Iliescu, A. Kushniarevich, Q. Ayub, C. Tyler-Smith, Y. Xue, B. Yunusbayev, K. Tambets, C. B. Mallick, L. Saag, E. Pocheshkhova, G. Andriadze, C. Muller, M. C. Westaway, D. M. Lambert, G. Zoraqi, S. Turdikulova, D. Dalimova, Z. Sabitov, G. Nurun Nahar Sultana, J. Lachance, S. Tishkoff, K. Momynaliev, J. Isakova, L. D. Damba, M. Gubina, P. Nymadawa, I. Evseeva, L. Atramentova, O. Utevska, F.-X. Ricaut, N. Brucato, H. Sudoyo, T. Letellier, M. P. Cox, N. A. Barashkov, V. Škaro, L. Mulahasanović, D. Primorac, H. Sahakyan, M. Mormina, C. A. Eichstaedt, D. V. Lichman, S. Abdullah, G. Chaubey, J. T. S. Wee, E. Mihailov, A. Karunas, S. Litvinov, R. Khusainova, N. Ekomasova, V. Akhmetova, I. Khidiyatova, D. Marjanović, L. Yepiskoposyan, D. M. Behar, E. Balanovska, A. Metspalu, M. Derenko, B. Malyarchuk, B. Voevoda, S. A. Fedorova, L. P. Osipova, M. Mirazón Lahr, P. Gerbault, M. Leavesley, A. Bamberg Migliano, M. Petraglia, O. Balanovsky, E. K. Khusnutdinova, E. Metspalu, M. G. Thomas, A. Manica, R. Nielsen, R. Villems, E. Willerslev, T. Kivisild, and M. Metspalu. 2016. Genomic Analyses Inform on Migration Events during the Peopling of Eurasia. *Nature* 538: 238–242.

Page, A. E., S. Viguier, M. Dyble, D. Smith, N. Chaudhary, G. Deniz Salali, J. Thompson, L. Vinicius, R. Mace, and A. Bamberg Migliano. 2016. Reproductive Trade-Offs in Extant Hunter-Gatherers Suggest Adaptive Mechanism for the Neolithic Expansion. *Proceedings of the National Academy of Sciences USA* 113: 4694–4699.

Panger, M. A., A. S. Brooks, B. G. Richmond, and B. Wood. 2002. Older Than the Oldowan? Rethinking the Emergence of Hominin Tool Use. *Evolutionary Anthropology* 11: 235–245.

Parfitt, S. A., N. M. Ashton, S. G. Lewis, R. L. Abel, G. R. Coope, M. H. Field, R. Gale, P. G. Hoare, N. R. Larkin, M. D. Lewis, V. Karloukovski, B. A. Maher, S. M. Peglar, R. C. Preece, J. E. Whittaker, and C. B. Stringer. 2010. Early Pleistocene Human Occupation at the Edge of the Boreal Zone in Northwest Europe. *Nature* 466: 229–233.

Parfitt, S. A., R. W. Barendregt, M. Breda, I. Candy, M. J. Collins, G. R. Coope, P. Durbridge, M. H. Field, J. R. Lee, A. M. Lister, R. Mutch, K. E. H. Penkman, R. C. Preece, J. Rose, C. B. Stringer, R. Symmons, J. E. Whittaker, J. J. Wymer, and A J. Steward. 2005. The Earliest Record of Human Activity in Northern Europe. *Nature* 438: 1008–1012.

Parfitt, S. A., and M. B. Roberts. 1999. Human Modification of Faunal Remains. In *Boxgrove: A Middle Pleistocene Hominind Site at Eartham Quarry, Boxgrove, West Sussex*, M. B. Roberts and S. A. Parfitt (eds.), pp. 395–415. London: English Heritage Archaeological Report 17.

Paris, E. H., S. Serafin, M. A. Masson, C. P. Lope, C. V. Guzmán, and B. W. Russell. 2017. Violence, Desecration, and Urban Collapse at the Postclassic Maya Political Capital of Mayapán. *Journal of Anthropological Archaeology* 48: 63–86.

Parker Pearson, M. 1998. Stonehenge for the Ancestors: The Stones Pass on the Message. *Antiquity* 72: 308–326.

Parker Pearson, M., A. Chamberlain, M. Jay, P. Marshall, J. Pollard, C. Richards, J. Thomas, C. Tilley, and K. Welham. 2009. Who Was Buried as Stonehenge? *Antiquity* 83: 23–39.

Parker Pearson, M., J. Pollard, C. Richards, J. Thomas, K. Welham, R. Bevins, R. Ixer, P. Marshall, and A. Chamberlain. 2011. Stonehenge: Controversies of the Bluestones. *Menga: Revista de prehistoria de Andalucía* 1: 219–252.

Parkington, J., D. Morris, and N. Rusch. 2008. *Karoo Rock Engravings*. Cape Town: Krakadouw Trust.

Parpola, A. 1986. The Indus Script: A Challenging Puzzle. *World Archaeology* 17(3): 399–419.

Parpola, A. 1994. *Deciphering the Indus Script*. Cambridge, UK: Cambridge University Press.

Paschou, P., P. Drineas, E. Yannaki, A. Razou, K. Kanaki, F. Tsetsos, S. Sampath Padmanabhuni, M. Michalodimitrakis, M.C. Renda, S. Pavlovic, A. Anagnostopoulos, J.A. Stamatoyannopoulos, K.K. Kidd, and G. Stamatoyannopoulos. 2014. Maritime Route of Colonization of Europe. *Proceedings of the National Academy of Sciences USA* 111: 9211–9216.

Pastó, I., E. Allué, and J. Vallverdú. 2000. Mousterian Hearths at Abric Romaní, Catalonia (Spain). In *Neanderthals on the Edge: Papers from a Conference Marking the 150th Anniversary of the Forbes' Quarry Discovery, Gilbraltar,* C. B. Stringer, R. N. E. Barton, and J. C. Finlayson (eds.), pp. 59–67. Oxford: Oxbow Books.

Patel, S. S. 2010. The Indus Enigma. *Archaeology* 63(2): 18, 58–60, 65–66.

Pauketat, T. R. 1992. The Reign and Ruin of the Lords of Cahokia: A Dialectic of Dominance. In *Lords of the Southeast: Social Inequality and the Native Elites of Southeastern North America,* A. W. Barker and T. R. Pauketat (eds.), pp. 31–51. Washington, DC: Archeological Papers of the American Anthropological Association Number 3.

Pauketat, T. R. 2003. Resettled Farmers and the Making of a Mississippian Polity. *American Antiquity* 68(1): 39–66.

Pauketat, T. R. 2004. *Ancient Cahokia and the Mississippians.* New York: Cambridge University Press.

Pauketat, T. R. 2007. *Chiefdoms and Other Archaeological Delusions.* Lanham, MD: Altamira Press.

Pauketat, T. R. 2013. An Archaeology of the Cosmos: Rethinking Agency and Religion in Ancient America. New York: Routledge.

Pauketat, T. R., L. S. Kelly, G. J. Fritz, N. H. Lopinot, S. Elias, and E. Hargrave. 2002. The Residues of Feasting and Public Ritual at Early Cahokia. *American Antiquity* 67(2): 257–279.

Pearce, D. G., and A. Bonneau. 2018. Trouble on the Dating Scene. *Nature Ecology & Evolution* 2: 925–926.

Pearsall, D. M. 2008. Plant Domestication and the Shift to Agriculture in the Andes. In *Handbook of South American Archaeology,* H. Silverman and W. H. Isbell (eds.), pp. 105–120. New York: Springer.

Pearsall, D. M., K. Chandler-Ezell, and J. A. Zeidler. 2004. Maize in Ancient Ecuador: Results of Residue Analysis of Stone Tools from the Real Alto Site. *Journal of Archaeological Science* 31(4): 423–442.

Pearson, G. A., and J. W. Ream. 2005. Clovis on the Caribbean Coast of Venezuela. *Current Research in the Pleistocene* 22: 28–31.

Pei, G. 1985. Microlithic Industries in China. In *Palaeoanthropology and Palaeolithic Archaeology in the People's Republic of China,* W. Rukang and J. W. Olsen (eds.), pp. 225–241. New York: Academic Press.

Perry, L., R. Dickau, S. Zarillo, I. Holst, D. M. Pearsall, D. R. Piperno, M. J. Berman, R. G. Cooke, K. Rademaker, A. J. Ranere, J. S. Raymond, D. H. Sandweiss, F. Scaramelli, K. Tarble, and J. A. Zeidler. 2007. Starch Fossils and the Domestication and Dispersal of Chili Peppers (*Capsicum* spp. L.) in the Americas. *Science* 315: 986–988.

Peters, J., and K. Schmidt. 2004. Animals in the Symbolic World of Pre-Pottery Neolithic Göbekli Tepe, South-Eastern Turkey: A Preliminary Assessment. *Anthropozoologica* 39(1): 179–218.

Peterson, C. E., and G. Shelach. 2012. Jiangzhai: Social and Economic Organization of a Middle Neolithic Chinese Village. *Journal of Anthropological Archaeology* 31: 265–301.

Peterson, D. M., and G. H. Haug. 2005. Climate and the Collapse of Maya Civilization. *American Scientist* 93: 322–329.

Phillips, D. A., Jr. 2009. Adoption and Intensification of Agriculture in the North American Southwest: Notes toward a Quantitative Approach. *American Antiquity* 74(4): 691–707.

Phillips, D. A., Jr., H. J. Wearing, and J. J. Clark. 2018. Village Growth, Emerging Disease, and the End of the Neolithic Demographic Transition in the Southwest United States and Northwest Mexico. *American Antiquity* 83(2): 263–280.

Phillipson, D. W. 2005. *African Archaeology,* 3rd ed. New York: Cambridge University Press.

Pike, A. W. G., D. L. Hoffman, M. Garía-Diez, P. B. Pettitt, J. Alcolea, R. De Balbín, C. González-Sainz, C. de las Heras, J. A. Lasheras, R. Montes, and J. Zilhão. 2012. U-Series Dating of Paleolithic Art in 11 Caves in Spain. *Science* 336: 1409–1413.

Pikirayi, I. 2001. *The Zimbabwe Culture: Origins and Decline of Southern Zambezian States.* Walnut Creek, CA: Altamira Press.

Pinhasi, R., M. G. Thomas, M. Hofreiter, M. Currat, and J. Burger. 2012. The Genetic History of Europeans. *Trends in Genetics* 28(10): 496–505.

Pinson, A. O. 2011. The Clovis Occupation of the Dietz Site (35LK1529), Lake County, Oregon, and Its Bearing on the Adaptive Divesity of Clovis Foragers. *American Antiquity* 76(2): 285–313.

Piperno, D. R. 2011. The Origins of Plant Cultivation and Domestication in the New World Tropics. Patterns, Process, and New Developments. *Current Anthropology* 52(Suppl. 4): S453–S470.

Piperno, D. R., and K. V. Flannery. 2001. The Earliest Archaeological Maize (*Zea mays* L.) from Highland

Mexico: New Accelerator Mass Spectrometry Dates and Their Implications. *Proceedings of the National Academy of Sciences USA* 98: 2101–2103.

Piperno, D. R., J. E. Moreno, J. Iriarte, I. Holst, M. Lachniet, J. G. Jones, A. J. Ranere, and R. Castanzo. 2007. Late Pleistocene and Holocene Environmental History of the Iquala Valley, Central Balsas Watershed of Mexico. *Proceedings of the National Academy of Sciences USA* 104: 11874–11881.

Piperno, D. R., A. J. Ranere, I. Holst, J. Iriarte, and R. Dickau. 2009. Starch Grain and Phytolith Evidence for Early Ninth Millennium B.P. Maize from the Central Balsas River Valley, Mexico. *Proceedings of the National Academy of Sciences USA* 106: 5019–5024.

Piperno, D. R., E. Weiss, I. Holst, and D. Nadel. 2004. Processing of Wild Cereal Grains in the Upper Paleolithic Revealed by Starch Grain Analysis. *Nature* 430: 670–673.

Pitblado, B. L. 2011. A Tale of Two Migrations: Reconciling Recent Biological and Archaeologial Evidence for the Pleistocene Peopling of the Americas. *Journal of Archaeological Research* 19: 327–375.

Pitblado, B. L. 2017. The Role of the Rocky Mountains in the Peopling of North America. *Quaternary International* 461: 54–79.

Pitulko, V. V., P. A. Nikolsky, E. Yu. Girya, A. E. Basilyan, V. E. Tumskoy, S. A. Koulakov, S. N. Astakhov, E. Yu. Pavlova, and M. A. Anisimov. 2004. The Yana RS Site: Humans in the Arctic before the Last Glacial Maximum. *Science* 303: 52–56.

Plog, S., C. C. Heitman, and A. S. Watson. 2017. Key Dimensions of the Cultural Trajectories of Chaco Canyon. In *The Oxford Handbook of Southwest Archaeology*, B. Mills and S. Fowles (eds.). New York: Oxford University Press. Oxford Handbooks Online: doi:10.1093/oxfordhb/9780199978427.013.15

Plog, S., and A. S. Watson. 2012. The Chaco Pilgrimage Model: Evaluating the Evidence from Pueblo Alto. *American Antiquity* 77(3): 449–477.

Plunket, P., and G. Uruñuela. 2010. Where East Meets West: The Formative in Mexico's Central Highlands. *Journal of Archaeological Research* 20(1): 1–51.

Pohl, M. E. D., D. R. Piperno, K. O. Pope, and J. G. Jones. 2007. Microfossil Evidence for Pre-Columbian Maize Dispersals in the Neotropics from San Andrés. *Proceedings of the National Academy of Sciences USA* 104: 6870–6875.

Pohl, M. D., K. O. Pope, J. G. Jones, J. S. Jacob, D. R. Piperno, S. D. deFrance, D. L. Lentz, J. A. Gifford, M. E. Danforth, and J. K. Josserand. 1996. Early Agriculture in the Maya Lowlands. *Latin American Antiquity* 7(4): 355–372.

Pokharia, A. K., J. S. Kharakwal, and A. Srivastava. 2014. Archaeobotanical Evidence of Millets in the Indian Subcontinent with Some Observations on Their Role in the Indus Civilization. *Journal of Archaeological Science* 42: 442–455.

Pollock, S. 1991. Of Priestesses, Princes and Poor Relations: The Dead in the Royal Cemetery at Ur. *Cambridge Archaeological Journal* 1(2): 171–189.

Pollock, S. 1999. *Ancient Mesopotamia. The Eden That Never Was.* New York: Cambridge University Press.

Pomeroy, E., M. Mirazón Lahr, F. Crivellaro, L. Farr, T. Reynolds, C. O. Hunt, and G. Barker. 2017. Newly Discovered Neanderthal Remains from Shanidar Cave, Iraqi Kurdistan, and Their Attribution to Shanidar 5. *Journal of Human Evolution* 111: 102–118.

Pope, G. 1989. Bamboo and Human Evolution. *Natural History* 98(10): 48–57.

Portal, J. (ed.). 2007. *The First Emperor: China's Terracotta Army.* London: British Museum Press.

Possehl, G. L. 1990. Revolution in the Urban Revolution: The Emergence of Harappan Urbanism. *Annual Review of Anthropology* 19: 261–282.

Possehl, G. L. 2002a. Harappans and Hunters: Economic Interaction and Specialization in Prehistoric India. In *Forager–Traders in South and Southeast Asia. Long Term Histories*, K. D. Morrison and L. L. Junker (eds.), pp. 62–76. New York: Cambridge University Press.

Possehl, G. L. 2002b. *The Indus Civilization. A Contemporary Perspective.* New York: Altamira Press.

Possehl, G. L. 2007. The Middle Asian Interaction Sphere: Trade and Contact in the 3rd Millennium BC. *Expedition* 49(1): 40–42.

Potter, B. A., J. D. Reuther, V. T. Holliday, C. E. Holmes, D. S. Miller, and N. Schmuck. 2017. Early Colonization of Beringia and Northern North America: Chronology, Routes, and Adaptive Strategies. *Quaternary International* 444: 36–55.

Potter, J. M. 1997. Communal Ritual and Faunal Remains: An Example from the Dolores Anasazi. *Journal of Field Archaeology* 24(3): 353–364.

Potter, J. M. 2011. Durango Basketmaker II Redux: New Data from the Animas-La Plata Project. *Kiva* 76(4): 431–452.

Potter, J. M., and S. G. Ortman. 2004. Community and Cuisine in the Prehispanic American Southwest. In *Identity, Feasting, and the Archaeology of the Greater Southwest*, B. J. Mills (ed.), pp. 173–191. Boulder: University Press of Colorado.

Potter, J. M., and E. M. Perry. 2011. Mortuary Features and Identity Construction in an Early Village Community in the American Southwest. *American Antiquity* 76(3): 529–546.

Potts, R. 1984. Home Bases and Early Hominids: Reevaluation of the Fossil Record at Olduvai Gorge Suggests That the Concentrations of Bones and Stone Tools Do Not Represent Fully Formed Campsites But an Antecedent to Them. *American Scientist* 72(4): 338–347.

Potts, R. 1991. Why the Oldowan? Plio-Pleistocene Toolmaking and the Transport of Resources. *Journal of Anthropological Research* 47(2): 153–176.

Potts, R., A. K. Behrensmeyer, and P. Ditchfield. 1999. Paleolandscape Variation and Early Pleistocene Hominid Activities: Members 1 and 7, Olorgesailie Formation, Kenya. *Journal of Human Evolution* 37: 747–788.

Power, R. C., D. C. Salazar-García, M. Rubini, A. Darlas, K. Harvati, M. Walker, J.-J. Hublin, and A. G. Henry. 2018. Dental Calculus Indicates Wide-Spread Plant Use Within the Stable Neanderthal Dietary Niche. *Journal of Human Evolution* 119: 27–41.

Powis, T. G., W. J. Hurst, M. del Carmen Rodríguez, P. Ortíz Ceballos, M. Blake, D. Cheetham, M. D. Coe, and J. G. Hodgson. 2007. Oldest Chocolate in the World. *Antiquity* 81(314). Project Gallery: http://www.antiquity.ac.uk/projgall/powis314/ (accessed July 28, 2018).

Pozorski, T., and S. Pozorski. 1993. Early Complex Society and Ceremonialism on the Peruvian North Coast. *Senri Ethnological Studies* 37: 45–68.

Pozorski, T., and S. Pozorski. 1994. Early Andean Cities. *Scientific American* 270(6): 66–72.

Prendergast, M. E., J. Yuan, and O. Bar-Yosef. 2009. Resource Intensification in the Late Upper Paleolithic: A View from Southern China. *Journal of Archaeological Science* 36: 1027–1037.

Preucel, R. W., and C. N. Cipolla. 2008. Indigenous and Postcolonial Archaeologies. In *Archaeology and the Postcolonial Critique*, M. Liebmann and U. Z. Rizvi, pp. 129–140. Lanham, MD: Altamira Press.

Price, T. D. 1989. Willow Tales and Dog Smoke. *Review of Archaeology* 10(1): 107–113 [reprinted from *The Quarterly Review of Archaeology* 3(1), 1982].

Price, T. D. 2000. The Introduction of Farming in Northern Europe. In *Europe's First Farmers*, T. D. Price (ed.), pp. 260–318. New York: Cambridge University Press.

Price, T. D., S. Plog, S. A. LeBlanc, and J. Krigbaum. 2017. Great House Origins and Population Stability at Pueblo Bonito, Chaco Canyon, New Mexico: The Isotopic Evidence. *Journal of Archaeological Science: Reports* 11: 261–273.

Pruetz, J. D., and P. Bertolani. 2007. Savana Chimpanzees, *Pan troglodytes* verus, Hunt with Tools. *Current Biology* 17(5): 412–417.

Pruetz, J. D., and P. Bertolani. 2009. Chimpanzee (*Pan troglodytes verus*) Behavioral Responses to Stresses Associated with Living in a Savanna-Mosaic Environment: Implications for Hominin Adaptations to Open Habitats. *PaleoAnthropology* 2009: 252–262.

Puleston, D. E., and D. W. Callender Jr. 1967. Defensive Earthworks at Tikal. *Expedition* 9(3): 40–48.

Pyburn, K. A. 2008. Pomp and Circumstance before Belize. Ancient Maya Commerce and the New River Conurbation. In *The Ancient City. New Perspectives on Urbanism in the Old and New Worlds*, J. Marcus and J. A. Sabloff (eds.), pp. 247–272. Santa Fe, NM: School for Advanced Research Press.

Quiles, A., H. Valladas, H. Bocherens, E. Delqué-Količ, E. Kaltnecker, J. van der Plicht, J.-J. Delannoy, V. Feruglio, C. Fritz, J. Monney, M. Philippe, G. Tosello, J. Clottes, and J.-M. Geneste. 2016. A High-Precision Chronological Model for the Decorated Cave of Chavet-Pont d'Arc, Ardèche, France. *Proceedings of the National Academy of Sciences USA* 113: 4670–4675.

Quilter, J. 1985. Architecture and Chronology at El Paraíso, Peru. *Journal of Field Archaeology* 12(3): 274–298.

Quilter, J. 2002. Moche Politics, Religion, and Warfare. *Journal of World Prehistory* 16(2): 145–195.

Quilter, J., and M. L. Koons 2012. The Fall of the Moche: A Critique of Claims for South America's First State. *Latin American Antiquity* 23(2): 127–143.

Rabinovich, R., and E. Hovers. 2004. Faunal Analysis from Amud Cave: Preliminary Results and Interpretations. *International Journal of Osteoarchaeology* 14: 287–306.

Radovčič, D., A. O. Sršen, J. Radovčič, and D. W. Frayer. 2015. Evidence for Neandertal Jewelry: Modified White-Tailed Eagle Claws at Krapina. *PLoS One* 10(3): e0119802.

Rae, T. C., T. Koppe, and C. B. Stringer. 2011. The Neanderthal Face Is Not Cold-Adapted. *Journal of Human Evolution* 60: 234–239.

Raff, J. A., and D. A. Bolnick. 2014. Genetic Roots of the First Americans. *Nature* 506: 162–163.

Raghavan, M., Po. Skoglund, K. E. Graf, M. Metspalu, A. Albrechtsen, I. Moltke, S. Rasmussen, T. W. Stafford Jr., L. Orlando, E. Metspalu, M. Karmin, K. Tambets, S. Rootsi, R. Mägil, P. F. Campos, E. Balanovska, O. Balanovsky, E. Khusnutdinova, S. Litvinov, L. P. Osipova, S. A. Fedorova, M. I. Voevoda, M. DeGiorgio, T. Sicheritz-Ponten, S. Brunak, S. Demeshchenko, T. Kivisild, R. Villems, R. Nielsen, M. Jakobsson, and E. Willerslev. 2014. Upper Palaeolithic Siberian Genome Reveals Dual Ancestry of Native Americans. *Nature* 505: 87–91.

Ranere, A. J., D. R. Piperno, I. Holst, R. Dickau, and J. Iriarte. 2009. The Cultural and Chronological Context of Early Holocene Maize and Squash Domestication in the Central Balsas River Valley, Mexico. *Proceedings of the National Academy of Sciences USA* 106: 5014–5018.

Rao, R. P. N., N. Yadev, M. N. Nahia, H. Joglekar, R. Adhikari, and I. Mahadevan. 2009. A Markov Model of the Indus Script. *Proceedings of the National Academy of Sciences USA* 106: 13685–13690.

Rasmussen, M., S. L. Anzick, M. R. Waters, P. Skoglund, M. De-Giorgio, T. W. Stafford Jr., S. Rasmussen, I. Moltke, A. Albrechtsen, S. M. Doyle, G. D. Poznik, V. Gundmundsdottir, R. Yadav, A.-S. Malaspinas, S. S. White V, M. E. Allentoft, O. E. Cornejo, K. Tambets, A. Eriksson, P. D. Heintzman, M. Karmin, T. S. Korneliussen, D. J. Meltzer, T. L. Pierre, J. Stenderup, L. Saag, V. M. Warmuth, M. C. Lopes, R. S. Malhi, S. Brunak, T. Sicheritz-Ponten, I. Barnes, M. Collins, L. Orlando, F. Balloux. A. Manica, R. Gupta, M. Metspalu, C. D. Bustamante, M. Jakobsson, R. Nielson, and E. Willerslev. 2014. The Genome of a Late Pleistocene Human from a Clovis Burial Site in Western Montana. *Nature* 506: 225–229.

Ratnagar, S. 2003. Theorizing Bronze-Age Intercultural Trade: The Evidence of the Weights. *Paléorient* 29(1): 79–92.

Rawson, J. in press. Ordering the Material World of the Western Zhou. *Archaeological Research in Asia*.

Ray, J. D. 1986. The Emergence of Writing in Egypt. *World Archaeology* 17(3): 307–316.

Raymond, J. S. 2003. Social Formations in the Western Lowlands of Ecuador during the Early Formative. In *Archaeology of Formative Ecuador*, J. S. Raymond and R. L. Burger (eds.), pp. 33–67. Washington, DC: Dumbarton Oaks.

Redding, R. W. 2013. A Tale of Two Sites: Old Kingdom Subsistence Economy and the Infrastructure of Pyramid Construction. In *Archaeozoology of the Near East X, Proceedings of the Tenth International Symposium on the Archaeozoology of Southwestern Asia and Adjacent Areas*, B. De Cupere, V. Linseele, and S. Hamilton-Dyer (eds.), pp. 307–322. Walpole, MA: Peeters.

Redmond, E. M., and C. S. Spencer. 2006. From Raiding to Conquest. Warfare Strategies and Early State Development in Oaxaca, Mexico. In *The Archaeology of Warfare. Prehistories of Raiding and Conquest*, E. N. Arkush and M. W. Allen (eds.), pp. 336–393. Gainesville: University Press of Florida.

Redmond, E. M., and C. S. Spencer. 2017. Ancient Palace Complex (300–100 BC) Discovered in the Valley of Oaxaca, Mexico. *Proceedings of the National Academy of Sciences USA* 114: 3805–3814.

Reents-Buder, D. 2006. The Social Context of *Kakaw* Drinking among the Ancient Maya. In *Chocolate in Mesoamerica. A Cultural History of Cacao*, C. L. McNeil (ed.), pp. 202–223. Gainesville: University Press of Florida.

Reich, D., N. Patterson, M. Kircher, F. Delfin, M. R. Nandineni, I. Pugach, A. M.-S. Ko, Y-C. Ko, T. A. Jinam, M. E. Phipps, N. Saitou, A. Wollstein, M. Kayser, S. Pääbo, and M. Stoneking. 2011. Denisova Admixture and the First Modern Human Dispersals into Southeast Asia and Oceania. *American Journal of Human Genetics* 89(4): 516–528.

Reid, J. J., R. Welch, B. K. Montgomery, and M. N. Zedeño. 1996. A Demographic Overview of the Late Pueblo III Period in the Mountains of East-Central Arizona. In *The Prehistoric Pueblo World, AD 1150–1350*, M.A. Adler (ed.), pp. 73–85. Tucson: University of Arizona Press.

Reimer, P.J., E. Bard, A. Bayliss, J. W. Beck, P. G. Blackwell, C. Bronk Ramsey, C. E. Buck, H. Cheng, R. L. Edwards, M. Friedrich, P. M. Grootes, T. P. Guilderson, H. Haflidason,

I. Hajdas, C. Hatté, T. J. Heaton, D. L. Hoffmann, A. G. Hogg, K. A. Hughen, K. F. Kaiser, B. Kromer, S. W. Manning, M. Niu, R. W. Reimer, D. A. Richards, E. M. Scott, J. R. Southon, R. A. Staff, C. S. M. Turney, and J. van der Plict,. 2013. IntCal13 and Marine13 Radiocarbon Age Calibration Curves, 0–50000 Years cal BP. *Radiocarbon* 55: 1169–1887.

Reinhard, J. 1998. Research Update: New Inca Mummies. *National Geographic Magazine* 194(1): 128–135.

Reinhard, J. 2016. Frozen Mummies of the Andes. *Expedition* 58(2) 8–12.

Reitz, E. J., H. E. McInnis, D. H. Sandweiss, and S. D. deFrance. 2016. Terminal Pleistocene and Early Holocene Fishing Strategies at Quebrada Jaguay and the Ring Site, Southern Peru. *Journal of Archaeological Science: Reports* 8, 447–453.

Relethford, J. H. 2001. Absence of Regional Affinities of Neandertal DNA with Living Humans Does Not Reject Multiregional Evolution. *American Journal of Physical Anthropology* 115: 95–98

Ren, X., X. Lemoine, D. Mo, T. R. Kidder, Y. Guo, Z. Qin, and X. Liu. 2016. Foothills and Intermountain Mountains: Does China's Fertile Arc Have 'Hilly Flanks'? *Quaternary International* 426: 86–96.

Rendu, W., C. Beauval, I. Crevecoeur, P. Bayle, A. Balzeau, T. Bismuth, L. Bourguignon, G. Delfour, J.-P. Faivre, F. Lacrampe-Cuyaubère, C. Tavormina, D. Todisco, A. Turq, and B. Maureille. 2014. Evidence Supporting an Intentional Neandertal Burial at La Chapelle-aux-Saints. *Proceedings of the National Academy of Sciences USA* 111: 81–86.

Renfrew, C. 1983. The Social Archaeology of Megalithic Monuments. *Scientific American* 249: 152–163.

Reno, P., R. Meindl, M. McCollum, and C. O. Lovejoy. 2003. Sexual Dimorphism in *Australopithecus afarensis* Was Similar to That of Modern Humans. *Proceedings of the National Academy of Sciences USA* 100: 9404–9409.

Restelli, F. B. 2001. *Formation Processes of the First Developed Neolithic Societies in the Zagros and the Northern Mesopotamian Plain*. Studi di Preistoria Orientale, Vol. 1. Rome: Visceglia.

"Rethinking the Origins of Agriculture" (all articles). 2009. *Current Anthropology* 50(5).

Revedin, A., B. Aranguren, R. Becattini, L. Longo, E. Marconi, M. M. Lippi, N. Skakun, A. Sinitsyn, E. Spiridonova, and J. Svoboda. 2010. Thirty Thousand-Year-Old Evidence of Plant Food Processing. *Proceedings of the National Academy of Science USA* 107(44): 18815–18819.

Rhode, D., Z. Haiying, D. B. Madsen, G. Xing, P. J. Brantingham, M. Haizhou, and J. W. Olsen. 2007. Epipaleolithic/Early Neolithic Settlements at Qinghai Lake, Western China. *Journal of Archaeological Science* 34: 600–612.

Rice, P. C. 1981. Prehistoric Venuses: Symbols of Motherhood or Womanhood? *Journal of Anthropological Research* 37(4): 402–416.

Rice, P. M. 2007. The Classic Maya "Collapse" and Its Causes: The Role of Warfare? In *Gordon R. Willey and American Archaeology: Contemporary Perspectives*, J. A. Sabloff and W. L. Fash (eds.), pp. 141–186. Norman: University of Oklahoma Press.

Rice, P. M. 2009. On Classic Maya Political Economies. *Journal of Anthropological Archaeology* 28: 70–84.

Richards, M. P., P. B. Pettitt, E. Trinkaus, F. Smith, M. Paunovic, and I. Karavanić. 2000. Neanderthal Diet at Vindija and Neanderthal Predation: The Evidence from Stable Isotopes. *Proceedings of the National Academy of Sciences USA* 97: 7663–7666.

Richerson. P. J., R. Boyd, and R. L. Bettinger. 2001. Was Agriculture Impossible during the Pleistocene but Mandatory during the Holocene? A Climate Change Hypothesis. *American Antiquity* 66(3): 387–411.

Richmond, B. G., and W. L. Jungers. 1995. Size Variation and Sexual Dimorphism in *Australopithecus afarensis* and Living Hominoids. *Journal of Human Evolution* 29: 229–245.

Richter, D., R. Grün, R. Joannes-Boyau, T. E. Steele, F. Amani, M. Rué, P. Fernandes, J.-P. Raynal, D. Geraads, A. Ben-Ncer, J.-J. Hublin, and S. P. McPherron. 2017. The Age of the Hominin Fossils from Jebel Irhoud, Morocco, and the Origins of the Middle Stone Age. *Nature* 546: 293–296.

Richter, D., and M. Krbetschek. 2015. The Age of the Lower Paleolithic Occupation at Schöningen. *Journal of Human Evolution* 89: 46–56.

Richter, J., and N. Noe-Nygaard. 2003. A Late Mesolithic Hunting Station at Agernæs, Fyn, Denmark. *Acta Archaeologica* 74(1): 1–64.

Richter, T., A. Garrard, S. Allcock, and L. Maher. 2011. Interaction before Agriculture: Exchanging Material and Sharing Knowledge in the Final Pleistocene Levant. *Cambridge Archaeological Journal* 21(1): 95–114.

Richter, T., L. Maher, A. Garrard, K. Edinborough, M. Jones, and J. Stock. 2013. Epipalaeolithic Settlement Dynamics in Southwest Asia: Radiocarbon Evidence from the Azraq Basin. *Journal of Quaternary Science* 28(5): 467–479.

Rick, J. W. 2005. The Evolution of Authority at Chavín de Huántar. In *The Foundations of Power in the Prehispanic Andes*, Vaughn, K. J., D. E. Ogburn, and C. A. Conlee (eds.), pp. 71–89. Washington, DC: American Anthropological Association Archeological Papers No. 14.

Rick, J. W., and D. Lubman. 2002. Characteristics and Speculations on the Uses of *Strombus* Trumpets at the Ancient Peruvian Center Chavín de Huántar. *Journal of the Acoustical Society of America* 112(5). https://doi.org/10.1121/1.4779586.

Rigaud, J.-P., J. Simek, and T. Ge. 1995. Mousterian Fires from Grotte XVI (Dordogne, France). *Antiquity* 69: 902–912.

Riggs, C. R. 2001. *The Architecture of Grasshopper Pueblo.* Salt Lake City: University of Utah Press.

Riggs, C. R. 2005. Late Ancestral Pueblo or Mogollon Pueblo? An Architectural Perspective on Identity. *Kiva* (70(4): 323–348.

Robb, J., and O. T. Harris. 2018. Becoming Gendered in European Prehistory: Was Neolithic Gender Fundamentally Different? *American Antiquity* 83(1): 128–147.

Roberts, F. H. H. 1929. *Shabik'eschee Village: A Late Basketmaker Site in the Chaco Canyon.* Washington, DC: Bureau of American Ethnology Bulletin No. 92 [reprinted: 1979; Lincoln, NE: J & L Reprint Company].

Roberts, M. B., and S. A. Parfitt. 1999. *Boxgrove: A Middle Pleistocene Hominind Site at Eartham Quarry, Boxgrove, West Sussex.* London: English Heritage Archaeological Report 17.

Roberts, R. G., K. E. Westaway, J. X. Zhao, C. S. M. Turney, M. I. Bird, W. J. Rink, and L. K. Fifield. 2009. Geochronology of Cave Deposits at Liang Bua and of Adjacent River Terraces in the Wae Racang Valley, Western Flores, Indonesia: A Synthesis of Age Estimates for the Type Locality of *Homo floresiensis. Journal of Human Evolution* 57: 484–502.

Robinson, A. 2015. Cracking the Indus Script. *Nature* 526: 499–501.

Roebroeks, W. 2005. Life on the Costa del Cromer. *Nature* 438: 921–922.

Rohn, A. H. 1977. *Cultural Change and Continuity on Chapin Mesa.* Lawrence: Regents Press of Kansas.

Rollefson, G. O. 1997. Changes in Architecture and Social Organization at 'Ain Ghazal. In *The Prehistory of Jordan II: Perspectives from 1997*, H. G. Gebel, Z. Kafafi, and G. Rollefson (eds.), pp. 287–308. Berlin: *ex oriente.*

Rollefson, G. O. 1998. 'Ain Ghazal (Jordan): Ritual and Ceremony III. *Paléorient* 24(1): 43–58.

Rollefson, G. O., and A. H. Simmons. 1987. The Life and Death of 'Ain Ghazal. *Archaeology* (November/December): 38–45.

Rolston, S. L. 1982. Two Prehistoric Burials from Qasr Kharaneh. *Annual of the Department of Antiquities of Jordan* 26: 221–229.

Roosevelt, A. C., M. Lima da Costa, C. Lopes Machado, M. Michab, N. Mercier, H. Valladas, J. Feathers, W. Barnett, M. Imazio da Silveira, A. Henderson, J. Silva, B. Chernoff, D. S. Reese, J. A. Holman, N. Toth, and K. Schick. 1996. Paleoindian Cave Dwellers in the Amazon: The Peopling of the Americas. *Science* 272: 373–384.

Rose, L., and F. Marshall. 1996. Meat Eating, Hominid Sociality, and Home Bases Revisited. *Current Anthropology* 37: 307–338.

Rosen, A. M. 2007. *Civilizing Climate. Social Responses to Climate Change in the Ancient Near East.* New York: Altamira Press.

Rosen, A. M., and I. Rivera-Collazo. 2012. Climate Change, Adaptive Cycles, and Persistence of Foraging Economies during the Late Pleistocene/Holocene Transition in the Levant. *Proceedings of the National Academy of Sciences USA* 109: 3640–3645.

Rosenswig, R. M. 2006. Sedentism and Food Production in Early Complex Societies of the Soconusco, Mexico. *World Archaeology* 38(2): 330–355.

Rosenswig, R. M., A. M. VanDerwarker, B. J. Culleton, and D. J. Kennett. 2015. Is It Agriculture Yet? Intensified Maize-Use at 1000 cal BC in the Soconusco and Mesoamerica. *Journal of Anthropological Archaeology* 40: 89–108.

Rossignol-Strick, M. 2002. Holocene Climatic Changes in the Eastern Mediterranean and the Spread of Food Production from Southwest Asia to Egypt. In *Droughts, Food and Culture. Ecological Change and Food Security in Africa's Later Prehistory*, F. A. Hassan (ed.), pp. 157–169. New York: Kluwer Academic/Plenum.

Roth, B. J., and A. Freeman. 2008. The Middle Archaic Period and the Transition to Agriculture in the Sonoran Desert of Southern Arizona. *Kiva* 73(3): 321–353.

Rothman, M. S. (ed.). 2001. *Uruk Mesopotamia and Its Neighbors: Cross-Cultural Interactions in the Era of State Formation*. Santa Fe, NM: School of American Research Press.

Rothman, M. S. 2004. Studying the Development of Complex Society: Mesopotamia in the Late Fifth and Fourth Millennium BC. *Journal of Archaeological Research* 12(1): 75–119.

Rothschild, N. A. 1979. Mortuary Behavior and Social Organization at Indian Knoll and Dickson Mouns. *American Antiquity* 44(4): 658–675.

Rothfield, L. 2009. *The Rape of Mesopotamia: Behind the Looting of the Iraq Museum*. Chicago: University of Chicago Press.

Rowley-Conwy, P. 1984. The Laziness of the Short-Distance Hunter: The Origins of Agriculture in Western Denmark. *Journal of Anthropological Archaeology* 3: 300–324.

Ruby, B. J., C. Carr, and D. K. Charles. 2005. Community Organizations in the Scioto, Mann, and Havana Hopewellian Regions. In *Gathering Hopewell: Society, Ritual, and Ritual Interpretation*, C. Carr and D. T. Case (eds.), pp. 119–176. New York: Kluwer Academic/Plenum.

Rudner, J. 1971. Painted Burial Stones from the Cape. *South African Journal of Science*, special issue 2: 54–61.

Ruff, C. B. 1993. Climatic Adaptation and Hominid Evolution: The Thermoregulatory Imperative. *Evolutionary Anthropology* 2: 65–107.

Ruggles, C., and N. J. Saunders. 2012. Desert Labrynith: Lines, Landscape and Meaing at Nazca, Peru. *Antiquity* 86: 1126–1140.

Rumold, C. U., and M. S. Aldenderfer. 2016. Late Archaic–Early Formative Period Microbotanical Evidence for Potato at Jiskairumoko in the Titicaca Basin of Southern Peru. *Proceedings of the National Academy of Sciences USA* 113: 13672–13677.

Russo, M. 2006. *Archaic Shell Rings of the Southeast U.S.* Tallahasse, FL: Southeast Archaeological Center, National Park Service. https://www.nps.gov/history/nhl/learn/themes/ArchaicShellRings.pdf (accessed July 28, 2018).

Russo, M. 2008. Late Archaic Shell Rings and Society in the Southeast U.S. *SAA Archaeological Record* 8(5): 18–22.

Rust, W. F., and R. J. Sharer. 1988. Olmec Settlement Data from La Venta, Tabasco. *Science* 242: 102–104.

Sabloff, J. 2008. *Archaeology Matters: Action Archaeology in the Modern World*. Walnut Creek, CA: Left Coast Press.

Sahlins, M. 1992. *Anahulu: The Anthropology of History in the Kingdom of Hawaii*. Vol. 1: *Historical Ethnography*. Chicago: University of Chicago Press.

Samuels, M. L., and J. L. Betancourt. 1982. Modeling the Long-Term Effects of Fuelwood Harvests on Piñon-Juniper Woodlands. *Environmental Management* 6: 505–515.

Samzun, A., and P. Sellier. 1985. First Anthropological and Cultural Evidences for the Funerary Practices of the Chalcolithic Population of Mehrgarh, Pakistan. In *South Asian Archaeology 1983*, Vol. 1, J. Schotsman and M. Taddei (eds.), pp. 91–119. Naples: Istituto Universitario Orientale.

Sanchez, G., V. T. Holliday, E. P. Gaines, J. Arroyo-Cabrales, N. Martínez-Tagüeña, A. Kowler, T. Lange, G. W. L. Hodgins, S. M. Mentzer, and I. Sanchez-Morales. 2014. Human (Clovis)-Gomphothere (*Cuvieronius* sp.) Association ~13,390 calibrated yBP in Sonora, Mexico. *Proceedings of the National Academy of Sciences USA* 111: 10972–10977.

Sanchez, J. L. J. 2005. Ancient Maya Royal Strategies: Creating Power and Identity through Art. *Ancient Mesoamerica* 16: 261–275.

Sanchez, M. G. 2001. A Synopsis of Paleo-Indian Archaeology in Mexico. *Kiva* 67(2): 119–136.

Sánchez-Quinto, F., L. R. Botigué, S. Civit, C. Arenas, M. C. Ávila-Arcos, C. D. Bustamante, D. Comas, and C. Lalueza-Fox. 2012. North African Populations Carry the Signature of Admixture with Neandertals. *PLoS One* 7(10): e47765.

Sanders, W. T. 2008. Tenochtitlan in 1519: A Preindustrial Megalopolis. In *The Aztec World*, E. M. Brumfiel and G. M. Feinman (eds.), pp. 67–86. New York: Harry N. Abrams.

Sandier, B., J.-J. Delannoy, L. Benedetti, D. L. Bourlès, S. Jaillet, J.-M. Geneste, A.-E. Lebatard, and M. Arnold. 2012. Further Constraints on the Chauvet Cave Artwork Elaboration. *Proceedings of the National Academy of Sciences USA* 109: 8002–8006.

Sandgathe, D. M., H. L. Dibble, P. Goldberg, and S. P. McPherron. 2011. The Roc de Marsal Neandertal Child: A Reassessment of its Status as a Deliberate Burial. *Journal of Human Evolution* 61(3): 243–253.

Sandweiss, D. H., H. McInnis, R. L. Burger, A. Cano, B. Ojeda, R. Paredes, M. del Carmen Sandweiss, and M. D. Glascock. 1998. Quebrada Jaguay: Early South American Maritime Adaptations. *Science* 281: 1830–1832.

Sarmiento, E. E. 2010. Comment on the Paleobiology and Classification of *Ardipithecus ramidus*. *Science* 328: 1105-b.

Sassaman, K. E. 2005a. Poverty Point as Structure, Event, Process. *Journal of Archaeological Method and Theory* 12(4): 335–364.

Sassaman, K. E. 2005b. The Social Contradictions of Traditional and Innovative Cooking Technologies in the Prehistoric American Southeast. In *The Emergence of Pottery: Technology and Innovation in Ancient Societies*, W. K. Barnett and J. W. Hoopes (eds.), pp. 223–240. Washington, DC: Smithsonian Institution Press.

Saunders, J. W., R. D. Mandel, C. G. Sampson, C. M. Allen, E. T. Allen, D. A. Bush, J. K. Feathers, K. J. Gremillion, C. T. Hallmark, H. E. Jackson, J. K. Johnson, R. Jones, R. T. Saucier, G. L. Stringer, and M. F. Vidrine. 2005. Watson Brake, a Middle Archaic Mound Complex in Northeast Louisiana. *American Antiquity* 70(4): 631–668.

Savard, M., M. Nesbitt, and R. Gale. 2003. Archaeobotanical Evidence for Early Neolithic Diet and Subsistence at M'lefaat (Iraq). *Paléorient* 29(1): 93–106.

Sayers, K., and C. O. Lovejoy. 2008. The Chimpanzee Has No Clothes. A Critical Examiniatino of *Pan troglodytes* in Models of Human Evolution. *Current Anthropology* 49(1): 87–114.

Scarre, C. 1996. The European Neolithic Period. In *The Oxford Companion to Archaeology*, B. Fagan (ed.), pp. 215–216. New York: Oxford University Press.

Scarre, C. 2013. Holocene Europe. In *The Human Past: World Prehistory & the Development of Human Societies*, 3rd ed., pp. 392–431. London: Thames & Hudson.

Schachner, G. 2010. Corporate Group Formation and Differentiation in Early Puebloan Villages of the American Southwest. *American Antiquity* 75(3): 473–496.

Scheinsohn, V. 2004. Hunter–Gatherer Archaeology in South America. *Annual Review of Anthropology* 32: 339–361.

Schmandt-Besserat, D. 2007. *When Writing Met Art. From Symbol to Story*. Austin: University of Texas Press.

Schmidt, K. 2001. Göbekli Tepe, Southeastern Turkey. A Preliminary Report on the 1995–1999 Excavations. *Paléorient* 26(1): 45–54.

Schmidt, K. 2002. The 2002 Excavations at Göbekli Tepe (Southeastern Turkey): Impressions from an Enigmatic Site. *Neo-Lithics* 2/06: 38–40.

Schmidt, K. 2006. Animals and a Headless Man at Göbekli Tepe. *Neo-Lithics* 2/02: 8–13.

Schoch, W. H., G. Bigga, U. Böhner, P. Richter, and T. Terberger. 2015. New Insights on the Wooden Weapons from the Paleolithic Site of Schöningen. *Journal of Human Evolution* 89: 214–225.

Schoeman, M. H. 2006. Imagining Rain-Places: Rain Control and Changing Ritual Landscapes in the Shashe–Limpopo Confluence Area, South Africa. *South African Archaeological Bulletin* 61: 152–165.

Schoeninger, M. J. 2009. Stable Isotope Evidence for the Adoption of Maize Agriculture. *Current Anthropology* 50(5): 633–640.

Schovsbo, P. O. 1983. A Neolithic Vehicle from Klosterlund, Central Jutland. *Journal of Danish Archaeology* 2: 60–70.

Schreiber, K. 2001. The Wari Empire of Middle Horizon Peru: The Epistemological Challenge of Documenting an Empire without Documentary Evidence. In *Empires*, S. E. Alcock, T. N. D'Altroy, K. D. Morrison, and C. M. Sinopoli (eds.), pp. 70–92. New York: Cambridge University Press.

Schriever, B. A. 2012. Mobility, Land Tenure, and Social Identity in the San Simon Basin of Southeastern Arizona. *Kiva* 77(4): 413–438.

Schurmans, U. A. 2007. *The Production of Small Flakes in the Middle Paleolithic: A New Look at Assemblage Variability*. PhD thesis. Philadelphia: University of Pennsylvania.

Schurr, T. G. 2000. Mitochondrial DNA and the Peopling of the New World. *American Scientist* 88(3): 246–253.

Schwarcz, H. P., R. Grün, B. Vandermeersch, O Bar-Yosef, H. Valladas, and E. Tchernov. 1988. ESR Dates for the Hominid Burial Site of Qafzeh in Israel. *Journal of Human Evolution* 17: 733–737.

Schwartz, D. W., A. L. Lange, and R. deSaussure. 1958. Split-Twig Figurines in the Grand Canyon. *American Antiquity* 23(3): 264–274.

Schwartz, M., and D. Hollander. 2016. The Uruk Expansion as Dynamic Process: A Reconstruction of Middle to Late Uruk Exchange Patterns from Bulk Stable Isotope Analyses of Bitumen Artifacts. *Journal of Archaeological Science: Reports* 7: 884–899.

Scott, G. R., K. Schmitz, K. N. Heim, K. S. Paul, R. Schomberg, and M. A. Pilloud. 2018. Sinodonty, Sundadonty, and the Berigian Standstill Model: Issues of Timing and Migrations into the New World. *Quaternary International* 466: 233–246.

Seeman, M. F., and J. L. Branch. 2006. The Mounded Landscapes of Ohio: Hopewell Patterns and Placements. In *Recreating Hopewell*, Charles, D. K., and J. E. Buikstra (eds.), pp. 106–121. Gainesville: University Press of Florida.

Semaw, S. 2000. The World's Oldest Stone Artefacts from Gona, Ethiopia: Their Implications for Understanding Stone Technology and Patterns of Human Evolution between 2.6–1.5 Million Years Ago. *Journal of Archaeological Science* 27: 1197–1214.

Sepulveda, M., F. Gallardo, B. Ballester, G. Caebllo, and E. Vidal. 2019. El Condor Mine: Prehispanic Production and Consumption of Hematite Pigments in the Atacama Desert, northern Chile. *Journal of Anthropological Archaeology* 53: 325–341.

Seymour, D. J. 1988. An Alternative View of Sedentary Period Hohokam Shell-Ornament Production. *American Antiquity* 53(4): 812–829.

Shafer, H. J. 2003. *Mimbres Archaeology at the NAN Ranch Ruin*. Albuquerque: University of New Mexico Press.

Shang, H., H. Tong, S. Zhong, F. Chen, and E. Trinkaus. 2007. An Early Modern Human from Tianyuan Cave, Zhoukoudian, China. *Proceedings of the National Academy of Sciences, USA* 104(16): 6573–6578.

Sharer, R. J. 2009. *Daily Life in Maya Civilization*, 2nd ed. Westport, CT: Greenwood Press.

Sharlach, T. M. 2005. Diplomacy and Rituals of Politics at the Ur III Court. *Journal of Cuneiform Studies* 57: 17–29.

Shaw, I. (ed.). 2000. *The Oxford History of Ancient Egypt*. New York: Oxford University Press.

Shea, J. J. 2003. The Middle Paleolithic of the East Mediterrean Levant. *Journal of World Prehistory* 17(4): 313–394.

Shea, J. J. 2006. The Origins of Lithic Projectile Technology: Evidence from Africa, the Levant, and Europe. *Journal of Archaeological Science* 33: 823–846.

Shea, J. J. 2008. Transitions or Turnovers? Climatically-Forced Extinctions of *Homo sapiens* and Neanderthals in the East Mediterranean Levant. *Quaternary Science Reviews* 27(23–24): 2253–2270.

Shea, J. J. 2017. Occasional, Obligatory, and Habitual Stone Tool Use in Hominin Evolution. *Evolutionary Anthropology* 26: 200–2017.

Sheehan, O., J. Watts, R. D. Gray, and Q. D. Atkinson. 2018. Coevolution of Landesque Capital Intensive Agriculture and Sociopolitical Hierarch. *Proceedings of the National Academy of Sciences USA* 115: 3628–3633.

Shelach, G. 2000. The Earliest Neolithic Cultures of Northeast China: Recent Discoveries and New Perspectives on the Beginning of Agriculture. *Journal of World Prehistory* 14(4): 363–413.

Shen, G., T.-L. Ku, H. Cheng, R. L. Edwards, Z. Yuan, and Q. Wang. 2001. High-Precision U-Series Dating of Locality 1 at Zhoukoudian, China. *Journal of Human Evolution* 41(6): 679–688.

Shennan, S. E. 1975. The Social Organization at Branč. *Antiquity* 49: 279–288.

Shennan, S. J. 1993. Settlement and Social Change in Central Europe, 3500–1500 BC. *Journal of World Prehistory* 7(2): 121–161.

Shipman, P. 2015. How Do You Kill 86 Mammoths? Taphonomic Investigations of Mammoth Megasites. *Quaternary International* 359–360: 38–46.

Showalter, P. S. 1993. A Thematic Mapper Analysis of the Prehistoric Hohokam Canal System, Phoenix, Arizona. *Journal of Field Archaeology* 20(1): 77–90.

Shreeve, J. 1996. Sunset on the Savanna. *Discover* 17(7): 116–125.

Shuler, K. A., S. C. Hodge, M. E. Danforth, J. L. Funkhouser, C. Stantis, D. N. Cook, and P. Zeng. 2012. In the Shadow of Moundville: A Bioarchaeological View of the Transition to Agriculture in the Central Tombigbee Valley of Alabama and Mississippi. *Journal of Archaeological Science* 31: 586–603.

Simanjuntak, T. 2001. New Insights on the Tools of *Pithecanthropus*. In *Sangiran: Man, Culture, and Environment in Pleistocene Times*, T. Simanjuntak, B. Prasetyo, and R. Handini (eds.), pp. 154–170. Jakarta: Yayasan Obor Indonesia.

Simmons, A. H. 2007. The Neolithic Revolution in the Near East. Transforming the Human Landscape. Tucson: University of Arizona Press.

Sinopoli, C. M. 2001. Empires. In *Archaeology at the Millennium: A Sourcebook*, G. M. Feinman and T. D. Price (eds.), pp. 439–471. New York: Kluwer Academic.

Skeates, R. 2002. The Neolithic Enclosures of the Tavioliere, South-East Italy. In *Enclosures in Neolithic Europe*, G. Varndell and P. Topping (eds.), pp. 51–58. Oxford: Oxbow Books.

Skoglund, P., E. Ersmark, E. Palkopoulou, and L. Dalén. 2015. Ancient Wolf Genome Reveals an Early Divergence of Domestic Dog Ancestors and Admixture into High-Latitude Breeds. *Current Biology* 25: 1515–1519.

Skoglund, P., H. Malmström, A. Omrak, M. Raghavan, C. Valdiosera, T. Günther, P. Hall, K. Tambets, J. Parik, K.-G. Sjögren, J. Apel, E. Willerslev, J. Storå, A. Götherström, and M. Jakobsson. 2014. Genomic Diversity and Admixture Differs for Stone-Age Scandanavian Foragers and Farmers. *Science Express Reports*. doi: 10.1126/science.1253448.

Slater, P. A., K. M. Hedman, and T. E. Emerson. 2014. Immigrants at the Mississippian Polity of Cahokia: Strontium Isotope Evidence for Population Movement. *Journal of Archaeological Science* 44: 117–127.

Smailes, R. L. 2011. Building Chan Chan: A Project Management Perspective. *Latin American Antiquity* 22(1): 37–63.

Smallwood, A. M. 2012. Clovis Technology and Settlement in the American Southeast: Using Biface Analysis to Evaluate Dispersal Models. *American Antiquity* 77(4): 689–713.

Smith, B. D. (ed.). 1992. *The Rivers of Change: Essays on Early Agriculture in Eastern North America*. Washington, DC: Smithsonian Institution Press.

Smith, B. D. 2005. Reassessing Coxcatlan Cave and the Early History of Domesticated Plants in Mexico. *Proceedings of the National Academy of Sciences USA* 102: 9438–9445.

Smith, B. D. 2011. A Cultural Niche Construction Theory of Initial Domestication. *Biological Theory* 6: 260–271.

Smith, F. H., J. C. M. Ahern, I. Janković, and I. Karavanić. 2017. The Assimilation Model of Modern Human Origins in Light of Current Genetic and Genomic Knowledge. *Quaternary International* 450: 126–136.

Smith, F. H., A. B. Falsetti, and S. Donnelly. 1989. Modern Human Origins. *Yearbook of Physical Anthropology* 32: 35–68.

Smith, H. L., and T. Goebel. 2018. Origins and Spread of Fluted-Point Technology in the Canadian Ice-Free Corridor and Eastern Beringia. *Proceedings of the National Academy of Sciences USA* 115: 4116–4121.

Smith, M. A., B. Fankhauser, and M. Jercher. 1998. The Changing Provenance of Red Ochre at Puritjarra Rock Shelter, Central Australia. *Proceedings of the Prehistoric Society* 64: 275–292.

Smith M. E. 2010. Regional and Local Market Systems in Aztec-Period Morelos. In *Archaeological Approaches to Market Exchange in Ancient Societies*, C. P. Garraty and B. L. Stark, pp. 161–182. Boulder: University Press of Colorado.

Smith, M. E. 2012. *The Aztecs*, 3rd ed. Malden, MA: Wiley-Blackwell.

Smith, R. J., and B. Wood. 2017. The Principles and Practice of Human Evolution Research: Are We Asking Questions That Can Be Answered? *Comptes Rendu Palevol* 16: 670–679.

Smyth, M. P. 2008. Beyond Economic Imperialism. The Teotihucan Factor in Northern Yucatan. *Journal of Anthropological Research* 64: 395–409.

Snitker, G., A. Diez Castillo, C. M. Barton, J. Bernabeu Aubán, O. García Puchol, and S. Pardo-Gordó. 2018. Patch-Based Survey Methods for Studying Prehistoric Human Land-Use in Agriculturally Modified Landscapes: A Case Study from the Canal de Navarrés, Eastern Spain. *Quaternary International* 483: 5–22.

Snodgrass, J. J., and W. R. Leonard. 2009. Neandertal Energetics Revisited: Insights into Population Dynamics and Life History Evolution. *PaleoAnthropology* 2009: 220–237.

Snoeck, C., J. Pouncett, P. Claeys, S. Goderis, N. Mattielli, M. Parker Pearson, C. Willis, A. Zazzo, J. A. Lee-Thorp, and R. J. Schulting. 2018. Strontium Isotope Analysis on Cremated Human Remains from Stonehenge Supports Links with West Wales. *Scientific Reports* 8: 10790.

Soffer, O., J. M. Adovasio, and D. C. Hyland. 2000. The "Venus" Figurines: Textiles, Basketry, Gender, and Status in the Upper Paleolithic. *Current Anthropology* 41(4): 511–537.

Soffer, O., J. M. Adovasio, N. L. Kornietz, A. A. Velichko, Y. N. Gribchenko, B. R. Lenz, and V. Y. Suntsov. 1997. Cultural Stratigraphy at Mezhirich, an Upper Paleolithic Site in Ukraine with Multiple Occupations. *Antiquity* 71: 48–62.

Soffer, O., P. Vandiver, B. Klima, and J. Svoboda. 1992. The Pyrotechnology of Performance Art: Moravian Venuses and Wolverines. In *Before Lascaux: The Complete Record of the Early Upper Paleolithic*, H. Knecht, A. Pike-Tay, and R. White (eds.), pp. 259–275. Boca Raton, FL: CRC Press.

Solecki, R. S. 1971. *Shanidar: The First Flower People*. New York: Knopf.

Somerville, A. D., M. Fauvelle, and A. W. Froehle. 2013. Applying New Approaches to Modeling Diet and Status: Isotopic Evidence for Commoner Resiliency and Elite Variability in the Classic Maya Lowlands. *Journal of Archaeological Science* 40: 1539–1553.

Sørensen, M. L. S. 2013. Identity, Gender and Dress in the European Bronze Age. In *The Oxford Handbook of the European Bronze Age,* H. Fokkens and A. Harding (eds.), pp. 216–233. Oxford: Oxford University Press.

Soressi, M., and F. d'Errico. 2007. Pigments, gravures, parures: les comportements symboliques controversies des Néandertaliens. In *Les Néandertaliens, biologie et cultures,* B. Vandermeersch and B. Maureille (eds.), pp. 297–309. Paris: C.T.H.S., Documents préhistoriques 23.

Soressi, M., S. P. McPherron, M. Lenoir, T. Dogandžić, P. Goldberg, Z. Jacobs, Y. Maigrot, N. L. Martisius, C. E. Miller, W. Rendu, M. Richards, M. M. Skinner, T. E. Steele, S. Talamo, and J.-P. Texier. 2013. Neandertals Made the First Specialized Bone Tools in Europe. *Proceedings of the National Academy of Sciences USA* 110: 14186–14190.

Special Issue: Archaeology and Heritage Tourism (various authors). 2005. *The SAA Archaeological Record* 5(3): 9–44.

Spencer, C. S. 1998. A Mathematical Model of Primary State Formation. *Cultural Dynamics* 10: 5–20.

Spencer, C. S., and E. M. Redmond. 2004. Primary State Formation in Mesoamerica. *Annual Review of Anthropology* 33: 173–199.

Speth, J. D. 2015. When Did Humans Learn to Boil? *PaleoAnthropology* 2015: 54–67.

Spikins, P. 2008. "The Bashful and the Boastful" Prestigious Leaders and Social Change in Mesolithic Societies. *Journal of World Prehistory* 21: 173–193.

Sponheimer, M., J. Lee-Thorpe, D. de Ruiter, D. Codron, J. Codron, A. T. Baugh, and F. Thackeray. 2005. Hominins, Sedges, and Termites: New Carbon Isotope Data from the Sterkfontein Valley and Kruger National Park. *Journal of Human Evolution* 48: 301–312.

Spooner, D. M., K. McLean, G. Ramsey, R. Waugh, and G. J. Bryan. 2005. A Single Domestication for Potato Based on Multilocus Amplified Fragment Length Polymorphism Genotyping. *Proceedings of the National Academy of Sciences USA* 102: 14694–14699.

Stanford, C. B. 1998. The Social Behavior of Chimpanzees and Bonobos: Empirical Evidence and Shifting Assumptions. *Current Anthropology* 39(4): 399–420.

Stanford, D., and B. Bradley. 2002. Ocean Trails and Prairie Paths? Thoughts about Clovis Origins. In *The First Americans: The Pleistocene Colonization of the New World,* N. G. Jablonski (ed.), pp. 255–271. San Francisco: Memoirs of the California Academy of Sciences No. 27.

Stanford, D., and B. Bradley. 2012. *Across Atlantic Ice. The Origin of America's Clovis Culture.* Los Angeles: University of California Press.

Stanford, D. J., and M. A. Jodry. 1988. The Drake Clovis Cache. *Current Research in the Pleistocene* 5: 21–22.

Stanish, C. 2001a. Regional Research on the Inca. *Journal of Archaeological Research* 9(3): 213–241.

Stanish, C. 2001b. The Origin of State Societies in South America. *Annual Review of Anthropology* 30: 41–64.

Stanish, C. 2017. *The Evolution of Human Co-Operation. Ritual and Social Complexity in Stateless Societies.* New York: Cambridge University Press.

Stanish, C., E. de la Vega, M. Moseley, P. R. Williams, C. Chávez J., B. Vining, and K. LaFavre. 2010. Tiwanaku Trade Patterns in Southern Peru. *Journal of Anthropological Archaeology* 29: 524–532.

Steegmann, A. T., F. J. Cerny, and T. W. Holliday. 2002. Neandertal Cold Adaptation: Physiological and Energetic Factors. *American Journal of Human Biology* 14: 566–583.

Stein, G. 1994. Economy, Ritual, and Power in 'Ubaid Mesopotamia. In *Chiefdoms and Early States in the Near East: The Organizational Dynamics of Complexity,* G. Stein and M. Rothman (eds.), pp. 35–46. Madison, WI: Prehistory Press.

Stein, G. 2001. Who Was King? Who Was Not King?: Social Group Composition and Competition in Early Mesopotamian State Societies. In *From Leaders to Rulers,* J. Haas (ed.), pp. 205–231. New York: Kluwer Academic/Plenum.

Steponaitis, V. P., and D. T. Dockery III. 2011. Mississippian Effigy Pipes and the Glendon Limestone. *American Antiquity* 76(2): 345–354.

Steponaitis, V. P., S. E. Swanson, G. Wheeler, and P. B. Drooker. 2011. The Provenance and Use of Etowah Palettes. *American Antiquity* 76(1): 81–106.

Steudel, K. 1996. Limb Morphology, Bipedal Gait, and the Energetics of Hominid Locomotion. *American Journal of Physical Anthropology* 99: 345–355.

Steudel-Numbers, K. 2003. The Energetic Cost of Locomotion: Humans and Primates Compared to

Generalized Endotherms. *Journal of Human Evolution* 44(2): 255–262.

Stevens, C. J., and D. Q. Fuller. 2017. The Spread of Agriculture in Eastern Asia. Archaeological Bases for Hypothetical Farmer/Language Dispersals. *Language Dynamics and Change* 7: 152–186.

Stevenson, C. M., I. Abdelrehim, and S. W. Novak. 2004. High Precision Measurement of Obsidian Hydration Layers on Artifacts from the Hopewell Site Using Secondary Ion Mass Spectrometry. *American Antiquity* 69(3): 555–568.

Steward, J. H. 1937. Ecological Aspects of Southwestern Society. *Anthropos* 32: 87–104.

Steward, J. H., and F. M. Setzler. 1938. Function and Configuration in Archaeology. *American Antiquity* 4: 4–10.

Stewart, R. M. 2010. *Archaeology: Basic Field Methods.* Dubuque, IA: Kendall Hunt.

Steyn, M. 2007. The Mapungubwe Gold Graves Revisited. *South African Archaeological Bulletin* 62: 140–146.

Stiner, M. C. 2002. Carnivory, Coevolution, and the Geographic Spread of the Genus *Homo. Journal of Archaeological Research* 10(1): 1–63.

Stiner, M. C., N. D. Munro, and T. A. Surovell. 2000. The Tortoise and the Hare: Small-Game Use, the Broad Spectrum Revolution, and Paleolithic Demography. *Current Anthropology* 41(1): 39–73.

Stoltman, J. B., and R. E. Hughes. 2004. Obsidian in Early Woodland Contexts in the Upper Mississippi Valley. *American Antiquity* 69(4): 751–759.

Stone, E., and P. Zimansky. 1995. The Tapestry of Power in a Mesopotamian City. *Scientific American* 269: 118–123.

Stone, G. D. 1984. Arizona D:11:2025. In *Excavations on Black Mesa, 1982, a Descriptive Report,* D. L. Nichols and F. E. Smiley (eds.), pp. 193–208. Carbondale: Southern Illinois University at Carbondale Center for Archaeological Investigations Research Paper No. 39.

Stone, T. 2009. Room Function and Room Suites in Late Mogollon Pueblo Sites. *Kiva* 75(1): 63–86.

Stothert, K. E., D. R. Piperno, and T. C. Andres. 2003. Terminal Pleistocene/Early Holocene Human Adaptation in Coastal Ecuador: The Las Vegas Evidence. *Quaternary International* 109–110: 23–43.

Straus, L. G. 2000. Solutrean settlement of North America? A Review of Reality. *American Antiquity* 63: 7–20.

Stringer, C. B., J. C. Finlayson, R. N. E. Barton, Y. Fernández-Jalvo, I. Cáceres, R. C. Sabin, E. J. Rhodes, A. P. Currant, J. Rodríguez-Vidal, F. Giles-Pacheco, and J. A. Riquelme-Cantal. 2008. Neanderthal Exploitation of Marine Mammals in Gibraltar. *Proceedings of the National Academy of Sciences USA* 105: 14319–14324.

Stringer, C., and C. Gamble. 1995. *In Search of the Neanderthals: Solving the Puzzle of Human Origins.* London: Thames & Hudson.

Stringer, C. B., R. Grün, H. P. Schwarcz, and P. Goldberg. 1989. ESR Dates for the Hominid Burial Site of Es Skhul in Israel. *Nature* 338: 756.

Sugiyama, N., A. D. Somerville, and M. J. Schoeninger. 2015. Stable Isotopes and Zooarchaeology at Teotihuacan, Mexico Reveal Earliest Evidence of Wild Carnivore Management in Mesoamerica. *PLoS One* 10(9): e0135635.

Sugiyama, N., S. Sugiyama, and S.G. Alejandro. 2013. Inside the Sun Pyramid at Teotihucan Mexico: 2008–2011 Excavations and Preliminary Results. *Latin American Antiquity* 24(4): 403–432.

Sun, Y. 2003. Bronzes, Mortuary Practice and Political Strategies of the Yan during the Early Western Zhou Period. *Antiquity* 77: 761–770.

Sutikna, T., M. W. Tocheri, M. J. Morwood, E. Wahyu Saptomo, Jatmiko, R. Due Awe, S. Wasisto, K. E. Westaway, M. Aubert, B. Li, J.-x. Zhao, M. Storey, B. V. Alloway, M. W. Morley, H. J. M. Meijer, G. D. van den Bergh, R. Grün, A. Dosseto, A.Brumm, W. L. Jungers, and R. G. Roberts. 2016. Revised Stratigraphy and Chronology for *Homo floresiensis* at Liang Bua in Indonesia. *Nature* 532: 366–369.

Summerhayes, G. R., M. Leavesley, A. Fairbairn, H. Mandui, J. Field, A. Ford, and R. Fullagar. 2010. Human Adaptation and Plant Use in Highland New Guinea 49,000 to 44,000 Years Ago. *Science* 330: 78–81.

Sutter, R. C., and R. J. Cortez. 2005. The Nature of Moche Human Sacrifice: A Bio-Archaeological Perspective. *Current Anthropology* 46(4): 521–549.

Svezhentsev, Y. S. 1993. Radiocarbon Chronology for the Upper Paleolithic Sites on the East European Plain. In *From Kostenki to Clovis. Upper Paleolithic—Paleo-Indian Adaptations,* O. Soffer and N. D. Praslov (eds.), pp. 23–30. New York: Plenum Press.

Svoboda, J., S. Péan, and P. Wojtal. 2005. Mammoth Bone Deposits and Subsistence Practices during the Mid-Upper Palaeolithic in Central Europe: Three Cases from Moravia and Poland. *Quaternary International* 126–128: 209–221.

Swenson, E. R. 2003. Cities of Violence: Sacrifice, Power and Urbanization in the Andes. *Journal of Social Archaeology* 3: 256–296.

Swenson, E. 2012. Warfare, Gender, and Sacrifice in Jequetepeque, Peru. *Latin American Antiquity* 23(2): 167–193.

Symons, D. 1979. *The Evolution of Human Sexuality.* Oxford: Oxford University Press.

Symonds, S. 2000. The Ancient Landscape at San Lorenzo Tenochtitlan, Veracruz, Mexico. In *Olmec Art and Archaeology in Mesoamerica,* J. E. Clark and M. E. Pye (eds.), pp. 55–74. Washington, DC: National Gallery of Art, and New Haven, CT: Yale University Press.

Tainter, J. A. 2006. Archaeology of Overshoot and Collapse. *Annual Review of Anthropology* 35: 59–74.

Tamm, E., T. Kivisild, M. Reidla, M. Metspalu, D. G. Smith, C. J. Mulligan, C. M. Bravi, O. Rickards, C. Martinez-Labarga, E. K. Khusnutdinova, S. A. Fedorova, M. V. Golubenko, V. A. Stepanov, M. A. Gubina, S. I. Zhadanov, L. P. Ossipova, L. Damba, M. I. Voevoda, J. E. Dipierri, R. Villems, and R. S. Malhi. 2007. Berengian Standstill and Spread of Native American Founders. 2007. *PLoS One* 7: e829.

Tang, J., Z. Jing, and G. Rapp. 2000. The Largest Walled Shang City Located in Anyang, China. *Antiquity* 74: 479–480.

Tankersley, K. B. 1998. Variation in the Early Paleoindian Economies of Late Pleistocene Eastern North America. *American Antiquity* 63(1): 7–20.

Tankersley, D. B., W. D. Huff, N. P. Dunning, L. A. Owen, and V. L. Scarborough. 2017. Volcanic Minerals in Chaco Canyon, New Mexico and Their Archaeological Significance. *Journal of Archaeological Science: Reports* 17: 404–421.

Tanner, C. L. 1976. *Prehistoric Southwestern Craft Arts.* Tucson: University of Arizona Press.

Taube, K. A. 2003. Tetitla and the Maya Presence at Teotihuacan. In *The Maya and Teotihuacan: Reinterpreting Early Classic Interaction,* G. E. Braswell (ed.), pp. 273–314. Austin: University of Texas Press.

Telecki, G. 1973. *The Predatory Behavior of Wild Chimpanzees.* Cranbury, NJ: Associated University Presses.

Texier, P.-J., G. Porraz, J. Parkington, J.-P. Rigaud, C. Poggenpoel, C. Miller, C. Tribolo, C. Cartwright, A. Coudenneau, R. Klein, T. Steele, and C. Verna. 2010. A Howeisons Poort Tradition of Engraving Ostrich Eggshell Containers Dated to 60,000 Years Ago at Diepkloof Rock Shelter, South Africa. *Proceedings of the National Academy of Sciences USA* 107(14): 6180–6185.

Thackeray, A. I., J. F. Thackeray, P. B. Beaumont, and J. C. Vogel. 1981. Dated Rock Engravings from Wonderwerk Cave, South Africa. *Science* 214: 64–67.

Thieme, H. 1997. Lower Palaeolithic Hunting Spears from Germany. *Nature* 385: 807–810.

Thomas, K. A., B. A. Story, M. I. Eren, B. Buchanan, B. N. Andrews, M. J. O'Brien, and D. J. Meltzer. 2017. Explaining the Origin of Fluting in North American Pleistocene Weaponry. *Journal of Archaeological Science* 81: 23–30.

Thomas, K. D. 2003. Minimizing Risk? Approaches to Pre-Harappan Human Ecology on the North-West Margin of the Greater Indus System. In *Indus Ethnobiology: New Perspectives From the Field,* S. A. Weber and W. R. Belcher (eds.), pp. 397–429. New York: Lexington Books.

Thomas, L. 2001. The Gender Division of Labor in Mississippian Households: Its Role in Shaping Production for Exchange. In *Archaeological Studies of Gender in the Southeastern United States,* J. M. Eastman and C. B. Rodning (eds.), pp. 27–56. Gainesville: University Press of Florida.

Thompson, V. D., and C. F. T. Andrus. 2011. Evaluating Mobility, Monumentality, and Feasting at the Sapelo Island Shell Ring Complex. *American Antiquity* 76(2): 315–343.

Thorne, A. G., and M. H. Wolpoff. 2003. The Multiregional Evolution of Humans. *Scientific American Special Editions: New Look at Human Evolution:* 46–53.

Thornton, E. K., and K. F. Emery. 2016. Patterns of Ancient Animal Use at El Mirador: Evidence for Subsistence, Ceremony and Exchange. *Archaeofauna* 25: 233–264.

Tobler, R., A. Rohrlach, J. Soubrier, P. Bover, B. Llamas, J. Tuke, N. Bean, A. Abdullah-Highfold, S. Agius, A. O'Donoghue, I. O'Loughlin, P. Sutton, F. Zilio, K. Walshe, A. N. Williams, C. S. M. Turney, M. Williams, S. M. Richards, R. J. Mitchell, E. Kowal, J. R. Stephen, L. Williams, W. Haak, and A. Cooper. 2017. Aboriginal Mitogenomes Reveal 50,000 Years of Regionalism in Australia. *Nature* 544, 180–184.

Tocheri, M. W., C. M. Orr, S. G. Larson, T. Sutikna, Jatmiko, E. W. Saptomo, R. A. Due, T. Djubiantono, M. J. Morwood, and W. L. Jungers. 2007. The Primitive Wrist of *Homo floresiensis* and Its Implications for Hominin Evolution. *Science* 317: 1743–1745.

Toll, H. W. 1991. Material Distributions and Exchange in the Chaco System. In *Chaco & Hohokam: Prehistoric Regional Systems in the American Southwest*, P. L. Crown and W. J. Judge (eds.), pp. 77–107. Santa Fe, NM: School of American Research Press.

Toll, H. W. 2001. Making and Breaking Pots in the Chaco World. *American Antiquity* 66(1): 56–78.

Toll, H. W. 2006. Organization of Production. In *The Archaeology of Chaco Canyon, an Eleventh Century Pueblo Regional Center*, S. H. Lekson (ed.), pp. 117–151. Santa Fe, NM: School of American Research Press.

Topic, J. R. 2003. From Stewards to Bureaucrats: Architecture and Information Flow at Chan Chan, Peru. *Latin American Antiquity* 243–274.

Toth, N. 1985. The Oldowan Reassessed: A Close Look at Early Stone Artifacts. *Journal of Archaeological Science* 12: 101–120.

Towers, J., J. Montgomery, J. Evans, M. Jay, and M. Parker Pearson. 2010. An Investigation of the Origins of Cattle and Aurochs Deposited in the Early Bronze Age Barrows at Gayhurst and Irthlingborough. *Journal of Archaeological Science* 37: 508–515.

Toyne, J. M., C. D. White, J. W. Verano, S. U. Castillo, J. F. Millaire, and F. J. Longstaffe. 2014. Residential Histories of Elites and Sacrificial Victims at Huacas de Moche, Peru, as Reconstructed from Oxygen Isotopes. *Journal of Archaeological Science* 42: 15–28.

Trigger, B. G. 2003. *Understanding Early Civilizations. A Comparative Study.* New York: Cambridge University Press.

Trigger, B. G. 2006. *A History of Archaeological Thought*, 2nd ed. New York: Cambridge University Press.

Trinkaus, E. 2012. Neandertals, Early Modern Humans, and Rodeo Riders. *Journal of Archaeological Science* 39: 3691–3693.

Trinkaus, E., and A. P. Buzhilova. 2018. Diversity and Differential Disposal of the Dead at Sunghir. *Antiquity* 92: 7–21.

Troy, C. S., D. E. MacHugh, J. F. Bailey, D. A. Magee, R. T. Loftus, P. Cunningham, A. T. Chamberlain, B. C. Sykes, and D. G. Bradley. 2001. Genetic Evidence for Near-Eastern Origins of European Cattle. *Nature* 410: 1088–1091.

Tung, T. A. 2007. Trauma and Violence in the Wari Empire of the Peruvian Andes: Warfare, Raids, and Ritual Fights. *American Journal of Physical Anthropology* 133: 941–956.

Tung, T. A., and K. J. Knudson. 2008. Social Identities and Geographical Origins of Wari Trophy Heads from Conchopata, Peru. *Current Anthropology* 49(5): 915–925.

Tung, T. A., and K. J. Knudson. 2011. Identifying Locals, Migrants, and Captives in the Wari Heartland: A Bioarchaeological and Biogeochemical Study of Human Remains from Conchopata, Peru. *Journal of Anthropological Archaeology* 30: 247–261.

Turchin, P., T. E. Curriec, H. Whitehouse, P. François, K. Feeney, D. Mullins, D. Hoyer, C. Collins, S. Grohmann, P. Savage, G. Mendel-Gleason, E. Turner, A. Dupeyron, E. Cioni, J. Reddish, J. Levine, G. Jordan, E. Brandl, A. Williams, R. Cesaretti, M. Krueger, A. Ceccarelli, J. Figliulo-Rosswurm, P.-J. Tuan, P. Peregrine, A. Marciniak, J. Preiser-Kapeller, N. Kradin, A. Korotayev, A. Palmisano, D. Baker, J. Bidmead, P. Bol, D. Christian, C. Cook, A. Covey, G. Feinman, Á. D. Júlíusson, A. Kristinsson, J. Miksic, R. Mostern, C. Petrie, P. Rudiak-Gould, B. ter Haar, V. Wallace, V. Mair, L. Xie, J. Baines, E. Bridges, J. Manning, B. Lockhart, A. Bogaard, and C. Spencer. 2018. Quantitative Historical Analysis Uncovers a Single Dimension of Complexity that Structures Global Variation in Human Social Organization. *Proceedings of the National Academy of Sciences USA* 115: e144-e151.

Tylor, E. B. 1920. *Primitive Culture*. New York: Putnam [originally published 1871].

Underhill, A. P. 2006. Warfare and the Development of States in China. In *The Archaeology of Warfare. Prehistories of Raiding and Conquest*, E. N. Arkush and M. W. Allen (eds.), pp. 253–285. Gainesville: University Press of Florida.

Underhill, A. P. 2018. Urbanization and New Social Contexts for Consumption of Food and Drink in Northern China. *Archaeological Research in Asia* 14: 7–19.

Urton, G. 2001. A Calendrical and Demographic Tomb Text from Northern Peru. *Latin American Antiquity* 12: 127–147.

Uyeoka, K. L. 2013. Huliau: A Time of Transformation in Hawaiian Cultural Resource Management. *The SAA Archaeological Record* 13(2): 33–35.

Valdés, J. A., and J. Kaplan. 2000. Ground-Penetrating Radar at the Maya Site of Kaminaljuyu, Guatemala. *Journal of Field Archaeology* 27: 329–342.

Valdés, J. A., and L. E. Wright. 2004. The Early Classic and Its Antecedents at Kaminaljuyu: A Complex Society with Complex Problems. In *Understanding Early Classic*

Copan, E. E. Bell, M. A. Canuto, and R. J. Sharer (eds.), pp. 337–355. Philadelphia: University of Pennsylvania Museum of Archaeology and Anthropology Publications.

Valla, F. R. 1975–1977. La sepulture H. 104 de Mallaha (Eynan) et le problem de la domestication du chien en Palestine. *Paléorient* 3: 287–292.

Valla, F. R. 1991. Les Natoufiens de Mallaha et l'espace. In *The Natufian Culture in the Levant,* O. Bar-Yosef and F. R. Vallay (eds.), pp. 111–122. Ann Arbor, MI: International Monographs in Prehistory.

Valladas, H., J. Evin, and M. Arnold. 1996. Datation par la method du carbone 14 des couches Obeid 0 et 1 de Tell el Oueili (Iraq). In *Oueili. Travaux de 1987 et 1989,* J. Huot (ed.), pp. 381–383. Paris: Éditions Recherche sur les Civilisations.

Vallet, R., J. S. Baldi, H. Naccaro, K. Rasheed, S. A. Saber, and S. J. Hamarasheed. 2017. New Evidence on Uruk Expansion in the Central Mesopotamian Zagros Piedmont. *Paléorient* 43(1): 61–87.

Van Andel, T. H., and W. Davies. 2003. *Neanderthals and Modern Humans in the European Landscape during the Last Glaciation.* Cambridge, UK: McDonald Institute for Archaeological Research.

van der Merwe, N. J,. and J. C. Vogel. 1978. ^{13}C Content of Human Collagen as a Measure of Prehistoric Diet in Woodland North America. *Nature* 276: 815–816.

Van Dyke, R. M. 1999. The Chaco Connection: Evaluating Bonito Style Architecture in Outlier Communities. *Journal of Anthropological Archaeology* 18: 471–506.

Van Dyke, R. M. 2004. Memory, Meaning, and Masonry: The Late Bonito Chacoan Landscape. *American Antiquity* 69(3): 413–431.

Vanhaeren, M., F. d'Errico, C. Stringer, S. L. James, J. A. Todd, and H. K. Mienis. 2006. Middle Paleolithic Shell Beads in Israel and Algeria. *Science* 312: 1785–1788.

Vandermeersch, B. 1970. Une sepulture moustérienne avec offrandes découverte dans la grotte de Qafzeh. *Comptes Rendues de l'Académie des Sciences Paris D* 268: 2562–2565.

Vandermeersch, B. 1993. Was the Saint-Césaire Discovery a Burial? In Context of a Late Neandertal: Implications for Multidisciplinary Research for the Transition to Upper Paleolithic Adaptations at Saint-Césaire, Charente-Maritime, France, F. Lévêque, A. M. Backer, and M. Guilbaud (eds.), pp. 129–131. Madison, WI: Prehistory Press.

Van den Bergh, G. D., Y. Kaifu, I. Kurniawan, R. T. Kono, A. Brumm, E. Setiyabudi, F. Aziz, and M. J. Morwood. 2016. *Homo floresiensis*-like Fossils from the Early Middle Pleistocene of Flores. *Nature* 534: 245–248.

Vanmontfort, B. 2008. Forager–Farmer Connections in an "Unoccupied" Land: First Contact on the Western Edge of LBK Territory. *Journal of Anthropological Archaeology* 27: 149–160.

Van Schaik, C. 2006. Why Are Some Animals so Smart? *Scientific American* 16(2): 30–37.

Van Tuerenhout, D. R. 2005. *The Aztecs. New Perspectives.* Denver, CO: ABC-CLIO.

van Willigen, S. 2018. Between Cardial and Linearbandkeramik: From No-Man's Land to Communication Sphere. *Quaternary International* 470: 333–352.

Vaughn, K. J. 2006. Craft Production, Exchange, and Political Power in the Pre-Incaic Andes. *Journal of Archaeological Research* 14: 313–344.

Vidale, M. 2011. P.G. 1237, Royal Cemetery of Ur: Patterns in Death. *Cambridge Archaeological Journal* 21(3): 427–451.

Villa, P., and W. Roebroeks. 2014. Neandertal Demise: An Archaeological Analysis of the Modern Human Superiority Complex. *PLoS One* 9(4): e96424.

Villmoare, B. 2018. Early Homo and the Role of the Genus in Paleoanthropology. *American Journal of Physical Anthropology* 165: 72–89.

Villmoare, B., W. H. Kimbel, C. Seyoum, C. J. Campisano, E. DiMaggio, J. Rowan, D. R. Braun, J. R. Arrowsmith, and K. E. Reed. 2015. Early *Homo* at 2.8 Ma from Ledi-Geraru, Afar, Ethiopia. *Sciencexpress.* doi: 10.1126/science.aaa1343.

Vivian, R. G. 1991. Chacoan Subsistence. In *Chaco & Hohokam: Prehistoric Regional Systems in the American Southwest,* P. L. Crown and W. J. Judge (eds.), pp. 57–75. Santa Fe, NM: School of American Research Press.

Vokes, A. W., and D. A. Gregory. 2007. Exchange Networks for Exotic Goods in the Southwest and Zuni's Place in Them. In *Zuni Origins: Toward a New Synthesis of Southwestern Archaeology,* D. A. Gregory and D. R. Wilcox (eds.), pp. 318–357. Tucson: University of Arizona Press.

Vranich, A. 2006. The Construction and Reconstruction of Ritual Space at Tiwanaku, Bolivia (A.D. 500–1000). *Journal of Field Archaeology* 31: 121–136.

Wadley, L. 1996. The Robberg Industry of Rose Cottage Cave, Eastern Free State: The Technology, Spatial

Patterns and Environment. *South African Archaeological Bulletin* 51: 64–74.

Wadley, L. 2001. What Is Cultural Modernity? A General View and a South African Perspective from Rose Cottage Cave. *Cambridge Archaeological Journal* 11: 201–221.

Wadley, L. 2005. Putting Ochre to the Test: Replication Studies of Adhesives That May Have Been Used for Hafting Tools in the Middle Stone Age. *Journal of Human Evolution* 49: 587–601.

Wadley, L., T. Hodgskiss, and M. Grant. 2009. Implications for Complex Cognition from the Hafting of Tools with Compound Adhesives in the Middle Stone Age, South Africa. *Proceedings of the National Academy of Sciences USA* 106: 9590–9594.

Wagner, G. E. 2000. Tobacco in Prehistoric Eastern North America. In *Tobacco Use by Native North Americans: Sacred Smoke and Silent Killer*, J. C. Winter (ed.), pp. 185–201. Norman: University of Oklahoma Press.

Waguespack, N. M., and T. A. Surovell. 2003. Clovis Hunting Strategies, or How to Make Out on Plentiful Resources. *American Antiquity* 68(2): 333–352.

el-Wailly, F., and Abu es-Soof. 1965. The Excavations at Tell es-Sawwan, First Preliminary Report (1964). *Sumer* 21: 17–32.

Walker, A., and R. Leakey (eds.). 1993. The *Narioko-tome Homo erectus Skeleton*. Cambridge, MA: Harvard University Press.

Walker, C. B. F. 1987. *Reading the Past. Cuneiform*. Los Angeles: University of California Press and the British Museum.

Walton, J. 1955. The Soapstone Birds of Zimbabwe. *South African Archaeological Bulletin* 10: 78–84.

Wang, G.-D., W. Zhai, H.-C. Yang, L. Wang, L. Zhong, Y.-H. Liu, R.-X. Fan, T.-T. Yin, C.-L. Zhu, A. D. Poyarkov, D. M. Irwin, M. K. Hytönen, H. Lohi, C.-I. Wu, P. Savolainen, and Y.-P. Zhang. 2015. Out of Southern East Asia: The Natural History of Domestic Dogs across the World. *Cell Research* 2015: 1–13.

Wang, J., L. Liua, T. Ball, L. Yu, Y. Li, and F. Xing. 2016. Revealing a 5,000-Y-Old Beer Recipe in China. *Proceedings of the National Academy of Sciences USA* 113: 6444–6448.

Wangping, S. 2000. The Longshan Period and Incipient Chinese Civilization. *Journal of East Asian Archaeology* 2(1–2): 195–226.

Warfe, A. R. 2003. Cultural Origins of the Egyptian Neolithic and Predynastic: An Evaluation of the Evidence from the Dakhleh Oasis (South Central Egypt). *African Archaeological Review* 20(4): 175–202.

Washburn, D. K. 2011. Pattern Symmetries of the Chaco Phenomenon. *American Antiquity* 76(2): 252–284.

Washburn, D. K., W. N. Washburn, and P. A. Shipkova. 2011. The Prehistoric Drug Trade: Widespread Consumption of Cacao in Ancestral Pueblo and Hohokam Communities in the American Southwest. *Journal of Archaeological Science* 38: 1634–1640.

Washburn, D. K., W. N. Washburn, and P. A. Shipkova. 2013. Cacao Consumption during the 8th Century at Alkali Ridge, Southeastern Utah. *Journal of Archaeological Science* 40(4): 2007–2013.

Wasylikowa, K. 2001. Site E-75–6: Vegetation and Subsistence of the Early Neolithic at Nabta Playa, Egypt, Reconstructed from Charred Plant Remains. In *Holocene Settlement of the Egyptian Sahara. Vol. 1: The Archaeology of Nabta Playa*, F. Wendorf, R. Schild, and Associates, pp. 544–591. New York: Kluwer Academic/Plenum.

Waters, M. R., and T. W. Stafford Jr. 2007. Redefining the Age of Clovis: Implications for the Peopling of the Americas. *Science* 315: 1122–1126.

Waters, M. R., T. W. Stafford Jr., B. Kooyman, and L. V. Hills. 2007. Late Pleistocene Horse and Camel Hunting at the Southern Margin of the Ice-Free Corridor: Reassessing the Age of Wally's Beach, Canada. *Proceedings of the National Academy of Sciences USA* 112: 4263–4267.

Watkins, T. 1992. Pushing Back the Frontiers of Mesopotamian Prehistory. *The Biblical Archaeologist* 55(4): 176–181.

Watkins, J. 2000. *Indigenous Archaeology: American Indian Values and Scientific Practice*. Walnut Creek, CA: Altamira Press.

Watkins, T. 2017. Architecture and Imagery in the Early Neolithic of Southwest Asia: Framing Rituals, Stabilising Meanings. In *Ritual, Play and Belief, in Evolution and Early Human Societies*, C. Renfrew, I. Morley, and M. Boyd (eds.), pp. 129–142. Cambridge, UK: Cambridge University Press.

Watkins, T., D. Baird, and A. Betts. 1989. Qermez Dere and the Early Aceramic Neolithic of N. Iraq. *Paléorient* 15(1): 19–24.

Watson, A. S., S. Plog, B. J. Culleton, P. A. Gilman, S. A. LeBlanc, P. M. Whiteley, S. Claramunt, and D. J.

Kennett. 2015. Early Procurement of Scarlet Macaws and the Emergence of Social Complexity in Chaco Canyon, NM. *Proceedings of the National Academy of Sciences USA* 112: 8238–8243.

Watts, I. 2002. Ochre in the Middle Stone Age of Southern Africa: Ritualised Display or Hide Preservative? *South African Archaeological Bulletin* 57: 1–14.

Weaver, T. 2003. The Shape of the Neandertal Femur is Primarily the Consequence of a Hyperpolar Body Form. *Proceedings of the National Academy of Sciences USA* 100: 6926–6929.

Webb, W. S. 1946. Indian Knoll Site, Oh 2, Ohio County, Kentucky. *University of Kentucky Reports in Archaeology and Anthropology* 4(3): 115–365 [reprinted in 1974 and in 2001 as *Indian Knoll*. Knoxville: University of Tennessee Press].

Webster, D. 2000. The Not So Peaceful Civilization: A Review of Maya War. *Journal of World Prehistory* 14(1): 65–119.

Webster, D. 2002. *The Fall of the Ancient Maya: Solving the Mystery of the Maya Collapse*. London: Thames & Hudson.

Webster, D. L. 2011. Backward Bottlenecks. Ancient Teosinte/Maize Selection. *Current Anthropology* 52(1): 77–104.

Webster, D., T. Murtha, K. D. Straight, J. Silverstein, H. Martinez, R. E. Terry, and R. Burnett. 2007. The Great Tikal Earthwork Revisited. *Journal of Field Archaeology* 32: 41–64.

Webster, L. D., and K. A. Hays-Gilpin. 1994. New Trails for Old Shoes: Sandals, Textiles, and Baskets in Basketmaker Culture. *Kiva* 60(2): 313–327.

Wegener, C. 2010. The Looting of the Iraq National Museum and the Future of Cultural Property during Armed Conflict. *The SAA Archaeological Record* 10(4): 28–30.

Weismantel, M. 2004. Moche Sex Pots: Reproduction and Temporality in Ancient South America. *American Anthropologist* 106(3): 495–505.

Weiss, E., M. E. Kislev, O. Simchoni, D. Nadel, and H. Tschauner. 2008. Plant-Food Preparation Area on an Upper Paleolithic Brush Hut Floor at Ohalo II, Israel. *Journal of Archaeological Science* 35(8): 2400–2414.

Welch, J. R., and D. Triadan. 1991. The Canyon Creek Turquoise Mine, Arizona. *Kiva* 56(2): 145–164.

Wells, P. S. 2016. Unique Objects, Special Deposits and Elite Networks in Bronze Age Europe. *Oxford Journal of Archaeology* 35(2): 161–178.

Wendorf, F., and H. Królik. 2001. The Megalithic Alignments. In *Holocene Settlement of the Egyptian Sahara.* Vol. 1: *The Archaeology of Nabta Playa*, F. Wendorf, R. Schild, and Associates, pp. 489–502. New York: Kluwer Academic/Plenum.

Wendorf, F., and J. M. Malville. 2001. Site E-96-1: The Complex Structures or Shrines. In *Holocene Settlement of the Egyptian Sahara.* Vol. 1: *The Archaeology of Nabta Playa*, F. Wendorf, R. Schild, and Associates, pp. 503–520. New York: Kluwer Academic/Plenum.

Wendorf, F., R. Schild, and Associates. 2001. *Holocene Settlement of the Egyptian Sahara.* Vol. 1: *The Archaeology of Nabta Playa*. New York: Kluwer Academic/Plenum.

Wendorf, F., R. Schild, and A. E. Close. 1984. *Cattle-Keepers of the Eastern Sahara: The Neolithic of Bir Kiseiba*. Dallas: Southern Methodist University Press.

Wendorf, F., R. Schild, and A. E. Close. 1989. *The Prehistory of Wadi Kubbaniya.* Vol. 3: *Late Paleolithic Archaeology*. Dallas: Southern Methodist University Press.

Wendt, W. E. 1976. "Art Mobilier" from the Apollo 11 Cave, South West Africa: Africa's Oldest Dated Works of Art. *South African Archaeological Bulletin* 31: 5–11.

Wenke, R. J. 2009. *The Ancient Egyptian State. The Origins of Egyptian Culture (c. 8000–2000 BC)*. New York: Cambridge University Press.

Weyrich, L. S., S. Duchene, J. Soubrier, L. Arriola, B. Llamas, J. Breen, A. G. Morris, K. W. Alt, D. Caramelli, V. Dresely, M. Farrell, A. G. Farrer, M. Francken, N. Gully, W. Haak, K. Hardy, K. Harvati, P. Held, E. C. Holmes, J. Kaidonis, C. Lalueza-Fox, A. de la Rasilla, A. Rosas, P. Semal, A. Soltysiak, G. Townsend, D. Usai, J. Wahl, D. H. Huson, K. Dobney, and A. Cooper. 2017. Neanderthal Behaviour, Diet, and Disease Inferred from Ancient DNA in Dental Calculus. *Nature* 544: 357–361.

Whalen, M. E., A. C. MacWilliams, and T. Pitezel. 2010. Reconsidering the Size and Structure of Casas Grandes, Chihuahua, Mexico. *American Antiquity* 75(3): 527–550.

Whalen, M. E., and P. E. Minnis. 2000. Leadership at Casas Grandes, Chihuahua, Mexico. In *Alternative Leadership Strategies in the Prehispanic Southwest*, B. J. Mills (ed.), pp. 168–179. Tucson: University of Arizona Press.

Whallon, R. 2006. Social Networks and Information: Non-"utilitarian" Mobility among Hunter–Gatherers. *Journal of Anthropological Archaeology* 25: 259–270.

Wheatley, P. 1971. *The Pivot of the Four Quarters*. Chicago: Aldine de Gruyter.

Wheeler, P. 1991. The Thermoregulatory Advantages of Hominid Bipedalsim in Open Equatorial Environments: The Contribution of Increased Convective Heat Loss and Cutaneous Evaporative Cooling. *Journal of Human Evolution* 21: 107–115.

White, A. A. 2013. Subsistence Economies, Family Size, and the Emergence of Social Complexity in Hunter–Gatherer Systems in Eastern North America. *Journal of Anthropological Archaeology* 32: 122–163.

White, M., P. Pettitt, and D. Schreve. 2016. Shoot First, Ask Questions Later: Interpretive Narratives of Neanderthal Hunting. *Quaternary Science Reviews* 140: 1–20.

White, R. 2003. *Prehistoric Art: The Symbolic Journey of Humankind*. New York: Abrams.

White, T., B. Asfaw, D. DeGusta, H. Gilbert, G. Richards, G. Suwa, and F. C. Howell. 2003. Pleistocene *Homo sapiens* from Middle Awash, Ethiopia. *Nature* 423: 742–747.

Whiteley, P. M. 2002. Archaeology and Oral Traditions: The Scientific Importance of Dialogue. *American Antiquity* 67(3): 405–415.

Whiten, A., J. Goodall, W. C. McGrew, T. Nishida, V. Reynolds, Y. Sugiyama, C. E. G. Tutin, R. W. Wrangham, and C. Boesch. 1999. Cultures in Chimpanzees. *Nature* 399: 682–685.

Whiten, A., V. Horner, and S. Marshall-Pescini. 2003. Cultural Panthropology. *Evolutionary Anthropology* 12: 92–105.

Whittaker, J. 2010. Weapon Trials: The Atlatl and Experiments in Hunting Technology. In *Designing Experimental Research in Archaeology: Examining Technology through Production and Use*, J. R. Ferguson (ed.), pp. 195–224. Boulder: University Press of Colorado.

Whittle, A. 1996. *Europe in the Neolithic: The Creation of New Worlds*. New York: Cambridge University Press.

Whittlesey, S. M., and J. J. Reid. 2001. Mortuary Ritual and Organizational Inferences at Grasshopper Pueblo. In *Ancient Burial Practices in the American Southwest*, D. R. Mitchell and J. L. Brunson-Hadley (eds.), pp. 68–96. Albuquerque: University of New Mexico Press.

Whittlesey, S. M., J. J. Reid, and S. H. Lekson. 2010. Introduction. *Kiva* 76(2): 123–140.

Wilcox, D. 1991. Hohokam Social Complexity. In *Chaco & Hohokam: Prehistoric Regional Systems in the American Southwest*, P. L. Crown and W. J. Judge (eds.), pp. 253–276. Santa Fe, NM: School of American Research Press.

Wild, E. M., P. Stadler, A. Häußer, W. Kutschera, P. Steier, M. Teschler-Nicola, J. Wahl, and H. J. Windl. 2004. Neolithic Massacres: Local Skirmishes or General Warfare in Europe? *Radiocarbon* 46(1): 377–385.

Wilkinson, R. H. 2003. *The Complete Gods and Goddesses of Ancient Egypt*. London: Thames & Hudson.

Wilkinson, T. A. H. 1999. *Early Dynastic Egypt*. London: Routledge.

Wilkinson, T. A. H. 2000. What a King Is This: Narmer and the Concept of the Ruler. *Journal of Egyptian Archaeology* 86: 23–32.

Williams, P. R. 2002. Rethinking the Disaster-Induced Collapse in the Demise of the Andean Highland States: Wari and Tiwanaku. *World Archaeology* 33(3): 361–374.

Wilmsen, E. N. 1974. *Lindenmeier: A Pleistocene Hunting Society*. New York: Harper & Row.

Willoughby, P. R. 2001. Middle and Later Stone Age Technology from the Lake Rukwa Rift, Southwestern Tanzania. *South African Archaeological Bulletin* 56: 34–45.

Willoughby, P. R. 2012. The Middle and Later Stone Age in the Iringa Region of Southern Tanzania. *Quaternary International* 270: 103–118.

Wills, W. H. 1988. *Early Prehistoric Agriculture in the American Southwest*. Santa Fe, NM: School of American Research Press.

Wills, W. H. 2000. Political Leadership and the Construction of Chacoan Great Houses, A.D. 1020–1140. In *Alternative Leadership Strategies in the Prehispanic Southwest*, B. J. Mills (ed.), pp. 19–44. Tucson: University of Arizona Press.

Wills, W. H., and P. L. Crown. 2004. Commensal Politics in the Prehispanic Southwest. In *Identity, Feasting, and the Archaeology of the Greater Southwest*, B. J. Mills (ed.), pp. 153–172. Boulder: University Press of Colorado.

Wills, W. H., B. L. Drake, and W. B. Dorshow. 2014. Prehistoric Deforestation at Chaco Canyon? *Proceedings of the National Academy of Sciences USA* 111: 11584–11591.

Wills, W. H., D. W. Love, S. J. Smith, K. R. Adams, M. R. Palacios-Fest, W. B. Dorshow, B. Murphy, J. O. Sturm, H. Mattson, and P. L. Crown. 2016. Water Management at Pueblo Bonito: Evidence from the National Geographic Society Trenches. *American Antiquity* 81(3): 449–470.

Wills, W. H., and T. C. Windes. 1989. Evidence for Population Aggregation and Dispersal during the Basketmaker III Period in Chaco Canyon, New Mexico. *American Antiquity* 54(2): 347–369.

Wills, W. H., F. S. Worman, W. Dorshow, and H. Richards-Rissetto. 2012. Shabik'eschee Village in Chaco Canyon: Beyond the Archetype. *American Antiquity* 77(2): 326–350.

Wing, E. 1986. Domestication of Andean Mammals. In *High Altitude Tropical Biogeography*, F. Vuilleumier and M. Monasterio (eds.), pp. 246–264. New York: Oxford University Press.

Winterhalder, B., and E. A. Smith. 2000. Analyzing Adaptive Strategies: Human Behavioral Ecology at Twenty-Five. *Evolutionary Anthropology* 9: 51–72.

Winters, H. D. 1974: Introduction to the New Edition. In *Indian Knoll* by W. S. Webb. Knoxville: University of Tennessee Press.

Wolpoff, M. H., J. Hawks, and R. Caspari. 2000. Multiregional, Not Multiple Origins. American *Journal of Physical Anthropology* 112(1): 129–136.

Wolpoff, M. H., J. Hawks, B. Senut, M. Pickford, and J. Ahern. 2006. An Ape or *the* Ape: Is the Toumaï Cranium TM 266 a Hominid? *PaleoAnthropology* 2006: 36–50.

Wood, B. 2002. Palaeoanthropology: Hominid Revelations from Chad. *Nature* 418: 133–135.

Wood, B., and M. Collard. 1999. The Human Genus. *Science* 284:65–71.

Wood, B., and T. Harrison. 2011. The Evolutionary Context of the First Hominins. *Nature* 470: 347–352.

Wood, M. 2000. Making Connections: Relationships between International Trade and Glass Beads from the Shashe–Limpopo Area. *South African Archaeological Society Goodwin Series* 8: 78–90.

Woods, W. I. 2004. Population Nucleation, Intensive Agriculture, and Environmental Degradation: The Cahokia Example. *Agriculture and Human Values* 21(2–3): 255–261.

Woolley, C. L. 1928. *The Sumerians*. Oxford: Oxford University Press [reprinted 1965, New York: Norton].

Woolley, C. L. 1934. *Ur Excavations*, Vol. 2: *The Royal Cemetery*. London: The British Museum and the University of Pennsylvania Museum.

Wright, L. E. 2012. Immigration to Tikal, Guatemala: Evidence from Stable Strontium and Oxygen Isotopes. *Journal of Anthropological Archaeology* 31: 334–352.

Wright, H. T. 1994. Prestate Political Formations. In *Chiefdoms and Early States in the Near East: The Organizational Dynamics of Complexity*, G. Stein and M. Rothman (eds.), pp. 67–84. Madison, WI: Prehistory Press.

Wright, R. P. 2010. *The Ancient Indus: Urbanism, Economy, and Society*. New York: Cambridge University Press.

Wroe, S., J. Field, R. Fullagar, and L. S. Jermin. 2004. Megafaunal Extinction in the Late Quaternary and the Global Overkill Hypothesis. *Alcheringa* 28: 291–331.

Wygal, B. T. 2018. The Peopling of Eastern Beringia and Its Archaeological Evidence. *Quaternary International* 466: 284–298.

Wymer, J. J. 1985. *Palaeolithic Sites of East Anglia*. Norwich: Geo Books.

Wynn, T., and F. L. Coolidge (guest eds.). 2010. Working Memory: Beyond Language and Symbolism. *Current Anthropology* 51(Suppl. 1): S1–S199.

Yamei, H., R. Potts, Y. Baoyin, G. Zhengtang, A. Deino, W. Wei, J. Clark, X. Guangmao, and H. Weiwen. 2000. Mid-Pleistocene Acheulean-like Stone Technology of the Bose Basin, South China. *Science* 287(5458): 1622–1626.

Yang, X. (ed.). 2004. *New Perspectives on China's Past: Chinese Archaeology in the Twentieth Century*, Vol. 2: *Major Archaeological Discoveries in Twentieth-Century China*. New Haven, CT: Yale University Press and Kansas City: The Nelson-Atkins Museum of Art.

Yarnell, R. A. 1978. Domestication of Sunflower and Sumpweed in Eastern North America. In *Nature and Status of Ethnobotany*, R. I. Ford (ed.), p. 289–299. Ann Arbor: Anthropological Paper 67, Museum of Anthropology, University of Michigan.

Yasin, W. 1970. Excavation at Tell Es-Sawwan, 1969 (6th season). *Sumer* 26: 4–11.

Yellen, J. E. 1998. Barbed Bone Points: Tradition and Continuity in Saharan and Sub-Saharan Africa. *African Archaeological Review* 15: 173–198.

Yerkes, R. W. 1983. Microwear, Microdrills, and Mississippian Craft Specialization. *American Antiquity* 48: 499–518.

Yerkes, R. W. 2002. Hopewell Tribes: A Study of Middle Woodland Social Organization in the Ohio Valley. In *The Archaeology of Tribal Societies*, W. A. Parkinson (ed.), pp. 227–245. Ann Arbor: International Monographs in Prehistory, Archaeology Series 15.

Yerkes, R. W. 2005. Bone Chemistry, Body Parts, and Growth Markers: Evaluating Ohio Hopewell and Cahokia Mississippian Seasonality, Subsistence, Ritual, and Feasting. *American Antiquity* 70(2): 241–265.

Yoffee, N. 2005. *Myths of the Archaic State*. New York: Cambridge University Press.

Yohe, R. M., and D. B. Bamforth. 2013. Late Pleistocene Protein Residues from the Mahaffy Cache, Colorado. *Journal of Archaeological Science* 40: 2337–2343.

Yung-Ti, L. 2003. On the Function of Cowries in Shang and Western Zhou China. *Journal of East Asian Archaeology* 5(1–4): 1–26.

Zagarell, A. 1986. Trade, Women, Class, and Society in Ancient Mesopotamia. *Current Anthropology* 27(5): 415–430.

Zagarell, A. 1989. Comment on the Uruk Expansion (by Guillermo Algaze). *Current Anthropology* 30: 600–601.

Zarillo, S., D. M. Pearsall, J. S. Raymond, M. A. Tisdale, and D. J. Quon. 2008. Directly Dated Starch Residues Document Early Formative Maize (*Zea mays* L.) in Tropical Ecuador. *Proceedings of the National Academy of Sciences USA* 105: 5006–5011.

Zazula, G. D., D. G. Froese, C. E. Schweger, R. W. Mathewes, A. B. Beaudoin, A. M. Telka, C. R. Harington, and J. A. Westgate. 2003. Ice-Age Steppe Vegetation in East Beringia. *Nature* 423: 603.

Zeanah, D. W. 2017. Foraging Models, Niche Construction, and the Eastern Agricultural Complex. *American Antiquity* 82(1): 3–24.

Zeder, M. A. 2006. A Critical Assessment of the Markers of Initial Domestication in Goats (*Capra hircus*). In *Documenting Domestication: New Genetic and Archaeological Paradigms*, M. A. Zeder, D. G. Bradley, E. Emshwiller, and B. D. Smith (eds.), pp. 181–208. Los Angeles: University of California Press.

Zeder, M. 2011. The Origins of Agriculture in the Near East. *Current Anthropology* 52(S4): S221–S235.

Zeder, M. A. 2012. The Broad Spectrum Revolution at 40: Resource Diversity, Intensification, and an Alternative to Optimal Foraging Explanations. *Journal of Anthropological Archaeology* 31: 241–264.

Zeder, M. A., D. G. Bradley, E. Emshwiller, and B. D. Smith (eds.). 2006. *Documenting Domestication: New Genetic and Archaeological Paradigms*. Los Angeles: University of California Press.

Zeder, M. A., and B. Hesse. 2000. The Initial Domestication of Goats (*Capra hircus*) in the Zagros Mountains 10,000 Years Ago. *Science* 287: 2254–225.

Zhang, F. 2000. The Mesolithic in South China. *Documenta Praehistorica* 27: 225–231.

Zhang, J., X. Xiao, and Y. K. Lee. 2004. The Early Development of Music: Analysis of the Jiahu Bone Flutes. *Antiquity* 78: 769–778.

Zhao, Z. 2011. New Archaeobotanic Data for the Study of the Origins of Agriculture in China. *Current Anthropology* 52(Suppl. 4): S295–S306.

Zilhão, J. 2001. Radiocarbon evidence for maritime pioneer colonization at the origins of farming in west Mediterranean Europe. *Proceedings of the National Academy of Sciences USA* 98: 14180–14185.

Zilhão, J. 2007. The Emergence of Ornaments and Art: An Archaeological Perspective on the Origins of "Behavioral Modernity." *Journal of Archaeological Research* 15: 1–54.

Zilhão, J., D. E. Angelucci, E. Badel-García, F. d'Errico, F. Daniel, L. Dayet, K. Douka, T. F. G. Higham, M. J. Martínez-Sánchez, R. Montes-Bernárdez, S. Murcia-Mascarós, C. Pérez-Sirvent, C. Roldán-García, M. Vanhaeren, V. Villaverde, R. Wood, and J. Zapata. 2010. Symbolic Use of Marine Shells and Mineral Pigments by Iberian Neandertals. *Proceedings of the National Academy of Sciences USA* 107: 1023–1028.

Zihlman, A. L. 1984. Body Build and Tissue Composition in *Pan paniscus* and *Pan troglodytes* With Comparisons to Other Hominoids. In *The Pygmy Chimpanzee*, R. L. Susman (ed.), pp. 179–200. New York: Plenum.

Zihlman, A. L., and D. R. Bolter. 2015. Body Composition in *Pan paniscus* Compared with *Homo sapiens* Has Implications for Changes during Human Evolution. *Proceedings of the National Academy of Sciences USA* 112: 7466–7471.

Zohar, I., T. Dayan, M. Goren, D. Nadel, and I. Hershkovitz. 2018. Opportunism or Aquatic Specialization? Evidence of Freshwater Fish Exploitation at Ohalo II—A Waterlogged Upper Paleolithic Site. *PLoS One* 13(6): e0198747.

Zorich, Z. 2011. Defending a Jungle Kingdom. *Archaeology* 64(5): 34–38.

Zuo, X., H. Lu, L. Jiang, J. Zhang, X. Yang, X. Huan, K. He, C. Wang, and N. Wu. 2017. Dating Rice Remains Through Phytolith Carbon-14 Study Reveals Domestication at the Beginning of the Holocene. *Proceedings of the National Academy of Sciences USA* 114: 6486–6491.

Zvelebil, M. 2006. Mobility, Contact, and Exchange in the Baltic Sea Basin 6000–2000 BC. *Journal of Anthropological Archaeology* 25: 178–192.

Zvelebil, M., and P. Pettitt. 2013. Biosocial Archaeology of the Early Neolithic: Synthetic Analyses of a Human Skeletal Population from the LBK Cemetery of Vedrovice, Czech Republic. *Journal of Anthropological Archaeology* 32(3): 313–329.

Credits

Chapter 1

Opening image: courtesy of Deborah I. Olszewski; **Figure 1.1:** courtesy of Deborah I. Olszewski; **Figures 1.2** and **1.3:** courtesy of the Abydos Survey for Paleolithic Sites and Deborah I. Olszewski; **Figure 1.4:** University of Pennsylvania Museum of Archaeology and Anthropology Photographic Archives image #206962; **Figure 1.5:** By U.S. National Park Service, U.S. Geological Survey [Public domain], via Wikimedia Commons; **Figure 1.6:** courtesy of Deborah I. Olszewski; **Figures 1.7** and **1.8:** courtesy of the Western Highlands Early Epipaleolithic Project and Deborah I. Olszewski; **Figure 1.9:** courtesy of Deborah I. Olszewski; **Figure 1.10:** courtesy of the Western Highlands Early Epipaleolithic Project and Deborah I. Olszewski; **Figures 1.11, 1.12, 1.13, 1.14, 1.15, 1.16:** courtesy of Deborah I. Olszewski

Chapter 2

Opening image: Pajac Slovensky/Shutterstock; **Figure 2.4:** courtesy of Deborah I. Olszewski; **Figure 2.5:** cast of *Sahelanthropus tchadensis* by Didier Descouens (Own work) [CC BY-SA 3.0 (http://creativecommons.org/licenses/by-sa/3.0/), via Wikimedia Commons [image has been cropped]; *Australopithecus sediba*, Photo by Brett Eloff. Courtesy Profberger and Wits University who release it under the terms below. (Own work) [GFDL (http://www.gnu.org/copyleft/fdl.html) or CC BY-SA4.0-3.0-2.5-2.01.0 (http://creativecommons.org/licenses/by-sa/4.0-3.0-2.5-2.0-1.0)], via Wikimedia Commons [image has been cropped]; *Homo habilis* by José-Manuel Benito Álvarez (España) → Locutus Borg (Own work) [Public domain], via Wikimedia Commons; *Australopithecus africanus* by José Braga; Didier Descouens (Own work) [CC BY-SA 3.0 (http://creativecommons.org/licenses/by-sa/3.0/)], via Wikimedia Commons [image has been cropped]; **Figure 2.7:** courtesy of William C. McGrew; **Figure 2.8:** redrawn from Leakey 1971

Chapter 3

Opening image: courtesy of Deborah I. Olszewski; **Figure 3.2:** by Claire Houck from New York City, USA (Turkana Boy) [CC BY-SA 2.0 (http://creativecommons.org/licenses/by-sa/2.0)], via Wikimedia Commons; **Figure 3.5:**
© Shannon P. McPherron; **Figure 3.6** and **3.7a:** courtesy of the Abydos Survey for Paleolithic Sites and Deborah I. Olszewski (photos by Laurent Chiotti); **Figure 3.7b:** courtesy of Professor Christopher Henshilwood, University of Bergen; **Figure 3.8:** courtesy of Harold L. Dibble; **Figure 3.9:** age fotostock / Alamy Stock Photo; **Figure 3.12:** courtesy of Ian Tattersall, The Strange Case of the Rickety Cossack and Other Cautionary Tales of Human Evolution, art by Jenn Steffey; **Figure 3.14:** by Ryan Somma [CC BY-SA 2.0 (http://creativecommons.org/licenses/by-sa/2.0)], via Wikimedia Commons; **Figure 3.15:** courtesy of Professor Christopher Henshilwood, University of Bergen; **Figure 3.16:** courtesy of Harold L. Dibble; **Figure 3.17:** redrawn from Lieberman 1991, Figures 2.2 and 2.4; **Figure 3.18:** Universal Images Group North America LLC / Alamy Stock Photo

Chapter 4

Opening image: CoreyFord/iStockphoto; **Figure 4.2a:** courtesy of Harold L. Dibble (photos by Vera Aldeias and Utsav Schurmans) for Smugglers; **Figure 4.2b:** courtesy of Francesco d'Errico; **Figure 4.3a:** courtesy of Deborah I. Olszewski (drawings by Bradley M. Evans); **Figure 4.3b:** Pierre Guenat © Musée des beaux-arts de Dole; **Figure 4.5:** courtesy of Harold L. Dibble (photos by Vera Aldeias and Utsav Schurmans); **Figure 4.6:** Photo: Hilde Jensen; © Tübingen University; **Figure 4.7:** HTO/Wikipedia; **Figure 4.8:** by Petr Novák, Wikipedia (guidance: Danny B. (che)) [CC BY-SA 2.5 (http://creativecommons.org/licenses/by-sa/2.5)], via Wikimedia Commons]; **Figure 4.9:** courtesy of Margherita Mussi; **Figure 4.10:** courtesy of John C. Whittaker; J. Lindow, photographer; **Figure 4.11:** RIA NOVOSTI/SCIENCE PHOTO LIBRARY; **Figure 4.12:** courtesy of Deborah I. Olszewski; **Figure 4.13:** Museo de Altamira y D. Rodríguez/Wikipedia; **Figure 4.15:** adapted from Maximilian Dörrbecker/Wikipedia; **Figure 4.20:** University of Pennsylvania Museum of Archaeology and Anthropology Photographic Archives image #151068 (Clovis point: Object #36-19-3; Folsom point: Object #36-19-16); **Figure 4.21:** University of Pennsylvania Museum of Archaeology and Anthropology Photographic Archives image #237277; **Figure 4.22:** courtesy of Deborah I. Olszewski; **Figure 4.23:** courtesy of Anna C. Roosevelt

Chapter 5

Opening image: Juan Aunion/Shutterstock; **Figure 5.3:** courtesy of the Western Highlands Early Epipaleolithic Project and Deborah I. Olszewski; **Figure 5.4:** courtesy of EFAP archive; **Figure 5.5:** excavations at Hilazon Tachtit Cave directed by Leore Grosman; photographed by Naftali Hilger; **Figure 5.7a:** By Teomancimit (Own work) [CC BY-SA 3.0 (http://creativecommons.org/licenses/by-sa/3.0)], via Wikimedia Commons; **Figure 5.7b:** Wikipedia; **Figure 5.8** and **5.9:** courtesy of Deborah I. Olszewski; **Figure 5.10:** photo © Nigel Goring-Morris; **Figure 5.14:** courtesy of Deborah I. Olszewski

Chapter 6

Opening image: PRISMA ARCHIVO / Alamy Stock Photo; **Figure 6.1:** courtesy of Deborah I. Olszewski; **Figure 6.4:** José-Manuel Benito Álvarez/Wikipedia; **Figure 6.5:** Einsamer Schütze/Wikipedia; **Figure 6.6:** carlos martin diaz/Shutterstock; **Figure 6.8:** Drone Explorer/Shutterstock; **Figure 6.9:** keith morris / Alamy Stock Photo; **Figure 6.10:** Portable Antiquities Scheme/flickr; **Figure 6.12:** Morphart Creation/Shutterstock; **Figure 6.13:** Wikipedia

Chapter 7

Opening image: courtesy of Deborah I. Olszewski; **Figure 7.1:** redrawn from http://www.delange.org/PuebloLaPlata/DSC04.jpg; **Figure 7.2** and **7.5:** courtesy of Deborah I. Olszewski; **Figure 7.6:** courtesy of Chaco Culture National Historical Park. Chaco Historic Photo Collection 0028/004-#28708. 29SJ1659, Shabik'eshchee Village, Pithouse. Florence Hawley Ellis, 1930; **Figure 7.7:** courtesy of Deborah I. Olszewski; **Figure 7.8:** redrawn from http://f.tqn.com/y/archaeology/1/S/n/n/1/Map_Chaco_Canyon2.png; **Figure 7.9:** courtesy of Deborah I. Olszewski; **Figure 7.10:** redrawn from https://davetzold.files.wordpress.com/2010/03/chaco-canyon-anasazi-ruins-map.jpg; **Figure 7.11:** courtesy of Deborah I. Olszewski; **Figure 7.12:** Image # 412070, American Museum of Natural History Library; **Figures 7.13** to **7.19:** courtesy of Deborah I. Olszewski; **Figure 7.20:** redrawn from Mimbres Archaeology at the NAN Ranch Ruin by Harry Shafer. Copyright © 2003 University of New Mexico Press, 2003; **Figure 7.21:** adapted from Multidisciplinary Research at Grasshopper Pueblo, Arizona, edited by William A. Longacre, Sally J. Holbrook, and Michael W. Graves © 1982 The Arizona Board of Regents.

Chapter 8

Opening image: adund/iStockphoto; **Figure 8.3:** redrawn from Sassaman (2005); **Figure 8.4:** redrawn from Heironymous Rowe 2010 (http://commons.wikimedia.org/wiki/File:Hopewell_Exchange_Network_HRoe_2010.jpg); subject to license: http://creativecommons.org/licenses/by-sa/3.0/deed.en; **Figure 8.5:** Rdikeman at the English language Wikipedia [GFDL (www.gnu.org/copyleft/fdl.html) or CC-BY-SA-3.0 (http://creativecommons.org/licenses/by-sa/3.0/)], from Wikimedia Commons; **Figure 8.6:** Cahokia Mounds State Historic Site; **Figure 8.7:** McClung Museum of Natural History and Culture, The University of Tennessee, Knoxville. 42/29RE17; **Figure 8.8:** Cahokia Mounds State Historic Site; **Figure 8.9** and **8.10:** courtesy of Deborah I. Olszewski

Chapter 9

Opening image: Fedor Selivanov/Shutterstock; **Figure 9.3:** courtesy of Deborah I. Olszewski; **Figure 9.4:** drawn after http://cdli.ox.ac.uk/wiki/lib/exe/fetch.php?w=400&h=369&tok=2af270&media=images:lateuruk02.jpg and http://4.bp.blogspot.com/_zBwAaY7HSjc/TK21G-GICyJI/AAAAAAAAACA/wEvs7SBb4N0/s320/uruk1.jpg; **Figure 9.5:** University of Pennsylvania Museum of Archaeology and Anthropology Photographic Archives image #225821 (object number 37-15-34); **Figure 9.6:** Royal Air Force official/Wikipedia: **Figure 9.7:** wikiwikiyarou/Wikipedia: **Figure 9.9:** University of Pennsylvania Museum of Archaeology and Anthropology Photographic Archives image #150014 (object number B14221); **Figure 9.10:** University of Pennsylvania Museum of Archaeology and Anthropology Photographic Archives image #171549; **Figure 9.11:** University of Pennsylvania Museum of Archaeology and Anthropology Photographic Archives image #184431; **Figure 9.12:** University of Pennsylvania Museum of Archaeology and Anthropology Photographic Archives image #190616

Chapter 10

Opening image: courtesy of Deborah I. Olszewski; **Figure 10.3:** The Calendar Circle of Nalota Playa (photograph by J. McKim Malville); **Figure 10.4:** drawn from the Narmer Palette; **Figure 10.5:** Wikipedia; Figure 10.6, 10.7, 10.8: courtesy of Deborah I. Olszewski; **Figure 10.9:** redrawn from Wilkinson (1999: Fig. 4.6); **Figure 10.10:** courtesy of Deborah I. Olszewski; **Figure 10.11:** University of Pennsylvania Museum of Archaeology and Anthropology Photographic Archives image #51179 (object number 40-19-2): photograph by Tom Jenkins

Chapter 11

Opening image: by Rosemania (http://www.flickr.com/photos/rosemania/4533297189) [CC BY 2.0 (http://creativecommons.org/licenses/by/2.0)], via Wikimedia Commons; **Figure 11.3:** based on Gurdjieff/Wikipedia; **Figure 11.4:** redrawn from Peterson and Shelach (2012: Fig. 1); **Figure 11.5:** reproduced by permission of Xu Hong; **Figure 11.6:** courtesy of Deborah I. Olszewski; **Figure 11.7:** redrawn from Campbell et al (2011: Fig. 1); **Figure 11.8:** based on Trigger (2003); **Figure 11.9:** BabelStone/Wikipedia; **Figure 11.10:** University of Pennsylvania Museum of Archaeology and Anthropology Photographic Archives image #151280 (object no. C352A); **Figure 11.11:** courtesy of Richard M. Leventhal

Chapter 12

Opening image: by Miya.m (Miya.m's file) [GFDL (http://www.gnu.org/copyleft/fdl.html) or CC BY-SA 3.0 (http://creativecommons.org/licenses/by-sa/3.0)], via Wikimedia Commons; **Figure 12.2:** redrawn from Law (2011: Fig. 2.1); **Figure 12.3:** © MAI / C. Jarrige; **Figure 12.4:** James P. Blair/National Geographic Creative; **Figure 12.5:** by Saqib Qayyum (Own work) [CC BY-SA 3.0 (http://creativecommons.org/licenses/by-sa/3.0)], via Wikimedia Commons; no changes were made to this image; **Figure 12.6:** courtesy of Deborah I. Olszewski; **Figure 12.7:** redrawn from Law (2011: Fig. 13.11); **Figure 12.8:** redrawn from Possehl (2002: Fig. 12.1); **Figure 12.9:** courtesy of Deborah I. Olszewski; **Figure 12.10:** redrawn from Marshall (1931); **Figure 12.11:** redrawn from Law (2011: Fig. 2.6D)

Chapter 13

Opening image: by chensiyuan (chensiyuan) [GFDL (http://www.gnu.org/copyleft/fdl.html) or CC BY-SA 4.0-3.0-2.5-2.0-1.0 (http://creativecommons.org/licenses/by-sa/4.0-3.0-2.5-2.0-1.0)], via Wikimedia Commons; **Figure 13.3:** University of Pennsylvania Museum of Archaeology and Anthropology Photographic Archives image #180670; **Figure 13.4:** redrawn from Marcus (1989: 171); **Figure 13.5:** POZZO DI BORGO Thomas/Shutterstock; **Figure 13.6:** Gianfranco Vivi/Shutterstock; **Figure 13.7:** drawn after http://elmiradorhike.blogspot.com/2010/11/el-mirador-centre-map.html; **Figure 13.8:** University of Pennsylvania Museum of Archaeology and Anthropology Photographic Archives image #237385; **Figure 13.9:** courtesy of Deborah I. Olszewski; **Figure 13.10:** Shellnut/Wikipedia; **Figure 13.11** and **13:13:** courtesy of Deborah I. Olszewski; **Figure 13.14:** redrawn from Schele Number 2033 (http://research.famsi.org/uploads/schele/hires/05/IMG0015.jpg); **Figure 13.15:** drawing by Linda Schele © David Schele. Photo courtesy Ancient Americas at LACMA (ancientamericas.org); **Figure 13.16:** University of Pennsylvania Museum of Archaeology and Anthropology Photographic Archives image #249496: photograph by E. H. Thompson; **Figure 13.18:** Miguel A. Muñoz Pellicer / Alamy Stock Photo; **Figure 13.19:** Julio Aldana/Shutterstock; **Figure 13.20:** Angus McComiskey / Alamy Stock Photo

Chapter 14

Opening image: courtesy of Meredith H. Keffer; **Figure 14.3:** courtesy of Tom D. Dillehay; **Figure 14.4:** © Rchphoto/Dreamstime.com; **Figure 14.5:** redrawn from Pozorski and Pozorski (1993: Fig. 2); **Figure 14.7:** © Reciprocity Images Editorial / Alamy; **Figure 14.8:** Naturalis Biodiversity Center/Wikimedia Commons; **Figure 14.9:** Diego Delso, delso.photo, License CC-BY-SA; **Figure 14.10:** Donna McClelland. The Christopher B. Donnan and Donna McClelland Moche Archive, Image Collections and Fieldwork Archives, Dumbarton Oaks, Trustees for Harvard University, Washington, DC; **Figure 14.11:** drawn after http://www.simo.ru/bolivia/map/bol-m-tiwanaku.jpg; **Figure 14.12:** University of Pennsylvania Museum of Archaeology and Anthropology Photographic Archives image #249497; **Figure 14.13:** redrawn from D'Altroy (2002: Fig. 6.2); **Figure 14.14:** Pi3.124/Wikipedia; **Figure 14.15:** redrawn from Jenkins (2001: Fig. 1); **Figure 14.17:** © Dumbarton Oaks, Pre-Columbian Collection, Washington, DC

Chapter 15

Opening image: evenfh/iStockphoto; **Figure 15.3:** redrawn from Huffman (2000); **Figure 15.4:** © University of Pretoria Museums; **Figure 15.5:** image taken by Jan Derk in 1997 in Zimbabwe. (en:Image:Great-Zimbabwe.jpg) [Public domain], via Wikimedia Commons; **Figure 15.6:** © University of Pretoria Museums; **Figure 15.7:** redrawn from Huffman (2008: Fig. 12); **Figure 15.8:** redrawn from Chirikure and Pikirayi (2008: Fig. 6) and Huffman (1984: Fig. 2); **Figure 15.9:** redrawn from Walton (1955: Fig. 2); **Figure 15.10:** redrawn from Chirikure and Pikirayi (2008: Fig. 2) and Huffman (1981: Fig. 7)

Epilogue

Opening image and **Figure E.1:** courtesy of Deborah I. Olszewski

Index

Note: Page references followed by a "*t*" indicate table; "*f*" indicate figure.